THE NEW
AMERICAN
COMMENTARY

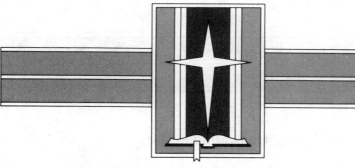

An Exegetical and Theological
Exposition of Holy Scripture

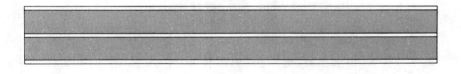

THE NEW AMERICAN COMMENTARY

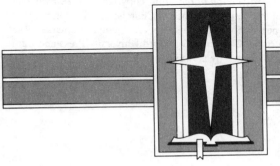

Volume
19A

HOSEA, JOEL

Duane A. Garrett

BROADMAN
& HOLMAN
PUBLISHERS

For *Patty*

With Love and Gratitude

הִנָּךְ יָפָה רַעְיָתִי הִנָּךְ יָפָה עֵינַיִךְ יוֹנִים:

Author's Preface

I would like to express my deep appreciation for the support and encouragement I have received from my colleagues at Bethel Theological Seminary, and in particular from Dean Leland Eliason, as I have endeavored to complete this project. I owe a special debt of thanks to Mr. Philemon Yong for his proofreading efforts. I also am certainly grateful to Ray Clendenen of Broadman & Holman Publishers for having the confidence in me to entrust this assignment to me. Above all, my deepest thanks go to my family, and especially to my wife, Patty, for their love, support, and patience.

—Duane A. Garrett
Bethel Theological Seminary

Editors' Preface

God's Word does not change. God's world, however, changes in every generation. These changes, in addition to new findings by scholars and a new variety of challenges to the gospel message, call for the church in each generation to interpret and apply God's Word for God's people. Thus, THE NEW AMERICAN COMMENTARY is introduced to bridge the twentieth and twenty-first centuries. This new series has been designed primarily to enable pastors, teachers, and students to read the Bible with clarity and proclaim it with power.

In one sense THE NEW AMERICAN COMMENTARY is not new, for it represents the continuation of a heritage rich in biblical and theological exposition. The title of this forty-volume set points to the continuity of this series with an important commentary project published at the end of the nineteenth century called AN AMERICAN COMMENTARY, edited by Alvah Hovey. The older series included, among other significant contributions, the outstanding volume on Matthew by John A. Broadus, from whom the publisher of the new series, Broadman Press, partly derives its name. The former series was authored and edited by scholars committed to the infallibility of Scripture, making it a solid foundation for the present project. In line with this heritage, all NAC authors affirm the divine inspiration, inerrancy, complete truthfulness, and full authority of the Bible. The perspective of the NAC is unapologetically confessional and rooted in the evangelical tradition.

Since a commentary is a fundamental tool for the expositor or teacher who seeks to interpret and apply Scripture in the church or classroom, the NAC focuses on communicating the theological structure and content of each biblical book. The writers seek to illuminate both the historical meaning and contemporary significance of Holy Scripture.

In its attempt to make a unique contribution to the Christian community, the NAC focuses on two concerns. First, the commentary emphasizes how each section of a book fits together so that the reader becomes aware of the theological unity of each book and of Scripture as a whole. The writers, however, remain aware of the Bible's inherently rich variety. Second, the NAC is produced with the conviction that the Bible primarily belongs to the church. We believe that scholarship and the academy provide an indispensable foundation for biblical understanding and the service of Christ, but the editors and authors of this series have attempted to communicate the findings of their research in a manner that will build up the whole body of Christ. Thus, the commentary concentrates on theological exegesis while providing practical, applicable exposition.

THE NEW AMERICAN COMMENTARY's theological focus enables the reader to see the parts as well as the whole of Scripture. The biblical books vary in content, context, literary type, and style. In addition to this rich variety, the editors and authors recognize that the doctrinal emphasis and use of the biblical books differs in various places, contexts, and cultures among God's people. These factors, as well as other concerns, have led the editors to give freedom to the writers to wrestle with the issues raised by the scholarly community surrounding each book and to determine the appropriate shape and length of the introductory materials. Moreover, each writer has developed the structure of the commentary in a way best suited for expounding the basic structure and the meaning of the biblical books for our day. Generally, discussions relating to contemporary scholarship and technical points of grammar and syntax appear in the footnotes and not in the text of the commentary. This format allows pastors and interested laypersons, scholars and teachers, and serious college and seminary students to profit from the commentary at various levels. This approach has been employed because we believe that all Christians have the privilege and responsibility to read and seek to understand the Bible for themselves.

Consistent with the desire to produce a readable, up-to-date commentary, the editors selected the *New International Version* as the standard translation for the commentary series. The selection was made primarily because of the NIV's faithfulness to the original languages and its beautiful and readable style. The authors, however, have been given the liberty to differ at places from the NIV as they develop their own translations from the Greek and Hebrew texts.

The NAC reflects the vision and leadership of those who provide oversight for Broadman Press, who in 1987 called for a new commentary series that would evidence a commitment to the inerrancy of Scripture and a faithfulness to the classic Christian tradition. While the commentary adopts an "American" name, it should be noted some writers represent countries outside the United States, giving the commentary an international perspective. The diverse group of writers includes scholars, teachers, and administrators from almost twenty different colleges and seminaries, as well as pastors, missionaries, and a layperson.

The editors and writers hope that THE NEW AMERICAN COMMENTARY will be helpful and instructive for pastors and teachers, scholars and students, for men and women in the churches who study and teach God's Word in various settings. We trust that for editors, authors, and readers alike, the commentary will be used to build up the church, encourage obedience, and bring renewal to God's people. Above all, we pray that the NAC will bring glory and honor to our Lord who has graciously redeemed us and faithfully revealed himself to us in his Holy Word.

SOLI DEO GLORIA
The Editors

Abbreviations

Bible Books

Gen	Isa	Luke
Exod	Jer	John
Lev	Lam	Acts
Num	Ezek	Rom
Deut	Dan	1, 2 Cor
Josh	Hos	Gal
Judg	Joel	Eph
Ruth	Amos	Phil
1, 2 Sam	Obad	Col
1, 2 Kgs	Jonah	1, 2 Thess
1, 2 Chr	Mic	1, 2 Tim
Ezra	Nah	Titus
Neh	Hab	Phlm
Esth	Zeph	Heb
Job	Hag	Jas
Ps (pl. Pss)	Zech	1, 2 Pet
Prov	Mal	1, 2, 3 John
Eccl	Matt	Jude
Song	Mark	Rev

Apocrypha

Add Esth	*The Additions to the Book of Esther*
Bar	*Baruch*
Bel	*Bel and the Dragon*
1,2 Esdr	*1, 2 Esdras*
4 Ezra	*4 Ezra*
Jdt	*Judith*
Ep Jer	*Epistle of Jeremiah*
1,2,3,4 Mac	*1, 2, 3, 4 Maccabees*
Pr Azar	*Prayer of Azariah and the Song of the Three Jews*
Pr Man	*Prayer of Manasseh*
Sir	*Sirach, Ecclesiasticus*
Sus	*Susanna*
Tob	*Tobit*
Wis	*The Wisdom of Solomon*

Commonly Used Sources

AASOR	Annual of the American Schools of Oriental Research
AB	Anchor Bible
ABR	*Australian Biblical Review*
ABD	*Anchor Bible Dictionary*
ABW	*Archaeology and the Biblical World*
AC	An American Commentary, ed. A. Hovey
AcOr	*Acta orientalia*
AEL	M. Lichtheim, *Ancient Egyptian Literature*
AJSL	*American Journal of Semitic Languages and Literature*
Akk.	Akkadian
AnBib	Analecta Biblica
ANET	J. B. Pritchard, ed., *Ancient Near Eastern Texts*
Ant.	*Antiquities*
AOAT	Alter Orient und Altes Testament
AOTS	*Archaeology and Old Testament Study,* ed. D. W. Thomas
ArOr	Archiv orientální
ATD	Das Alte Testament Deutsch
ATR	*Anglican Theological Review*
AusBR	*Australian Biblical Review*
BA	*Biblical Archaeologist*
BAGD	W. Bauer, W. F. Arndt, F. W. Gingrich, and F. W. Danker, *Greek-English Lexicon of the New Testament*
BALS	Bible and Literature Series
BARev	*Biblical Archaeology Review*
BASOR	*Bulletin of the American Schools of Oriental Research*
BDB	F. Brown, S. R. Driver, and C. A. Briggs, *Hebrew and English Lexicon of the Old Testament*
BETL	Bibliotheca ephemeridum theologicarum lovaniensium
BFT	Biblical Foundations in Theology
BHS	*Biblia hebraica stuttgartensia*
Bib	*Biblica*
BibRev	*Bible Review*
BKAT	Biblischer Kommentar: Altes Testament
BO	*Bibliotheca orientalis*
BSac	*Bibliotheca Sacra*
BSC	Bible Study Commentary
BT	*Bible Translator*
BurH	*Buried History*
BZ	*Biblische Zeitschrift*

HAT	Handbuch zum Alten Testament
HBT	*Horizons in Biblical Theology*
HDR	Harvard Dissertations in Religion
Her	Hermeneia
HKAT	Handkommentar zum Alten Testament
HSM	Harvard Semitic Monographs
HT	Helps for Translators
HTR	*Harvard Theological Review*
HUCA	*Hebrew Union College Annual*
IB	*Interpreter's Bible*
ICC	International Critical Commentary
IDB	*Interpreter's Dictionary of the Bible,* ed. G. A. Buttrick, et al.
IDBSup	Supplementary volume to *IDB*
IBHS	B. K. Waltke and M. O'Connor, *Introduction to Biblical Hebrew Syntax*
IEJ	*Israel Exploration Journal*
IES	Israel Exploration Society
Int	*Interpretation*
INT	Interpretation: A Bible Commentary for Teaching and Preaching
ITC	International Theological Commentary
IOS	*Israel Oriental Society*
ISBE	*International Standard Bible Encyclopedia,* rev. ed. G. W. Bromiley
IJT	*Indian Journal of Theology*
ITC	International Theological Commentary
JANES	*Journal of Ancient Near Eastern Society*
JAOS	*Journal of the American Oriental Society*
JBL	*Journal of Biblical Literature*
JBR	*Journal of Bible and Religion*
JCS	*Journal of Cuneiform Studies*
JEA	*Journal of Egyptian Archaeology*
JETS	*Journal of the Evangelical Theological Society*
JJS	*Journal of Jewish Studies*
JNES	*Journal of Near Eastern Studies*
JNSL	*Journal of Northwest Semitic Languages*
JPOS	*Journal of Palestine Oriental Society*
JSJ	*Journal for the Study of Judaism in the Persian, Hellenistic, and Roman Period*
JSOR	*Journal of the Society for Oriental Research*
JSOT	*Journal for the Study of the Old Testament*

JSOTSup	JSOT—Supplement Series
JSS	*Journal of Semitic Studies*
JTS	*Journal of Theological Studies*
JTSNS	*Journal of Theological Studies, New Series*
JTT	*Journal of Translation and Textlinguistics*
KAT	Kommentar zum Alten Testament
KB	L. Koehler and W. Baumgartner, *Lexicon in Veteris Testamenti libros*
LBBC	Layman's Bible Book Commentary
LBI	Library of Biblical Interpretation
LCC	Library of Christian Classics
LLAVT	E. Vogt, *Lexicon Linguae Aramaicae Veteris Testamenti*
LTQ	*Lexington Theological Quarterly*
MT	Masoretic Text
NAC	New American Commentary
NB	*Nebuchadrezzar and Babylon,* D. J. Wiseman
NBD	*New Bible Dictionary*
NCBC	New Century Bible Commentary
NIBC	New International Biblical Commentary
NICOT	New International Commentary on the Old Testament
NJPS	New Jewish Publication Society Version
NKZ	*Neue kirchliche Zeitschrift*
NovT	*Novum Testamentum*
NTS	*New Testament Studies*
Or	*Orientalia*
OTL	Old Testament Library
OTP	*The Old Testament Pseudepigrapha,* ed. J. H. Charlesworth
OTS	*Oudtestamentische Studiën*
OTWSA	*Ou-Testamentiese Werkgemeenskap in Suid-Afrika*
PCB	*Peake's Commentary on the Bible,* ed. M. Black and H. H. Rowley
PEQ	*Palestine Exploration Quarterly*
POTT	*Peoples of Old Testament Times,* ed. D. J. Wiseman
PTR	*Princeton Theological Review*
Pss. Sol.	*Psalms of Solomon*
RA	Revue d'assyriologie et d'archéologie orientale
RB	*Revue biblique*
ResQ	*Restoration Quarterly*
RevExp	*Review and Expositor*
RSR	Recherches de science religieuse
SANE	Sources from the Ancient Near East
SBLDS	Society of Biblical Literature Dissertation Series

SOTI	*A Survey of Old Testament Introduction,* G. L. Archer
SBT	Studies in Biblical Theology
SJT	*Scottish Journal of Theology*
SP	Samaritan Pentateuch
SR	Studies in Religion/Sciences religieuses
ST	*Studia theologica*
STJD	Studies on the Texts of the Desert of Judah
Syr	Syriac
TDOT	*Theological Dictionary of the Old Testament,* ed. G. J. Botterweck and H. Ringgren
Tg	Targum
TJNS	Trinity Journal—New Series
TLZ	*Theologische Literaturzeitung*
TOTC	Tyndale Old Testament Commentaries
TrinJ	*Trinity Journal*
TS	*Theological Studies*
TWAT	*Theologisches Wörterbuch zum Alten Testament,* ed. G. J. Botterweck and H. Ringgren
TWOT	*Theological Wordbook of the Old Testament*
TynBul	*Tyndale Bulletin*
UF	*Ugarit-Forschungen*
Vg	Vulgate
VT	*Vetus Testamentum*
VTSup	Vetus Testamentum, Supplements
WBC	Word Biblical Commentaries
WEC	Wycliffe Exegetical Commentary
WTJ	*Westminster Theological Journal*
WMANT	Wissenschaftliche Monographien zum Alten und Neuen Testament
ZAW	*Zeitschrift für die alttestamentliche Wissenschaft*
ZDMG	*Zeitschrift der deutschen morgenländischen Gesellschaft*
ZDPV	*Zeitschrift des deutschen Palätina-Vereing*
ZTK	*Zeitschrift für katholische Theologie*

Contents

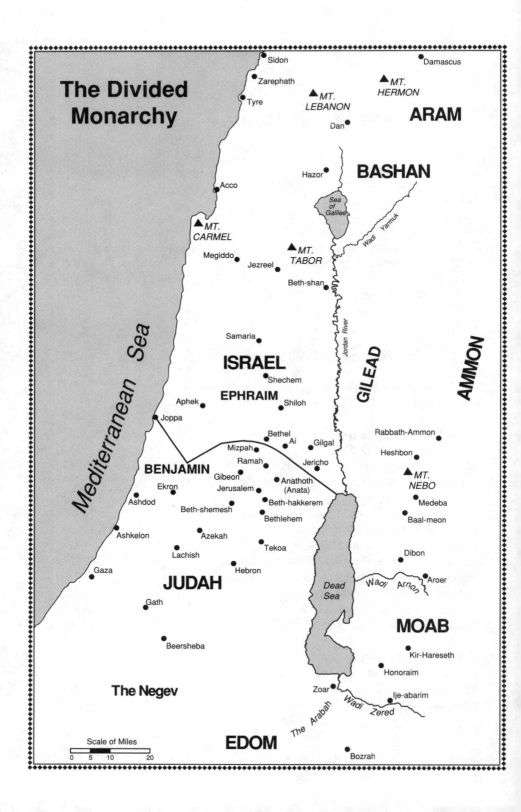

Hosea

━━━━━━━━━━ **INTRODUCTION** ━━━━━━━━━━

Hosea is not an easy book. It begins with a prophet receiving a command to marry a prostitute and promptly describes the births of his three children, each of whom is given a bizarre but significant name. From here the book swiftly plunges into a maze of warnings, microsermons, poems, and laments, and through them all it swiftly and evasively alludes to biblical texts and incidents, mixes metaphors, and changes topics, seemingly at random. To say that the Hebrew is perplexing sounds like a scholar's whine; the English reader might better appreciate how precarious the task of interpreting Hosea really is by comparing how the various versions have handled the book (and even that only

21

tells a small part of the story).

But though Hosea is a difficult book, it is also a great book. It is like a tree whose roots go down deep into the Torah and whose branches bear the fruit of a discourse that became the grammar of biblical prophecy. Many of the themes, and much of the vocabulary, of the great literary prophecies of Isaiah, Jeremiah, and Ezekiel originate in Hosea. It also is a book that jolts the reader; it refuses to be domesticated and made conventional. It does comfort the afflicted, but it most surely afflicts the comfortable. It is as startling in its presentation of sin as it is surprising in its stubborn certainty of grace. It is as blunt as it is enigmatic. It is a book to be experienced, and the experience is with God.

1. The Historical Background of the Book of Hosea

We know virtually nothing about Hosea himself. We know nothing of his ancestral family beyond the name of his father, Beeri. We do not know where his home was, what events were formative in his early life, or how he was educated. His remarkable familiarity with the Torah, Joshua, and Judges suggests that he was thoroughly trained in the Scriptures (as they existed in his day). Similarly, the self-consciously enigmatic nature of his book[1] suggests a high degree of intelligence and a subtle mind. We do not know how close he was to the political events of his lifetime. Was he, like Isaiah, on familiar terms with members of the aristocracy and the central government, or was he outside the circles of power? We do not know how or where he died. He became a prophet prior to his marriage because it was by divine command that he chose the woman he did, but his marriage to Gomer may have been the first act of his prophetic career (see commentary at 1:2). This, combined with the fact that 1:1 implies that his ministry lasted quite a long time, suggests that he became a prophet at a reasonably young age.[2]

We know more about the age in which he lived. Hosea 1:1 tells us that he ministered "during the reigns of Uzziah, Jotham, Ahaz and Hezekiah, kings of Judah, and during the reign of Jeroboam son of Jehoash king of Israel." Evidence suggests that Hosea ministered during the latter part of Jeroboam's reign (793–753 B.C.) and for some years following. The title verse says that he prophesied as late as the reign of Hezekiah of Judah (716–686) B.C. Assuming that Hosea began his ministry fairly late in Jeroboam II's reign and ended fairly early in Hezekiah's reign, we conclude that his prophetic career went from about 760 to 710 B.C., or roughly fifty years. The fact that he lived into Hezekiah's reign is especially significant because it tells us that he lived to see

---

[1] See the commentary on 14:9.

[2] Cf. J. L. Mays, *Hosea,* OTL (Philadelphia: Westminster, 1969), 2.

the fall of Samaria (722 B.C.). It is not unreasonable to assume that he ended his days in Hezekiah's Jerusalem and that his book was preserved there, but we have no direct evidence to that effect.

Jeroboam II, who reigned from about 790 to 750 B.C., came to power while Israel's two enemies to the north, Syria and Assyria, were weakened by internal conflicts. Jeroboam II was a long-lived and capable ruler; Amos 6:13 alludes to two victories won under his reign.[3] After the death of Ben-Hadad II of Syria, Jeroboam extended the domain of Israel as far north as the city of Damascus itself (2 Kgs 14:25–26).[4] Renewed success on the battlefield restored the prosperity of the nation as well; the economy boomed. But this was to be the Indian Summer of Israel. Dark days were ahead.

Even in Jeroboam's lifetime evidence of social trouble was apparent. A two-class system developed; the lower class suffered increasingly under oppression and poverty while the upper class enjoyed power and excess. After the political stability afforded by Jeroboam II's long life, moreover, Israel entered a time of political chaos. Soon after his death the situation approached anarchy; almost every king of Israel died by assassination at the hands of his successor. Israel's internal weakness, combined with the rise of an invigorated Assyria under Tiglath-pileser III (745–727 B.C.) and his successors Shalmaneser V (727–722 B.C.) and Sargon II (722–705 B.C.), sealed the fate of the Northern Kingdom.

Jeroboam II was succeeded by his son Zechariah (753 B.C.). Almost immediately, however, Zechariah was struck down by the assassin Shallum. This ended the dynasty of Jehu (841–814 B.C.). Shallum had little chance to savor his moment, however, for after a single month he was in turn assassinated by Menahem (752–742 B.C.). Israel's downward spiral continued under his reign; Menahem's most noteworthy act was to send a thousand talents of silver to Tiglath-pileser III (Pul) of Assyria in return for Assyria's support for his claim to the throne (2 Kgs 25:17–22). Menahem's son Pekahiah succeeded him, but his reign also was cut short by assassination. Pekah, son of Remaliah, a high-ranking military officer, killed him after Pekahiah had held the throne for only about two years (741–739 B.C.).

The chronology of Pekah's reign is difficult because 2 Kgs 15:27 says he reigned for twenty years. This is not possible if one dates the beginning of his reign to around 739 B.C. because the kingdom itself ended in 722. It may be that the Kings text has a scribal error, or it may be that Pekah headed a rival government beginning around 752 B.C. and that with the murder of Pekahiah he became sole monarch. Either way, his reign lasted until about 732 B.C. Unlike Menahem, Pekah was hostile to the Assyrian Empire (this may explain why he led a rival government). After he had seized power, Pekah, along with

---

[3] J. Bright, *A History of Israel,* 2d ed. (Philadelphia: Westminster, 1975), 254.
[4] See E. H. Merrill, *Kingdom of Priests* (Grand Rapids: Baker, 1987), 374–75.

Rezin of Syria, formed a coalition aimed at resisting the growing power of Assyria. Jotham of Judah refused to join the coalition, as did his successor, Ahaz. The Syro-Ephraimite coalition could not risk having a hostile force in their rear and invaded the south with an intention of replacing Ahaz with a certain ben Tabeel as a puppet king (Isa 7:6). Ahaz appealed to Tiglath-pileser for aid, and the Assyrian king quickly routed the forces of the coalition. Hoshea son of Elah then assassinated Pekah and took the crown for himself. He saved Samaria from destruction by a hasty submission to Assyria, but he also carried on secret negotiations with Egypt for support against Assyria. When this treachery was discovered, Assyria, now under Shalmaneser V, invaded the land and took Hoshea captive. Samaria held out for about two years, during which time Shalmaneser died; but his successor, Sargon II, completed the destruction of Israel's capital city. According to Assyrian records, 27,290 Israelite citizens were deported to Mesopotamia.

One cannot easily correlate any text in Hosea with any known event of history. Some scholars assert that Hosea 5 reflects the period of the Syro-Ephraimite war (735–733 B.C.).[5] This is unlikely. Isaiah 7 shows that Judah was on the defensive, desperately seeking allies in this war. In Hosea, Judah is the aggressor (5:10). The Hosea text may refer to border disputes in the reign of Uzziah of Judah,[6] but even this is not certain (see commentary). In general, however, Hosea describes the volatile political situation following the death of Jeroboam II, a chaotic time in which power changed hands rapidly and self-styled kings made claims of royalty that were as hollow as they were ignored by the people (e.g., 7:3–7; 8:4; 10:3). Probably most of Hosea's extant messages come from the last three decades of Israel's history.

2. The Authorship and Compilation of Hosea

Most scholars today affirm that the bulk of the book comes from the sermons of Hosea himself, but many attribute the actual writing of the book to a group of disciples.[7] The notion that the prophetic books stem from schools of disciples, though common, is not founded on solid evidence. We know from the example of Jeremiah 36 that prophets sometimes employed scribes, but that text also informs us that the prophets had a direct hand in producing written versions of their proclamations. In addition, the Book of Hosea, albeit a text that is notoriously difficult to analyze and seemingly a series of fragments, is best understood when treated as a literary work, a complex whole, and not as

---

[5] E.g., H. W. Wolff, *Hosea,* Her (Philadelphia: Fortress, 1974), xxi.

[6] F. I. Andersen and D. N. Freedman, *Hosea,* AB (New York: Doubleday, 1980), 34–35.

[7] Cf. Mays, *Hosea,* 16; B. W. Anderson, *Understanding the Old Testament,* 3d ed. (Englewood Cliffs, N.J.: Prentice-Hall, 1975), 284; Wolff, *Hosea xxix–xxxii;* and Andersen and Freedman, *Hosea* 53.

an anthology of many separate parts. There is no reason to doubt that the messages of Hosea come from the prophet himself.

Many scholars, even those who believe that the bulk of the book is from Hosea, argue that the book has a significant number of redactional interpolations. Interpreters commonly attribute the references to Judah to secondary hands. Some say that these are from two separate redactions of the book; the first was a "pro-Judah" redaction designed to distance Judah from the condemnation pronounced against Israel (e.g., 1:7; 3:5). The second was a redaction that took oracles of condemnation originally delivered against Israel and redirected them toward Judah (e.g., 5:5; 6:11).[8] Evidence for this redaction history is minimal; it stems more from a century-old habit of scholarship than from significant anomalies in the text. Hosea regarded the Davidic king in Jerusalem the legitimate one anointed of Yahweh and hoped that Judah would reject the apostasy of their northern counterparts (e.g., 4:15). He also knew that the house of David would be the source of Israel's salvation (3:5). Nevertheless, he understood that apostasy was deeply rooted in Judah and knew that harrowing days lay ahead for the south as well. There is nothing here that demands even one "Judah" redaction, much less two. Furthermore, references to Judah can often be shown to be integral to the structure or message of the texts in which they appear.[9]

A few scholars maintain that the "optimistic" oracles do not stem from Hosea, but this comes from a tendency to regard the prophets as incapable of delivering complex messages. The selfsame prophet could give messages of both doom and hope. In Hosea's case the sayings of condemnation and the sayings of salvation are so thoroughly intertwined, and the style is so self-evidently uniform, that the notion that the salvific statements are secondary should be abandoned.[10]

In short, the Book of Hosea should be treated as a literary unity and not as a pastiche of short sayings and messages redacted by disciples. No text is demonstrably secondary, and none should be treated as such. The book is extremely difficult, but uniformly so, and attempts to demarcate secondary material frequently have as their true aim the removal of texts that contradict the theses of modern scholars. The prophet probably used a scribe, but there is no reason to suppose that anyone other than Hosea is responsible for the contents of this book.

---

[8] Cf. B. S. Childs, *Introduction to the Old Testament as Scripture* (Philadelphia: Fortress, 1979), 377–78; Wolff, *Hosea xxxi–xxxii;* W. H. Schmidt, *Introduction to the Old Testament* (London: SCM Press, 1979), 204.

[9] See, e.g., this commentary on 4:15–5:15.

[10] Cf. G. Fohrer, *Introduction to the Old Testament* (Nashville: Abingdon, 1968), 422.

3. The Hebrew Text of Hosea

Hosea contains possibly the most difficult Hebrew in the Bible (although many scholars would give that distinction to Job). Hosea is frequently elliptical, at times apparently ungrammatical, and often contains passing allusions to historical incidents and other texts of the Bible that are almost bewildering. Its logic is sometimes paradoxical. It also contains a fairly high number of obscure or rare words, the meanings of which scholars must struggle to recover.[11] The difficulty of the Hebrew of Hosea naturally makes it inviting territory for those who wish to invade it with an arsenal of techniques for emendation.[12] Critical scholars of a previous generation believed that the text had been severely corrupted[13] and were sublimely confident in their ability to recover the text, but few scholars today feel free to rearrange, delete, and modify Hosea at will.[14] For the most part, our confusion with the text of Hosea is a matter both of our ignorance of his dialect and of the intentionally elliptical and obscure nature of the book. It is not in most cases a matter of the text having been badly transmitted.[15]

On the other hand, some emendation may be necessary. The versions and manuscripts contain enough divergence to convince us that at least some passages may have suffered in transmission. In a few texts emendations commend themselves so obviously or have such strong manuscript or versional support that an inflexible commitment to the Masoretic tradition is unreasonable.

Nevertheless, it is easy to resort to emendation too quickly. The problem, simply, is this: the more one emends, the less one can claim to be interpreting the Book of Hosea. The more one emends a passage, the less likely it is that one's interpretation of the text will be persuasive. Many proposed emendations of Hosea have attained nothing like scholarly consensus.[16] One is thus left to the imagination of the individual scholar. An overly emended text is not the text of Hosea at all but is really a new book, the work of a scholar (or commit-

---

[11] Hapax legomena appear at 2:12,15; 3:2; 5:2,13; 7:9; 8:6,13; 9:14; 10:6,7,10; 12:5; 13:5,14,15. Add to this the number of other rare words and the number of verbs, the parsings of which are controversial, and the translation of Hosea becomes challenging indeed.

[12] Cf. J. A. Soggin, *Introduction to the Old Testament* (Philadelphia: Westminster, 1989), 293.

[13] Cf. W. R. Harper (*Amos and Hosea,* ICC [New York: Scribner, 1905], clxxiii), who asserts that Hosea "is one of the most corrupt [texts] in the O.T."

[14] The high-water mark for this kind of approach relative to Hosea may be G. R. Driver, "Linguistic and Textual Problems: Minor Prophets I," *JTS* 39 (1938): 154–66.

[15] The LXX, we should note, reflects a Hebrew text that is in basic agreement with the Masoretic tradition, while some of the distinctive readings of the LXX arise from specific concerns on the part of the translators. Cf. S. Pisano, " 'Egypt' in the Septuagint Text of Hosea," in *Tradition of the Text,* ed. G. J. Norton and S. Pisano (Fribourg, Switzerland: Vandenhoeck & Ruprecht Göttingen, 1991), 301–8.

[16] Cf. the enormous number of proposed emendations for Hos 4:4 cited in E. Tov, *Textual Criticism of the Hebrew Bible* (Minneapolis: Fortress, 1992), 359.

tee) who has ceased to be an interpreter and has become a redactor. A number of recent scholars have fallen into this trap, and the average reader of modern translations of the English Bible would be surprised at how much of a given translation of Hosea is based on emendation, especially since some translations do not footnote emended readings.

It thus becomes a matter of balance. The best approach is to try to stay with the Masoretic text unless compelling reasons present themselves for emending. This obviously allows for some subjectivity in what is generally regarded as a relatively objective discipline, since what seems to one person to be a "compelling reason" may seem like slim justification to another. But it cannot be otherwise. In an area such as this, simple rules for knowing when to emend—rules that can be applied with mathematical precision—do not exist. Nevertheless, if one conscientiously seeks to follow a conservative *modus operandi*, the number of emendations will be kept to a minimum. In the commentary that follows, I have tried to show that many proposed emendations, including many followed by the NIV, are unnecessary and obscure the flow of the argument of Hosea.[17] The reason for this approach, again, is not some notion that the text has been perfectly handled by the Masoretic scribes but a desire to interpret the Hosea that we have rather than create a new Hosea. The Masoretic text is still our primary and best witness to what the prophet actually wrote.

4. The Imagery, Style, and Literary Background of Hosea

Obviously Hosea was familiar with the literary motifs of the (pagan) world around him. Some scholars see parallels between Hosea and the Mari prophets.[18] It is also possible that Hosea's language reflects concepts found in Akkadian incantations.[19] One might contend that there are elements of tragedy and comedy, analogous to the Aristotelian categories, integrated in Hosea.[20] Even so, these external, non-Israelite parallels to Hosea are of limited use and certainty.

(1) Hosea and the Torah

By contrast, it is impossible to analyze Hosea without a thorough reckoning with his allusions to the Torah[21] and to Israelite history. Hosea stood squarely

---

[17] There are, of course, exceptions to this. An example is at 5:2, where the NIV does not emend but offers a translation that is, in my view, so full of hypothesis that it has little to commend it.

[18] Cf. M. J. Buss, "Mari Prophecy and Hosea," *JBL* 88 (1969): 338.

[19] W. G. E. Watson, "Reflexes of Akkadian Incantations in Hosea," *VT* 34 (1984): 242–47.

[20] In my view this is an implausible and unfruitful avenue for research into Hosea, but see Buss, "Comedy and Tragedy in Hosea," *Semeia* 32 (1984): 71–82.

[21] The pioneering work in this area is U. Cassuto, "The Prophet Hosea and the Books of the Pentateuch," in *Biblical and Oriental Studies* (Jerusalem: Magnes Press, 1973), 1:79–100.

within the traditions of Israel as he addressed the crises facing his generation.[22] In particular, the stories of Genesis and the exodus event dominate the Book of Hosea. To Genesis, for example, Hosea makes among others the following allusions.[23]

HOSEA TEXT	GENESIS REFERENCE
1:10	22:17, blessing on Abraham
2:18	1:20–25, creation of wild animals
4:3	1:20–25, creation of wild animals
6:7	3:6, sin of Adam
6:9	34:1–31, destruction of Shechem
9:6	47:29, burial in Egypt
9:14	49:25, blessings of the breasts and of the womb
11:8	14:2 (and Gen 19), destruction of cities of the plain
12:2–5	25:19–35:15, story of Jacob
12:12–13	30:25–31:16, Jacob's sheep
13:15	41:2,18, pharaoh's dream

Examples of passing references to the exodus are at 7:13; 8:4–6; 9:10; 10:9–10; 11:1–4; 12:9–10; 13:4–6. Examples of allusions to other biblical texts could easily be multiplied. For example, Hos 2:9–10 alludes to the curses of Deuteronomy 28; and Hos 4:2 all but cites the Decalogue. Hosea 9:9 looks back to the bizarre history of Judges 19–21. Most significantly, the foundational metaphor of Hosea, Israel as an adulterous wife, is founded upon the Pentateuchal depiction of apostasy as whoredom.[24]

In short, Hosea's critique of his generation is founded entirely upon the Pentateuch. Against this evidence it is difficult to resist the implication that the Pentateuch (including supposed P texts) preexisted the Book of Hosea. For our

---

[22] Cf. W. Brueggemann, *Tradition for Crisis: A Study in Hosea* (Richmond: John Knox, 1968).

[23] On first reading it may not be self-evident that all the Hosean texts mentioned here allude to texts in Genesis, but the links between the Hosean and Genesis passages are described in the commentary on the specific verses.

[24] See Exod 34:11–16; Lev 17:7; 20:4–6; Deut 31:16; Judg 2:16–17; and R. C. Ortlund, Jr., *Whoredom: God's Unfaithful Wife in Biblical Theology* (Grand Rapids: Eerdmans, 1996), 25–45.

purposes, however, it is important to recognize that the interpretation of Hosea is impossible without reckoning with how he used the Torah as his canon.

(2) The Style and Imagery of Hosea

Hosea uses striking images. He can announce that Israel's love is like a morning mist: it quickly disappears in the heat of the day (6:4). He can portray Ephraim as a senseless bird fluttering between Egypt and Assyria in search of a place of safety and wandering far from God (7:11). He can also describe Ephraim as a diseased, dried-up plant that bears no good fruit (9:16), a metaphor that condemns the Baal cult for failure to provide fertility in terms of both good harvests and strong children. Sometimes Hosea's imagery turns on a Hebrew wordplay.[25]

Yahweh comes to the reader in many guises in Hosea; some of them are conventional,[26] but others definitely are not. Indeed, some metaphors for God are astonishing to the point of seeming irreverence. In addition to the traditional husband (2:2), father (11:1), and physician (14:4) images, Yahweh is also a fowler (7:12[27]), a lion or leopard (13:7), a bear (13:8), dew (14:5), a green tree (14:8), and even maggots or gangrene (5:12[28]). Employment of such language to describe God, as harsh as it is surprising, served to jolt and possibly awaken his jaded audience.

Hosea also turns his images in unexpected directions. In 7:4–7 the nation is likened to a hot oven, with the meaning that Israel is hot with debauchery and intrigue. In 7:8, however, instead of being the oven that produces the heat, Israel is dough in the oven and is sure to be burned.

Hosea brings penetrating pathos to his message through the use of rhetorical questions. A particularly strong example is 11:8: "How can I give you up, Ephraim? How can I hand you over, Israel? How can I treat you like Admah? How can I make you like Zeboiim? My heart is changed within me; all my compassion is aroused." Through the anthropomorphism of God seeming to be at wit's end about his people's stubborn sinfulness, Hosea transforms the abstraction of divine compassion into vivid reality. (See also 6:4 and 8:5.)[29]

---

[25] In 8:9 the image of Ephraim as a wild donkey is based on a wordplay with פֶּרֶא and אֶפְרָיִם. In 9:16 the prophet states that Ephraim (אֶפְרַיִם) yields no fruit (פֶּרִי). For further examples see P. A. Kruger, "Prophetic Imagery: On Metaphors and Similes in the Book of Hosea," *JNSL* 14 (1988): 143–51.

[26] For a sustained attempt to describe the conventional ways in which Hosea presents God (as Judge, King, Savior, etc.), see G. Östborn, *Yahweh and Baal* (Lund: C. W. K. Gleerup, 1956).

[27] For further discussion of this metaphor, see P. A. Kruger, "The Divine Net in Hosea 7:12," *ETL* 68 (1992): 132–36.

[28] See commentary.

[29] On the other hand, these questions do not have the significance that J. G. Janzen ascribes to them ("Metaphor and Reality in Hosea 11," *Semeia* 24 [1982]: 7–44). Janzen is operating in the framework of process theology and sees here evidence of existential development in God.

Hosea 11:8 also illustrates another rhetorical tendency of Hosea; he is at times very obscure, and one must conclude that this obscurity is often deliberate. It is extraordinary that in 11:8 Hosea, alone among the prophets, refers to the destruction of the cities of the plain not by mention of Sodom and Gomorrah but with a reference to Admah and Zeboiim . These cities are not even mentioned in Genesis 19, although they are linked to Sodom in Gen 14:2. One can hardly escape the sense that the prophet has intentionally referred to Genesis 19 in an obscure manner. Elsewhere the text makes use of riddles (e.g., 12:11), and the language is frequently ambiguous. From the peculiar chronology at 1:1, to the partially told and heavily veiled account of Hosea's marriage, to the final notice in 14:9, Hosea is a book that places high demands on the reader.

At times the sayings seem self-contradictory. In 13:14–16, for example, the text promises that God will redeem Israel and then abruptly declares that he will have no compassion on the nation and that their children will be slain and their pregnant mothers ripped open. The prophet forces the reader to assimilate each short declaration in sequence, without transitions, so that he jars the reader with these paradoxical pronouncements. Rather than distill his message down to a logically consistent whole, he confronts the reader with diverse truths presented in a form that is as stark and unqualified as possible. It is a rhetorical strategy—a strategy similar to that found in Wisdom Literature—that forces the reader to reckon with the full impact of every word.

A final difficulty in interpreting Hosea is his tendency to use pithy declarations rather than longer speeches. Large-scale rhetorical structure is not as obvious in Hosea as in some other prophetic books. Nevertheless, Hosea is not without structure.

5. The Structure of Hosea

(1) A Survey of Analyses of the Structure of Hosea

The analysis of the structure of Hosea seems to be one of the great pitfalls of Old Testament study. It has produced little unity or consensus, and the various proposals have little in common besides noting that there is an apparent break between 3:5 and 4:1. We will not attempt an exhaustive discussion of the proposals regarding the structure of Hosea[30] but will describe a few representative positions.

---

[30] For additional proposals and discussion, see G. R. Driver, *An Introduction to the Literature of the Old Testament* (Gloucester, Mass.: Peter Smith, 1972), 302–4; G. V. Smith, *The Prophets as Preachers: An Introduction to the Hebrew Prophets* (Nashville: Broadman, 1994), 75; Schmidt, *Introduction,* 202–3; R. K. Harrison, *Introduction to the Old Testament* (Grand Rapids: Eerdmans, 1969), 859; G. Morris, *Prophecy, Poetry, and Hosea,* JSOTSup 219 (1996): 103–31; D. B. Wyrtzen, "The Theological Center of Hosea," *BSac* 141 (1984): 315–29.

W. R. Harper.   Writing for the *International Critical Commentary* (1936), Harper represents the older liberal school that felt free both to excise verses and to rearrange the text according to the scholar's whims. Thus, for example, in the Hebrew text of Hosea 1–3, Harper treats 1:1,7; 2:1–3,4b,6,8–9,12,16–17,18,20–25; 3:5 as secondary additions. He considers the original text to have been (in this order) 1:2–6,8–9; 3:1–4; 2:1–7,10–14,15,19.[31] Few scholars today are willing to follow such fanciful arrogance. We need give no refutation here except to note that no evidence except for the scholar's personal aesthetic judgments supports such radical reconstructive surgery on the text. The outcome of such procedures is not a commentary on the Book of Hosea but a commentary on an artificial book newly created by the scholar's scissors and paste. For us the warning is to be careful about reshaping the book in order to support our theories of how it should read.

M. J. Buss.   M. J. Buss has developed an analysis of the structure of Hosea based on the criteria of the repetition of catchwords and a common formal pattern. Like most interpreters he sees a major division in the book between chaps. 1–3 and 4–14. He says that there are twenty-two oracles in Hosea, the first three being in chaps. 1–3 and the rest in the remainder of the book. He argues that the prophetic oracles of chaps. 4–14 are collected in a series of five "cycles." Each of the cycles works around central concepts or catchwords. The cycles are: "Cult Ruin" (4:1–5:7, catchword = "whoredom"), "The disorder of Politics and Society" (5:8–8:10, catchwords = "kings" and "princes"), "Religious Chaos" (8:11–9:9, catchwords = "sacrifices" and "return to Egypt"), "Israel's Sin in History" (9:10–11:11, catchwords = "fruit" and "hill"), and "The Overthrow of Sacred Traditions" (12:1–14:10, catchwords = "Egypt," "Assyria," and "Yahweh your God"). Each cycle contains several of the aforementioned twenty-two prophetic oracles (e.g., the oracles of "Cult Ruin" are 4:1–11a; 4:11b–14; 4:15–19; and 5:1–7). Words related to the catchword concept appear throughout a cycle. For example, "Religious Chaos" has such words as "sacrifice," "altar," "sin offering," "Egypt," and "prophet" scattered throughout (e.g., 8:11,13; 9:3,4,6,7). In regard to the smaller units, the individual prophetic oracles, Buss asserts that each one begins with a call in the second person or an announcement of a day of judgment or historical reference. He also says that they end with a word either of disaster or of hope.[32]

Buss has used form-critical methods to analyze Hosea, and his analysis has several weaknesses. First of all, on reading the texts, it is not at all clear that the catchwords he has chosen actually have that function in the texts. The passages in question do not especially focus on the themes he has attached to them, and

---

[31] Harper, *Amos and Hosea,* clx.

[32] Buss, *The Prophetic Word of Hosea: A Morphological Study,* BZAW 111 (Berlin: Verlag Alfred Töpelmann, 1969), 6–37. Buss also notes other catchwords in the texts.

he has not adequately defended his text boundaries. Also the catchwords are not all confined to the designated texts. That is, while it is true that words such as "prince" or "king" appear in what he calls "The disorder of Politics and Society" (5:8–8:10), these words also appear frequently enough elsewhere in Hosea.[33] This is of course not fatal to his theory—it is not fair to claim that none of the catchwords should appear in any other texts. The real point, however, is that there is no clear reason to suppose that these words have special significance in one part of the book over against the remainder of the book. They are scattered throughout the text. Simply put, this catchword analysis is arbitrary and insufficient to sustain a thesis regarding the book's structure. Finally, his formal analysis of the prophetic oracle has too many variables to be helpful or persuasive. That is, Buss allows for such a variety of beginnings and endings to oracles that one cannot feel confident that he has adequately established his demarcation of text boundaries. The book contains numerous second-person addresses, historical references, and statements of judgment. It is not clear why some of these are marked as the starting points for new oracles while others are not.[34] For that matter, it is equally unclear why these begin oracles, but statements of doom or hope end them. One could just as well begin an oracle with a statement of doom and then move to a second-person address (e.g., to an appeal to repent).

H. W. Wolff. H. W. Wolff, in his magisterial Hosea commentary, divides the book into three "transmission complexes" (1–3; 4–11; 12–14). The three are similar in that each moves from accusation to threats of punishment and then promises of salvation. Each transmission complex is made up of individual units of text ("kerygmatic units") that can be classified form critically (e.g., the *memorabile,* the "messenger speech," the "historico-theological accusation," the "prophetic summons," the "penitential prayer"). In my view this analysis is of limited value. Although the prophets (including Hosea) generally follow the pattern of accusation—punishment—salvation, Wolff's analysis does not do justice to the complexity of Hosea. Promises of salvation are interwoven with threats of judgment in the text, and they can occur at any point (not just at the end of units). Expressions of hope for a glorious future occur as early as 1:7,10–11, and 6:1–3 (the last text found in the middle of the second "transmission complex"). Hosea 11, on the other hand, is not uniformly a promise of salvation but mingles together accusations, threats, and statements of mercy; it is not necessarily the end of a major "transmission complex." The whole form-critical exercise, moreover, is virtually fruitless in Hosea. Classi-

---

[33] E.g., שַׂר ("prince") is found in the Hb. text at 3:4; 9:15; 13:10. מֶלֶךְ ("king") occurs in 1:1; 3:4,5; 10:3,6,7,15; 11:5; 13:10,11.

[34] E.g., Buss treats 10:9–15 as a single oracle, but one could just as easily say that 10:9–10 meets his criteria since it begins with a historical reference and ends with a statement of disaster. Similarly, 10:12–15 begins with a second-person address and ends with a statement of doom.

fying texts as "messenger speeches" or "historico-theological accusations" has done little to explain the meaning of the various units or even to demarcate text boundaries.

G. Yee.   G. Yee has created a complex redaction history of Hosea that reminds one of the older source criticism of Harper. She believes the book came together in four stages: the Hosean tradition (H) being the earliest level of material; the Collector (C), who created the first written edition of the Hosean material and reshaped some of the material by adding a number of verses in chaps. 1 and 2; the first redactor (R1), a Judean of the Josianic period who, like the Deuteronomistic Historian, was especially critical of the shrines of Jeroboam I; and finally, the second redactor (R2), who gave the book its present shape. To get a sense of the complexity of her model, one need only look at how she divides chaps. 1–3. The texts are (following Hb. versification): H = 2:4aA; 2:4b–5; 2:7b; 2:12. C = 1:2–4; 1:6abA; 1:8–9; 2:4aB; 2:6–7a; 2:18aBb; 2:21–22a. R1 = 2:10a; 2:11; 2:13–15a. R2 = 1:1; 1:5; 1:6bB–7; 2:1–3; 2:8–9; 2:10b; 2:15b–18aA; 2:19–20; 2:22b–25; 3:1–5. Like Wolff, Yee divides the text into three parts, but she sees a chiastic structure: 1–3, following the wife/Israel motif; 4–11, following the youth/Israel motif; and 12–14, again following the wife/Israel motif.[35]

Yee's redaction history is impossibly complex and detailed. Evidence is far too scanty to sustain her model. The assignment of individual verses and fragments from throughout the book to the four stages Yee creates requires an omniscience that few scholars today are willing to claim. It is difficult, in fact, to take proposals like this seriously anymore. Furthermore, her division of the final product into three parts is not persuasive. Chapters 12–14, although they do at a few points return to the motif of wife and mother, are not dominated by this imagery. Chapters 4–11, moreover, are not dominated by the youth motif, although it is present.

F. I. Andersen and D. N. Freedman.   Andersen and Freedman, in their exhaustive Hosea commentary, divide the text into four sections: (1) 1:1–3:5, "Hosea's Marriage"; (2) 4:1–7:16, "The State of the Nation"; (3) 8:1–11:11, "The Spiritual History of Israel"; (4) 12:1–14:10, "Retrospect and Prospect." Each major section is then further subdivided into smaller texts.[36] In addition, their commentary distinctively uses syllable counting as a guide to the meter of Hosea's poetry. Few scholars have followed this procedure, and probably it is fair to say that most would not regard it as the key that opens the door to the mysterious structure of this book. Beyond that, the macrostructural analysis of Andersen and Freedman is not particularly remarkable in comparison to those of McComiskey, Hubbard, and others. In addition, the headings "The State of

---

[35] G. Yee, *Composition and Tradition in the Book of Hosea* (Atlanta: Scholars Press, 1985).
[36] Andersen and Freedman, *Hosea*, xii–xiii.

the Nation," "The Spiritual History of Israel," and "Retrospect and Prospect" seem arbitrary. The book does not neatly divide into sections describing these themes; allusions to Israel's spiritual history, for example, occur throughout the book.

T. E. McComiskey, J. L. Mays, D. A. Hubbard, and J. M. Ward.   Each of these four scholars has produced a commentary on Hosea, and each has given an outline of the book.[37] The four outlines these scholars constructed are by no means in agreement. Rather, if anything, they illustrate well the difficulty of finding the structure of Hosea. McComiskey divides Hosea into seventeen discreet units, most of these being further subdivided into smaller blocks of text. Mays has no hierarchical structure at all; he simply divides Hosea into thirty-seven units of text. Of the four commentaries under discussion here, Hubbard's is the most hierarchical. He divides the text into three major sections (1–3; 4–11; and 12–14), each of which is further divided into subsections and sub-subsections. Ward also divides the book into three major units (1–3; 4–10; and 11–14), each divided into subsections that for the most part simply follow the chapter divisions of the English Bible. To be sure, occasionally all of these commentaries are in agreement about the boundaries of a given text unit, but often they are not. Looking at all of them together, one has little reason to feel reassured about any specific proposal regarding the outline of Hosea.

(2) A New Proposal Regarding the Structure of Hosea

If any analysis of Hosea's structure is to command the attention of readers, that analysis must demonstrate that some strategy governs the book. Simply to propose boundaries for individual units of text is fairly meaningless if the final result is a miscellany of poems, sermons, and sayings. It is of course possible that the book has no strategy and that in fact sayings were inserted at random. But there are too many indications of care, precision, and artistry in this book for me to find this solution satisfactory. Analyses that are nothing more than generalizations of the most sweeping kind, moreover, are also of limited value (e.g., that Hosea begins with judgment and ends with a promise of salvation).

Hosea's rhetorical strategy may be derived from chaps. 1–3. The observation that Hosea 1–3 is programmatic for the whole book should startle no one. But in what sense is it programmatic? Several observations are in order. First, the account of Hosea 1 is dominated by the births of three children, and these children are symbols of Israel's future for both woe and weal. Second, Hosea describes his domestic life in two parts, the first being in the third person

---

[37] T. E. McComiskey, *The Minor Prophets,* 3 vols., ed. T. E. McComiskey (Grand Rapids: Baker, 1992), 4–6; Mays, *Hosea,* v–vi; D. A. Hubbard, *Hosea,* TOTC (Downers Grove: InterVarsity, 1989), 49–50; J. M. Ward, *Hosea: A Theological Commentary* (New York: Harper & Row, 1966), vii–viii.

(chap. 1) and the second being in the first person (chap. 3). Third, the text portrays Israel as an adulterous woman who must undergo exile and deprivation but who will eventually experience restoration (chap. 2).

The shape of chaps. 1–3 demands attention. Chapter 1, with its account of the births of the three children, is fairly straightforward. Chapter 3, moreover, despite extensive debate over the meaning of these five verses, is structurally fairly simple. What is more confusing is chap. 2, which seems to interrupt the account of Hosea's personal life with a prophetic sermon. This, however, misreads the text. In chap. 1 the accounts of the births of the three children become progressively longer. The account of first child, Jezreel, simply contains a mention of his birth and naming with an explanation of how his name represents the future punishment of Israel (1:3b–5). The story of the birth of Lo-Ruhamah includes the account of her birth, naming, and an explanation of how her name represents Israel's doom; but it adds a reversal, a promise that God would one day restore Israel to its honored place (1:6–7). The account of Lo-Ammi's birth is still longer. It includes all that was in Lo-Ruhamah's birth account (birth, naming, significance of name as a sign of judgment, and reversal; 1:8–11), but it presses on to give a much more complete account of how Hosea's family represents Israel. The first reversal in the Lo-Ammi text (1:10–11) is answered by a second, more detailed statement of restoration and reversal of judgment in 2:14–23. Between these two reversals stand a warning of punishment (2:2–4) and a prediction of a new exile as a redemptive punishment (2:6–13); 2:1 and 5 are transitional verses. Thus the Lo-Ammi oracle leads into a chiasmus:

A Restoration (1:10–11)
  B Punishment (2:2–4)
  B′ Punishment (2:6–13)
A′ Restoration (2:14–23).

This leads to the conclusion that chap. 2 is not an interruption but is the completion of the Lo-Ammi oracle. Drawing together all the symbolism of Hosea's family, it asserts that the adulterous nation can be made faithful again and that Lo-Ammi, "not my people," can again be made into the people of God. Chapter 3 then returns to Hosea's domestic life to demonstrate in a living parable how Israel can be restored.

When we turn to chaps. 4–14, we discover that these same features are subtly shaping chaps. 4–14 as well. The most noteworthy feature of chaps. 4–7 is the astonishing frequency of the number three.[38] The first general accusation is threefold (4:1). The book then indicts three specific groups of people (religious leadership, 4:4–10; common people, 12–13a; and women, 13b–14). In 4:14–5:15, the text gives three extended warnings to Israel and Judah, and 6:1–3 fol-

---

[38] For a detailed defense of the threefold patterns in the texts cited here, see commentary.

lows this with a threefold call to repent. In 5:1 the text addresses three groups: the priests, the house of Israel, and the house of the king; and in 5:1–2 one reads of traps at Mizpah, Tabor, and Shittim.[39] In 5:8 signals ring out at three places: Gibeah, Ramah, and Beth Aven. Yahweh then laments Israel's incapacity to repent and in particular cites the sins at Adam, Gilead, and Shechem (6:7–9) and the unforgiven status of Israel, Ephraim, and Samaria (7:1). In a book that bears strong resemblance to wisdom (see 14:9), focus on the number three cannot be considered accidental. The most reasonable explanation is that this pattern reflects the number of Hosea's children—three. Indeed, as this commentary seeks to demonstrate, 4:1–5:15 deliberately builds upon the three oracles of Jezreel, Lo-Ruhamah, and Lo-Ammi. Thus, 4:1–7:16 is shaped by the symbolism of Hosea's three children, and the text moves from a series of accusations and predictions of woe to a call to repent (6:1–3). It ends, however, in frustration, with Yahweh's recognition that this people is too deep in sin to repent (6:4–7:16).

In 8:1–14:8, however, a different motif shapes the text. Here, instead of the heavy focus on the number three, Yahweh and the prophet distinctly make antiphonal proclamations. That is, the text moves back and forth between first person (Yahweh speaking) and third person (Hosea speaking). In many cases, Hosea will pick up a theme or idea introduced by Yahweh and carry it further. Although it is not hard to find passages in the prophets where first person and third person proclamations are mixed together—sometimes seemingly at random—the movement between Yahweh as speaker and Hosea as speaker is too systematic and regular in this part of the book to be meaningless or accidental (for details, see outline on p. 37). The explanation for this phenomenon seems to be that it echoes the pattern established in chaps. 1–3, in the account of Hosea's marriage: the first text is third person (1:2ff.) and the second is first person (3:1–5).

When this pattern is recognized, the significance of the structure almost explains the whole book: *Hosea's experience with the promiscuous Gomer has legitimated his call to be Yahweh's prophet.* This is not to say that the whole purpose of Hosea is to defend the legitmacy of Hosea's claim to the prophetic office. Still, what many would consider a disqualification for the office—a prophet whose own wife was morally out of control—serves in this case as his *credentials.* This is because Yahweh and Hosea have shared the same experience—that of marriage to an unfaithful spouse. Thus the book tells the stories of Hosea's and Yahweh's marriages in both first and third person texts—each "husband" speaks for himself and has the other speak in his behalf. It is for this reason, moreover, that historical retrospective frequently surfaces in these chapters (e.g., 9:15; 10:9; 11:1–4; 12:3–4; 12:12–13:1). *Like 1–3, these chap-*

---

[39] Emended text.

ters are story driven, and each recounts the history of a marriage from the perspectives of both the husband and an observer.

The antiphonal proclamations come in three distinct series. First, at 8:1–10:15, the book assails the false security and false prosperity of Israel. The nation relies upon her "lovers," being foreign nations and foreign gods, as well as upon her own military might. Images of fertility (e.g., that Israel is a wild vine, 10:1) also emerge here. In a manner reminiscent of 2:2–7, these passages promise that Israel will lose everything. Their allies, their gods, and their fertility will fail.

The second series is at 11:1–13:16. Chapter 11 is often regarded as the end of a series of texts because it includes statements of future restoration, and scholars assume that the prophets followed a scheme of sin—punishment—restoration. In Hosea, however, proleptic promises of restoration appear very early (e.g., 1:7). Furthermore, careful reading of chap. 11 reveals that it is not a uniform prophecy of healing; to the contrary, the dominant motif is the vexation of God over what to do about Israel. God is here a perplexed parent at wit's end, vacillating between leniency and severity toward a wicked son. Hosea, in his proclamations, responds to Yahweh's torment over his son with two reflections on the story of Jacob as set over against the story of the children of Israel (12:1–8; 12:12–13:3). By the end of this series, Yahweh has determined and Hosea has affirmed that Israel must be severely punished.

The third and final series is a call to repentance and grace, first by the prophet and then by Yahweh (14:1–8). This corresponds to the appeal to repent in 6:1–3; but two differences are that this appeal is expanded to eight verses and that it lacks the despairing commentary of 6:4–7:16, in which Yahweh declares that Israel will not repent. Like many prophets, Hosea ends in hope.

The movement of the book is thus: first, linkage is established between Yahweh and his prophet in the account of the marriage to Gomer, and the major themes of apostasy, judgment, and restoration are developed (1–3). Second, using the three children of Hosea to shape the text, the book presents a series of accusations dominated by the number three, but ends this section with a threefold call to repent; nevertheless, it asserts that at this stage repentance is impossible (4–7). Third, in three series of antiphonal proclamations, Hosea presents a distressed Yahweh torn over what to do with his people but finally resolves upon exile as the solution; this is followed by a final, more optimistic, call to repent (8–14). In outline form, the structure of the book is as follows:

The Volume of Gomer and Her Children (1:1–3:5)
    Title (1:1)
        I. Hosea's Three Children (1:2–2:23)
            1. The Command to Marry Gomer (1:2–3a)
            2. Naming the Three Children (1:3b–2:23)

(1) Jezreel (1:3b–5)
(2) Lo-Ruhamah (1:6–7)
(3) Lo-Ammi [leads into chiastic structure] (1:8–2:23)
  II. Gomer's Restoration (3:1–5)
    1. Yahweh's Command (3:1)
    2. Hosea's Response (3:2–3)
    3. Explanation: Punishment and Reversal (3:4–5)
The Volume of Accusation and Redemption (4:1–14:8)
  III. The Threefold Complaints (4:1–7:16)
    1. Accusation (4:1–5:15)
      (1) Jezreel: General Complaint (4:1–3)
      (2) Lo-Ammi: The Three Guilty Groups (4:4–14)
      (3) Lo-Ruhamah: Three Warnings for Israel and Judah
        (4:15–5:15)
    2. Exhortation for Future Grace (6:1–7:16)
      (1) The Prophet's Threefold Call to Repent (6:1–3)
      (2) Yahweh's Sorrow [Inclusio Pattern with Parallelism]
        (6:4–7:16)
  IV. Antiphonal Proclamations by Yahweh and His Prophet (8:1–14:8)
    1. First Series: False Security and False Prosperity
      (8:1–10:15)
      (1) Opening Divine Complaint: False Security of Israel
        (8:1–14)
      (2) Opening Prophetic Complaint: The Barren Prostitute
        (9:1–9)
      (3) Divine Complaint: Barrenness Instead of Fruit (9:10–17)
      (4) Prophetic Complaint: The Vine and the Bull (10:1–8)
      (5) Divine Complaint: Military Arrogance (10:9–15)
    2. Second Series: Judgment on Apostate Israel (11:1–13:16)
      (1) Divine Complaint: Divine Vexation over Apostate Israel
        (11:1–12) [A]
      (2) Prophetic Complaint: Jacob and His Heirs (12:1–8) [B]
      (3) Divine Complaint: Divine Resolve over Apostate Israel
        (12:9–11) [A′]
      (4) Prophetic Complaint: Jacob and His Heirs
        (12:12–13:3) [B′]
      (5) Divine Complaint and Decision (13:4–14) [C]
      (6) Prophetic Announcement of Judgment (13:15–16) [C′]
    3. Third Series: Exhortation for Future Grace (14:1–8)
      (1) The Prophet's Call to Repent (14:1–3)
      (2) Yahweh's Promise (14:4–8)
  V. Wisdom Postscript: The Riddle of Hosea (14:9)

We should note that a hierarchical outline, as a device of Western interpretation, is by nature somewhat alien to an Old Testament text. Also there are many catchwords and recurrent themes that serve as crosslinks to hold Hosea together, although they do not necessarily have a macrostructural function. Nevertheless, I believe that the above outline is a fair representation of the inner logic of Hosea.

6. The Message of Hosea

It is a truism to say that Hosea presents the apostasy of Israel under the metaphor of an unfaithful wife. But this analysis only tells half of the story. Hosea did not just have a wife; he also had three children who were themselves signs and symbols to Israel. It is reasonable to suppose that the wife and the three children do not all simply represent "Israel," as though there were no difference between mother and children. But wherein lies the distinction? As this commentary will try to demonstrate, Israel the wayward wife is the leadership, institutions, and culture of Israel. The children are the ordinary men and women who are trained and nurtured in that culture.[40] Behind these two metaphors lies a story.

Mother Israel is the shrines and sacrifices, the sacred blessings, the royal symbols and trappings, the armies, and the official teachings that are passed from generation to generation. Especially, Mother Israel is the priests and kings and other members of the ruling class who shape, direct, and exploit the people. Mother Israel is that which gives the people their identity. She is the institution that forms every Israelite generation.

The children, again, are the common people. They are the farmers who want good crops, the mothers who want many children, and the common folk who want security and divine blessing. But something has gone terribly wrong. Mother Israel has abandoned Yahweh, her husband. She has embraced a new lover, Baal, because he claims to be able to enrich her with jewels and clothe her in the finest materials. She has also pursued other lovers—nations who can supposedly protect her and enrich her with trade. So enticed, Mother Israel has taught her children to serve Baal at the shrines. In doing this, she does not imagine that she has broken her marriage vows but supposes that she is faithful to the real meaning of those vows. Looking at the bulls of the shrines, she declares, "These are your gods, who brought you out of Egypt!" (cf. Exod 32:4).

The children have followed their mother. Superstitious and fearful while at the same time captivated by that alluring benefit of Baalism, the cult prostitute, they know nothing of their father, Yahweh. Indeed, one cannot even say that

---

[40] To be sure, not all of Hosea is governed by the metaphor of the mother and her children. Sometimes the whole nation is portrayed as a single entity, e.g., as Yahweh's son (Hos 11:1).

Yahweh is their father. They are a lost generation, the children of Baal. They possess none of the three basic qualities that should mark the chosen people: integrity, compassion, and the knowledge of God. Their only hope of salvation is to turn from Mother Israel and go back to the one real Father, Yahweh. That is, to be true children of God they would have to abandon Mother Israel, for she is not his wife, and her children are Lo-Ammi, "Not-my-people." But this they cannot do. She has too well instructed them in her ways, and they belong to Baal. What shall Yahweh do with a people who can neither repent, nor even understand the need for it, nor recognize that Baal is a lie, nor divorce themselves from their mother and her ways? He must strip Mother Israel of all she has. That is, the institutions of Israel must die. The shrines must burn, the crops must fail, the kings and army must perish, the priests and princes must fall into disgrace, and Mother Israel and her children must once again wander in the wilderness. When this happens, at last, they will see both the truth and the lies for what they are and return to Yahweh, Husband and Father.

There is, of course, a great deal more one could say about the theology of Hosea. One could speak of the future kingdom under David, or of the nature of true repentance, or of the theology of history that the book develops. Still, the story gives the real message of Hosea. It is also the message of the other Old Testament prophets and, in its essence, the message of Jesus, another prophet who lamented over a lost generation of Jews whose way had been perverted by Mother Israel. Knowing that the nature of human institutions and of humans themselves has changed very little over the last three millennia, we can only hope that we will heed Hosea and apply his message to Mother Church. *Ecclesia reformata semper reformanda.*[41]

---

[41] "The reformed church always needs to be reformed."

TITLE (1:1)
THE VOLUME OF GOMER AND HER CHILDREN
I. HOSEA'S THREE CHILDREN (1:2–2:23)
    1. The Command to Marry Gomer (1:2–3a)
    2. Naming the Three Children (1:3b–23)
        (1) Jezreel (1:3b–5)
            Birth (1:3b)
            Name and Explanation of Punishment (1:4–5)
        (2) Lo-Ruhamah (1:6–7)
            Birth (1:6a)
            Name and Explanation of Punishment (1:6b)
            Reversal (1:6c–7)
        (3) Lo-Ammi (1:8–2:23)
            Birth (1:8)
            Name and Explanation of Punishment (1:9)
            Reversal (1:10–11) **[A]**
            Transitional Verse (2:1)
            Warning of Judgment (2:2–4) **[B]**
            Second Transitional Verse (2:5)
            Redemptive Punishment (2:6–13) **[B′]**
            Prophecy of Restoration: Reversal of Adultery
               (2:14–23) **[A′]**

TITLE (1:1)

Hosea lived a pain-filled life and preached in a troubled time. This may seem to be something of a cliché and hardly worth pointing out for an Israelite prophet; they *all* lived through harrowing days and soul-testing controversies.[1] Nevertheless, Hosea may have special claim to this unenviable distinction. His family life uniquely qualified him for the title of suffering prophet. In addition to that, however, was the sorrow he felt as a result of the political upheaval and disaster he saw in his lifetime (see introduction on the history of this period).

---

[1] Isaiah lived through the Assyrian invasion of Judah, Jeremiah saw the fall of Jerusalem, Ezekiel was taken to exile, etc.

¹**The word of the LORD that came to Hosea son of Beeri during the reigns of Uzziah, Jotham, Ahaz and Hezekiah, kings of Judah, and during the reign of Jeroboam son of Jehoash king of Israel:**

The strange thing about the chronology that v. 1 provides is that the reigns of the kings do not fully overlap. That is, the dates for the reign of Jeroboam II of Israel are approximately 793–753 B.C. This does overlap with the first king of Judah mentioned, Uzziah (792–740 B.C.). However, the verse also mentions three subsequent kings of Judah (Jotham, Ahaz, and Hezekiah) whose reigns go from approximately 750[2] to 686 B.C. without any mention of the kings of Israel that reigned at the same time (Zechariah, Shallum, Menahem, Pekahiah, Pekah, and Hoshea, going from 753 to 722 B.C.).[3] This might not be surprising if Hosea had been a prophet to the kingdom of Judah, but his message was for the Northern Kingdom.

At the very outset of this disorienting book, therefore, we find ourselves confronting a riddle. Why did Hosea neglect to mention the rest of the kings of Israel? The reason appears to be twofold. First, he regarded Jeroboam II as the last king of Israel with any shred of legitimacy. Those after him were a pack of assassins and ambitious climbers who had no right to the title "king." Hosea's assessment of the kings of Israel appears in texts like 7:1–7. Second, he hoped for better things from Judah. At times he criticized the south as heavily as the north (5:5,12), but he also prayed that they not follow Israel's lead (4:15). Most importantly, he looked for salvation and reunification in the line of David (3:5).

The superscript of the book is therefore extraordinary. It has given us in cryptic form something of the theology of the prophet. It has also warned us that the interpretive task ahead will not be easy.[4]

---

[2] Jotham was co-regent with Uzziah from 750 to 740 B.C.

[3] I have here followed the dates of E. R. Thiele, *The Mysterious Numbers of the Hebrew Kings,* rev. ed. (Grand Rapids: Zondervan, 1983), 217. Some scholars follow slightly different chronologies.

[4] The heading may also provide hints regarding the process of collecting and canonizing the four books of Amos, Hosea, Isaiah, and Micah. For an intriguing suggestion that works from the headings of these four books, see D. N. Freedman, "Headings in the Books of the Eighth Century Prophets," *AUSS* 25 (1987): 9–26. Freedman argues that the headings indicate the process of collecting these works began with Amos, during the reign of Uzziah, and concluded in Hezekiah's reign after Jerusalem was rescued from the army of Sennacherib.

──────── **I. HOSEA'S THREE CHILDREN (1:2–2:23)** ────────

Following the outline of Hosea described in the introduction, 1:1–3:5 constitutes the first major division of the book. On this point scholars are fairly unanimous. What is much less clear is the place of chap. 2, which appears to abandon the biographical details of chaps. 1 and 3 and to contain only prophecy concerning the nation. This misreads the text. Chapter 2 continues the Lo-Ammi oracle and is the climax of a progression Hosea has already begun. The oracle of Jezreel is very brief and is entirely negative; none of the judgments against Israel are reversed. The oracle of Lo-Ruhamah is longer and does contain a reversal. The oracle of Lo-Ammi is longer still and, after a brief introduction, develops the theology of judgment and reversal in a chiastic pattern. Through the whole, many catchwords link the thoughts of this oracle and the whole text together, until at last we have a reversal of all three judgments (i.e., of Jezreel, of Lo-Ruhamah, and of Lo-Ammi). The concluding text, 3:1–5, maintains the reversal-of-judgment pattern but reverts to much more concise language, and it makes no allusion to the three children.

The reversal of the Lo-Ammi judgment in 1:10–11 cannot be separated from the explanation of the name (1:9). Moreover, it cannot be separated from the material that follows because of the chiastic pattern of the text and because of the numerous catchwords that crisscross these passages (see commentary). The Lo-Ammi oracle is not, therefore, to be disconnected from chap. 2. Rather, it is the climactic judgment in which the Israelites not only suffer punishment but lose their status as the people of God. Yet it also includes the climactic reversal, in which Jezreel becomes a fruitful land, Lo-Ruhamah receives love, and Lo-Ammi becomes again the covenant nation. We thus have a single, unified text in two parts (1:2–2:23 and 3:1–5) rather than two biographical sections with a prophetic excursus sandwiched in between the two.

1. The Command to Marry Gomer (1:2–3a)

[2]When the LORD began to speak through Hosea, the LORD said to him, "Go, take to yourself an adulterous wife and children of unfaithfulness, because the land is guilty of the vilest adultery in departing from the LORD." [3]So he married Gomer daughter of Diblaim,

The book begins with its major interpretive problem. Why is a prophet of God commanded to marry an immoral woman? What can the story mean, and what really happened? Adultery is a major theological metaphor in this book. That being the case, how one answers these questions will shape not only how one interprets Hosea's life and ministry but one's analysis of the prophecy as well as.

The problem of interpreting chap. 1 is made more difficult by the even more obscure chap. 3, which describes Hosea's relationship to an unnamed immoral woman. Is this woman Gomer or someone else? Although there is risk of oversimplification, there are eight major interpretations of these texts:

1. Chapters 1–3 are a parable or allegory with no historical basis. Or the whole story is a vision and has no relationship to Hosea's actual marriage and family life. The latter, that it is a vision, was the view of Ibn Ezra and of Calvin.[5] One could equally well claim that it was a parable that Hosea devised in order to illustrate his message, as though he had said, "Now suppose I had a wife—we'll call her Gomer—who did this to me ..." or the like. In this interpretation chaps. 1 and 3 are either variant versions of the same parable or two parts of one parable.[6]

2. Gomer was Hosea's real but faithful wife. Chapter 1 is only a metaphor of Israel's sin. In chap. 3 Hosea shows kindness to a wretched prostitute (not his wife) as a prophetic symbol of God's compassion on Israel, but this had nothing to do with his real married life.[7] This view is obviously similar to the first except that it regards Gomer and the prostitute of chap. 3 as historical people. The story of Gomer's infidelity, on the other hand, is regarded as a fabrication to make a point.[8]

3. Chapters 1 and 3 are historical but refer to two different women. Hosea first married the prostitute Gomer, at the beginning of his prophetic ministry, to illustrate Israel's sin against God.[9] Later in his ministry he married a second woman, also a prostitute, to illustrate God's compassion and the

---

[5] A. Lipshitz, *The Commentary of Rabbi Ibn Ezra on Hosea: Edited from Six Manuscripts and Translated with an Introduction and Notes* (New York: Sepher-Hermon, 1988), 19–21. Ibn Ezra at least does not sidestep. He plainly states that his reason for taking this view is that the literal reading is too offensive to be true. See also J. Calvin, *Commentaries on the Twelve Minor Prophets* (Grand Rapids: Baker, n.d.), 1:43–45.

[6] C. F. Keil takes the whole affair to be parabolic (he calls it an "internal event"). He argues that Gomer and the woman of chap. 3 cannot be one and the same and thus that, if taken literally, Hosea had to marry two prostitutes in succession, a notion that is too outlandish for anyone to accept (*Hosea* [Grand Rapids: Eerdmans, n.d.], 26–36). Of course, this argument only works if one is persuaded that the text requires two separate women and if one is as offended at the idea as Keil was.

[7] R. H. Pfeiffer, *Introduction to the Old Testament* (New York: Harper & Brothers, 1941), 567–70.

[8] A novel variant of this theory is the hypothesis of Y. Kaufmann, who imagines that Hosea, Gomer, and the children put on a theatrical performance for the benefit of the Israelites (*The Religion of Israel* [New York: Schocken, 1960], 370–71). He compares 1 Kgs 20:35–43; Isa 20:2; Jer 27:2. His analogies fail because all the texts speak of the prophets altering their appearance to portray some message. Neither Hosea nor Gomer are ever told to put on items (e.g., the jewelry of a prostitute) in order to act out roles. God commanded Hosea to do something (marry an immoral woman) and not to pretend to do something. By analogy Jeremiah at God's command actually remained unmarried (Jer 16:2); he did not pretend to be unmarried.

[9] See, e.g., D. Stuart, *Hosea–Jonah,* WBC (Dallas: Word, 1987), 64–65.

hope of salvation.[10] This interpretation is similar to the second except that it asserts that Gomer actually committed adultery against Hosea.

4.   God commanded Hosea to marry Gomer, who was already an immoral woman. He did so, and she gave him one son but soon returned to her old ways and bore two additional children, possibly of doubtful paternity (1:2–9). Hosea then separated from her or was abandoned by her (2:2a). She fell into poverty and disgrace and eventually into slavery. Hosea bought her out of slavery and restored her to the family (3:1–3).[11] This interpretation is like the third except that it treats Gomer and the unnamed immoral woman of chap. 3 as one and the same. It also interprets chaps. 1 and 3 sequentially. That is, the events of chap. 3 took place some time after the events of chap. 1.

5.   A variant interpretation of the fourth seeks to avoid the scandal of God commanding Hosea to marry a flagrantly immoral woman. It asserts that the reference to Gomer's immorality in 1:2 is proleptic,[12] or that when he married her she had "tendencies" to immorality but had not yet actually engaged in extramarital sex.[13] Alternatively, one may argue that Hosea did not deliberately marry a wanton woman but only retrospectively realized that his unhappy marriage was actually, in the providence of God, a portrayal of God's relationship to Israel.[14] This interpretation agrees with the fourth, that Hosea did actually marry Gomer, that she was an adulteress, that Gomer was also the woman of chap. 3, and that chaps. 1 and 3 should be read sequentially.

6.   Chapters 1 and 3 are historical and not parabolic, but they are variant accounts of the same event; no sequence is intended.[15] One could argue that Hosea was commanded to marry a prostitute (1:2), he purchased Gomer from a slave market (1:3; 3:1–3), and then had children by her before she returned to her immorality (1:3–9). This interpretation differs

---

[10] G. Fohrer, *Introduction to the Old Testament* (Nashville: Abingdon, 1961), 420–21.

[11] E.g., J. Limburg, *Hosea–Micah,* IBC (Atlanta: John Knox, 1988), 8–15.

[12] Cf. R. I. Vasholz attempts to defend this interpretation on the grounds that the text uses the "explicative *Waw*" ("Gomer—Chaste or Not?" *Presbyterion* 19 [1993]: 48–49). The argument is not cogent. See also J. H. Johansen, "The Prophet Hosea: His Marriage and Message," *JETS* 14 (1971): 179–84.

[13] Thus W. R. Harper, *Amos and Hosea,* ICC (Edinburgh: T & T Clark, 1936), 207.

[14] F. I. Andersen and D. N. Freedman, *Hosea,* AB (New York: Doubleday, 1980), 155–70. Cf. G. Archer, *A Survey of Old Testament Introduction* (Chicago: Moody, 1974), 323.

[15] Cf. R. Gordis, who takes Gomer to be a historical woman but defiled by virtue of her association with Israel (*HUCA* 25 [1954]: 9–35). He argues that chaps. 1 and 3 are doublet accounts of the same event. He believes that Gomer was not guilty of adultery. Rather, she was regarded as guilty of adultery by virtue of identification with the people of Israel. Gordis's argument for guilt by association is particularly weak, and his claim that עוֹד in 3:1 means "on the same theme" cannot stand. See also the discussion in C. H. Bullock, *An Introduction to the Old Testament Prophetic Books* (Chicago: Moody, 1986), 91.

from 4 and 5 in that they see a sequence of events from chap. 1 through chap. 3, whereas this regards chaps. 1 and 3 as giving two versions of one story.

7. Chapter 3 is from a later hand—that is, it is an interpolation—and should not be taken into account when reconstructing Hosea's life or interpreting chap. 1.[16] On this view one could still explain chap. 1 as allegory or history.

8. Gomer was truly Hosea's wife, but her sin was not literal adultery against Hosea but spiritual adultery against God. That is, she was an idol worshiper like the people to whom Hosea preached. Hence the account of her adultery was both allegorical, in that she was not a true adulteress, and historical, in that she was guilty of abandoning Yahweh.

Other variations are possible as well. In what follows we will give only a general argument in favor of one of these views and against the other seven. The exegesis that follows will examine in more detail specific issues in specific verses.

View 7 should be rejected out of hand; we have no grounds for treating chap. 3 as an interpolation or from a later date.[17] No manuscript evidence, from the Hebrew or the versions, supports its excision. The style of the chapter does not look remarkably different from the rest of Hosea, and at any rate the chapter is too short for a meaningful stylistic analysis. The whole idea seems to be little more than an easy way around the interpretive problems that chap. 3 poses.

Although it was a favorite of older interpreters, we should also reject the first option, that the whole account is a vision or parable. The obvious incentive to adopt this reading is to save the text from itself. Surely, some may think, Hosea could not have meant what he said. Unfortunately, there is not the slightest hint that the text is anything other than a straightforward account of what actually happened. Calvin argues that there is no reason it could not have been a vision,[18] but in making this argument he obscures the point entirely. The onus is on him to show that it was a vision; no one has to show that it was not, since the form is that of a simple narrative with no indication of its being parabolic or hypothetical. By itself chap. 3 is obscure, but chap. 1 is not.

One may argue that God could not have told Hosea to marry an immoral woman since Lev 21:14 prohibits the marriage of a priest to a prostitute, but nothing in Hosea indicates that he was a priest. The Leviticus text, moreover, demands that a priest marry a virgin; a priest could not even marry a widow. The ordinary Israelite was not subject to such requirements.

Furthermore, it is difficult to imagine Hosea's story having any impact on an

---

[16] E.g., F. S. North, "Solution of Hosea's Marital Problems by Critical Analysis," *JNES* 16 (1957): 128–30.

[17] See Harper, *Amos and Hosea*, cxliv.

[18] Calvin, *Twelve*, 1:43–45.

audience who knew that none of it was true. A parable can be pure fiction (e.g., the prodigal son), but if one creates fiction while purporting to give one's own life story, those who know the truth will reject the whole concoction with disdain. Also this text does not in any sense resemble the vision accounts of the prophets (e.g., Ezek 1; Isa 6; Amos 7:7–9). It also gives, in a matter-of-fact manner, too many specific details of Hosea's home life—the births of three children and the weaning of Lo-Ruhamah—for it to be read as a vision.

Surely it is not correct to say that Hosea and Gomer were a happily married couple and that Hosea made up the whole story of her adultery in order to make a point to his congregation (interpretation 2). Apart from the fact that the deed would have made him the cruelest of husbands, such a strategy would have failed entirely to have its intended rhetorical effect. He could not possibly have preached about how Israel's apostasy parallels his wife's adultery when everyone present would have known that Gomer had done none of it.[19] If anything, such behavior would have convinced the people that Hosea was a religious fanatic. "Here is a man so judgmental that he wrongly accuses his own wife of adultery! Why then," the Israelites could have asked themselves, "should we pay attention to him when he points an accusing finger at us?"[20] This interpretation is little more than an impossible halfway house between a historical reading and a parabolic reading.

Interpretation 8, that Gomer was guilty of idolatry but was not an adulteress, is clever but unlikely. Again the problem is that such preaching would have only confused his audience. "Even if Gomer has worshiped the Baals," they might have reasoned, "why does Hosea regard this as unfaithfulness against himself? Has he begun to think of himself as God?" A variant of this interpretation argues that Gomer and the children bore the taint of adultery by virtue of being members of a depraved society. But if such was sufficient reason for him to call her and the children a "woman of promiscuity" and "children of promiscuity," then could not the same be said of Hosea himself? In fact, there is no reason to suppose that the text means anything other than what the ordinary sense of the words "promiscuous woman" indicates. It is of course possible that Gomer became promiscuous as a result of involvement in the Baal cult,[21] but it is not credible that she was in the cult but was faithful to Hosea.

We should also reject interpretation 3, that Gomer and the woman of chap. 3 are two different women. Even though the Hebrew of 3:1 only calls her "a woman" and not "your wife,"[22] context implies that Gomer is meant. First of

---

[19] Cf. J. A. Soggin, *Introduction to the Old Testament* (Philadelphia: Westminster, 1976), 249.

[20] Note also that Deut 22:13–19 imposes penalties on a man who wrongly accuses his wife of adultery.

[21] Cf. Andersen and Freedman, *Hosea*, 69.

[22] Although I agree that Gomer is meant, the NIV is somewhat free with 3:1 in translating אִשָּׁה as "your wife." It only means "a woman." See commentary below.

all, she is the only immoral woman we know anything about in the book. It seems odd that Hosea, after speaking of Gomer as the paradigm of faithlessness, would suddenly refer to some other immoral woman without even mentioning her name. Also the word "again" implies continuity. A question here is whether "again" in 3:1 goes with "the LORD said" or with "go, love." If "the LORD said to me again, 'Go, love …'" is correct, it is possible (but not certain) that a second woman is meant. If the correct interpretation is "the LORD said, 'Go again and love a woman …'" then it is much more likely that he was to love Gomer again. In my view the former is preferable. Even so, as we will try to show, chap. 3, unlike chap. 1, does not concern the taking of a new wife but the recovery and correction of a wayward wife.[23]

For similar reasons interpretation 6 (that chap. 3 is a doublet of chap. 1) also fails. The word "again" in 3:1 especially undermines this position since it implies that the events of chap. 3 *follow* those of chap. 1. Thus one has to excise "again" as an editorial insertion to maintain this interpretation, and textual surgery is a fairly clear sign that the interpretation contradicts the sense of the text itself.[24] Furthermore, reading chap. 3 as the second half of the story rather than as a second account is congruent with the message of Hosea. If chap. 3 is merely a doublet, then Gomer simply disappears from the story after her adultery, and the story ends there. But if, as we will argue, Hosea sought her out and redeemed her, then her life story mirrors the message of sin, punishment, and redemption that is the essence of Hosea's prophecy. On the doublet reading of Hosea 3, the story of Gomer is in fact a poor analogy for the prophecy, since it implies that the result of Israel's sin will be irreconcilable and irrevocable divorce.

We are thus left with interpretations 4 and 5, which differ only in that 4 asserts that Gomer was already a promiscuous woman when Hosea married her, whereas 5 states that she was not yet immoral at the time of their marriage. The latter perhaps seems more attractive since it avoids having to explain why God would demand that his prophet marry an immoral woman—perhaps even a prostitute. On further investigation, however, interpretation 5 cannot stand.

First, the comfort that interpretation 5 gives is very cold. Would it really have been easier on Hosea to marry a woman that he knew was *going to* be promiscuous over against a woman who already was? If anything, the torment of this story seems worse. Furthermore, ᵓēšet zĕnûnîm ("an adulterous wife," 1:2) cannot be credibly translated "a woman with immoral tendencies." It is difficult to imagine how Hosea would have gone about seeking a woman who was still chaste but who had tendencies toward promiscuity, and the whole idea is if anything more offensive than just saying that he married a prostitute.

---

[23] See also Andersen and Freedman, *Hosea,* 293.

[24] Both the LXX and the Vg attest to the word.

On the other hand, the view that a brokenhearted Hosea saw the hand of God in his marriage to Gomer only *after* she had broken faith with him is even more troubling. It suggests that the divine call to marry Gomer may have been no more than the rationalization of a man trying to make sense of his shattered life. Most significantly, the text clearly states that first Hosea received a command to marry an immoral woman and then did so (1:2–3).

By process of elimination, we have arrived at interpretation 4, which asserts that Hosea, having been commanded to marry an immoral woman, took Gomer as his wife. After some time and the birth of three children, she abandoned him for other lovers. Then apparently she fell into destitution. Again at God's direction Hosea went after her and found her, redeemed her (perhaps from slavery), and took her home. Proponents of this view have often regarded it as another example of a prophetic "speech-act" in which the prophet does something strange or shocking to carry home his message. Isaiah walked about naked and barefoot for three years as a sign of the coming exile of Egypt and Cush (Isa 20:3–5). Ezekiel lay on his side for over a year near a small model of Jerusalem under siege (Ezek 4–5); he also was forbidden to mourn when his wife died (24:15–18). Jeremiah did not marry (Jer 16:2).

While it is true that Hosea's marriage was a speech-act—indeed, it is the most extreme example in the Bible—this alone is not sufficient to explain this astonishing history. Deuteronomy 24:1–4 forbids a man to remarry his wife after a divorce if she has married another man in the interim. Although probably not technically in violation of this law, because it does not seem that she had remarried in the interim,[25] Hosea's action of taking Gomer back pushes the envelope. If it was wrong for a man to take back a woman after she had been married to another man, what was Hosea doing taking Gomer back after she had been with countless men?

Surprisingly, however, the very offense of Hosea's action strongly confirms that this is indeed the correct interpretation. God has divorced Israel just as Hosea has divorced Gomer, but in both cases grace triumphs over righteous jealousy and the demands of the law. Like the cross itself, Hosea's action is a stumbling block. A man does not normally take back a woman who has behaved the way Gomer did. But we must acknowledge this as a revelation of grace through suffering.

Hosea's sad story is important in another equally paradoxical way. One would think that having married an immoral woman, and then having the marriage collapse because of the wife's gross infidelity, would be enough to disqualify anyone from claiming the role of God's spokesman. But the oppo-

---

[25] Also we do not know with certainty if he ever gave her a bill of divorce or if the two resumed sexual relations after she returned to him. See the exegesis at 2:2 and 3:3.

site is true. Hosea offers his private tragedies as his *credentials* for serving as God's spokesman.[26] As we have seen in the introduction to this commentary, Hosea and God echo one another in this book. First one speaks, and then the other. The human serves as advocate for God, but as the two speak, they speak common words from a common experience. Hosea has endured as husband the same treatment God has endured as covenant Lord of Israel. More than any other, Hosea has the right to speak in God's name. He has shared in God's experiences and therefore can speak with God's heart.

1:2   The opening phrase, "when God began to speak," implies that this command is among the first, if not the very first, revelation God gave to Hosea. The Hebrew here is somewhat unusual but not so much so that its meaning is in doubt, and the NIV translation is appropriate.[27] What the NIV rendering fails to communicate, however, is that the phrase reads almost like a title and could be translated as "The Beginning of the Lord's speaking to Hosea."[28] Whether or not it was the first word Hosea ever received from Yahweh, it is clear that he marks this revelation as the real beginning of his prophetic ministry. His call came in the form of a command to marry a wanton woman! This language also implies that the command to marry a prostitute was the first of two similar commands, the second being in 3:1.[29] Hubbard notes that it is curious that Hosea tells us nothing of how he felt about this command or how he went about making his arrangements to marry Gomer.[30] But Hosea has done something much more significant than this. By telling us that this command was the initiation of Yahweh's revelation to him, he shows us that it was the pivotal theological moment of his life.[31] This is more than a tragic episode; it is the foundation of Hosea's ministry and his qualification to speak for God. We cannot understand Hosea's book if we do not take into account his own interpretation of his ministry.

---

[26] Much as Paul offered his suffering as the proof of his apostleship (2 Cor 11:16–33).

[27] The phrase תְּחִלַּת דִּבֶּר־יְהוָה has a construct followed by a finite verb. Literally translated this is, "The beginning of Yahweh spoke …" McComiskey notes that this construction is rare but sufficiently well attested that it need not be emended ("Hosea," 1:11). See GKC §130d.

[28] Cf. Andersen and Freedman, who observe that this "amounts to his call to the prophetic office" (*Hosea*, 154–55).

[29] On the relationship between תְּחִלַּת דִּבֶּר־יְהוָה in 1:2 and וַיֹּאמֶר יְהוָה אֵלַי עוֹד in 3:1, see D. Grossberg, who notes that the wording indicates that the two events are a pair ("Multiple Meaning: Part of a Compound Literary Device in the Hebrew Bible," *East Asia Journal of Theology* 4 [1986]: 77–86).

[30] D. A. Hubbard, *Hosea*, TOTC (Downers Grove: InterVarsity, 1989), 59.

[31] So profound was this event that prophets after Hosea could routinely speak of and develop the metaphor of Israel the immoral wife. Cf. M. Greenburg, "Ezekiel 16: A Panorama of Passions," in *Love and Death in the Ancient Near East,* ed. J. H. Marks and R. M. Good (Guilford, Conn.: Four Quarters, 1987), 143–50, esp. p. 146.

The NIV properly translates that she was to be his "wife."[32] Hosea was to be bound to this immoral woman in covenant union. For better or for worse, the path of his life would join hers. He would be like Yahweh, who also bound himself in covenant with a willful and wayward people (Deut 9:6).

Scholars have long pondered whether the phrase "adulterous wife" means that she was a prostitute or simply immoral. The Hebrew phrase simply means "promiscuous woman." Some scholars have suggested that if Hosea had meant that she was a prostitute, he would have plainly said so and that "promiscuous woman" implies only that she had immoral tendencies.[33] This suggestion fails for several reasons. First, "promiscuous woman" does not describe what she might do but what she actually does. Therefore, whether or not she was a prostitute, she was not simply a girl whom one might suspect would someday turn immoral.[34] Second, the word found here, zĕnûnîm ("promiscuity"), is a favorite of Hosea's,[35] and its use here implies that he was more interested in conveying her behavior and character than her profession. Hence he did not use the more common word zônâ, "prostitute."[36] Third, the whole question of whether she was a prostitute or simply sexually loose reflects more of modern social realities than ancient Israelite social realities. In our society of female independence a woman might be sexually loose but not receive payment for it. In ancient Israel this would have been the exception.[37] An immoral woman would generally not have been married or have any other means of support, so she naturally would take payment for her sexual favors. Such women might not have worked in brothels, but if prostitution is defined as giving sex for payment, they certainly were prostitutes. Fourth, evidence elsewhere in the book suggests that she was a prostitute.[38] Even so, we must not think of her as a prostitute in modern terms—a call girl or streetwalker—but should think of her more as an immoral girl who depended on gifts from her lovers.

Although the evidence is not conclusive, it also is possible that her immo-

---

[32] The phrase לָקַח אִשָּׁה means "to marry." In a sexual context without אִשָּׁה it implies illicit sexual relations (Gen 20:3; 34:2; Lev 18:17; 20:17; 2 Sam 11:4; Ezek 16:32). If the command were קַח זוֹנָה, it would imply sexual relations with a harlot without marriage. See McComiskey, "Hosea," 1:12–13.

[33] E.g., Harper, *Amos and Hosea*, 207.

[34] The phrase אֵשֶׁת זְנוּנִים is comparable to אִישׁ לָשׁוֹן ("slanderer") and אֵשֶׁת מִדְיָנִים ("contentious woman") and thus simply means a promiscuous woman. A אֵשֶׁת מִדְיָנִים is not someone who might someday become contentious but someone who already is; the same is true of אֵשֶׁת זְנוּנִים. See GKC §128s-v and *GBH* §129f.

[35] Of the twelve occurrences of זְנוּנִים in the OT, six are in Hosea.

[36] G. I. Davies, *Hosea*, NCBC (Grand Rapids: Eerdmans, 1992), 50–51.

[37] The exception is illustrated by Potiphar's wife—the sexually free wife of a wealthy man.

[38] Comparing ANE customs, P. A. Kruger observes that 2:5b refers to the fee paid a prostitute and that 2:2b may allude to ornaments worn by prostitutes ("Israel, the Harlot," *JNSL* 11 [1983]: 107–16).

rality resulted from devotion to the cult of Baal, a thesis that Andersen and Freedman have developed.[39] Wolff argues that the text does not mean that she was unusually immoral but that she had participated in a specific rite of sexual initiation prior to her marriage. He argues that a young woman attached to the fertility cults presented herself in the shrine prior to marriage. There she lost her virginity in sexual union with strangers. Afterward she wore symbolic jewelry that gave proof that she had been initiated. This could have been a one-time event, and Gomer may not have been habitually promiscuous.[40] Intriguing as this reconstruction may be, it really has very little evidence to substantiate it.[41] Besides the fact that we do not know if any such ritual really existed, Hosea never says Gomer took part in it. Rather, he implies that she was habitually licentious.[42]

A more difficult question is the meaning of "children of unfaithfulness." The Hebrew phrase could be interpreted as "promiscuous children," but this seems *prima facie* unlikely.[43] Hosea never accuses his children of sexual immorality, and they never appear in the book as anything other than children. At the same time, there may be some significance to this ambiguity, which we will explore below.

A second possibility is that if Gomer was attached to a fertility shrine, her children would be thought to belong to Baal. Here again it is not clear that

---

[39] Andersen and Freedman argue that Gomer participated in the sexual rites of the fertility cult (*Hosea,* 158–59). They build their case primarily on the fact that the text uses זְנוּנִים for Gomer's behavior instead of זוֹנָה, "prostitute." They further argue on the basis of Deut 18:10–11; 2 Chr 33:6; and Jer 27:9 that the fertility rites of the ancient world combined sexual immorality, magic, and idol worship. They maintain that the women involved in such rites were typically married or betrothed and thus were committing adultery but that these women were not ordinary prostitutes. Against Andersen and Freedman, we must note that neither Deut 18:10–11; 2 Chr 33:6; nor Jer 27:9 contain זְנוּנִים or any reference to sexual activity and really add little to their case (although it is true that זְנוּנִים is linked to כְּשָׁפִים ["sorcery"] in 2 Kgs 9:22 and Nah 3:4). Furthermore, if Gomer regularly engaged in sexual intercourse as part of the Baal cult, one wonders why she is not called a קְדֵשָׁה ("cult prostitute"). While Gomer may have been involved in the Baal cult, זְנוּנִים basically refers to sexual immorality, not participation in a cult, and the text is silent regarding religious aspects of her life.

[40] H. W. Wolff, *Hosea, Her* (Philadelphia: Fortress, 1974), 14–15, 33–34.

[41] This highly speculative reconstruction depends upon limited and ambiguous evidence. While it is clear from the Bible and extrabiblical sources that the fertility cults involved prostitution and immorality, unequivocal evidence for an initiatory rite on the model that Wolff has described is wanting. Jer 3:6–10 and Ezek 16:23 (two texts Wolff cites), e.g., imply orgiastic rites and sacred prostitution but say nothing about any rite of initiation.

[42] It is difficult to imagine how אֵשֶׁת זְנוּנִים could mean "woman who has completed the rite of sexual initiation."

[43] The phrase וְיַלְדֵי זְנוּנִים is grammatically identical to אֵשֶׁת זְנוּנִים. One might therefore argue that they have the same meaning, but this places grammatical parallelism above common sense in that it ignores context. A woman and a child are not the same, and זְנוּנִים does not necessarily relate to them in the same way.

Hosea's own children were in any way consecrated to Baal, and we must be careful about reading these details into the text.

A third suggestion is that these children were the result of promiscuity, born out of wedlock. An obvious problem here is that Hosea's three children were born after his marriage to Gomer and thus were not illegitimate. Of course, one might argue that one or more of the three were not really his, a possibility we will consider at 1:9. But these could also be other children of Gomer (not Jezreel, Lo-Ruhamah, and Lo-Ammi) whom Gomer had already given birth to prior to her marriage to Hosea. That is, when Hosea married her, he also took in her children by her previous lovers.

T. McComiskey champions this view. He argues that "children of promiscuity" can only mean "children born out of wedlock" and that this implies that Gomer brought children with her into the marriage. McComiskey sees further support for this in 2:1, where Hosea speaks of his children having "brothers" and "sisters," something which is not possible if there were only one daughter.[44] This interpretation, however, is improbable. Although "children of promiscuity" could mean "illegitimate children," in this context it seems to mean "children who bear the disgrace of their mother's behavior." That is, this phrase anticipates that Jezreel, Lo-Ruhamah, and Lo-Ammi would bear the reproach of their mother's conduct (see 2:4–5 [Hb. 2:6–7]). In short, v. 2 commands Hosea to build a family with an immoral woman,[45] but it does not necessarily mean she already has children.[46] Also the use of "brothers" and "sisters" in 2:1 (Hb. 2:3)[47] is not specifically a reference to the size of Hosea's immediate family. Rather, in Hosea's theological symbolism his children in 2:1 have already begun to merge into their counterparts, the Israelite people, who are metaphorically the children of Yahweh and his unfaithful wife, Israel. In Hosea's imagery Israel is an adulterous mother, and individual Israelites are her children. Thus "brothers" and "sisters" in 2:1 are also the Israelites and not just Hosea's children.

This helps us understand why Hosea used the striking phrase "children of promiscuity" to describe his three children. They were more than his children; they were signs for the Israelite people. Put another way, Hosea's children bore the stigma of immorality, but the people were *themselves promiscuous* and were in that sense *just like their mother*, Israel. The culture and social mores of that abstraction known as the nation of Israel had worked

---

[44] McComiskey, "Hosea," 1:15–16, 32.

[45] An expanded paraphrase of God's command to Hosea would be, "Go, get yourself a wife of promiscuity and children of promiscuity—marry a woman who is immoral and beget children who will bear the stigma."

[46] See Andersen and Freedman, *Hosea*, 162, 167–68.

[47] Note that the LXX has the singular ἀδελφῷ and ἀδελφῇ here. Although I would still consider the MT reading preferable, this further weakens McComiskey's case.

itself out in the concrete lives of individual Israelites. They were truly the "promiscuous children" of a "promiscuous woman." Through the use of powerful and multifaceted language, Hos 1:2 has already brought us into the complexities of his theological metaphor. But we should not use this language to try to flush out more details about his family life or Gomer's background than he actually tells us.

The reason for God's astonishing command to Hosea is that "the land is guilty of the vilest adultery in departing from the LORD." In other words, God specifically tells Hosea to enter into the same kind of marriage that Yahweh himself is in. Hosea is to experience the sorrows of God and thus speak in God's place to the nation. The Hebrew also implies that Israel's acts of adultery against God have taken the people progressively further away from him. Every act of apostasy and immorality has driven a wedge more deeply between them and their God.[48]

The "land" here is of course not the soil but the nation itself abstractly conceived to be the wife of Yahweh. We may well wonder why Hosea did not say that the "people" or "Israel" is promiscuous, since land cannot be promiscuous. Such language, however, would mislead the reader into supposing that Hosea's primary concern was in sexual immorality. This is far from the case. The "promiscuity" of the "land" is itself metaphorical for apostasy. On the other hand, had the text read, "For Israel is apostate," then the link between Gomer's promiscuity and Israel's apostasy would be unclear. The term "promiscuity" looks back to the analog, Gomer's behavior, and also forward to its final referent, the apostasy of Israel. The term "land" here refers not so much to individuals as to the culture, institutions, and ethic that filled the land.[49]

1:3a "Gomer" and "Diblaim" are simply personal names; they do not have any hidden significance.[50] Hosea could scarcely have said less about his wife (unless he had left her anonymous). But it is precisely this, the fact that she is not anonymous but a real person with a real name and a real father, that tells us we have been given a glance, however slight, of a real and painful story in the life of a man of God. She was no vision or hypothetical construct but was a flesh-and-blood human being.

---

[48] The infinitive absolute with finite verb construction זָנֹה תִזְנֶה focuses attention on the act of adultery (spiritual and literal). The phrase מֵאַחֲרֵי יְהוָה ("from after Yahweh") implies that each act moved them further from Yahweh. It is not just that they committed fornication against the Lord but that they fornicated themselves away from the Lord. See also McComiskey, "Hosea," 1:17.

[49] The noun הָאָרֶץ ("the land") is well suited to the marriage metaphor since it is a feminine noun. "Israel," on the other hand, is a masculine noun.

[50] "Gomer" appears as a personal name on Samaria ostracon 50 and is comparable to "Gemariah" in Jer 29:3. Some have suggested that Diblaim is either a place name or the dual form of דְּבֵלָה ("fruitcake"). The latter suggestion implies that Gomer was devoted to the rituals in which the gods were offered cakes (cf. Hos 3:1). Both theories are highly unlikely; Diblaim is almost certainly no more than her father's name. See Davies, *Hosea,* 53.

2. Naming the Three Children (1:3b–23)

Hosea had three children. It goes without saying that this was important to him as a father, but the significance of these three children for him went beyond normal, parental love. Although Isaiah also regarded his children as "signs and symbols in Israel from the LORD Almighty" (Isa 8:18), Hosea makes the births and naming of his children the beginning of the entire prophecy. He devotes more attention to their births than he does to his marriage to Gomer, and he records the significance Yahweh ascribed to each child's name. The children are themselves oracles, and they are the theological framework of Hosea's message (see introduction). The report of their births should not be passed over as a sad but merely incidental prologue to the actual prophecy; *in a real sense, they are the prophecy, and everything else is just exposition.*

(1) Jezreel (1:3b–5)

and she conceived and bore him a son.
⁴Then the LORD said to Hosea, "Call him Jezreel, because I will soon punish the house of Jehu for the massacre at Jezreel, and I will put an end to the kingdom of Israel. ⁵In that day I will break Israel's bow in the Valley of Jezreel."

BIRTH (1:3b).   **1:3b**   Hosea has just taken a wife and, as is often the case in the Bible, an account of taking a wife is here followed by a report of the birth of the first child (Gen 30:4–5; 38:2–3; Exod 2:1–2; 6:25).

NAME AND EXPLANATION OF PUNISHMENT (1:4–5).   **1:4**   He gave the boy the name Jezreel. As a personal name it apparently was quite uncommon; it appears only one other time as such in the Bible (1 Chr 4:3). A town in Judah had the name Jezreel; one of David's wives, Ahinoam, came from there (1 Sam 25:43).

But for Hosea's audience Jezreel signified the town and valley of the same name located between Galilee and Samaria (the town of Jezreel was in the valley and just northwest of Mount Gilboa). This area was the scene of many significant—and violent—events in Israel's history. There Israelite forces mustered in preparation for a disastrous battle with the Philistines (1 Sam 29:1). It was part of the abortive kingdom of Ishbaal (or Ishbosheth) according to 2 Sam 2:8. Jezreel was where Naboth had his vineyard until he was framed and murdered by the agents of Jezebel (1 Kgs 21:1). It was here also that Jehu killed Joram, Jezebel, and the rest of Ahab's household and supporters (2 Kgs 9:24–10:11). The valley of Jezreel, moreover, was the scene of battles fought by Deborah (Judg 4–5) and Gideon (Judg 6–7). In the mind of an Israelite, Jezreel may have signified bloodshed in the same way that Chernobyl signifies nuclear disaster to a modern person.

Another curious fact about this name, however, is that it means "May God sow" and thus associates God with the productivity of the land. In this it

addresses the fertility cults that figure so heavily in the background of the
Book of Hosea. For the prophet no doubt the name contrasts Yahweh, the
true giver of life, with the false fertility god Baal.[51] We thus have in this
name associations of both death by violence and of a prayer to God, the giver
of bountiful harvests.

God explains the name by saying that he will soon punish the house of Jehu
and bring Israel to an end. As the NIV (and most versions) translate it, however,
there is something troubling about the statement "because I will soon punish
the house of Jehu for the massacre at Jezreel." The problem is that elsewhere in
the Bible the prophetic word commends Jehu for his zeal in finishing off the
dynasty of Omri and in particular for the slaughter of the priests of Baal (2 Kgs
10:30). In fact, Jehu had obeyed a word from the Lord (2 Kgs 9:7).[52]

Why now would the dynasty be punished for the same act? Modern readers,
offended by the sheer volume of blood Jehu spilled, perhaps do not find this
troubling,[53] and some scholars even suggest that Hosea's pronouncement represents a major step forward in the evolution of Israel's understanding of God:
the religious pogrom once commended by the prophets now stands condemned. But, as Andersen and Freedman remark, such analysis "seems
detached from the realities of the ninth–eighth centuries B.C.E. in the Near
East."[54] Hosea himself described the wrath of God in the goriest of terms (e.g.,
13:7–8), and he certainly does not distance himself—even a little bit—from his
predecessors Elijah, Elisha, and the other prophets.[55]

Another possibility is that Jehu was right to destroy the house of Omri but
that the way he went about it was overly zealous and bloodthirsty. One might
compare this to Isa 10:5–12, in which God condemns Assyria for the arrogant
manner in which it went about fulfilling its God-given task of punishing the
nations. But this too fails for two reasons. First, Hosea never accuses Jehu of
having too much pride or of being overly zealous—he simply mentions the
"bloodshed of Jezreel." Second, again in 2 Kgs 10:30 God unconditionally
approves of what Jehu did at Jezreel. This is something we never hear about the
exploits of Assyria.

We must take another look at the phrase "because I will soon punish the
house of Jehu for the massacre at Jezreel." In all probability this misrepresents

---

[51] Cf. Andersen and Freedman, *Hosea,* 173.

[52] One might argue that the young prophet whom Elisha sent to Jehu had wrongly expanded
the original word of Elisha (2 Kgs 9:3), but this seems unlikely since the young man himself was
a prophet (v. 4) and his word did come to pass (vv. 10,36). Rather, it seems that v. 3 simply abbreviates Elisha's message.

[53] Limburg (*Hosea–Micah,* 9) observes that "Jezebel died a cruel death" at Jezreel and does not
reckon with the fact that elsewhere the Bible considers the manner of her death to be no more than
her just deserts.

[54] Andersen and Freedman, *Hosea,* 178–79.

[55] Contrary to Wolff, *Hosea,* 18.

what the Hebrew means here. The word translated "punish" *pāqad* has a wide variety of meanings ("attend to," "appoint," "visit," "muster," etc.), and its specific meaning in any verse is dependent on context. In some cases, to be sure, it can be translated "punish," as when "I will visit their iniquity upon them" means "I will punish them for their iniquity."[56] We should not conclude from this, however, that *pāqad* is the semantic equivalent to the English "punish." In addition, this verse is unusual in that it is the only verse in the Bible with this particular construction, using *pāqad* with *dāmîm* ("bloodshed," "massacre," NIV) as its object. Nothing in the text requires that we understand this to mean "punish" in the sense that the house of Jehu would receive retribution for what he did to the house of Omri at Jezreel. Rather, it seems to mean "visit upon" in the sense that God would bring upon Jehu's dynasty the same violent destruction that befell Omri's dynasty.[57] It should be translated, "And I will bring the bloodshed of Jezreel upon the house of Jehu."

This is not punishment for Jehu's zeal in the slaughter at Jezreel; rather it is punishment *for not learning the lesson of Jezreel*. Jehu himself had been the agent of God's fury and personally had seen how terribly it fell upon an apostate dynasty. But he and his household went on to repeat the apostasy of the Omrides and their predecessors (2 Kgs 10:31; 13:1). God visited the bloodshed of Jezreel on the house of Jehu because, in the final analysis, his dynasty's rule was little better than that of Jeroboam I or of Ahab and Jezebel. Jehu's actions at Jezreel were, if anything, the main reason God did not eliminate his dynasty sooner (2 Kgs 10:30).

1:5 Mays and Wolff both argue that this verse is an independent but authentic saying of Hosea,[58] but it is difficult to understand how such a small saying could have survived independently, or on what grounds we can say it is authentically Hoseanic if it once circulated separately from this book.[59] Also the structure of the oracle requires that this verse not be omitted. The following diagram demonstrates the structure of the poem:

Call his name <u>Jezreel</u> (A)
   For it is just <u>a little while</u> (B)
      And I will <u>bring the bloodshed</u> of Jezreel (C) upon the <u>house of Jehu</u> (D)

---

[56] The idiom of פָּקַד with עָוֹן as the direct object and עַל with a personal indirect object appears in Exod 20:5; 34:7; Lev 18:25; Num 14:18; Deut 5:9; Isa 13:11; 26:21; Jer 36:31; Lam 4:22; Amos 3:2.

[57] For an example of where פָּקַד + X as direct object + עַל with Y as personal indirect object means "to bring X upon Y," see Jer 15:3. Even where עָוֹן is the direct object, I suspect that the root metaphor is bringing someone's iniquity down on his own (or his offspring's) head, as in Exod 20:5; 34:7. It is not simply to punish as we understand the concept. For further discussion see McComiskey, "Hosea," 1:20–21.

[58] J. L. Mays, *Hosea: A Commentary,* OTL (Philadelphia: Westminster, 1969), 28, and Wolff, *Hosea,* 19.

[59] Cf. Andersen and Freedman, *Hosea,* 174–75.

> And I will <u>put an end</u> (C) to the kingdom of the <u>house of Israel</u> (D)
> [5] And it will be <u>in that day</u> (B)
> And I shall <u>break</u> (C) the <u>bow of Israel</u> (D)
> In the valley of <u>Jezreel</u>. (A)[60]

"Jezreel" forms an inclusion pattern at the beginning and end of the oracle (lines marked "A"), within which there is an incomplete parallel structure composed of temporal clauses (lines "B") followed by statements of doom for Israel and the house of Jehu ("C" and "D"). Each of these statements of doom is composed of two parts, a verb phrase that describes God's action ("C" = "bring the bloodshed of Jezreel," "bring an end," "and I shall break") and a noun phrase identifying the objects of God's judgment ("D" = "house of Jehu," "kingdom of the house of Israel," and "bow of Israel"). The parallel structure is incomplete because the first half has two "C–D" lines but the second has only one. But there appears to be a reason for this. In the first half "house of Jehu" describes the royal house, and "kingdom of the house of Israel" describes the nation as a whole.[61] In the second half, however, the metaphor "bow of Israel" jointly describes both the military power of the nation as a whole and the king as its head.[62] In short, king and nation will fall as one. The entire structure is lost, however, if v. 5 is omitted.

We cannot be sure precisely what event constituted the fulfillment of this prophecy. Wolff argues that it refers to the events of 733 B.C., when Tiglath-pileser III, in response to Judah's pleas for help, subjugated the Israelite territory in the valley of Jezreel (2 Kgs 15:29).[63] Others, however, argue that Jehu's dynasty specifically ended when Shallum assassinated Zechariah, the last king of Jehu's dynasty.[64] If an ancient Greek translation of 2 Kgs 15:10 is correct, Shallum killed Zechariah at Ibleam, a town located in a southern part of the valley of Jezreel.[65] This is appropriate. It implies that the dynasty ended, as it

---

[60] I have set out the poem in this manner in order to clarify parallel structure among the cola. For a good metrical analysis of the poem's structure, see BHS. I do not follow the syllable-counting method advocated in Andersen and Freedman (*Hosea,* 174) and feel that their analysis loses the inclusion pattern built around "Jezreel."

[61] It is not possible that מַמְלְכוּת here refers to the reign of the house of Jehu instead of the kingdom of Israel. See McComiskey, "Hosea," 1:20–21. The translation suggested by Andersen and Freedman, "I will also put an end to its rule over the state of Israel" (*Hosea,* 3; see also pp. 183–84), is unlikely for וְהִשְׁבַּתִּי מַמְלְכוּת בֵּית יִשְׂרָאֵל. The noun phrase is a simple construct chain meaning "the kingdom of the house of Israel," and this verse is not grammatically similar to קָרַע יְהוָה אֶת־מַמְלְכוּת יִשְׂרָאֵל מֵעָלֶיךָ ("Yahweh will tear away the kingdom of Israel from you") in 1 Sam 15:28.

[62] The king was the chief warrior of the nation and the embodiment of its military power; see 1 Sam 8:20 and Isa 7:8–9.

[63] Wolff, *Hosea,* 19–20.

[64] E.g., Andersen and Freedman, *Hosea,* 177, and McComiskey, "Hosea," 1:21.

[65] Where the MT has the curious קׇבׇל־עׇם, the Lucianic recension of the LXX here has ἐν Ιεβλααμ. See BHS note *a* on 2 Kgs 15:10.

had begun, with the assassination of the ruling house in the valley of Jezreel. Not only was poetic justice done to Jehu's line,[66] but Hosea's prophecy was completely fulfilled. Perhaps we should best understand the verse to mean that the environs of the valley of Jezreel relate to both the fall of the dynasty and to the destruction of the nation.

(2) Lo-Ruhamah (1:6–7)

[6]Gomer conceived again and gave birth to a daughter. Then the LORD said to Hosea, "Call her Lo-Ruhamah, for I will no longer show love to the house of Israel, that I should at all forgive them. [7]Yet I will show love to the house of Judah; and I will save them—not by bow, sword or battle, or by horses and horsemen, but by the LORD their God."

BIRTH (1:6a). **1:6a** The account of the daughter's birth is very terse; in fact, throughout this chapter Hosea economizes on words wherever possible. The text tells us nothing of the circumstances of her birth.

NAME AND EXPLANATION OF PUNISHMENT (1:6b). **1:6b** The name Lo-Ruhamah means "not loved." It is a dreadful name to give to a little girl. It communicates rejection by her father and says that he has abandoned her to all the troubles of the world. For a culture as child-centered as Israel was, it is difficult to imagine a name more scandalous and offensive. Whenever her name was spoken, it commanded the attention of the people around and invited the question, *Why would anyone call his daughter that?*

Why, indeed? We should not assume that this name communicates Hosea's true feelings or behavior toward the girl. The name is, again, a sign to the people of Israel. Furthermore, we should not jump to the conclusion that she was not really his daughter but was the product of one of Gomer's liaisons. It is true that the text merely says that Gomer "gave birth to a daughter" here in apparent contrast to "she bore him a son" in v. 3. But v. 6 is more abbreviated than vv. 3–4, and it does not repeat the obvious. Where v. 4 says, "The LORD said to Hosea," the Hebrew of v. 6 merely says, "And he said to him," omitting both "the LORD" and "Hosea" as understood speaker and addressee.[67] Thus, while it is always possible that Lo-Ruhamah was not Hosea's, the text says nothing to this effect.

But what was figurative and a subject for popular speculation on a personal level was brute reality for the people of Israel. They were the children of a nation that had gone after Baal. They could not expect grace from Yahweh. The startling name Lo-Ruhamah calls attention to this estrangement between Yahweh and the people. The little girl was the text of Hosea's sermons. The people

---

[66] Note also that Jehu fatally wounded Ahaziah of Judah near Ibleam (2 Kgs 9:27).
[67] The NIV supplies these.

heard that terrible name and no doubt whispered to one another, "Hosea's wife is unfaithful; he must doubt that this child is his. He has rejected the poor thing!" and Hosea could respond something like: "Do you trouble yourself over Lo-Ruhamah? I tell you, you are Lo-Ruhamah! Yahweh has turned his back on you!" He would be like Nathan with David: "You are the man!" (2 Sam 12:7).

REVERSAL (1:6c–7). **1:6c–7**　The precise meaning of 1:6c–7 is much debated. The main difficulty is the end of v. 6, which the NIV renders "that I should at all forgive them." This is a very questionable, and one might even say impossible, translation of the Hebrew. The most obvious meaning of the line is, "But I will certainly forgive them." This, of course, would be a complete non sequitur after the previous line, a pronouncement that God would no longer show compassion on Israel.

Scholars have dealt with the problem in various ways. The first, found not only in the NIV but also the RSV, is to try to make this line somehow explanatory of "I will no longer show love to the house of Israel." This approach translates the difficult line as a modal construction, as in, "I will no longer show Israel love *by forgiving them.*"[68] But if the Hebrew here means this, it is unlike any other Hebrew in the Bible.[69] We should not follow the NIV rendition here.

Another explanation is to argue that the negative in "I will no longer" controls everything that follows. Following this theory, one might retranslate this part of the oracle, "I will no longer show love to the house of Israel, nor will I forgive them at all, nor will I show love to the house of Judah, nor will I save them by Yahweh their God." In this interpretation the whole of vv. 6–7 is an oracle of doom for Israel and Judah. Here again, however, the grammar of the text does not lend itself to this kind of interpretation; the "I will no longer" controls only the single phrase "show love to the house of Israel," not what follows.[70]

---

[68] I.e., this is a modal (or perhaps resultative) translation of כִּי־נָשֹׂא אֶשָּׂא לָהֶם. Cf. Harper, *Hosea,* 214.

[69] There are no grounds for giving an infinitive absolute with a *yiqtol* verb following כִּי, a modal translation. See below and cf. McComiskey, "Hosea," 1:24.

[70] See Andersen and Freedman, *Hosea,* 188–94, for a defense of this interpretation. Their translation is based on their analysis of the poetic structure of the oracle. They argue that there are two major clauses, the first begun by כִּי לֹא in v. 6 and the second by וְלֹא in v. 7. They argue that this implies that כִּי לֹא אוֹסִיף עוֹד controls everything after it until וְלֹא אוֹשִׁיעֵם begins the next major clause. Their argument fails for two reasons. First, they have not demonstrated that כִּי לֹא אוֹסִיף עוֹד can span the clause-level break implied by the כִּי and infinitive absolute phrase of כִּי־נָשֹׂא אֶשָּׂא לָהֶם. None of the analogies they offer (Jer 3:2; 22:10; Num 23:19) has anything like the kind of difficulties of what they are proposing. Jer 22:10, e.g., is a simple negated *yiqtol* (imperfect) plus *weqatal* (converted perfect) construction: לֹא יָשׁוּב עוֹד וְרָאָה אֶת־אֶרֶץ. It means "He will no longer return and see the land …" and is by no means "exactly the same as" Hos 1:6 (p. 190). Second, they fail to include the first colon, קְרָא שְׁמָהּ לֹא רֻחָמָה ("call her name Lo-Ruhamah") in their analysis of the poem. If included, this suggests a different metrical analysis of the poem, one in which כִּי לֹא and וְלֹא do not govern the whole piece. See below.

Another approach is to seek a different translation for the word that the NIV renders "forgive." This word *(nāśāʾ)* has the root meaning of "lift," but it also means "forgive" in many contexts. A number of scholars, feeling that it is absurd that the text should say "I will absolutely forgive them" immediately after having pronounced that God no longer will show love to the people, argue that the word here must mean something like "carry away." Thus, McComiskey says that it means "I will surely take them away" (i.e., into exile).[71] Wolff takes it to mean that God will remove his compassion and so translates it, "I will withdraw it from them."[72] Once again, however, this stratagem forces the Hebrew to say something one would not naturally take it to mean.[73] As it stands, *nāśāʾ* can only mean "forgive."

We are thus left with the astonishing possibility that the text means exactly what it says: "I will completely forgive[74] them." How is it possible that Hosea (speaking for God) could in the same breath say, "I will no longer show love to the house of Israel" and "I shall completely forgive them"? It is jolting, but it is not unusual for an author who routinely sets assertions about God's terrible wrath directly and without transition beside statements of his absolute love. The very next oracle does the same thing in vv. 9–10: "I am not your God. Yet Israel shall be like the sand on the seashore ..." See also, for example, 13:14.

The structure of the oracle, I suggest, supports this reading. Although the meter is irregular, I read the poem as composed of three tricola, as follows:

Call her name Not-Loved

Thus I shall no longer let it happen[75]

That I should love the house of Israel.

---

[71] McComiskey, "Hosea," 1:21. Also Mays, *Hosea,* 22.

[72] Wolff, *Hosea,* 8.

[73] There is no analogy for taking נָשָׂא with לְ to mean "carry [someone] away [into exile]" in the Hebrew Bible. נָשָׂא can mean "take away," but the direct object is always explicit and is not marked with a לְ. See Gen 40:19; Num 16:15; Judg 21:23; 1 Sam 17:34; 2 Sam 14:14; 1 Kgs 15:22; 18:12; Isa 40:24; 41:16; Jer 49:29; Mic 2:2; Job 32:22; Lam 5:13. Furthermore, there are no grounds for reading "compassion" into this line as the object of נָשָׂא in the sense of, "I will take my compassion away from them." Neither scholar offers any persuasive analogy for the meaning he proposes; in fact, in every analogous text that McComiskey cites but one (Jer 49:29, which is not a true analogy), נָשָׂא means "forgive" (e.g., Josh 24:19)! נָשָׂא without a direct object can mean "forgive," and לְ is used to mark the person or group forgiven. Usually, but not always, some word for sin with a לְ preposition and a personal pronoun suffix is the object, as in לֹא יִשָּׂא לְפִשְׁעֲכֶם ("He will not forgive your rebellion," Exod 23:21). Wolff, however, wrongly says that the meaning "forgive" requires the accusative instead of לְ. See Gen 18:26: וְנָשָׂאתִי לְכָל־הַמָּקוֹם בַּעֲבוּרָם ("then I shall forgive the whole place for their sake"). See also Num 14:19; Isa 2:9; Ps 99:8.

[74] The infinitive absolute construction makes the act of forgiving the topic of the clause and implies that sin will be entirely removed.

[75] I translate כִּי לֹא אוֹסִיף עוֹד as "I shall no longer let it happen" to bring out the fact that כִּי לֹא אוֹסִיף עוֹד and אֲרַחֵם אֶת־בֵּית יִשְׂרָאֵל are in different cola in Hebrew. This is not possible if we simply translate the two cola as "I shall no longer love ...," although linguistically this is a perfectly acceptable translation of the verse.

But[76] I shall completely forgive them
　[7] And I shall show love to the house of Judah
　　And I shall save them by Yahweh their God.[77]
And I shall not save them
　By bow, or by sword, or by war[78]
　　By horses, or by horsemen.

Perhaps Hosea's audience sensed that the name "Not-Loved" was an impossibility. Of course Hosea loved Lo-Ruhamah! Could God abandon his love for Israel? On one level the answer is yes—he could give them over to the most terrible suffering—but on a deeper level it is impossible: "How can I give you up, Ephraim? How can I hand you over, Israel? ... My heart is changed within me; all my compassion is aroused" (Hos 11:8). This inconsistency is the language of the vexation of a broken heart—and it also reflects the mystery of a God whose ways are above our ways.

A number of scholars have registered surprise at the sudden mention of the house of Judah here, but this too characterizes the Book of Hosea. Although the Northern Kingdom of Israel was his primary audience, he could not forget about Judah and the house of David (see Introduction). Also scholars who treat this verse as an interpolation operate from the faulty assumption that this text contains only woe for Israel. As I have just suggested, the text has already made a dramatic change in proclaiming that God will forgive Israel. Since Hosea links the salvation of Israel to the house of David (3:5), it is not surprising that he turns his attention briefly to Judah here. There is no reason to regard this as a secondary addition.[79]

The final tricolon of this poem adds one more paradox. Immediately after saying, "I shall save them," he says, "I shall not save them." This can mean, as translated above, that God *will* deliver them but not *by* military means. On the other hand, it could equally well mean "I shall not save them *from*"[80] bows and cavalry and warfare. And both statements are true! God will abandon Israel to the cruelty of the Assyrian war machine and will not deliver them. And yet God will make them to be a new people, "Not by might nor by power, but by my Spirit" (Zech 4:6).

---

[76] It is well known that כִּי can be adversative with the meaning "except" or the like (e.g., 1 Sam 18:25), and the LXX (ἀλλά) and the Vg *(sed)* support an adversative translation here. Even so, my interpretation of this verse does not depend upon translating this כִּי as "but" because, in my view, the text deliberately astounds the reader.

[77] Note the assonance of the final syllables of לָהֶם, אֲרַחֵם, and אֱלֹהֵיהֶם at the end of the three lines.

[78] The unexpected asyndeton at וּבְמִלְחָמָה בְּסוּסִים implies a colon break here.

[79] Contrary to Mays, *Hosea*, 29.

[80] Although the preposition בְּ can mean "by" or "from," context favors "by" (because of וְהוֹשַׁעְתִּים בַּיהוָה אֱלֹהֵיהֶם, "and I shall save them by Yahweh their God"). But in a text as disorienting as this, it is easy to suppose that the ambiguity is deliberate.

Excursus: Hosea 1:6 and Theological Hermeneutics

Modern physics, more than any other area of study, has revolutionized our understanding of reality and of the nature of knowledge. For example, we now know that light has both particle and wave characteristics. This is inconceivable from our frame of reference, and all attempts to conceptualize what light "really" is fail, except to say that light is simply light and that it has characteristics that most of us cannot reconcile. It is a paradox.

We could give many other such examples from physics. How is it possible for electromagnetic waves to travel through the vacuum of space? How can a wave exist without something waving—a medium? It was for this reason that nineteenth-century physicists understandably but wrongly postulated that the ether was the medium of light and electromagnetic fields. We now also know that the speed of light is a constant regardless of the speed and direction of the observer relative to the light. This does not make sense, but it is true. So strange have the laws of physics turned out to be that the greatest scientific minds of our time are engaged in a quest to understand how the laws of the quantum world of the atom and the laws of relativity and gravity can coexist in the same universe. The point of all this is that reality, when we understand it on its deepest level, can be profoundly nonintuitive and can even appear to jettison the law of noncontradiction.

This commentary argues that scholars and translators have not correctly handled Hos 1:6. In this text God tells Hosea to give his daughter the terrible name Lo-Ruhamah, which means "Not loved." He explains that Lo-Ruhamah is a type for Israel and that he, God, will no longer show love to Israel. The next line, which of itself is not particularly difficult, simply means "I will completely forgive them." The problem is that it is astonishing that Hosea as God's spokesperson would in one breath say, "I will no longer love them" and in the next, "I will completely forgive them." As argued above, attempts to find an alternative translation for this line fail.

God, through his spokesman Hosea, astonishes us by declaring first that he will no longer love Israel and then by asserting without a hint of explanation or transition that he will completely forgive them. This is not the only time, however, we see such incongruity in Hosea. In the very next oracle at 1:9–10, that about Lo-Ammi, he declares: "Call him Lo-Ammi, for you are not my people, and I am not your God. Yet the Israelites will be like the sand on the seashore." Here the translation "yet" is not incorrect, but it does convey a stronger sense of contrast and transition than is really present in the Hebrew text, which could easily be translated "*and* the Israelites will be like the sand on the shore."[81] In other words, immediately after declaring Israel no longer to be his covenant people, God reaffirms the covenant in the terms of the promise to Abraham of Gen 22:17, "I will surely bless you and make your descendants as numerous as the stars in the sky and as the sand on the seashore." And these are not even the most extreme examples of Hosea's non sequiturs. Hosea 13:14–16 is a text that begins by declaring God's determination to redeem Israel, then suddenly asserts that God

---

[81] Translating וְהָיָה מִסְפַּר בְּנֵי־יִשְׂרָאֵל כְּחוֹל הַיָּם.

will have no compassion, and ends by foretelling that their pregnant women will be ripped open.

Hosea presents Israel with two contrary realities. On the one side is God's rejection of them as an apostate people as well as their certain doom, and on the other side is his covenant faithfulness. But Hosea does not try to reconcile these two because to reconcile them would be to subordinate one to the other. Either that or both concepts would be rendered tame and would lose their power. In Hosea absolute rejection and destruction are set alongside complete restoration and forgiveness with no transition or explanation. These are, like the particle function and the wave function that is light, simply two autonomous realities. Each side of Hosea's paradox appropriately describes God's response to Israel.

We may feel that we can reconcile the two by saying that God loves his children but must take them through a period of discipline for their own good. But this is not how Hosea presents the matter. God's intent is not to "discipline" these children and so teach them a lesson; his intention is to *kill* them—and then, incomprehensibly, to restore them. Our term "discipline" connotes something of a spanking, but we should recall that what Israel really faced was prolonged siege, massive starvation, slaughter of the people, rape of the women as a means of further annihilating their culture, and taking away the few surviving captives naked and in chains for a march across the desert in which many more would perish. This was racial and cultural genocide; it was holocaust. It was nothing less than the death of the nation. So horrible and complete is this kind of conquest that Ezekiel could only conceive of its reversal as a *resurrection*, and not as a simple restoration, in his vision of the valley of dry bones (Ezek 37:1–14). And yet at the same time God says, "I will completely forgive them."

But what does this tell us about hermeneutics and theology? It tells us that if we must accept paradox in our understanding of the nature of light, we should much more be willing to have paradox in the nature of God and his dealings with human beings. God, after all, is far more profound than light, which is after all still part of this universe. Whereas the word "paradox" is something of a cliché, we must acknowledge that sometimes two seemingly contradictory truths stand side-by-side, that both are equally valid, and that it is more important that we *accept* the two than it is that we *reconcile* them. Indeed, the very act of reconciling the two may cause us to obscure one or both truths.

Thomas Aquinas was arguably the greatest philosopher of the Christian faith. He was the quintessential natural theologian, meaning that he sought to show that right analysis of the natural world inevitably leads us to God. He fully engaged the greatest philosophers of his age, both Christian and non-Christian, in order to establish that the catholic faith provides the only satisfying answers to human inquiry.

We know Aquinas best for his fivefold proof for the existence of God.[82] He is truly a marvel for answering the objections to the Christian concept of God. One small example should suffice. In part 1a, question 16, article 7, of the *Summa Theologiae*, Aquinas asserts that truth resides solely in the intellect and not in things. He states: "Truth in statements is not apart from truth in mind. Hence if no intellect were eternal, no truth would be eternal. But since the divine intellect alone is eternal, truth has eternity in it alone. Nor does it follow from this that anything other than God is eternal; because truth in the divine intellect is God himself, as we have shown. Hence, the idea of circularity, and that two and three make five, possess eternity in the divine mind."[83]

Why is this so insightful? Many philosophers assert that certain axioms, especially mathematical axioms, are independent of God. Even God cannot make a four-sided triangle or make 2 + 3 to equal 4, they say. To say that an axiom is eternally true apart from God in effect makes it independent of God, and from this one can say that the only eternal truths that we can be sure of, and that we really need, are the axioms. Some modern physicists have taken this a step further and have made the laws of physics into a surrogate God.[84] We can respond with the argument that axioms do not make for a satisfying God, but Aquinas has given us an answer that is far more intellectually satisfying.

Axioms do not exist at all apart from the mind. We cannot say that 2 + 3 = 5 is true whether or not minds exist because numbers have no existence apart from minds. Axioms cannot be eternally true unless they are sustained by an eternal mind, and thus all truth is subordinate to God. Mathematical axioms and laws are in no sense equal to God.

Today some of the greatest intellectuals are saying things that are quite troubling to theism—S. Hawking, for one, comes immediately to mind. But this thirteenth-century Dominican friar, Aquinas, still has much to say to the questions of our day. All who engage in apologetics, except the most radically presuppositional, are followers of Aquinas whether or not they agree with his specific conclusions. Indeed, if you believe that all truth is God's truth, you are to some degree a Thomist.

An Augustinian monk, Martin Luther, took a very different view of things. Although we naturally celebrate Luther's proclamation of justification by grace through faith, perhaps his two foundational discoveries were of the bondage of the will and most especially of the theology of the cross. In his *Heidelberg Disputations* numbers nineteen and twenty, he wrote: "The man who looks upon the invisible things of God as they are perceived in created things does not deserve to be called a theologian. The man who perceives the visible backside of God as seen in suffering and the cross does deserve to be called a theologian."

Martin Luther reacted against scholasticism and issued a call to return to the gospel of Christ. He had no place for natural theology. For him, anyone who tried to discern God through philosophy, nature, and reason was trying to see the

---

[82] I would not call Aquinas's teaching on this point a "proof" in the sense that there is a proof for the Pythagorean theorem, but I do think that, on the basis of reason and nature, he has given us a strong argument for the existence of God; and I do not believe that Hume and Kant have overturned his position. Cf. M. Adler, *Ten Philosophical Mistakes* (New York: Collier, 1985).

[83] Aquinas, *Summa Theologiae: Latin Text and English Translation, Introductions, Notes, Appendices and Glossaries,* Blackfriars ed. (New York: McGraw-Hill, 1963), 4:93.

[84] Cf. M. W. Worthing, *God, Creation, and Contemporary Physics* (Minneapolis: Fortress, 1996).

Father directly, without the aid of Christ. Rather, drawing on Exodus 33, where Moses sees only God's back as he passes by, Luther proclaimed that *we* can only see God's "backside"; that is, we can only see God in the suffering and humiliation of the cross. God comes to us not as we expect him, as glorious Creator, but in a form in which we cannot recognize, as a man broken by the weight of sin and oppression. Luther considered anyone who tries to see God directly through logic and nature to be a "theologian of glory." The theology of glory is deceitful and is founded on human works. The only real theology is the theology of the cross. We only see God when we have been crushed by the law and in absolute despair look up to the crucified God. The theology of glory depends on reason; the theology of the cross depends on faith. The theology of glory builds up pride; the theology of the cross brings a person to his knees.[85]

In this understanding of Christianity Luther is followed by Blaise Pascal, who declared that he had found the God of Abraham, Isaac, and Jacob and not the God of the philosophers. More recently, Karl Barth, with a thundering no, rejected entirely natural theology and contended that God is revealed only in Christ. We have in Aquinas and Luther, therefore, two incompatible ways of looking at Christianity. And they really are incompatible, as Luther understood full well.

I would contend, however, that they are both true.

Christianity really is the supreme philosophy, and it can engage whatever school of thought holds sway in any generation. The church can live in Athens, and not only in Jerusalem. And if God really is our Creator and if we have been given minds to comprehend this world around us, then surely honest reason should lead us to God. Recent calls for evangelicals to start making significant contributions in the arts, sciences, and humanities[86] make no sense if we reject the natural theology.

At the same time, we know nothing of Christianity if we are strangers to the power and the offense of the cross. Dead to God as we are, our eyes are blinded by a thousand lies. Unless our hearts are broken, our wills surrendered, our sin exposed, and our cool logic abandoned, we are only imitation Christians who are aliens to the life of grace, who mimic true faith through learning and practice. The crucified God offends both reason and religion, both Jew and Greek, but the folly of God is wiser than human wisdom.

Those who think that they can readily reconcile Aquinas and Luther may not understand either. More than that, the very act of harmonizing the two robs both of their essentials. If paradox in theology is troubling, we should consider that the fundamental doctrine of Christianity, that of the Trinity, goes very hard on human reason.

The doctrine of the Trinity really *explains* very little; it simply sets out what the data of Scripture on the Godhead are. There is one God, but he exists eternally not as three modes of existence but as three persons. These are the facts about God. But being able to assert these facts and even to describe the history of the development of the doctrine does not mean that we can conceptualize God him-

---

[85] Cf. A. E. McGrath, *Luther's Theology of the Cross* (Grand Rapids: Baker, 1985), 148–52.
[86] E.g., M. A. Noll, *The Scandal of the Evangelical Mind* (Grand Rapids: Eerdmans, 1994).

self in a way that is comfortable for human reason. It is axiomatic in theology that no true analogy for the Trinity exists, and since all our God-talk is analogical, this means that the Trinity is not something we positively understand.

Outside of the teaching of the Bible itself, this is the greatest argument that the doctrine is true. If the nature of light, an aspect of the physical universe, is so far above normal modes of thinking as to be beyond our ability to conceptualize, surely the nature of the Maker of heaven and earth is much more so! A God who is easy to understand is likely to be the product of human reason, and indeed if I were inventing a doctrine of God from my own imagination, that God would be more like the God of Islam than the God of the Bible. Here Tertullian's famous quip *Credo quia absurdum* ("I believe because it is absurd") is truly applicable—not that absurdity is itself a mark of truth but that a God who is not in some sense beyond human comprehension is no God at all, but is an idol.

Many aspects of biblical truth, particularly those truths that pertain to God and the ways of God with people, are beyond the ability of human reason to comprehend fully. Biblical truths are sometimes paradoxical either in the sense they seem to violate the law of noncontradiction or in the sense that they are beyond our ability to form meaningful analogies. Furthermore, following the rhetorical strategy of Hosea, it is often better to let these truths simply stand side-by-side than it is to saddle them with an artificial harmonization or with misleading analogies. Most importantly of all, we should never choose one truth over another or subordinate one truth to another. Frankly admitting that we see through a glass darkly is the greatest safeguard to remaining true to the faith.

Having said this, it is perhaps important to state what this does *not* mean and then conclude by suggesting some implications and applications.

This does not mean that systematic theology is invalid or that all theological synthesis is wrong. We can do a great deal of synthesis. Nevertheless, although we can systematize and synthesize, we must recognize that synthesis is not always possible or even beneficial.

Second, *this does not mean* that we should read Scripture naively or fail to apply standard methods of hermeneutics. I especially have in mind here what the Antiochene school called "condescension," a valid principle of interpretation. This is the fact that God comes down to our level when he speaks to us in Scripture because if he did not, we could not understand anything at all. He speaks to us on a human level, and we should be careful about taking biblical language in its most literal sense.[87] Similarly, we must take into account poetic imagery, social context, and genre when reading the Bible.

Third, *this does not imply* anything that might be called epistemological pluralism or cultural relativism. These assert first that truth is not absolute and second that no person has the right to call another person's vision of the truth wrong. The *hermeneutics of paradox* builds upon the profound richness and variety of truth that is in God; *pluralism* builds upon the variety of opinions that exist in people. To go back to physics, under a pluralistic model I would not only have to

---

[87] See D. A. Garrett, *An Analysis of the Hermeneutics of John Chrysostom's Commentary on Isaiah 1–8 with an English Translation* (Lewiston, N.Y.: Edwin Mellen, 1992), 22–23.

speak of light as a wave and a particle but would also have to say that those who believe that light travels through the ether are entitled to their own truth. Or if Hosea were pluralistic rather than paradoxical, he would have to say that those who equated Yahweh with Baal were simply fellow pilgrims taking a different road to God. Hosea did not say this.

Fourth, *this does not necessarily imply* that there are various theologies in the Bible—for example, the notion that a wisdom school stands against the prophetic movement or that there is one theology of Paul, another of James, another of John, and so forth. Whatever one may say for or against this idea, this hermeneutical stance simply is not related, although the principles described here could be useful in reconciling James and Paul if one had already concluded that they described different aspects of the gospel.

Fifth, *this does not mean that* in the *final* analysis truth is self-contradictory. Certainly God is not in the least perplexed by the nature of light, and he fully comprehends the Trinity. Still, we often try to synthesize where we ought simply to believe, and some of our attempts to synthesize spring from a disobedient spirit, or a proud intellectualism, and are harmful to the gospel.

What then are the implications and applications of this stance?

First, we must carefully and honestly interpret Scripture. As far as we are able, we must not place a theological grid over Scripture. It is better to *proclaim* the Bible than to *explain* the Bible. It is only in this that we unleash the power of the Word. *We must proclaim the unfettered Word.* We should not rob it of its power with rationalizing commentary, explanation, and modification. In so far as we are able, we should not subordinate it to our systems.

Perhaps a more pointed example is needed: Where the Bible proclaims predestination, we should preach it. Where the Bible declares that God desires all people to repent and come to a knowledge of the truth, we should preach that too. We should not defile either truth with private modifications.

To give another example, consider Jesus' command to be perfect as our Father in heaven is perfect (Matt 5:48). If we teach this without holding in tension the fact of human depravity, we may become like those deranged souls who reckon themselves sinless. But we should not water Jesus' command down with the idea that he just wants us to be "mature." Our standard, according to Jesus' analogy, is God, who is *perfect* and not just mature.

Or we might consider Exodus 32, where God announces his decision to destroy Israel and start over again, Moses intercedes, and God relents. If we proclaim this text without holding in tension the fact that God has perfect foreknowledge and that his character is unchanging, we proclaim a god who is more pagan than Christian. And we should remember that the language of Scripture condescends to us. But we should not so interpret and qualify and modify the text that it loses its simple power. *Moses prayed, and God changed his mind.* What a marvelous picture of prayer! We should not deface it with our exegesis but remember that Jesus himself was willing to portray God as a judge whom a widow nagged until he acted in her behalf (Luke 18:2–7). Only by choosing to live with the tension that arises from our limited understanding can we proclaim the unfettered Word.

Second, this hermeneutic is necessary for Christian unity. This is an over-simplification, but I believe that much denominational division simply springs from Christians preferring one truth over another. Christ prayed that we should be one, but we say "I am of Calvin," or "I am of Wesley," or of Aquinas, or of Luther. We do not need to surrender all convictions but must recognize that God is not only greater than our hearts but also than our minds.

Finally, this hermeneutic is helpful for spiritual life. Spirituality and prayer do not necessarily coexist well with a rationalistic view of God. To the contrary, prayer requires that we acknowledge our inability to comprehend, explain, and control ultimate truth. The secret things belong to God (Deut 29:29). God is in heaven and we are on earth (Eccl 5:2). The Christian faith is not all mystery, nor is it irrational. But just as surely as God is above us, so also much that we believe is above human reason. No one will learn how to walk by faith while clinging only to that which can be seen with the eye and comprehended with the mind. There are things about God and his ways that we *believe* but do not fully *understand*.

It is a difficult thing to hold truths in tension. Hosea knew this. It is perhaps for this reason that he concludes his book with a proverb that describes the limitations of human understanding and the necessity of a submissive response to the multifaceted Word of God (14:9).

(3) Lo-Ammi (1:8–2:23)

⁸After she had weaned Lo-Ruhamah, Gomer had another son.

BIRTH (1:8). **1:8** It is curious that the text mentions the weaning of Lo-Ruhamah; it implies that Lo-Ammi was born some three years after Lo-Ruhamah since children nursed longer in the ancient world than today.[88] It may be that Gomer lived faithfully with Hosea for a number of years. Notwithstanding the speculations of some interpreters,[89] however, it probably is best to take this as an incidental detail and not as a moral allegory.

⁹Then the LORD said, "Call him Lo-Ammi, for you are not my people, and I am not your God.

NAME AND EXPLANATION OF PUNISHMENT (1:9). **1:9** The name Lo-Ammi simply means "Not my people." This has given rise to further speculation about whether these children were really his. If a man will call his son "Not my people," is he saying that the child is "not mine"? The direct answer is that we do not know. It is possible, but the text does not directly say anything about it.

With the naming of the child "Not my people," God declares the covenant

---

[88] Cf. Davies, *Hosea,* 58.

[89] Following Calvin, some see here a portrayal of the patience of God. Ibn Ezra, however, takes this to mean that the Israelites would bear children in exile (Lipshitz, *Ibn Ezra,* 22).

between himself and Israel to be null and void. The line "You are not my people, and I am not your God" reverses the familiar covenant language of Exod
6:7 and Lev 26:12. God is rejecting Israel and abandoning her people.

The NIV has slightly supplemented the text in its translation "and I am not
your God" in this verse. The Hebrew only says, "And I am not yours" and
omits the word "God," but the addition of the word "God" here is justifiable.
Some scholars argue that the Hebrew actually means "And I am not 'I AM' to
you." In other words, they argue that with these words God has relinquished the
title of I AM for Israel (Exod 3:14); he shall no longer be the God of Moses that
they knew.[90] This interpretation is possible.[91] It is, however, open to question.
The text nowhere else makes reference to the name "I AM" or to the burning
bush episode.[92] We also have to wonder whether the ancient Hebrew reader
would take this clause to mean "And I am not 'I AM' to you."[93] It is probably
enough to see that God has reversed the covenant bond of Exod 6:7 without
straining for an allusion to Exod 3:14.

---

[90] See Hubbard, *Hosea,* 65, Wolff, *Hosea,* 21–22; and especially Andersen and Freedman, *Hosea,* 198–99.

[91] To take וְאָנֹכִי לֹא־אֶהְיֶה לָכֶם to mean "I am not I AM to you" requires that one treat it as a verbless clause in which אֶהְיֶה functions not as a verb but substantivally as a proper name in the predicate position. The order [subject + לֹא + predicate noun] can be used for a negative verb-less clause. Examples include this verse (אַתֶּם לֹא עַמִּי "you are not my people"), Hos 2:4 (Eng. 2:2), and Jer 2:11 (= 16:20). On the other hand, we also see the pattern [לֹא + predicate + subject], as in Amos 7:14 לֹא־נָבִיא אָנֹכִי ("I am not a prophet"). See also Jer 5:10 and 51:5. If the statement is a negative rhetorical question, the normal order is [הֲלֹא + subject + predicate], as in Exod 4:11; 14:12; Num 22:30; Deut 3:11; Isa 45:21.

[92] The only other occurrence of אֶהְיֶה in Hosea is at 14:6 ("I shall be as the dew to Israel"), where it is simply a verb and cannot allude to Exod 3:14.

[93] We have several reasons for reading the phrase with אֶהְיֶה as a normal verb ("I am not your [God]"). First of all, וְאָנֹכִי לֹא־אֶהְיֶה לָכֶם is normal Hebrew grammar. That is, we have many examples of a [subject pronoun + לֹא + imperfect verb] pattern (to cite but a few, Jer 15:19; 23:14; 38:18; Ezek 5:11; 11:11; Hos 5:13). The Hebrew reader probably would take אֶהְיֶה in its ordinary sense as a verb and not as a proper name. The lack of the word אֱלֹהֵיכֶם ("your God") is not all that surprising; we saw that Hosea omitted both יהוה and הוֹשֵׁעַ in v. 6 (saying only "and he said to him"). Also there may be another reason for Hosea's choice of וְאָנֹכִי לֹא־אֶהְיֶה לָכֶם over something like וְאָנֹכִי לֹא אֱלֹהֵיכֶם ("I am not your God") at this early stage of the oracle. By simply saying "and I am not yours," the text continues to operate at two levels. On one side is God's relationship to Israel, but on the other is Hosea's estrangement from his own family. "I am not yours" allows for this ambiguity in a way that "I am not your God" would not. See especially 3:3, where Hosea tells Gomer, "Then indeed I shall be yours" (וְגַם־אֲנִי אֵלַיִךְ), a reversal of the line in 1:9. Finally, as mentioned above, there is no other reference to Exod 3 or to the I AM in this oracle. It seems strange that the text would slip in such a significant allusion and then do nothing with it. Instead, the oracle ends at 2:25 (Eng. 2:23) with Lo-Ammi saying, "You are my God" (אֱלֹהָי), which implies that the reader was simply to understand אֱלֹהֵיכֶם (or, אֱלֹהֶיךָ) at 1:9. If an allusion to Exod 3:14 were the point of the text, we may have expected the reversal also to include אֶהְיֶה in some fashion (i.e., "You are I AM to me"). For further discussion see C. S. Ehrlich, "The Text of Hosea 1:9," *JBL* 104 (1985): 13–19.

[10]"Yet the Israelites will be like the sand on the seashore, which cannot be measured or counted. In the place where it was said to them, 'You are not my people,' they will be called 'sons of the living God.' [11]The people of Judah and the people of Israel will be reunited, and they will appoint one leader and will come up out of the land, for great will be the day of Jezreel.

REVERSAL (1:10–11) [A].   The Lo-Ammi oracle follows exactly the same pattern as the Lo-Ruhamah oracle. It includes the birth of the child, his or her name, the explanation of the name with warnings of God's rejection of the people, and also an unexpected reversal of the punishment. In this, both Lo-Ruhamah and Lo-Ammi expand on Jezreel, which does not include the gracious reversal.[94] Lo-Ammi, however, dramatically expands the pattern further by detailing in chap. 2 the sins of the mother (Israel) and her punishment and restoration. As described in the introduction, moreover, chap. 2 is so closely woven into the Lo-Ammi oracle that it cannot be considered a separate message.

1:10 [2:1]   Having stated that Israel has forfeited their status as the people of God, the text turns around without warning or transition and reaffirms the ancient covenant promise to Abraham (Gen 22:17). To recall this promise is to reaffirm their status as God's people. It is pointless to resist Hosea's style as incongruous or his text as in need of repair. The sin of the people and the faithfulness of God are two realities he simply treats as equally true. The affirmation that they would become as numerous as the sand on the seashore was almost laughable in Hosea's day. Wolff observes that in 738 B.C., according to 2 Kgs 15:19–20, Israel had about sixty thousand free landholders and that the nation was puny compared to the expanding Assyrian Empire.[95] Only faith in God could foresee a reversal of this reality.

"Israelites" is actually *bĕnê yiśrāʾēl*, the phrase traditionally rendered "children of Israel." Hosea uses the term seven times, and all are within chaps. 1–3 except for one occurrence at 4:1, which is perhaps transitional.[96] The reason is not hard to fathom; in these chapters Hosea especially draws on the analogy between his own children and the *bĕnê yiśrāʾēl*. This may explain the ambiguous reference to "the place" where they were called "not my people." Scholars have suggested that the place may be the wilderness, where Israel would return to Yahweh,[97] or the valley of Jezreel, the scene of so many of their

---

[94] The name Jezreel, "God sows," does implicitly contain the idea of reversal. H. G. May ("An Interpretation of the Names of Hosea's Children," *JBL* 55 [1936]: 285–91) contends that Lo-Ruhamah and Lo-Ammi can be easily reversed to אֵל רַחוּם ("merciful God") and אֵל עַמִּי ("God with me"). One may question whether Hebrew readers would have seen the double entendres that May sees.
[95] Wolff, *Hosea,* 26.
[96] בְּנֵי יִשְׂרָאֵל appears at (Hb. text) 2:1,2 (twice); 3:1,4,5; and 4:1.
[97] Andersen and Freedman, *Hosea,* 203. See 2:3,14 (Hb. 5,16).

failures.[98] Again, however, the ambiguity of "place" opens it up to refer not just to the children of Israel but also to Hosea's children. In his own community Hosea's son carried the odious name "Not my people"; Hosea perhaps here promises Lo-Ammi that God would acknowledge him as his son. The people as a whole will also one day experience vindication as God's people. For them "place" need not refer to any specific location at all. Like the English idiom "in place of," it may mean no more than "instead."[99]

The phrase "sons of the living God" is important for three reasons.[100] First, it obviously asserts that they have regained their status and are now acknowledged by God as his own. Second, the title "living God" often appears in a context of military conflict between Israel and the nations. In this "living God" virtually means the "true God" who is able to give victory, in contrast to dead idols (see Deut 5:26; Josh 3:10; 1 Sam 17:26; 2 Kgs 19:4; Jer 10:10–11; Dan 6:26).[101] Third, "living God" also means that he is Lord of life and able to give life, as in Pss 42:2; 84:2).[102] As giver of victory and life, Yahweh will cast out the usurper, Baal, and regain his family (see 2:5–8).[103]

1:11 [2:2] Hosea believes the division of the twelve tribes into two nations to be fundamentally perverse. Israel and Judah are one people and should be one nation. This, along with his conviction that the house of David must lead the people, accounts for this expansion on the previous mention of Judah in the Lo-Ruhamah oracle. Curiously, Hosea says that the united nation will appoint a leader rather than that God would give them a leader. This should not be taken to mean that democracy will replace divine authority; rather, it stresses unanimous spirit of the redeemed people. The old conflict between the house of David and the kings of Israel will end.[104] The reunification of the nation under one leader, specifically the Davidic messiah, was to become a major element of the prophetic hope. Ezekiel, in particular, would develop it (Ezek 37:18–25).

---

[98] Mays, *Hosea,* 32.

[99] Thus Wolff, *Hosea,* 27.

[100] Mays observes that the title "living God" is unique to the OT (*Hosea,* 32).

[101] The term אֵל חַי is found only here and in Josh 3:10; Pss 42:3 (Eng. 2); 84:3 (Eng. 2). Other forms include אֱלֹהִים חַיִּים (e.g., Deut 5:23; 1 Sam 17:36; Jer 10:10) and אֱלֹהִים חַי (Isa 37:4,17). The names are interchangeable and should not be regarded as conveying different meanings. The choice of the specific title אֵל חַי may reflect a desire to contrast Yahweh with the gods of Canaan. Cf. Andersen and Freedman, *Hosea,* 205–6.

[102] Wolff explains that they are not simply renamed "My people" here because that would only imply restoration of the covenant, but not necessarily the future, abundant population (*Hosea,* 27).

[103] The term has nothing to do, however, with the concept of a dying and rising god. But it is used against idolatry to assert that Yahweh is really present and active. See H. Ringgren, "חָיָה chāyāh," *TDOT* 4:324–44, esp. pp. 338–39.

[104] Hosea avoids the word מֶלֶךְ ("king") here and instead uses the word רֹאשׁ ("head"), perhaps because he believes that the new leadership will transcend the old institution of monarchy. See Davies, *Hosea,* 62.

The translation "they ... will come up out of the land" is accurate but perhaps misleading. It implies that Hosea is talking about a return from exile in a new exodus, and this is indeed how many scholars take it.[105] The problem is that it is unprecedented in the Old Testament that Hosea would call foreign nations "the land" *(hā˒āreṣ)*. It is more likely that "they will come up from the land" develops the metaphor of the plant growing up from the earth on the basis of the name Jezreel ("God sows"), the name with which Hosea ends this verse.[106] Growing up out of the land like grass is another way of describing the vast population for Israel that Hosea foresees in the previous verse. Ezekiel also develops this concept in 36:9–11:

> I am concerned for you and will look on you with favor; you will be plowed and sown,[107] and I will multiply the number of people upon you, even the whole house of Israel. The towns will be inhabited and the ruins rebuilt. I will increase the number of men and animals upon you, and they will be fruitful and become numerous.

This does not exhaust, however, the implications of this line. To come up out of the earth also implies resurrection, in which the redeemed break out of the subterranean tomb.[108] If this seems too far-fetched, we should observe that here again Ezekiel combines the idea of a reunited Israel under David to the idea of resurrection (chap. 37).[109] The decimated population of Israel will rebound. On the metaphorical level the verse describes how the people spring up like the grass of the field; on the theological level it asserts that they will rise again from the grave.[110] The ultimate fulfillment of the text is when the united Israel of God stands again under their one head, Christ.[111] This is the great day of Jezreel, when God sows.[112]

[1]"Say of your brothers, 'My people,' and of your sisters, 'My loved one.'

TRANSITIONAL VERSE (2:1).   **2:1 [2:3]**   This verse looks both backward and forward. It is optimistic in tone and concludes the reversal of the three

---

[105] E.g., Andersen and Freedman, *Hosea,* 209.

[106] See McComiskey, "Hosea," 1:30; Hubbard, *Hosea,* 68. Cf. Gen 2:6; 41:5,22.

[107] וּזְרַעְתֶּם, using the same root as Jezreel.

[108] See Job 10:21–22.

[109] Even those who do not regard the dry bones vision as a statement of a literal resurrection must concede that resurrection is the operating metaphor there.

[110] This is true typology, in which the ultimate fulfillment (resurrection) is implicit in the language of a nearer fulfillment (restoration of the population). It is not allegorism, nor are we waffling on the meaning of the phrase. In my view the dry bones prophecy of Ezek 37 functions in the same way.

[111] See Wolff, *Hosea,* 29.

[112] We cannot but wonder if there is an intended reversal of the Baal myth here. Instead of a myth of a dying and rising god who releases the fertility of the earth, we have a metaphor of fertility for resurrection of the people of Israel.

names. Just as Jezreel would become a name of salvation, so Lo-Ruhamah and
Lo-Ammi would be transformed into "My loved one" *(rûḥāmâ)* and "My people" *(ʿammî)*. On the other hand, it also looks ahead to the next verse in that it
begins with an imperative and directly addresses Hosea's children. The transitional, Janus-nature of this verse binds what precedes to what follows. It is
impossible to sever chap. 2 [Hb. 2:3–25] from the Lo-Ammi oracle.

The change of name reflects a real change of status. It can be negative (cf.
Ruth 1:20) or positive (cf. Gen 17:5,15; Isa 62:4; Jer 3:17; Matt 16:18). Here
the name change reflects an authentic act of grace and is no insignificant label,
as is implied in Juliet's pouty question: "What's in a name? That which we call
a rose / By any other name would smell as sweet."[113]

> 2"**Rebuke your mother, rebuke her,**
> **for she is not my wife,**
> **and I am not her husband.**
> **Let her remove the adulterous look from her face**
> **and the unfaithfulness from between her breasts.**
> 3**Otherwise I will strip her naked**
> **and make her as bare as on the day she was born;**
> **I will make her like a desert,**
> **turn her into a parched land,**
> **and slay her with thirst.**
> 4**I will not show my love to her children,**
> **because they are the children of adultery.**

WARNING OF JUDGMENT (2:2–4) [B].   Formally, the imperative
addressed to the children (2:2aα) links this section to the previous section via
the transitional 2:1, as described above. Again, however, the text is incongruous. Hosea first tells the children that they are beloved and "my people" and
then tells them that he will not show love to them. Again he sets two opposed
but equally true realities alongside each other.

This passage is in two parts (2:2a and 2:2b–4, with the second part joined to
the beginning of the second transitional verse (2:5a) in a chiasmus, as the following diagram illustrates.

A   Children must denounce their mother (2:2aa)
     B   Because she has lost her status as wife (2:2ab)
A′ Wife must abandon adultery (2:2b)
     B′   She will be abandoned (2:3)
     B″   Children will be rejected (2:4a)
A″ Wife is an adulteress and conceived children in shame (2:4b–5a)

The A lines describe the wife as an adulteress and tell what she and the chil-

---

[113] *Romeo and Juliet,* act 2, sc. 1.88.

dren must do, and the B lines describe the rejection she and the children suffer as a result of her adultery. It begins with Hosea's call for the children to renounce her (2:2aα) and ends with the explanation that they were conceived with the shame of adultery on their heads (2:4b,5aβ).

2:2 [2:4] The translation "rebuke" is accurate for the Hebrew *rîbû*, but it does not fully convey what is meant here and may be misleading. "Rebuke" seems to imply that the children would be speaking from a position of moral superiority, as though they were prophets censuring the nation. This is not correct; the children were not (yet) a righteous remnant; they were themselves the "children of adultery" who were in danger of falling with their mother.[114] And *rîbû* cannot mean "plead,"[115] as some have it, because the word does not describe an appeal for someone to amend his or her ways.[116] Nor is "accuse" a particularly good translation here, if from that we take the setting to be a courtroom, since nothing else in the context implies that at this point we have a trial in progress.[117] The word is at most quasi judicial here. Hosea is not calling upon the children to testify against their mother in a trial; rather, they are to repudiate her behavior. Not every accusation is a courtroom accusation, even metaphorically; people often accuse one another of misdeeds outside courts of law. Thus *rîbû* here means to "find fault with," to "contend against," or to "denounce." In saying that the children must denounce their mother, Hosea is not calling on them to testify formally. He is saying that they must set themselves apart from their mother lest they suffer the same fate she does.[118]

"For she is not my wife, and I am not her husband"[119] explains why they must denounce their mother. The Israelites believed that they were God's people

---

[114] Cf. Andersen and Freedman, *Hosea*, 219.

[115] Cf. NRSV. McComiskey argues for "plead" since, he says, the children are appealing for her to put away her adulteries ("Hosea," 1:32). But "let her remove …" is not spoken by the children. Yahweh is the speaker, and he is telling the children what the mother should do; he is not giving them words that they are to repeat to her.

[116] Cf. Davies, *Hosea*, 69. He notes that 4:4 sets רָב in parallel with יוֹכַח ("accuse").

[117] The word רִיב can be used in a judicial setting, but it does not require it. See Andersen and Freedman (*Hosea*, 219), who observe that none of the formal characteristics of a trial are present (e.g., a summons to witnesses or a call for a vindicator). Mays (*Hosea*, 37–38) defends the translation "accuse," but the image implied, that of children standing up in court to bring charges of adultery against their mother, is unnatural and does not illuminate the rest of the text. Furthermore, כִּי does not introduce indirect discourse here. Mays renders it "make complaint that she is not my wife." Stuart (*Hosea–Jonah*, 44) is similar. But "she is not my wife" is not a legal complaint or accusation. Also I have not found any occurrence of כִּי with רִיב that functions in the way Stuart describes. כִּי simply means "because" here.

[118] We should not interpret Hosea's call to the children as an ancient counterpart to a divorced couple competing for the allegiance of their children.

[119] The line כִּי־הִיא לֹא אִשְׁתִּי וְאָנֹכִי לֹא אִישָׁהּ appears deliberately constructed to create two parallels to לֹא עַמִּי (לֹא אִשְׁתִּי and לֹא אִישָׁהּ). This again shows that we are still in the Lo-Ammi oracle.

solely because they were Israelites. God was in covenant with this nation, and their identity as Israelites assured them of their special place before God. Now God declares that the bond between himself and their "mother" is void. Israelites can become God's people only by renouncing Israel! The identity in which they trusted had become the greatest impediment between them and God.[120] This is as great a blow to their religious underpinnings as is John the Baptist's claim that God could raise up children of Abraham from the stones (Matt 3:9). It is common, we should note, for interpreters to treat this language as a divorce decree on the basis of certain parallels from the ancient Near East.[121] While there may be divorce language here, however, this should not be regarded as the dominant metaphor of the text. One does not divorce a wife and then in the same breath call on her to abandon her waywardness and return, as this verse does.

It is, to say the least, a harsh thing to call upon a child to denounce his own mother. We cannot know how this may have played itself out in Hosea's family life. Is it possible that Jezreel and his siblings turned their backs on Gomer? One might hope that they did reject her way of life, but Hosea's personal life is not the real point of this verse. It concerns what Hosea expected of the Israelites. They were to recognize and denounce their culture for what it was—apostate, cruel, and selfish. This, too, is no easy task. No one wants to admit that he is part of a society that is decadent *and that he himself is decadent along with it*. This culture had nurtured a generation of Israelites, and now they were to declare the core values they had received to be fundamentally wrong. The children of Israel were not a righteous remnant, but Hosea called on his audience to become a righteous remnant by rejecting their own perverse society. They must follow Isaiah in his confession, "I am a man of unclean lips, and I dwell among a people of unclean lips" (Isa 6:5). Modern readers of Hosea need to ask whether their culture, including that subculture that identifies itself as Christian, is leading toward or away from God.

---

[120] A number of scholars have wondered whether "she is not my wife, and I am not her husband" is an official divorce decree. Cf. C. H. Gordon, "Hos 2.4–5 in the Light of New Semitic Inscriptions," *ZAW* 54 (1936): 277–80, and M. A. Friedman, "Israel's Response in Hosea 2:17b: 'You are my Husband,'" *JBL* 99 (1980): 199–204. Gordon cites an intriguing Nuzi document in which a man can send his sons to fetch his ex-wife's clothing should she take up with another man. In that case, however, the sons do not accuse in court; they simply recover the estranged husband's property. "She is not my wife ..." cannot be a legal proceeding here since it is addressed to the children; the children do not address some imaginary court. The text does, on the other hand, assert that the marriage bond is broken. Thus it speaks of the fact of a divorce, but it does not necessarily relate to legal proceedings of divorce. But again we are in the realm of theological metaphor here. We cannot know whether Hosea and Gomer legally divorced. See also Andersen and Freedman, *Hosea*, 223–24.

[121] For a defense of interpreting this language as a divorce decree, see W. D. Whitt, "The Divorce of Yahweh and Asherah in Hos 2,4–7.12 ff," *Scandinavian Journal of the Old Testament* 6 (1992): 31–67. Whitt develops the most improbable thesis that in Hosea, Yahweh divorces his wife, the goddess Asherah, on the grounds that she has committed adultery with Baal (i.e., that the people have been worshiping Asherah as consort of Baal instead of as consort of Yahweh).

The translation "Let her remove the adulterous look from her face and the unfaithfulness from between her breasts" gives one interpretation of what in Hebrew is a difficult text. The Hebrew actually calls on the woman to remove "promiscuity" (not an "adulterous look") from her face. A number of scholars take the "promiscuity" and "adultery" that are on the woman's face and between her breasts to be some kind of jewelry, either cultic trinkets that mark her consecration to a shrine[122] or the characteristic jewelry of a prostitute.[123] The "promiscuity" on her face could then be the cosmetics that characterized prostitutes. Some have even suggested (less plausibly) that tattoos or lacerations on the flesh from orgiastic sex are meant.[124] Probably "promiscuity" and "adultery" are deliberately ambiguous, referring to the promiscuity itself and anything that pertains to promiscuity, including perhaps ornamentation.

More significant here are the words "face" and "breasts." "Face" suggests intent and personality, and "breasts" by metonymy represents the body with particular emphasis on sexuality. In short, the woman is called upon to turn her whole person away from lewd and faithless behavior. She must abandon her old ways and everything that went along with them.

2:3 [2:5] Two metaphors work together here. The first is of an adulterous woman being stripped naked by her husband, and the second is the desertification of the land. The naked woman here is not sensual; she is humiliated before all and abandoned to her fate with nothing to protect her. "As on the day she was born" connotes not just nakedness but also helplessness (cf. Ezek 16:4–5). The denuded land is incapable of supporting life and is deserted by those who once dwelt there. God will leave the people to their fate, and the land will revert to wilderness. The two metaphors merge when the woman of the first metaphor dies of thirst in the desert of the second metaphor.[125] The point is that Israel will lose everything, the land will be emptied, and the people will go into exile. In the ancient world captives were often taken away naked.

Gordon has argued that in some ancient cultures stripping the wife was a normal part of divorce and thus that the same probably was true in Israel.[126]

---

[122] Mays, *Hosea,* 38. Also Hubbard (*Hosea,* 73), who compares Jer 4:30 and Song 1:13.

[123] This is not as far-fetched as it may seem to the English reader. The abstract plurals זְנוּנֶיהָ and נַאֲפוּפֶיהָ lend themselves to being taken concretely as objects associated with promiscuous behavior. Still it is far from certain that this is the meaning.

[124] The latter suggestion is made by Wolff, *Hosea,* 34.

[125] McComiskey ("Hosea," 1:33) points out other metaphor shifts in Hosea at 7:4,8; 10:11–12; 13:13; 14:5–7.

[126] Gordon, "Hos 2.4–5," 277–80. He cites a Kassite text from *Ḫana,* two Nuzi texts, a Jewish exorcism text from pre-Islamic Nippur, and a German custom described by Tacitus in Germanica 19. The Tacitus text describes the punishment for an adulterous woman and is not properly a divorce proceeding (it rather supports Gordis's view below). The Mesopotamian practice appears to be more of a way of declaring that the woman has no right to carry property from her ex-husband's home. E.g., when a man sends his sons to the home of his ex-wife's new lover to get her clothes, it seems to reflect the fact that the man himself could not go into the other man's home, and it appears to be more a fetching of property than a public humiliation of the woman.

Gordis, however, replies that in Israel an outraged husband could publicly strip his adulterous wife but that this was not the routine for ordinary divorce.[127] Neither scholar has compelling arguments. Judging from similar threats in other prophets (Jer 13:22–27; Ezek 16:37–39; Nah 3:4–5), it is conceivable that something like public exposure for prostitution happened in Israelite society, but the evidence is far from certain. We cannot be sure whether the Israelites actually had such a practice or whether stripping adulterous Israel is simply a prophetic motif. The Torah prescribes the death penalty for both guilty parties in adultery (Lev 20:10; Deut 22:22) but does not call for a public exposure of the woman. Deuteronomy 24 simply describes divorce procedure as the writing of a "bill of divorce," again with no hint that a woman would be sent out naked. The prophets' metaphorical warnings that Yahweh would strip Israel (Jer 13:22–27; Ezek 16:37–39; this text) do not necessarily tell us anything about Israelite divorce practices. Furthermore, we cannot be sure that supposed parallels from other ancient cultures tell us much about Israelite society. Behind the metaphor of nakedness in the prophets is the threat that the people will go into exile, and ancient art work routinely portrays exiles naked. Thus the nakedness of the woman in these passages probably has more to do with the realities of conquest in the ancient world than with their divorce laws.

The most telling detail is the nature of the exposure in Hos 2:10 and Ezek 16:37–39. Yahweh does something that no injured husband would do—he arranges for a private showing of his naked wife before her lovers, before the very men who made him a cuckold! Clearly, the imagery has moved out of the realm of actual Israelite customs for dealing with an adulteress and into an artificial, parabolic world in which metaphors are molded to suit the prophet's message. The "lovers" are the foreign nations and their gods, and the exposure of the woman is the abandonment of Israel to foreign domination. The irony in the image is that one willingly strips naked in order to commit adultery. Israel once voluntarily committed adultery through reliance on foreign powers and their gods, but now she would be forcibly stripped by these same powers in conquest.[128]

We have no grounds for asserting that Hosea cast Gomer naked out of his house, much less that he called in her former clients and stripped her in their presence. Clearly he did not have her executed, which the Law did permit. Unlike 1:2–3 or 1:8, 2:3 is not autobiographical; its real focus is the exile and

---

[127] Gordis, in "Hosea's Marriage," argues on p. 20 (n. 30a) that stripping the woman was not part of Israelite divorce proceedings but was a punishment for adulterous women. He cites the Mishnah (*Sanhedrin* 6:3), but this text only says that a woman should not be naked when stoned to death but that a man could be stripped naked. It does not specifically concern adultery and does not assert that an adulterous woman should be or ever was publicly stripped.

[128] In Ezek 16:37–39 the movement from "exposure" to violent conquest to exile is self-evident.

devastation that is ahead for the nation. All we can say with any confidence regarding Hosea's family is that Gomer was unfaithful and that at some point after the birth of Lo-Ammi she departed.

2:4 [2:6] This verse is a commentary on the names Lo-Ruhamah, "not loved," and Lo-Ammi, "not my people."[129] He calls the children "her children" rather than "my children," which again begs the question of whether Lo-Ruhamah and Lo-Ammi were really Hosea's and again demands that we confess ignorance. Hubbard lists three possible explanations for the punishment of the children: (1) they are illegitimate, that is, not Hosea's; (2) they are themselves adulterers; (3) they participate in her guilt via "corporate solidarity."[130] But none of these solutions is satisfactory, and such reasoning misses Hosea's point entirely.

The important point here is the *metaphor*, which presents the Israelite people as illegitimate claimants to the title of the people of God. The culture of Israel, particularly its political and religious leadership, is here metaphorically the prostitute mother of the Israelite people. This culture has given birth to a generation that has no right to call Yahweh their father. In contemporary terms we might say the people of Hosea's time were the "Generation X" of Israelite history. They had lost all connection with what it meant to be the keepers of the covenant. Their "mother" had taught them nothing but greed, immorality, and idolatry. Yahweh looked at this misbegotten generation and in effect declared them to be Baal's offspring and not his.

> [5]Their mother has been unfaithful
>   and has conceived them in disgrace.
> She said, 'I will go after my lovers,
>   who give me my food and my water,
>   my wool and my linen, my oil and my drink.'

SECOND TRANSITIONAL VERSE (2:5).   **2:5 [2:7]** This verse, like 2:1, looks both backward and forward.[131] It looks back to the previous section in that it explains why Israel's children were "children of adultery," and it looks ahead in that it describes the sin for which she would be punished according to 2:6–13. But the verse is a unity and cannot be split down the middle because 2:5b expounds on the meaning of 2:5a.

Once again we face the questions about the paternity of Hosea's children;

---

[129] Note the self-evident play on the name Lo-Ruhamah in אֲרַחֵם לֹא ("I will not show love"). This again throws doubt on the notion that Hosea was speaking of his step-children, other children of Gomer (McComiskey, "Hosea," 1:33–34).

[130] Hubbard, *Hosea,* 74.

[131] C. Westermann analyzes 2:5–7 form-critically as an "announcement of judgment against Israel" but does not observe that v. 5 looks backwards as well as forward (*Basic Forms of Prophetic Speech* [Philadelphia: Westminster, 1967], 174).

here suspicions arise from the assertion that their mother "conceived them in disgrace." Again we do not know; the verse only tells us that she was in the status of disgrace when she conceived the children, and the Israelite people are again the focus of the message. However, we should not miss the rhetorical effect of these accumulated doubts over the paternity of Hosea's family. Just as neighbors must have asked themselves if these children could possibly be Hosea's, so Hosea sowed doubt about Israel's spiritual paternity—Is Yahweh really our God, or are we the children of Baal?

This text subtly alludes to the principal alleged benefit of Baalism, fertility. It tells us that the woman conceived children, and the woman contends[132] that she received all kinds of agricultural bounty from her lovers. Numerous offspring and agricultural prosperity were the two compensations that the fertility cults promised their devotees. It may even be that the line "who give me my food and my water, my wool and my linen, my oil and my drink" is a fragment of a fertility cult hymn that Hosea's contemporaries sang.[133] If Gomer was a follower of these cults, she probably considered the three children to be her rewards. Also, of course, the "lovers" refer to foreign nations with whom Israel formed alliances for the benefits they supposedly could offer.[134]

> [6]**Therefore I will block her path with thornbushes;**
> **I will wall her in so that she cannot find her way.**
> [7]**She will chase after her lovers but not catch them;**
> **she will look for them but not find them.**
> **Then she will say,**
> **'I will go back to my husband as at first,**
> **for then I was better off than now.'**
> [8]**She has not acknowledged that I was the one**
> **who gave her the grain, the new wine and oil,**
> **who lavished on her the silver and gold—**
> **which they used for Baal.**
>
> [9]**"Therefore I will take away my grain when it ripens,**

---

[132] The *qatal* form (perfect tense) אָמְרָה expresses the deluded thinking of Israel. Cf. Keil, *Hosea*, 54. It should be translated in the present tense, "she says."

[133] Some contend that וּפִשְׁתִּי should be vocalized as a plural (וּפִשְׁתַּי) on the analogy of the pattern of the other two word pairs (singular followed by plural). See Wolff, *Hosea*, 30, and Andersen and Freedman, *Hosea*, 232. The word פֵּשֶׁת ("flax") appears as both a singular and plural. But the term with a first-person suffix is found only in one other place, Hos 2:11 (Eng. 9), where it is singular. We should not revocalize on the basis of what is aesthetically pleasing to us. See K. A. Tångberg, "A Note on *pištî* in Hosea II, 7, 11," *VT* 27 (1977): 222–24, who rejects the revocalization and makes the suggestion that this is a hymn fragment.

[134] It is not certain, in my view, that this text establishes that the Israelites celebrated a *hieros gamos* ("sacred marriage") ritual, although it is possible. Cf. H. Ringgren, "The Marriage Motif in Israelite Religion," in *Ancient Israelite Religion,* ed. P. D. Miller, Jr., P. D. Hanson, and S. D. McBride (Philadelphia: Fortress, 1987), 421–28.

and my new wine when it is ready.
I will take back my wool and my linen,
   intended to cover her nakedness.
[10]So now I will expose her lewdness
   before the eyes of her lovers;
   no one will take her out of my hands.
[11]I will stop all her celebrations:
   her yearly festivals, her New Moons,
   her Sabbath days—all her appointed feasts.
[12]I will ruin her vines and her fig trees,
   which she said were her pay from her lovers;
I will make them a thicket,
   and wild animals will devour them.
[13]I will punish her for the days
   she burned incense to the Baals;
she decked herself with rings and jewelry,
   and went after her lovers,
   but me she forgot,"

declares the LORD.

REDEMPTIVE PUNISHMENT (2:6–13) [B′].   Structural analysis of Hosea
is difficult because he carefully interweaves his texts and does not simply work
with discrete blocks. For our purposes we must divide the text into separate
units, but we must observe how Hosea breaks these boundaries and ties texts
together at many different points. This passage is in two parts. The first part
actually includes the second half of v. 5, the transitional verse, and describes
how Yahweh will block her off from the lovers she has sought. This part ends
at 2:7b, which anticipates that she will return to Yahweh. The pattern is thus sin,
punishment, and redemption. The second part focuses on Israel's refusal to
acknowledge that Yahweh is the source of fertility and agricultural prosperity,
for which the punishment is depravity and starvation. This repeats the sin and
punishment pattern and leads the reader to look for a second redemption text.
But Hosea first concludes the sin and punishment theme with a summary verse
(2:13) and then devotes a larger section to redemption (2:14–23).

A   Sin = going after lovers for agricultural bounty (2:5b)
 B   Punishment [135] = walling her in (2:6–7a)
  C   Anticipated redemption = she will seek her husband (2:7b)
A′   Sin = refusal to acknowledge Yahweh as source of bounty and
            fertility (2:8)
 B″   Punishment = she will be destitute (2:9–12)
A″   Summary of sin = devotion to Baal and to decadence (2:13)
  C′   Redemption = Yahweh will draw her back and restore her (2:14–23)

---

[135] Note use of לְכֵן in vv. 6 and 9 (Hb. 8 and 11).

2:6–7a [2:8–9a]   The imagery here implies entrapment and frustration. Does the walling in imply a metaphor of Israel as a wanton heifer (4:16)? Does it anticipate exile? It is possible but unlikely that this has a literal counterpart in the isolation of an immoral woman from society in a kind of imprisonment. The context describes agricultural prosperity, so the walls could be garden walls. Thorns were also used as a hedgerow to keep wild animals out of garden land. The idea might be that she was like a wild animal or a thief trying to get food that did not belong to her. But blocking "paths" is not a garden metaphor, so we should not press any interpretation too far.[136] The main point is that Israel's attempts to get what she needed from the foreign nations and their gods would come to naught.

2:7b [2:9b]   This verse does not specifically promise redemption, but it anticipates it. We do not see here any assurance that Yahweh will forgive Israel, only the expectation that Israel will seek him. But such a change in attitude on her part is preparatory to the redemption in 2:14–23. The fact that she will seek her "husband" anticipates the promise of 2:16, "You will call me 'my husband'; you will no longer call me 'my Baal.'"[137]

2:8 [2:10]   The verbs here should be translated in the present tense.[138] "She does not know that I am the one who gives her the grain and the wine and the fresh oil; / And I make her silver[139] increase, but she makes gold into Baal."[140] The point is that this is an ongoing activity that Yahweh must put a stop to; it is not some prior offense for which he must punish them. Yahweh is the true fertility God—not in the lecherous sense in which they perceived Baal to give fertility but in the sense that harvests, wealth, and indeed children come from the Lord. Year by year Yahweh gives them plenty, and year by year they attribute their fortune to Baal and honor him out of their prosperity. In the Feast of Harvest Israel was supposed to acknowledge that all the bounty of the land came from God (Lev 23:10–20; Deut 26:10–11).

2:9–10 [2:11–12]   Behind the threat of deprivation stands the curses for

---

[136] The figurative use of גָּדֵר ("to wall off") to describe God blocking a person's alternatives appears in Job 19:8 (with אֹרַח, "path") and Lam 3:9 (with דֶּרֶךְ, "way"). This may have been a stock metaphor for God's activity of frustrating human plans, and if so, we should not seek a specific context for the metaphor.

[137] Note the use of אִישִׁי ("my husband") in both places.

[138] The perfective aspect of the *qatal* form is not necessarily past action, and it certainly is not always "completed action." This is particularly true in prophetic discourse. E.g., Isa 1:14: "My soul hates [שָׂנְאָה] your new moons and festivals; they are [הָיוּ] a burden upon me that I am tired of bearing [נִלְאֵיתִי נְשֹׂא]."

[139] Hubbard (*Hosea*, 77) states that in ancient Israel silver was more valuable than gold.

[140] The idiom עשׂה ל usually means to "make into" and would imply that they made their gold into images of Baal. McComiskey ("Hosea," 1:36) states that the term may include the idea of making idols but is not limited to that, since the term Baal here has the article and thus is the god, and not merely an idol. He thinks it means that they used the gold for Baal.

apostasy found in Deuteronomy 28. For example, "The fruit of your womb will be cursed, and the crops of your land, and the calves of your herds and the lambs of your flocks" (Deut 28:18). The list of staples in v. 9 obviously recalls the lists in vv. 5 and 8. We should also observe, however, the items that Yahweh will take away from the people, food and clothing, are necessities and not luxuries. The punishment is dramatic and severe. At the same time, Yahweh is only taking back what is rightfully his. He is a husband retrieving[141] his property from his wayward wife. To take away the grain "when it ripens" implies a failure of the harvest and is the means by which Yahweh will refute Baal's pretensions of being a god of fertility.

Once again the text uses the image of stripping the woman. It operates on three levels: as a warning of coming captivity,[142] as a depiction of destitution,[143] and as a mark of public humiliation.[144] Verse 10 focuses on the shaming of the woman through public disgrace.[145] Shame played a large role in the ancient world, and we should not underestimate the trauma involved in defeat and economic setbacks, which all would interpret as outer signs of moral and spiritual failure (see 2 Sam 19:3; Pss 6:10; 83:17; Isa 1:29; Jer 48:13–14; Mic 7:16–17). The line "no one will take her out of my hands" does not mean that the false gods will try to help but fail.[146] If anything, the other gods are the "lovers" who join in shaming the woman when she is exposed. Rather, Hosea contrasts the power of God to lay waste Israel with human[147] inability to protect her. Neither military strength nor even prayer will be effective; and no one, by cunning, effort, or saintliness, can allay the coming disaster (cf. Ezek 14:13–14, which declares that even Noah, Daniel, and Job could not turn aside God's wrath).

2:11 [2:13]   We can easily miss the significance of the Israelite ritual life. Ward remarks: "No institution of modern public life occupies a comparable role as a molder of human behavior. The functions analogous to those of

---

[141] The phrase וְלָקַחְתִּי אָשׁוּב is idiomatic and means "I shall retrieve." See Deut 24:4,19; and Jer 36:28. Deut 24:4, e.g., states that if a man divorces a woman, then she remarries and divorces her second husband, the first husband is not free to take her back (לָשׁוּב לְקַחְתָּהּ). One should not follow Andersen and Freedman, *Hosea*, 244, in their translation, "I reverse myself," for אָשׁוּב. On the other hand, they are correct that there is an ironic link between this אָשׁוּב and the woman's וְאָשׁוּבָה in v. 9 (Eng. 7).

[142] As in Isa 20:1–6, where Isaiah walks naked as a sign of coming captivity.

[143] As mentioned above, v. 9 describes the removal of the necessities of life, food and clothing.

[144] The word עֶרְוָתָהּ ("her nakedness," v. 11 [Eng. 9]) probably refers specifically to exposure of the genital area; cf. *HALAT*, 882. In v. 12 (Eng. 10) נַבְלֻתָהּ ("her shame") also might refer to the genitals. See S. M. Olyan, " 'In the Sight of her Lovers': On the Interpretation of *nablūt* in Hos 2,12," *BZ* ns 36 (1992): 255–61, *HALAT*, 664, and Andersen and Freedman, *Hosea*, 248.

[145] Again, however, there are no grounds for seeing this as normal punishment inflicted on an adulteress, or for supposing that Hosea stripped Gomer in front of her lovers. See comments on 2:3.

[146] Contra Harper, *Amos and Hosea*, 231.

[147] The word וְאִישׁ ("and a man") in this verse focuses on human limitations vis-à-vis God.

church, school, press, and theatre resided in the single instrumentality of the annual covenantal celebration."[148] The festivals had been corrupted by Baalism, and Wolff may be correct that some of the rites had degenerated to sexual orgies.[149] On the other hand, we should not exaggerate this possibility since Hosea does not here describe any such behavior in the cult. It is important to recognize that these festivals were all essential parts of Israel's covenant life. They were Israel's expressions of love and gratitude to Yahweh and were to be occasions of joy (Lev 23:40; Deut 26:11). For us it is noteworthy that their apostasy had not caused them to abandon the routines of life under the covenant. They could carry on the outward duties the faith required without realizing that God had rejected them and was determined to put this pretense to an end.[150] The tragedy is not that so many were desperately licentious but that so many had fallen so far from God and did not know it.

2:12 [2:14]   Structurally, this verse looks back to vv. 5b and 8. Once again a present-tense translation is more appropriate than "she said": "I will ruin her vines and fig trees, about which she says, 'These are my rewards which my lovers give me,' and I will turn them into a wilderness, and the beasts of the field will eat them." The loss of vineyards and fruit trees is catastrophic; grains could be replanted and bear fruit in a single year, but these could not. This reflects a total reversion to wilderness and not just a temporary setback, as might occur because of drought or locusts. The fact that wild animals could freely take whatever crops remain implies that the people would be too few to resist them. Also the reference to beasts here is reversed by the covenant with the animals in 2:18.

We should not miss the tone of religious devotion in the woman's words. She—Israel—really believed that she was practicing sound principles of religion and that she was receiving the appropriate rewards.[151] Fixation on the adultery metaphor and on erotic aspects of the fertility cult can prevent us from recognizing the sincere devotion—and spiritual blindness—that had seized the people. Perhaps this is because we too feel vindicated by the external trappings of success and take this to be the validation of our theology and practice. Could

---

[148] J. Ward, *Hosea: A Theological Commentary* (New York: Harper & Row, 1966), 31.

[149] Wolff, *Hosea,* 38.

[150] Note the irony of וְהִשְׁבַּתִּי ("I shall bring to a halt") and וְשַׁבַּתָּה ("her Sabbath"). Also Andersen and Freedman (*Hosea,* 250) observe that this verse contains discontinuous hendiadys with כָּל־מְשׂוֹשָׂהּ and וְכֹל מוֹעֲדָהּ. We might translate it, "And I shall put an end to all her celebrations—her holy days, new moons, and Sabbaths—and all her festivals."

[151] Wolff (*Hosea,* 38) sees the use of the hapax legomenon אֶתְנָה instead of the more common אֶתְנַן ("prostitute's fee," Deut 23:19; Mic 1:7; Hos 9:1) to be simply a wordplay on תְּאֵנָה ("fig tree"). While he is no doubt correct that there is a pun here, I am inclined to agree with Andersen and Freedman (*Hosea,* 254) that the avoidance of a term that simply means a prostitute's hire is deliberate. We should not allow the sexual metaphor to dominate the text entirely, or we may miss its deeper meaning.

we go back to Hosea's time, we might be shocked to discover that the spiritual decadence of Hosea's day was no more severe than that of our own. Worse yet, we might find ourselves wondering why Hosea was so upset with his generation because we have more in common with them than with him.

2:13 [2:15]   This verse is better translated, "And I will bring upon her the days of the Baals, when she burns incense to them, and adorns herself with rings and jewelry, and goes after her lovers, but me she forgets, says Yahweh." Once again all the verbs but the first describe ongoing action.[152] Also, although "punish" in the NIV is not incorrect, this translation loses the sense of fitting retribution that is implied here.[153] The idea is that Yahweh will turn his back on Israel just as she has turned her back on him. Yahweh, the jilted husband, will jilt desperate Israel when they call to him. It is in this sense that they will experience the "days of the Baals,"[154] which the text has here defined as the time when she turns from her husband to flirt with paramours.

The "Baals" here are either different deities who all carry the name Baal or are one deity as he is honored at various shrines throughout the land. Ugaritic literature has given us a better understanding of Baal Hadad,[155] who in some sense is behind all the Baals. According to the texts, he defeated the sea god Yamm, who represents chaos and destruction. Also, with the aid of his sister-consort Anat, he annually overcame Mot, the god of death who was manifested in the summer drought. It was in this capacity that Baalism attracted the Israelites—they believed that he could bring the rains necessary for a good harvest. The myth exists only in a fragmentary condition, but in it Baal dies at the hand of Mot, and during his sojourn in the grave the earth "dies" with the summer

---

[152] This verse is something of a textbook case for the use of finite verb forms in prophetic discourse. As is typical in such texts, the *weqatal* form (וּפָקַדְתִּי) here indicates future action. However, all the verbs after אֲשֶׁר are a series of subordinate clauses that modify יְמֵי הַבְּעָלִים. The *yiqtol* תַּקְטִיר cannot be future or past tense—it must be regarded as a description of present action. See Andersen and Freedman, *Hosea,* 258. Two *wayyiqtols* then follow, וַתַּעַד and וַתֵּלֶךְ. In historical narrative *wayyiqtols* describe past action and carry the foreground action of the narrative. This, however, is prophetic discourse, in which they do not have this function. Rather, in this case at least they can only be construed as continuing the time frame of the prior *yiqtol*, which as we have seen is present. Here the text could not have used *weqatal* phrases because, in prophetic discourse, that implies future tense. The same time frame continues, but strong contrast and focus on "me" (אֹתִי) appears in the *waw X qatal* phrase וְאֹתִי שָׁכְחָה.

[153] The phrase וּפָקַדְתִּי עָלֶיהָ אֶת־יְמֵי הַבְּעָלִים ("and I will visit upon her the days of the Baals") recalls וּפָקַדְתִּי אֶת־דְּמֵי יִזְרְעֶאל עַל־בֵּית יֵהוּא ("and I will visit the blood of Jezreel upon the house of Jehu") from 1:4. In both cases it is not precisely punishment but forcing someone to experience what he or she has done to others. The NIV should not break up the construct chain אֶת־יְמֵי הַבְּעָלִים ("the days of the Baals"), as it does.

[154] One also has to wonder, in light of the cultic setting, whether we should here recall the familiar theme of the "sacrifice of Yahweh" when he slaughters his enemies. See Isa 34:6; Jer 46:10; Ezek 39:17; Zeph 1:7.

[155] See *ANET,* 129–42.

heat. His return and defeat of Mot, however, brings the autumn rains. The mythological texts contain practices that no doubt were repeated in the actual rituals of the devotees of the cult. For example, after the death of Baal, his father, El, and sister-consort, Anat, gashed and cut themselves from grief (see 1 Kgs 18:28). Prior to entering the underworld, moreover, Baal had intercourse with a cow (probably Anat in this form), and she gave birth to Baal's son, Math. This may represent the season of calving in Palestinian agriculture and helps us to understand how the Canaanites could have thought that ritual sex in the Baal shrines was necessary to insure healthy breeding of the flocks and herds. Thus in Hosea 2 Israel attributes all her agricultural bounty to Baal.

As does so much else in this chapter, the woman putting on jewelry and going after lovers functions on at least two levels. It is Israel going after her paramours, but it is also probably the women of Israel wearing sacred jewelry and going to the Baal shrines.

> **14"Therefore I am now going to allure her;**
>   **I will lead her into the desert**
>   **and speak tenderly to her.**
> **15There I will give her back her vineyards,**
>   **and will make the Valley of Achor a door of hope.**
> **There she will sing as in the days of her youth,**
>   **as in the day she came up out of Egypt.**
>
> **16"In that day," declares the LORD,**
>   **"you will call me 'my husband';**
>   **you will no longer call me 'my master.'**
> **17I will remove the names of the Baals from her lips;**
>   **no longer will their names be invoked.**
> **18In that day I will make a covenant for them**
>   **with the beasts of the field and the birds of the air**
>   **and the creatures that move along the ground.**
> **Bow and sword and battle**
>   **I will abolish from the land,**
>   **so that all may lie down in safety.**
> **19I will betroth you to me forever;**
>   **I will betroth you in righteousness and justice,**
>   **in love and compassion.**
> **20I will betroth you in faithfulness,**
>   **and you will acknowledge the LORD.**
>
> **21"In that day I will respond,"**
>   **declares the LORD—**
> **"I will respond to the skies,**
>   **and they will respond to the earth;**
> **22and the earth will respond to the grain,**
>   **the new wine and oil,**

and they will respond to Jezreel.
²³I will plant her for myself in the land;
  I will show my love to the one I called 'Not my loved one.'
I will say to those called 'Not my people,' 'You are my people';
  and they will say, 'You are my God.'"

PROPHECY OF RESTORATION: REVERSAL OF THE ADULTERY (2:14–23) [A']. Hosea concludes the Lo-Ammi oracle with a triumphant declaration of saving grace. Although somewhat disconcerting—once again Hosea moves from the final consequences of rebellion to complete redemption with no transition or explanation—this tense coexistence of judgment and grace parallels the Christian concept of salvation in one important particular. As the Spanish theologian Juan de Valdes (ca. 1509–1541) discovered, the only true knowledge of God is the knowledge of Christ, and this presupposes the experiences of the knowledge of sin through the law and the knowledge of grace through the gospel.[156] Although it jolts what we might intuitively suppose, our experience not only of guilt but also of condemnation and despair is integral to knowing God. But of course there is no gospel at all if there is no redemption, and it is to this that Hosea now turns.

The structure of this text is a parallel structure within an inclusio, as follows:

A: Reversal: Wooing in the wilderness (2:14–15)
  B: A new marriage covenant (2:16–17)
    C: Return to Eden (2:18)
  B': A new marriage covenant (2:19–20)
    C': Return to Eden (2:21–23a)
A': Reversal: The names of the children are changed (2:23bc).

By such structuring, Hosea not only unifies this text but brings about redemption of both the mother and her children. The mother, Israel, experiences the tender love of Yahweh and is reunited to him in an eternal covenant, whereas the children experience the security of a new Eden and have their accursed names turned into names of blessing.

2:14–15 [2:16–17] When Hosea says "Therefore" after what he had said in the previous verse, we can no longer harbor doubts that he is deliberately dealing in non sequiturs.[157] "Therefore" should introduce the logical consequence of what Hosea had just stated, that God would abandon his wife as she had abandoned him. Rather, God promises a new and tender courtship of the wayward woman and holds forth the possibility of a regeneration of the rela-

---

[156] J. Houston, "Knowing God: The Transmission of Reformed Theology," in *Doing Theology for the People of God,* ed. D. Lewis and A. McGrath (Downers Grove: InterVarsity, 1996), 223–44, p. 230.

[157] The word לָכֵן clearly means "therefore." Rather than seek some alternative meaning for לָכֵן, we should acknowledge that Hosea here is deliberately being paradoxical.

tionship through a return to the wilderness. Just as Jeremiah would later foresee a new covenant written on the heart (Jer 31:31–34) and Ezekiel would promise that God would remove their heart of stone and replace it with a heart of flesh touched by the Spirit of God (Ezek 36:26–27), so Hosea sees God speaking tenderly to the heart of his beloved. Not only this, but he pledges himself to restore all the possessions he had just declared that she had forfeited! By metonymy "her vineyards" stands for the orchards, grains, livestock, wool, and flax that Hosea had declared God would strip her of in vv. 3–12.

The return to wilderness here picks up the theme of desolation from these previous verses, moreover, and transforms it into a way of redemption. Later prophets developed this idea too: the wilderness is not only a place of deprivation but is also a place of renewal and innocence (see Jer 2:2; 31:2; Ezek 20:10–38). The annual Festival of Tabernacles (Lev 23:33–43; Deut 16:13–15; Num 29:12–40) also contributes to this metaphor. It took place in what is now mid-October on Tishri 15, five days after the Day of Atonement. For seven days the Israelites lived in huts made from palm fronds and leafy branches of trees while elaborate offerings were made to God. This temporary return to a nomadic way of life recalled the sojourn of the Israelites after the exodus (Lev 23:43). The week was to be a time of joy as a final celebration and thanksgiving for that year's harvest (Deut 16:14–15). This of itself should have acted as an antidote to the Baal cult; the festival was a reminder that they were aliens in the land and that all the bounty they received from it was a gift from Yahweh, who had conquered the gods of Canaan.

Excursus: The Ideal of the Wilderness

Yahweh threatens to turn Israel into a wilderness (Hos 2:3) but then promises to allure Israel into the wilderness and there win her love (2:14). In this, the text of Hosea draws together two theological concepts that are founded on the idea of wilderness. Ancient Israel sat precariously at the edge of a great desert, and this neighboring, hostile world so impressed itself on the minds of the inhabitants that the prophets and other biblical writers repeatedly returned to the ideal of wilderness in order to present the great themes of the Bible.

The basic and most obvious fact about the desert is that it is hostile to human and most other forms of life. It represents, in a sense, the lifeless chaos that existed prior to God's creative work (Gen 1:2). Job 38:26–27 speaks of the wilderness as a "desert wasteland" and a place "where no man lives." For this reason the desert could toughen a person while at the same time making him to be an outcast. Ishmael was a man of the wilderness; he was both adept at survival and lived apart from all ordinary people (Gen 16:7–12; 21:14–21). For the average person wilderness was something to avoid. The Israelites of the exodus complained that they would have preferred to have died in Egypt than to suffer in the wilderness (Exod 14:12; see also Prov 21:19). The wilderness stands in contrast to the city, the place of human habitation.

For this reason the wilderness is the place of punishment, and the archetype for this ideal is the forty years of wandering Israel suffered as punishment for lack of obedience (Num 32:13). Ezekiel 29:5 (here speaking against Egypt) portrays abandonment in the wilderness in terms that bring out what a fearful place it was: "I will leave you in the desert, you and all the fish of your streams. You will fall on the open field and not be gathered or picked up. I will give you as food to the beasts of the earth and the birds of the air."

Frequently the prophets used the image of reversion to wilderness to describe God's rejection of a city. Isaiah 27:10 is typical: "The fortified city stands desolate, an abandoned settlement, forsaken like the desert; there the calves graze, there they lie down; they strip its branches bare." Jeremiah's vision of Yahweh's wrath was similar: "I looked, and the fruitful land was a desert; all its towns lay in ruins before the LORD, before his fierce anger" (Jer 4:26). Joel 2:3, speaking of the northern army, has a similar theme: "Before them fire devours, behind them a flame blazes. Before them the land is like the garden of Eden, behind them, a desert waste—nothing escapes them" (see also Isa 14:17; 33:9; 64:10; Jer 22:6; 50:12; 51:43; and Mal 1:3).

By contrast the prophets promise that God will fructify the wilderness in the eschatological salvation. Isaiah 32:14–17 gives the most complete statement of this aspect of Israel's hope:

The fortress will be abandoned,
  the noisy city deserted;
citadel and watchtower will become a wasteland forever,
  the delight of donkeys, a pasture for flocks,
till the Spirit is poured upon us from on high,
  and the desert becomes a fertile field,
  and the fertile field seems like a forest.
Justice will dwell in the desert
  and righteousness live in the fertile field.
The fruit of righteousness will be peace;
  the effect of righteousness will be quietness and confidence forever.

Isaiah, in fact, makes more of this idea than any other prophet (35:6; 41:18–19; 43:19–20; 51:3), although one does see it elsewhere, as in Ps 107:33–38; Joel 2:22; Ezek 47:1–12.

None of this implies that the Old Testament uniformly treats the wilderness as evil. One could more accurately say that it portrays the desert as harsh and dangerous. The wilderness forces the individual to rely upon God, and the Bible often attributes survival in the wilderness to his grace. The archetype here is the feeding of the nation with manna (Exod 16:11–16), when Yahweh miraculously sustained Israel in the wilderness. One sees reflections of this throughout the Old Testament. An example is Jer 2:6: "They did not say, 'Where is the LORD who brought us up from the land of Egypt, who led us in the wilderness, in a land of deserts and pits, in a land of drought and deep darkness, in a land that no one passes through, where no one lives?'" (see also Deut 8:15–16). Hosea 13:5 alludes to this tradition. In fact, so great was Yahweh's ability to protect his people from the rigors of the wilderness that even their clothes did not wear out (Deut 29:5). When Jesus fed the four thousand in the wilderness (Matt 15:33–34), he demonstrated that he possessed the power of the God of the exodus.

Because God is able to sustain his people in the wilderness, it is also a place of sanctuary in times of danger. David retreated to the wilderness when pursued by his enemies (e.g., 1 Sam 23:14). Elijah was sustained by ravens at the Wadi Kerith (1 Kgs 17:4–6). Psalm 55:6–8 reflects this longing for the security of the wilderness:

I said, "Oh, that I had the wings of a dove!
    I would fly away and be at rest—
I would flee far away
    and stay in the desert;
I would hurry to my place of shelter,
    far from the tempest and storm."

This idea appears again in Jer 31:2, where Israel seeks sanctuary in the wilderness, and in Rev 12:6,14, where the woman flees from the dragon into the wilderness.

As a place of refuge it is also a place where one learns complete reliance on God. The wilderness is therefore also the place of testing, repentance, and spiritual growth. Deuteronomy 8:2 declares that God left Israel in the wilderness for forty years "in order to humble you, testing you to know what was in your heart, whether or not you would keep his commandments." Thus the time of Israel's punishment was redeemed in that it became a time of cleansing and renewal, and Jer 2:2 remembers it not as a time of apostasy but of special devotion to Yahweh. John the Baptist, fulfilling Isa 40:3, preached the message of repentance from the wilderness (Matt 3:1–3). Jesus, moreover, had to confront temptation in the wilderness as the final act of preparation for his ministry (Matt 4), perhaps because it was there he especially confronted the weakness of what it means to be human. Paul also appears to have spent time in the wilderness prior to his missionary work (Gal 1:17).

The wilderness is therefore the place for encountering God, albeit that encounter might involve wrestling with the devil as well. Jacob, alone in the night on the other side of the Jordan, wrestled with the Angel of the Lord (Gen 32:24–31). It was there that Moses saw his great vision at the burning bush (Exod 3) and there that Israel met God and received the Torah (Exod 19–20). In the wilderness Elijah had his greatest encounter with the word of God (1 Kgs 19:10–18). Hosea draws upon this idea in 2:14, where God promises to come to his people in the wilderness.

The idea of wilderness also is prominent in romantic literature, and this, too, fits in well with Hosea. Song of Songs, for example, is replete with pastoral language and images from the wilderness (e.g., Song 4:8; 7:11). In Hosea, Yahweh is taking his beloved back to the paradise of Eden.

The wilderness is therefore a threat to life and is the opposite of the subdued land, the city. It can represent rejection by God, and the eternal peace of God will mean an end to wilderness. But it is also the place of abandoning the world, wealth, and pretense and of depending entirely upon God for life. It is thus the place of grace and the training ground of spirituality. It is no surprise that Christians through the centuries have sought out the desert as the place to learn discipleship and to meet God. Israel, separated from Baal, the nations, and the material allurements of the city, can find herself again in the wilderness.

The references to the "valley of Achor" and the "door of hope" look back to the conquest narrative. After Achan wrongfully took plunder from Jericho, the Israelite conquest of Canaan temporarily failed as the wrath of God came upon them. God's favor returned, and the conquest resumed only after Joshua found out Achan's sin and the man was executed. The text tells us that Achan's grave was marked with a pile of rocks and the location named the valley of Achor ("trouble") as a memorial (Josh 7:26). Achan's sin, we recall, was in seizing riches that God had declared taboo. By analogy the Israel of Hosea's day went after the "gifts" of her lovers. But the grace of God here reverses the meaning of Achor; instead of signifying punishment for greed, it has become a place of restoration.

The phrase "door of hope" is, as Andersen and Freedman comment, unusually abstract.[158] The word translated "hope" is fairly common in Proverbs and Job and occasionally appears elsewhere. Curiously, however, its homonym occurs in Josh 2:18,21, with the meaning "cord," in reference to the scarlet cord Rahab put out as a sign of her allegiance to Israel during the siege of Jericho. Rahab, of course, was the prostitute who sheltered the Israelite scouts and became a mother of the royal line of Israel (cf. Matt 1:5). It is possible that in promising "hope" to fallen Israel, Hosea is making a wordplay that alludes to the salvation of another prostitute, Rahab.

2:16–17 [2:18–19]   The phrase translated "my master" is literally "my Baal." The familiar "in that day" formula looks ahead to the eschatological restoration of Israel (cf. Joel 3:18). What is significant, however, is that the hope of future salvation is the basis for current reformation. In the prediction Hosea says that someday, when God restores his people, they will forever banish the name Baal from their religious life. The very meaning of the term *ba'al*—"lord" or "husband"—made it easy to interject the word into Israelite worship. One could call Yahweh "my Baal" and justify it on the grounds that the term means no more than "my lord." But since the word was also the name of the Canaanite deity, the devotees of Baal could make use of this semantic overlap to smuggle their cult into Yahweh's worship. We see how completely Baalism would be removed in the promise that God would "remove the names of the Baals from her lips; no longer will their names be

---

[158] Andersen and Freedman, *Hosea,* 276.

invoked."[159] Hosea, by declaring that the pure worship of the future would be purged of this term, in effect forbade its use in his own generation. Christians would do well to consider what demands the hopes of the future make upon the present. If the unity of all believers and the removal of all evil will characterize the consummated kingdom of God (Rev 7:9; 22:15), it is surely the case that we should seek to attain those ideals, however imperfectly, in the church today.

2:18 [2:20] This verse looks back to two previous texts in these oracles. First, the promise that God would "make a covenant[160] for them with the beasts of the field and the birds of the air and the creatures that move along the ground" reverses the threat of 2:12. Instead of the wilderness being a place of exposure to the dangers of the wild animals, the animals themselves are brought into covenant relation with the redeemed people. This promise also clearly echoes the description of God's creatures found in Gen 1:21,24.[161] Yahweh therefore mediates between humanity and the rest of creation to end the estrangement between the two (see Gen 3:17–19; Rom 8:20–21). What Hosea has in view, therefore, is a restoration of the creation order—a paradise regained.[162] It is the same vision that Isaiah has in 11:6–7,[163] and that has its fulfillment in the new heaven and new earth of the Rev 21:1.

Second, this verse looks back to 1:7b, which we have already seen is delib-

---

[159] The translation "no longer will their names be invoked" is justifiable but needs comment. The Hb. reads, וְלֹא־יִזָּכְרוּ עוֹד בִּשְׁמָם (which could be rendered "and they shall no longer be remembered by their names"). The root זכר in the *niphal* stem normally means simply "to be remembered" (e.g., Ezek 25:10; Ps 109:14; Jer 11:19). However, in Semitic thought causing someone's name to be remembered was another way of describing the honoring of that person. Similarly, one would desire to see the names of one's enemies forgotten. Making the name of a deity to be remembered therefore implied the praise and invocation of that deity. See Josh 23:7; Isa 26:13; 48:1 (all in *hiphil* stem). In Zech 13:2 Yahweh declares that he will "banish the names of the idols from the land, and they will be remembered no more [וְלֹא יִזָּכְרוּ עוֹד]." To this he adds, "I will remove both the prophets and the spirit of impurity from the land," implying that "remembering" the names of the gods here includes all that is done in honor of these gods, including invocation and prophecy.

[160] McComiskey ("Hosea," 1:44) notes that "covenant" need not imply that the creatures agree as though they had free will. See Jer 33:20.

[161] We might notice that references such as this call into question persistent claims that the preexilic writers knew nothing of the Mosaic Law. See, e.g., W. S. LaSor, D. A. Hubbard, F. W. Bush, *Old Testament Survey,* 2nd ed. (Grand Rapids: Eerdmans, 1996), 9. Hosea's allusion to Gen 1 (and to 8:19), regarded by standard critical theories as among the latest texts of Genesis, is too clear to be doubted. For further discussion see D. A. Garrett, *Rethinking Genesis* (Grand Rapids: Eerdmans, 1991), 54–55.

[162] Despite the similarities between this text and Gen 9:8–17, as pointed out by Davies (*Hosea,* 84), this does not seem to be the real connection Hosea is making. See Andersen and Freedman, *Hosea,* 281.

[163] Cf. B. V. Malchow, "Contrasting Views of Nature in the Hebrew Bible," *Dialog* 26 (1987): 40–43.

erately ambiguous about whether God would save Israel from warfare. Here there is no ambiguity. Hosea promises an end to warfare, a promise that would be developed in Isa 2:4 and Mic 4:3 and which has its fulfillment in Rev 21:2–4.[164] The final promise that all would "lie down in safety" unites both the ideas of peace with the animals and peace with the nations. Sleep here is a metaphor for security.[165] The image of children sleeping[166] peacefully in the midst of animals that had been hostile and nations who had been hostile recalls Isa 11:8.

2:19–20 [2:21–22]   These verses obviously reverse God's declaration that Israel was no longer his wife (2:2). The marriage between Yahweh and Israel is the covenant, but this particular analogy for covenant implies more than either of the other two standard analogies, a contract and a treaty. A simple contract (where business and property is at the heart of the relationship) and a treaty between two nations (where cessation of hostilities or the subordination of one state to another is the issue) can both be executed without any love at all between the two parties. But a marriage—especially as Hosea describes it here—is an act of love. This is no mere reestablishment of the covenant rights of Israel; it is the beginning of a relationship of love between God and his people such as they had not known before. It is a *new* covenant.

As the NIV has it, the four qualities described here go together in two pairs, "in righteousness and justice, in love and compassion."[167] In the analogy of betrothal Yahweh gives righteousness, justice, love, and compassion as the bride-price, the means by which he obtains his bride.[168] What is especially important here is that it is *God's* "righteousness and justice," *not Israel's*, that redeem Israel. As Luther discovered, this throws our whole conception of righteousness on its head. We naturally think of righteousness as the moral quality that we must bring with us if we are to have a relationship with God. It was for this reason that the young Luther hated both righteousness and God. But he says that meditating on Rom 1:17, "I began to understand that 'righteousness of God' as that by which the righteous lives by the gift of God, namely by faith, and this sentence, 'the righteousness of God is revealed,' to refer to a passive righteousness, by which the merciful God justifies us by faith."[169] So too here

---

[164] Wolff (*Hosea*, 51) draws the wrong conclusion when he observes that אֶרֶץ in Hosea always refers to the land, and not to the whole world, and that therefore this is no promise of universal peace. Peace between Israel and the nations, together with the turning of the nations to the worship of the God of Israel, are all part of the final consummation that the prophets discern in the future.

[165] See Job 5:23–24 and Andersen and Freedman, *Hosea,* 282.

[166] The plural suffix on וְהִשְׁכַּבְתִּים implies that the children, not the mother, are in view here.

[167] The term "compassion" (רִחַמִים) implies a reversal of the curse in the name Lo-Ruhamah.

[168] See the use of בְּ with the price paid for a bride when used with אָרַשׂ, "betroth," in 2 Sam 3:14.

[169] Luther's account of his conversion appears in his preface to the first volume of his collected works, first published in 1545. This translation comes from McGrath, *Luther's Theology,* 96–97. See his pp. 95–147 for a full account of Luther's discovery of the righteousness of God.

in Hosea, the righteousness of God is not the moral perfection by which he judges the world but the perfection of compassion by which he saves and communicates his righteousness to his people. God pays the coin of grace to obtain the bride he loves.

"Faithfulness"[170] has a special place in this series because "I will betroth you in faithfulness" repeats the verb and so sets this quality apart from the other four. It would seem, in fact, that faithfulness sums up the other four qualities in a single word. Because God is consistently good ("righteousness and justice"), one can rely upon him to do good consistently to his people. And because God is consistently merciful ("love and compassion"), one can rely upon him to show mercy consistently to his people. The consistent goodness of God, his faithfulness (in contrast to the capriciousness of Baal), is the basis for Israel's salvation.

"You will acknowledge the LORD" is better translated simply as "you shall know the LORD." This is a reversal of God's complaint in 2:13, "but me she forgot." The goal of God's wooing of the people, and the point of the whole text, is that they should know him. To know God implies the deepest relationship with him.[171] It is to love him, to be one of his people, to abandon all other gods, and to be eternally wedded to him. The promise of these two verses anticipates the new covenant promise of Jer 31:31–34.[172] Israel will be bound to Yahweh in an unbreakable covenant, and all the people from least to greatest will know him.

2:21–23a [2:23–25a] The basic sequence of thought in these verses is plain enough: God will address the heavens, and the heavens in turn will send rain to the earth, which in turn will produce the fruit of the soil, which in turn will meet the need of Israel, which had been turned into a wilderness. Thus Hosea gives us another reversal: a good harvest returns to Israel (contrast 2:9). But we need to answer a number of questions. Why does Hosea here use the verb "respond"? Why is Israel called "Jezreel"? Why does God "plant her" in the land?

"Respond" conveys two ideas. It is first of all a positive answer to a call for

---

[170] The basic meaning of אֱמוּנָה is "that which can be relied upon." The word "conveys the idea of inner stability, integrity, conscientiousness, cleanliness, which is essential for any responsible service" and thus basically means "conscientiousness" when used of humans (A. Jepsen, "אָמַה ʾemeth," TDOT 1:317). Used in reference to God, אֱמוּנָה basically emphasizes God's faithfulness to show compassion and to honor the covenant. It is sometimes set parallel to חֶסֶד ("kindness, grace"), as in Ps 89:2. Deut 32:4 calls Yahweh the אֵל אֱמוּנָה. In context this means that Yahweh can always be trusted to do right and is never capricious.

[171] It is well known that יָדַע ("to know") is sometimes used of sexual intercourse (e.g., Gen 4:1). When used in this sense, however, the man is the subject, and there is no erotic implication here in Hosea. Nevertheless, this usage of יָדַע illustrates the kind of intimacy that the verb can carry.

[172] Cf. Mays, Hosea, 50–51.

help.[173] The people are in a desolate land and call for help, the land calls to the heavens for rain, and the heavens look to God for direction. In short, "respond" conveys the idea that the prayers of the people will be answered.[174] Second, "respond" emphasizes the power of the word of God, the same power that acted in creation (Gen 1). In contrast to Baal, Yahweh does not go through some elaborate conflict with death in order to secure a harvest for his people, nor does he need to be rescued by his consort. He simply speaks the word.

"Jezreel" obviously alludes to the name of Hosea's firstborn and looks back to the beginning of the text. It anticipates the name changes in 2:23bc and tells us that we are approaching the end of this section. The name Jezreel had meant calamity for Israel (1:4–5), but now it implies salvation and prosperity. Jezreel means "God sows." Previously Hosea had associated the name with bloodshed (1:4), but now he takes the same name and uses its meaning to teach that God will provide for his people. What had been hidden at first is now revealed: "Jezreel" has a double meaning, and for this reason it, unlike the other two names, need not be changed.

In light of the meaning of "Jezreel," it is clear why God declares that he will "plant" Israel in her land. The word "plant" is the Hebrew word *zāraʿ*, the same word that is part of the name "Jezreel." This brings out another aspect of Jezreel's name. God will not only plant crops, he will also plant a people.[175]

We should notice that the agricultural items specified ("grain, the new wine and oil") do not constitute an exhaustive list of all the crops that the land will produce. On the other hand, two of the items (wine and oil) are associated with celebration and wealth. The point here is that Israel will not only have food and shelter but will have an abundance of the best. Furthermore, by describing their

---

[173] In 1 Kgs 18:26 the priests of Baal call for him to act with the cry, "Baal, answer us!" (הַבַּעַל עֲנֵנוּ).

[174] We should note also that עָנָה is not used in precisely the same way at every point. God "answers" heaven by giving it the command to send rain; heaven "answers" earth with rain; but the grain, new wine, and oil themselves are the answer that the land gives to Jezreel. The produce of earth "answers" Jezreel by meeting the need of the people for food. See also Davies, *Hosea,* 89–90.

[175] The use of the feminine suffix in וּזְרַעְתִּיהָ ("I will plant her") is hardly a problem (contrast Wolff [*Hosea,* 54], who suggests that a protasis has dropped out). Hosea freely moves between describing Israel as the wife of Yahweh and using the names of his children as representatives for the people of Israel. In saying "I will plant her," he both builds a wordplay on the name יִזְרְעֶאל and implies that the days of Israel's suffering in the wilderness (2:3, "I will make her like a desert") are over. To "plant her," we should add, is to describe Israel under the metaphor of the tree that is established, well watered, and secure (as in, e.g., Ps 1:3). It does not mean "I shall sow her" in the sense, "I shall impregnate her." Although the metaphor of a pregnant woman as a field sown with seed is well known (as in the cases cited in Andersen and Freedman, *Hosea,* 288), the text has nowhere threatened the woman Israel with inability to have children. As we have seen, the blessings Yahweh promises to Israel are all reversals of previous curses. Also, although the text speaks of Yahweh wooing and betrothing Israel, to speak of him actually impregnating her, that is, having sexual relations with her, is too close to the Baal cult Hosea himself opposes.

salvation in such cosmic terms, with heaven and earth participating in their deliverance, God in effect declares that he will move the whole universe to bring this about. The ramifications go well beyond the concerns of a small nation on a small piece of land. The return of the exiles is a type for a new order of eternal celebration in a new heaven and earth.

2:23b–c [2:25b–c]   Hosea concludes this extended oracle with a final reversal, the reversal of the names Lo-Ruhamah and Lo-Ammi. This reversal had already been anticipated in 1:6c and 1:10, but here the reversal is made permanent by changing the name "Not my people" to "My people" *('ammî)*. The people's response, "You are my God," fulfills the prophecy of 2:20, that they will know the Lord, and reverses the rejection described in 1:9, "I am not your God." To affirm that Yahweh is their God is to confess that he is their Savior, to submit to him as their only King, to worship him as the One who alone is worthy, and to awaken the truth that they had once rejected.

II. GOMER'S RESTORATION (3:1–5)
1. Yahweh's Command (3:1)
2. Hosea's Response (3:2–3)
3. Explanation: Punishment and Reversal (3:4–5)

——————— **II. GOMER'S RESTORATION (3:1–5)** ———————

As indicated already, the interpretation of this section is much debated. We must answer two major questions. (1) Is the woman of this section Gomer or another woman? (2) If the woman is Gomer, is this a doublet account—that is, is it a second version of the story already told in chap. 1—or does it complete the story begun in chap. 1? The position defended earlier in general terms is that the woman here is Gomer and that the events of this chapter are subsequent to the events of chap. 1. Here we will consider these questions in detail as they arise in the exegesis of the text.

1. Yahweh's Command (3:1)

¹The LORD said to me, "Go, show your love to your wife again, though she is loved by another and is an adulteress. Love her as the LORD loves the Israelites, though they turn to other gods and love the sacred raisin cakes."

The structure of this passage is straightforward. First, Yahweh issues a command to Hosea (v. 1); second, Hosea carries it out (vv. 2–3); and third, Yahweh explains the message behind these actions (vv. 4–5). We should notice that this pattern is the same one the book has already followed. In chaps. 1 and 2 Yahweh commanded Hosea to marry Gomer, which he did; then Yahweh explained the significance of this act for Israel. The major difference is that Hosea's act of marrying Gomer is subdivided into three subordinate events (the birth of the three children) with the result that three suboracles explain the full significance of Hosea's marriage. In chap. 3, however, no new children are born, and children do not play a role in the metaphor of chap. 3. Therefore we have only a single explanation of the events (vv. 4–5).

One other difference between chap. 1 and chap. 3 is that whereas chap. 1 describes Hosea's life from the standpoint of a third person narrator, Hosea himself speaks in chap. 3. This does not demand that we take either text as a secondary addition by disciples or redactors.[1] Instead, we should notice how the movement between third person and first person discourse characterizes the prophecies of Hosea, especially in 8:1–14:8. In that section we move back and forth between a prophet speaking *for God* (and thus speaks of God in the third person) and complaints spoken *by God* himself (e.g., 8:1–14, God speaks; 9:1–9, the prophet speaks for God). Thus, both Hosea's experience and Yahweh's are recounted in both third and first person. Even in formal presentation, therefore, Hosea's experience mirrors Yahweh's. As one who has endured faithlessness by a spouse, Hosea has earned the right to speak for God. The very structure of the text points to the sympathy between Yahweh and Hosea that arises from shared experience.

3:1 The NIV translation paraphrases a good deal here. The verse might more literally be rendered: "And the LORD said to me again, 'Go, love a woman loved by another and committing adultery, just as the LORD loves the children of Israel even though they are turning to other gods and love raisin sweetmeats.'" With the translation "show your love to your wife again," the NIV has removed the ambiguity from the Hebrew entirely.[2]

But ambiguity is here in abundance. The text does not say "your wife" but only "a woman." Also, the location of the word "again" is a matter for debate; the NIV has made it a modifier of "show your love," but it probably modifies "the LORD said to me."[3] In other words, we merely have here a statement that Yahweh spoke to Hosea again; the text does not necessarily mean that Hosea was told to love the same woman again, which would demand that the woman be Gomer.

Nevertheless, there are good reasons to believe that the anonymous woman of 3:1 is in fact Gomer. Hosea probably felt no need to give his audience the name of this woman precisely because the reader already knows who she is. In narration new information needs to be specified; old information does not. To

---

[1] Contra J. L. Mays, *Hosea: A Commentary*, OTL (Philadelphia: Westminster, 1969), 24, 54.

[2] Although אִשָּׁה can also mean "wife," in this text the translation "your wife" reads quite a bit into the text. "Your wife" in Hb. is אִשְׁתְּךָ (e.g., Gen 3:17; 6:18; 8:16). F. I. Andersen and D. N. Freedman (*Hosea*, AB [New York: Doubleday, 1980], 296) point out that "I procured her" in v. 2 tells us that this is a specific woman and not just any woman, but we cannot read v. 2 back into the translation of v. 1.

[3] The adverb עוֹד could go with either the preceding clause, וַיֹּאמֶר יְהוָה אֵלַי, or with the following clause, לֵךְ אֱהַב־אִשָּׁה. On balance וַיֹּאמֶר יְהוָה אֵלַי seems preferable because לֵךְ, as it often does, functions here as an auxiliary to another imperative (אֱהַב). It is odd for עוֹד to modify אֱהַב, from in front of לֵךְ. Sometimes there is an adverb before לֵךְ, usually וְעַתָּה ("now," e.g., Gen 31:44; Exod 3:10; 4:12), but in these cases עַתָּה modifies לֵךְ and not the following verb. We do have the example of Zech 11:15, which is similar to Hos 3:1. Unfortunately, עוֹד is as ambiguous in Zech 11:15 as it is in Hos 3:1. Also the Zechariah text lacks the intervening לֵךְ, so it is not a true parallel. We would expect that if the meaning were "Go, love a woman again," the text would have something like לֵךְ אֱהַב־אִשָּׁה עוֹד.

put it another way, those who believe that this is a different woman must explain why she is unnamed, but there is no such onus on those who take this to be the woman already introduced in the text. Most important, however, is the fact that this woman is called an "adulteress," which implies that she is married but faithless to her husband (see Lev 20:10; Jer 3:8–9; Ezek 16:32). There is no reason for Hosea to "show love" to the adulterous wife of another man; such a command comes near to demanding Hosea commit adultery himself! The command only makes sense if the woman in adultery is his own wife.

We still have to ask, however, why Hosea describes Gomer in anonymous terms, not to defend our conclusion that this woman is Gomer but as a simple matter of exegesis. The answer seems to be that she has forfeited her identity through her adultery. She can no longer claim the title "wife of Hosea" just as Israel can no longer claim the title "people of God." Israel in apostasy is not Israel. By analogy adultery does not enhance a person's identity; it destroys it.

Is it possible that the woman is Gomer but that this text is merely a doublet of what we have in chap. 1—in other words, that this is not the rest of the story of Hosea and Gomer but only a rehash of what we already know? Here the placement of "again" with "the LORD said to me" is helpful because it clearly implies sequence: Yahweh spoke to Hosea *a second time*. Furthermore, the details of the narrative oppose reading chap. 3 as a doublet. Chapter 1 reads like the initiation of a marriage: Hosea hears the command to marry an immoral woman; he finds and marries Gomer, and she has children. Chapter 3, however, is the resumption of a relationship: the Lord "again" tells Hosea to love a woman; he finds her, buys her, and warns her to abandon her prior behavior, and this time no children are mentioned. Here again the fact that she is called an "adulteress" (where before she was simply a promiscuous woman, 1:2[4]) is important. An unmarried woman can be promiscuous, but only a married woman can be an adulteress. Thus, we must regard 3:1–5 as subsequent to the events of chap. 1.

Several phrases in the verse call for comment. The command "love a woman," in contrast to "take a wife" (1:2), implies that the woman he is to love already is his wife. She has forfeited her right to his love, but he is to give it anyway, just as Yahweh will again show love to Israel. Also, the phrase "loved by another" does not mean that some other man is in love with her; it simply means that she has had sexual encounters with other men.

The phrase "love the sacred raisin cakes" again paraphrases the Hebrew— "sacred" is not part of the original text. But it is almost comical to modern readers that Yahweh is distressed because the Israelites "love raisin cakes." Yahweh's grief over Israel has nothing to do with their choice in desserts. It is

---

[4] The NIV translation at 1:2, "an adulterous wife," is particularly unfortunate. It obscures the difference between a promiscuous woman (אֵשֶׁת זְנוּנִים) and an adulterous woman (וּמְנָאָפֶת).

possible, but unlikely, that the subject of "love the sacred raisin cakes" is not the Israelites but the gods whom they honor.[5] It is more probable that the Israelites themselves are the ones who love the raisin cakes but that the significance of these cakes lies in their context and purpose.

The eating of raisin cakes was not of itself evil, even when eaten as part of a religious ceremony. According to 2 Sam 6:19, David, at the end of his celebration of the return of the ark to Jerusalem, distributed raisin cakes and other sweetmeats to the people (this was also the occasion that "David, wearing a linen ephod, danced before the Lord with all his might").[6] Raisins were for the Israelites a form of high energy food and were consumed by those who were faint with hunger (1 Sam 30:12; Song 2:5). Song 2:5 may also imply that raisin cakes were thought to have an aphrodisiac quality. We can surmise from these examples and from the context that the raisin cakes Hosea describes were used in pagan worship (since he says that "they turn to other gods"), may have been part of ecstatic or wild celebrations, and may have played a role in the promiscuity of the fertility cult.

2. Hosea's Response (3:2–3)

²So I bought her for fifteen shekels of silver and about a homer and a lethek of barley. ³Then I told her, "You are to live with me many days; you must not be a prostitute or be intimate with any man, and I will live with you."

3:2   The precise amount of barley Hosea paid for Gomer is unknown because we do not know how large a "homer" or a "lethek" was. A homer probably was about six bushels or about two hundred liters, and a lethek may have been half a homer.[7] Thus, a figure of about three hundred liters probably is not far off the mark. The translation "I bought her" is open to question,[8] but it is

---

[5] See F. I. Andersen and D. N. Freedman (*Hosea*, AB [New York: Doubleday, 1980], 298), who consider but reject this possibility on the grounds that for the Israelite prophets the gods are nonentities and therefore incapable of loving or hating anything.

[6] See also 1 Chr 12:40, where raisin cakes are associated with the celebration of David's inauguration.

[7] The word לֶתֶךְ is a hapax legomenon, although an improbable conjecture has the word present in the phrase בְּכֹר לֶתֶךְ ("for a kor and a lethek") in Isa 57:8. See *HALOT* 2:537.

[8] The Hb. has וָאֶכְּרֶהָ, but the *dagesh forte* in the *kaph* is peculiar if the root is כרה, "to buy." This is often explained as a *dagesh forte dirimens*, i.e., a *dagesh* meant to make the *shewa* vocal rather than silent. See *GKC* §20h. However, Andersen and Freedman (*Hosea,* 298) comment that the *shewa* should be silent and that if this is *dagesh forte dirimens,* it is the only occurrence of it with a letter *kaph* in the Hebrew Bible. Scholars have proposed various suggestions and emandations (e.g., that the root is נכר in the *hiphil,* meaning "to acknowledge"; cf. L. Waterman, "Hosea, Chapters 1–3, in Retrospect and Prospect," *JNES* 14 [1955]: 100–109), but none is convincing. See also T. E. McComiskey, who observes that *dagesh forte dirimens* frequently appears before *resh* ("Hosea," in *The Minor Prophets,* 3 vols., ed. T. E. McComiskey [Grand Rapids: Baker, 1992], 1:51). All in all, the best solution is that this is indeed כרה.

almost certainly correct because the text states specifically what price was paid.[9] That the payment is both in money and in kind is curious; it suggests that Hosea had difficulty in coming up with enough money to purchase her. This possibility receives further support from the fact that the Hebrew word translated "bought" includes the idea of haggling.[10]

The real problem here is why he had to buy her at all. The traditional interpretation is that she had fallen into slavery and that he bought her from her owner. Another possibility, that he bought her from a second husband, is most unlikely because we have no indication that Israelite men could buy and sell their wives. If Gomer had fallen into slavery, we do not know the legal mechanism whereby this change in her status came about. It is conceivable that Hosea sent her out of the house, she fell into poverty, and finally gave herself over to slavery in order to survive (see 2:2–3), but neither the scanty details of this text nor our scant knowledge of Israelite legal and social customs allows us to make this claim with great confidence.[11] H. W. Wolff suggests that she could have been either someone's personal slave or a temple prostitute;[12] we are unlikely to get much closer to the true story than that.[13]

3:3 Hosea's charge to Gomer is distressingly terse. His words can be, and have been, taken in a variety of ways. The NIV's "You are to live with me many days; you must not be a prostitute or be intimate with any man, and I will live with you" actually takes something of a middle ground and again paraphrases at the point "and I will live with you."[14] Alternative interpretations of this verse include: (1) Hosea remarried Gomer and resumed conjugal relations with her; (2) Hosea brought Gomer home but never again had conjugal relations with her; and (3) Hosea brought Gomer home, imposed a probationary period on her in which he had no conjugal relations with her, but afterwards resumed the nor-

---

[9] The preposition בְּ on בַּחֲמִשָּׁה indicates price paid; it does double duty here for both the price in coin and in grain.

[10] Mays, *Hosea,* 57. Assuming that כרה is indeed the root, its specific nuance may include the idea of haggling over a purchase (see Job 6:27; 40:30 [Eng. 41:6]).

[11] Another possibility is that Hosea reacquired legal possession of Gomer as his wife by giving the payment to Gomer herself. If so, then the money, grain, and wine serve as tokens for the restoration of Israel, when Yahweh will restore prosperity to the nation (see 2:8). Cf. W. Vogels, "Hosea's Gift to Gomer (Hos 3,2)," *Bib* 69 (1988): 412–21. But this interpretation is built on a very doubtful analysis of וָאֶכְּרֶהָ (taking it from נכר and interpreting it to mean "take legal possession"). It would help a great deal if the text plainly stated that Hosea gave this payment to Gomer, which of course it does not.

[12] H. W. Wolff, *Hosea,* Her (Philadelphia: Fortress, 1974), 61.

[13] McComiskey ("Hosea," 1:51) regards the רֵעַ of v. 1 as the implied owner from whom Hosea bought her, but this only works if one regards רֵעַ as a reference to a single person. If the phrase אֲהֻבַת רֵעַ simply means "who has been loved by another," i.e., who has had sex with other men, then we have no reason to suppose that she was living with a paramour who is here called the רֵעַ.

[14] The verb "live" is not in the original here; it simply reads וְגַם־אֲנִי אֵלָיִךְ (which most literally but not necessarily most accurately means "and also I to you").

mal relations of husband and wife. There is something unpleasantly voyeuristic about modern readers trying to determine whether the prophet and his wife resumed a sexual relationship; we must, however, understand these words in order to comprehend Hosea's message.

The view that Hosea immediately resumed conjugal relations with her is improbable for two reasons. First, "many days" in this verse has an obvious parallel in the "many days" of v. 4, which speaks of Israel having to undergo a period of cleansing deprivation. By analogy the "many days" of v. 3 must also be a period of deprivation; it does not make sense for the "many days" of v. 3 to be a positive period but the corresponding period of v. 4 to be negative and probationary. Second, the injunction that Gomer should not "be intimate with any man" would have to include Hosea himself—otherwise, we should expect something like "except me" to be included.[15] We might add that it would seem quite unnatural for Hosea and Gomer immediately to resume conjugal relations.

The second view, that Hosea and Gomer never resumed sexual relations, depends upon translating the end of the verse ("and I will live with you" in the NIV) as something like "and I also shall behave in the same way toward you" (i.e., "I shall live a life of celibacy too").[16] This interpretation also has at least two problems. First, it is doubtful that the Hebrew can have the meaning that this view requires.[17] Second, this line, which might legitimately be translated "and then I shall be yours," probably is a reversal of the threat in 1:9, "and I shall no longer be yours"[18] (the NIV has "I am not your God"; see commentary above). It is most unlikely that Hosea would develop in this verse a Hebrew line that recalls "I shall no longer be yours" and yet intend an entirely different meaning, "I, like you, shall be celibate."

The best interpretation is that Hosea means that she should live with him in total abstinence of sexual relations for "many days" until at last the two of them could resume the normal life of husband and wife. This interpretation most naturally parallels the explanation of the symbolism given in vv. 4–5, and it also

---

[15] The NIV "be intimate with any man" is a legitimate translation here of the Hb. וְלֹא תִהְיִי לְאִישׁ. See, e.g., Ruth 1:12. For a good discussion of the idiom used here, see Andersen and Freedman, *Hosea*, 302–3.

[16] McComiskey ("Hosea," 1:53) supports this interpretation and argues that the literal translation "is clear enough." The literal translation, in McComiskey's view, is "you shall not belong to another man, and also I to you." In fact, this is not clear at all, and McComiskey seems to have been so sure of how he read the words that he thought the meaning he saw coincided with the literal translation.

[17] I have yet to see any analogy for taking אֲנִי אֵלַיִךְ to mean "I will do the same as you." Otherwise, one must emend the text by inserting a negative (W. R. Harper, *Amos and Hosea*, ICC [New York: Scribners, 1905], 216; Wolff, *Hosea*, 56; Mays, *Hosea*, 54) to obtain the desired translation.

[18] The Hb. of 1:9 (וְאָנֹכִי לֹא־אֶהְיֶה לָכֶם) can be seen to parallel the Hb. of 3:3 (וְגַם־אֲנִי אֵלַיִךְ).

maintains the reversal of 1:9 mentioned above. The goal of Hosea is the resumption of the covenant relationship between Yahweh and Israel. If Gomer only lives in the home of Hosea as something of a guest (or a prisoner) and never enjoys the full status of wife (which includes sexual relations), then the covenant between Hosea and Gomer is never truly mended. The verse should be translated, "And I said to her, 'Many days you shall remain with me, and you shall neither prostitute yourself nor be with any man, and then[19] I shall be yours."

3. Explanation: Punishment and Reversal (3:4–5)

[4]For the Israelites will live many days without king or prince, without sacrifice or sacred stones, without ephod or idol. [5]Afterward the Israelites will return and seek the LORD their God and David their king. They will come trembling to the LORD and to his blessings in the last days.

3:4 The reader should notice that the list of things Israel will lose for "many days" includes both licit and illicit items. Only the "idol"[20] is fundamentally evil; all the rest could be good or evil depending on context. Preference for a government of kings and princes can reflect rejection of Yahweh's leadership (1 Sam 8:7), but the idea of a monarchy over God's people receives final approval in the Davidic covenant (2 Sam 7). "Sacrifice" could be good or evil, depending on to whom and with what attitude the sacrifice was made. Sacrifice to Yahweh with a broken heart is good, but sacrifice to Baal is always evil, and even sacrifice to Yahweh without true faith is corrupting (1 Sam 15:22). The phrase "sacred stones" *(maṣṣēbâ)* refers to a stone pillar. Ancient peoples often raised these in honor of pagan gods, and the term carried pagan implications (Exod 23:24; Deut 16:22). Nevertheless, even Jacob could raise up a *maṣṣēbâ* (Gen 28:18; cf. Isa 19:19). "Ephod" refers to the sacred garments of the priests (Exod 28:28–30). By metonymy absence of ephod and sacrifice implies absence of priests and temple worship. Although most of the items on this list are not intrinsically evil, probably all are to be understood as corrupted through participation in idolatry.

The analogy between Gomer's probation and Israel's is complete. Gomer is to abstain from prostitution and even from sexual relations with any man, but this does not mean that after the probation she can resume prostitution. She can, however, return to true conjugal love with her husband. By analogy Israel

---

[19] The phrase וְגַם here implies sequence. See, e.g., Exod 19:9: "And the Lord said to Moses, 'I am coming to you in a thunderhead of clouds so that the people will hear when I speak to you, and then they will trust you unshakably'" (וְגַם־בְּךָ יַאֲמִינוּ לְעוֹלָם).

[20] The term used here, תְּרָפִים, refers to household gods. Wolff (*Hosea,* 62) suggests that the term could also refer to cultic masks. The priestly ephod is associated with תְּרָפִים in Judg 17:5; 18:14–20.

will be for a time without monarchy, priesthood, and idols. When her probation ends, idolatry will never return, but a purified monarchy and true worship will return (Ezek 37:24; Mal 3:3).[21]

3:5 In this text Israel plays the part of the prodigal son. She returns in fear and yet is received in love. By analogy the destitute Gomer might have viewed her purchase by Hosea with terror. Would he now extract revenge on her as his slave? But Yahweh had commanded Hosea to love her, and Hosea gave her dignity, a new start, and an opportunity to regain her status as the prophet's wife. Israel is to "return to" and "seek" (two words that connote repentance) Yahweh. In fear they call on him to restore the blessing they have squandered.

The prophecy that they would seek "David their king" is messianic. The phrase does not mean simply that the Israelites would again submit to the Davidic monarchy and so undo Jeroboam's rebellion. Had that been the point, we would expect the text to say that they would return to the "house of David." Instead we see "David their king" set alongside of Yahweh as the one to whom the people return in pious fear.[22] This "David" cannot be the historical king, who was long dead, but is the messianic king for whom he is a figure. As D. A. Hubbard states, returning to David implies the reunion of the two kingdoms (1:11), an end to dynastic chaos (8:4), and an end to seeking protection through alliances with pagan states (7:11).[23] Unity and security can come to Israel only when they seek God and his Christ. "And if they do not persist in unbelief, they will be grafted in, for God is able to graft them in again" (Rom 11:23).

The eschatological fulfillment of all this is in the "last days." This phrase is better translated "at the end of the days." The "end" (*ʾaḥărît*) is the time of fulfillment, when the final outcome of God's program is realized. The word creates a distance between the age of fulfillment and the age of the prophet himself[24] and is often associated with hope.[25] It implies that the people of God must live in expectation of redemption and vindication.

---

[21] Hos 3:4 had some significance as an eschatological text for Qumran. Cf. M. Black, "The Theological Appropriation of the Old Testament by the New Testament," *SJT* 39 (1986): 1–17, esp. p. 4.

[22] Andersen and Freedman (*Hosea,* 307) observe that the "close linkage of Yahweh and David is unacceptable to many scholars." While we might smile at the scholar's notion that he or she is in a position to find anything in Hosea "unacceptable," this comment points out how striking is the position that "David their king" occupies in the text.

[23] D. A. Hubbard, *Hosea,* TOTC (Downers Grove: InterVarsity, 1989), 94–95.

[24] Davies, *Hosea,* 105.

[25] Andersen and Freedman, *Hosea,* 308. תִּקְוָה ("hope") is associated with אַחֲרִית in Jer 29:11; 31:17; Prov 23:18; 24:14.

THE VOLUME OF ACCUSATION AND REDEMPTION (4:1–14:8)
  III. THE THREEFOLD COMPLAINTS (4:1–7:16)
    1. Accusation (4:1–5:15)
      (1) Jezreel: General Complaint (4:1–3)
        No Faithfulness, No Love, No Knowledge of God (4:1)
        List of Crimes (4:2)
        Result (4:3)
      (2) Lo-Ammi: The Three Guilty Groups (4:4–14)
        Religious Leadership (4:4–10)
        Transition: Proverb on Debauchery [A] (4:11)
        Superstition of Common People (4:12–13a)
        Women [Charges Dismissed for Rhetorical Purposes]
          (4:13b–14)
      (3) Lo-Ruhamah: Three Warnings for Israel and Judah
          (4:15–5:15)
        Israel's Apostasy a Warning to Judah (4:15–19)
        Israel Leads Judah into Sin (5:1–7)
        Israel and Judah Face the Wrath of God (5:8–15)
    2. Exhortation for Future Grace (6:1–7:16)
      (1) The Prophet's Threefold Call to Repent (6:1–3)
        Healer Instead of a Sickness or a Lion (6:1–2)
        Dawn Instead of New Moon (6:3a)
        Rain Instead of Wind (6:3b)
      (2) Yahweh's Sorrow [Inclusio Pattern with Parallelism]
          (6:4–7:16)
        Yahweh's Frustration (6:4–6) [A]
        Sins of Adam, Gilead, Shechem (6:7–9) [B]
        Apostasy of Ephraim–and Judah (6:10–11a) [C]
        Unforgiven Sins of Israel, Ephraim, and Samaria
          (6:11b–7:7) [B′]
        Folly of Ephraim (7:8–12) [C′]
        Yahweh's Lament (7:13–16) [A′]

──────── **III. THE THREEFOLD COMPLAINTS (4:1–7:16)** ────────

In 1:2–3:15 we have what this commentary has called "The Volume of Gomer and Her Children." There Hosea's family served as a type for the relationship between God and his people. In 4:1–13:6 the Book of Hosea gives its arguments (*rîb*, 4:1) against Israel. The tone is that of a prosecutor laying out his charges against the accused. At the same time, however, the metaphor of a court of law is not developed or maintained, and it would be a mistake to interpret all of the book or even a major part of it as though it were a presentation of a lawsuit.[1] Once again "accusation" in this context need not be judicial, even metaphorically so. One can accuse another outside of a courtroom setting. Throughout this material, moreover, promises of redemption appear as suddenly and unexpectedly as did the reversals of judgment in 1:2–3:15. Thus this is not simply a book of accusation, but also of redemption.

1. Accusation (4:1–5:15)

Everything in 4:1 gives the appearance of a major division heading: (1) it begins with a call to listen, (2) it announces that what follows is the "word of the LORD," (3) it identifies the addressees as the whole people of Israel, (4) it gives the reason (*rîb*) that they should listen, that the Lord has a complaint (*rîb*) to bring against them, and (5) it describes, in summary fashion, the complaint God is bringing.[2] From this point on we have nothing of Hosea's biography. In fact, we do not even have any indication of when or under what circumstances Hosea preached the following material. Having given us a glimpse of the most intimate details of his personal life, the prophet recedes entirely into the background. Attempts to identify the "setting" for each text of Hosea[3] are futile and misleading.

Today scholars customarily regard prophets as charismatic preachers who attracted bands of followers. The prophets themselves, according to the reigning reconstruction, did not write down their prophecies or oversee the editorial process whereby their oral proclamations were transformed into literary works. That process was left first to their disciples and then to redactors who

---

[1] Cf. D. R. Daniels, "Is There a 'Prophetic Lawsuit' Genre?" *ZAW* 99 (1987): 339–60, and P. N. Franklyn, "Oracular Cursing in Hosea 13," *HAR* 11 (1987): 69–80.

[2] Elsewhere in the prophets we find a similar pattern often appears at the head of a new section. E.g., Isa 1:2 includes the introductory שִׁמְעוּ, identifies the addressees (heaven and earth), gives the reason for this address with a כִּי clause, and declares that Yahweh speaks. Similar (but not identical) patterns occur in Isa 48:1–2; 49:1; 51:1; Jer 2:4; 10:1; 11:2; Hos 5:1; Joel 1:2; Amos 3:1,13; 4:1; 5:1; 8:4; Mic 1:2; 3:1,9; 6:1–2. In all of these a new section begins with the imperative שִׁמְעוּ.

[3] E.g., as is done by H. W. Wolff, *Hosea,* Her (Philadelphia: Fortress, 1974).

worked in later generations of the "schools" of individual prophets. Thus, for example, the school of Isaiah first committed the oracles of the great prophet to writing, then later generations of the Isaianic school supplemented the original oracles with fresh prophecies and in the process redacted all of this material into a single book.

This hypothesis makes too much of the disciples of the prophets and too little of the prophets themselves. It is clear from the examples of Baruch (Jer 32) and the "sons of the prophets" (e.g., 2 Kgs 2) that the prophets could employ amanuenses and that many had disciples. It is not clear that these disciples were responsible for the creation of the prophetic books (beyond the purely mechanical task of transcribing) or that eponymous "schools" of prophets continued for generations to develop the work of their masters in a manner analogous to the work of the Franciscans or Benedictines. Baruch, for one, appears to have been no more than a secretary taking dictation; he does not seem to have had any control over the creative process (Jer 36:4).

In regard to the Book of Hosea, a few pieces of data stand out. First, as is self-evident, none of the material of Hosea is dated in the text (contrast, for example, Ezekiel and Haggai). Second, as is universally acknowledged, the sayings of Hosea do not readily subdivide into discrete oracles. Although there is room for disagreement among scholars, the oracular divisions in Isaiah, Micah, or Amos are fairly straightforward. Hosea, by contrasts, comes to us en masse. Third, Hosea is nevertheless a literary masterpiece with intricate and subtle divisions among the texts that weave the whole into a unified piece. The point here is that we should analyze Hosea as a conscious literary production and not as an anthology, however craftily redacted, of discrete sermons.

No doubt Hosea did preach the material found in this book on various occasions. Nevertheless, the recovery of separate sermons and their original *Sitzen im Leben* is now almost entirely beyond us. Form critical analysis of Hosea, whereby we isolate a text and assert when, to whom, and under what circumstances the prophet (or some disciple) proclaimed that message, is futile. Furthermore, the quest for original versus secondary material is hopeless in a book of this nature. Form criticism has its place, but that place is not Hosea 4–14.[4] We should instead seek the structure of Hosea and, via that structure, its message (for structure see outline on p. 105).

As described in the introduction, the recurrence of a threefold pattern in this structure indicates that Hosea's three children continue to dominate the pattern of his prophecy. There is also again the pattern of reversal, whereby the disaster spoken of in the first part is reversed if the people repent.

---

[4] Cf. the following from F. I. Andersen and D. N. Freedman: "And, without denying that Gunkel could be correct about the presentation of oracles as brief spoken messages, Hosea 4–14 has been preserved as a literary composition, and it is all of a piece" (*Hosea,* AB [New York: Doubleday, 1980], 316).

Throughout this material, Hosea subtly employs standard techniques of
Hebrew poetry, such as wordplay, chiasmus, and inclusion.

(1) Jezreel: A General Complaint (4:1–3)

> ¹**Hear the word of the LORD, you Israelites,**
> **because the LORD has a charge to bring**
> **against you who live in the land:**
> **"There is no faithfulness, no love,**
> **no acknowledgment of God in the land.**
> ²**There is only cursing, lying and murder,**
> **stealing and adultery;**
> **they break all bounds,**
> **and bloodshed follows bloodshed.**
> ³**Because of this the land mourns,**
> **and all who live in it waste away;**
> **the beasts of the field and the birds of the air**
> **and the fish of the sea are dying.**

As described above, this passage marks a major division in the text. More
than that, it sets the tone for what follows. By giving a summary accusation
(v. 1), a list of the evidence (v. 2), and an account of the results of Israel's
offenses (v. 3), this passage prepares the reader for a full rebuke of Israel.

NO FAITHFULNESS, NO LOVE, NO KNOWLEDGE OF GOD (4:1).
4:1 At the outset this verse gives us an enigma. The opening line of 4:1
should be translated, "Hear the word of the LORD, Children of Israel, for the
LORD has a complaint against the inhabitants of the land." The NIV is quite
misleading; by adding the word "you" (in "you who live in the land") it
obscures the fact that Hosea speaks of the "children of Israel" and the "inhabitants of the land" as though they were two distinct groups. This passage to
some degree follows what is supposedly the normal pattern of the "covenant
lawsuit" (rîb) and yet, when compared to an analogous text in Mic 6:2, it
appears that Hosea is calling upon the people of Israel to serve as both jury
and defendant. The Micah text reads: "Hear, O mountains, the Lord's accusation; listen, you everlasting foundations of the earth. For the LORD has a case
against his people; he is lodging a charge against Israel." The mountains and
the foundations of earth here seem to serve as the jury who hear God's case
against Israel (see also Isa 1:2). Hosea, in a speech pattern that is similar to
Micah's, makes the Israelites the audience of the charges and then declares
that Yahweh has a complaint against the "inhabitants of the land." It is not possible to treat the "inhabitants of the land" as a separate, non-Israelite, group.
Clearly, the sinful people that Yahweh accuses are Israelites. If Hosea is giving
us a lawsuit, then the Israelites are serving as both the jury and the accused.
This too is obviously impossible.

The best solution is to recognize that accusations do not necessarily make for a courtroom setting even if the word "complaint" *(rîb)* is used.[5] Furthermore, the reader should recall that in 2:2 Hosea called on his children/the Israelites to denounce *(rîbû)* their mother/Israel. Hosea was calling on the people to turn back to Yahweh and to reject Israel and its culture because it had become "not my people." Here, he essentially does the same thing. In calling the children of Israel[6] to hear his grievances against the inhabitants of the land, he is calling for a remnant to acknowledge that Yahweh's complaints are valid so that they would become true Israel, in contrast to the rest of the people, who, although Israelites, have forfeited their place as the Israel of God and been demoted to the status of being "inhabitants of the land." In 1:2 it is the "land" (metonymy for Israelite culture) that prostitutes itself.

Hosea summarizes God's charges in three short statements: "There is no faithfulness, no love, no acknowledgment of God in the land." This line might be better rendered, "There is no integrity; there is no compassion; there is no knowledge of God in the land."[7] This is the first and briefest of the many threefold accusations of 4:1–5:15.[8] As the introduction has already argued, we should not view this pattern as fortuitous but as a deliberate rhetorical strategy that is modeled on the three children of Hosea.

The first charge is that the people lacked "faithfulness" *(ʾĕmet)*. This word, which also means "truth," is perhaps best translated here as "integrity." It is not merely loyalty, although it often includes that, but it is instead the wholesomeness of soul that comes from a life that follows principle rather than expediency. It is a determination to know the truth and live by it.[9] The person of *ĕmet* is to the person without *ĕmet* as sound wood is to rotten wood or as a

---

[5] The supposed form for the lawsuit motif can be found in H. B. Huffmon, "The Covenant Lawsuit in the Prophets," *JBL* 78 (1959): 285–95. Even if one accepts this as a legitimate prophetic *Gattung*, Hos 4:1ff. does not really follow it.

[6] Note that 4:1 calls them the בְּנֵי יִשְׂרָאֵל, the term "children" (בְּנֵי) providing a conceptual link to the three children of Hosea. In addition, the term בְּנֵי יִשְׂרָאֵל occurs elsewhere only in 2:1–2 (Eng. 1:10–11); 3:4–5. All of these texts are salvific in tone, although 3:4 does speak of the exile as a period of cleansing. This use of בְּנֵי יִשְׂרָאֵל fits well with the idea that Hosea in 4:1 is calling upon a remnant to emerge that will reject the behavior of their fellow Israelites, behavior that has transformed them from the status of בְּנֵי יִשְׂרָאֵל to the status of יוֹשְׁבֵי הָאָרֶץ.

[7] The threefold use of אֵין, "there is no/not," is striking and should be reflected in the translation.

[8] Wolff treats אֱמֶת and חֶסֶד as a word pair that reinforce each other, as if it were hendiadys (*Hosea*, 67). This is not correct. As T. E. McComiskey points out, each has its own negative particle and stands in relation to each other as both do to דַּעַת אֱלֹהִים ("Hosea," in *The Minor Prophets*, 3 vols., ed. T. E. McComiskey [Grand Rapids: Baker, 1992], 1:56).

[9] Prov 29:14, e.g., promises that a king will have a secure throne if he judges, בֶּאֱמֶת, "in truth," i.e., without partiality and without distorting the facts for his own or his favorite's benefit. Similarly, in Exod 18:21 Jethro counsels Moses to choose אַנְשֵׁי אֱמֶת שֹׂנְאֵי בָצַע ("men of integrity who hate bribes").

genuine diamond is to paste.[10] To say that the people are without ĕmet is to say that they are all living a lie and thus are without moral integrity. The word ĕmet "denotes the nature of the man who is said to be faithful to his neighbor, true in his speech, and reliable and constant in his actions."[11]

The second charge is that they lacked "love" or "compassion" (ḥesed). This word connotes consistently doing good for another based on a prior commitment to love, and it often means "mercy" or "grace." The quality of ḥesed is not simply a matter of fulfilling one's duties to a covenant obligation; it is going beyond legal obligations to give kindness freely to those with whom one relates.[12] When Lot proclaimed that the angels had shown him great ḥesed in saving his life, he meant that they had given him mercy that he did not deserve, not that they merely fulfilled some kind of duty to him (Gen 19:19). When Ruth offered herself in marriage to Boaz, he called it a great act of ḥesed, not meaning that she had fulfilled an obligation to him or to Naomi, but that she had gone far beyond what was required (Ruth 3:10). The common thread here is that people are in relationship with one another, but that the person who shows ḥesed goes beyond basic requirements and freely gives kindness to the other.[13] Thus ḥesed exists in a marriage when the husband goes beyond the minimal requirements of a husband's obligations and shows real kindness to his wife. In the community one person can show ḥesed to another by being compassionate to the other, even if that person is a stranger. In saying that Israel was without ḥesed, Hosea asserts that they are a cruel, self-centered people.

The third charge is that Israel was without knowledge of God. Knowing God has both objective and subjective poles. Objectively, it is correct doctrine about God—for example, objective knowledge of God includes the fact that God abhors the cult of Baal and the fertility religion that surrounds it. Subjectively, it is the personal relationship one has with God whereby one can honestly say, "You are my God" (Hos 2:23). In 4:6 Hosea mourns the lack of objective knowledge of God among the people; the priests have not taught them, and so they stumble in error. In 6:3 Hosea calls for them to pursue a subjective, personal knowledge of God. It is evident that 6:3 refers more to relationship than to doctrine because the parallel, 6:1, calls on them to "return" to Yahweh, a term that describes repentance. A people without knowledge of God are a people who have embraced false teaching about God and/or who have no living connection to God.

---

[10] Jer 2:21 speaks of זֶרַע אֱמֶת, i.e., good seed that does not come from inferior stock or have other kinds of seed mixed in with it. In context it is used metaphorically for Israel.

[11] A. Jepsen, "אָמַת ᵓᵉmeth," TDOT 1:313.

[12] Cf. G. Farr, "The Concept of Grace in the Book of Hosea," ZAW 70 (1958): 98–107.

[13] The covenant between David and Jonathan does not contradict this understanding of ḥesed. See TWOT, s.v., "חֶסֶד (ḥsd)," by R. L. Harris.

We could rightly describe these three elements—integrity, compassion, and the knowledge of God—as describing the meaning of the Christian faith. All of Hosea's accusations sprang from the fact that these were lacking in his people.

LIST OF CRIMES (4:2). **4:2** Numerous scholars have pointed out the parallel between this list of offenses and the Decalogue. Using five single words, Hosea alludes to the people's violations of Commandments three, nine, six, eight, and seven.[14] The first, "cursing," is related to the Third Commandment. The word means to "swear or to bring down a curse on someone in the name of a god."[15] The word does not actually appear in the Third Commandment, but "cursing" is the nearest one-word equivalent to what that command prohibits.[16]

The second word, "lying," relates to the Ninth Commandment.[17] The word used here means to "deny something, to keep a secret, or to deceive." It covers any attempt to evade responsibility or detection through falsehood as well as lying in general. It is the word used in Gen 18:15 to describe Sarah's attempt to conceal the fact that she had laughed at Yahweh's announcement that she would soon bear a son. In short Hosea means that the Israelites of his age could not be trusted.

The Hebrew words behind "murder, stealing and adultery" are the same three words used in the Decalogue for those sins. It is significant that Hosea here lists primarily the social crimes of the Ten Commandments rather than the more theological evils (worshiping other gods, making idols, or Sabbath breaking) or the more domestic or private sins (failure to honor parents and

---

[14] The order Hosea uses is not necessarily significant because he does not claim to be establishing the proper order for the Decalogue. We should note, however, that the order of commands six, seven, and eight is not entirely certain: the MT has murder, adultery, and theft; the LXX order for Exod 20:13–15 is adultery, theft, and murder. In Jer 7:9 the order is stealing, murder, and adultery. The NT order is adultery, murder, and theft in Luke 18:20 and Rom 13:9. For a discussion of this and other issues related to the prophetic use of the Ten Commandments, see M. Weiss, "The Decalogue in Prophetic Literature," in *The Ten Commandments in History and Tradition,* ed. B.-Z. Segal and G. Levi (Jerusalem: Magnes, 1985), 67–81.

[15] The clearest example of the meaning of אלה in the *qal* stem is Judg 17:2, in which a woman utters a curse on whoever stole eleven hundred silver shekels from her. When her son confesses and returns the money, she rejoices and appears to seek to reverse the curse by declaring, "Blessed be my son by Yahweh!"

[16] There is no single word in Exod 20:7 ("who takes his name in vain," RSV) that Hosea could have used that would have communicated that he was referring to this command. The Third Commandment prohibits both taking an oath falsely and using the name of God for cursing or profanity. The word Hosea uses, אלה, focuses more on the latter.

[17] One may wonder why Hosea used כחֹש instead of a word that actually appears in the Ninth Commandment, שֶׁקֶר. The reason may be that the form in which it appears in Exod 20:16, עֵד שֶׁקֶר ("false witness"), appears to relate more to the specific crime of perjury but that Hosea wants to describe a more general trait of deceitfulness.

coveting). The point is not that he regarded these as less important—if anything, the whole burden of Hosea is that the fundamental evil in Israel is that the people have abandoned their God. Rather, Hosea is here describing the social manifestations of their apostasy, and these manifestations then serve as proof of their apostasy. They have no knowledge of God and thus civil life is in disintegration.

The translation "they break all bounds" is one way to deal with a difficult problem in the Hebrew text, but it is probably not correct.[18] A more likely interpretation is that the five crimes heading v. 2 are the collective subject of this verb: "Cursing, lying, murder, stealing, and adultery break out (in the land)."[19]

The final line, "bloodshed follows bloodshed," implies that violence and recrimination dominate society. The emphasis on "bloodshed," however, has caught scholars' attention primarily because it seems unnecessary; the verse has already condemned murder. It is therefore noteworthy that "bloodshed" has already appeared in 1:4, where Yahweh declares, "I will bring the bloodshed of Jezreel upon the house of Jehu."[20] Hosea's condemnation of the pervasive violence within Israel looks back to the Jezreel oracle, just as the next two sections (4:4–14 and 4:15–5:15) look back respectively to Lo-Ammi and Lo-Ruhamah.

RESULT (4:3). **4:3** This text implies that the land is suffering drought. Hosea sees the entire population, including wildlife,[21] withering away. One might wonder how a drought would affect the "fish of the sea," but it could be that shortage of food has caused overfishing of the coastline or that changes in weather patterns have caused fish stocks to move further out to sea, beyond where ancient fishermen could pursue them. Although the NIV translation does not reflect this, Hosea himself seems to regard the decline of the seafood catch as surprising.[22]

In declaring that land animals, birds, and fish are disappearing, Hosea has

---

[18] The verb פָּרַץ usually has a direct object (e.g., Eccl 10:8), but it can be used intransitively as in the case of Prov 3:10, in which wine bursts out of its vats. In no other case, however, does it have the meaning "to violate established ethical norms" as the translation "they break all bounds" implies.

[19] Cf. J. L. Mays, *Hosea: A Commentary*, OTL (Philadelphia: Westminster, 1969), 60, and Wolff, *Hosea*, 65. This interpretation requires that we disregard the Masoretic punctuation, but this is not a significant emendation. The LXX adds ἐπὶ τῆς γῆς ("in the land"), which may have been lost by homoioteleuton with v. 1.

[20] It is not possible to regard דָּמִים as a favorite term of Hosea; outside of 1:4 and 2:1 it only appears in 12:15 (Eng. 12:14).

[21] Scholars have pointed out that the use of the preposition בְּ in בְּחַיַּת and וּבְעוֹף is unexpected. One could take this to mean "along with" (cf. Wolff, *Hosea*, 65) or, perhaps better, treat it as a partitive, meaning that some of the wild animals and the birds are dying.

[22] Note וְגַם ("and even"), here used only with "fish of the sea."

presented all of creation (earth, sky, and sea) as suffering the wrath of Yahweh. This is the familiar prophetic theme of the undoing of creation, and the language recalls Genesis 1. The wrath of God has a cosmic dimension; if the people of God are disobedient, then all creation suffers.[23] As a type this anticipates the final judgments on creation.

(2) Lo-Ammi: The Three Guilty Groups (4:4–14)

[4]"But let no man bring a charge,
    let no man accuse another,
for your people are like those
    who bring charges against a priest.
[5]You stumble day and night,
    and the prophets stumble with you.
So I will destroy your mother—
[6] my people are destroyed from lack of knowledge.
"Because you have rejected knowledge,
    I also reject you as my priests;
because you have ignored the law of your God,
    I also will ignore your children.
[7]The more the priests increased,
        the more they sinned against me;
    they exchanged their Glory for something disgraceful.
[8]They feed on the sins of my people
    and relish their wickedness.
[9]And it will be: Like people, like priests.
    I will punish both of them for their ways
    and repay them for their deeds.
[10]"They will eat but not have enough;
    they will engage in prostitution but not increase,
because they have deserted the LORD
    to give themselves
[11]to prostitution, to old wine and new,
    which take away the understanding

[12]of my people.
They consult a wooden idol
    and are answered by a stick of wood.
A spirit of prostitution leads them astray;
    they are unfaithful to their God.
[13]They sacrifice on the mountaintops

---

[23] For a good study of creation reversal in Hosea, see M. DeRoche, "The Reversal of Creation in Hosea," *VT* 31 (1981): 400–409. As DeRoche notes, the use of the verb אסף is characteristic of creation reversal, as in Jer 8:13 and Zeph 1:2–3. DeRoche also comments that recognition of this motif repudiates the notion that this text is a "covenant lawsuit."

> and burn offerings on the hills,
> under oak, poplar and terebinth,
> 　where the shade is pleasant.
> Therefore your daughters turn to prostitution
> 　and your daughters-in-law to adultery.
>
> [14]"I will not punish your daughters
> 　when they turn to prostitution,
> nor your daughters-in-law
> 　when they commit adultery,
> because the men themselves consort with harlots
> 　and sacrifice with shrine prostitutes—
> a people without understanding will come to ruin!

Three times in this passage, in 4:6,8,12, Hosea alludes to the name Lo-Ammi ("not my people"). In v. 6 he declares that "my people" *(ʿammî)* perish for lack of sound teaching from the priests. In v. 8 he declares that the priests feed upon the sins of "my people" *(ʿammî)*. In vv. 11–12 he asserts that the religious life of "my people" *(ʿammî)* consists in the most primitive form of superstition. But in v. 4 he asserts that "your people" (that is, the priests' people) can rightly blame the priests for their condition. The overall meaning is clear; the ordinary men and women of Israel, who should have been the pious people of God, had lost that status due to the greed and negligence of the priesthood. Instead, they had become the priests' people.

In addition, Hosea singles out three classes of people who stand guilty before Yahweh: the priests, the common people, and the women. Only the priests, however, receive severe reprimand. The complaint against the common peasants is very brief and is more sorrowful than angry (vv. 12–13a), and the women, although guilty of prostitution, are exonerated on the grounds that the men led them into it. Therefore Hosea in this text looks back to the Lo-Ammi oracle and maintains the threefold pattern while at the same time focusing on the guilt of a single group, the religious leadership.

RELIGIOUS LEADERSHIP (4:4–10).　　Verse 4 changes the apparent direction of the complaint entirely. Hosea appears to be headed into a diatribe against the whole nation (vv. 1–3), but he abruptly narrows his focus to the priesthood in v. 4, which serves as the heading to this text. This passage repeats the same basic pattern four times, with variation, and uses inclusion to bracket the borders of the text. The basic pattern is: (1) Yahweh accuses the priesthood and (2) he announces appropriate punishment. The inclusion is the proverb on debauchery (v. 11) in conjunction with the stumbling of the leadership (v. 5). Its structure, given here in more detail, is:

A　　Guilt: Religious leaders are really to blame for moral decline (4:4)
B　　Punishment: Leadership "stumbles"; "I will destroy" (4:5)
A'　　Guilt: People are not instructed because leadership rejects Torah (4:6a)

B'   Punishment: "I will reject" priesthood (4:6bc)
A″   Guilt: Increased influence of priests leads to more sin in the nation (4:7a)
B″   Punishment: loss of all prestige (4:7b)
A‴   Guilt: Priests use position for Greed (4:8)
B1‴   Punishment: They shall share the fate of commoners (4:9) and
B2‴   Punishment: Frustration and fruitlessness (4:10ab)
A‴′   Concluding statement of guilt: Apostasy of religious leaders (4:10c)
B‴′   Proverb on debauchery [inclusio with "stumbling" in B] (4:11).

As described below, this reading of the text implies that at certain points
the NIV translation, particularly at 4:11–12, should not be followed.

4:4 The text maintains the language of accusation,[24] yet with a negative
twist ("let no man bring a charge, let no man accuse another") it indicates that
this verse begins a new section.[25] Hosea is not continuing the description of
the complaint of vv. 2–3 but is turning the accusation in a new, unexpected
direction.

Indeed, this verse takes the message in such an entirely new direction that
scholars are not sure what to do with it. Why would Hosea suddenly say, "Let
no man bring a charge"? Furthermore, it is difficult to know what to do with
"for your people are like those who bring charges against a priest." One solution is to assert that Hosea is here quoting one of his opponents, a priest, who
is demanding that the prophet stop criticizing the spiritual health of the nation.
This interpretation supposes that Hosea here alludes to a confrontation similar
to that between Amos and Amaziah in Amos 7:10–17. The problem, however,
is that this text, unlike Amos 7, contains no evidence that it is a citation from
one of Hosea's adversaries or that any such incident took place. This interpretation would be helpful if we had any reason to be confident that it is accurate;
in fact, we do not. Unless more convincing arguments appear, we must reject
it and assume that this verse represents the viewpoint of the prophet/
Yahweh.[26]

Another possibility is simply to emend the text, a path chosen by Wolff,[27]

---

[24] Note אַל־יָרֵב ("let him not accuse") and כִּמְרִיבֵי כֹהֵן ("like those who accuse a priest").

[25] Also the use of אַךְ (here meaning "but") indicates that this is a new section. Cf. Andersen
and Freedman, *Hosea*, 345. See Mays, *Hosea*, 67; Andersen and Freedman, *Hosea*, 345–46.

[26] Another approach is that of McComiskey, who takes it to mean that Hosea is rebuking the
people for failure to submit to the teaching of their religious leadership ("Hosea," 1:60). In light of
Hosea's unwavering opposition to the priesthood of Israel, especially in this context, this interpretation is not possible.

[27] Wolff emends to read, "No, not just anyone <should be accused>, / nor should just anyone
<be reproved>, but <my lawsuit is with you>, O priest" (*Hosea*, 70) . This is a major reconstruction
of the text, and it is without evidence.

the NRSV,[28] and Harper.[29] The problem with this is that although the significance of the verse is debatable, the Hebrew itself is quite clear.[30] The LXX and Vulgate do not support emendation.[31] Another approach is to propose a novel translation for the Hebrew text, as Lundbom does, but this too fails.[32]

Taking the text as it stands, we observe that Hosea has just accused Israel of being a perversely criminal society (v. 2). In this light the comment "let no man bring a charge, let no man accuse another" means that even though the nation has violence and injustice in every corner, the prophet does not want the reader to regard the people themselves as primarily responsible for this situation. The next line, "For your people are like those who bring charges against a priest," read in context, means that the people are bringing evidence against the priesthood.

More exactly, the people are evidence against the priests. We have already seen that in 4:6,8,12, using the sobriquet "my people," Hosea brings against the priests charges of official misconduct and failure to perform their duty. The superstition and lawlessness of the peasants—whom he here calls "your people"—is proof enough that the priests are not doing their job. It is the reverse of Paul's boast with the Corinthians, "You yourselves are our letter, written on our hearts, known and read by everybody" (2 Cor 3:2). Thus giving this verse an expanded paraphrase, we can take it to mean: "Even though this nation is full of blasphemers, liars, murderers, thieves, and adulterers (v. 2), there is no point in one person accusing or pointing the finger of blame at another. When they accuse one another, your people are really[33] bringing charges against a priest—they are evidence for what a poor job the priests have done." This

---

[28] The NRSV follows the *BHS* note ᵃ and reads, "For with you is my contention, O priest." This would be helpful if it had any supporting evidence.

[29] W. R. Harper strangely translates v. 4b as, "Since my people are but like their priestlings" (*Amos and Hosea,* ICC [New York: Scribner, 1905], 253).

[30] Notwithstanding the extended discussion in Andersen and Freedman (*Hosea,* 346–50) and numerous proposals by other scholars, there is no reason to take כִּמְרִיבֵי as anything other than a *hiphil* masculine plural construct participle of רִיב with the preposition כְּ, meaning "like the accusers of." See 1 Sam 2:10.

[31] The LXX translation "for my people are like a priest who speaks in opposition" probably represents an attempt to make sense of the present Hb. text, or at most implies that the final י of כִּמְרִיבֵי had fallen from the Vorlage, making it a singular rather than a plural participle. It is not evidence for a substantially different Hebrew reading.

[32] J. R. Lundbom, "Contentious Priests and Contentious People in Hosea IV 1–10," *VT* 36 (1986): 52–70. Lundbom argues that וְעַמְּךָ כִּמְרִיבֵי כֹהֵן means "and your people are like the contentions of a priest," but no noun meaning "contentions" exists that would have a plural construct מְרִיבֵי. In addition, it really does not make sense to say that people are like "contentions of a priest," and Lundbom's explanation is not satisfactory.

[33] The preposition כְּ in כִּמְרִיבֵי כֹהֵן could be regarded as a כְּ *veritatis,* meaning that the people are in fact accusing the priests when they accuse one another. On the כְּ *veritatis,* see *GBH* §133g.

interpretation agrees with what we have already seen in Hosea, that the culture and institutions of Israel (metaphorically, the mother) are the greatest impediment to spiritual integrity in the people (metaphorically, the children).

4:5 Hosea enters his discourse against the priests by claiming, curiously, that they "stumble." As Wolff comments, stumbling must be the consequence of their sins rather than the sins themselves.[34] The image is of a person who can no longer function or who has a downfall. "Day" and "night" are here merismus for "all of the time" (and not only at night, when one might be expected to take a tumble), and the priest and prophet represent the religious leadership. No explanation is given of why they stumble, nor of why this particular metaphor is used here. The solution appears to be in v. 11, part of a proverb on debauchery. It teaches that prostitution and wine make one senseless. An obvious link between the two verses is that drunkenness causes stumbling. Stumbling here perhaps connotes a drunken stupor and alludes to the image of Yahweh making his enemies drink wine on the day of his wrath. In Jer 25:15–28, for example, the nations must drink the cup of God's wrath, get drunk and stagger, and fall to rise no more.[35]

The association between stumbling and the wrath of God explains what appears to be a non sequitur, the clause, "I will destroy your mother."[36] The "mother" is again the representation of institutional Israel, the entity that corrupts the ordinary people, the "children," and that empowers the hierarchy.[37] Destroying the "mother" refers to the overthrow of the power and prerogatives of the religious leadership. In short, assertions that the clergy stumbles and that God is destroying their mother both imply destruction of Israel's institutions.

4:6 Hosea asserts first that the people perish because of ignorance of God and his Torah. The word "destroy" links this verse with the preceding one[38] but moves in a different direction. In v. 5 "destroy" refers to the judgment of

---

[34] Wolff, *Hosea*, 77. Hosea also uses כשׁל ("stumble") in 5:5 and 14:2,10 (Eng. = 1,9). In every case the sin is what causes the guilty party to stumble.

[35] The word כשׁל does not appear in this text, but other terms adequately convey the idea of stumbling. The association between suffering divine wrath and drunkenness is perhaps in the stumbling of the drunkard as a metaphor for terrified people fleeing enemy soldiers. Nah 3:3 describes the defeated Ninevites stumbling over dead bodies in their flight, but v. 11, asserting the certainty of their defeat, simply says that they will be "drunken."

[36] "So" in the NIV translation is not justified; it is simply "and" (וְ in a *weqatal* construction in prophetic discourse).

[37] The supposition that v. 4 is a quotation of a priestly enemy of Hosea has led many scholars to suppose that "your mother" refers to some anonymous priest's anonymous mother. See Wolff, *Hosea*, 78, Andersen and Freedman, *Hosea*, 351. Contra Hubbard, *Hosea*, 100–101.

[38] The catchwords are נִדְמוּ and וְדָמִיתִי, both from the root דמה ("destroy"). Nevertheless, contrary to the *BHS*, we should not read וְדָמִיתִי אִמֶּךָ: נִדְמוּ עַמִּי מִבְּלִי הַדָּעַת as a single poetic line. The use of the *qatal* נִדְמוּ (instead of a *weqatal*) indicates that they are rightly placed in separate verses in the MT.

God against a corrupt institution, the "mother." In this verse it refers to the pitiable folly of the ill-instructed laity, "my people." They perish because they do not know God, a point Hosea has already made in his general complaint in v. 2. Failure to teach the people rightly is a grievous offense (Matt 18:6; Jas 3:1). The preacher or teacher who sins in this way is not only responsible for his own misdeeds, but also of those whom he misled.

Anticipating vv. 9–10, Hosea here asserts that the judgments the priests suffer will be entirely appropriate. As they have disowned God's teaching, so he will disown them. The "knowledge" the priests reject is not, of course, knowledge in general or a "liberal education," but specifically the knowledge of God in both its objective and subjective senses. Thus, the priests will lose their rights to serve any longer in that capacity, much as Eli's family did (1 Sam 3:11–14). In this light we should understand the threat against "your children" in this verse as having a dual significance. On the one hand it is a threat to the priestly families, that they shall lose their status. On the other hand, it is a warning that all the people, the "children" in Hosea's now well-established metaphor,[39] have been misled by false teaching and will fall with their religious leaders.

One may ask whether "the law of your God" is specifically the Torah—that is, the Pentateuch—or whether it is merely a general term for religious teaching. Many scholars today, because they believe that the Torah was not in anything like its final form until after the Josianic reformation of 622 B.C. (2 Kgs 22–23) and was not finished until after the exile, would consider it highly unlikely that "the law of your God" is canonical Scripture, much less the full Torah. On the other hand, while it is true that we cannot know precisely what constituted the "law" for Hosea, we should be reminded that v. 2 makes a fairly certain allusion to the Decalogue. Furthermore, U. Cassuto has already documented the many references to the Torah in Hosea.[40] The point of Hosea's complaint is that the priest had rejected God's revelation; hence a canonical body of teaching is implied.

4:7 Scholars who see a specific conflict between Hosea and a single priest in vv. 4–6 note with surprise the sudden shift to the plural in this verse.[41] Such surprise is unnecessary; Hosea's conflict throughout this text is with the whole priesthood and not some individual.[42] "The more the priests increased" apparently refers to the fact that during a time of prosperity the number of people free to enter a religious vocation increases. Israel experi-

---

[39] Hence there is a link between בָּנֶיךָ in this verse and עַמְּךָ in v. 4.

[40] "The Prophet Hosea and the Books of the Pentateuch," reprinted in U. Cassuto, *Biblical and Oriental Studies,* trans. I. Abrahams (Jerusalem: Magnes, 1973), 1:79–100.

[41] E.g., Wolff, *Hosea,* 80, who concludes that this is a saying added by the "traditionist."

[42] The use of singular forms in vv. 4–6 is unremarkable. Even the שְׁמַע of Deut 6:4–5 uniformly uses singular forms, even though all the people in the nation are addressed.

enced such prosperity under Jeroboam II, and no doubt many considered the increased numbers of priests, their increased power, and the increased interest in formal worship to be signs of spiritual vitality. To the contrary, Hosea retorts, the more religious leadership the nation had, the worse they became.[43]

The line "they exchanged their Glory for something disgraceful" actually says, "I will change their glory into disgrace." Although there is some justification for the emendation the NIV employs,[44] it should be rejected. If one accepts the emendation, the "glory" that the priests have abandoned is Yahweh himself (thus the NIV capitalizes the word). On the other hand, following the present Hebrew text, the "glory" is the status and privileges of the priesthood. The latter is preferable[45] both because it fits the context of Hosea's denunciation of the priesthood for misleading the people and because it continues the formal pattern seen throughout this text: an accusation is followed by a promise of judgment spoken in the first person. The judgment is that someday God will bring the priests into disgrace in that he will cause the people to recognize them for the frauds they are and to despise them.[46]

4:8 Understandably, readers puzzle over the line "They feed on the sins of my people and relish their wickedness." The word translated "sins" can also mean "sin offerings,"[47] and thus many interpreters argue that this verse means that the priests were greedy for the people's sin offerings, the meat of which they had the right to eat (Lev 6:26).[48] On the other hand, the parallel word, "wickedness," never refers to a sacrifice, and thus some commentators reject this interpretation.[49] However, Hosea possibly is here uniquely using "wickedness" as a term to describe the sacrificial system of Israel's religion.[50] Understood this way, he regards the whole system of sacrifice as corrupted

---

[43] Andersen and Freedman (*Hosea,* 354) argue that כְּרֻבָּם refers to their pride, and not their numbers, and so translate, "As they grew proud, so they sinned against me" (p. 342). This is incorrect because the relationship between the increase of the priesthood and the increase of the sin is here ironic (cf. Hos 11:2). There is nothing ironic about people sinning more as their pride increases.

[44] The Tg. and the Syr. have a third plural here, and this is one of the (traditionally) eighteen *Tiqqune sopherim,* emendations suggested by the Masoretes. See E. Würthwein, *The Text of the Old Testament* (Grand Rapids: Eerdmans, 1979), 18–19, and *BHS* note [b].

[45] Cf. Hubbard, *Hosea,* 102.

[46] For a good example of how a hypocritical religious authority can fall into disgrace in the eyes of the common people, see N. Cohn, *The Pursuit of the Millennium* (London: Pimlico, 1957), especially pp. 80–84.

[47] The word חַטָּאת means "expiation" or "sin offering" in, e.g., Exod 29:36; 30:10; Lev 4:8,20; Ezek 43:21.

[48] E.g., Mays, *Hosea,* 70.

[49] E.g., Davies, *Hosea,* 120.

[50] Cf. Wolff, *Hosea,* 81. If it seems odd that Hosea would use the word עָוֹן to refer to the sacrificial system, note that only a few verses later, in 4:15, he calls Bethel ("house of God") בֵּית אָוֶן (Beth Aven, "house of deception").

and of having lost its original intent. Instead of being a means of confession and grace, it had become a means of permissiveness for the people and of gluttony for the priests. In addition, the "wickedness" of the laity only increases the power of the religious professionals because the people's guilt gives the leaders a means of manipulation. Finally, the wickedness of their religion may also have included the practice of sacred prostitution. Decadent religious authority leads ironically to cheap grace and immorality as well as to domineering by a clergy that knows how to play upon the fear and superstition of a poorly instructed people.

4:9 What the religious leaders were to suffer would be entirely appropriate. First, they should in no manner receive better treatment than the most coarse and unlettered peasant. They were themselves responsible for the wretched state of the religious life of the commoners, and thus they had no right to expect favoritism from God. Second, "I will punish both of them for their ways and repay them for their deeds" implies that what they did to the commoners would be done to them.[51] They will become outcasts, uncared for, suffer deprivation, and themselves be led astray by false hopes.

4:10 The translation of this verse is difficult. The first problem is relatively minor; it concerns the meaning of the word translated "increase" in the NIV. The word basically means to "break out," but in this context, and in keeping with usage elsewhere, it probably means to increase their possessions. Assuming that this is sacred prostitution and not just ordinary indulgence in sexual license, the priests had apparently supposed that fulfilling the requirements of the sacred rites would insure that they would become more prosperous—their wives would bear children, their livestock would calve, and they would enjoy the life of plenty.[52] This hope would fail; only Yahweh, not Baal, could give fertility and prosperity.

A second, more difficult problem is at the end of this verse. The NIV takes "prostitution" from v. 11, attaches it to v. 10, and translates "because they have deserted the LORD to give themselves to prostitution." This rendering,

---

[51] Note the use of פָּקַד, which here as in 1:4 does not so much mean "punish" as to "bring someone's actions back on his own head."

[52] In parallel with "they will not have enough" (וְלֹא יִשְׂבָּעוּ) in the first line, it is possible that וְלֹא יִפְרֹצוּ means "they will not have sexual satisfaction," but this meaning is not attested for פָּרַץ. Following texts such as Gen 28:14, it is often taken to mean "multiply" (RSV, NRSV). However, in Gen 28:14 the context clearly indicates that Jacob would expand via his offspring. In this text it is those who go to prostitutes, not their children, who presumably hope to פָּרַץ. Also "multiply" seems to imply that they hope to have children by prostitutes, but men do not go to prostitutes for the sake of having children by them. It is possible, however, to see an analogy to this text in Gen 30:43, "The man grew exceedingly prosperous [פָּרַץ] and came to own large flocks, and maidservants and menservants, and camels and donkeys." If the prostitution here is sacred prostitution as part of the fertility cult, the idea is that they hope to secure their prosperity through the cult.

although it appears to fit the context, is not possible.[53] Because of the difficulty of this line, scholars have emended the text in some fairly extravagant ways; but that very extravagance, coupled with the lack of textual evidence, makes it impossible for us to have any confidence that these reconstructions are anything other than exercises of scholarly imagination.[54] All in all, it is best to deal with the present text without emending or relocating words.

The end of v. 10 can be translated, "For they have abandoned keeping faith with Yahweh."[55] In short, this summarizes all the misdeeds of the priesthood in a single line: they are apostate. Their failure to give sound teaching, their greed, and their promotion of sin are all at root rejection of God.

TRANSITION: A PROVERB ON DEBAUCHERY (4:11). **4:11** As in the KJV and NASB, this verse should be translated, "Prostitution, wine, and new wine take away the heart."[56] The words "my people" in v. 12 are not part of this verse; although there is an argument for doing as the NIV has done in moving those words here, this is a mistake (see further discussion at v. 14c). This verse reads like a simple proverb that Hosea has inserted as closure for this section. It has no distinct connection to its context; but a connection is suggested, as mentioned above, by the warning in v. 5 that the religious leaders will "stumble." It also anticipates the next section, in which the prophet mourns the degenerate state of the people.[57] The word "heart" describes a per-

---

[53] The issue is that לִשְׁמֹר in v. 10 appears to need an object. The main problem is that if זְנוּת is moved to v. 10, then v. 11 begins, וְיַיִן וְתִירוֹשׁ ("and wine and new wine"), which implies that another noun stands in front of וְיַיִן. Translators' attempts to overcome this have not been successful. The NIV translation of v. 11 with יִקַּח־לֵב taken as a relative clause ("which take away understanding") is out of the question. The NRSV simply deletes the conjunction on וְיַיִן, but this is unwarranted. Verse 11 makes good sense as it stands and should not be emended to solve a problem in v. 10. Also the idea of "keeping prostitution" (reading לִשְׁמֹר זְנוּת) is itself quite unnatural and never appears in the Bible. We should add that the LXX, although its translation anticipates the path taken by the NRSV (Πορνείαν καὶ οἶνον καὶ μέθυσμα ἐδέξατο καρδία λαοῦ μου), actually implies that the present Hb. text is correct. Mays solves the dilemma by adding זְנוּת to the end of v. 10 but retaining it at the beginning of v. 11 (*Hosea*, 72). This would solve the problem wonderfully if we had any reason to think that it were right.

[54] See, e.g., Wolff, *Hosea*, 72, Andersen and Freedman, *Hosea*, 343, 363–64.

[55] This translation of כִּי־אֶת־יְהוָה עָזְבוּ לִשְׁמֹר takes לִשְׁמֹר as epexegetical of אֶת־יְהוָה עָזְבוּ and thus could be given more literally as "they abandon Yahweh—that is, they abandon keeping faith." The problem translators have had concerns whether it is possible to translate לִשְׁמֹר absolutely since it normally has an object. However, שָׁמַר often means "to fulfill one's obligations," and in this sense it often appears in phrases such as "to keep justice" (מִשְׁפָּט) as in Hos 12:7; Isa 56:1. Sometimes, however, שָׁמַר can mean "to keep [God's commands]" even when used absolutely. See BDB. An example is Deut 4:6, וּשְׁמַרְתֶּם וַעֲשִׂיתֶם כִּי הִוא חָכְמַתְכֶם, "You shall keep and you shall do [the Law] because this is your wisdom."

[56] See the discussion in the previous notes. Of itself this verse has no real difficulties in it and should be left as is.

[57] Note references to prostitution in both verses. In addition the foolhardy oracle seeking in v. 12 illustrates the depraved heart of which v. 11 speaks.

son's reasoning ability, character, and strength of will. The proverb means that debauchery ruins the soul and clouds the mind, and it is a fitting conclusion to the diatribe against the priests and a fitting introduction to the condition of the common people.

An unusual feature of this proverb, however, is that it is a monocolon (most are bicola). This peculiar feature and the apparent isolation of this line demands further investigation; the explanation is provided in v. 14c (see discussion below).

SUPERSTITION OF COMMON PEOPLE (4:12–13a). **4:12–13a** Verses 12 and 13a form a poem of two couplets. Both lines of v. 12 are chiastically structured. In v. 13a the first line has simple parallelism, but the second line, which serves to end the poem, has no parallelism. The poem begins with the people consulting a "tree" and ends with them offering sacrifices underneath trees because the shade "is good." It should be regarded as a prophetic lamentation:

> My people[58] consult their[59] tree[60]
> and their rod gives an answer[61] to them.
> For a spirit of prostitution leads them astray,
> and they prostitute themselves away from their God[62] (v. 12)
> On the tops of the mountains they sacrifice
> and on the hills they burn food offerings[63]
> Under oak, and poplar, and terebinth,
> for their shade is good (v. 13).

The "tree" (translating literally) that the people consult may be a wooden

---

[58] As in the MT, עַמִּי must be regarded as part of this verse and not the previous. First, עַמִּי clarifies who is the subject of the verb יִשְׁאָל (which is particularly important since the second half-line has a different subject, וּמַקְלוֹ). In addition, the line has a chiastic structure that is lost if עַמִּי is moved:

A עַמִּי
  B בְּעֵצוֹ יִשְׁאָל
  B′ וּמַקְלוֹ יַגִּיד
A′ לוֹ

But see also discussion of v. 14c.

[59] Translating the singulars in this line as plurals because עַמִּי is a collective.

[60] The word עֵץ basically means "tree," and in this context it possibly refers either to a wooden idol (as in the NIV) or to a wooden divining rod, in parallel with וּמַקְלוֹ. Even so, it is important that Hosea used עֵץ here since it indicates a deliberate inclusion pattern with the trees mentioned at the end of the fourth line.

[61] There is no reason for the change the NIV has made here. The "rod" is the subject, and the verb is active. The NIV has made the people the subject and the verb passive.

[62] Another chiastic line; here the noun phrases form the outer parts of the chiasmus, and the verbs (הִתְעָה and וַיִּזְנוּ) form the inner elements.

[63] The verb קטר here probably implies more than incense burning; it may indicate the burning of all kinds of food offerings. See D. Edelman, "The Meaning of *qiṭṭēr*," *VT* 35 (1985): 395–404.

idol or a sacred branch or staff (as in the NIV), or it could literally be a sacred tree.[64] Hosea has deliberately used the word "tree," however, to link this line to the trees mentioned in the last line, in the inclusion pattern mentioned above. The terms used here are representative; they stand for the many types of omen taking employed in the ancient world. Casting arrows into the air and observing the pattern formed when they fell to earth, examining the liver of an animal, observing the flight of birds, and many other means were also used to determine the future and the will of a god. Images of gods sometimes gave special prominence to the Adam's apple in order to convey the idea that the god was able to answer the queries of the seeker.[65] Hosea focuses on taking omens from a tree and sticks because it has a link to the other lamentation of this poem, going to sacred groves. He sees this omen seeking as foolish and as debasing for a human.

The "spirit of prostitution" they followed was both literal, in the acts of sacred prostitution, and metaphorical, in the act of giving love to other gods. Going to the temple prostitutes only took the Israelites further from God. Interestingly, the characteristic act for the priests would be "stumbling," a reference to their downfall (v. 5), but the characteristic act of the laity is passive, that they are led astray. Hosea again holds the religious leadership accountable for the moral state of the laity while not excusing the latter from all responsibility.

The closing of the poem, that the shade is "good" where they worship, is not an accidental comment but implies that the cults were in some ways truly appealing to the average person. In order to appreciate fully the lament concerning their going to hills and shade trees to offer sacrifices, we need to understand how this activity could be attractive. The "sacrifices" were not simply for the gods but were eaten by human participants. In a beautiful setting in the hills and under trees, the people could experience something that combined a picnic with "sacred mysteries." Also in these mountain shrines they enjoyed freedom from the restraints of the strict morality imposed by orthodox Yahwism (thus Josiah found it necessary to close down all rural shrines, 2 Kgs 23:8–9). This, combined with a belief that these gods and their rites had the power to insure good crops and healthy births in their flocks and herds, made for a religion as irresistible as it was corrupting. The real tragedy, however, was not merely that these rites led to various kinds of immorality; it was that people went to the shrines and consulted trees and stones with a sense of piety and reverence.

Also we note in passing that the number three is significant again in Hosea. Here it is the three types of trees under which they practiced their rites.

---

[64] Wolff, *Hosea,* 84.

[65] Andersen and Freedman, *Hosea,* 366.

WOMEN (4:13b–14).   **4:13b–14b**   "Therefore" is transitional and leads into a second poem, a kind of commentary on the first.[66] When women in significant numbers no longer value their virginity before marriage or their chastity after it, society is in trouble. The point that these women would not suffer punishment is more rhetorical than literal; the women were not spared the horrors that engulfed Israel when it fell to Assyria. The rhetorical effect, however, is powerful. Those in the ancient Near East took adultery by women very seriously and often applied a double standard, as in Gen 38:24, where Judah, who had recently made use of the services of a prostitute, demanded that Tamar be burned to death for prostituting herself. Here Yahweh is in effect saying: "Why should I be outraged when young women commit adultery? They only learned it from their husbands!"

In this passage Hosea makes his plainest assertion that the Israelites were engaging in sexual intercourse as part of the worship at the shrines. Wolff, in his commentary, cites Herodotus's account of the prostitution in the temple of Aphrodite in Babylon. He claimed that every woman at least once in her life had to sit in the temple and wait for a man to come, cast money in her lap, and claim her in the name of the goddess. No woman of any social status was exempt, and she was required to have sexual relations with the first man who claimed her.[67] While we have no way of knowing if the Israelites followed this practice, the example tells us something of what sacred prostitution was like, and it also explains Hosea's rhetorical exoneration of the women.

Excursus: Feminism and Hosea

Feminists approach the chief interpretive problem of Hosea, that of the prophet's relationship to his wife, via two hermeneutical presuppositions. The first is that the Bible reflects the oppressive ideology of patriarchy, which is the dominance of men over women. This bias is supposed to have so skewed the worldview of the biblical writers that even the best of them supported this form of injustice. Because this attitude pervades the entire Bible, moreover, it cannot be expunged by means of the traditional liberal method of a "canon within canon." Instead, many assert that the entire text must be deconstructed in order to find the subversive voice that liberates the text.

Second, feminists view it as the responsibility of the reader who is committed to liberation to approach the text from a standpoint of advocacy rather than from the standpoint of a supposed (but phony) neutrality and objectivity. They sometimes display little patience with the objection that a proposed interpretation contradicts the text or context, and especially the argument that a given interpretation cannot have been the author's intent. It is daunting indeed to engage an inter-

---

[66] Note that after עַל־כֵּן the line תִּזְנֶינָה בְּנוֹתֵיכֶם וְכַלּוֹתֵיכֶם תְּנָאַפְנָה is a perfect chiasmus, similar to the two chiastic lines that began the previous poem. עַל־כֵּן is a bridge between the two, but it also separates the two. These are two poems, not one.

[67] Wolff, *Hosea,* 86–87, citing Herodotus I.199.

preter who has declared objectivity to be not just an impossible ideal but a tool of oppression as well. Even so, feminist interpreters, in order for their analyses to have claim to a hearing, also allow for certain "fixed points" in the text that are "non-negotiable,"[68] and these provide a basis for interaction.

Not surprisingly, Hosea comes in for some severe criticism from feminist readers. After all, he threatens to humiliate the woman by stripping her naked (2:3,9–10), he plans to imprison her (2:6), and he appears to be infuriated by her wearing of jewelry (2:13). Thus a feminist reader might conclude that this is the work of a deranged stalker of his ex-wife, and not the work of a messenger of justice. A number of feminist readers assert that the book condones violence against women as a means of controlling them.[69]

A more creative if less convincing interpretation is that of F. van Dijk-Hemmes. She argues that Hosea gives us distorted fragments of Gomer's love poetry—love songs that were analogous to the woman's parts in Song of Songs. In this reconstruction these love songs extolled the erotic and nurturing power of the woman/goddess, but Hosea intentionally misconstrued them and condemned Gomer to silence in the text in order to crush the religion of the mother-goddess and maintain patriarchal, oppressive religion.[70] Apart from the fact that the representation of Gomer singing love songs analogous to Song of Songs is pure hypothesis, one should note that Song of Songs does not endorse or in any way deal with goddess religion.[71] The idea that Gomer used such songs to promote such a religion is fragile hypothesis built upon fragile hypothesis. In addition, the prophet Hosea was not so much in a struggle against the goddess as he was in a contest against Baal, the metaphorical rival of Yahweh (2:16–17).[72]

Y. Sherwood has given us a more complete feminist analysis of Hosea in a book which, whatever one may think of her conclusions, is a model of research. She forthrightly shuns any notion that hers is an "objective" reading of the text and instead claims to represent the marginalized viewpoint of the woman.[73] She expertly details flaws in the evasive and clumsily created interpretations of Hosea

---

[68] The terms are from Y. Sherwood, *The Prostitute and the Prophet: Hosea's Marriage in Literary-Theological Perspective,* JSOTSup 212 (Sheffield: Academic Press, 1996), 33. She compares the fixed points in a text to stars in the sky which the reader must respect but in which she is free to draw whatever constellation lines she chooses (p. 34). While I believe that this analogy gives too much control to the reader, it is helpful that she allows for the fixed points.

[69] Cf. R. J. Weems, "Gomer: Victim of Violence or Victim of Metaphor?" *Semeia* 47 (1989): 87–104, and T. D. Setel, "Prophets and Pornography: Female Sexual Imagery in Hosea," in L. Russell, *Feminist Interpretation of the Bible* (Philadelphia: Westminster, 1985), 86–95.

[70] F. van Dijk-Hemmes, "The Imagination of Power and the Power of Imagination: An Intertextual Analysis of Two Biblical Love Songs," *JSOT* 44 (1989): 75–88.

[71] Cf. D. A. Garrett, *Proverbs, Ecclesiastes, Song of Songs,* NAC (Nashville: Broadman, 1993), 361–63.

[72] Cf. Mays, *Hosea,* 11–12.

[73] Sherwood, *Prostitute,* 39. It would not be fair, however, to argue prematurely that Sherwood uniquely ignores the text except where it suits her. She correctly points out that a host of earlier scholars have made what they wanted of this story, often inventing details with little or no support from the text (e.g., pp. 54–57).

that apologetics-dominated commentaries have propagated through the centuries.[74] As a semiotic analysis she focuses on the signifier rather than the signified and on how the text achieves meaning instead of what it means.[75] Using the strategy of deconstruction developed by Derrida, she argues that the book undermines itself.

In her semiotic analysis she demonstrates that Hosea is capable of using signs in a remarkable manner. His children are "defamiliarized" by the astounding names they receive, but this improper naming has the effect of commanding the reader's attention. More than that, Hosea exercises the principal of "transformability" in making the names represent the opposite of what they signify: Lo-Ammi becomes "My people."[76] By the horrible image of a daughter named Lo-Ruhamah (Not-loved), the text prepares the reader for Yahweh himself to recoil from his decree of judgment.[77] She further contends that Hosea debunks the illusion that a text can provide direct access to its historical referents by turning its own signs back upon themselves.[78] Hosea 1, she asserts, is self-consciously a text of signs and makes no claim of taking us into the historical situation itself. Without explicitly saying so, we should add, Sherwood has demonstrated that Hosea is an author of extreme sophistication.

In a very thorough survey of the history of the interpretation of Hosea, Sherwood repeatedly makes the point that traditional interpreters of the book have refused to face the blunt assertion that Hosea married a prostitute. Some have created a romantic fiction out of the text, in which Hosea the heartbroken but compassionate prophet laments the behavior of his wife, who was once pure but became wayward.[79] Male interpreters of this sort, she complains, are unified in their portrayal of Hosea the victim who nevertheless was the epitome of grace. Gomer herself is either romanticized as a fallen beauty or demonized as a monster of depravity. If not that, male interpreters flee from the stark reality of the text into the sanctuary of interpreting the marriage of a prophet to a prostitute as pure vision, parable, or as a metaphor for idolatry. She correctly insists that these interpreters, defenders of Jewish or Christian orthodoxy, have obscured the text with fantasies of their own creation.[80]

Sherwood finds the feminine voice of compassion hidden away in this text. For example, she writes: "As soon as Gomer gives birth to the children her right to name them is denied and she is silenced, but although it is given no voice, the

---

[74] Ibid., 40–82. E.g., that the marriage account is just a vision, that Gomer was really a virtuous woman, and so forth.

[75] Ibid., 83–149.

[76] Sherwood, *Prostitute,* 117–20.

[77] Ibid., 145.

[78] Ibid., 121–22.

[79] For an example see W. E. Crane, "The Prophecy of Hosea," *BibSac* 89 (1932): 480–94, an introduction that fairly dodges the question of Hosea's marriage altogether, except to speak of "true love blighted by unchaste unfaithfulness" (p. 481).

[80] Sherwood, *Prostitute,* 40–79. But not all traditional interpreters are as unbalanced as she contends. See H. L. Ellison, "The Message of Hosea in the Light of His Marriage," *EvQ* 41 (1969): 3–9, especially p. 6.

maternal force within the text is not eradicated, but continues to exert a strong and silent force. Hosea (under the instruction of Yhwh) names the second child Not-Loved; Gomer, in a silent and rebellious dumb-show of love, is depicted as weaning her. Weaning implies a prior act of suckling, a gesture of love, that counters the father's harsh decree."[81]

A sustained example of deconstructive analysis is Sherwood's treatment of the relationship between Yahweh and Baal according to Hosea 2. She asserts that Yahweh's starting point is the pristine love that once supposedly existed between himself and Israel but which Israel has abandoned, and she debunks this myth of lost innocence on the basis of deconstructionist categories. She further argues that Yahweh is playing the role of a desperate cuckold, who at one point imprisons his ex-wife and at another point seeks to love her tenderly. The result is that the reader instinctively recoils at Yahweh's irrational behavior. She then contends that Yahweh seeks to supplant Baal by reinventing himself in Baal-like categories. As Baal is lover and provider, so shall Yahweh be lover and provider. She argues that Yahweh is here a sexual god trying to oust Baal, his rival, and gain the favors of Israel, but that in order to do this he must plagiarize the Baal cult and become a surrogate Baal.[82]

In a remarkable piece of psychosexual analysis of Hosea, Sherwood contends that Hos 2:2–3 "focuses lasciviously on the act of stripping and on the woman's breasts." In doing this, the text deconstructs itself and reveals the distorted sexuality of its male author.[83] That is, Hosea demands moral purity in his wife while he is himself luridly fascinated with erotic images. At the same time, Hosea is terrified of the female power represented by Gomer's immoral behavior and her freedom to divorce. Hosea/Yahweh attempts to imprison the woman in order to thwart this most dangerous, antipatriarchal phenomenon, the woman who is free, financially independent, and who might find her mate unsatisfactory and so leave to find another.[84]

Finally, prostitution is itself the means of Gomer's liberation. Sherwood argues that the woman's contention that her possessions are the "wages" she received from her lovers "seems to imply a surprisingly modern view of the economics of prostitution: the woman speaks in terms of contracts rather than subordination and suggests that she strikes her own bargain with a society ruled by men and deities." That is, her sexual and economic freedom undermines the entire patriarchal system. Through prostitution she can give male society what it wants and maintain her own freedom.[85]

In short, the Book of Hosea is a text whose signifiers both arise from and seek to establish the patriarchy in which men are dominant, independent, and provid-

---

[81] Sherwood, *Prostitute,* 146.

[82] Ibid., 207–35.

[83] Ibid., 316. "The location of the offenses on her face and on her breasts makes the reader aware of an otherwise invisible presence, the male author and his desires." This confused author "revels in female sexuality even as he condemns it."

[84] E.g., Sherwood, *Prostitute,* 310, 314–21.

[85] Ibid., 319–20.

ers but women are submissive, dependent, and weak because of their more sexual nature. Deconstructed, however, the book reveals a patriarchy that is powerless, voyeuristic, and desperately seeking to maintain control in the presence of a woman who is both loving and independent. This is, to say the least, a distinctively feminist interpretation. At several points, however, one must call it into question.

First, the text of Hosea gives scant support to Sherwood's assertions of vicious misogyny. It is difficult to see, for example, how 2:2–3 has the kind of voyeuristic quality that Sherwood wants us to find here:

Let her remove the adulterous look from her face
and the unfaithfulness from between her breasts.

Otherwise I will strip her naked
and make her as bare as on the day she was born.

For a book that takes prostitution as its starting point, it is remarkable how little Hosea really says about the subject and about female sexuality in particular (contrast Prov 7; Ezek 16; 23). Hebrew writers and poets routinely refer to the woman's breasts as an area of sexuality—a fact that often is celebrated as a positive thing (Prov 5:19; Song 1:13; 4:5; 7:3,7,8; 8:1,8)—but Hosea's comments here are minimal. Furthermore, the plea that the woman should remove the unfaithfulness from between her breasts neither leers at nor condemns female sexuality. These words are hardly "lascivious." It is clear that Sherwood has in reality read Ezekiel 16 and 23—and her own ideology—into the Book of Hosea.[86]

Hosea 2:9–10 is more violent in nature: God will remove the wool and linen with which Israel covered her nakedness and expose her lewdness[87] before her lovers. The language ironically turns sexual imagery on its head. In the analogy of Israel the adulteress, nakedness is the situation she chose for herself with her lovers. In the retribution nakedness is dire poverty (v. 9) and exile (v. 10). The irony is similar to that found in Rev 2:22, in which Christ threatens to throw "Jezebel" into a bed. She had voluntary gone into bed with her lovers, but she would involuntarily be bedridden because of disease. But the threat to cast her into bed does not represent some kind of lurid sexuality on John's (or Jesus') part.

In her fixation on the signifier, however, Sherwood wants the reader to see real abuse of a woman here, an abuse tinged with sadism. But what she fails to deal with is that Hosea, for his theological purposes, has deliberately constructed an unnatural, artificial response by the outraged husband. In ancient Israel an offended husband might have sought to destroy the woman's paramour (Prov 6:32–35) or to have both the woman and the paramour put to death (Lev 20:10). One might even concede that he could have had her publicly stripped, but solid evidence for this in ancient Israel is lacking. What no outraged husband would

---

[86] These two chapters are genuinely astonishing in their sexual bluntness; even here, however, one can maintain that this is not the work of a decadent, religious voyeur. Nevertheless, regardless of what one does with Ezekiel, one cannot read these texts into the Book of Hosea.

[87] The word נַבְלוּת could mean either "genitals" or "stupidity."

do, however, is give the woman's paramours the pleasure of another private display of his naked wife,[88] as Yahweh does in Hos 2:10. But if one recognizes that the root "strip" in another stem means "send into exile"[89] and that the "lovers" are not just gods but foreign nations, the significance of the act is clear. Israel adulterated herself—lost her true identity—with the foreign nations and their gods, and now she would forcibly go into exile among them. And it is the thing signified, not the signifier, that is the real point. By focusing on the signifier Sherwood has sought to contend with an injustice as unreal as those committed by the unjust steward and by the unusual vineyard owner of Jesus' parables (Matt 20:1–16; Luke 16:1–9). To focus on the imaginary misdeeds of artificial literary constructs is not to read perceptively but perversely and indeed to miss the point entirely.

Second, the violence of Hosea's metaphors are deliberate and serve to stun his readers. Sherwood herself realizes this and goes to great lengths to demonstrate it.[90] What she does not see is that this undermines her whole thesis that Hosea needs to be deconstructed. Hosea does not seek to establish a world where violence and rape rule. To the contrary, he uses abhorrent images precisely because they are abhorrent—to himself no less than to his readers. He does this not in order to make the abhorrent acceptable but to establish the fact that Israel had almost lost the ability to distinguish between what is acceptable and what is abhorrent. Put another way, Hosea could not stun his audience with horrible images if the images themselves constituted acceptable behavior to him or to his readers.

Thus, when he declares that Yahweh is like "maggots" or "rot" to Israel (5:12),[91] he uses language that one could not describe as befitting God. By using terms for God that one can hardly imagine, he seeks to break through Israelite intransigence and force them to recognize how completely the relationship between themselves and Yahweh has degenerated. Israel, he says, is related to God in the same way that wounded, dying flesh is related to gangrene! This is not evidence that Hosea believed that decay was good and proper in living flesh.

In the same way, when Hosea declares that God would strip Israel naked, imprison her, and destroy her, he is not thereby asserting that this is the proper way for a man to deal with his wife; nor is the literary stripping of the woman the act of a self-righteous voyeur or a sadist. Rather, Hosea portrays this as a relationship without love or compassion (Lo-Ruhamah). It is a stunning perversion of a marriage, and the abhorrent language is a jolt for the jaded audience of the prophet. But it no more establishes the rules for the conduct of a real marriage than Jesus' hyperbole about casting out one's right eye gives the proper method for dealing with lust (Matt 5:29). Yahweh has the right to "strip" apostate Israel and humiliate the nation before the whole world, but this does not demonstrate that Hosea believed men could do the same to their wives. The signifier has shock

---

[88] Note that this is not humiliation before the community; it is only for the eyes of the lovers.
[89] The root גלה means to "strip" in the *piel* stem and to "send into exile" in the *hiphil* stem.
[90] E.g., Sherwood, *Prostitute,* 148.
[91] See commentary on this verse.

value only if it is shocking; it has no such value if it follows the norms of an entrenched mentality. Sherwood cannot have it both ways; she cannot explore the semiotic depths of a Hosea who skillfully disorients the reader through non-traditional and abhorrent signs and at the same time denounce him as a man who ferociously if stupidly seeks to maintain traditional chauvinism.[92]

Third, Hos 4:14 goes a long way in exonerating Hosea of misogyny: "I will not punish your daughters when they turn to prostitution, nor your daughters-in-law when they commit adultery, because the men themselves consort with harlots and sacrifice with shrine prostitutes." No deranged husband—outraged at the adultery of his wife, fearful of the power that female sexuality represents, and in a mood to crush her spirit by any means necessary—could utter such words. If anything, the adultery of the women is tertiary in Hosea's mind. He gives more attention to the paganism of the people in general, and far more attention to the sins of the religious leadership, than he does to literal adultery committed by Israelite women. And he says absolutely nothing about divorce (contrast Mal 2:16). If Hosea had been driven to distraction by fear of feminine power in the freedom to divorce, it is astounding that he did not use his prophetic office to condemn it. Plainly put, "We must whip these women into line!" is not the message of Hosea. In fact, he does not see the promiscuity of the women as a rebellion against male leadership at all; rather, he laments the fact that the women are following the men into promiscuity.[93]

Fourth, Hosea's metaphors remain that—metaphors. Hosea himself never indicates that he was violent toward his wife, nor does he advocate such behavior. Rather, his language indicates how the Israelite people (male and female) would suffer for their apostasy. Many feminist readers, to be sure, dismiss the "it's-only-a-metaphor" argument out of hand. Sherwood, for example, goes so far as to say that it is not the woman who represents the land but the land who represents the woman.[94] This is completely misguided.

It is clear from the beginning (1:2) that the "land" is metonymy for apostate Israel[95] and that the wayward wife represents the land and not vice-versa. More than that, "Israel" in the Book of Hosea often represents the culture and power structure that misleads the people. When Hosea pleads with the "children" to

---

[92] The obvious response here is that deconstruction does not imply that the author is stupid (cf. Sherwood, *Prostitute*, 167); but if we follow a feminist analysis, we not only have a stupid Hosea but two Hoseas. The one Hosea skillfully disorients the reader in order to expose the self-contradiction in the violence, oppression, and lasciviousness of their culture, while the other zealously but crudely seeks to preserve it.

[93] The obvious counterattack here (cf. Sherwood, *Prostitute*, 273) is that 4:14 subordinates women by making them follow the leadership of the men. But Hosea is not here prescribing anything about the roles of the sexes in society; he is merely describing what he sees—and that with disapproval. The point is that Hosea cannot be terrified of women's sexual freedom and at the same time speak of them in the terms he does in 4:14—terms that indicate that female sexuality is far from being Hosea's primary concern.

[94] Ibid., 137–38.

[95] Notwithstanding her tortured attempts to turn 1:2 into a tautology; cf. Sherwood, *Prostitute*, 120–21.

denounce their "mother" (2:2), he is really calling on the people to abandon these corrupt power structures. "Israel" is the religious leadership who drives the poor into superstition in order that they may more easily consume them (4:4–11), and who have turned the shrines of Israel into traps in order to control the people (5:1). The political leadership that is "Israel" includes a government that makes fraud and oppression instruments of policy.[96] When Sherwood deconstructs Hosea and defends the "woman" of Hosea 1–3, she is actually defending the wealthy, hierarchical, male-dominated institutions of Israel that oppressed the poor and drew the women into prostitution! Deconstruction has a way of biting the hand that feeds it.

Hosea is actually the champion of opposition to abusive authority. His critique of the religious power structure and rhetorical exoneration of the women indicates that he has more sympathy for those who are weak and who must follow the path laid down for them and less (or no) sympathy for those who have power over others. His promise to "strip" the woman (2:3) is not polemic against women who divorce their husbands. It is polemic against the priests, prophets, and governors who controlled, consumed, and abandoned the peasants and the women. His call is for the people to escape this hierarchy and so become part of the true Israel of God. In view of 4:14, one can make the case that Hosea viewed Gomer more as a casualty of Israelite culture than as an insolent woman against whom he wanted vengeance for his hurt sexual pride.[97]

The interpretive method Sherwood follows is itself seriously flawed. It goes without saying that deconstructionism takes the text in strange directions; it would not be "subversive" if its readings were naturally suggested by the text. This poses a problem, however, for deconstructive reading: How can one get others to take seriously an interpretation that is so far removed from what the text itself rather plainly states? In a curious manner feminist-deconstructionist analysis of Hosea follows the logic of Alexandrian allegorism. Allegorizers, in order to justify their hermeneutics, used the following strategy:

• They would take a text with a self-evident metaphor but refuse to read it as a metaphor. Instead, they would take it in its most crudely literal sense.

• They would then assert that the literal meaning of the text is impossible.

• They would therefore assert that their allegorization of the text was legitimate and necessary.

Feminist-deconstructionist analysis of Hosea functions as follows:

• They announce that a self-evident metaphor, in which the punishment of the "woman" represents the punishment of Israel, is not a metaphor at all, or they claim that the signifier is more important than the signified.

---

[96] Especially at 7:1–7 (see commentary).

[97] This does not imply that Hosea presents Gomer as an innocent girl corrupted by the ways of the world or as a child, not responsible for her own decisions. She, like the rest of the Israelites, was still responsible for her own actions, and Hos 4:14 does not patronize women any more than 4:12–13 patronizes the ordinary people who had been misled by the priests. This text does imply, however, that Hosea does not speak out of hostility to all women or to Gomer in particular.

• They assert that this is spousal abuse by a deranged husband and that it represents the dominant voice of patriarchal culture.

They therefore conclude that the text must be read subversively, or deconstructed, in order to hear the woman's voice.

In both cases the new reading only gives us a pseudotext that gives a pseudolegitimacy for an orthodoxy that is extraneous to the real text.

In this way it is not Hosea but Sherwood who disorients (or rather misleads) the reader. A case in point is her understanding of 1:2, which she claims is tautologous and does not reveal anything. She asserts that the signified, the land that commits adultery, is confusedly obscure because it has turned itself back into the signifier, the adulterous woman. She must do this in order to convince us that the signifier is the real focus of the text. To carry out this strategy she must persuade us that the signified is an impossibility because land does not literally prostitute itself.

In fact, the text is not nearly so difficult. To work backwards, the apostasy of Israel is metaphorically adultery against Israel's covenant husband, Yahweh. Hosea marries a promiscuous woman as an analogy for that relationship. "The land prostitutes itself" is self-evidently metaphorical; Sherwood has tried to pull the wool over our eyes by claiming that its signified meaning is impossible. The linguistic movement in 1:2, moreover, is not an eternal circle of movement between signifier to signified; it is linear, from analog to metaphor to signified. The signified, not the signifier, remains the focus of the text. Sherwood cannot successfully instruct us in "how" the text means when she has so thoroughly distorted "what" it means.

This distorted hermeneutic reveals itself in other ways. Feminists complain that Hosea has "silenced" Gomer and refused to give her a voice. This observation obscures the fact that Hosea has equally silenced himself about the relationship. Hosea never claims that he was deceived by or about her or that she betrayed his trust. In fact, he never blames Gomer for anything. He simply states that God told him to marry a promiscuous woman, and he did so. She was what she was before the marriage, and he knew it. He never appeals for the reader's sympathy, builds a case against her, or reveals details of their domestic life. So effectively has he muzzled himself in this matter that it is only with difficulty, and with much disagreement among scholars, that we can piece together the barest outline of their story. Regarding Hosea's marriage, we do not have only one side of a domestic dispute; we have neither side, and we don't know that there ever was what we would call a domestic dispute. We do not know if Hosea divorced Gomer, or if Gomer divorced Hosea, or if there was a divorce at all, or if Gomer simply abandoned Hosea, or if there was a period of mutually agreed separation, or if they ever argued about her behavior. We know nothing about her behavior during the marriage, in fact, except that she had three children. Otherwise all we know is that when Hosea married her, she was a "woman of promiscuity" and that 3:1 apparently indicates she somehow separated from him and for a time became the salable property of some other person or institution.

It is clear too that Sherwood's portrayal of Gomer the loving mother is itself as much a romantic reconstruction by an overactive imagination as is any of the reconstructions of Hosea the heart-broken prophet that she lampoons. As described above, Lo-Ruhamah (Not-Loved) is an abhorrent name. Contrary to Sherwood's analysis, however, we do not have any grounds for supposing that Hosea had issued a "decree" that no love should be given to Lo-Ruhamah any more than that he had decreed that Jezreel should be murdered or that Lo-Ammi should be cast out of the household. Furthermore, the fact that Gomer suckled Lo-Ruhamah (i.e., she did not allow the baby to starve to death) does not mean that Gomer was an especially good or loving mother. If she was a loving mother, we have no grounds for claiming that Hosea disapproved of her love or did not love Lo-Ruhamah himself. In attributing the name of the girl to Yahweh, Hosea distances himself from the naming process. In short, a doctrine of feminist orthodoxy, the woman as loving nurturer who resists the cruel patriarchy, has been imposed on the text just as surely as medieval allegorists imposed the orthodox teachings of the church on Old Testament texts.

Finally, we must say a word about the moral deception that feminist readers have introduced into the text. By exalting Gomer as a kind of protofeminist, they have asserted that her immorality and paganism were expressions of freedom from patriarchal bondage. This itself is absurdly anachronistic, but it is also dangerous because it conveys the impression that promiscuity or even prostitution is a legitimate tool of women in the struggle for equality. But promiscuity never frees; it only enslaves. No person is liberated whose soul is destroyed or whose life is decadent. Such thinking is like the notion that girls can achieve equality with boys by smoking cigarettes, taking drugs, and resorting to violence and crime. Girls who do this only achieve the equality of a miserable life and an early death while giving themselves over to abusive power structures (tobacco companies, drug dealers, pornographers, organized crime, etc.). It is the real Hosea, not the deconstructed Hosea, who opposes this kind of hierarchy and stands for true liberation of women and men.

TRANSITION: A PROVERB ON DEBAUCHERY (4:14c). **4:14c** The line has no logical connection to the poem that precedes it, although it is an apt comment on the social situation Hosea describes. It reads like the second line of a proverb;[98] one might hypothesize about what the original full proverb looked like.[99] Outside of this text the word translated "come to ruin" only appears in Proverbs, which reinforces the probability that this is a proverb fragment that Hosea has used for concluding this section.[100] This line is well suited as a closing for 4:4–14 because it begins with ʿām, "a people," which alludes to the emphasis here on ʿammî, "my people," in vv. 6 and

---

[98] It seems to be the second line because it begins with the conjunction (וְעָם).

[99] Cf. Prov 10:8: "The wise in heart accept commands, but a chattering fool comes to ruin."

[100] The word לבט (niphal stem) appears only here and in two identical clauses in Prov 10:8,10. The unusually terse style of Hos 14:4c, with two yiqtol (imperfect) verbs side by side, is also the kind of grammar one would find in a proverb (cf. Prov 4:6). Also note the emphasis on "understanding" (בִּין) in this line, which is another characteristic of wisdom.

12.[101] It is as though Israel is demoted from being "my people" to simply being "a people," one of the nations. It also comments appropriately on the situation the text has described. The priests were not teaching the truth, the people were being led astray, and the men were educating the women in the ways of promiscuity. Thus they were truly a people without understanding.

But what might the original full proverb have been? I would propose that the first half of the proverb was v. 11, so that the full proverb read, "Prostitution, wine, and new wine take away the heart, and a people without understanding come to ruin."[102] Structurally, this line functions as a response to the previous line at v. 11. The first proverb speaks of how immoral behavior makes people senseless, and the second declares that a senseless nation faces ruin.[103] If this hypothesis is valid, Hosea has split a proverbial couplet and inserted between the two lines a description of the debauchery of his own people, as if Israel were a living illustration of the decadence the proverb describes.

(3) Lo-Ruhamah: Three Warnings for Israel and Judah (4:15–5:15)

The number of Hosea's children, three, continues to dominate the text. This section is made up of three warnings to Israel, in each of which a message goes to Judah as well. As we will see, items come in groups of three throughout this passage. Formally, each of the three sections below consists of an opening threefold exhortation (4:15; 5:1–2; 5:8), various indictments of the people (4:16–18; 5:3–7; 5:9–11), and a powerful or unusual metaphor for the wrath that Yahweh will bring upon them (whirlwind, 4:19; new moon, 5:8; rot and a lion, 5:12–14). These metaphors of destruction are reversed in the call to repent in 6:1–3. A transitional verse, 5:15, continues the metaphor of Yahweh as a lion but introduces the topic of repentance, a theme taken up in 6:1–7:13.

Most significantly, words to Judah are woven into texts directed against

---

[101] The phrase וְעָם לֹא־יָבִין ("and a people does not understand") also looks back to 4:6, where Yahweh grieves that עַמִּי ("my people") perish מִבְּלִי הַדָּעַת ("from lack of knowledge").

[102] The probability of this hypothesis is reinforced by the Hb. text, as reconstructed:

זְנוּת וְיַיִן וְתִירוֹשׁ יִקַּח־לֵב
וְעָם לֹא־יָבִין יִלָּבֵט

Note the assonance with the consonants לֵב at the ends of the two lines.

[103] A case can be made for placing עַמִּי at the end of v. 11, as in the NIV, in that the line at the end of v. 11 would thus end with עַמִּי just as the proverb at the end of v. 14 begins with וְעָם. Cf. J. R. Lundbom, "Poetic Structure and Prophetic Rhetoric in Hosea," VT 29 (1979): 300–308. Even so (for reasons stated above), I believe that עַמִּי belongs with v. 12 and not with v. 11. If the full proverb is as I have proposed, in fact, there is no reason at all to place עַמִּי with v. 11, although its presence as the very next word in the text is no doubt deliberate. If the Israelites knew the proverb "Prostitution, wine, and new wine take away the heart, and a people without understanding come to ruin" but Hosea began "My people consults a tree …" right where they expected to hear "and a people …," the homiletical effect would be striking.

Israel. A progression is evident. First, Hosea warns Judah not to imitate Israel
(4:15). Next, Hosea claims that Judah was stumbling into sin along with Israel
(5:5). Finally, he says that Judah bore the same guilt as Israel (5:9–11). These
are not interpolations added by pro- and anti-Judah redactors.[104] Rather, they
present Hosea as a prophet to all of Israel and not to the northern tribes alone.
More than that, they complete the pattern begun in 4:1–14, in which Hosea
gives oracles that allude to the interpretations of his three children's names.
The "bloodshed" of 4:1–3 looked back to the bloodshed of Jezreel (1:4), and
the repeated use of "my people" looked back to Lo-Ammi. Here the surprising
words to Judah correspond to the equally surprising first mention of Judah in
1:7, in the Lo-Ruhamah oracle. In addition, the meaning of the name Lo-
Ruhamah, "no compassion," is reflected in the harsh and violent language used
to describe the penalties Yahweh would inflict on the people (e.g., 4:12–15).

15"Though you commit adultery, O Israel,
   let not Judah become guilty.
"Do not go to Gilgal;
   do not go up to Beth Aven.
   And do not swear, 'As surely as the LORD lives!'
16The Israelites are stubborn,
   like a stubborn heifer.
 How then can the LORD pasture them
   like lambs in a meadow?
17Ephraim is joined to idols;
   leave him alone!
18Even when their drinks are gone,
   they continue their prostitution;
   their rulers dearly love shameful ways.
19A whirlwind will sweep them away,
   and their sacrifices will bring them shame.

ISRAEL'S APOSTASY A WARNING TO JUDAH (4:15–19).   **4:15**   At the
very beginning, Hosea informs the reader that this section will address Judah
also and not Israel alone. The passing reference to prostituting themselves
(NIV, "commit adultery") provides a catchword link between this section and
the previous,[105] but it is clear we are in a new section. In addition to the unexpected mention of Judah, the prophet here uses the name "Israel" for the first
time since 1:11, but he drops the use of the term "my people" until it reappears
at 7:1. The prayer for Judah reflects Hosea's belief that the salvation of the
nation and its true royal line is in the Davidic dynasty (Hos 3:5). The assertion

---

[104] Wolff, who does not see the progression here, makes the unwarranted claim that Hosea
made no distinction between Israel and Judah (*Hosea,* 89). He regards "Judah" in 4:15 to be the
work of a glossator and strangely regards the LXX as support for his position.
[105] The word זָנָה here looks back to prior uses of the root זנה in 4:13–14.

that the nation was prostituting itself again refers both to the nation's apostasy and their sexual immorality.[106]

After the prayer for Judah, Hosea gives his first threefold alarm in the form of three negative commands.[107] Although the Bible mentions a number of sites called Gilgal, it appears that the Gilgal of this verse is the location near the Jordan that Joshua made his first base of operations after crossing into Canaan (Josh 4:19). There the men of the nation were circumcised in preparation for Israel's first Passover in the land (Josh 5:7–12), and from there Jericho was taken. Gilgal was on Samuel's annual circuit (1 Sam 7:16), and it is the setting for much of the story of Samuel and Saul (e.g., 1 Sam 11:14–15). The people of Judah welcomed David back at Gilgal after the war with Absalom (2 Sam 19:15). A group of Elisha's disciples resided there (2 Kgs 4:38). Thus one can say that Gilgal was a place of great significance in the spiritual history of Israel, and the people had every reason to consider it sacred. Unfortunately, it went from being a shrine for pilgrims to a center of apostasy, and by the eighth century not only Hosea but Amos as well was counseling people to stay away from there (Amos 4:4; 5:5).

Beth Aven is almost certainly Bethel; Amos also associates Gilgal with Bethel, and employing the same pun that Hosea uses, he declares that Bethel would become "nothing" (*ʾāwen*). Amos ministered in the reigns of Uzziah of Judah and Jeroboam II of Israel and thus overlaps and slightly precedes Hosea. It appears that Amos's use of this wordplay is original, and that Hosea is following patterns Amos had already set.[108]

Bethel was, if anything, even more sacred than Gilgal. Abraham camped there (Gen 12:8), and while sleeping there Jacob saw his vision of the stairway into heaven and gave the place its name, "house of God" (*bêt-ʾēl;* Gen 28:11–18; 31:1–15). Later God revealed himself to Jacob as the "God of Bethel" (Gen 31:13). Jacob confirmed the status of the site by building a memorial pillar and an altar there. Jeroboam I took advantage of the sacred traditions associated with Bethel to turn it into a shrine to rival Solomon's temple in Jerusalem. He thereby put an end to his people's religious pilgrimages to Jerusalem (1 Kgs 12:29), an act immediately condemned by the prophets as apostasy (1 Kgs 13). The term *ʾāwen* basically means "disaster," "nothingness," or "deception," and it is a polemical term used by the prophets to describe idolatry (e.g., Isa 66:3). Psalms often speaks of the "doers of *ʾāwen*,"

---

[106] It is unusual to find זֹנֹה as a masculine participle, but the gender of the participle simply agrees with the gender of יִשְׂרָאֵל, which is a masculine noun although in Hosea's metaphor it is feminine. There is no need to emend; it is the same metaphor first employed in 1:2.

[107] These three negative commands are distinct from יֶאְשַׁם יְהוּדָה אַל־ ("let not Judah become guilty") in that they are all second person while אַל־יֶאְשַׁם יְהוּדָה is third person. As is normal for Hb., *yiqtol* (imperfect) forms (rather than imperatives) are used for negative commands.

[108] Also the use of the threefold warning, so significant in Hosea's literary setting, seems to be adapted from Amos (see, e.g., Amos 5:5).

and this term may refer to idol makers or sorcerers.[109] Hosea's wordplay implies that the house of God had become the house of deception—the deception being the religious fraud that is idolatry.

The third warning is distinctive in that it does not mention a place name. The oath formula, "As the LORD lives," is very common in the Old Testament, and it was used by many of the heroes of the faith, including Boaz (Ruth 3:13), David (1 Sam 20:3), Solomon (1 Kgs 2:24), and Micaiah (2 Chr 18:13). Jeremiah 12:16 promises that God will establish those who learn to say, "as the LORD lives," instead of swearing by Baal. On the other hand, Jer 5:2 declares that the people often perjure themselves when they use this oath. Nothing comparable to Hosea's prohibition of this oath formula would occur again until Jesus forbade oaths (Matt 5:34). Hosea's opposition to the oath must be seen in light of the previous two warnings, both of which relate to places that were legitimately regarded as sacred in Israel. The point is that the people had so profaned things that were once good in their tradition that they could no longer use them rightly. Like Moses' serpent image, they had become snares (2 Kgs 18:4). The only recourse was their abandonment. The phrase "as the LORD lives" had either lost all significance or had become itself associated with the fertility cult.[110]

It appears that these three warnings are directed not to Israel but to Judah, which is urged not to imitate the ways of their northern neighbors. The two shrines of Gilgal and Bethel were near Judah, and the people of Judah could have been accustomed to making pilgrimages north to these places. Interestingly, Hosea departs from Amos 5:5 in that Amos warns people away from Bethel, Gilgal, and Beer-sheba, but Beer-sheba is far to the south, in Judah. Hosea substitutes the warning about swearing "as Yahweh lives" for an injunction against going to Beer-sheba. The warning about oath taking is appropriate here since the name Beer-sheba means "well of the oath."

4:16–18 The fundamental charge in these verses is that Israel is incorrigible in its evil ways. This is shown (1) in the simile of the stubborn heifer, (2) in their unbreakable attachment to idols, and (3) in their habitual debauchery of drunkenness and promiscuity. A stubborn heifer was a cow that refused to go where her owner led (cf. Jer 31:18).[111] The stubbornness of the people made it impossible for God to give them peace and prosperity.

---

[109] Andersen and Freedman, *Hosea,* 372. Examples of the phrase פֹּעֲלֵי אָוֶן are found in (Hb. text) Pss 5:6; 6:9; 14:4; 28:3; 36:13; 53:5; 59:3; 64:3; 92:8).

[110] Cf. Mays, *Hosea,* 78.

[111] The line translated, "How then can the LORD pasture them like lambs in a meadow?" could be translated, "Now the LORD will pasture them like lambs in a meadow," but the NIV translation is preferable. Nothing in the clause specifically marks it as a question, but in this context it probably is. Although Hosea sometimes in unexpected ways casts promises of hope as oracles of doom, this does not seem to be such an example. However, to translate the line more accurately, one should render it, "Will Yahweh now shepherd them ...?" instead of adding "how," as the NIV has done.

The line "Ephraim is joined to idols" (which implies that Israel has formed a political alliance[112] with idols) could instead be rendered, "Ephraim is spellbound of idols." The latter interpretation implies that Israel is bewitched by idols, and it is preferable.[113] Following such an interpretation, "Leave him alone!" implies that the nation is in a trance from which no one may arouse them.

The NIV translation of v. 18a implies that the people continued to engage in promiscuity, even when sober and not under the inhibition-removing effects of alcohol. This probably is not correct; the line seems to mean, "When their liquor runs out, they engage prostitutes,"[114] meaning that they drink all they can and then turn to sex.

The last line of v. 18 (NIV: "their rulers dearly love shameful ways") is very difficult in the Hebrew,[115] but one can literally translate it (with one emendation), "Her shields absolutely love shame,"[116] or, alternatively with a second minor emendation, "They absolutely love the shame of her shields."[117] Many interpreters (including the NIV) take "shields" to be the subject and understand it to be a metaphor for "leaders" on the basis of Pss 47:9 and 89:18. This is questionable, however, because while Ps 89:18 indicates that the "king" is metaphorically the "shield" of the nation, it does not imply that Hebrew readers would routinely understand "shield" to mean "leader"—the

---

[112] See Gen 14:3.

[113] Many interpreters take חָבוּר here to mean "bound in a political alliance," but this does not suit the context. Ps 58:6 (Eng. 5) says that an enchanter (חוֹבֵר) can (under normal circumstances) paralyze a cobra, which indicates complete hypnosis, a condition one would not want to interrupt. There is no reason to "leave alone" someone in an alliance. An enchantment under the spell of a strange cult is intrinsically more likely.

[114] There is no basis for a concessive translation ("even when") here. Probably סָבְאָם is the subject of סָר, which normally means to "turn aside" or "depart." Here it apparently means to "run out" or "stop"; cf. Amos 6:7, "the revelry of the carousers shall cease" (וְסָר מִרְזַח סְרוּחִים). One cannot account for the change in number from the singular verb סָר to the plural הִזְנוּ, unless there is a change of subject. Cf. NRSV: "When their drinking is ended, they indulge in sexual orgies." The LXX is radically different (ᾑρέτισεν Χαναναίους, πορνεύοντες ἐξεπόρνευσαν, "he has chosen Canaanites, they practice sexual immorality").

[115] The LXX adds to the uncertainty about this verse. It reads ἐκ φρυάγματος ("from their snorting") for מָגִנֶּיהָ and is behind the proposed emendation to מִגְּאוֹנָם, which the RSV translates, "They love shame more than their glory." While ingenious, this is a doubtful translation for a hypothetical מִגְּאוֹנָם.

[116] The first difficulty in אָהֲבוּ הֵבוּ קָלוֹן מָגִנֶּיהָ is the imperative הֵבוּ ("give!") that all interpreters agree is impossible. Left unemended the text reads, "They love—give disgrace!—her shields." The best explanation is that אָהֲבוּ הֵבוּ should be emended to אָהֹב אָהֲבוּ ("they absolutely love") in agreement with Symmachus (see Wolff, Hosea, 73; Mays, Hosea, 76). For other possibilities see McComiskey, "Hosea," 1:72–73.

[117] For this one would need to emend קָלוֹן to קְלוֹן, a construct form. The motivation for such an emendation is that it is somewhat unusual for a subject to be separated from its verb by the object.

context of Psalm 89, a celebration of the Davidic covenant, is highly specific, and the psalm uses parallelism to elucidate the meaning of "shield." Also, it is not at all clear that the "shields" of Psalm 47 are leaders—the term could be a metaphor for God's authority over the earth, a quality that the Psalm proclaims.[118]

In Hos 4:18 the reader is unprepared to recognize "leaders" as the meaning of the term "shields." Rather, vv. 15–19 describes the pagan worship and debauchery that the Israelites stubbornly refused to give up. This being the case, one might hypothesize that the "shields" are either objects associated with the worship of the gods or are the gods themselves. As justification for this assumption, we note that "shield" is routinely used as an appellation for Yahweh (Gen 15:1; 2 Sam 22:3; Pss 3:3; 7:10; 18:30; etc.). In addition, shields could be used for decorative purposes (1 Kgs 10:16–17; Song 4:4). Possibly, the fertility cult used ornamental shields of some kind[119] or, in the same manner that the orthodox described Yahweh as their shield, its liturgy called the gods their "shields." The feminine suffix ("her shields") perhaps indicates that these were items sacred to a goddess. Thus, the line would either mean that their gods loved the shameful deeds the people practiced, or more likely, that the people loved the shamefulness that the cultic "shields" represented.[120]

4:19 The first line of this verse is literally, "a wind binds her[121] in its wings," but the NIV could be correct in taking this to be a whirlwind that will sweep Israel away.[122] On the other hand, the word "bind" is associated with binding up waters in Job 26:8, and wind is associated with drought in Isa 49:10. It may also be that this is a theophany of God in a whirlwind, a motif that is common in the Old Testament and often associated with judgment.[123] Thus the wind could bind or afflict the land through drought, a condition that

---

[118] If anything, Ps 47:9 [Hb. 10] implies that the Gentile leaders will submit to Yahweh because he possesses the shields, not that they themselves are the shields.

[119] If these are some kind of ceremonial shields, it explains the unusual use of the feminine suffix on מָגִנֶּיהָ ("her shields"). I.e., these could be the shields of a goddess. Cf. G. I. Emmerson, "A Fertility Goddess in Hosea IV 17–19?" *VT* 24 (1974): 492–97, who emends to "They love the shame of her wantonness."

[120] There is, ironically, a third possibility, that the word here is actually *māgān*, analogous to a Punic word for "suzerain," if Dahood's musings are correct (M. Dahood, *Psalms,* AB [Garden City: Doubleday, 1965], 16–18). Even so, I would suggest that a religious meaning is present in Hosea, since that is also the meaning in Psalms.

[121] A number of scholars puzzle over the feminine pronoun here. It probably refers to the metaphor of Israel as the mother of the people. The text need not be emended.

[122] Cf. Wolff, who compares 2 Sam 22:11; Ps 18:11 (Eng. 10); 104:3 (*Hosea,* 92). "Wings of the wind" seems to be a storm (LXX συστροφὴ πνεύματος). We cannot help but wonder why Hosea chose the word צרר ("bind") here. The answer seems to be that it is a wordplay on סרר ("stubborn") in v. 16 and סר ("turn away, stop") in v. 18.

[123] For a major study of this motif, see J. J. Niehaus, *God at Sinai* (Grand Rapids: Zondervan, 1995).

Hos 4:3 has already alluded to. In any case the wind is in some way a meta-phorical agent of affliction. The people would be "ashamed" of their sacrifices because the gods would fail them and the people in turn would realize how disgraceful their worship has been. The thrust of this passage is therefore that Judah should not follow Israel into apostasy and promiscuity. The people of Judah should abandon religious shrines and practices of Israel because they had become hopelessly defiled by paganism. The Israelites were like a stubborn cow in their apostasy—entranced by idols, debauched, in love with their cults, but destined to be swept away as by a storm and to be sadly disappointed by the failure of their gods.

> [1]"Hear this, you priests!
>   Pay attention, you Israelites!
> Listen, O royal house!
>   This judgment is against you:
> You have been a snare at Mizpah,
>   a net spread out on Tabor.
> [2]The rebels are deep in slaughter.
>   I will discipline all of them.
> [3]I know all about Ephraim;
>   Israel is not hidden from me.
> Ephraim, you have now turned to prostitution;
>   Israel is corrupt.
>
> [4]"Their deeds do not permit them
>   to return to their God.
> A spirit of prostitution is in their heart;
>   they do not acknowledge the LORD.
> [5]Israel's arrogance testifies against them;
>   the Israelites, even Ephraim, stumble in their sin;
>   Judah also stumbles with them.
> [6]When they go with their flocks and herds
>   to seek the LORD,
> they will not find him;
>   he has withdrawn himself from them.
> [7]They are unfaithful to the LORD;
>   they give birth to illegitimate children.
> Now their New Moon festivals
>   will devour them and their fields.

ISRAEL LEADS JUDAH INTO SIN (5:1–7). This text, like the previous, follows the basic pattern of threefold warning, complaint, and punishment. It has, however, a chiastic structure, as follows:

A   Threefold Warnings (5:1–2)
    B   Prostitution/apostasy of Israel/Ephraim (5:3)

    C Impossibility of repentance (5:4)
      D Stumbling of Israel, Ephraim, and Judah (5:5)
    C′ Impossibility of repentance (5:6)
   B′ Prostitution/apostasy [of Israel] (5:7a)
A′ Punishment (5:7b)

Here, instead of one, there are two threefold warnings (vv. 1–2; see below). Verse 3 declares that Israel was guilty of the apostasy of "prostitution," and this is balanced by v. 7a, which accuses them of both apostasy, in being faithless to Yahweh, and prostitution, in bearing "foreign" children. Verse 4 asserts that the fertility cults had such a strong hold on Israel that the nation could not return to God, and this is answered by v. 6, which asserts that God refused to pay heed to their hollow ceremony even when it was directed at him. In the center of the structure v. 5 declares that not only Israel but Judah as well had stumbled. Coming at this pivotal point in the text, this implies that Hosea foresaw disaster ahead for Judah as well. The announcement of punishment in v. 7b concludes the text and in the structure of the passage is the answer to vv. 1–2.[124]

5:1–2 In this strophe Hosea continues to describe the defection of Israel to the sexual allure of the fertility cult, but he condemns all three leading segments of Israelite society. The religious leadership, the leaders of the common people, and the governmental authorities each had a role to play in the expiration of the nation's spiritual life.

We obviously have another threefold warning here, but the identity of "Israelites" (lit., "house of Israel") is problematic. This could be a reference to the common people in general, except that the thrust of this passage appears to be to bring charges against the leadership. One might argue that although in form the text addresses three groups, in reality it addresses only two—the religious hierarchy and the royal house—and that the term "house of Israel" describes both.[125] A better solution, however, is to take "house of Israel" to refer to the landed middle and upper classes. These were the men who thought of themselves as, and actually were, the social backbone of the country. They were not the political or religious elite, but neither were they the impoverished peasants and landless laborers.[126] A parallel text is Jer 2:26, which refers to the "house of Israel ..., they, their kings and their officials, their priests and their prophets."

---

[124] For a rhetorical analysis of this text, see Y. Mazor, "Hosea 5:1–3: Between Compositional Rhetoric and Rhetorical Composition," *JSOT* 45 (1989): 115–26.

[125] Thus Andersen and Freedman, *Hosea,* 383.

[126] Wolff observes that in view of Mic 3:1,9; 1 Sam 11:3; 1 Kgs 21:8; Deut 19:12, this text appears to be an abbreviation for something like זִקְנֵי בֵּית יִשְׂרָאֵל, "elders of the house of Israel" (*Hosea,* 97). He remarks that this group would not include the שָׂרִים ("princes"), who were part of the house of the king, or the נְבִיאִים ("prophets"), who were part of the religious leadership.

The line "This judgment is against you" is more literally "for the judgment belongs to you." It is ambiguous, and the ambiguity is deliberate. Although it can refer to accusation and conviction against the leaders of the nation, it can also mean "for you possess the power of judgment." That is, the leadership had control of the institutions of Israel and gave guidance to the ordinary peasants. They gave "judgment"—leadership—in the same sense that the "judges" gave leadership prior to the monarchy. Although the commoners were responsible for their apostasy, the social leaders had shown them the way. Because they had the responsibility of passing judgment over the common people, divine judgment on the nation began with them.

The NIV translation, "the rebels are deep in slaughter," is possible but depends heavily on hypothetical translations of some very unusual Hebrew.[127] A better solution is to emend the text and render it "and a pit they have dug for Shittim" (see NRSV and REB). This involves two modifications[128] but fits the context well. The last two lines of v. 1 speak of a "snare at Mizpah" and a "net spread on Tabor." The proposed "pit" obviously parallels "snare" and "net" just as the proposed "Shittim" parallels "Mizpah" and "Tabor." "I will punish all of them" (5:2b) could be taken to refer to Mizpah, Tabor, and Shittim together.

By contrast, the translation, "the rebels are deep in slaughter" does not suit this context well. The rest of this strophe describes how the apostate leadership takes the people into the decadence of the fertility cult ("prostitution") with the result that their worship of Yahweh is hollow and without repentance. That is, the topic of this strophe is religious apostasy and not violence or civic disorder. Although Hosea elsewhere speaks of the violence in the community of Israel, that is not the case here, and the peculiar image of rebels deep in slaughter does not fit this text.[129] As emended, vv. 1–2 read as follows:

---

[127] The noun שַׁחֲטָה occurs only here, but it could be regarded as a feminine noun from שׁחט and thus could mean "slaughter." The word שֵׂטִים might be translated "rebels" on the basis of the root שׂוּט found in Ps 40:5 and the word סֵטִים ("deeds that swerve [?]") in Ps 101:3. The verb עמק (hiphil stem) means "they make deep," although it might be taken adverbially to mean "they are in deep." Andersen and Freedman (*Hosea,* 386–88) support this translation although they admit that the text is "largely unintelligible in its present form." It goes without saying that a translation of the unemended MT is itself fraught with doubtful meanings and hypothesis. Cf. LXX.

[128] One must read שַׁחַת, "pit," for שַׁחֲטָה and בַּשִּׁטִּים, "in Shittim," for שֵׂטִים. Also favoring these emendations are Wolff (*Hosea,* 94), Mays (*Hosea,* 79), and D. Stuart (*Hosea–Jonah,* WBC [Waco: Word, 1987], 88–89).

[129] One could follow Andersen and Freedman in the proposal that the slaughter here is not ordinary violence but child sacrifice (*Hosea,* 386). This interpretation depends on the use of שׁחט in Isa 57:5; Ezek 16:21; 23:39. The difficulty with this is that these other passages are unambiguous about the slaughter of children, while the reader of Hosea is expected to make the connection to child sacrifice with no guidance other than the presence of the hapax legomenon וְשַׁחֲטָה.

Hear this, O priests!
Listen, House of Israel!
    And royal house, pay attention!
    For the judgment belongs to you.
For a trap you have been for Mizpah,
    And a net is spread out at Tabor, (v. 1)
    and a pit they have dug for Shittim,
    But I am fetters for all of them. (v. 2)

This gives us two A-A-A-B patterns, quatrains in both of which the first three cola parallel one another and the fourth is a threat of judgment.[130] Once again, the use of threefold patterns dominates this portion of Hosea.

Several towns in Palestine had the name Mizpah, but the one mentioned here probably is the most important one, the Mizpah in Benjamin located some ten kilometers north of Jerusalem. Like Gilgal and Bethel, Mizpah was one of the principal cities on Samuel's normal itinerary (1 Sam 7). As Mays observes, "It was an important centre for the tribes before the monarchy and probably contained a sanctuary."[131] A number of Astarte figurines dating to the eighth century B.C. have been found there. Shittim was on the other side of the Jordan and was the last staging area before the invasion of the land (Josh 2:1), and is thus similar to Gilgal, the first campsite for the nation after crossing the Jordan. It was under Israel during the reign of Jeroboam II. Tabor was a mountain much further in the north, some twenty kilometers southwest of the Sea of Galilee. We know of no specific incidents that may link this site to the others, but it rose above the Jezreel valley, a place quite important for Hosea. It was probably the location of a "high place," a cult shrine to the fertility gods.[132] These three locations were apparently sacred to the people and sponsored by the leaders. They were all traps in the sense that they induced the ordinary people into apostasy.

The last line of v. 2 could be translated either, "I am discipline for all of them" or, "But I am fetters for all of them."[133] The NIV, "I will discipline all of them," is either a paraphrase of the first interpretation or is based on an emendation.[134] The interpretation that God would be "discipline" for them

---

[130] See Mazor, "Hosea 5:1–3: Between Compositional Rhetoric and Rhetorical Composition," 119–20, which shows that in the emended version of the text, 5:1c–2 has precisely the same rhetorical structure as 5:1ab.

[131] Mays, *Hosea,* 81.

[132] Wolff, *Hosea,* 98.

[133] Reading מוֹסֵר, "fetters," for מוּסָר, "discipline." Wolff's objection that Hosea usually adds לְ before such an expression does not seem to be decisive (*Hosea,* 94). Cf. Stuart, who observes that on the basis of the vocalization in Job 12:18, no emendation is necessary to read "fetters" here (*Hosea–Jonah,* 88–89).

[134] The NIV is similar to Wolff (*Hosea,* 94) in emending מוּסָר to מְיַסֵּר, a *piel* participle of יסר.

certainly makes sense, but it is somewhat banal after such colorful metaphors. More than that, the idea that God would become "fetters" for the leadership after they had used traps, nets, and pits to ensnare the people is wonderfully ironic. What they had done to others would happen to them (cf. 4:9). Finally, "fetters" implies captivity,[135] which was indeed the fate of Israel.

5:3 Yahweh "knows" Israel in the sense that he is aware of their wicked behavior. They cannot hide their paganism from him. On the other hand, Israel does not "know" God in the sense of belonging to him or having a relationship with him (v. 4).[136] Thus God only knows them to the extent that he is cognizant of their sins; but he could at the same time say, in the words of Jesus, "I never knew you" (Matt 7:23).

The use of both "Israel" and "Ephraim" in this verse reinforces the impression that this text especially has the leadership of the nation in view. Already, Hosea has tended to use "Israel" to refer to the mother (the institutions and culture of the nation) as he has used "children" to refer to the ordinary people. Although the prophets often used "Ephraim" as a virtual synonym for "the northern kingdom," this was because Ephraim was the leading tribe, and it is this cultural hegemony that Ephraim represents here. The second person address to Ephraim indicates that Yahweh was addressing Ephraim as cultural leader of Israel: now that Ephraim practiced prostitution, all of Israel was defiled. "Israel" and "Ephraim" in this text are not simply the nation and one of its tribes, nor are they two separate kingdoms,[137] nor do they strictly represent all the people, but they are the corporate body, institutions, and cultural ideals that make up the northern kingdom. They stand in contrast to Judah, the Davidic state, which ideally ought to have had greater devotion to Yahweh.

The "prostitution" of Israel is again the apostasy and the immorality of the pagan cults. The term used here, however, seems to imply that Ephraim led the nation into prostitution[138] (i.e., into paganism and the fertility cults). Again this is not so much an indictment of one tribe as it is of the cultural leadership of the Northern Kingdom. Ever since Jeroboam I had installed calf-idols in Dan and Bethel, the institutions of Israel had been guiding the people into apostasy and immorality, with the result that they had all become defiled (the word translated "corrupt" means "unclean" and implies that the

---

[135] Cf. Isa 52:2, where fetters (מֹוסֵר) are a symbol of captivity.

[136] Hb. uses the same word (יָדַע) in both texts.

[137] Contra H. J. Cook, "Pekah," *VT* 14 (1964): 121–35.

[138] The verb זנה is used in the *hiphil* stem here and in 4:10,18. In the other two verses, however, the verb is plural and means that men engage the services of prostitutes. Here, in the singular with "Ephraim" as the subject, it appears instead to express true causality: Ephraim causes the people to prostitute themselves.

nation had become loathsome to God[139]).

5:4 The Bible holds two truths in tension: first, that repentance is always a possibility, and second, that corruption can so enslave a soul that repentance becomes a practical impossibility. This verse focuses on the latter truth. As Wolff comments, "Total apostasy takes away freedom."[140] Long years of training in paganism had had its effect; the nation had become unable to return to Yahweh. The point that they no longer knew God looks back to the original indictment on the nation, that it lacked the knowledge of God (4:1). We should note that Hosea uses a number of catchwords to link v. 4 to v. 3. God knows about them (v. 3), but they do not know him (v. 4); Ephraim led them into prostitution (v. 3), and a spirit of prostitution now filled their hearts (v. 4); they were unclean (v. 3), and thus they could not enter God's presence (v. 4).

5:5 Hosea's introduction of "arrogance" in this context seems somewhat incongruous unless one bears in mind that the upper classes are the real focus of this text.[141] Since they were sure of their power and their right to rule, the political, social, and religious leaders of Israel felt no need to be constrained by the limits of orthodoxy and morality. And as surely as pride goes before a fall, so the institutions of Israel and Judah would collapse. Here, as in 4:5, "stumble" is the result of their sin; it is not the sin itself.

We must ask, however, what is meant by "Israel's arrogance testifies against them" in this context.[142] The word "judgment" in v. 1 could imply that this is a courtroom setting, but "stumble" is not appropriate as a courtroom metaphor.[143] It appears, therefore, that the word picture Hosea draws here is not strictly of a courtroom in which guilt or innocence is determined. Rather, the arrogance of Israel testifies against them less technically in the sense that when the kingdom and its religious institutions collapse, people will readily see why that collapse occurred. Perhaps a translation, "speaks against" is preferable to "testifies against," because the former, unlike the latter, does not strictly connote legal proceedings. Put another way, it appears that the court here is not Yahweh's court but the court of public opinion.

---

[139] The word טמא in the *niphal* stem means to be "defiled" (as by eating unclean food; Lev 11:43), but it is also used in Num 5:13 to describe a wife who has "defiled herself" by committing adultery. As the jealous husband of Num 5 cannot love his wife, so Yahweh cannot love defiled Israel.

[140] Wolff, *Hosea,* 99.

[141] The NIV somewhat obscures this by translating ישראל in v. 5b as "the Israelites."

[142] The difficulty would be removed entirely if we could follow the LXX (καὶ ταπεινωθήσεται ἡ ὕβρις) and translate this line "their arrogance shall be humbled" (reading this as ענה II, "to cringe"). However, the idiom ענה ב indicates that this is ענה I, meaning "testify against." On the other hand, the versions universally take ענה ב in Ruth 1:21 to mean "afflict" (Yahweh is subject).

[143] Stuart asserts that the legal setting of this text is implicit throughout, but actually legal terminology is scarcely used at all (*Hosea–Jonah,* 93).

This verse, uniquely in this passage, is a triplet, and everything here indicates that the third line, "Judah also stumbles with them," is artificially added on.[144] This does not mean, however, that it is not original to the text or not from Hosea himself. To the contrary, the very appendage-like quality of this line makes it prominent. It is as though Hosea composed an elegant poem and then added his own gloss: "by the way, Judah is going the same route as Israel." In the context of the progression in 4:15–5:15, the point is that although Hosea longs for Judah to avoid destruction, he knows that his hope is vain. This passage anticipates Ezekiel 23.

5:6 This verse, with v. 4, could be an example of a figure or pattern of thought called pseudosorites, as described by Andersen and Freedman: "Although their doings will not let them return to Yahweh, even if they try, they will not find him."[145] A more certain example of this rhetorical technique is found in 9:11–12. This verse probably does not refer to a heartfelt seeking of Yahweh but the formal invocation of him in liturgy and sacrifice. Amos 5:4–5 contrasts authentic returning to Yahweh with pilgrimages to shrines. Mays is probably correct here that Israel was treating Yahweh like Baal, as another deity to be placated through sacrifice and offerings.[146] In this context, coming to God with sheep and cattle implicitly contrasts with coming to God with a contrite heart.

5:7a Israel's faithless dealings with the Lord resulted in her giving birth to illegitimate children. This metaphor looks back to the prostitution that 5:3 mentions.[147] It also implies that the apostasy of Israelite culture and their leaders had given rise to a generation that could more accurately be called children of Baal than children of Yahweh. They were "not my people" but Baal's. The term "illegitimate" is literally "foreign," which can refer to sexual liaison outside of marriage or, as in the English, another nation or culture. Hosea employs both senses. They were the children of apostasy/adultery, and they were the children of foreign gods.

5:7b The line "Now their New Moon festivals will devour them and their fields" has mystified interpreters. The term "new moon" is often taken to refer to new moon sacrifices to other gods, so that the point is that they will waste their resources on sacrifices to other gods. The problem with this is that the new moon specifically consumes real estate ("their fields") and not livestock. It is difficult to see how animal sacrifices could accomplish this. The LXX

---

[144] The line וְעָנָה גְאוֹן־יִשְׂרָאֵל בְּפָנָיו וְיִשְׂרָאֵל וְאֶפְרַיִם יִכָּשְׁלוּ בַּעֲוֹנָם is a complete bicolon by itself with an inclusion formed by the assonance of וְעָנָה and בַּעֲוֹנָם.

[145] Andersen and Freedman, *Hosea*, 394. See also M. O'Connor, "The Pseudo-sorites in Hebrew Verse," in *Perspectives on Language and Text*, ed. E. W. Conrad and E. G. Newing (Winona Lake: Eisenbrauns, 1987), 239–53, especially pp. 242–43.

[146] Mays, *Hosea*, 84.

[147] Cf. Jer 3:20, which also uses בגד to describe the deception of an adulterous wife.

suggests emending the text; it asserts that a "red blight" would devour their property.[148] It is not clear, however, how such a corruption could have occurred in the text. Another possibility is that the word "new moon" should be translated (with minor emendation to *ḥādāš*) as "someone else."[149] This would play on the fact that their children were "foreigners" (v. 7a), and imply that the punishment would fit the crime: they consorted with outsiders, and outsiders would take their property.

The unemended text, however, yields good sense. "New moon" connotes religious festivals, as in Isa 1:13: "New Moons, Sabbaths and convocations—I cannot bear your evil assemblies." This looks back to the corruption of the religious leadership and the fact that the shrines had become snares (5:1–2). By metonymy new moon could be taken to mean that the religious practices of Israel would be their downfall. This still does not explain, however, how new moons consume the property. The solution appears to be that a new moon is literally a time that the moon is invisible and the night is black. The prophets spoke of the moon going dark as a sign of the day of Yahweh (e.g., Joel 2:10; 3:15). The new moon therefore represents eschatological darkness, a darkness that would envelop the land. There could also be a pun based on the assonance between *ḥōdeš* ("new moon") and *ḥādāš* ("someone else") as described above. In Hosea's usage the eschatological darkness of the new moon is primary, the cultic significance is secondary, and the wordplay on "someone else" is (if present at all) tertiary.

> [8]"Sound the trumpet in Gibeah,
>   the horn in Ramah.
>   Raise the battle cry in Beth Aven;
>   lead on, O Benjamin.
> [9]Ephraim will be laid waste
>   on the day of reckoning.
>   Among the tribes of Israel
>   I proclaim what is certain.
> [10]Judah's leaders are like those
>   who move boundary stones.
>   I will pour out my wrath on them
>   like a flood of water.
> [11]Ephraim is oppressed,
>   trampled in judgment,
>   intent on pursuing idols.
> [12]I am like a moth to Ephraim,

---

[148] The LXX has ἡ ἐρυσίβη for חֹדֶשׁ ("new moon"). The LXX of Joel 1:4 translates הֶחָסִיל as ἡ ἐρυσίβη, and this suggests to Wolff (*Hosea*, 95) that the text should be emended to הֶחָסִיל ("the locust").

[149] Reading חָדָשׁ, as suggested by Andersen and Freedman, *Hosea*, 397.

like rot to the people of Judah.

¹³"When Ephraim saw his sickness,
    and Judah his sores,
then Ephraim turned to Assyria,
    and sent to the great king for help.
But he is not able to cure you,
    not able to heal your sores.
¹⁴For I will be like a lion to Ephraim,
    like a great lion to Judah.
I will tear them to pieces and go away;
    I will carry them off, with no one to rescue them.
¹⁵Then I will go back to my place
    until they admit their guilt.
And they will seek my face;
    in their misery they will earnestly seek me."

ISRAEL AND JUDAH FACE THE WRATH OF GOD (5:8–15).   The progression in 4:15–5:7 reaches its climax in this text. First, Hosea prayed that Judah would not imitate Ephraim (4:15–19), and then he warned in what was almost a gloss that Judah stumbled with Ephraim (5:5). In this text Ephraim and Judah are indistinguishable in their guilt. Both alike commit the same crimes and both receive the same punishment.

Progression is also evident in the structure of the passage, which, in contrast to the previous texts, gives almost all its attention to warnings and punishment and gives only passing reference to their actual offenses. Like 5:1–7 it begins with two quatrains, each containing a threefold warning (vv. 8–10), but to this it adds two complaints and punishments (vv. 11–14). The passage here has an A–B–A–B pattern of complaint (v. 11), punishment (v. 12), complaint (v. 13), and punishment (v. 14). Both complaints refer to a different kind of apostasy—dependence upon a foreign nation (see commentary on v. 11). Verse 14 describes the punishment coming upon them under the metaphor of the lion, and v. 15, a transitional verse, builds upon this metaphor to open the way to repentance and restoration.

Scholars frequently read 5:8–6:6, and this section in particular, against the backdrop of the war between Judah and the Syro-Ephraimite coalition. According to Isaiah 7 and 1 Kgs 16:1–7, a coalition of forces under Rezin of Syria and Pekah of Israel formed an alliance in order to free themselves from servitude to Assyria. They hoped that Judah would join the coalition, but Ahaz, fearing the power of Assyria, refused to join. Not wanting to begin a war with Assyria while unsure of their southern flank, the coalition first launched a campaign to overthrow Ahaz, put a puppet on the throne of Judah, and proceeded with their struggle against Assyria. Ahaz, terrified of the combined forces of his two northern neighbors, appealed to Assyria for help. Isaiah supported the refusal to join the coalition but considered an appeal to Assyria to be desertion of Yahweh. He sought to encourage Ahaz to stand firm in faith that Yahweh would save them but was rebuffed by the king. In the aftermath both Syria and Israel were crushed by Assyria, and the land of Judah itself was razed by foreigners.[150]

At least two details of this text, however, militate against seeing these events as the background to Hos 5:8–15. First, Hosea presents Judah as the aggressor (v. 10, taking, as advocates of the Syro-Ephraimite war interpretation usually do, the moving of boundary stones to refer to encroaching on the territory of the northern tribes[151]). But in the Syro-Ephraimite war Judah was on the defensive, and joining the anti-Assyrian coalition, not minor territorial gains, was the issue in the war against the Syro-Ephraimite coalition. Isaiah tells us that at this time "the hearts of Ahaz and his people were shaken, as the trees of the forest are shaken by the wind" (7:2). Second, in the Syro-Ephraimite war it was Judah that appealed to Assyria for help against Israel, in contrast to what we see in Hos 5:13, which says that Ephraim turned to Assyria for help. Those who seek to maintain that the war is the background of this text can only do so by appealing to incidents that took place before or after the war.[152] It is more likely that this passage refers in general to political events of the latter half of the eighth century, but not especially to the events of this particular war.[153]

5:8 The language of this quatrain is exceedingly brief and elliptical.[154] The "trumpet" was the ram's horn, or shofar, and the "horn" is a metal trumpet

---

[150] Scholarly attempts to tie Hos 5:8–15 to this period build upon A. Alt, "Hosea 5.8–6.6. Ein Krieg und seine Folgen in prophetischen Beleuchtung," *NKZ* 30 (1919): 537–68, which depends heavily upon emendations of the text. Alt's essay was highly influential, extending even to the *BHS* apparatus and the RSV. See Andersen and Freedman, *Hosea*, 401–2 and P. N. Franklyn, "Oracular Cursing in Hosea 13," *HAR* 11 (1987): 69–80.

[151] In my view, however, this is at most petty aggression. See commentary below.

[152] E.g., Mays, *Hosea*, 86–91. Hubbard dates this text to shortly after 733, after the war with the Syro-Ephraimite coalition and after Assyria had subdued Syria and Ephraim (*Hosea*, 118–20; see also Stuart, *Hosea–Jonah*, 99–106). This makes better sense because it could explain the minor territorial aggression by Judah (Israel being in a severely weakened state) implied in v. 10. Hubbard takes v. 13, in which Ephraim goes to Assyria, to refer to the submission of Hoshea to Assyria. This is less convincing; Hoshea formally submitted to Shalmaneser, but he actually went to Egypt for help (2 Kgs 17:1–4). It seems more likely that v. 13, if it refers to any event of which we have knowledge, refers to Menahem's payment of tribute to Tiglath-pileser III of Assyria (a.k.a. Pul) in return for Assyria's support for his claim to the throne (2 Kgs 15:19), in about 752.

[153] For a good defense of reading the Syro-Ephraimite war as the background for this text, see P. M. Arnold, "Hosea and the Sin of Gibeah," *CBQ* 51 (1989): 447–60. Even so, Arnold must resort to special pleading, e.g., that v. 10 originally read "the rulers of Israel act like men who move boundary stones."

[154] The verb תִּקְעוּ does double duty, the preposition בְּ is dropped from בֵּית אָוֶן, and the terse אַחֲרֶיךָ בִּנְיָמִין lacks a verb.

of some kind.[155] These instruments had various uses (e.g., to call the people into sacred assemblies, Num 10:1–10), including use as military signals. The three towns mentioned here, Gibeah, Ramah, and Bethel (= Beth Aven), are all located in Benjamin more or less in a line directly north of Jerusalem. The sequence, from the southernmost (Gibeah) to the northernmost (Bethel), could indicate that a military expedition from Judah was moving northward to take control of these cities.[156] We must be careful about such conjectures, however, because we do not know if the alarm to be sounded in these cities is one of defensive or offensive warfare. The line "Lead on, O Benjamin" (lit., "Behind you, Benjamin") might be a traditional battle cry for mounting an attack[157] and perhaps reflects the fact that Benjamin had a tradition of military leadership.[158] It is possible that Hosea used the battle cry "Behind you, Benjamin" because all three towns are in Benjamin. The reverse is equally possible, that he mentions these specific three towns because this war cry calls upon Benjamin. If there is a war in view here, we do not know if Ephraim and Judah are fighting each other over Benjamite territory or if they are allied in resisting outside enemies. A military interpretation of this passage only implies there was some kind of conflict in the territory between Judah and Ephraim. It is possible that Hosea may have simply chosen this area as the locus of his prophecy because it had associations with both Israel and Judah, and both were destined for destruction. But we do not really know that battles are behind this text at all. It is possible that the blowing of the horn and the raising of shouts are not war cries at all but are liturgical shouts of the fertility cults.[159] It seems more likely that these are military alarms, but either way, Hosea's call for trumpet blasts and shouts is sarcastic. Whether they are battle alarms or calls to sacred assemblies at the shrines, they are futile. Neither the gods of the shrines nor their own arms will save them.

5:9–10 Scholars generally interpret these two verses as two separate cou-

---

[155] Cf. "horns of silver (חֲצוֹצְרֹת כֶּסֶף) in Num 10:2.

[156] Mays, *Hosea,* 88.

[157] We must confess that this too is uncertain. אַחֲרֶיךָ בִּנְיָמִין could be taken to mean "Benjamin is behind you" or even "(Look out) behind you, Benjamin!" Cf. NRSV. A number of scholars emend to some form of חרד, "to terrify" (e.g., Wolff, *Hosea,* 104). The line אַחֲרֶיךָ בִּנְיָמִין is already found in the Song of Deborah (Judg 5:14), however, and in this context it appears to indicate that Benjamites were at the head of the Israelite military formation. By the time of Hosea the phrase may have become a formulaic battle cry with no specific assertion of Benjamite leadership. Amid all these possibilities, therefore, we probably are on the safest ground if we take the line as a war cry that, in the course of time, became divorced from a concrete historical setting, somewhat like "Remember the Alamo!"

[158] Cf. Ps 68:28 (Eng. 27). Saul was a Benjamite (1 Sam 9:1–2); it is conceivable that this battle cry was used in his reign.

[159] The verb הָרִיעוּ simply means "shout" and does not necessarily imply a military context. For a presentation of the view that this text is cultic and not military in nature, see E. M. Good, "Hosea 5:8–6:6: An Alternative to Alt," *JBL* 85 (1966): 273–86.

plets. What many do not recognize, however, is that vv. 9–10 together have the same A–A–A–B pattern as v. 8, which we already saw in 5:1–2. In v. 8 three calls to sound the alarm in various towns are followed by a fourth phrase that breaks the pattern, "Behind you, Benjamin!" In vv. 9–10 three lines that refer to the Hebrew nations (Ephraim [metonymy for Israel, it is here used to create a threefold pattern], Israel, and Judah) are also followed by a fourth line that breaks the pattern. As mentioned above, v. 8 uses very short, military-like (or liturgical) phrases, but vv. 9–10 use full lines. Thus the structure of vv. 8–10 is:

A1	Blow the shofar in <u>Gibeah</u>,
A2	the horn in <u>Ramah</u>,
A3	Raise the cry in <u>Beth Aven</u>,
B	Behind you, Benjamin!
A1′	<u>Ephraim</u> shall become a desolation on the day of punishment,
A2′	Among the tribes of <u>Israel</u> I make known a certainty,
A3′	The rulers of <u>Judah</u> are like boundary-stone movers,
B′	Upon them I shall pour out like water my fury.

As is the case in the rest of this text, Ephraim in v. 9 refers to the Northern Kingdom. The meaning of v. 9a is self-evident: the land would be ravaged. The cause for this calamity is not specified; either natural disaster or an invading army is possible. It is more probable that Hosea means that a foreign army will ransack the land. The phrase "among the tribes of Israel" is deliberately archaic. It hearkens back to the days of the judges, when all twelve tribes were held together by the common bond of being the "children of Israel." If v. 10a describes encroachments of Judah against Israelite territory, it may imply a rebuke for a lack of unity among the tribes of Israel. It is more likely, however, that he means that he is giving a certain prophecy that all the tribes of Israel, north and south, will suffer terribly at the hands of foreigners.

The line "Judah's leaders are like those who move boundary stones" is generally taken to mean that Judah encroaches upon Israelite territory, since it seems odd that Hosea would here describe internal violations of the property rights of private citizens. Interpreted thus, the "boundary markers" are not markers between private plots of land but boundaries between the tribes. Advocates of this interpretation, however, are unable to point to evidence for significant expansionism from Judah at this time. To the contrary, Judah itself was nearly swept away by the flood that was Assyria (cf. Isa 7:17–25). Furthermore, 5:8–15 does not single out Judah in its accusations; to the contrary, the one verse that explicitly describes covenant faithlessness only mentions Ephraim (v. 13). Furthermore, in the punishment both Ephraim and Judah suffer together, although the text is rather more explicit about the destruction facing Ephraim (vv. 9,11). In short, the standard interpretation of this text as an incrimination of Judah for territorial aggrandizement is not a good fit with what we know of the history of the period or with this context.

Three facts stand out about the reference to moving boundary stones. First, moving boundary stones is not a good way of describing military aggression; it is rather a petty, furtive, and cowardly means of stealing land. Second, Deut 27:17 declares anyone who commits such a crime to be under God's curse. Third, if this is an official act of the Jerusalem government, it is odd that the text mentions only "leaders" (or "princes") and not the king as instigating the action. The plural subject might mean that we have here a series of minor incidents. The line therefore reflects not an invasion but minor, contemptible attempts to grab at parcels of land in the midst of the crises of the latter part of the eighth century. This verse is not even the main accusation of this passage; this comes in v. 13, which describes the apostasy of seeking help from Assyria instead of God. This is simply a portrait of a land whose leaders are debased and which, like its northern neighbor, has harrowing days ahead. We also have to consider the possibility that "like those who move boundary stones" simply means that Judah's aristocracy is under a curse (Deut 27:17) and that the text does not assert that they literally moved boundary stones at all. The phrase may mean no more than that they are as contemptible as common thieves.

The line "I will pour out my wrath on them like a flood of water" is very similar to Isaiah's description of the Assyrian invasion (Isa 8:5–10), and it connotes the same thing. The Assyrian army will plunder the land as effectively as if a flood had passed through.

5:11 This verse is quite difficult, but the NIV translation "intent on pursuing idols" is based upon an emendation. A more likely interpretation is: "Ephraim is oppressed, justice is crushed,[160] for he willingly went with the policy."[161] The "policy" here is not a command of God but the stipulations laid down by the Assyrian government for its vassals. The complaint of v. 13, that Ephraim went (using the same as verb 5:11b, *hālak*) to Assyria for aid, is

---

[160] Rather than supply a preposition בְּ for מִשְׁפָּט, it is better simply to take מִשְׁפָּט as the subject of the clause. Cf. Mays, *Hosea,* 85.

[161] The word I translate as "policy" is צָו, a word for which there is an enormous variety of interpretations. Some simply emend it to צָר, "enemy," which fits my interpretation well but lacks textual support. Cf. *BHS* note ᵇ. Another possibility is to emend to שָׁוְא, "vanity," after the LXX ὀπίσω τῶν ματαίων. From this one may take שָׁוְא to refer to idols (thus the NIV). The word צָו also appears in Isa 28:10,13, but this is scarcely any help since that text is an infamous conundrum. Andersen and Freedman (*Hosea,* 410) take it to mean "filth" or feces on the basis of the root צֹאָה (cf. BDB), which could again refer to idols. Apart from this being speculative, it is not clear why the א would disappear if the root were צֹאָה. Contrary to Andersen and Freedman, this does not require an emendation because the word also appears in Isa 28 without the א. To me, therefore, the best solution is still to take it from the root צָוָה, to "command," and understand it to mean a rule or policy. Cf. KJV, NKJV, and NASB. This admirably fits the context since v. 13 also declares that Ephraim followed (הלך in both verses) Assyria.

the only possible way to understand this otherwise enigmatic line. Thus the point of this verse is that Ephraim followed the policies that Assyria demanded that its client states follow. This most likely refers to Menahem's submission to the Assyrian government in return for their support (2 Kgs 15:19–20: "Then Pul king of Assyria invaded the land, and Menahem gave him a thousand talents of silver to gain his support and strengthen his own hold on the kingdom. Menahem exacted this money from Israel. Every wealthy man had to contribute fifty shekels of silver to be given to the king of Assyria. So the king of Assyria withdrew and stayed in the land no longer"). The annals of Tiglath-pileser III also mention Menahem's tribute.[162] In this circumstance Ephraim was under oppression, and the right role of Israel's monarchy was perverted.

5:12 The precise definitions of the words rendered "moth" and "rot" are uncertain, but this verse plainly describes God's opposition to Israel/Judah in the harshest, most astonishing language possible. The word translated "moth" could also refer to a "maggot" in an open wound or to "pus" from the wound.[163] The word for "rot" does describe something that causes decay. Since the metaphor as extended into v. 13 relates to a diseased or wounded body (and not to clothing), "moth" is probably not the intended sense here. We therefore should envisage here a wounded man, left unattended, whose injuries fester in the most horrible manner. A good translation would be, "I am like the maggot to Ephraim, and like the gangrene to the house of Judah." We should not obscure the fact that it is Yahweh whom these metaphors describe; nor should we miss the point that he is exacerbating, not reversing, the effects of their injuries.

5:13 This verse, like 5:5 in the preceding text, is to some extent the focal verse of the passage and like it is a triplet. The three lines follow a simple logic: (1) Israel and Judah realize that they are grievously ill, (2) they send to Assyria for help, but (3) Assyria cannot help them. This verse does not in any way attack Assyria as cruel or oppressive and thus not the appropriate people to go to for help; the entire thrust is that Israel has done wrong simply by virtue of seeking the aid of a foreign power. In not seeking Yahweh, they committed apostasy.

The "sickness" and "sores" describe the precipitous loss of power and wealth that Israel and Judah experienced in the latter part of the eighth century. Contrary to some interpreters, however, these terms are too general to permit us to attach a specific date to this verse.[164] The NIV translation "the

---

[162] *ANET,* 283.

[163] Cf. Andersen and Freedman, *Hosea,* 412, and *HALOT,* 895.

[164] Cf. Wolff, *Hosea,* 115.

great king" is based on an emendation, but it probably is correct.[165] The word translated "heal" occurs only here in the Hebrew Bible, and its meaning must be surmised from context.

Many regard Hoshea's payment of tribute to Shalmaneser to be the incident to which this text alludes,[166] but this is not certain. As noted earlier, Hoshea appears to have been subjugated by Shalmaneser rather than to have gone to him for help. The only nation to which Hoshea voluntarily turned for help was Egypt (2 Kgs 17:1–4). We know that Menahem, on the other hand, did seek support from the Assyrians (2 Kgs 15:19). Furthermore, it is curious that Hosea explicitly says that Ephraim sought Assyria's aid, but one can only infer, and that not with certainty, that Hosea is also accusing Judah of seeking Assyrian assistance.[167] In view of the disastrous consequences of Ahaz's appeal to Assyria, the failure to mention Judah here is extremely odd if the text dates to the reign of Hoshea, shortly after the Syro-Ephraimite war.

5:14 The Hebrew here strongly emphasizes the pronoun "I."[168] It does this to contrast the power of Assyria to deliver with the power of Yahweh to destroy (this itself is an ironic reversal of what one would expect). It is hopeless to turn for human help to save what God has determined to demolish. Thus the text affirms that no one can "rescue them." The metaphor for Yahweh has shifted from a flesh-eating decay (v. 12) to a flesh-eating lion.[169] This may be significant; "decay" implies a prolonged demise, but "lion" implies a sudden, violent end. The Israelite states were already in a lengthy state of decay and had suffered ravages of various kinds, but the final conquest would come

---

[165] The phrase מֶלֶךְ יָרֵב probably does not mean "King Yareb" (notwithstanding the LXX βασιλέα Ιαριμ) because it is unusual for the anarthrous מֶלֶךְ to precede the proper name of a king in this fashion. It could mean "the king of Yareb." Thus McComiskey ("Hosea," 1:85) suggests that it is some kind of sign-name, "the king of let-him-contend" (taking יָרֵב as the jussive of רִיב). This seems far-fetched. It is best to stay with the interpretation that this should be read as מלכי רב, the *yod* being *yod compaginis* and not a sign of a construct chain. The meaning would then be "great king," and מכלי רב would serve as the Hb. equivalent to the Akk. *šarru(m) rabû(m)*. Cf. Wolff, *Hosea,* 104. Regardless of how one understands the grammar, the parallel indicates that it must somehow refer to the king of Assyria.

[166] E.g., Stuart, *Hosea–Jonah,* 105.

[167] Scholar's have noted the lack of a specified subject in the line וַיִּשְׁלַח אֶל־מֶלֶךְ יָרֵב. A common argument is that יְהוּדָה has been omitted for metrical reasons (e.g., Andersen and Freedman, *Hosea,* 413), but this is not necessarily the case. Many lines in Hosea are unbalanced, but the explicit pairing of Ephraim and Judah is unnaturally broken at this point (contrast vv. 12–13a,14). The NIV probably is correct to read Ephraim as the subject of this clause.

[168] Placing אָנֹכִי at the beginning of the verse already makes it the focus of the text, but this is doubly reinforced through the repetition אֲנִי אֲנִי.

[169] As far as we can tell, the linking of שַׁחַל to כְּפִיר has no significance beyond the poetic pairing of two synonyms. Both mean "lion," but the semantic distinction between the two is lost on us.

upon them with the ferocity of a lion.

5:15 Continuing the metaphor of the lion, Yahweh declares that he will turn back and go to his "place," that is, his "lair."[170] After Yahweh has destroyed the nations, he will await Israel's repentance. This, of course, turns the metaphor of the lion in an unnatural direction; a lion, after it has devoured its prey, cannot return to its den and offer a new chance at life to its prey. Hosea, however, is not bound by convention. More than that, in the language of Hosea, "Israel" and "Judah" refer more to the political and religious institutions of those nations than to the people. With the corrupt governments and priesthoods overthrown, a possibility of return now presents itself. It is noteworthy that in this verse he has abandoned the motif of Ephraim and Judah as collective entities. After the conquest these will no longer exist. When the verse says: "until *they* admit their guilt. And *they* will seek my face; in their misery *they* will earnestly seek me" (emphasis added), the plural verbs do not refer to institutional Ephraim and Judah but to the people of these former states. After the conquests the distinction between the two kingdoms will have no significance. Once again it will simply be the children of Israel who return to God. Put another way, killing Israel is the means of offering salvation to the Israelites.

2. Exhortation for Future Grace (6:1–7:16)

As described earlier, this section is in two parts, 6:1–3 and 6:4–7:16. The whole serves as closure to 4:1–5:15 and as the introduction to 8:1–13:16. As 4:1–5:15 contains the principal charges against Israel, so 6:1–3 calls for repentance while 6:4–7:16 laments the stubbornness of the nation. Links to the preceding material include the reversal of previously described punishments and the continuation of the theme that Israel and Judah are alike in sin. On the other hand, 6:1–7:16 anticipates the antiphonal manner in which Yahweh and Hosea address the nation throughout 8:1–13:16. In addition, 6:4–7:16 introduces the tone of lamentation and retrospection that characterizes the remainder of the book.

(1) The Prophet's Call to Repent (6:1–3)

¹**"Come, let us return to the LORD.**
 He has torn us to pieces
 but he will heal us;
he has injured us
 but he will bind up our wounds.
²**After two days he will revive us;**

---

[170] Thus Andersen and Freedman, *Hosea,* 415. Cf. Wolff, *Hosea,* 116.

on the third day he will restore us,
 that we may live in his presence.
 ³Let us acknowledge the LORD;
  let us press on to acknowledge him.
 As surely as the sun rises,
  he will appear;
 he will come to us like the winter rains,
  like the spring rains that water the earth."

Hosea here identifies himself with the people and calls on them to join him in returning to Yahweh. The placement of 6:1–3, a call to repent, immediately after Yahweh's declaration that he would retire to his place and await a positive response from the people cannot be accidental. Nevertheless, scholars often treat this text as a secondary addition, or at least as a spurious repentance on the part of Israel. Some argue that this text is a citation of a liturgy given by the wayward religious leadership, which Hosea or a redactor has inserted in order to illustrate their artificial piety and their arrogant presumption that Yahweh would save them.[171] So interpreted 6:1–3 is ironic; it is not a true call to repentance. The justification for such a reading is that Yahweh's response in 6:4 indicates exasperation with the transitory piety of Israel and Judah. In that response, however, Yahweh specifically chides the people for hollow cultic ceremony and for a want of true repentance (6:6). Verses 1–3, however, are entirely in keeping with what God desires: the verses recognize that God has punished the people (v. 1) and express a desire

---

[171] Wolff, e.g., denies that this text contains the kind of repentance Hosea desires and instead claims 6:1–3 contains "a penitential song the priests sung during these very times of danger," which the "traditionist" later added to Hosea's material (*Hosea,* 116–17). He admits that 6:1–3 has catchwords with the preceding text but dismisses this evidence as unimportant. Hubbard, similarly, calls this a "song of feeble repentance" on the grounds that it does not contain an explicit statement of guilt (*Hosea,* 124–26). But "return to Yahweh" (6:1), using שׁוּב, is standard OT terminology for true, not feeble, repentance. E. R. Wendland argues that the prayer of 6:1–3 reflects pagan thinking, as opposed to 14:1–3 (Hb. 2–4) (*The Discourse Analysis of Hebrew Prophetic Literature* [Lewiston, N.Y.: Mellen Biblical Press, 1995], 204–21). This is certainly wrong. Both texts focus on the critical aspect of repentance (שׁוּב). It is true that 14:1–3 gives specific attention to confession of sin, but this does not mean that 6:1–3 is somehow deficient. Of itself, turning back to God (שׁוּב) implies that one recognizes that one's present course of life is wrong. Nothing in 6:1–3 indicates a placing of confidence in ritualized appeasement of God along pagan lines. In addition, 6:1–3 stresses something 14:1–3 omits: active pursuit of the knowledge of God. This is a quality Hosea declares from the very beginning to be an essential aspect of the true people of God (4:1). As Stuart comments: "The song is Hoseanic in style and not disruptive of the context. Its placement follows the alternating doom-hope pattern that characterizes the entire book. It represents a faithful presentation of covenant teaching because its orientation is eschatological, not immediate" (*Hosea–Jonah,* 107).

for them to attain to the knowledge of God.[172] One could only read 6:1–3 as false piety if it expressed the things 6:4ff. condemns, specifically, a desire to appease God through ritual. In fact, the desiderata of 6:1–3 and 6:4–6 are exactly the same. Therefore 6:4 should not be read as a rejection of 6:1–3 but as despair over whether the people would ever heed the call of 6:1–3.

The exhortations to repent include promises that reverse the punishments described in 4:15–5:15. These punishments were a wind (4:19), the darkness of the new moon (5:7), disease and infection (5:12), and a lion (5:15). In structure this text brings together exhortations and the reversals of these afflictions and incorporates all into a short song of two strophes, as follows:

Strophe 1
 Exhortative: Return to Yahweh (1a)
  Result: Heal injuries, bind wounds (1b–c)
  Result: Resurrection on third day (2a–b)
 Outcome: Life in his presence (2c)

Strophe 2
 Exhortative: Know Yahweh (3aα)
 Exhortative: Pursue knowledge of Yahweh (3aβ)
  Result: Salvation certain as the dawn (3b)
  Result: Rains appear on earth (3c–d).

Observe that the two strophes do not follow the same pattern. Instead the first has an inclusion structure, in which returning to Yahweh is fulfilled by dwelling in his presence, between which are two couplets. The second is a couplet followed by a triplet.[173]

Strophe 1
 Come, and let's return to Yahweh
 For he has torn us that he may heal us,
  He has struck us that he may bandage us. (v. 1)
 He will restore life after two days,
  On the third day he will raise us,
 That we may live in his presence. (v. 2)

Strophe 2   And let us know [Yahweh],[174]
 let us pursue knowledge of Yahweh.

---

[172] Compare the call in 6:3 (נִרְדְּפָה לָדַעַת אֶת־יְהוָה, "let us pursue the knowledge of Yahweh") to the complaint in 6:6 (וְדַעַת אֱלֹהִים מֵעֹלוֹת, "[he desires] knowledge of God more than burnt offerings").

[173] I.e., a monocolon (in two parallel *hemistichoi*) followed by a tricolon.

[174] Some think that this verb (וְנֵדְעָה) goes with the preceding line (cf. BHS), perhaps on the strength of the conjunction. However, the inclusion pattern of vv. 1–2 speaks against this interpretation. Furthermore, if וְנֵדְעָה is separated from v. 3, it has no object since לְפָנָיו does not properly supply the object.

> Like the dawn, sure is his coming forth,
> [He shall be] like the rain to us,
> Like the spring rains, he will water the earth. (v. 3)

Here, as elsewhere, Hosea has asymmetrical patterns that challenge the interpreter.

6:1–2   Every time the word "return" is used with Israel as the subject and Yahweh as the one to whom return is made, it indicates a true repentance and not a pseudoreturn. In fact, returning to Yahweh is a major theme of the book.[175] The structure of this short song develops a basic theme of the Bible, that repentance necessarily precedes reception of divine favor.

The first reversal is that God will heal what he has torn to pieces, an allusion to the lion metaphor of 5:14.[176] The second reversal is that God will bandage the injuries of Israel, a reversal of 5:12, in which Yahweh is like gangrene in their wounds.[177] We should observe that these promises not only reverse the former punishments but reverse the sequence as well. A surprising addition, however, is the promise to restore life: "After two days he will revive us; on the third day he will restore us." On the other hand, it is not an inappropriate reversal; 5:14 had declared that Yahweh would tear apart Israel as a lion tears apart her prey; this implies that the prey is slain.

It is impossible for the Christian to read this text and not wonder if it foreshadows Christ's resurrection on the third day. Wolff attempts to eliminate the idea of resurrection here, which he casts in a pagan light, and asserts that this text only describes recovery from illness.[178] The language Hosea employs, however, renders this view impossible.[179] Besides that, recovery after a two-day illness, as opposed to two days in the grave, is hardly significant. The New Testament does not explicitly cite this verse, but 1 Cor 15:4 asserts that Christ arose on the third day "in accordance with the Scriptures," and no other text speaks of the third day in the fashion that Hos 6:2 does.

It is clear that in its original context this passage describes the restoration

---

[175] In 2:9 (Eng. 2:7) Israel declares that she will return (שׁוּב) to her husband, and in 3:5 the children of Israel return (שׁוּב) and seek Yahweh. In 5:4 their deeds do not allow them to return (שׁוּב) to Yahweh, and 7:10,16 states that Israel refuses to return (שׁוּב) to Yahweh. Hos 11:5 combines two uses of שׁוּב; the nation will return to Egypt and captivity because they refuse to return to Yahweh. At the end of the book the demands for repentance reach a crescendo: Israel must return (שׁוּב) to Yahweh (12:7 [Eng. 6]; 14:2–3 [Eng. 1–2])! Involvement in the cult is not a pseudoreturn but a refusal to return; it does not permit any שׁוּב at all, except to captivity.

[176] The verb טָרַף is used with a lion as subject in 5:14 and elsewhere; e.g., Ps 7:3 (Eng. 7:2).

[177] The verb נָכָה with God as subject often means to strike someone with disease, as in Num 14:12; 1 Sam 5:6,12.

[178] Wolff, *Hosea,* 117–19.

[179] As Stuart points out, the use of the verbs חָיָה and קוּם here has a strong parallel in Ezek 37 (*Hosea–Jonah,* 108). See also J. Wijngaards, "Death and Resurrection in Covenantal Context (Hos. VI 2)," *VT* 17 (1967): 226–39.

of Israel, the people of God; and for many interpreters this is proof enough that the resurrection of Christ is not in view here. Such interpretation, however, understands messianic prophecy too narrowly as simple, direct predictions by the prophets of what the Messiah would do. In fact, the prophets almost never prophesied in that manner. Instead, they couched prophecy in typological patterns in which the works of God proceed along identifiable themes. Furthermore, Christ in his life and ministry embodied Israel or recapitulated the sojourn of Israel. Thus, for example, Christ's forty days in the wilderness paralleled Israel's forty years of wandering, and his giving of his Torah on a mountain (Matt 5–7) paralleled the Sinai experience.

Another great event in Israel's history was its restoration after captivity, an event that was almost a bringing of the nation back from the dead. Ezekiel develops this concept in his dry bones vision (Ezek 37:1–14). From this we can conclude that Christ's resurrection, in addition to its profound soteriological aspects, was a typological embodiment of the "resurrection" of Israel in its restoration. We should add that this is not artificially reading New Testament history into the Old Testament (as in allegorization) because it follows the established pattern of the parallel between the history of Israel and the life of Christ. Furthermore, as so often happens in texts of this kind, the details of the passage work themselves out in different ways. The "two days" are for Israel metaphorical for a relatively short captivity but have a literal fulfillment in the resurrection of Christ. Similarly, the raising to life is literal in the case of Christ, but in the case of Israel it is a metaphor for restoration. On the other hand, there is also a literal fulfillment for the Israel of God, when all who are Christ's shall be raised at his coming (1 Thess 4:13–17).

6:3 The two great calls of Hosea are that Israel must return to Yahweh (i.e., repent) and "know" Yahweh (NIV, "acknowledge"). Lack of knowledge of God is one of the primary failings of the people (4:1).

The next line, "As surely as the sun rises, he will appear," is literally, "As the dawn is certain, [so is] his coming forth."[180] The surface meaning is moderately clear; we can count on Yahweh to come (and save us) just as surely as we can count on the rising of the sun. Through the metaphor, however, Yahweh's advent is portrayed as a time of joy, like the dawn after a dark night. This language is not accidental. Rather, it is a reversal of the punishment in the second oracle, the devouring of the land by the new moon (5:7). As described there, the operating metaphor is the darkness that consumes the land during the new moon; dawn is an obvious reversal of the image.

The final reversal is the coming of rain. We have already suggested that the unusual phrase "the wind shall bind her in her wings," in 4:19, might

---

[180] It is difficult to know whether the NIV translation is a paraphrase of כְּשַׁחַר נָכוֹן מוֹצָאוֹ or is based on an emendation of מוֹצָאוֹ.

refer to drought, but in any case 4:3 has already described drought and 2:9 (Hb. 2:11) describes the effects of drought. Thus the return to Yahweh reverses all the afflictions that had come upon the people. The terrors of the lion, disease, darkness, and drought disappear in healing, bandaging, dawn, and seasonal rains.

(2) Yahweh's Sorrow (6:4–7:16)

> [4]"What can I do with you, Ephraim?
> 　What can I do with you, Judah?
> Your love is like the morning mist,
> 　like the early dew that disappears.
> [5]Therefore I cut you in pieces with my prophets,
> 　I killed you with the words of my mouth;
> 　my judgments flashed like lightning upon you.
> [6]For I desire mercy, not sacrifice,
> 　and acknowledgment of God rather than burnt offerings.

YAHWEH'S FRUSTRATION (6:4–6) [A].　In this text Yahweh speaks of his frustration with the transitory devotion of Israel (v. 4). He then declares this is the reason for issuing judgments against them (v. 5) and proclaims that what he really wants is true piety, expressed as love for others and knowledge of God, and not outward shows of religious zeal (v. 6).

6:4　In the previous progression of texts, Judah was brought down to Israel's level of depravity, and this verse introduces the two together as equals in hollow devotion to God. "What can I do?" obviously is a cry of frustrated love, borne of their refusal to "return" to God and pursue the knowledge of him. Here, for the first time, we see clearly the attitude behind the sudden, often inexplicable shifts between harsh, unmerciful judgment and complete pardon in the Book of Hosea: it is the frustration of Yahweh that arises from his unwavering love and from their constant wavering and outright apostasy. Clouds and dew describe that which is fleeting. Unsteadiness in love, that is, the inability to love consistently, not only shows itself in the cult prostitution but increases because of the immorality associated with the cults. An immoral soul loses the capacity for intimacy, loyalty, and love.

6:5　The translation of the third line of this verse, rendered in the NIV as, "my judgments flashed like lightning upon you," is unlikely. The Hebrew text means, "And as for your judgments, light shall go forth."[181] The Greek, however, with the Syriac and Targum, has "And my judgment shall go forth as a light."[182] This is good support for emending, but the difficulty with this alter-

---

[181] Taking וּמִשְׁפָּטֶיךָ in וּמִשְׁפָּטֶיךָ אוֹר יֵצֵא to be accusative of respect. אוֹר must be the subject.

[182] Cf. BHS note e.

native reading is that it is not entirely clear how "light," generally a positive thing, functions as the analogue for divine judgments. Perhaps this is why the NIV translated "light" as "lightning," something that naturally suits divine judgment. This interpretation, however, is almost certainly wrong. The word for "light" in Hebrew rarely means "lightning," and should only be understood to refer to lightning in very specific contexts.[183] Furthermore, there is no basis for adding "upon you," as the NIV has done. The MT need not be emended. Perhaps translators are misled by the violence of the metaphors in "Therefore I cut you in pieces with my prophets, I killed you with the words of my mouth," and suppose that this verse describes the actual punishment God is inflicting on Israel. Close reading of the text shows that it in fact describes prophetic pronouncements against Israel, and not the substantive inflicting of punishment. Thus, "your judgments" here are not actual famines and wars, but the verbal decrees—the declarations of "guilty"—that God makes against Israel. Understood in this way, "And as for your judgments, light goes forth," can be expansively paraphrased as, "And here is what your judgments—the prophetic pronouncements against you—mean: light goes forth—it shines into the darkness of your apostasy." This fully agrees with what the first two lines assert, namely, that God verbally slays the nation through the prophets. Put another way, the prophets continually assail the people with their guilt because the people are so fickle and faithless (v. 4).

6:6 This is one of the great texts of the prophets—Jesus used it to expose the hypocrisy of his opponents (Matt 9:13; 12:7). Here, again, the two great desiderata of Hosea, love and the knowledge of God, reappear. We should not fail to notice that the polemics against prostitution, violence, and corruption, although not unimportant, are secondary. Hosea is not a religious reactionary who simply desires to stamp out social sins and impose religious duty on people. To the contrary, he desires that his reader acquire the loving and compassionate heart that comes from a transformational life with God. In Hosea's context the shrines and rituals of Israel had become impediments to true spirituality, and Hosea called upon the people to denounce them. This does not mean that Hosea regarded sacrifice or ritual worship as intrinsically bad, and it should not prompt us to suppose that the path to spirituality is to overthrow all liturgy and formal worship. In modern language one might appropriately rephrase this verse as, "I desire devotion and not hymn-singing, service and not sermons," without thereby concluding that hymns and sermons were evil.

---

[183] *HALOT* 1:24–25 does not list "lightning" as a possible meaning of אוֹר, but BDB 21 understands it to mean "lightning" in Job 36:32; 37:3,11,15. This passage, however, is a description of a thunderstorm, and "lightning" is demanded by context. Perhaps the author of Job has used אוֹר for "lightning" for some specific poetic purpose. The normal word for lightning is בָּרָק. Andersen and Freedman, *Hosea,* 429, in translating אוֹר here as "sun," are as arbitrary as the NIV.

⁷Like Adam, they have broken the covenant—
  they were unfaithful to me there.
⁸Gilead is a city of wicked men,
  stained with footprints of blood.
⁹As marauders lie in ambush for a man,
  so do bands of priests;
they murder on the road to Shechem,
  committing shameful crimes.

SINS OF ADAM, GILEAD, SHECHEM (6:7–9) [B]. **6:7** To what does "Adam" refer? Candidates include the following. (1) Adam is the first man, the original sinner, and thus the model for Israel's unfaithfulness. But "there" implies that "Adam" is a place, as do the parallels "Gilead" and Shechem," and this seems to rule out this interpretation. (2) Adam is the city of that name on the Jordan river.[184] The problem with this interpretation is that the city is mentioned only in Josh 3:16 as the place where the waters of the Jordan heaped up prior to Israel's invasion of Canaan. Otherwise, it seems to have no significance. (3) Adam should be emended to Admah, the city of the plain that perished along with Sodom and Gomorrah (Gen 19:29). Hosea does mention Admah in 11:8. Otherwise, this emendation has little to commend it since Admah did not break any covenant of which we know.[185] (4) The text should be translated something like, "They have walked on my covenant like dirt." This involves several unusual interpretations of the Hebrew, so that it cannot be considered probable.[186]

We thus appear to be at an impasse. A solution is possible, however, if one takes note of the unusual language the text employs. When it says, "like Adam,"[187] the reader naturally assumes that it refers to the most famous transgressor in the Bible, the man Adam. But when it says "there," the reader's reference point shifts, and he must assume that "Adam" is a place name. Inasmuch as there were shrines throughout Israel at the time of Hosea, we need not be surprised that the town of Adam would have had a shrine, nor need we suppose that the shrine there was in any respects unusual.[188] It

---

[184] This view is held, e.g., by M. A. Eaton, *Hosea* (Fearn, Great Britain: Christian Focus, 1996), 108.

[185] One could also emend אָדָם to אֲרָם, "Aram," but again it is not clear how Aram would serve as the model for covenant–breaking.

[186] See, e.g., Stuart, *Hosea–Jonah,* 99, who takes אָדָם to mean "dirt," הֵמָּה to mean, "look!" and שָׁם to mean, "see."

[187] The text should not be emended to בְאָדָם ("in Adam"), contrary to Hubbard, *Hosea,* 128. Note that the LXX has ὡς ἄνθρωπος, which supports the MT.

[188] J. Day, "Pre-Deuteronomic Allusions to the Covenant in Hosea and Psalm LXXVIII," *VT* 36 (1986): 1–12, argues (pp. 5–6) that the offense at Adam was the coup d'état of Pekah against Pekahiah, on the grounds that Pekah had fifty Gileadites with him according to 2 Kgs 15:25, and Adam was in the vicinity of Gilead.

appears that Hosea singled out the shrine at Adam not because of some peculiarity about the town, but because of its namesake. The prophet has made a pun on the name of the town and the name of the original transgressor. His meaning is, "Like Adam (the man) they break covenants; they are faithless to me there (in the town of Adam)."

6:8 Gilead was in the Transjordan region and was famous for a number of incidents in the Bible. Laban caught up with Jacob there and accused him of treachery (Gen 31:25–26). Then, at Mahanaim in the region of Gilead, Jacob prepared to face Esau and had his wrestling encounter with the angel of the Lord (Gen 32). Jephthah was from Gilead, and he fought to save the city from the Ammonites (Judg 11).

The Hebrew of the last part of this verse is unusual.[189] It means, as in the NIV, "stained with footprints of blood."[190] The choice of such a peculiar word and image must be deliberate, and the reason is in the fact that the root of the word for "footprints" is also the root of the name "Jacob." Another curiosity of this verse is that it describes the inhabitants of Gilead as "doers of wickedness," using the word ʾāwen, the same word that is used for the wordplay for Bethel, "Beth Aven." Bethel was the place where Jacob as he fled Esau in Canaan, met God (Gen 28:11–22). Gilead, therefore, as the place where he was caught by Laban as he returned to Canaan, and as the region where he met the angel of God while preparing to face Esau, corresponds to Bethel as the end of Jacob's flight corresponds to its beginning. It is evident, therefore, that Hosea is working the story of Jacob into his prophecy; he will return to this story in 12:2–4.[191] The point here appears to be that the Israelites have taken on the worst characteristics of Jacob—selfishness and cunning—without having his redeeming experiences—encounters with God. They had no knowledge or experience of God comparable to Jacob's, who had a vision at Bethel and was renamed Israel in the region of Gilead. His descendants, instead of being transformed into Israel, into people of God, remained Jacob, a name that Hosea has transformed into the grim phrase, "stained with footprints of blood."

6:9 This verse is quite difficult in Hebrew. It might be better translated, "Like members of marauding bands, so is a gang of priests along the way, /

---

[189] The word עֲקֻבָּה appears only here in the Hebrew Bible.

[190] The word עֲקֻבָּה obviously is from the root עָקַב, which means something like "grab by the heel." See *HALOT* 2:872. A cognate is the noun עָקֵב, "heel." In this verse it basically has a passive adjective pattern (McComiskey, "Hosea," 1:96), and is rendered in BDB, 784, as "foot-tracked." Contrary to Andersen and Freedman, the phrase here does not mean, "deceitful, because of bloodshed" (*Hosea*, 440). דָּמִים, not דָּם, is generally used for "bloodshed." דָּם simply means "blood," and it is not clear why blood would cause deceit.

[191] Note that he again uses the verb עָקַב in 12:4 (Eng. 12:3).

they commit murder at Shechem, for they carry out a wicked plan."[192] Once
again, Hosea looks back to Genesis for his wordplay. Shechem was a city in
north central Palestine. It, too, had its share of historical incidents. For example, Rehoboam was crowned there (1 Kgs 12:1). The most notorious incident
involving Shechem, however, was the slaughter of its inhabitants by Simeon
and Levi in retaliation for the rape of Dinah (Gen 34). In this verse Hosea
describes the priests as a gang of thugs who lie in wait for unsuspecting victims. This is a metaphor of ambush, and it cannot be accidental that Hosea
alludes to a place where Levi, father of the priesthood, was guilty of treachery and mass murder. Furthermore, the assertion that the priests "carry out a
wicked plan" appropriately describes the deceit of Simeon and Levi at
Shechem (Gen 34:13).

Hosea has therefore once again used a threefold pattern involving places
in Israel, but this time with a peculiar twist. Each place recalls the worst
characteristics of one of the patriarchs. At Adam they broke faith with God as
did Adam; at Gilead the people, unlike Jacob, are entirely without grace; and
at Shechem the sons of Levi renew the history of treacherous slaughter.

¹⁰I have seen a horrible thing
   in the house of Israel.
   There Ephraim is given to prostitution
   and Israel is defiled.

¹¹"Also for you, Judah,

APOSTASY OF EPHRAIM—AND JUDAH (6:10–11a) [C].   **6:10–11a** This
text self-evidently looks back to previous accusations against Israel (e.g.,
4:12), and it renews the link between Israel and Judah. The "harvest" for
Judah is evidently a day of judgment (cf. Hos 10:13 and Isa 63:3). A number
of scholars comment that 6:11a looks like a gloss.[193] This is undeniable, but it
does not necessarily mean that it is an addition by a later hand. As suggested at
5:5, one can regard this line as an authentic Hoseanic text meant to read like
an added comment.[194] The purpose behind such a rhetorical strategy—the use

---

[192] This verse should probably be divided as follows:

וּכְחַכֵּי אִישׁ גְּדוּדִים/ חֶבֶר כֹּהֲנִים דֶּרֶךְ // יְרַצְּחוּ־שֶׁכְמָה/ כִּי זִמָּה עָשׂוּ:

The form חַכֵּי should be read as a *piel* infinitive construct with י where one normally sees ה
(McComiskey, "Hosea," 1:96; GKC §231). דֶּרֶךְ can be interpreted simply as "along the way" and
need not be connected to שֶׁכְמָה. זִמָּה means "evil plan"; the NIV translation "committing shameful crimes," is not particularly good.

[193] E.g., Mays, *Hosea,* 102.

[194] Cf. Andersen and Freedman: "The great difficulty of this verse speaks against its being a
conventional gloss" (*Hosea,* 443).

of an aside—is actually to highlight the fact that Judah, too, is headed down the road to apostasy and destruction.[195]

> **a harvest is appointed.**
> [1]**"Whenever I would restore the fortunes of my people,**
>   **whenever I would heal Israel,**
> **the sins of Ephraim are exposed**
>   **and the crimes of Samaria revealed.**
> **They practice deceit,**
>   **thieves break into houses,**
>   **bandits rob in the streets;**
> [2]**but they do not realize**
>   **that I remember all their evil deeds.**
> **Their sins engulf them;**
>   **they are always before me.**
>
> [3]**"They delight the king with their wickedness,**
>   **the princes with their lies.**
> [4]**They are all adulterers,**
>   **burning like an oven**
> **whose fire the baker need not stir**
>   **from the kneading of the dough till it rises.**
> [5]**On the day of the festival of our king**
>   **the princes become inflamed with wine,**
>   **and he joins hands with the mockers.**
> [6]**Their hearts are like an oven;**
>   **they approach him with intrigue.**
> **Their passion smolders all night;**
>   **in the morning it blazes like a flaming fire.**
> [7]**All of them are hot as an oven;**
>   **they devour their rulers.**
> **All their kings fall,**
>   **and none of them calls on me.**

UNFORGIVEN SINS OF ISRAEL, EPHRAIM, AND SAMARIA (6:11b–7:7) [B']. All scholars agree that 6:11b belongs with 7:1. This unit begins with three proper names for the nation, that is, Israel, Ephraim, and Samaria. Two general threefold accusations follow in 7:1b and v. 2. This serves to link this text with the previous threefold accusation at 6:7–9. After this, 7:3–7, a chiastic text, focuses on the crimes of the leading members of society under the

---

[195] One can regard this strategy as a variant of the familiar numeric pattern frequently employed in wisdom texts: "There are three things Yahweh hates, four he detests..." The purpose is to draw the reader's attention to the fourth thing on the list. Even in modern rhetoric, a person might say something like, "Oh, there is one more thing I would like to add," in order to make the "one more thing" all the more emphatic.

metaphor of a hot oven.

6:11b–7:1a   Although all major modern translations agree with the NIV in translating this as a kind of contrary–to–fact statement (meaning, "Although I have many times wanted to heal Israel, I could not do it because of their iniquity"), there is little support for such an interpretation in the Hebrew, which contains a temporal clause followed by a future tense.[196] Together, 6:11b and 7:1a form a couplet: "When I restore the fortunes of my people, when I heal Israel, / the sins of Ephraim will be exposed and the crimes of Samaria revealed." This is not a lamentation by Yahweh, but a promise that the restoration of the nation will involve exposure and healing of their sins.

7:1b–2   This is another pair of threefold accusations. The first recalls the opening complaints at 4:2, that crime is rampant in society. People cheat one another, thieves burglarize, and gangs mug people in the streets (one wonders whether Hosea is here speaking of ancient Israel or modern America). Like 4:2, this verse also recalls the Ten Commandments and makes the point that the Law is forgotten and civil justice is nowhere to be found.[197] As a result, Yahweh says that when he looks at Israel all he sees is guilt; there is no atonement to cover their sin. "Their sins engulf them" (literally, "their deeds surround them") in the context of v. 2 does not mean that crime is overwhelming society (v. 1b has already established that). Rather, it means that no matter from what angle Yahweh looks at Israel, all he sees is their evil doings.

7:3–7   This is without question among the most vexing texts in the Hebrew Bible. The language is extremely obscure, and even its main point is not entirely clear. Not surprisingly, many interpreters resort to numerous emendations.[198] We should shun this approach, however, simply because we have no clear direction in which to go with our emendations. That is, if we have a text that is for the most part clear except for an obvious anomaly, the larger context may provide guidance for improving the one odd feature in the text. But in a passage such as this, emendation only leaves us at the mercy of the creativity and ingenuity of scholars. The emended text might be very pleasing and consistent, but we have no grounds for knowing if it in any way reflects the original. Thus, we do better to try making sense of the unemended text. Following that principle, one can defend an interpretation of this text as

---

[196] The pattern is an infinitive construct temporal clause followed by a *weqatal* pattern. For example, Ezek 18:23: הֲלוֹא בְּשׁוּבוֹ מִדְּרָכָיו וְחָיָה ("Is it not that when he turns from his ways that he shall live?"). See also Andersen and Freedman, *Hosea*, 432. On the other hand, there is no reason to link this bicolon to the preceding context since Andersen and Freedman admit that infinitive constructions like this usually begin paragraphs (p. 444).

[197] Note the use of שֶׁקֶר and the root גנב; cf. Exod 20:15–16.

[198] Cf. the extensive emendation in Wolff, *Hosea*, 106–7, Stuart, *Hosea–Jonah*, 116, and Mays, *Hosea*, 103–4.

eight uneven verses (not corresponding to the verse divisions we have received) arranged in chiastic fashion.

A With their evil they gladden a king,
> By their deception (they gladden) princes. (v. 3)

B All of them commit adultery.
> It (adulterous passion)[199] is burning like a baker's[200] oven;
> He desists from stirring, from kneading the dough, till it is leavened. (v. 4)

C By day,[201] princes incapacitate[202] our king (by) poisoned wine.[203]
> D He draws in[204] mockers (with) his hand. (v. 5)
> D' For they bring (him) near[205] —their hearts are like an oven[206] —

---

[199] One would expect the participle with תַנּוּר ("oven," a masculine noun) to be masculine instead of the unusual feminine בֹּעֵרָה. One can only assume that while the "oven," תַנּוּר, is the analogue, the thing that is actually heated is something else, signaled by the feminine. Since the preceding line declares that they are all "adulterers," it is reasonable to suppose that the thing that is heated is adulterous passion.

[200] The word מֵאֹפֶה means "from a baker." In the analogy this means either that the oven is heated by a baker who stokes the fire, or, what is more likely, that it is an oven "from a baker," i.e., of the kind used by bakers. The NIV apparently moves מֵאֹפֶה to the next line (against MT accentuation) and emends מֵאֹפֶה to אֹפֶה, thereby eliminating the preposition in order to make אֹפֶה the subject of the verb יִשְׁבּוֹת. It also supplies the words, "whose fire," which it understands to be the object of מֵעִיר. As it stands in the MT, מֵעִיר and מִלּוּשׁ are both objects of יִשְׁבּוֹת.

[201] Taking יוֹם absolutely and not as a construct with מַלְכֵּנוּ. The "day of our king" makes little sense here, but "by day" naturally contrasts with "all night" and "at morning" in v. 6. Also, the transitive הֶחֱלוּ, requires a direct object, and no other word is available unless it be שָׂרִים, "princes." In position directly after הֶחֱלוּ, however, שָׂרִים appears to be the subject of the verb. Thus, I take מַלְכֵּנוּ to be the object.

[202] The verb הֶחֱלוּ should be translated in its normal sense of "make ill" and not exceptionally as "be ill."

[203] The phrase חֲמַת מִיָּיִן is odd because it appears to have a construct before a word beginning with the preposition מִ. Andersen and Freedman read this as an enclitic mem (*Hosea*, 458). The word חֵמָה means "heat," but it can also mean "poison." Since it appears that someone deliberately incapacitated the king, it is best to regard this as poisoned, drugged, or at least very potent wine.

[204] It is very unlikely that מָשַׁךְ יָדוֹ means "to join hands with." The verb מָשַׁךְ means "to pull or drag"; thus, מָשַׁךְ יָדוֹ אֶת־לֹצְצִים simply means, "He pulls in mockers (with) his hand," unless, as is rarely the case, יָד is treated as a masculine noun, so that it means, "His hand pulls in mockers."

[205] The verb קֵרְבוּ (*piel* stem) means to "bring (something or someone) near" and not to "approach" (NIV). This should not be emended since it immediately follows and parallels מָשַׁךְ, to "pull in." Lacking another object, one might assume that לֹצְצִים must be the direct object here as well. On the other hand, it seems more probable that the action of the two verbs "draws in" and "bring near" is reciprocal—that is, that the king and the "mockers" draw one another into conspiracy. Thus, one may easily supply "him" for the verb "bring near." What the king does not know, however, is that his fellow conspirators are planning to betray and "ambush" him.

[206] The phrase כַתַנּוּר לִבָּם must be regarded as a parenthesis here.

in their ambush.[207]
C' All night their baker sleeps,
   At morning it (the fire in the oven)[208] burns like a raging fire. (v. 6)
B' All of them will be hot like an oven
   And they will consume their judges.
A' All their kings fall;
   Not one of them calls on me. (v. 7)

In structure the evil and deception of the king and princes (A) corresponds to the spiritual stubbornness and demise of the kings in A'. The passionate sin that burns like a fire in "all of them"[209] links B to B'. C begins by describing the crime that is perpetrated "by day," and C' begins by describing how the "baker" sleeps "all night." D tells how the king "draws in" mockers, and D' tells how they in turn entice him, only to destroy him.

This text describes the debauchery and especially the intrigue of court life. It uses the image of the baker and the oven throughout. At the opening, A (v. 3), it declares that some unspecified group "gladdens" the king and the princes. This could be the priesthood, but it is more likely that the lack of specificity here is deliberate and should be respected.[210] The subject here is simply everyone who is in a position of power in the nation, including the priesthood, the military, and members of the royal court. The term "gladden" here has a double edge. On the one hand, it means that leading members of society join the king and higher aristocrats in debauchery, but on the other hand, it means that they flatter them while preparing to stab them in the back, as the rest of the text makes clear. The central lines of the chiasmus, D and D', succinctly state the problem: the king and his rowdy companions attract one another into debauchery; but unknown to him, they are plotting his demise. Thus, the text describes a court life that is both debased and filled with intrigue.

The adultery in B (v. 4) is probably literal and not metaphorical; it is an indication of the kind of decadence that goes on at the center of power. The adulterous passions of the leaders of society burn with the heat not of an ordinary oven but of a baker's oven, which apparently would be a larger oven than that used in an ordinary household. Here we first encounter the oven and the baker.

---

[207] The noun אֶרֶב appears elsewhere only in Jer 9:7 (Eng. 8) where it means "ambush" ("they set an ambush," יָשִׂימוּ אָרְבּוֹ) and not "intrigue" (NIV). The point is that the "mockers" draw the king into their midst only to ambush him.

[208] This word (הוּא) could be translated "he." The interpreter must decide if the burning thing here is the baker or the fire in the oven. Although one might make the case that it is the former, the latter makes more sense.

[209] Observe that B (v. 4) and B' (v. 7a) both begin with כֻּלָּם.

[210] A number of scholars develop the idea that "priestly treachery" lies behind this text (thus, Hubbard, *Hosea,* 134). If so, it is strange that Hosea does not in any way identify the priests as the culprits, not even by using a metaphor that might specifically apply to them.

The baker is a mysterious figure. In B he lets the dough rest while it rises (which is, of course, the normal thing for a baker to do). In C′ (v. 6), however, he sleeps all night. This is something that bakers probably did not do, since they had to keep their fires alive and under control. Also, if ancient bakers were anything like their modern counterparts, they probably had to work in the dark hours of the morning to have bread ready for the day. This baker, however, sleeps all night but in the morning discovers not that his fire has died but that (contrary to what would normally be the case) it is a raging inferno. We thus find that this baker is noted primarily for his inactivity—he desists from kneading the dough while the leaven does its work, and sleeps all night while the fire in the oven gets larger and larger. It would seem, therefore, that the baker is the king who, by inattentiveness due to his debauchery with wine and "sleep" (which may allude to the adulteries of v. 4), allows evil and conspiracy to flourish. If leaven in B (v. 4) is metaphorical, as it often is, for the pervasive influence of evil, we can understand why Hosea included this picture of a baker who does nothing while leaven spreads through the dough. This is a king who does nothing while evil (leaven) spreads through society and the court.

"By day" in C corresponds to "at night" in C′. The point is that the king willingly lets himself be diverted from his duties at all hours by those who seek to overthrow him. "His hand draws mockers" (D) means that the king attracts the most reprobate kind of people into his service. These are people who not only do the nation no good but will undo the king as well. They "bring him near" in the sense that they gain his trust. These ambitious and debauched aristocrats are aflame with both revelry and palace intrigue (D′ [v. 6a]). The lack of strong government brings about an atmosphere of chaos and self-promotion unchecked by honor or integrity. The same ovenlike burning that characterized passions for adultery in B also characterizes lust for power (D′–C′–B′ [vv. 6–7a]). The result is that society is in chaos and decent government is swallowed up by those who only want power (B′ [v. 7a]). In the end the king himself is destroyed in a political world that has abandoned God (A′ [v. 7b]).

> 8"Ephraim mixes with the nations;
>   Ephraim is a flat cake not turned over.
> 9Foreigners sap his strength,
>   but he does not realize it.
> His hair is sprinkled with gray,
>   but he does not notice.
> 10Israel's arrogance testifies against him,
>   but despite all this
> he does not return to the LORD his God
>   or search for him.

¹¹**"Ephraim is like a dove,**
  easily deceived and senseless—
now calling to Egypt,
  now turning to Assyria.
¹²**When they go, I will throw my net over them;**
  I will pull them down like birds of the air.
When I hear them flocking together,
  I will catch them.

FOLLY OF EPHRAIM (7:8–12) [C′].   Reference to Ephraim and Israel
links this passage to 6:10–11a. Furthermore, Hosea has indicated that a new
strophe begins here through a subtle change in metaphor; the operative metaphor of 6:11b–7:7 was the oven, but in v. 8 it is the thing that is cooked, a
cake. This text divides into two parts. The first, vv. 8–10, under the metaphor
of the unturned cake, declares that Israel's leadership is not attending to their
duties. The second, vv. 11–12, under the metaphor of the senseless dove, portrays the leadership frantically seeking for help from a foreign power.

7:8–10   Israel mixed with the nations on religious, political, and cultural
levels. This mixing was religious in that they adopted the gods and rituals of
foreigners, political in that they entered into alliances with or became vassals
of other powers, and cultural in that they adopted the values of these nations.
The metaphor of the unturned cake, however, does not specifically describe
foreign influences on Israel. Rather, it looks back to the previous image, that
of the baker, and implies negligence of duty on the part of the officials who
were charged with preserving Israel. It is this laxity that has allowed foreign
influence to become so prevalent.

Verse 9 specifies two areas in which the leader's neglect of duty was evident, both under the metaphor of the cake. The first is that foreigners are eating it. This could mean that foreigners have taken away the material
resources of the nation (cf. 2 Kgs 15:20). Or it could be more metaphorical,
that foreigners are drawing the people into their religion and ways. While the
translation "His hair is sprinkled with gray" in 9b is possible, it is not clear
why Hosea would present having gray hair as a tragic situation. A gray head
was highly regarded in ancient Israel (Prov 16:31; 20:29). A better interpretation is that this is the gray fuzz of mold that appears on bread.[211] The line
can be translated, "It is sprinkled with gray, but he does not know it." It is
another picture of Israel as a diseased, weakened state, and is comparable to
5:12. It also further develops the idea of official delinquency of duty, since
bread turns moldy when people let it sit before they get around to eating

---

[211] Andersen and Freedman point out that זָרַק, "to sprinkle," is not suited to a description of
human hair and that שֵׂיבָה here is probably analogous to the Akk. word *šîbu*, "mold"(*Hosea*, 467).

it.[212] The repeated line "he does not know it" further describes the failure of the leadership to oversee properly the affairs of state.

Verse 10a repeats exactly a line from 5:5, "Israel's arrogance testifies against him." Again this does not necessarily mean that the setting is a court-room with Yahweh as judge, since there are no other signs of a lawsuit meta-phor in this text. "Speaks against" might be better here than "testifies against." The end of this verse, looking back to the prophet's appeal in 6:1–3, states that the people have dismissed all calls to repentance.

7:11–12 Hosea abruptly changes the operative metaphor from a cake to a dove.[213] Here, the point is not that the leaders neglect their duty, but that they are frantic to find help. Perhaps the one, a desperate search for aid, arises from the other, failure to do one's duty in the first place. The dove here is probably a homing pigeon, but it is an especially stupid one, since it cannot find its way home. In the metaphor Yahweh is the home to which it should fly. It is probably unwise to try to isolate one specific historical incident as the occasion for this charge (e.g., 2 Kgs 17:4);[214] Hosea here speaks of the habitual behavior of Israel's leadership.[215] When Yahweh declares that he will snare the bird, the point is that he will frustrate Israel's attempts to find outside help (cf. 2:6–7) and put an end to their freedom by making them captives.

The last line, "When I hear them flocking together, I will catch them," is more literally translated, "I will discipline them when a report (comes) to their assembly." The NIV rendering is an imaginative attempt to tie this line to the fowler imagery, but it is difficult to justify.[216] A number of scholars emend the text.[217] As McComiskey has demonstrated, however, the text is best left as is.[218] The "report" that is to come to the assembly is probably a report of a diplomatic failure in negotiations with a foreign power.

---

[212] Hubbard is not correct that the operative metaphor is that the bread is inedible, since in fact foreigners are eating it (*Hosea*, 136–38). Under the one image of bread, Hosea has three separate pictures of neglect: unturned cakes, foreigners eating it, and mold.

[213] In Hb. וַיְהִי אֶפְרַיִם ("And Ephraim is") signals the reader that the text is moving to a new section.

[214] Wolff isolates this text to the year 733 B.C. (*Hosea*, 127).

[215] This probably accounts for his use of plural verb forms here (e.g., הָלְכוּ and קָרְאוּ).

[216] The NIV is apparently emending כְּשֵׁמַע ("like a report") to כְּשָׁמְעִי ("as soon as I heard" [infinitive construct of שָׁמַע with first singular suffix and preposition כְּ). Also "catch" is a peculiar translation for the root יָסַר I, which always has the idea of teaching or chastising.

[217] E.g., Stuart takes it to mean "I will punish them sevenfold for their evil," with three emendations, on the basis of Lev 26:28 (*Hosea–Jonah*, 115–16). Wolff (*Hosea*, 107) emends to לְרָעָתָם and thus translates "according to the report of their wickedness." See also Mays, *Hosea*, 107. Andersen and Freedman (*Hosea*, 471) emend to עֵדוּתָם, "their covenant," and take it to mean "I will chastise them according to report of their treaties."

[218] McComiskey, "Hosea," 1:112, who compares Isa 23:5.

¹³Woe to them,
   because they have strayed from me!
Destruction to them,
   because they have rebelled against me!
I long to redeem them
   but they speak lies against me.
¹⁴They do not cry out to me from their hearts
   but wail upon their beds.
They gather together for grain and new wine
   but turn away from me.
¹⁵I trained them and strengthened them,
   but they plot evil against me.
¹⁶They do not turn to the Most High;
   they are like a faulty bow.
Their leaders will fall by the sword
   because of their insolent words.
For this they will be ridiculed
   in the land of Egypt.

YAHWEH'S LAMENT (7:13–16) [A′]. **7:13–16** This text closes off 6:4–7:16 in that it gives a divine lamentation which, forming an inclusion, corresponds to the divine frustration of 6:4–6. In addition it closes off the larger unit of 6:1–7:16 in that it focuses on the refusal of the people to repent (*šûb*), which is the very thing the prophet exhorts the nation to do in 6:1–3. This text also gives closure to all of 4:1–7:16 in that it brings down judgment on the two institutions that Hosea assails throughout this text, the religious and political leadership of Israel. Finally, however, its tone of lamentation looks ahead to the antiphonal messages of Yahweh and his prophet in 8:1– 14:8, which contain a great deal of the kind of lamentation we see here.

Once again the Hebrew of this section is extremely difficult. Still it is possible to make sense of the text and to see how it all fits together as a single unit in two parts:

First Strophe	**Paganism and Apostasy**
1A General statement of apostasy and judgment	Woe to them, for they wander from me;
	Destruction to them, for they rebel against me.
1B Israel rejects grace.	I ransomed them,²¹⁹ but against me they speak lies.
	(v. 13)
1C Refusal to repent.	They do not cry to me from their hearts,

---

²¹⁹ It is difficult to know how to translate אֶפְדֵּם here. One could make a case for a subjunctive mood ("I would ransom them" [but the NIV is reading quite a bit into this verbal form with the rendition "I long to redeem them"]), or for a simple future tense, or for a past tense. Andersen and Freedman (*Hosea*, 473) make a compelling case that this verb alludes to the exodus event and should be translated in the past tense. See Deut 7:8; 9:26; 13:6 (Eng. 5); 21:8.

1D	Pagan ritual.	Rather, they howl upon their beds,
1D′	Pagan ritual.	For grain and wine they slash themselves. (v. 14)[220]
1C′	Refusal to repent.	They turn away from me.
	Second Strophe	**Political Failure**
2B	Israel rejects grace.	And I trained, I strengthened their arms, but against me they plot evil. (v. 15)
2C	Profane worship.	They will turn (to) Not–on–High,[221]
2D	Leaders fail.	They are like a slack[222] bow.
2D′	Leaders fail.	Their leaders will fall by the sword,
2C′	Profane speech.	Because of the cursing[223] of their lips.

---

[220] One should read יִתְגּוֹדָדוּ ("they cut themselves") on the basis of a number of manuscripts and the LXX κατετέμνοντο. The received text, יִתְגּוֹרָרוּ, is a *hithpolel* of גּוּר, which means, to "dwell as a resident alien" or to "be a guest." The NIV "They gather together" apparently reads root גדד II (see Ps 94:21). Since context and the LXX support taking this to mean "they cut themselves," this interpretation is preferable to the NIV rendering.

[221] The line יָשׁוּבוּ I לֹא עַל is obscure. The NIV takes עַל substantively and translates, "They do not turn to the Most High." This probably is wrong because: (1) the translation of "the Most High" for עַל is suspect, and (2) if the verb were negated, לֹא should precede it. Support for taking עַל to mean "Most High" comes primarily from Hos 11:7, וְאֶל־עַל יִקְרָאֻהוּ, if one should render it "They call to the Most High," as NIV does. But this translation probably is wrong (see below). At any rate, even if עַל sometimes means "the Most High," 7:16 should be something like לֹא יָשׁוּבוּ אֶל־עַל if its meaning were "They do not turn to the Most High." One might follow Wolff (*Hosea*, 108) in reading either לֹא עָדַי or לֹא אֵלַי here (thus, "they do not turn to me"). The *BHS* hypothesis that the original text is לְבַעַל, "(they turn) to Baal," is also appealing. But it, like Wolff's emendation, is purely conjectural. More plausibly, Andersen and Freedman (*Hosea*, 477) take לֹא עַל as a negated divine name and so translate, "They turned to a no–god." We would expect to see a preposition with שׁוּב, as in Isa 44:22; Jer 31:21; Hos 14:3; Joel 2:13; etc., although Hosea does sometimes drop prepositions. The LXX is suggestive here. It reads, ἀπεστράφησαν εἰς οὐθέν ("they have turned [it] back toward nothing"), which suggests that for לֹא עַל the original may have been לְאָוֶן, employing a favorite word of Hosea's, a word that means "nothingness" and by extension, idolatry. The LXX does not translate אָוֶן consistently in Hosea. Even so, it is difficult to account for the corruption from לְאָוֶן to לֹא עַל. But at 11:3 this commentary suggests that Yahweh rejects the title that the Israelites have applied to him, ʾēl ʿal (God on High). If this is correct, then לֹא עַל could be a derisive wordplay on ʾēl ʿal, one achieved by simple metathesis of א and ל. So understood, לֹא עַל means "Not-on-High." Thus, לֹא עַל is to ʾēl ʿal as Beth aven is to Bethel. Either way, "nothingness" or "Not-on-High," the reference here is to unacceptable, idolatrous worship.

[222] There are two meanings to the word רְמִיָּה, (1) treachery and (2) slackness. If "treachery" is the meaning here, then it is a "defective bow." However, the idea of slackness corresponds so well with a bow that it probably is a "slack" bow (i.e., one that is not strung or that even when strung is not sufficiently taut to function properly). According to Ps 78:57, such a bow twists when one tries to use it.

[223] Andersen and Freedman (*Hosea*, 479) observe that elsewhere the noun זַעַם always refers to divine wrath, and thus, with some distinctive (and perhaps far-fetched) interpretations of the Hebrew text, render this line "out of the rage of the One who mocked them—in the land of Egypt." It appears rather that one should regard זַעַם here as meaning "cursing," on the analogy of the use of the verb זעם in, e.g., Num 23:7: זֹעֲמָה יִשְׂרָאֵל ("curse Israel!").

| 2A Specific statement of humiliation in Egypt. | This shall become the taunt about them in the land of Egypt. (v. 16) |

As can be seen, this text is in two strophes that parallel each other and are bound by an inclusion. The inclusion is made up of a general statement of woe and destruction to come (1A) and a specific statement of humiliation in Egypt (2A). Statements 1B and 2B both have the same conceptual structure, that Yahweh has shown grace to Israel in providing for their salvation, but they in response have been hostile to him. Both strophes then have chiastic patterns. In 1C and 1C′ refusal to repent forms the outer elements. In 2C and 2C′ the false worship and the "cursing" represents rejection of true turning to Yahweh, because they do "turn" (*šûb*), but not to Yahweh. In 1D and 1D′ the inner elements of the chiasmus describe the paganism of the apostate cults. In 2D and 2D′, however, the point is that the military leadership of Israel will fail before the enemies of the state. The first strophe focuses on the apostasy of the religious leadership, and the second strophe focuses on the failures of the military and political leadership.

Verse 13, as indicated above, laments in general terms Israel's refusal to repent and the calamities that this is sure to bring upon them. The text does not specify what "lies" the priesthood was telling against Yahweh, but context indicates that they were religious or theological lies. Hence, we can assume that the lies involved a misrepresentation of Yahweh as approving of their syncretistic and paganlike worship.[224]

In v. 14 the fact that the people "do not cry to" Yahweh from their hearts but "turn away" from him restates the point that they would not repent but would only go further from Yahweh. The fact that they "howl upon their beds" is subject to various interpretations (e.g., that they are in such need that they wail at night rather than sleep). It is more likely, however, that this line refers to ritual wailing for the deceased Baal as part of fertility rites.[225] Details of the rituals of the cults are lost to us, but they certainly included both prostitution at the shrines and ceremonial lamentation (see Ezek 8:14). The cultic setting for this verse is implied by the yearning for the products promised by the fertility cult, grain and wine, and by the self-laceration the text describes (see 1 Kgs 18:28).

In v. 15 the training of Israel's army refers to how God fought for Israel and taught Israel to defend itself, perhaps especially in the conquest of Canaan. The phrase "against me they plot evil" implies treason against God

---

[224] Andersen and Freedman (*Hosea,* figures X and XI, before p. 463) vividly illustrate the kind of apostasy Hosea confronted in Israel. The figures depict an Iron Age jug with crude drawings of two males with exposed genitals and a seated female, with the inscription, "May you be blessed by Yahweh, our guardian, and by his Asherah."

[225] Cf. Hubbard, *Hosea,* 141.

and is well suited to the political and military setting of the second strophe. God, in effect, describes Israel as a vassal state and accuses them of committing the same kind of rebellion against him that they committed against Assyria (see 2 Kgs 17:3–5).

Verse 16 declares that the political leaders were idolatrous and profane. They turned to idols and cursing rather than blessing the name of Yahweh. They also cursed the prophets of Yahweh, who sought to persuade them to repent.[226] On the other hand, "curse" may be used here not literally but sarcastically, as a parody of the blessings pronounced in the sanctuaries. What is meant to be a blessing or doxology is in reality, the text asserts, a curse.

Hosea obviously employed two related terms in the "bow" and the "sword," but he used them in different ways. The slack bow is metaphorical for the lack of diligence and hence the military uselessness of the Israelite leadership. The sword more literally speaks of defeat and death in warfare. The point is that Israel's political leadership was apostate, ineffective, and doomed. The closure of the text probably speaks of Egypt because "I ransomed them" in v. 13 looks back to the exodus from Egypt. Thus the victory of the exodus would be reversed. "Egypt" by metonymy also represents all the gentile powers that would mock Israel when catastrophe befell her.

---

[226] Cf. Wolff, *Hosea,* 128. The best example of this kind of behavior is seen in Amos 7:10–17.

IV. ANTIPHONAL PROCLAMATIONS BY YAHWEH AND HIS
     PROPHET (8:1–14:8)
  1. First Series: False Security and False Prosperity (8:1–10:15)
     (1) Opening Divine Complaint: False Security of Israel
         (8:1–14)
     (2) Opening Prophetic Complaint: The Barren Prostitute (9:1–9)
     (3) Divine Complaint: Barrenness Instead of Fruit (9:10–17)
     (4) Prophetic Complaint: The Vine and the Bull (10:1–8)
     (5) Divine Complaint: Military Arrogance (10:9–15)
  2. Second Series: Judgment on Apostate Israel (11:1–13:16)
     (1) Divine Complaint: Divine Vexation over Apostate Israel
         (11:1–12) [A]
     (2) Prophetic Complaint: Jacob and His Heirs (12:1–8) [B]
     (3) Divine Complaint: Divine Resolve over Apostate Israel
         (12:9–11) [A']
     (4) Prophetic Complaint: Jacob and His Heirs (12:12–13:3) [B']
     (5) Divine Complaint and Decision (13:4–14) [C]
     (6) Prophetic Announcement of Judgment (13:15–16) [C']
  3. Third Series: Exhortation for Future Grace (14:1–8)
     (1) The Prophet's Call to Repent (14:1–3)
     (2) Yahweh's Promise (14:4–8)

IV. ANTIPHONAL PROCLAMATIONS BY YAHWEH AND HIS PROPHET (8:1–14:8)

From 8:1 to near the end of the book, Yahweh and Hosea antiphonally speak in lamentation over Israel's sin. As indicated in the introduction, this antiphonal structure is anticipated in chaps. 1–3, in which chap. 1 describes in the third person Hosea's marriage to Gomer; but chap. 3 takes up the tale in the first person. Thus the pattern is set in which the aggrieved husband in part tells his own story and in part has a third party tell it for him via the artifice of a third-person narrator in chap. 1. This further establishes the legitimacy of Hosea as the prophet of Yahweh. Both he and Yahweh have had the experience of unfaithful wives, and both give their stories to the reader by means of alternating first- and third-person accounts. The structure of this part of the book is presented in the above outline.

We should observe that this section has the same general structure as 4:1–

7:16 in that both begin with a series of complaints against Israel (4:1–5:15; 8:1–13:16), and both end with an exhortation to receive grace (6:1–7:13; 14:1–8). A difference is that the exhortation to receive grace in 6:1–7:13 is frustrated by Israel's refusal to repent, while 14:1–8 concludes the book with a promise of final salvation.

A leitmotif (or dominant recurring theme) of the divine complaints in chap. 8 is the historical perspective provided by Yahweh's reminiscences of Israel's former days, especially the days of the exodus (8:4–6; 9:10; 10:9–10; 11:1–4; 12:9–10; 13:4–6). The prophet answers these with two reflections on the story of Jacob, ancestor of Israel (12:2–5,12–13). These historical reflections serve at least two purposes. First, they add pathos to the divine lamentations and develop the analogy of Yahweh as an aggrieved husband/father who recalls happier days with his wife/children. Second, conversely, they indicate that the present rebellion of Israel against Yahweh is not a new thing but is the outworking of bad character that was in Israel from the beginning.

1. First Series: False Security and False Prosperity (8:1–10:15)

The texts of this section (8:1–10:15), using a wide variety of images, drive home two major points. First, Israel has depended on the fertility cults and on military power for its prosperity and security. Second, both of these are proving to be hollow. Israel's military establishment is soon to be overwhelmed, and the land already is suffering the effects of famine. These texts look back to Hosea 2, which predicted deprivation and a return to the wilderness.

(1) Opening Divine Complaint: False Security of Israel (8:1–14)

> [1]"Put the trumpet to your lips!
>   An eagle is over the house of the LORD
> because the people have broken my covenant
>   and rebelled against my law.
> [2]Israel cries out to me,
>   'O our God, we acknowledge you!'
> [3]But Israel has rejected what is good;
>   an enemy will pursue him.
> [4]They set up kings without my consent;
>   they choose princes without my approval.
> With their silver and gold
>   they make idols for themselves
>   to their own destruction.
> [5]Throw out your calf-idol, O Samaria!
>   My anger burns against them.
> How long will they be incapable of purity?
> [6]They are from Israel!

> This calf—a craftsman has made it;
>   it is not God.
> It will be broken in pieces,
>   that calf of Samaria.

> [7]"They sow the wind
>   and reap the whirlwind.
> The stalk has no head;
>   it will produce no flour.
> Were it to yield grain,
>   foreigners would swallow it up.
> [8]Israel is swallowed up;
>   now she is among the nations
>   like a worthless thing.
> [9]For they have gone up to Assyria
>   like a wild donkey wandering alone.
> Ephraim has sold herself to lovers.
> [10]Although they have sold themselves among the nations,
>   I will now gather them together.
> They will begin to waste away
>   under the oppression of the mighty king.

> [11]"Though Ephraim built many altars for sin offerings,
>   these have become altars for sinning.
> [12]I wrote for them the many things of my law,
>   but they regarded them as something alien.
> [13]They offer sacrifices given to me
>   and they eat the meat,
>   but the LORD is not pleased with them.
> Now he will remember their wickedness
>   and punish their sins:
>   They will return to Egypt.
> [14]Israel has forgotten his Maker
>   and built palaces;
>   Judah has fortified many towns.
> But I will send fire upon their cities
>   that will consume their fortresses."

The opening text alternately complains on the one hand over how Israel has sought artificial political protection and lives in a world of artificial piety, and on the other hand it asserts that the result will be military disaster and famine conditions. The text is structured in the following fashion:

A The Coming Conquest (8:1a)
  B Artificial Piety: Vain Reliance on the Covenant (8:1b–3)
    C Artificial Political Protection: Choosing Their Own Kings (8:4a)

    B′ Artificial Piety: The Calf-idol (8:4b–6)
A′ The Coming Deprivation (8:7)
    C′ Artificial Political Protection: Seeking Foreign Help (8:8–10)
    B″ Artificial Piety: Unintended Results of Worship (8:11–13)
      C″ Artificial Political Protection: Fortresses (8:14)

This structure presents a picture of an Israel that, in its religion, had a presumptive confidence in the covenant and repeated the sin of the golden calf and whose worship had results that were the opposite of what they supposed. In the political realm they chose their own leaders rather than seek Yahweh's direction, they sought help from other nations rather than from God, and they relied on their walls and military power to defend them.

    8:1a The opening call to "Put the trumpet to your lips! An eagle is over the house of the LORD" is literally, "To your palate, shofar, like the vulture[1] over the house of Yahweh." Scholars have naturally wondered over the meaning of this elliptical line. One does not play the shofar with the palate; there is no verb (such as "put") with shofar; it is not clear exactly what is supposed to be "like the vulture"; and it is unusual that Israel would be called "house of Yahweh," a term that almost always refers to the tent of meeting or the Jerusalem temple. The most widely accepted interpretation is that it means something like, "Set the shofar to your mouth! Someone is over the house of Yahweh like a vulture!" (taking "palate" here to represent the entire mouth and taking "house of Yahweh" to be not the temple but Israel on the basis of the phrase "house of the LORD" in 9:4 and "house of his God" in 9:8).[2] So interpreted, the line means that watchmen should sound the alarm because an enemy is swooping down on Israel like an eagle or vulture.

    Andersen and Freedman have argued that v. 1a could mean something like, "As the shofar is for the mouth, so the eagle is for the house of Yahweh."[3] Although this interpretation is inviting, it requires slightly emending the text and does not make for an entirely logical comparison. In what sense is an eagle (or vulture) appropriate for the house of Yahweh in the same way that a shofar is appropriate for the mouth?

    To resolve this enigma we must assume with most scholars that "palate" here refers to the mouth generally and that some verb such as "put" is implied. Thus we have a situation in which watchmen should alert the people of an invading army. However, it is not at all clear that "like the vulture" can

---

[1] Either "eagle" or "vulture" is possible for נֶשֶׁר.

[2] E.g., J. L. Mays, *Hosea: A Commentary,* OTL (Philadelphia: Westminster, 1969), 113; T. E. McComiskey, "Hosea," in *The Minor Prophets* (Grand Rapids: Baker, 1992), 118.

[3] F. I. Andersen and D. N. Freedman, *Hosea,* AB (New York: Doubleday, 1980), 485. This interpretation moves the כּ from the end of חִכְּךָ to the beginning of שֶׁפָר. So emended the line has a chiastic pattern.

mean "someone like a vulture." It seems more probable that "like the vulture over the house of Yahweh" means "as when a vulture is on the house of Yahweh." Furthermore, in light of the fact that "house of Yahweh" elsewhere is always a sanctuary dedicated to Yahweh, it seems impossible that it here means the land of Israel (we will argue for the same interpretation at 9:4 and 9:8). In short, the point is not that an enemy is coming "like a vulture" but that one should blow trumpets and sound alarms as vigorously as one would do when a vulture, a notoriously unclean bird, had lighted on the roof of the temple. When such a thing happened, we presume, the priests made all the noise they could to get this bird, as grotesque as it is ill-omened, off of the temple roof. This does not exclude the idea that an invading army is coming since the sounding of alarms implies that an enemy is about to attack; the idea of a vulture on the temple is only an analogy for how vigorously one should sound the alarm. On the other hand, this analogy also presents the reader with a picture of something hideously unclean at the very temple of God. This image implicitly compares the Israelite priests or perhaps the pagan deities to vultures at the shrines of Yahweh, and it prepares the reader to understand that the apostasy of the nation is linked to its coming military collapse.

8:1b–3 As does 4:1–3, this text describes the rejection of Yahweh as Israel's fundamental sin. Covenant violation and nonobservance of the Torah constitute the general terms under which all other accusations fall (cf. 4:2, where violations of the Decalogue open the accusations of 4:1–7:16). Contrary to Wolff, there is no reason to regard Hosea's concept of covenant and Torah as anything other than the Sinai tradition.[4]

Verse 2 might be better translated, "They cry out to me, 'My God!' (and) 'We know you!' (and) 'Israel!'"[5] "That is, "My God!" and "We know you!" and "Israel!" are three fragments of the liturgical prayers offered at the shrines. The outcry "Israel" refers to their confidence that they were the people of the covenant and therefore the special recipients of his favor (cp. John 8:39). This confidence was misplaced, of course, as were their claims to know Yahweh. In the texts that follow, Yahweh and Hosea will demonstrate that the people did not know Yahweh or have him as their God and that they embodied the worst, not the best, of what it meant to be Israelites.

"Good" in v. 3 is a very general word and should be treated as such; it refers to God himself as the ultimate good, the good teachings of the Torah, the right way of living, and the benefits that come from faithfulness to God. "Enemy" is also somewhat general and here is the opposite of "good" as to

---

[4] Cf. H. W. Wolff, *Hosea,* Her (Philadelphia: Fortress, 1974), 138.

[5] יִשְׂרָאֵל at the end of the line is not likely the subject of the third masculine plural יִזְעָקוּ at the beginning of the line. A number of scholars omit יִשְׂרָאֵל with the LXX, but cf. the Vg.

"reject" is the opposite of "pursue." Thus those who forsake the good find themselves chased by something or someone hostile to them and to what is good for them. Here pursuit by enemies includes but extends beyond military defeat; it can also imply that Yahweh himself hunts them down as an enemy would.[6]

8:4a Here the text briefly alludes to abandonment of Yahweh in the political realm; later on the text will give more attention to this matter. Israel's political instability in the latter half of the eighth century is behind this verse. This line is better translated, "It is they who make kings—kings who are not from me; they appoint rulers [whom] I do not know."[7] The complaint here is twofold. First, the Israelites appoint leaders without consulting Yahweh, and second, those whom they appoint are themselves strangers to Yahweh in the sense that they are untouched by grace and outside the covenant (much as what "I never knew you" implies in Matt 7:23). More is implied by this than simply that God did not give "consent" (as in the NIV) to their decision. The point is that God should have been the one to initiate the choice. They had wrested the whole process from him, and the result is that they had chosen the worst possible leaders.

8:4b–6 This is another very difficult text of Hosea. The language is more like rhetoric than poetry, and the grammar is challenging. Even so, one can make sense of its structure and message. The topic is an idol called the "calf of Samaria," a bovine representation of Baal or of Yahweh himself, which Yahweh rejects in what one may reverently call almost apoplectic anger. The broken grammar and uneven lines portray Yahweh as vexed in the extreme over the perversity of Israel's representation of their God in a fashion that both mixes Yahwism with Baalism and reenacts the sin of the golden calf (Exod 32:4). One might best understand the text as follows:

---

[6] Cf. Andersen and Freedman, *Hosea*, 491. They probably are correct that this is a parody of "she pursues her lovers" in 2:9 (Eng. 2:7). On the other hand, it is most unlikely that זָנַח יִשְׂרָאֵל טוֹב should be translated, as they suggest, "The Good One has rejected Israel." See G. I. Davies (*Hosea*, NCBC [Grand Rapids: Eerdmans, 1992], 199), who also notes that the unusual suffix on יִרְדְּפוֹ may reflect a northern dialect.

[7] The line הֵשִׂירוּ וְלֹא יָדָעְתִּי is lit., "They appoint princes but I do not know." The implied object of "know" is the leaders whom the Israelites appoint. The NIV's "without my approval" is an odd translation for יְדִע.

A1	Israel makes idols	Their silver and their gold they make for themselves into idols—so that[8] it might be cut off! (v. 4b)
A2	Calf of Samaria	Your calf is rejected,[9] Samaria! (v. 5a)
B1	Wrath of Yahweh	My anger burns hot against them! (v. 5b)
B2	Guilt of people	How long will they be inept at innocence? (v. 5c)
A1′	Israel makes idols	For (it is) from Israel, and it[10]—a craftsman made it and it is not God! (v. 6a)
A2′	Calf of Samaria	For the calf of Samaria shall be shattered! (v. 6b)[11]

In A1 (v. 4b) the translation "so that it might be cut off" is preferable to the NIV's "to their own destruction," which is not possible.[12] The word "it" apparently refers to the wealth of Israel, their silver and gold, that they would lose as a result of their apostasy. It was not literally the purpose of the people that they lose their wealth—to the contrary, health and wealth was the whole point of the fertility cult; "so that it might be cut off" should be read as sarcasm. They worshiped idols in the hope that they would receive riches and protection, but the opposite would come about. Making idols—that is, making gods—is conceptually linked to making kings for themselves in v. 4a.

The real focus of Yahweh's attention here, however, is the "calf of Samaria," a bull-god comparable to the golden calf of Exodus 32. It may be that the "idols" mentioned in v. 4b include both the archetype "calf of Samaria" as well as smaller replicas of it that people kept at private shrines (cp. the many replicas of Artemis of Ephesus mentioned in Acts 19:24–29). The calf of Samaria is probably the calf-idol that Jeroboam set up at Bethel (1 Kgs 12:28–29), which Hos 10:5–6 states that the people of Samaria

---

[8] The word לְמַעַן indicates purpose, although it obviously was not literally the case that the Israelites made idols in order that they or their wealth might be destroyed. The broken grammar here should be taken as sarcasm and as a rhetorical sign of the depth of Yahweh's dismay.

[9] The Hb. זָנַח עֶגְלֵךְ שֹׁמְרוֹן literally means "your calf has rejected Samaria," which is obviously impossible. The LXX and Theodotion have ἀπότριψαι (aorist imperative, "reject!"), implying that we should read זְנַח, "reject!" (as in the NIV). Symmachus has ἀποβλήθη (aorist passive, "it is cast out"), which implies זֻנַּח ("rejected"). Either is possible, but in the OT God is usually the subject of זנח (v. 3 is exceptional in this regard). Especially apropos here are Lam 2:7 ("The Lord has rejected [זָנַח] his altar") and 2 Chr 11:14, which states that Jeroboam had the Levitical priests excluded [זָנַח] from service at the altars. In these texts זנח describes rejection of something from cultic service. Thus when Yahweh declares that the calf of Samaria is "rejected," he means that it is banned as unfit for sacral use.

[10] We have in כִּי מִיִּשְׂרָאֵל וְהוּא חָרָשׁ עָשָׂהוּ a simple case of anacoluthon, in which the speaker abruptly changes his sentence midstream. In light of the suffix on עָשָׂהוּ, it is clear that הוּא must refer to the idol and not a person.

[11] Following the suggestion of BDB, 985, that שְׁבָבִים means "splinters."

[12] The singular form of the verb יִכָּרֵת should not be smoothed out in translation and made into a plural, as the NIV does. Since the text uses the plural עָשׂוּ ("they made") to refer to the Israelites, the singular יִכָּרֵת must refer to something else, and the abstraction "wealth," from the aforementioned "silver and gold," is the most logical choice.

revered. As Wolff observes, the calf-sanctuary was active as an official shrine and was sponsored by the throne right up to the end of Israel. Furthermore, as he notes, the calf was sacred to Baal, and its image would have been regarded as a statue of the god himself and not merely as a pedestal for the god or as a representation of one of his attributes, as some scholars have contended.[13] A calf—that is, a young bull conveys power and fertility.

The central section (B1 and B2) describes in general terms the anger of Yahweh and the moral obtuseness of the people. In a word, they have lost all decency.

The third section, A1' and A2', forms an inclusion with A1 and A2. Verse 6a is particularly broken; Yahweh is almost speechless with anger! "This calf—a craftsman has made it; it is not God!" is another case in which the speaker abruptly changes what he is saying in the middle of a thought for rhetorical effect. The idea that Israel, after all her experiences, could embrace such idolatry is beyond comprehension. Israel had to learn the same lesson over again. Just as the calf that Aaron made was ground to powder (Exod 32:20), so would this idol be smashed to pieces.

8:7   The first part of this verse is usually taken as a proverb directed against people who pursue a foolish course of action. Interpreters take the sowing of wind to be stirring up trouble, with the outcome being that those who sow wind bring far greater trouble upon themselves: they reap a storm. On the other hand, the image of "sowing wind" is quite unnatural. Perhaps a better interpretation is that the wind and storm are not the objects of the verbs but are adverbial; they are the conditions in which sowing and reaping takes place. Thus one could render it, "For in wind they sow, and they shall reap in a storm."[14] The point is that they will have no harvest, as when one attempts to sow seed or harvest crops in the worst conditions. Ancient farmers sowed seed by hand, scattering it on the ground, as Jesus' parable indicates. Anyone who cast out seed in a high wind would have all his seed blown away. Similarly, gale winds would scatter the sheaves of a farmer who tried to cut and bundle them in a windstorm.

The second part of this verse is a pseudosorites, a rhetorical device in which the speaker says that event A will not happen but that even if it did, it would be undone by event B (see the discussion at 5:6). In this case Hosea says that there will be no harvest of grain but that even if there were one, foreigners would take it.[15] In this connection the stalk that has no head probably

---

[13] See Wolff, *Hosea*, 140–41.

[14] We take רוּחַ יִזְרָעוּ וְסוּפָתָה יִקְצֹרוּ to mean "they sow in a wind and they reap in a gale," with D. Stuart, *Hosea–Jonah*, WBC (Dallas: Word, 1987), 133, and Andersen and Freedman, *Hosea*, 496–97. The latter note that Hosea frequently drops prepositions. Furthermore, in this interpretation the ending on the form סוּפָתָה need not be taken as an old accusative on סוּפָה but more plausibly as a locative ending.

[15] Cf. M. O'Connor, "The Pseudosorites: A Type of Paradox in Hebrew Verse," JSOTSup 40 (1987): 161–72.

not only represents literal fields of wheat that will yield no harvest but also
metaphorically the religious and political ideology on which Israel had placed
its trust, especially the fertility cults. These would not give them the prosperity they seek.

8:8–10 Once again we are confronted with exceptionally difficult
Hebrew in this passage. Nevertheless, the main thrust of the text in all the versions is fairly clear: Israel has sought for help among the nations but has
failed and is left alone. Hosea uses three images to convey the message that all
of Israel's efforts to gain the favor of the nations only resulted in Israel being
made helpless before the nations.

A Israel an empty cup, ready to be discarded	Israel is swallowed up! Now they are among the nations like a cup[16] nobody wants! (v. 8)[17]
B Israel a lone donkey.	For they went up to Assyria. Ephraim[18] is a wild donkey wandering by itself. (v. 9a)
C All the tribute Israel has paid will do them no good.	They paid the prostitutes' fees (v. 9b).[19] Although they have hired (prostitutes) among the nations, I will gather them; and they have begun[20] to decline[21] because of the burden of king (and) officials.[22] (v. 10)

Israel is first compared to a cup or container that has been emptied of all its
drink. Thus the cup is no longer of value to anyone, and those who drank
from it are ready to throw it away. The meaning of the metaphor is self-

---

[16] The word כְּלִי refers to a pottery vessel, a tool, a weapon, or any kind of "thing." Here, in
light of the metaphor of Israel being swallowed, it seems to be a cup or container.

[17] אֵין־חֵפֶץ בּוֹ is more literally "there is no pleasure in it," but in context it means that it is
something no one wants.

[18] Contrary to the NIV, אֶפְרַיִם should be regarded as the subject and פֶּרֶא as the predicate in
a verbless clause. אֶפְרַיִם is not the subject of הִתְנוּ, a plural verb. In Hosea אֶפְרַיִם always takes
a singular verb (e.g., 12:15 [Eng. 14]) unless it is part of a compound subject (e.g., 12:1 [Eng.
11:12]). Also note the evident wordplay on פֶּרֶא and אֶפְרַיִם in the line פֶּרֶא בּוֹדֵד לוֹ אֶפְרַיִם.

[19] The verb תנה means to "hire." It appears to mean to "pay the fee of hiring" in the *hiphil* stem
in v. 9 and simply to "hire someone" in the *qal* stem in v. 10. Contrary to the NIV it does not mean
to sell oneself. The noun אַהַב means "love gifts" (cf. *HALOT*, 18) and in this context must mean
the fee required by prostitutes. Some interpreters emend to אֹהֲבִים, "lovers" (e.g., Stuart,
Hosea-Jonah, 128), but the sense of the text—hiring prostitutes—remains the same.

[20] Many translators render וַיָּחֵלּוּ as something like "they writhe," as though the form were
וְיָחִילוּ (from חיל), or as "they become sick," as though the form were וְיֶחֱלוּ (from חלה). But the
text as it stands is a *hiphil* stem from חלל and means "to begin." Cf. Wolff, *Hosea,* 133.

[21] It is difficult to make sense of this word, מְעַט if one reads it as the adverb מְעַט, "little," as
most interpreters do. It makes better sense to take it as an infinitive construct of the verb מעט. Cf.
NASB and C. F. Keil, *Hosea* (Grand Rapids: Eerdmans, n.d.), 116.

[22] The NIV takes מֶלֶךְ שָׂרִים to mean "the mighty king" presumably because a "king of
princes" would be a mighty king. However, in light of how often Hosea attacks the מֶלֶךְ and שָׂרִים
of Israel, it is doubtful that this expression denotes the Assyrian king. We probably have asyndeton
here, and not a construct chain. Thus Hosea refers to the "king" and "princes" of Israel.

evident. The nations were only interested in draining from Israel all the
wealth they could get in the form of tributary payments. Once that was
exhausted, they had no interest in protecting Israel but were happy to discard
it. Yahweh's point is that all the money that Israel has doled out to Assyria,
Egypt, and other nations has done them no good. Instead of taking Yahweh's
protection for free, they paid exorbitantly and received only disdain from
those to whom they gave payment.

The second comparison is between Israel and the solitary donkey of the
desert. Here the point is that Israel went to mighty Assyria for aid, but instead
of gaining an alliance with a great power, it remained a lonely creature left to
fend for itself.[23]

The third metaphor is of paying the fees of prostitutes to gain their favors.
Some might object that the dominant metaphor of the book is that Israel
itself is the wanton prostitute and that the nations are her clients. The prophets, however, freely altered their metaphors to suit their messages, and one
need not follow the NIV in its translation "they have sold themselves." Here
Yahweh compares Israel to a man who tries to gain love by giving money to
prostitutes, only to discover that he has both squandered his money and
gained no love in return. The nations are like prostitutes in that they offer
their friendship and protection for a price. In this light "I will gather them" in
v. 10 probably does not mean that Yahweh will gather together the Israelites
from the nations, which implies salvation, but that he will gather the nations
together to make war against Israel. Finally, Yahweh says, Israel has already
begun to decline under the burden of the royal house's demands on the people. In context this refers to the money that the government demanded of the
people to buy off other governments,[24] the most striking example being the
tax imposed by Menahem (2 Kgs 15:19–20). Israel's leadership had already
sapped the nation's wealth and given it to foreign powers long before the
final blow was delivered by the Assyrian army.

8:11–13 Here Yahweh returns to the religious sins of Israel and attacks
the cultic life of the nation with three ironies. First, the altars they make to
expiate sin only increase sin; second, the people treat Yahweh's laws as if they
were the teachings of a foreign religion; third, the effect their sacrifices have
on Yahweh is the reverse of what they intended.

The translation of v. 11 is disputed, but the NIV probably is correct even

---

[23] An alternative interpretation, based on emending פֶּרֶא בּוֹדֵד to פֶּרֶא בָּדָד, is, "Ephraim
has sprouted up on his own." See S. A. Irvine, "Politics and Prophetic Commentary in Hosea 8:8–
10," *JBL* 114 (1995): 292–94.
[24] The word "burden" in v. 10 (מַשָּׂא) means "tribute" in 2 Chr 17:11. Cf. also the usage of
מַשְׂאֵת (also from the root נשׂא) for "tribute."

though it involves an emendation.[25] The point is that the people built altars for expiating their sins. But these altars became at best emblems for a false theology of easy grace and at worst sites for the immorality of the fertility cults.

The second ironic charge, in v. 12, is especially incriminating. Yahweh had given the nation an abundance of principles and regulations regarding every aspect of life, including sacrifices, feasts, religious practices, diet, military and political life, and the family. The priests had so little respect for the Torah, however, and the people were so poorly taught (cf. 4:6) that some regarded the Torah as the religious laws of some foreign land! The principles of Baal had been accepted as orthodox and indeed as the genuine expression of the Israelite faith. For modern readers the lesson is that we need to beware of how easy it is to substitute culture and prevalent opinions for true Christianity. It is possible to regard true examples of Christian spirituality as alien.

The beginning of v. 13 is difficult; the NIV translation, "They offer sacrifices given to me," although it follows several other versions, is hypothetical.[26] A better translation of v. 13 might be:

> As for my choice sacrifices[27]: They sacrifice flesh[28] and they eat it.
> "The LORD does not accept them.
> He will remember their iniquity and punish their sins.
> They shall return to Egypt."

This verse clearly involves the offering of sacrifice in order to appease Yahweh. The result, however, is the opposite of what the people want. God rejects them (rather than accept them), remembers their sin (rather than forget it), and sends them away into exile, which is the ultimate expression of his displeasure. The portion of the text that I have put in quotation marks ("The LORD does not accept them. He will remember their iniquity and punish their

---

[25] The line is redundant: כִּי־הִרְבָּה אֶפְרַיִם מִזְבְּחֹת לַחֲטֹא הָיוּ־לוֹ מִזְבְּחוֹת לַחֲטֹא׃ is literally, "For Ephraim multiplied altars for sinning; they are for him altars for sinning." Wolff (*Hosea*, 133) makes a case for translating this as: "Ephraim has multiplied altars. He uses them for sinning. Altars for sinning!" It probably is better to follow Mays (*Hosea*, 114) and Stuart (*Hosea-Jonah*, 128) and emend the first occurrence to לַחֲטֹא, "to remove sin."

[26] The NIV follows the suggestion that the hapax legomenon הַבְהָב means "gift." Cf. BDB 396. Many scholars consider this unlikely and offer alternative interpretations. Some emend to זֶבַח אָהֲבוּ וַיִּזְבְּחוּ ("sacrifice they love and they make sacrifice"). See Mays, *Hosea*, 114, and Wolff, *Hosea*, 133. Note that the LXX at the end of v. 12 has τὰ ἠγαπημένα ("loved").

[27] The interpretation "my choice sacrifices" is, I think, the best we can do with זִבְחֵי הַבְהָבַי. The phrase seems to be a technical term within the cult for some kind of offerings. On הַבְהָב see *HALOT*, 236, and E. W. Nicholson, "Problems in Hosea VIII 13," *VT* 16 (1966): 355–58. The word either means "roasted" or something like "ardent love." Either way it seems to refer to sacrifices that the people supposed to be especially pleasing to Yahweh. It is here *casus pendens*.

[28] "Flesh" (בָּשָׂר) is the object of יִזְבָּחוּ, a point established by the conjunction on וַיֹּאכֵלוּ. As an object of "they sacrifice," "flesh" is surprising. But that is the point. What the people suppose to be a sacrifice acceptable to God is in Yahweh's eyes just meat for human consumption.

sins. They shall return to Egypt.") is distinctive here for speaking of Yahweh in the third person. This is not, however, prophetic discourse as I have described it; we are still in Yahweh's discourse. Instead, this appears to be a parody of a priestly blessing that might have been pronounced at a sacrifice. The priestly benediction may have been something like: "Yahweh has accepted them. He will not remember their iniquity but will pardon their sins. He is Yahweh, who brought them out of Egypt." In other words, this pronouncement reverses what the priests and people expected to gain from their sacrifices.[29]

Reference to "Egypt" here does not mean that all the people would literally return to Egypt (although some did). It is a reversal of the exodus and implies removal from the land and nullification of covenant promises. It also serves as a counterpoint to v. 9, "They have gone up to Assyria." Together Egypt and Assyria are the two nations to which apostate Israel turned for help, and they were the two nations to which exiled Israel would go.

8:14   Yahweh concludes his first complaint with another lamentation over Israel's desire to find security through political and military means.[30] The nation "forgets" God when it supposes that it must resort to military buildup in order to provide security for itself. In this context "palaces" probably are not especially places of luxury but fortified residences analogous to Herod's residence at Masada.[31] Together with fortified towns and garrisons, these were to be a security network that both protected the nation and in particular preserved the lives and wealth of the upper classes. The "fire" that Yahweh sends is metonymy for invasion and siege work by enemy nations, but the language recalls the destruction of Sodom and Gomorrah by fire.

> [1]**Do not rejoice, O Israel;**
>   **do not be jubilant like the other nations.**
> **For you have been unfaithful to your God;**
>   **you love the wages of a prostitute**
>   **at every threshing floor.**
> [2]**Threshing floors and winepresses will not feed the people;**
>   **the new wine will fail them.**
> [3]**They will not remain in the LORD's land;**

---

[29] Note that רצה ("accept") is used in Deut 33:11, where Moses prays that God will accept the work of Levi, i.e., the sacrifices of the priests. See also Pss 51:18 (Eng. 16); 119:108; Amos 5:22; Mal 1:10,13. Especially note Isa 43:25, which promises that Yahweh "remembers your sins no more" and contrasts with this verse.

[30] A number of scholars consider this verse to be secondary, but the alternating pattern of false security in religion and false security in political life establishes that 8:14 fits the larger pattern of the text. Contra Wolff, *Hosea*, 147, and Andersen and Freedman, *Hosea*, 511.

[31] Davies comments that palaces were often heavily fortified and cites excavation reports from Hazor and Samaria (*Hosea*, 210).

     Ephraim will return to Egypt
       and eat unclean food in Assyria.
[4]**They will not pour out wine offerings to the LORD,**
       nor will their sacrifices please him.
Such sacrifices will be to them like the bread of mourners;
       all who eat them will be unclean.
This food will be for themselves;
       it will not come into the temple of the LORD.

[5]**What will you do on the day of your appointed feasts,**
       on the festival days of the LORD?
[6]**Even if they escape from destruction,**
     Egypt will gather them,
     and Memphis will bury them.
Their treasures of silver will be taken over by briers,
       and thorns will overrun their tents.
[7]**The days of punishment are coming,**
       the days of reckoning are at hand.
       Let Israel know this.
Because your sins are so many
       and your hostility so great,
the prophet is considered a fool,
       the inspired man a maniac.
[8]**The prophet, along with my God,**
       is the watchman over Ephraim,
yet snares await him on all his paths,
       and hostility in the house of his God.
[9]**They have sunk deep into corruption,**
       as in the days of Gibeah.
God will remember their wickedness
       and punish them for their sins.

OPENING PROPHETIC COMPLAINT: THE BARREN PROSTITUTE (9:1–9). Form-critical attempts to specify a *Sitz im Leben* for individual units of Hosea are for the most part ill-advised. The text rarely gives us enough information to make such judgments, and in any case Hosea has shaped his material into a unified literary work. This is not an anthology of sermons, each of which can be studied in isolation. The redaction of Hosea's previous oral messages has been so thorough that attempts to identify the original oral settings of individual units are usually as artificial as they are forced.

Nevertheless, in this text it is reasonable to suppose that Hosea has adapted a message that he first delivered on the occasion of a failed harvest. The opening, "Do not rejoice," reads like an inversion of what would have been a typical harvest proclamation (something like, "Rejoice, Israel, for Yahweh has given you a harvest!"). Joel 2:23–24, for example, reads: "O children of Zion, be glad and rejoice in the LORD your God; for he has given the early rain for your vindication, he has poured down for you abundant rain, the early and the later rain, as before. The threshing floors shall be full of grain, the vats shall overflow with wine and oil." Thus it seems that Hosea is turning what should be a proclamation of joy into one of lamentation. Israel the harlot thought that the fertility cult would give her prosperity, but she received only barrenness.

Hosea interprets the failed harvest under three points. The first is that the bad harvest, as a sign of Yahweh's displeasure, indicates that greater calamities—military defeat and exile—are on the horizon (vv. 1–3). Second, he draws the people's attention to another adversity that accompanies famine conditions, namely, the inability of the people and priesthood to make suitable offerings to God (vv. 4–6). Third, he asserts that the people had dismissed the prophets when they warned that such troubles were coming (vv. 7–9). In linking a failed harvest to military defeat, and in regarding the famine as especially calamitous because it brought about the end of sacrifice and offering to Yahweh, Hosea's words call to mind Joel's prophecy.[32] In confronting an Israelite establishment that was dismissive of Yahweh's prophets, Hosea's experience paralleled that of Amos and many other prophets.[33]

9:1 The NIV has made a number of modifications to the text that are not immediately apparent to the English reader. It follows most scholars in emending the beginning of the verse, which literally reads, "Do not rejoice, Israel, to jubilation like the nations." The emendation "do not be jubilant" is supported by the LXX and the Vulgate and possibly is correct.[34] On the other hand, the Hebrew text as it stands may reflect an idiom and be legitimately translated something like, "Do not work yourself into a joyful frenzy."[35] Also the translation "you have been unfaithful" may mislead the English reader, since the Hebrew actually says, "You have committed prostitution."[36] Finally, this verse ends with the word "grain," which the NIV has suppressed but which should either be translated here or moved to v. 2 (see below).[37]

Israel had tried to be like other nations by seeking wealth and good harvests by the same means that the nations employed, the fertility cult. But Israel could not become one of the nations, and the lost harvest served as evidence that, whether or not they wanted it, they were the elect of Yahweh.

---

[32] See especially Joel 2:1–11 and the analysis in this commentary. See also Joel 1:13 regarding the loss of food for sacrifice and offerings.

[33] See Amos 7:10–17.

[34] The usual emendation involves changing אֶל־גִּיל to אַל־תָּגֵל; the LXX has μηδὲ εὐφραίνου and the Vg has *noli exultare*. It is possible that גִיל is here an infinitive absolute serving (with אַל) as a negative command; see Andersen and Freedman, *Hosea*, 522.

[35] See Job 3:22, הַשְּׂמֵחִים אֱלֵי־גִיל, which usually is rendered "who rejoice exceedingly."

[36] Using זנה.

[37] It is also possible, but in my view not likely, that דָּגָן refers to the god Dagon, a suggestion made by J. M. Ward, *Hosea: A Theological Commentary* (New York: Harper & Row, 1966), 159.

When Israel embraced pagan religious ideals, it was behaving in a way inconsistent with its own identity. In the same manner the church cannot do itself or anyone else any good if it tries to be what it is not. When salt loses its flavor, it becomes entirely worthless (Matt 5:13).

Because their harvest has failed, they cannot rejoice, and their harvest has failed because of their "prostitution" against God. Here Hosea only briefly alludes to the metaphor of the prostitute, but that allusion is sufficient for the reader to call to mind the entire image of Israel the wayward wife that Hosea has already developed. The "wages of a prostitute at every threshing floor" probably carries a double meaning. It is literally the immoral acts that often accompanied the party atmosphere at harvest, but it is also figuratively the large harvest that the fertility cult was intended to insure. The supposed benefits of the cult were both sexual license and agricultural prosperity.

9:2 The NIV, like many versions, emends the Hebrew to create the reading "the new wine will fail them." This emendation is unnecessary, however, and the text can be understood to mean, "Threshing floor and wine vat shall not sustain them; and new wine fails in her," with "her" referring to the land.[38] It is possible in fact that "grain" from the end of v. 1 should be connected with this verse to give it the meaning: "Grain (threshing floor and wine vat shall not sustain them) and new wine fails in the land."[39] Although this interpretation inserts an entire clause between "grain" and "new wine," it makes sense because grain is to the threshing floor as new wine is to the wine vat. At any rate, a bad harvest is obviously behind this text.

9:3 The conceptual leap from v. 2 to v. 3 seems unnatural unless one recognizes that Hosea, like Joel, regarded famine to be a precursor for military defeat and exile. Behind this text stands Deut 28:38–41, where famine conditions are the last stroke of divine punishment prior to the departure of the people into captivity. The two phrases "Yahweh's land" and "unclean food" relate to each other. Rejected from "Yahweh's land," the people will eat "unclean food." Because they have defiled themselves, they will be unfit for residence in the holy land and will instead eat defiled food in a foreign land.

9:4 Although "nor will their sacrifices please him" is a traditional translation, this clause might be taken to mean "they shall not bring their sacrifices to him" in parallel with "they will not pour out wine offerings to the LORD."

---

[38] Interpreters emend בָּהּ to בָּם; cf. Davies, who notes that the supposed scribal error here is not easy to explain (*Hosea*, 215). The very next phrase concerns the יהוה אֶרֶץ; that being the case, it is best simply to take the feminine pronoun as a reference to the land. At any rate, the picture of the land/Israel as a woman dominates the Book of Hosea.

[39] This proposal builds upon but modifies a proposal by Andersen and Freedman, who note that "grain and must" is something of a stock phrase in the Hebrew Bible (*Hosea*, 519). Also the phrase גָּרְנוֹת דָּגָן ("threshing floors of grain") is odd; it occurs only here in the Hebrew Bible.

Still, evidence seems to support the traditional translation here.[40] In either case context makes clear that the point is that either they would offer sacrifices that were unacceptable for use in the house of God or that they would have nothing at all to give in sacrifice. If the traditional translation is correct, the point is that they have no offerings to give that would be suitable for use in worship. Any offerings they made in the shrines during times of drought would be of very poor quality and thus be unusable as offerings. The phrase "like the bread of mourners" refers to the fact that those who are in mourning, and who must deal with the burial of a dead body, contaminate the food they touch with uncleanness. Such bread is unfit for offering to God (see Deut 29:12–14). This food could be eaten by laypeople but was not to be used in the house of the Lord. In this sense whatever food the Israelites could gather during times of famine would be "like the bread of mourners" and useful only for providing the necessities of survival.[41]

9:5 Some readers might suppose that Israel's embracing Baalism would mean they had also chosen to reject Yahweh. This is not correct. Although apostate they considered themselves still to be orthodox and desired Yahweh's favor. Hosea has already made the point that he does not necessarily regard their keeping of the feasts to be a good thing (2:11–13), since their feasts were occasions more for false security and sin than for true repentance before God. This is not because festivals are by nature bad but because the Israelites had come to regard the observation of the festivals as sufficient to appease Yahweh and, worse, had contaminated these festivals with pagan ideals. So he confronts them with the fact that other than maintaining a form of ceremonial worship, they have nothing to recommend themselves to God. Even this fig leaf of piety would be stripped away when famine made continuation of the rituals impossible.[42]

---

[40] Cf. *HALOT,* 877; G. R. Driver, "Difficult Words in the Hebrew Bible," in *Studies in Old Testament Prophecy,* ed. H. H. Rowley (Edinburgh: T & T Clark, 1950), 64; Stuart, *Hosea-Jonah,* 140; Mays, *Hosea,* 124. But Wolff (*Hosea,* 150) stays with the traditional "shall not please him" on the basis of the LXX, Targum, and Vg. Andersen and Freedman (*Hosea,* 526) argue that the verb here, יֶעֱרְבוּ, should be read as a *hiphil* stem of the root ʿrb, which is attested in Ugaritic with the meaning "to enter" and thus in the *hiphil* stem would presumably mean "to cause to enter" or "to offer (sacrifice)." They cite Ugaritic text KRT 159–60 in support of this interpretation, which reads ʿrb bzl ḥmt lqh / imr dbḥ bydh. It is not clear to me, however, that ʿrb means "offer" here. The line appears to mean "he entered the shade of a tent, he took / a sacrificial lamb in his hand" (cf. *ANET,* 144). I.e., ʿrb simply means "enter" here, notwithstanding that it is in a cultic context. Also if Ugaritic ʿrb in a causative stem can mean "offer," one would expect to see it in the Š stem with this meaning. Finally, Jer 6:20, וְזִבְחֵיכֶם לֹא־עָרְבוּ לִי ("and your sacrifices are not pleasing to me"), plainly supports the traditional interpretation.

[41] The word לְנַפְשָׁם is best taken to mean "for their survival" instead of simply "for themselves" (NIV). The נֶפֶשׁ is literally the throat and by extension "breath" or "life."

[42] A number of scholars read this verse to mean that they would no longer be able to keep the feast because of the coming exile. See Stuart, *Hosea-Jonah,* 144; Hubbard, *Hosea,* 158. This is not correct; although Hosea sees exile as the next stage of punishment to come, his point is that already they have lost the means of properly celebrating the feasts because of the famine.

It is possible that the specific feast Hosea has in mind is the festival of the fifteenth day of the eighth month that was established by Jeroboam I in order to insure the loyalty of the Israelites to the northern shrines (1 Kgs 12:32). Since Hosea refers to this as a "feast of Yahweh," the feast may also have been a variant on the Festival of Booths (Lev 23:39–43, where it is twice called a "feast of Yahweh"), which was supposed to be observed on the fifteenth day of the seventh month. Jeroboam's festival was inherently improper, and it is not surprising that it would generate only artificial piety and would amalgamate with Baalism.

9:6 The first line of v. 6, "Even if they escape from destruction," is difficult. The NIV translation, although in agreement with many other versions, is open to question. First, the word translated "escape" (and which other versions render as "flee") simply means to "go." It does not in itself carry the idea of flight or escape.[43] Second, the translation, "Even if" (other versions have "Although") is very doubtful; the words are most naturally taken to mean "For, behold."[44] Thus the line means "For, behold, they come from destruction." This would seem to mean that the Israelites (or their foodstuff) come from a famine situation in which death is prevalent and uncleanness is everywhere. It reinforces the previous point that their bread was like mourners' bread, and it is a transition from v. 5 to v. 6. It speaks of people suffering from the plight of famine whose food is unfit to offer to God because of its poor quality and because it comes from an environment where death and contact with the dead are common. At the same time, it introduces a situation in which economic refugees, people who "come from devastation," would go down to Egypt just as Abraham had once done.

Following this interpretation, "Egypt will gather them, and Memphis will bury them" describes how famine-ravaged Israelites would seek for deliverance in Egypt. The Egyptians would receive them, but the outcome would not be as the Israelites had supposed. They would not survive but would die in Egypt and be buried there. This probably alludes to Jacob's determination not to be buried in Egypt (Gen 47:29) and, since the Northern Kingdom was dominated by the tribe of Ephraim, to Joseph's body being placed in a coffin in Egypt to await removal to the promised land (Exod 13:19). Unlike their ancestors, the Israelites of Hosea's day would forfeit their Israelite heritage in seeking refuge in Egypt.

The following line, however, is very difficult in Hebrew. "Their treasures

---

[43] The word is simply הלך, "to go/come." Hebrew has other words that mean "flee" or "escape," such as נוס, ברח, and פלט.

[44] The word כי by itself can under certain circumstances mean "although," but the particle הִנֵּה points to reality and virtually excludes a concessive meaning, although by itself הִנֵּה can occasionally describe a simple protasis (e.g., Exod 3:13). The number of cases where כִּי הִנֵּה means "For, behold" are legion; e.g., Judg 13:15; Isa 3:1; 26:21; 60:2; 65:17–18; 66:15; Jer 1:15; 8:17; 25:29; 30:3,10; 34:7; 45:5; 46:27; 49:15; 50:9; Joel 4:1 (Eng. 3:1); Amos 4:2.

of silver will be taken over by briers" makes little sense. If "treasures of silver" were lying around in a place where briers could grow up around them, surely someone would carry the silver off. One might speak of cities and palaces being left in ruin and overrun with weeds, but not treasures. The troublesome line actually reads, "A prized possession for their silver."[45] Rather than try to connect this to the weeds mentioned in the following line, one should take this to be a sarcastic response to seeking safety in Egypt: the prized possession that the refugees obtained for silver (that they presumably gave to the Egyptians) was burial in Egypt. This also serves as a reversal of the "plundering of the Egyptians" in the exodus story (Exod 12:35–36). Indeed, this entire text can be taken to be an undoing of the exodus and thus an erasure of Israel's redemption history. Also the statement that Memphis (the Egyptians) would bury Israelites may imply that opportunists, taking advantage of the desperation of the refugees, would actually kill them after they had stolen all they could. The "tents" that would be overrun with weeds and thistles refer to the tents that were used in their flight to Egypt, tents that would be abandoned when the owners had died. One might therefore suggest the following translation for this strophe:

> Do not pour out libations to Yahweh!
>> And their sacrifices will not be pleasing to him,
> Their (offerings) are like the bread of mourners,
>> All who eat it spread uncleanness.[46]
> For their bread is for their survival;
>> It shall not enter the house of Yahweh. (v. 4)
> What will you do for the day of assembly,
>> or the day of Yahweh's festival? (v. 5)
>> For behold, they come from devastation.
> Egypt will gather them, and Memphis will bury them:
>> A prized possession for their silver!
> Weeds will possess them, and thorns will overrun their tents. (v. 6)

9:7–9 Once again Hosea has taxed translators to the limit with his elliptical style, a style that is at the same time both allusive and elusive. Interpreters differ over the syntactical structure of parts of this text, and some propose emendations.[47] On the other hand, this is one text where Hosea has given us

---

[45] This simply translates מַחְמַד לְכַסְפָּם literally. Scholars have naturally proposed emendations for this text. E.g., Ward (*Hosea,* 160) emends מחמד to מעמד and takes it to mean "a pedestal for their silver (idol)."

[46] The *piel* stem of טמא means to "spread uncleanness," not to be defiled, although obviously it is those who are defiled who spread it.

[47] E.g., Stuart reads יָרִיעוּ ("they cry out") for MT יָדְעוּ ("they know") in v. 7 and reads עַם ("people") for עַם ("with") in v. 8 (*Hosea-Jonah*). Wolff deletes נָבִיא ("prophet") from v. 8 (*Hosea,* 157).

clear parallelism, which helps when trying to clarify its meaning. One should begin with the structure of the text and develop the interpretation of difficult lines from there. The structure, if one follows the accentuation of the MT, is as follows:

A1   Days of punishment have come,
A2   Days of retribution have come.
    —Let Israel know—
B1   The prophet is a fool
B2   The man of the Spirit is mad,
C1   because your iniquity is abundant,
C2   and (because of) the abundance of your hatred. (v. 7)
B1′ Ephraim's watchman is with my God,[48]
B2′ And a prophet is a fowler's snare upon all his [Ephraim's] ways.
C1′   Hatred is in the house of his God! (v. 8)
C2′   They have deeply corrupted themselves
    —as in the days of Gibeah.
A1′ He shall remember their iniquity,
A2′ He shall deal with their sin. (v. 9)

In this text we have six couplets arranged in a pattern A-B-C-B′-C′-A′. The two couplets A1-A2 and A1′-A2′ are both general assertions that punishment is coming. In both the second line closely parallels the first. The two couplets B and B′ both concern the prophet, who is described as a "prophet," a "man of the Spirit," and a "watchman of Ephraim." The NIV, like many other modern versions, has obscured this parallel structure by making "prophet" in B2′ the subject of line B1′ and then attaching B2′ to C1′. This has the effect of destroying the parallelism in each of the three bicola B1′- B2′, C1′- C2′, and A1′-A2′ (cp. KJV).

The two bicola C1-C2 and C1′-C2′, as presented here, both concern the depravity of Israel, variously described as "hatred" (using the same word in C2 and C1′), "iniquity," and deep corruption. The phrase "as in the days of Gibeah," which has no parallel elsewhere in the text, provides ballast to match the extra clause, "Let Israel know," in v. 7. Taking the text in this way, we see strong parallels within each bicolon and between each of the three pairs of matched bicola. Also B1-B2 and B1′-B2′ together give us the chiastic structure "prophet . . ., man of the Spirit . . ., watchman . . ., prophet." Similarly, C1- C2 and C1′-C2′ have the pattern "iniquity . . ., hatred . . ., hatred . . ., corrupted."

---

[48] Although it is grammatically conceivable that נָבִיא in this verse is the subject of a verbless clause with צֹפֶה אֶפְרַיִם עִם־אֱלֹהָי as the predicate, the sense is quite unnatural. Keil (*Hosea*, 123) observes that "the idea of a prophet standing with Jehovah upon a watchtower is not only quite foreign to the OT but is irreconcilable with the relation in which the prophets stood to Jehovah." Adhering to the MT, נָבִיא is joined to what follows it and not to what precedes it.

It appears that the people widely regarded the prophets as mad because of their trances and ecstasies (cf. 1 Sam 10:11; 2 Kgs 3:15) and that "the prophet is a fool, the man of the Spirit is mad" was a popular taunt of the prophets. Hosea, however, takes this taunt and turns it around against Israel. He in effect says: "Yes, the prophets are crazy. You have driven them to it with your sin and hostility!" In the parallel couplet, B1'- B2', he affirms that notwithstanding the appearance that the prophets are crazy, God is with them. Thus they will be vindicated. The term "watchman," as a metaphor for a prophet, is quite familiar from the prophetic corpus (Jer 6:17; Ezek 3:17; 33:2,6–7). Similarly, prophets are described metaphorically as tools or weapons of Yahweh. In Jer 15:20 Jeremiah is called a "wall of bronze" against the people. In Isa 8:14 Yahweh himself is called a "snare and a trap" for the inhabitants of Jerusalem. The point in this text is that the prophets, in speaking to the unrepentant people, would not be the means of their salvation but of their downfall, similar to Paul's understanding of his own ministry as the "smell of death" to those who are perishing (2 Cor 2:15–16). The prophets are a snare to the people (and not the other way around, as the NIV indicates).

The phrase "as in the days of Gibeah" apparently alludes to the grisly story of Judges 19–21, in which a Levite's concubine was raped and murdered at Gibeah. The Levite, to obtain vengeance, cut her body into twelve pieces, sent the pieces to the tribes of Israel to provoke their outrage, and so began a civil war and a series of grotesque atrocities. Hosea declares that the people of his day have fallen to the level of this most corrupt generation of Israel's history.

> ¹⁰"When I found Israel,
>   it was like finding grapes in the desert;
> when I saw your fathers,
>   it was like seeing the early fruit on the fig tree.
> But when they came to Baal Peor,
>   they consecrated themselves to that shameful idol
>   and became as vile as the thing they loved.
> ¹¹Ephraim's glory will fly away like a bird—
>   no birth, no pregnancy, no conception.
> ¹²Even if they rear children,
>   I will bereave them of every one.
> Woe to them
>   when I turn away from them!
> ¹³I have seen Ephraim, like Tyre,
>   planted in a pleasant place.
> But Ephraim will bring out
>   their children to the slayer."
>
> ¹⁴Give them, O LORD—
>   what will you give them?

Give them wombs that miscarry
    and breasts that are dry.

¹⁵"Because of all their wickedness in Gilgal,
    I hated them there.
Because of their sinful deeds,
    I will drive them out of my house.
I will no longer love them;
    all their leaders are rebellious.
¹⁶Ephraim is blighted,
    their root is withered,
    they yield no fruit.
Even if they bear children,
    I will slay their cherished offspring."

¹⁷My God will reject them
    because they have not obeyed him;
    they will be wanderers among the nations.

DIVINE COMPLAINT: BARRENNESS INSTEAD OF FRUIT (9:10–17). In this text Yahweh declares his dismay at the apostasy of Israel to the Baal of the shrine of Baal Peor and his anger over the sins at Gilgal. Infertility and the death of children dominate this section. This emphasis reflects the Baal cult, a religion that was purported to guarantee fertility for people, their livestock, and their crops alike. This text thus reflects the warnings in 2:4–9, which say that Yahweh would have no pity on Israel's children and that he would eradicate the agricultural benefits supposedly conferred by Baal. Following 9:1–9, which describes famine conditions, this text goes a step further and foresees not just the ruin of crops but the obliteration of the next generation of Israelites.

In structure this text is made up of two parts that parallel each other, as follows:

A Sin of Baal Peor (v. 10)
   B1 Ephraim saying (vv. 11–12)
   B2 Ephraim saying (v. 13)
      C Prophetic interjection (v. 14)
A′ Sin of Gilgal (v. 15)
   B′ Ephraim saying (v. 16)
      C′ Prophetic interjection (v. 17)

In both parts Yahweh begins with a condemnation of Israel for sins at a certain location and with a promise of punishment to come ("A" sections). Then each of the "B" sections describes the coming barrenness of "Ephraim," each giving that name prominence in the Hebrew text. Finally, both of the "C" sections are prophetic interjections that consent to Yahweh's decree. Verse 17, in addition, serves as a transition from this account of Yahweh's complaints to the next passage, 10:1–8, containing a prophetic complaint.[49]

On the other hand, it is a measure of the complexity of Hosea's literary technique that this section also has an underlying chiastic structure, as follows:

A Israel found in the desert (v. 10a)
  B Israel apostatizes from God (v. 10b)
    C Ephraim barren; even if they bear children, God will slay them
        (vv. 11–12)
      D Comparison to Tyre; children go to "slayer" (v. 13)
        E Prophet's prayer (v. 14)
      D′ Sin at Gilgal; people expelled and leaders stubborn (v. 15)
    C′ Ephraim barren; even if they rear children, God will slay them (v. 16)
  B′ Israel disobeys God and is rejected (v. 17a)
A′ Israel a wanderer among the nations (v. 17b)[50]

Here the prophet's prayer is the pivotal point of the chiasmus, which implies that the prayers of the prophets played a significant role in the extent and timing of God's judgments on Israel and the nations. The prophets were more than mere spokesmen, who only announced what Yahweh told them, but were also partners with Yahweh in ministry and judgment (see also Amos 7:1–9).

9:10 One does not expect to find edible grapes in the desert, and such a discovery would make a real feast for a Bedouin traveler. Similarly, the first fruits of a fig tree in spring would be especially delicious to people in the ancient world. This is because they did not transport produce over long distances, as we do, and could not enjoy any fruit except when it was locally in season. Figs would have been especially delightful to people who had not had any for almost a year; by the end of the season, when everyone had eaten their fill of figs, the pleasure would have worn off.[51] The point of both metaphors is that Israel in her youth was a special source of delight to God.

The mood of the verse abruptly turns: the people went to Baal Peor and consecrated themselves to "shame" (NIV paraphrases this as "that shameful idol"). The Hebrew word for "shame," *bošet*, is a contemptuous sobriquet that Hebrew scribes came to substitute regularly for the name Baal. For example, the scribes transformed the name Ish-baal ("man of Baal," found in 1 Chr 8:33) into Ish-bosheth ("man of shame," found in 2 Sam 2:8). Possibly it was

---

[49] Note that in the MT both vv. 16 and 17 end with the paragraph marker ס. This peculiar isolation of v. 17 indicates its transitional status.

[50] This chiastic analysis is a modification of that found in Andersen and Freedman, *Hosea*, 539.

[51] There is thus no need to delete by emendation the pleonastic בְּרֵאשִׁיתָהּ, "at her beginning." The text is emphasizing that this is the first of the harvest. The words may mean that this is the first crop this particular tree has ever given, a fact that would make the crop all the more special.

this text of Hosea that gave rise to this practice.[52] At any rate, there is little doubt that the cult of Baal is in view here.

Baal Peor was the location of a shrine to Baal in the plains of Moab some twenty kilometers (twelve miles) northeast of the Dead Sea. According to Num 25:1–9, after Balaam failed in his efforts to bring a curse down on Israel, the Israelites brought one down on themselves by yielding to the enticement to have sexual relations with Moabite women who were sacred prostitutes in the cult of Baal Peor. A plague began in Israel, and the plague did not come to a stop until the priest Phinehas took a spear and ran it through the bodies of an Israelite man and a Moabite woman whom he had apparently caught *flagrante delicto*. The biblical allusion serves at least two purposes here. First, it reminds the reader that Israel had already begun its apostasy to Baal before it even entered the promised land.[53] Second, it shows the kind of drastic steps that had to be taken to put this kind of immorality to a halt.[54]

Many interpreters emend the Hebrew text to obtain a reading such as, "They became as vile as their lover." This is not appropriate here.[55] On the other hand, the NIV rendering, "They became as vile as the thing they loved," is difficult to justify. A better translation is, "They became vile, like their love."[56] That is, their love was itself vile; the more they loved the cult and its prostitutes, the more depraved they became. There was a direct relationship between how far a man became involved with Baal Peor and how apostate and decadent he became.

Psalm 106:28–30 also tells the story of apostasy at Baal Peor. It states: "They yoked themselves to the Baal of Peor / and ate sacrifices offered to life-

---

[52] Cf. Wolff, *Hosea,* 165.

[53] This implies that for Hosea the conflict between Baal and Yahweh was a theological struggle for the soul of the nation that had existed as long as Israel itself. This implication contradicts some modern reconstructions that argue that rejection of Baalism as an essentially religious issue did not emerge until Elijah issued his challenge, "Yahweh or Baal!" Cf. F. E. Eakin, Jr., "Yahwism and Baalism Before the Exile," *JBL* 84 (1965): 407–14.

[54] G. R. Boudreau argues that Hos 9:10 does not refer to the Num 25 incident primarily on the basis of a formal analysis, which to me is not persuasive ("Hosea and the Pentateuchal Traditions," JSOTSup 173 [Sheffield: Academic Press, 1993]: 121–32).

[55] E.g., Mays (*Hosea,* 131) and Stuart (*Hosea-Jonah,* 149) emend to כְּדֹדָם, "their lover." This is an unlikely emendation. Since the subject הֵמָּה is masculine plural, it would require a feminine plural participle for "lovers" rather than the masculine singular of the emendation. Of course, one can argue that the "lover" is Baal, but this would require that Baal's counterpart be "Israel," construed metaphorically as a woman, and not the masculine plural הֵמָּה. In addition, the allusion to the Baal Peor incident implies that the text has in view individual men who went to prostitutes, and not Israel viewed collectively as a woman.

[56] The infinitive construct כְּאָהֳבָם does not refer to a person or thing that was loved but to the act of loving itself, and the suffix must be considered subjective, not objective. Hence the preposition כְּ sets up a proportional relationship here. Alternatively, it could be a temporal clause meaning "they became vile as soon as they loved (prostitutes)."

less gods; // they provoked the Lord to anger by their wicked deeds, / and a plague broke out among them. // But Phinehas stood up and intervened, / and the plague was checked." It is curious that the sin the psalmist chose to specify was not sacred prostitution but eating food offered as a sacrifice to the dead. Furthermore, the psalm goes on to describe the child sacrifice associated with the Baal cults in vv. 36–38: "They worshiped their idols, / which became a snare to them. // They sacrificed their sons / and their daughters to demons. // They shed innocent blood, / the blood of their sons and daughters, // whom they sacrificed to the idols of Canaan, / and the land was desecrated by their blood." The psalm thus brings out the hideous paradox of the fertility cult: a major objective of the cult was to enable women to give birth to many healthy children, but that same cult consumed children in ritual sacrifice. Hosea, however, does not explicitly charge the Israelites with conducting child sacrifice, although one might suggest that the judgment of barrenness, v. 11, is a response to such atrocities.

9:11–12   The opening line should be translated, "Ephraim! Just as a flock of birds scatters in flight,[57] so their glory (shall depart)."[58] One might suppose that the "glory" that will depart from Israel is their wealth and power or even their children, but context implies that it is Yahweh himself. These two verses themselves are a minichiasmus, as follows:

A   Ephraim's glory departs (v. 11a)
   B   No successful pregnancies (v. 11b)
   B′ Even if they raise children, God will take them (v. 12a)
A′ God will turn from[59] them (v. 12b)

This being the structure of the text, it is certain that the "glory" in v. 11 is Yahweh himself who will abandon them. The metaphor of birds flying away implies that Yahweh's departure will be as sudden and as impossible to prevent as is the abrupt taking to the air of a startled flock of birds. The text emphasizes the departure of Yahweh in order to make the point that it is he, not Baal, who has given them successful pregnancies[60] and healthy, thriving children. Without God's aid their children will languish.[61] Once again Hosea uses the rhetorical device of the pseudosorites (see comments at 5:6 and 8:7):

---

[57] The word עוֹף is here collective for a flock of birds and is not a single bird. The curious *hitpolel* יִתְעוֹפֵף seems to mean "to scatter in flight." See *HALOT*, 801.

[58] The NIV's somewhat paraphrasing translation, while not incorrect, has obscured the grammatical parallels between v. 11a and v. 13. See discussion below.

[59] The form שׁוּר probably is an alternative for the verb סוּר, "turn aside."

[60] With virtually all commentaries and translations, it is best to take the מִן in the line מִלֵּדָה וּמִבֶּטֶן וּמֵהֵרָיוֹן as privative. Note that the sequence "no giving birth, and no gestation, and no getting pregnant" reverses the natural order of things.

[61] Cf. Hubbard: "It is Yahweh's vital presence that makes possible the cycles of life" (*Hosea*, 166).

the Israelites will not have successful pregnancies, and even if they do, the children will not survive.[62]

9:13 This verse is extremely difficult in Hebrew, and various emendations have been proposed.[63] The NIV also seems to work from an emended text.[64] But the verse can be translated without emendation as, "Ephraim! Just as I saw of[65] Tyre—(that it was a fig tree[66]) planted in a meadow, so too, Ephraim [is] to lead out his children to the slayer." Another possibility that avoids emendation is: "Ephraim! As when I provided for[67] Tyre (that it be) planted in a meadow, / so too Ephraim (is) to lead out his children to the slayer."[68] Either way the verse is highly elliptical, but it draws a comparison between Tyre and Ephraim, and the structure implies that each half of the verse supplies missing information for the other so that what is true of one is also true of the other. Both Tyre and Ephraim were "planted" in advantageous circumstances, but both embraced the Baal cult, and both would receive due punishment.

Tyre was "planted in a meadow" in the sense of having been placed in very favorable conditions (this is a metaphor and not a description of the geography of Tyre). In the same way, Ephraim had been favored by God. But now

---

[62] Cf. Andersen and Freedman, *Hosea,* 538.

[63] E.g., Mays, following the LXX ὃν τρόπον εἶδον, εἰς θήραν παρέστησαν τὰ τέκνα αὐτῶν, translates the line as, "Ephraim, as I have seen, has made his sons a hunter's prey" (*Hosea,* 131). So too Wolff, *Hosea,* 160. But Stuart, on the basis of a series of emendations, translates, "Ephraim will be like a man who sees a siege set for him and for his children" (*Hosea-Jonah,* 148–49). Andersen and Freedman take לְצוֹר to mean "by the Rival," on the grounds that צוּר here means "rock" and stands for Baal as Yahweh's rival (*Hosea,* 544). They also take "planted in a meadow" to be a resumption of v. 10a. All in all, it is difficult to have confidence in these emendations and unusual translations.

[64] It is difficult to see how אֶפְרַיִם כַּאֲשֶׁר־רָאִיתִי לְצוֹר could mean "I have seen Ephraim, like Tyre," as in the NIV, although the full line could possibly be taken to mean "Ephraim, just as I have seen of Tyre, was planted in a meadow." However, the fact that שְׁתוּלָה is feminine implies that צוֹר is its antecedent since city names are generally feminine (*GBH* §134g), but אֶפְרַיִם is considered to be masculine here (note the suffix on בָּנָיו). The alternative (see below) is to supply another antecedent for שְׁתוּלָה. The NIV translators appear to have emended to something like אֶפְרַיִם רָאִיתִי כְצוֹר.

[65] Taking the לְ on לְצוֹר to be genitive.

[66] Taking תְּאֵנָה ("fig tree") to be the implied antecedent of שְׁתוּלָה; cf. v. 10, which also uses רָאִיתִי in a similar metaphor.

[67] לְ + רָאָה means "provide for." See Gen 22:8; 1 Sam 16:1,17. Cf. McComiskey ("Hosea," 1:150), who takes it to mean "choose for." See also McComiskey, "Hos 9:13 and the Integrity of the Masoretic Tradition in the Prophecy of Hosea," *JETS* 33 (1990): 155–60.

[68] This verse has the same elliptical style of v. 11a: "Ephraim! Like a flock of birds scatters in flight, so their glory (shall depart)." Here the words also begin with "Ephraim" in *casus pendens,* also move directly into a comparison, and also omit the finite verb in the main clause (in v. 11a we have no finite verb governing כְּבוֹדָם, and in this verse we have only the infinitive לְהוֹצִיא in the second line).

both states are sending their children to the "slayer," a term that refers primarily to Baal, to whom they were sacrificing their children. Tyre and the Phoenicians generally became notorious for their practice of child sacrifice, and Israel perhaps followed in their path. Secondarily, the "slayer" is the Assyrian army[69] and represents the judgment God gave these peoples for engaging in such a contemptible practice. That is, just as Tyre and Ephraim handed their children over to Baal for sacrifice, so God would hand these peoples over to their enemies. Shalmaneser V of Assyria laid siege to both Tyre and Samaria in about 724 B.C.; both cities fell to Sargon II in 722. We might give this verse a Targum-like paraphrase, as follows: "Ephraim! Just as I saw of Tyre *that it was well situated like a fig tree* planted in a meadow, *and yet it became a place of child sacrifice,* so too Ephraim, *although it was equally well situated,* will give its children to the 'slayer'—*first to their god, Baal, and then to the Assyrians.*"

9:14 Because they attributed their fertility to Baal, barrenness is the only appropriate judgment for Israel. Wolff takes the question, "What will you give them?" to mean that after deliberation, Hosea chose to ask God to punish Israel with the lesser of various punishments that he has laid out for the people.[70] But Andersen and Freedman probably are correct that it is a purely rhetorical question and virtually means "I know what you should give them."[71] Hosea is not trying to assuage Yahweh or dissuade him from punishing Israel. The curse on the breasts and the wombs of the women of Ephraim reverses the blessing of Jacob upon the Joseph tribes (Gen 49:25). The patriarch had called upon the God of the Fathers to give to Joseph's heirs "blessings of the breasts and of the womb." Hosea rhetorically undoes that blessing. This is not in any sense a prayer for mercy.[72]

9:15 The Hebrew of the first line of this verse reads, "All their evil is at Gilgal, for there I (came to) hate them."[73] The NIV, perhaps to avoid the misunderstanding that Yahweh by hating Israel caused them to sin at Gilgal, has inserted "because" at the beginning of the verse. Actually the verse means that Gilgal is the quintessential city of Israel—it contained every evil that the book of Hosea condemns. The text asserts that one can grasp how much evil was there when one recognizes that this was the city that prompted Yahweh to

---

[69] The term "slayer" (הֹרֵג) seems uniquely appropriate for describing both Baal and the Assyrians. In addition, the ambiguity of the elliptical infinitive לְהוֹצִיא indicates that we should seek layers of meaning in this line.

[70] Wolff, *Hosea,* 166. Mays also sees this as intercession (*Hosea,* 134–35).

[71] Andersen and Freedman, *Hosea,* 544.

[72] See D. Krause, "A Blessing Cursed: The Prophet's Prayer for Barren Womb and Dry Breasts in Hosea 9," in *Reading Between the Texts: Intertextuality and the Hebrew Bible,* ed. D. N. Fewell (Louisville: Westminster/John Knox, 1992), 191–202.

[73] Note the position of כִּי, preceding the second clause, not the first as required by the NIV rendering.

declare Israel his enemy. Gilgal is described as a cult center in 4:15 and 12:11. It was also the place where Saul's reign was inaugurated (1 Sam 11:15), and God's rejection of Saul probably serves here as a type for God's rejection of the northern monarchy. In effect, this part of the verse means "Every kind of evil that Israel practices can be found at Gilgal; you see,[74] that is where I came to hate them."

The statement that God would cast Israel out of his house and no longer love them because of their sin looks back to the metaphor of Israel the adulterous wife. The final line, "all their leaders are rebellious," seems incongruous. However, Gilgal's role as a type for the northern monarchy because of its historical significance in the reign of Saul, as described above, probably explains why the text would suddenly say a word about Israel's leaders. In addition, the word translated "rebellious" is found in one other text of Hosea, at 4:16, in another context that concerns Gilgal.[75]

9:16 Again a metaphor of Hosea has a double meaning. The words "Ephraim is blighted,[76] their root is withered, they yield no fruit,"[77] taken literally, describe famine conditions and the failure of the Baal cult to secure a good harvest. Metaphorically, however, "fruit" refers to children, as is made explicit in the second half of the verse.[78] This verse echoes vv. 11–13.

9:17 As described above, "they will be wanderers among the nations," in the chiastic structure of this passage, corresponds to Yahweh's finding of Israel like grapes in the desert. In effect, they have been returned to their original status as outsiders and wanderers (Deut 26:5).

[1]**Israel was a spreading vine;**
   he brought forth fruit for himself.
As his fruit increased,
   he built more altars;
as his land prospered,
   he adorned his sacred stones.
[2]**Their heart is deceitful,**
   and now they must bear their guilt.
The LORD will demolish their altars

---

[74] In other words, the כִּי here is explanatory and not causal. It serves to notify the reader of the notorious position Gilgal occupies among the cities of Israel.

[75] See 4:15 for Gilgal. In 4:16 סָרַר is generally translated "stubborn."

[76] In context the NIV is correct to translate הֻכָּה אֶפְרַיִם ("Ephraim has been struck") in an agricultural sense.

[77] Wolff (*Hosea,* 168) points out that there is a pun here on אֶפְרַיִם ("Ephraim"), that it will bear no פְּרִי ("fruit").

[78] A curiosity here is that "womb" has a masculine plural suffix (בִטְנָם). The point seems to be that this is not a punishment directed specifically at the women but at all the people. Cf. Andersen and Freedman, *Hosea,* 546.

and destroy their sacred stones.

[3]Then they will say, "We have no king
  because we did not revere the LORD.
But even if we had a king,
  what could he do for us?"
[4]They make many promises,
  take false oaths
  and make agreements;
therefore lawsuits spring up
  like poisonous weeds in a plowed field.
[5]The people who live in Samaria fear
  for the calf-idol of Beth Aven.
Its people will mourn over it,
  and so will its idolatrous priests,
those who had rejoiced over its splendor,
  because it is taken from them into exile.
[6]It will be carried to Assyria
  as tribute for the great king.
Ephraim will be disgraced;
  Israel will be ashamed of its wooden idols.
[7]Samaria and its king will float away
  like a twig on the surface of the waters.
[8]The high places of wickedness will be destroyed—
  it is the sin of Israel.
Thorns and thistles will grow up
  and cover their altars.
Then they will say to the mountains, "Cover us!"
  and to the hills, "Fall on us!"

PROPHETIC COMPLAINT: THE VINE AND THE BULL (10:1–8).   In this text Hosea condemns Israel first under the metaphor of the destructive vine (vv. 1–4) and then with his focus on the bull-image at Bethel (vv. 5–8). Idolatry dominates both halves of the passage; this is not a text that primarily concerns social disorder, although there are references to the king. The central issues are Baalism and apostasy at the shrine of Bethel. Once again the meaning of the Hebrew is quite controversial. In order to facilitate the reader's understanding of the interpretations advocated in this commentary, a separate translation and outline are again useful.

Israel the Destructive/Poisonous Plant

A Sin = bad fruit:	Israel is a destructive vine; it makes fruit for itself.	
B Pagan worship:	The more there was for its fruit, the more abundant were its altars.	

| | | As it went well for its land, they enhanced their sacred pillars. (v. 1) |

C Cunning hearts: Their hearts are wily; the time has come for them to bear their guilt.

D Punishment: He shall break their altars and shall demolish their sacred pillars. (v. 2)

E Israel says: Indeed, they now are saying,

F "No" king: "We have no king!
                    For we do not fear Yahweh!
                    And a king, what will he do for us"? (v. 3)

E Israel says: They speak words—

G Empty devotion: hollow oaths to make a covenant!

H Wild plants: Like a poisonous plant in furrows of a field, (Israel's) "justice" sprouts up. (v. 4)

The Bull of Bethel

A Sin = bull idol: The populace of Samaria trembles at the bull of Beth Aven.

B Pagan worship: Indeed, my people mourn over it, and their shamans exult over it, over its glory.

D Punishment: Surely it shall go into exile from them. (v. 5)
                    Yes, (they shall take) it to Assyria.
                    It shall be carried as an offering to the Great King.

C Cunning plan: Ephraim shall get disgrace, Israel shall be ashamed of its counsel. (v. 6)

F Weak king: Samaria is destroyed; her king is like a stick on the surface of water. (v. 7)

D Punishment: The high places of Aven, the Sin of Israel, will be exterminated.

H Wild plants: Thornbush and thistle will grow up on their altars,

E Israel says: And they shall say to the mountains,

D Punishment: "Cover us!"

E Israel says: And to the hills (they shall say),

D Punishment: "Fall on us!" (v. 8)

10:1–4 Verses 1–4 describe Israel as a vine that fails to give good fruit and that instead serves only itself. This image is another version of the familiar metaphor of Israel the vineyard of Yahweh. The most famous example of this image is the "Song of the Vineyard" in Isa 5:1–7, in which Yahweh looks for good grapes from his vineyard but gets only bad ones. Seeking "justice" *(mišpāṭ)* and "righteousness," he found only violence. As a result he will destroy his vineyard. Hosea's text begins with Israel described as a "destructive vine" that yields fruit only for itself. Specifically, Israel uses its fruit to build altars and shrines to the fertility cult, has a hollow devotion to Yahweh, and refuses to acknowledge him as king. The text ends (v. 4) with the vine yielding only poisonous fruit as its "justice" *(mišpāṭ)*.

At the beginning of v. 1 most translations (like the NIV) say that Israel was a "spreading" or "luxuriant" vine. This interpretation is based on the Greek translation[79] and an Arabic cognate, and it is the only place in the Old Testament where *bāqaq* is translated this way. It normally means to "lay waste."[80] Translators no doubt feel that the rendering "lay waste" is impossible here, but in fact vines can be very destructive of other flora, as residents of the southeastern United States who are familiar with kudzu know well. In this sense there is not much difference between a "luxuriantly growing" vine and a "destructive" vine. Furthermore, gardeners understand that a luxuriantly growing plant is not necessarily the one that produces the best or most abundant fruit (hence the need for pruning). In the context of this verse, moreover, this line is part of Yahweh's complaint against Israel, and a negative sense is appropriate. Whether one takes this clause to mean "destructive" or "luxuriantly growing," the point is not that the plant was very fruitful.

This is made clear in the second clause, which many versions render as something like "which yields its fruit." In fact, the line means that the vine yields fruit "for itself."[81] Even translated this way, however, it is easy to miss the significance of the metaphor. A vintner does not look for a vine to yield fruit for the benefit of the vine but for the benefit of the harvest he will receive. A vine that yields fruit "for itself" is only taking up space that should be used by productive plants, as in Jesus' parable of the fig tree in Luke 13:7. Thus Israel is a destructive vine in that it takes up valuable soil, crowds out productive plants, and gives benefit only to itself and not to its owner.

Hosea develops the point of this analogy in what follows: "The more there was for its fruit, the more abundant were its altars." Here most translations

---

[79] The LXX has Ἄμπελος εὐκληματοῦσα ("luxuriantly growing vine").

[80] בקק has this meaning in the *qal* stem at Isa 24:1; Nah 2:3; Jer 19:7, and in the *piel* stem at Jer 51:2. In the *niphal* stem it means "to be laid waste" at Isa 19:3 and 24:3.

[81] On לוֹ meaning "for himself/itself" see Gen 14:11; Exod 21:8; Lev 9:8; Deut 17:16–17.

have something like the NIV, "As his fruit increased." The Hebrew, however, does not say that the "fruit" increased but that the conditions for bearing fruit improved.[82] That is, the point of the verse is that circumstances for fruit production were optimal; it was good soil, weeded and fertilized, and rain and other weather conditions were just right. But instead of good fruit, Israel yielded bad, self-serving fruit: the altars to Baal and the fertility cults. Thus the main point is not that the altars were built and improved because Israel had a good harvest and used their disposable income on shrines (although this might be implied as well); rather, it is that *the shrines are themselves the fruit that Israel (metaphorically) yielded.*

Verse 2, which has as its premise that the heart of the people is deceitful, is a non sequitur unless one reads v. 1 as described above. That is, it is difficult to see any connection between an "abundant harvest" (implied in the traditional interpretation) and false hearts. However, if one takes v. 1 to describe Israel as a false vine that deceives its owner by yielding false fruit, then the complaint about their false hearts makes sense. God will thus destroy their "fruit"—that is, their shrines and sacred pillars. Although the Hebrew does not require this interpretation, it is possible that here the pillars (*maṣṣēbâ*; NIV, "sacred stones") are the kind of phallic images common to fertility cults throughout the ancient world.

In v. 3 the primary thing that the people are saying is, "We have no king." This should not be taken to refer exclusively or even primarily to a human king, nor does it imply that the setting for these words is after the destruction of the monarchy by the Assyrians, as the NIV implies ("We have no king because we did not revere the Lord"). Taken that way, the Israelites seem to be confessing that Yahweh was just to demolish their kingdom; but what follows, "And a king, what will he do for us?" indicates that the Israelites are indifferent about the matter of having a king. These are not words of regret but of rejection of authority. The words "For we do not fear[83] Yahweh" mean that they also do not speak of Yahweh as their king because they have no reverence for him. It appears that the setting for these words is not after the fall of Samaria but the chaotic years after the death of Jeroboam II, when one Israelite general vied with another for control of the country and none could

---

[82] The phrase כְּרֹב לְפִרְיוֹ ("as there was abundance for its fruit") should not be taken to mean "as his fruit became abundant." Although one might argue that the לְ marks a genitive here, there is no reason at this point not to use an ordinary construct chain if that were the meaning. Wolff (*Hosea*, 170) takes both רֹב and טוֹב to be infinitives in order to sustain the common translation, but this strikes me as most unnatural and at any rate leaves the לְ on פְּרִי and אֶרֶץ unexplained. Andersen and Freedman recognize that the standard translation of this line is inadequate, but their attempt to take Yahweh as the implied subject (thus, "the more Yahweh multiplied his fruit") seems forced upon the Hebrew and does not yield good sense (*Hosea*, 550).

[83] The *qatal* (perfect) form יָרֵאנוּ should not be here taken as a past tense. Like יָדַע often does, יָרֵא in the *qatal* form here describes current action.

make any claim to being the legitimate ruling dynasty over Israel. In such a situation, no doubt, many people became cynical and considered this succession of royal pretenders to have no legitimate claim to the title of king. Even so, rather than become alarmed at the political instability, they simply declared that they were free of all royal rule, be it divine or human. In connection to the vineyard metaphor, this line constitutes the people's rejection of Yahweh's claim to their "fruit" and is analogous to the conspiracy of the workers in the vineyard in Jesus' parable (Matt 21:33–46).

Verse 4, in the NIV, indicates that Hosea is attacking the people for fraudulently making agreements and thus being very litigious toward one another. However, this interpretation depends upon translating *mišpāṭ* as "lawsuits" here, which is indefensible.[84] Rather, the word has its more common meaning, "justice." Also v. 4a should be rendered, "They speak words—hollow oaths to make a covenant!"[85] Contrary to what the NIV appears to imply, this verse has nothing to do with making legal contracts and business agreements. Rather, it is talking about the hollow repetition of covenant formulae before Yahweh. "They speak words" here contrasts verbal pretense with actual devotion of the heart (the NIV rendering, "They make many promises," reads far too much into the text). They go through the liturgical declarations of fealty to Yahweh, but these mean nothing to them. They do not fear him.

In this situation the "justice" they yield, the fruit that Yahweh seeks (as in Isa 5:1–7), turns out to be not good fruit but poisonous fruit. The metaphor of the poisonous plant is not of a plant that proliferates rapidly, like the supposed lawsuits of the NIV, but of a plant that gives dangerous, inedible fruit. The simile describes a farmer who goes out to the field he has plowed and planted expecting to find a good crop but finds a poisonous plant growing there instead. The word used for "poisonous plant" here *(rō'š)* is generic, but it may refer to the poisonous gourd plant of 2 Kgs 4:39, *Citrullus colocynthis L.* This plant is a trailing vine whose fruit is dangerously purgative; it may be mentioned also in Deut 32:32 as the "vine of Sodom" with "grapes of poison."[86] Israel is thus a destructive, deceptive vine, serving only itself and

---

[84] The word מִשְׁפָּט can mean "lawsuit"; but for "lawsuits" to be the intention here, it should have been plural rather than singular. The translation "a lawsuit springs up," as though Hosea had some specific lawsuit in mind, is most unlikely.

[85] In דִּבְּרוּ דְבָרִים אָלוֹת שָׁוְא כָּרֹת בְּרִית there is only one finite verb; דִּבְּרוּ. אָלוֹת and כָּרֹת are often taken as infinitive absolute forms serving as finite verbs, but it would seem that if this were the intent, two more finite forms would be employed in parallel to דִּבְּרוּ. Furthermore, interpreted in this manner the line literally means "They speak words, they swear vainly, they make a covenant," and this makes little sense unless it is subjected to paraphrase or expansion. The NIV paraphrase, "They make many promises, take false oaths and make agreements," is typical. It is better to take אָלוֹת as a plural of the noun אָלָה in apposition to דְּבָרִים. The infinitive absolute כָּרֹת serves as a gerund.

[86] *ISBE*, rev., s.v. "Poison," 899–900.

yielding the false fruit of impiety, hypocrisy, and paganism.

10:5–8   The second part of the passage turns to the bull-image[87] at Bethel, before which, the text says, Israel trembles in reverence. But the bull can only lead the people into Assyrian exile. From the outline of this passage given in the chart on p. 205, one can see that vv. 5–8 have a number of parallels to vv. 1–4. Both begin with a general statement of the sin of the nation; first it is the vine analogy, but here it is the bull-idol. Both then describe the pagan worship of Israel and the punishment that shall come. Furthermore, both assert that the cunning of the Israelites will be exposed (vv. 2,6b). Also, whereas in the vine text the people declare that they have no king (v. 3), v. 7 similarly presents them as a nation under a weak king. In addition, both texts describe what the people are saying: first, it is cynicism and hypocrisy (vv. 3–4), and second, it is panic and despair (v. 8b). Finally, the desolation of the pagan altars in v. 8a, when they are covered with weeds and thistles, appropriately looks back to the metaphor of vv. 1–4: Israel had been a well-plowed, carefully managed field, but it yielded only the poisonous fruit of paganism. As a result, God would allow the field to be overrun with weeds that would consume the destructive vine of the fertility cult.

In v. 5, in the NIV (and some other translations), the people are in a panic over the fate of their calf-idol because it has been taken into exile. This is almost certainly incorrect. The text should be rendered: "The populace of Samaria trembles at the bull of Beth Aven. / Indeed, my people mourn over it, and their shamans[88] exult over it, over its glory." The terms "tremble," "mourn," and "exult" do not describe anxiety over the well-being of their idol. Instead, they are here part of the vocabulary of the fertility cult. The people were in awe of Baal[89] but ritually mourned for him in commemoration of his battle with Mot (death) and his descent into the underworld.[90] Self-mutilation may well have accompanied this mourning. Then they gave themselves over to ecstasies,

---

[87] Following the Gk. text (τῷ μόσχῳ) and almost all modern interpreters, it probably is best to read לְעֵגֶל ("to the bull") instead of the MT לְעֶגְלוֹת ("to heifers"). Note also that the relevant pronouns are masculine singular (e.g., עָלָיו). It is possible that עֶגְלוֹת is not a scribal error (which is somewhat difficult to explain) but is a deliberate use of a diminutive meant to cast contempt on the bull-image.

[88] I have chosen the translation "shaman" for כֹּמֶר because the word is used of pagan and not orthodox priests.

[89] The term גּוּר means to "fear" and can be used for ceremonial worship (Ps 22:24, Eng. 23; 33:8). See also Wolff, *Hosea,* 175. The term is also used for the religious fear one might experience before a false prophet in Deut 18:22. Furthermore, the place name Gur-Baal (גּוּר־בָּעַל, 2 Chr 26:7), although taken by some to mean "sojourner of Baal," seems more likely to mean "the dread of Baal."

[90] The term אבל basically means to "mourn," as for a deceased loved one; but here, with the bull-idol as its object, it should be taken as cultic mourning and not as anxiety over what the Assyrians would do to the idol. The closest parallel in the OT is in Ezek 8:14, where the women of Jerusalem "weep for Tammuz," who was the Mesopotamian equivalent to Baal.

orgies, and Bacchic frenzy in order to awaken and celebrate the return of the god and of fertility.[91] Thus the mourning and the frenzied celebration describe the paganism for which the nation would be punished; it does not describe the response of the people to an exile that has already taken place.

The last clause of v. 5 should be translated, "Surely[92] it shall go into exile from them" and should be connected with v. 6, which concerns exile. This verse begins highly elliptically with a disconnected direct object "it," and one must supply something like "they shall take" to govern "it."[93] As in 5:13, Assyria is linked to the "great king."[94] Little is said here about the military subjugation of Samaria or the Assyrians' cruelty; all the emphasis is on the removal of the bull-idol. This would be of great disgrace to Israel because the bull of Bethel was to them such a significant religious object. Its removal signified more than the loss of wealth and treasures that paying tribute ordinarily entailed; its departure was a sign that their religion had failed them. Their response is not anxiety (as the NIV and other translations of v. 5 imply) but shame because their carefully crafted belief system has failed.[95]

The bull as a religious symbol has deep roots in ancient Near Eastern mythology. From Egypt statues of a bull represent Apis, god of fertility. Among the Canaanites, El, the high god of the pantheon, is often described as a bull. The bull was also sacred to the storm god Hadad, later worshiped as Baal; and here, too, the bull represented fertility. The most famous single incident of apostasy in the Old Testament concerns the making of the golden calf (Exod 32), a bull-image that was made of wood and overlaid with gold. Scholars have debated whether to the Israelites the bull represented Yahweh or an Egyptian god. It probably is best to regard the calf as an image of Yahweh that nevertheless reflected how heavily Israel had been influenced by the

---

[91] The term גּיל means to "rejoice" but, according to *HALOT*, 189, it is also a technical term of the Canaanite fertility cult. Here, with the subject being וּכְמָרָיו ("and his shamans"), a cultic meaning is virtually certain. None of the other attempts to deal with גּיל here is satisfactory. A number of scholars emend the verb (e.g., to יְלַל, "to howl"), but as Wolff observes, this runs counter to the unanimous transmission of the word (*Hosea*, 171). Andersen and Freedman argue that גּיל has a polar meaning, "to be in agony," but they have no credible evidence to support this peculiar translation (*Hosea*, 556–57). The word means "to celebrate" (usually in a religious sense). The NIV pluperfect, "those who had rejoiced over its splendor," is inappropriate for the *yiqtol* (imperfect) found here; one might also note that this cannot be a relative clause.

[92] The word כִּי need not be translated "because," and it does not here indicate that the exile of the bull is the cause for the mourning and celebration of the people and their priests. כִּי is a favorite particle of Hosea's (it appears some sixty-nine times in the book), and it by no means always carries the meaning "because." E.g., in v. 5 כִּי־אָבַל does not mean that their mourning (אבל) is the cause of their awe (גּור) over the idol. In כִּי־גָלָה it is deictic and "emphatic" (cf. *HALOT*, 470).

[93] Cf. Wolff, *Hosea*, 171. אוֹתוֹ cannot be connected with וּבָל, which is a passive verb. אוֹתוֹ here stands for the bull and not for כְּבוֹדוֹ ("its glory"). See McComiskey, "Hosea," 1:167.

[94] See 5:13 for a discussion of the title מֶלֶךְ יָרֵב.

[95] The NIV has needlessly emended עֵצָה ("counsel") to עָצָב ("idol"). The LXX has ἐν τῇ βουλῇ αὐτοῦ ("in his counsel"). See also comments on 10:13b.

environment of Egypt. Jeroboam's golden calves (1 Kgs 12:28–33) at Dan and Bethel appear in the Bible as the counterpart to the apostasy of the exodus generation. Some scholars, because the Decalogue explicitly forbids making an image of Yahweh, postulate that the bulls did not represent Yahweh himself but were simply his pedestals. While it is possible that such an interpretation may have provided the original rationale for making the bulls, it is quite clear in Hosea that the bulls are treated as representations of God and not merely as pedestals. One may wonder again whether the bulls represented Yahweh or Baal, and the answer probably is that the people merged the two in their minds. Thus they could worship at the bull shrines according to the theology of the Baal cult, but in their own minds they remained loyal to Yahweh.

That Hosea did not concern himself with the northern bull-shrine at Dan is curious. The priests of this shrine claimed descent from Moses' grandson Jonathan, and the shrine apparently remained active until the captivity (Judg 18:30). It fell with the rest of the northern territories before the armies of Tiglath-pileser (2 Kgs 15:29).

Verse 7 is another difficult verse. The verb found here, *dāmâ*, can be from one of three roots meaning either "to be similar," "to be silent," or "to destroy." It is difficult to know which to choose because the second line, "like a twig on the surface of the waters," does little to elucidate the text. A number of translators take the verse to mean "Samaria is destroyed; their king (is swept away) like a stick on the surface of the water."[96] On the other hand, nothing in the text implies that a verb such as "swept away" should be supplied, and "like a twig on the surface of the waters" is a bewildering metaphor for the defeat of a king or the destruction of a city. And the word "twig" is also questionable here.

Nevertheless, it appears that the best translation is, "Samaria is being destroyed, her king[97] [is] like a twig[98] on the surface of water." The point of

---

[96] See Wolff, *Hosea,* 171. Mays, *Hosea,* 138, reads, "From Samaria its king shall be eliminated / like a broken branch upon the torrent." The LXX translation, ἀπέρριψεν Σαμάρεια βασιλέα αὐτῆς ὡς φρύγανον ἐπὶ προσώπου ὕδατος ("Samaria has thrown away her king like tinder on the surface of water"), appears to be as speculative as many of its modern counterparts.

[97] Of itself נִדְמֶה שֹׁמְרוֹן מַלְכָּהּ appears to mean "Samaria resembles her king." BDB does not allow for דמה I, "to resemble," in the *niphal* stem; but see *HALOT,* 225; cf. Ezek 32:2. Neither דמה II ("be silent") nor דמה III ("be destroyed") makes any sense in conjunction with the noun מַלְכָּהּ ("her king") after שֹׁמְרוֹן. On the other hand, attestation for taking a *niphal* stem דמה in the sense "resemble" is slim, and one would expect to see כְּ before מַלְכָּהּ if that were the meaning (see Ezek 32:2). But one can disregard the MT accentuation and move מַלְכָּהּ to the second line, take דמה to mean "destroyed," and so translate, "Samaria is destroyed; her king is like a stick on the surface of water." Furthermore, the use of the *niphal* stem of דמה in Hos 10:15 all but requires that it here also mean "be destroyed." Andersen and Freedman (*Hosea,* 558) advocate that the clause means "The king of Samaria has been destroyed," but this requires that Hosea used some peculiar grammar (one would expect מֶלֶךְ שֹׁמְרוֹן if this were the meaning). The NIV "Samaria and its king will float away like a twig on the surface of the waters" is hard to justify and appears to be highly paraphrastic.

[98] This is the only place where קֶצֶף is translated "twig" or the like in the Bible. Elsewhere it always means "wrath" and generally refers to God's wrath. But "like wrath on the surface of water" leaves the reader entirely at a loss. Also the versions support the translation "twig" or "stick."

the metaphor is difficult to determine. A twig or branch can of course float on the surface of water, but floating of itself seems to have no relevance for Samaria and its king. As mentioned earlier, nothing in the text implies flood-waters or rapids; it simply says that the stick is "on the surface" of water. On the other hand, one thing that characterizes a stick on water, regardless of how rapidly the water moves, is that the stick is simply moved along with the water. That is, the stick is entirely subject to movements over which it has no control. Understood this way, both Samaria (the capital city) and the king within her have no power to affect historical events. The city will fall because its king is entirely subject to powers outside of his control. Taken this way, the line parallels the earlier assertion by the Israelites that they have "no king" (v. 3). Their point was not that they literally were without anyone on the throne but that the king had no real legitimacy and little power or hope of success. Such a king is like a stick on water in that he can exercise no con-trol over events.[99] A nation with such leadership is doomed.

In v. 8 Hosea's complaint concludes with a promise that Bethel (here called Aven or "wickedness") and its associated shrines[100] would be annihi-lated. The designation "the sin of Israel" for the Bethel shrine is similar to the constant refrain in Kings that the shrines at Dan and Bethel were the means by which Jeroboam son of Nebat "made Israel sin" (e.g., 2 Kgs 3:3). Thorns and thistles overrunning the altars remind the reader of the same fate that would befall the tents of the Israelites (9:6). The final, frantic call of the people for the hills to cover them, so familiar in apocalyptic texts, under-scores the folly of seeking protection from the bull of Bethel.

> [9]"Since the days of Gibeah, you have sinned, O Israel,
>   and there you have remained.
> Did not war overtake
>   the evildoers in Gibeah?
> [10]When I please, I will punish them;
>   nations will be gathered against them
>   to put them in bonds for their double sin.
> [11]Ephraim is a trained heifer
>   that loves to thresh;
> so I will put a yoke
>   on her fair neck.
> I will drive Ephraim,

---

[99] Cf. Stuart, *Hosea–Jonah*, 163.

[100] The plurals בָּמוֹת ("high places") and מִזְבְּחוֹתָם ("their altars") have been the occasion of some commentary. They probably refer to a cluster of local shrines that were associated with the main shrine of the bull at Bethel. The plurals do not require that one take אָוֶן in the ordinary sense "nothingness" nor as a reference to Bethel (contra Davies, *Hosea*, 240).

Judah must plow,
  and Jacob must break up the ground.
[12]Sow for yourselves righteousness,
  reap the fruit of unfailing love,
and break up your unplowed ground;
  for it is time to seek the LORD,
until he comes
  and showers righteousness on you.
[13]But you have planted wickedness,
  you have reaped evil,
  you have eaten the fruit of deception.
Because you have depended on your own strength
  and on your many warriors,
[14]the roar of battle will rise against your people,
  so that all your fortresses will be devastated—
as Shalman devastated Beth Arbel on the day of battle,
  when mothers were dashed to the ground with their children.
[15]Thus will it happen to you, O Bethel,
  because your wickedness is great.
When that day dawns,
  the king of Israel will be completely destroyed.

DIVINE COMPLAINT: MILITARY ARROGANCE (10:9–15). Yahweh concludes the first series of antiphonal complaints with a three-part text that draws together the warnings and accusations of 8:1–10:8 and reveals that Israel has nothing to look forward to but a complete military collapse. As befits a concluding text, however, it also appeals to the nation to repent and "sow righteousness" (v. 12). Yahweh claims that judgment must come because of two evils (10:10), although he does not specify what these are. Judging from this passage and the larger context, those two evils must be, first, an incompetent but arrogant and ambitious military and political establishment and, second, paganism and religious apostasy. Yahweh describes both evils in this text in an A-B-A pattern, as follows:

A	Israel's violent	From the days of Gibeah you have sinned, Israel; there you
	history and trust	remain.
	in military power	(They think that) war shall not reach them in Gibeah. (v. 9)
	and their defeat.	I come upon an unjust[101] people to punish them
		—and nations shall be gathered against them when they are

---

[101] With most interpreters, taking עַלְוָה (v. 9) to be a corruption by metathesis for עַוְלָה, "injustice," and taking בְּאַוָּתִי (v. 10) to be a corruption of בָּאתִי (LXX: ἦλθεν). The resulting line should be taken together to mean, "I come upon an unjust people." לֹא־תַשִּׂיגֵם (v. 9) already has an object and it should not be connected to עַל־בְּנֵי עַוְלָה.

punished[102]— for their two crimes. (v. 10)

B Israel a heifer;   Ephraim is a trained heifer that loves to thresh; I yoked[103] her
   an exhortation to   fine neck.
   righteousness.   I harness[104] Ephraim; Judah plows; Jacob does his tilling.
                              (v. 11)
                           Sow righteousness for yourself, and harvest a crop that befits
                              compassion!
                           Prepare the soil for yourselves—yes, it is time to seek
                              Yahweh—
                           until he comes that he may pour forth righteousness on you!
                              (v. 12)

A′ Israel's violent   You have plowed wickedness and reaped injustice. You eat
   history and trust   false fruit.
   in military power,   For you trust in your system,[105] and in the massive number
   and their defeat.   of your soldiers. (v. 13)
                           Calamity shall come upon your people, and all your
                              fortifications will be demolished,
                           Like Shalman's destruction of Beth Arbel, (where) mothers
                              were bludgeoned with (their) children. (v. 14)
                           Thus shall he do to you, Bethel, because of your absolute evil.
                           At dawn, the king of Israel will be totally destroyed. (v. 15)

10:9–10   The text again returns to Gibeah. In 5:8 Gibeah is the site of battle, where the military alarm resounds. In 9:9, in an allusion to Judges 19–20, Gibeah is remembered as the place of depravity and civil war. This text combines both features; the city typifies both the decadence of Israel and its dependence on military strength. The association of Gibeah with Saul, a king who relied heavily on force of arms but lacked David's devotion to Yahweh, reinforces this association.

Saul's Gibeah was a fortress-palace. The first major archaeological campaign there was conducted by W. F. Albright (1922, 1923, 1933), and further work was done by P. Lapp in 1964. The fortress had a wall some 1.2 millimeters thick, possibly of casemate type, and a tower.[106] The fortress fell into decay after the reign of David, and it does not seem to have had great mili-

---

[102] Most modern interpreters (e.g., Mays, *Hosea,* 143) emend the text here to a passive of יסר ("when they are punished"). Of itself בְּאָסְרָם can mean "when they capture." It is possible that the pointing should be emended to read a *pual* infinitive of אסר ("when they are captured"). Nevertheless, a passive of יסר appears to fit the context best.

[103] Reading עֲבַרְתִּי עֹל עַל for עָבַרְתִּי עַל. Cf. Stuart, *Hosea–Jonah,* 166.

[104] The *hiphil* of רכב means to "harness" when used of draft animals. See *HALOT,* 1233.

[105] The word בְדַרְכְּךָ ("in your way"), because it is all-inclusive as a description of the religious and political philosophy they had adopted, can well be translated "in your system."

[106] See E. M. Blaiklock and R. K. Harrison, eds., *The New International Dictionary of Biblical Archaeology* (Grand Rapids: Zondervan, 1983), s.v. "Gibeah," 212–13.

tary significance during Hosea's lifetime. Nevertheless, Gibeah's role as a type for dependence on military might is vital for the message of this passage.

The line "there you remain"[107] metaphorically asserts that Israel has maintained the Gibeah mind-set, which can be described as reliance on violence and military power. Israel looks to walls and arms for its security, and the city of Samaria has in effect become New Gibeah, a city behind whose walls the king and his soldiers can feel smug in their power. The NIV translates the next line as, "Did not war overtake the evildoers in Gibeah?" The line does not look to the past, however, and the NIV translation is quite unusual.[108] The line could be a rhetorical question that looks to a future event, as in, "Shall war not overtake them in Gibeah?" (see NRSV). The line probably is a description of what the people believe, that war will not overtake them and that they are safe in "Gibeah," which here stands for military force generally and probably for Samaria in particular.[109] Thus "(They think that) war shall not reach them in Gibeah" is appropriate.

Verse 9 ends with three Hebrew words that mean "against an unjust people." These words do not fit well with v. 9, as the KJV illustrates. Its rendering, "the battle in Gibeah against the children of iniquity did not overtake them," makes no sense in this context. Furthermore, the Hebrew of v. 10 begins with a noun phrase that means "in my desire." This, too, makes for a scarcely intelligible text (the NIV's "when I please" is such a free rendering that it is not persuasive). Greek manuscript evidence, however, suggests that this should be translated "I shall come," which, combined with "against an unjust people" from the previous line, makes excellent sense.[110]

Unfortunately, more problems remain in this verse. The next phrase (NIV, "I will punish them") also contains some odd Hebrew, and emendation seems necessary. The line could mean "I will capture them," but "I will punish

---

[107] There is no need to emend עמרו ("they remained") to אמרו, "they said," contrary to Ward, *Hosea*, 174–75.

[108] Although Hosea's use of verb tense is often difficult, it is quite doubtful that לֹא־תַשִּׂיגֵם looks to a past event. Also the NIV translation eliminates the pronoun suffix on תַשִּׂיגֵם and treats עַל־בְּנֵי עַלְוָה as the direct object of the verb. This is not a good strategy with the Hb. text.

[109] While one could take לֹא־תַשִּׂיגֵם בַּגִּבְעָה מִלְחָמָה as a rhetorical question, nothing in context implies that it is. In fact, even if it is a rhetorical question, one could safely argue that the question is a response to a common assumption that "Gibeah" can provide protection for the people. Either way, the text would appear to imply they supposed that walls and soldiers gave them security.

[110] The copula on וְאֶסְרֵם goes against taking it with בְּאַוָּתִי. Thus for the MT עַל־בְּנֵי עַלְוָה: בְּאַוָּתִי one should read עֲלֶה בָאתִי עוֹלָה עַל־בְּנֵי. Note that not only בְּאַוָּתִי but also the unknown עַלְוָה requires emendation, which further indicates that the MT is corrupted here (the change from עולה to עלוה appears to be simple metathesis). The LXX has the third person ἦλθεν ("he came"), but it still implies reading the verb בוֹא.

them" probably is correct.[111] This translation is more natural, however, if it is connected to "for their two crimes" at the end of the verse. This implies that "and nations shall be gathered against them when they are punished" is parenthetical (and thus I have isolated this line with dashes in my translation). This creates a vivid metaphor in a context that describes Israel as smug behind the walls of fortress "Gibeah"; Yahweh will punish them for their two crimes by bringing enemy armies to entrap Samaria in a siege.

In short, these two verses describe Israel as a nation with a violent history and which now relies on military power for security, and "Gibeah" symbolizes this trait. Samaria thinks it is safe behind its walls, but God will punish them for their two sins of apostasy and militarism. This will come about when enemy nations entrap the people behind the walls of their cities.

10:11–12 These verses return to the metaphor of Israel as a farm. In 10:1–4 Israel was an aggressively growing vine in good soil that yielded only poisonous fruit. Here Israel is a strong heifer that is capable and willing to plow but which only plants bad seed in the land she has prepared. (The fact that draft animals did not actually do the sowing of seed is not germane here; the text juxtaposes the picture of Israel the farm animal with that of Israel sowing the seed of evil without regard for maintaining a fully consistent metaphor.) In 10:1 Hosea declared that no matter how good conditions were for growing, Israel bore only the fruit of idolatry. Here (with v. 13) Yahweh asserts that although the heifer Israel has a good, strong neck, she uses it only for plowing wickedness and reaping injustice.

Nevertheless, Yahweh exhorts Israel the strong heifer to produce fruit worthy of the people of God. The promise that God would come and rain down righteousness on the nation is an oracle of salvation. Similar promises appear elsewhere in the prophets (e.g., Joel 2:23–27), where a link is made between the agricultural healing of the land by rain and the spiritual healing of the people.[112] Thus Yahweh appeals to Israel to return to sowing a crop of righteousness and mercy. The appeal comes here because this text ends a major section of Hosea, and the author apparently did not want to close on a note of unmitigated condemnation and doom. This also prepares the way for the final appeals and promises, at the end of the second series of complaints, at 14:1–8.

Yahweh's challenge is for Israel to seek righteousness, mercy, and God himself. This takes us all the way back to the initial complaint against Israel, that it lacked moral integrity, compassion, and the knowledge of God (4:1).

---

[111] The verb וְאֶסֳרֵם is quite difficult. If it is a *qal* imperfect first person singular from סר, the doubling of the ס is difficult to explain. If it is a *piel* of the same root, the vowels are anomalous. The same holds true if one takes it to be from אסר. The LXX reads יסר (παιδεῦσαι). I take it to be יסר in conjunction with the phrase לְשְׁתֵּי עוֹנֹתָם: (reading the *qere* here).

[112] Ward misses this point when he contends that the line should be translated "he will teach you justice" (*Hosea,* 176).

These three things describe the fundamental characteristics of life in God and also imply repentance from apostasy.

10:13–15 Still using the agricultural metaphor as a transition, Yahweh again returns to the false faith of Israel and here especially to their military establishment. This movement is similar to that seen in 6:4, where immediately after an appeal to repent Yahweh declares that the people are incurably evil. The fruit Israel grows and eats is "false fruit" (not "fruit of lies"[113]), which is here similar to the poisonous fruit of v. 4. That is, it appears to be good and edible, but it actually is poison. In light of the context of 10:1–4, the "false fruit" probably is idolatry, but it also includes the dependence on military power. The phrase "your system" (NIV: "your own strength") implies everything that Israel had built itself upon, including the fertility cult, political alliances, military fortifications, and raw violence. Above all, it was the pride and glory of an ancient state, their army. The term also looks back to the "counsel" of 10:6, of which Israel would become ashamed.

Neither "Shalman" nor "Beth Arbel" is known to us, although some have postulated that "Shalman" is the Assyrian monarch Shalmaneser, and others suggest that the text refers to a person mentioned in the Assyrian annals of Tiglath-pileser III named Salamanu of Moab.[114] Beth Arbel may be the modern Irbid, located some thirty kilometers (about eighteen miles) southeast of the Sea of Galilee. We can only assume that the text is referring to some terrible siege that was known to Hosea's audience. The fall of "Beth Arbel" may be specifically cited here because the name sounds like "Bethel."

Mention of Bethel links to 10:5–8, the polemic against the bull shrine of Bethel. Here it is called the place of "absolute evil"[115] (NIV: "your wickedness is great"). That is, Bethel was the place where everything that was abhorrent had its center. Throughout the book Bethel and the other shrines are described as places of apostasy, immorality, false piety, and hostility to God. It was the heart of Israel's darkness.

As is appropriate for a people who placed arrogant faith in military power, their fall will involve unmitigated military defeat. The king, the symbol of their power but also, in 10:1–8, a figure greatly weakened, would be utterly undone. He would perish "at dawn," that is, at the very beginning of battle.[116]

---

[113] The phrase פְּרִי־כַחַשׁ, although literally "fruit of deceit," means "false fruit" in the same way that הַר־קָדְשִׁי means "my holy mountain."

[114] See the discussion in Mays, *Hosea,* 149.

[115] The construct רָעַת רָעַתְכֶם would seem to mean more than that evil was "great" there. Like expressions such as "king of kings," it implies quintessence.

[116] Thus Wolff, *Hosea,* 188; Mays, *Hosea,* 150. Andersen and Freedman see this as a description of some specific assassination, but this is not convincing (*Hosea,* 572).

(2) Second Series: Judgment on Apostate Israel (11:1–13:16)

The second series of complaints has the structure:

A Divine Complaint: Divine Vexation over Apostate Israel (11:1–12)
  B Prophetic Complaint: Jacob and His Heirs (12:1–8)
A′ Divine Complaint: Divine Resolve over Apostate Israel (12:9–11)
  B′ Prophetic Complaint: Jacob and His Heirs (12:12–13:3)
    C Divine Complaint and Decision (13:4–14)
    C′ Prophetic Announcement of Judgment (13:15–16)

In parallel sections God grieves and expresses his vexation over the apostasy of Israel (A) and finally resolves the matter by determining to give them a new wilderness experience (A′). The prophet for his part gives two accounts of Jacob and his heirs, which both emphasize how Israel has taken on only the worst qualities of their ancestor (B and B′). Finally, in two parallel sections (C and C′), both Yahweh and Hosea make their final proclamations of judgment against Israel. Thus the text begins with a dismayed Yahweh grieving over what to do with his wayward people and ends with the issue of their punishment decided but with the possibility of future salvation still ahead.

¹"When Israel was a child, I loved him,
    and out of Egypt I called my son.
²But the more I called Israel,
    the further they went from me.
They sacrificed to the Baals
    and they burned incense to images.
³It was I who taught Ephraim to walk,
    taking them by the arms;
but they did not realize
    it was I who healed them.
⁴I led them with cords of human kindness,
    with ties of love;
I lifted the yoke from their neck
    and bent down to feed them.

⁵"Will they not return to Egypt
    and will not Assyria rule over them
    because they refuse to repent?
⁶Swords will flash in their cities,
    will destroy the bars of their gates
    and put an end to their plans.
⁷My people are determined to turn from me.
    Even if they call to the Most High,
    he will by no means exalt them.

⁸"How can I give you up, Ephraim?

How can I hand you over, Israel?
How can I treat you like Admah?
How can I make you like Zeboiim?
My heart is changed within me;
all my compassion is aroused.
⁹I will not carry out my fierce anger,
nor will I turn and devastate Ephraim.
For I am God, and not man—
the Holy One among you.
I will not come in wrath.
¹⁰They will follow the LORD;
he will roar like a lion.
When he roars,
his children will come trembling from the west.
¹¹They will come trembling
like birds from Egypt,
like doves from Assyria.
I will settle them in their homes,"
declares the LORD.

¹²Ephraim has surrounded me with lies,
the house of Israel with deceit.
And Judah is unruly against God,
even against the faithful Holy One.

DIVINE COMPLAINT: DIVINE VEXATION OVER APOSTATE ISRAEL
(11:1–12) [A]. This chapter contains an oracle from Yahweh on the apostasy
of Israel that draws heavily on two components of Israel's sacred history,
Israel's exodus and the destruction of Sodom and Gomorrah. The first strophe,
vv. 1–5, focuses on the exodus and ends with the warning that God will undo
the exodus and send Israel to a new Egypt, Assyria, and into servitude to a
new Pharaoh, the Assyrian king. The second strophe, vv. 6–12, concerns the
possibility that Israel will become like the cities of the plain, that is, eternally
annihilated. Yahweh recoils from this and promises a new exodus.

11:1 The childhood of Israel, the period of history when the nation was
young, was when Israel was in Egypt. This verse self-evidently refers to the
exodus event, and in particular to Exod 4:22, where Yahweh declares to Pharaoh, "Israel is my firstborn son." The word translated "child" *(naʿar)* can
refer to a boy anywhere in the age range from infancy (Exod 2:6) to adoles-
cence (Gen 21:12). The presentation of Israel as a male child here distin-
guishes it from Ezek 16:1–6, which describes the young nation as a female
child. In a number of passages God calls the people of Israel his "children,"[117]

---

[117] Using the masculine בָּנִ generically, as in Deut 14:1; Isa 1:2; 30:9; Jer 3:14,19,22; Hos 2:1
(Eng. 1:10).

but it is not extremely common for God to speak of the nation as a whole as his son.[118] The metaphor of Israel as God's son is distinct from the earlier terminology (Hos 1:10) in which the text describes the people as Yahweh's children but describes the corporate nation, with its culture and institutions, as Yahweh's adulterous wife. Here the corporate nation is Yahweh's son. Wolff argues that the metaphor of "son" implies that Yahweh raised up and educated Israel. Also, although he finds a few parallels to this text in non-Israelite sources, he sees no evidence that Hosea has borrowed the metaphor from another culture.[119] Thus it is fair to say that this metaphor, although founded on Exod 4:22, is a striking and unexpected move on Hosea's part. The "love" of God for Israel here implies divine election.

Excursus: The Use of Hosea 11:1 in Matthew 2:15

In the context of Hosea 11, v. 1 plainly concerns the exodus from Egypt. Matthew 2:15, however, asserts that Jesus fulfilled this verse when the holy family returned from Egypt after the death of Herod: "And so was fulfilled what the Lord had said through the prophet: 'Out of Egypt I called my son.'" One cannot but wonder, therefore, whether Matthew has wrenched Hos 11:1b from its context and applied it gratuitously to Jesus. Or, to put it in perhaps gentler terms, whether Matthew has engaged in a bit of midrashic exegesis, reading back into the text something that is not really there but which might nevertheless be justified on theological grounds.

It is noteworthy that Matthew chose a translation that reflects the Hebrew text over against the LXX, which reads, "And out of Egypt I called his children."[120] Assuming he was aware of the LXX, Matthew's choice of the Hebrew reading over the Greek must be regarded as deliberate.

In determining how Matthew came to interpret Hos 11:1 in the way that he did, scholars have observed that the apostle may have been influenced by the LXX rendition of Num 24:7–8,[121] which reads, "A man shall come forth from his seed, and he shall rule many nations. And his kingdom shall be raised up higher than Gog, and his kingdom shall increase. God brought him out of Egypt." The Hebrew text of Num 24:7–8 is quite different. If Matthew was aware of this text, which in the LXX is explicitly messianic, this could explain how he came to regard Hos 11:1 as messianic as well. On the other hand, if Matthew did accept the LXX of Num 24:7–8, why did he not cite it instead of or in addition to the more obscure Hos 11:1? Since he chose not to use it, one could argue that he

---

[118] God calls Ephraim his "firstborn" (בְּכֹר) in Jer 31:9 and his "son" (בֵּן) in Jer 31:20. The LXX substitutes a plural (τέκνα) for the MT singular in Hos 11:1.

[119] Wolff, *Hosea*, 198–99.

[120] The LXX has ἐξ Αἰγύπτου μετεκάλεσα τὰ τέκνα αὐτοῦ, but the MT is supported by Aquila. This probably implies that Matthew followed the Hebrew, unless one postulates the existence of either an earlier Jewish translation similar to Aquila or a pre-Matthean Christian testimony book. See W. D. Davies and D. C. Allison, *Matthew*, ICC (Edinburgh: T & T Clark, 1988), 262.

[121] E.g., D. Hill, *Matthew*, NCB (London: Oliphants, 1972), 85.

actually considered the LXX of Num 24:7–8 to be unreliable. In that case it is hard to see how the Numbers text would have governed his reading of Hos 11:1.

Many interpreters observe that the idea that Jesus fulfilled Hos 11:1 corresponds to the typology that one finds throughout Matthew, in which Jesus recapitulates the story of Israel.[122] Jesus was forty days in the wilderness, just as Israel was there for forty years. Jesus gave his law on a mountain, just as God gave the Torah at Sinai. Jesus miraculously fed his followers in the wilderness, just as Moses gave the people manna. As such it hardly is surprising that Matthew could see a parallel between Jesus' departure from Egypt and the striking line of Hosea, "Out of Egypt I called my son." The benefit of this approach to Matthew, aside from the fact that it fits not only with this passage but with the whole of his gospel, is that it does not require us to suppose Matthew was unaware of or sought to obscure the Old Testament context of Hos 11:1. To the contrary, for Matthew to have asserted that Jesus, in his return from Egypt, recapitulated the exodus experience, of necessity requires that Matthew understood the context and original meaning of Hos 11:1 to be Israel's exodus. Nevertheless, although this approach to the text of Matthew is in my view correct, it still leaves one wondering whether Matthew has rightly appropriated Hos 11:1 or has simply applied his hermeneutic to the Old Testament verse.

One can always appeal to *sensus plenior* (Latin, "fuller meaning"), the hermeneutical principal that says that Old Testament writers sometimes wrote better than they knew because the Holy Spirit led them to use vocabulary that had a significance of which the writers themselves were unaware. This aspect of inspiration, while helpful if used carefully, actually fails to resolve the fundamental question of whether Matthew has rightly made use of Hosea. To say that God caused Hosea to frame his words in such a way that Matthew could appropriate them does not tell us anything about whether the text of Hos 11:1 really has anything to do with the Messiah's return from Egypt.

To put it more pointedly, did Hosea suppose that this verse looked ahead to the Messiah? It is, of course, difficult if not impossible to show that Hosea intended readers to discern from this passage that the Messiah would come out of Egypt. This question, however, is the wrong question to ask of Hos 11:1. The real issue is not, Did Hosea intend this verse to be read messianically? but What did Hosea understand to be the nature of prophecy? In answer to this question, we must assert that Hosea, like all biblical prophets, saw prophecy not so much as the making of specific, individual predictions (which are actually quite rare among the writing prophets), but as the application of the Word of God to historical situations. In doing this the prophets brought to light certain patterns that occur repeatedly in the relationship between God and his people. These patterns or themes have repeated fulfillments or manifestations until the arrival of the final, absolute fulfillment. Thus, for example, the conquest of the land "fulfilled"

[122] Cf. W. F. Albright and C. S. Mann, *Matthew,* AB (New York: Doubleday, 1971), 18; D. A. Carson, "Matthew," EBC (Grand Rapids: Zondervan, 1984), 8:91–93; Hill, *Matthew,* 85; D. A. Hagner, *Matthew,* WBC (Dallas: Word, 1993), 36–37; Davies and Allison, *Matthew,* 262–64; C. L. Blomberg, *Matthew,* NAC (Nashville: Broadman, 1992), 67.

the promises to the patriarchs but did not fulfill those promises finally or in their ultimate form. The inheritance of the "new earth" is the ultimate conclusion of this prophetic theme. All of the prophets were, to some degree, "like Moses" (Deut 18:5), but the ultimate prophet like Moses can only be the Messiah. Each of the kings of the line of David was a fulfillment of the promise that God would build him a "house" (2 Sam 7), but the Messiah is again the final fulfillment of this theme. Thus prophecy gives us not so much specific predictions but types or patterns by which God works in the world. We need look no further than Hosea 11 to understand that Hosea, too, believed that God followed patterns in working with his people. Here the slavery in Egypt is the pattern for a second period of enslavement in an alien land (v. 5), and the exodus from Egypt is the type for a new exodus (vv. 10–11). Thus the application of typological principles to Hos 11:1 is in keeping with the nature of prophecy itself and with Hosea's own method. Understood in this way, we can regard the wording of Hos 11:1 not as fortuitous but as a work of God. Whether or not Hosea himself understood the ultimate fulfillment of his words, he knew that his words had significance that transcended his own time. We should note, however, that the surprising shift of metaphor from Israel as mother and children to Israel as son gives us further reason to regard this as a deliberate move and not as happy coincidence.

11:2   The NIV, like most modern versions, follows the LXX in its translation, "But the more I called Israel, the further they went from me."[123] Interpreters generally suppose that the Hebrew text, which translates to "they called to them, that is how they went from them," makes no sense. On the other hand, the MT reading appears in the Vulgate,[124] which implies that the MT has ancient support. Furthermore, although the emended text is intelligible, it actually does not fit the context as well as the more difficult Hebrew text. The emendation "But the more I called Israel, the further they went from me" seems to be a reflection on the history of the prophetic movement in Israel and in particular on how the people through the centuries disregarded the prophets' message. This passage, however, focuses not on prophetic history but on the exodus, when God called his "son" out of "Egypt." Against this background the line "they [Israel] called to them [Egypt], that is how they [Israel] went from them [Egypt]" means that in the exodus itself Israel was already committing apostasy by yearning for Egypt (e.g., Num 11:4–6) and carrying Egyptian paganism with them.[125]

---

[123] The LXX has καθὼς μετεκάλεσα αὐτούς, οὕτως ἀπῷχοντο ἐκ προσώπου μου. This suggests an emendation to כְּקָרְאִי for MT קָרְאוּ and to הֶם מִפְּנֵי for MT מִפְּנֵיהֶם.

[124] The Vg reads *vocaverunt eos sic abierunt a facie eorum.*

[125] The line "they called to them, that is how they went from them" is of course ambiguous regarding subject and object, but following v. 1b it appears that Israel was "calling" to Egypt as they departed. At the same time it seems that the vocabulary (and ambiguity) of this verse is influenced by Num 25:2, וַתִּקְרֶאןָ לָעָם לְזִבְחֵי אֱלֹהֵיהֶן ("The [Moabite] women called to the people and invited them to the sacrifices of their gods").

The following words, "They sacrificed to the Baals and they burned incense to images," should be taken to refer to the continued practice of paganism in the Israelite camp. The idea that Israel in the exodus was already embracing Baalism may be to some degree anachronistic (i.e., Hosea describing the apostasy of the exodus generation in terms more relevant to the cults of his own day), but it is not an unreasonable charge. After all, the exodus began with the golden calf (Exod 32), a cultic item that Hosea could easily identify with the fertility cults of his generation, and it ended with Israelites falling into the fertility cult of Baal of Peor (Num 25). In short this verse teaches that the apostasy of Hosea's generation was a continuation of what they began as early as the exodus.

11:3 The NIV rendering of the first line, "It was I who taught Ephraim to walk,[126] taking[127] them by the arms," is preferable to the emendation to "taking them in my arms" found in a number of translations (e.g., NRSV). The picture is of a father teaching his child to walk; one does this by bending over and holding the child's arms, not by picking up the child.[128] The metaphor of teaching to walk appears to relate to Israel's walking out of Egypt.

The line "but they did not realize it was I who healed them" also alludes to the story of the exodus. In particular it looks back to Exod 15:22–26, the story of the bitter water at Marah, which Moses miraculously purified after praying to Yahweh. God then commented on this incident, "If you listen carefully to the voice of the LORD your God and do what is right in his eyes, if you pay attention to his commands and keep all his decrees, I will not bring on you any of the diseases I brought on the Egyptians, for I am the LORD, who heals you" (Exod 15:26). Yahweh thus compared the bitter water of Marah to the plagues on the Egyptians and made the point that he would continue to be Israel's healer so long as they were faithful. Hosea's allusion to this incident implies that the Israelites quickly forgot both how the Egyptians were

---

[126] Scholars have long noted the peculiar form תִרְגַּלְתִּי and have postulated that it may be some kind of ת preformative stem. Be that as it may, it is apparently similar in meaning to a *hiphil* stem here, with "I made walk" meaning "I taught to walk." Cf. Stuart, *Hosea-Jonah,* 175, and Wolff, *Hosea,* 191. Andersen and Freedman reject this interpretation on the grounds that a נַעַר cannot be so young a child, but see Exod 2:6 (*Hosea,* 579). Also the metaphors of Hosea shift suddenly and unexpectedly, and it is not clear that נַעַר should determine the meaning of תִרְגַּלְתִּי. The LXX translation συμποδίζω ("tie the feet together") appears speculative. It is of course possible that the meaning is not that Yahweh taught Israel to walk but that he made Israel walk out of Egypt in the sense that one might lead an older child who already knows how to walk, taking that child by the hand. In this case, however, we would have expected "hand" instead of "arms" in this verse.

[127] *HALOT,* 534 regards קָחָם as a textual error, but the morphology of לקח is unusual, and this form may be dialectal. It clearly is not what it appears to be, an imperative. This form may be an infinitive, or it could be emended to either a perfect (*qatal*) or imperfect (*yiqtol*) form. See *BHS* notes.

[128] The use of the preposition עַל here is perhaps surprising, but prepositions are notoriously fluid, and one should not emend זְרוֹעֹתָיו to זְרוֹעֹתָי, notwithstanding the support in the versions.

afflicted and how God repeatedly restored health to Israel in the wilderness
(e.g., Num 21:6–10).

11:4 The text continues to reflect upon the exodus as a type for all of
Israel's future behavior, but it here changes the metaphor from Israel as a
child to Israel as a draft animal. Israel is an ox whose yoke God loosened and
whom God gently led to the promised land, hand-feeding it along the way.
The NIV translation, "I led them with cords of human kindness," paraphrases
the Hebrew, which actually reads, "I led them with cords of a human." The
meaning of this phrase is not self-evident, since every cord is presumably a
cord made by humans. In parallel with the next phrase, "ropes of love,"
"human" is often taken to mean "humane" here, but the Hebrew word
"human" does not carry the connotation "humane."[129]

Two possibilities present themselves. First, "human" here may stand in
contrast to "God" and imply that Yahweh did not make use of the full power
or majesty of his deity in leading Israel through the wilderness. Taken this
way the metaphor connotes gentleness, as the NIV paraphrase indicates. The
second possibility is perhaps more far-fetched, but it should not be ruled out
without some consideration. The "human" rope between Yahweh and the ox
Israel may in fact be Moses, the intermediary between God and the nation.
Throughout the exodus experience, and especially at Sinai, Moses had the
role of being God's human face for Israel. That is, the people preferred to deal
with Yahweh through the man Moses rather than to face Yahweh directly (the
most illustrative incident being at Sinai as recounted in Deut 5:22–33). In this
capacity, moreover, Moses was the voice of compassion who repeatedly inter-
ceded with Yahweh to be merciful to Israel (e.g., Exod 32:11–14). Although
this interpretation is not self-evident, it is the only one that explains how
"cords of a human" can also be "ropes of love," and it also provides a specific
referent for the metaphor of the rope as a mediator between Yahweh and Israel
rather than seeing it simply as a description of gentleness.

The meaning of the next line, "I lifted the yoke from their neck," is subject
to some debate. The REB takes it to mean "I lifted them like a little child to
my cheek" (see also NRSV).[130] In this case, however, the NIV translation is
preferable because the image of leading by a rope tells us that the operative
metaphor has changed from Israel the child to Israel the draft animal. It is too
harsh, even for Hosea, to have the text jump back and forth between two metaphors. Nevertheless, the Hebrew text actually says, "I became like those who

---

[129] Thus some speculate that אָדָם here means "leather." See *HALOT,* 14; but the parallel "with
ropes of love" (בַּעֲבֹתוֹת אַהֲבָה) excludes this possibility. See Davies, *Hosea,* 256, and R. S. Hess,
"ʾādām as 'Skin' and 'Earth': An Examination of Some Proposed Meanings in Biblical Hebrew,"
TynBul 39 (1988): 143–49.

[130] This interpretation, followed by a number of interpreters, asserts the Masoretic pointing is
incorrect; instead of עֹל ("yoke") it would read עוּל ("baby"). Cf. Ward, *Hosea,* 192.

raise up a yoke that (was) on their jaws." The metaphor does not necessarily mean that Yahweh removed their yoke altogether, as though Israel suddenly became freed from all restraint, like a wild ox. The point is rather that Yahweh was like farmers who ease the burden of the yoke that is on their oxen.[131] The term "jaws" here implies that farmers needed to adjust some kind of bit or harness device that either went into the animal's mouth or around its jaws. Hence the line describes an adjustment of the yoke and an easing of the burden, not a complete removal of the yoke. The point is not liberation from all duties but liberation from the harsh conditions Israel experienced in Egypt.

The last line of this verse, "and bent down to feed them," probably could be better translated "and gently I would give to him his food."[132] Either way the point is that Yahweh fed Israel throughout the exodus, a fact that is well documented in the Pentateuch. The alert reader will recall how Israel complained about the lack of variety in the diet of manna, and in particular remember the episode at Kibroth Hattaavah, in which there was a plague after the people gluttonously consumed quail (Num 11).

11:5 This verse should be translated, "He shall not return to the land of Egypt, but Assyria shall be his king, for they did not return (to me)." The NIV regards the opening line as a rhetorical question ("Will they not return to Egypt?") in agreement with a number of other recent translations. Instead, with the KJV and NASB, it is better to take the first line as a simple negative.[133] The meaning is that the exodus will be undone and Israel will return to its former condition of slavery but that this time the captivity will not be in Egypt but in Assyria. It is true that Hosea does sometimes speak of a return to Egypt (e.g., at 8:13 and in this text at 11:11), but that does not require us to read this passage with that sense. Although some Israelites did flee to Egypt, and God would call them back from there, the large majority were taken by the Assyrians. Perhaps the distinction here is between Egypt, to which some Israelites voluntarily fled, and Assyria, that took many away by force. The king of Assyria here supplants the pharaoh of the exodus as the new lord of Israel. The text introduces a wordplay at the end using the verb *šûb:* Israel

---

[131] If the complete removal of the yoke had been the point, one would have expected מֵעַל ("from upon") and not simply עַל ("upon"). See McComiskey, "Hosea," 1:185.

[132] At issue is whether וְאַט should be regarded as a *hiphil* imperfect from נטה (thus, e.g., Wolff, *Hosea,* 191) or as the adjective אַט ("gentle") here used adverbially. I prefer the latter because it appears that if the meaning were "and I would bend down to feed them," אוֹכִיל should either have a conjunction or instead take the form of an infinitive construct with the לְ preposition. More importantly, נטה in the *hiphil* requires an object; it is not intransitive. In the *qal* it can be intransitive and mean "bow down," but reading this as a *qal* would require modifying the vowel pointing to אַט. See also McComiskey, "Hosea," 1:185–86.

[133] A rhetorical question is always a possibility on a clause introduced with לֹא, but it should not be the reader's first choice. The line that follows, וְאַשּׁוּר הוּא מַלְכּוֹ, is contrastive. Cf. the outcry of the people in 1 Kgs 18:39: יְהוָה הוּא הָאֱלֹהִים ("[Not Baal but] Yahweh, he is God!").

would not *return* to Egypt but instead would go to Assyria because they refused to *return* to Yahweh (i.e., repent).

11:6 The opening line of this verse, literally "a sword will whirl about in his cities," poetically portrays the fury of the Assyrian army as a sword slashing through the cities of Israel. The second line, translated in the NIV as "will destroy the bars of their gates," probably means "it will put an end to his boasting." The Hebrew word *bad* can mean a "pole," "a priest," or "a boast";[134] and the NIV evidently takes it to mean "pole" here and from that makes the connection that the pole is the bar of a city gate. The correlation between "pole" and the bars of a gate is far-fetched, however; it is unlikely that a Hebrew reader would have taken *bad* in that sense.[135] Some versions, such as the NRSV, take it to mean "priest" ("it consumes their oracle-priests"). Nevertheless, although the Book of Hosea has a great deal to say about the Israelite priesthood, this is not the focus of this text. In parallel with the following line, "consume[136] their plans," one should take *bad* here to mean "empty talk" or "boasting." Elsewhere Hosea says that Yahweh will frustrate the plans or counsels of Israel (e.g., 10:6).

11:7 This verse should be rendered, "My people are depending upon apostasy from me, and they call him *ʾēl ʿal* [God on High], but he will not raise them at all." The word that the NIV translates as "determined to" is literally "hang upon." With other versions the NIV takes "hang upon" to mean "bent upon" and thus "determined to." It seems more likely, however, that the metaphor of hanging upon something implies pinning one's hopes on it rather than implying determination.[137] Thus "depending upon" is a better translation. Also instead of "even if they call to the Most High," which involves considerable emendation, one should translate, "They call him *ʾēl ʿal* [God on High]"[138] and understand that the Israelites had taken to worshiping God

---

[134] The word בַּד can also mean "solitude" or "linen," but neither of these meanings seems possible here.

[135] The word בַּד with the sense of "pole" is taken to refer to the bars of a gate only in one other passage, Job 17:16, which speaks of the בַּדֵּי שְׁאֹל ("bars of Sheol" in the NRSV). This text should almost certainly be emended to fit the context. See R. L. Alden, *Job,* NAC (Nashville: Broadman, 1993), 193, and M. Pope, *Job,* AB (New York: Doubleday, 1965), 131, who calls the translation "bars of Sheol" a "poor guess."

[136] We should note that the NIV has unnecessarily emended the Hb. from וְאָכְלָה ("and she [the sword] shall consume") to some form of כלה, "put an end to." Hebrew idiom often speaks of swords "devouring" things (Deut 32:34; 2 Sam 2:26; 11:25; 18:8; Jer 2:30; 12:12). Thus the line means "and it shall consume their plans."

[137] The root תלא appears elsewhere only in 2 Sam 21:12 and Deut 28:66, neither of which illuminate the present text. Nevertheless, the text should not be emended, contrary to Ward, *Hosea,* 193 (cf. LXX and Wolff, *Hosea,* 192).

[138] The line וְאֶל־עַל יְקְרָאֻהוּ is literally "and to ʿal they are calling him," which makes no sense. However, with a very minor change in pointing, from אֶל to אֵל, one can take it to be the divine name *ʾēl ʿal,* and so translate "and they call him *ʾēl ʿal.*" The NIV translation requires that one delete the pronoun suffix and treat עַל alone as a divine name, both of which are unlikely.

under the name of ʾēl ʿal, but that Yahweh rejected that title and considered it to be the name of another god (i.e., Baal). That is, the Israelites depended upon an apostate theology in which they assimilated the worship of Yahweh to the Canaanite cults under the ambiguous title "God on High," or ʾēl ʿal. As this commentary has already indicated, Hosea apparently makes a parody of this name with the term "Not-on-High" in 7:16.

11:8 Abruptly, Yahweh enters what can only be described as distraught self-questioning. Like a father who is at wit's end over what to do with a wayward child, Yahweh is here at a loss as he tries to resolve his compassion for Israel and the punishment demanded by their sin. One may of course regard this as metaphor, as language that somehow puts divine love into terms that a human can understand, even though God himself does not really experience self-doubt and anxiety over issues of justice and mercy. This is certainly true, and we should not press the language too strongly, as do some advocates for the "openness" of God. Still we should not be overhasty to correct the image that the text gives us. While accepting the fact that God transcends our metaphors and that theological doctrines about the impassability and foreknowledge of God should never be jettisoned, texts such as this should be allowed to speak to us in the power of their raw emotion. It is precisely in texts such as this that the love of God becomes a vivid reality and not a barren abstraction.[139]

Zeboiim and Admah, together with Bela, were the other cities of the plain in addition to the more famous Sodom and Gomorrah (Gen 14:2). That is, these cities represent the depravity that God annihilated in the destruction that is recounted in Genesis 19 and is recalled in Deut 29:23. One may fairly ask why the text mentioned the relatively obscure Zeboiim and Admah as opposed to the more famous Sodom and Gomorrah (contrast Isa 1:9–10; 3:9; 13:19; Jer 23:14; 49:18; 50:40; Lam 4:6; Ezek 16:46–56; Amos 4:11; Zeph 2:9). Answering that question, it is hard to avoid the conclusion that Hosea is at times deliberately obscure, elusive, and demanding of his reader. Certainly many of the problems in reading Hosea cannot be dismissed as scribal errors or even as obscurities that result from it being written in a northern dialect. This book is highly elliptical and allusive, and in this case it requires the reader to recognize the allusion to the destruction of Sodom and Gomorrah by mentioning their far less famous sister cities.

11:9 This verse should be translated, "I will not carry out the fury of my wrath; I will not again destroy Ephraim; for I am God and not man (I am) holy in your midst,[140] and I shall not enter the city." The NIV translation, "nor will

---

[139] For further discussion of this text, see J. L. McKenzie, "Divine Passion in Osee," *CBQ* 17 (1955): 287–99.

[140] The line כִּי אֵל אָנֹכִי וְלֹא־אִישׁ בְּקִרְבְּךָ קָדוֹשׁ could be translated, "For I am holy deity, and not human, in your midst." Cf. יְהוָה אֱלֹהֵינוּ יְהוָה אֶחָד (Deut 6:4), which should probably be translated, "Yahweh, Yahweh is our one God," and not "Yahweh is our God, Yahweh is one."

I turn and devastate Ephraim," fails to render accurately a common Hebrew idiom meaning "to do again." In this case it means "I will not again destroy Ephraim."[141] Furthermore, the Hebrew at the end of the verse plainly states, "I shall not enter the city"; it does not mean "I will not come in wrath."[142] This translation of the verse prompts three questions: (1) Why does Yahweh say here that he will not execute his wrath when everything else in the book implies that he will in fact destroy Ephraim?[143] (2) What does he mean by saying that he will not destroy Ephraim "again" if the Assyrian conquest of Samaria had not yet taken place (as seems certain)? (3) Why does Yahweh say that he will not enter the city?

The answer to all three questions arises from the fact that the text presents Israel as a city in danger of repeating the history of Sodom, Gomorrah, and the cities of the plain. "I will not carry out the fury of my wrath" does not mean that Ephraim is going to escape punishment. Rather, it means that Yahweh will not give full vent to his fury, as he did in the case of Sodom. In other words, Israel will not suffer the total, irreversible annihilation that Sodom experienced. Furthermore, because Yahweh has come to regard Ephraim as a second Sodom, the reverse is also true: Sodom is the original Ephraim. Yahweh can therefore declare that he will not come back and obliterate Ephraim "again." The implied first destruction of "Ephraim" was the destruction of the cities of the plain. In this the text of Hosea anticipates Isaiah's declaration that Jerusalem is a kind of "New Sodom" (Isa 1:10) and Ezekiel's characterization of Jerusalem, Samaria, and Sodom as three sisters (Ezek 16:46). In Hosea, however, Yahweh's point is again that he will not annihilate Ephraim in the way that he annihilated Sodom. Also, "I will not *enter* the city" looks back to the account of Genesis 19, in which Yahweh (or his angels) enter Sodom to see how bad the evil there really is and conclude that the city must be wiped off the face of the earth. If he were to *enter* Samaria in the same way he entered Sodom, the text implies, he would have to destroy Samaria as completely as he did Sodom. Finally, God's inner debate over whether to make Israel like the cities of the plain may allude to Abraham's negotiations with Yahweh, in which he called upon divine mercy and forbearance (Gen 18:22–

---

[141] The idiomatic use of שׁוּב: with an infinitive meaning "to do X again," is well established. See Mays, *Hosea*, 151, Wolff, *Hosea*, 193, and BDB, 998.

[142] The justification for translating עִיר in this text as "wrath" is Jer 15:8, "I caused anguish [עִיר] and terror suddenly to fall upon her." This is the only place where עִיר has this meaning in the OT, but, significantly, it is a quality of the victim of an attack; it is not a quality of an attacker. The Hebrew reader would naturally take וְלֹא אָבוֹא בְּעִיר to mean "I will not enter the city." Cf. the LXX (καὶ οὐκ εἰσελεύσομαι εἰς πόλιν) and Vg (*et non ingrediar civitatem*).

[143] Andersen and Freedman consider the negatives here to be so intolerable that they treat them as asseveratives (*Hosea*, 589). Again one must always consider this to be a possibility, but it is not the first choice. Unless there are compelling reasons to the contrary, a negative should be treated as a negative.

33). That is, what God ultimately could not do with the cities of the plain, save them from total annihilation, he is determined to do for Israel.

In this regard the point that Yahweh is "God and not man, holy in your midst" is remarkable. The holiness of God recalls the enormous number of texts in Exodus, Leviticus, Numbers, and Deuteronomy in which God either declared himself to be a holy person in the camp of Israel or demanded that the people of Israel be holy. Thus, for example, Israel had to keep everything that was defiled away from Yahweh's tent (Deut 23:14). Holiness is therefore not a trait associated with mercy but with judgment. Precisely because Yahweh was a holy God in the midst of Israel, he chose to avoid entering the city, lest he should have to destroy it entirely. This refusal to enter the city is an act both of judgment and of mercy.

11:10–11 Here Yahweh takes upon himself the ferocity of the lion, not to destroy Israel but to restore it. The image, like many in the prophets, is disorienting: a lion roars, but birds *come to it* rather than flee. This metaphor recalls Num 24:8–9:

> "God brought them out of Egypt;
>   they have the strength of a wild ox.
> They devour hostile nations
>   and break their bones in pieces;
>   with their arrows they pierce them.
> Like a lion they crouch and lie down,
>   like a lioness—who dares to rouse them?"

> "May those who bless you be blessed
>   and those who curse you be cursed!"[144]

One could take the lion of this text to be Israel, as at Num 23:24. In Num 24:8–9, however, God himself is the ferocity of Israel, and Israel is addressed in the second person; thus the lion appears to describe God and not Israel. Hosea's point here is that there is to be a new exodus in which God will again play the part of the lion and deliver his people from their enemies and into a new Promised Land. In contrast to 7:11, Israel will no longer be a silly dove wandering to and fro; it will fly directly to Yahweh. This text envisages a general return of the people, not only from Egypt and Assyria but also from the west, the regions around the Mediterranean.

11:12 [12:1] The first half of 11:12 is straightforward in meaning, although the text does not specify what particular "lies" Yahweh has in mind. These terms probably represent false ideology and apostasy generally. On the

---

[144] One could also argue for a link between Hos 11:10–11 and Isa 31:4–5, as does G. Eidevall, "Lions and Birds as Literature: Some Notes on Isaiah 31 and Hosea 11," *Scandinavian Journal of the Old Testament* 7 (1993): 78–87.

other hand, the image of Yahweh being surrounded is striking and quite unusual.[145] One cannot but wonder if this text refers to some shrine or altar, ostensibly and perhaps originally dedicated to Yahweh, which the Israelites have literally surrounded with images sacred to the fertility cult.

Verse 12b is subject to various interpretations.[146] The NRSV, for example, renders it, "But Judah still walks with God, and is faithful to the Holy One," thus taking this to be a positive assessment. The NIV, however, is correct to read this as a criticism of Judah that parallels the criticism of Ephraim in v. 12a (and see especially the assessment of Judah in 12:2a[147]). It appears, however, that a more accurate translation would be "and Judah still wanders with deity, and is faithful with the holy gods." The word here translated "deity" is ʾēl, also the name of the high god of the Canaanite pantheon. The word can, in a proper context, be used of the one God, Yahweh.[148] To "wander," however, implies apostasy.[149] Judah wanders off into the religious worship of ʾēl, perhaps using the justification that ʾēl is merely another term for Yahweh. This generic and semipagan term, however, invites a pagan interpretation. Judah is also faithful to the "holy ones," a term that might also be used of Yahweh but that in a context such as this is better taken to refer to

---

[145] The speaker here is Yahweh, not Hosea. Cf. Hubbard, *Hosea,* 199. Andersen and Freedman puzzle over the picture of Yahweh being surrounded and note that in Psalms the verb סבב is often used of one who is terrified, surrounded by wild beasts (*Hosea,* 600–601). But of itself, סבב implies neither fear nor a hostile situation.

[146] Cf. R. B. Coote, "Hosea XII," *VT* 21 (1971): 389–402, especially pp. 389–92.

[147] Wolff, who reads 12:1 (Eng. 11:12) as a positive assessment of Judah, excises Judah from 12:2 (Eng. 12:1) as redactional (*Hosea,* 206).

[148] El appears as the Canaanite high god in the Ug texts. When used of the one God in the Bible, אֵל is almost always qualified in some way (e.g., אֵל עֶלְיוֹן [Gen 14:18] אֵל שַׁדַּי [Gen 17:1], אֵל הַשָּׁמָיִם [Ps 136:26], etc.). The term אֵל can appear in parallel with another phrase that indicates that Yahweh is meant (e.g., Num 23:8). It often refers to a pagan god, as in אֵל זָר ("a strange god"; Ps 44:21). Of itself, however, אֵל simply means "deity" or "a god," as in Micah's question at 7:18 מִי־אֵל כָּמוֹךָ ("who is a god like you?"). Thus Yahweh can claim אֵל אָנִי ("I am [the true] God") in Isa 43:12, but Tyre can make almost the exact same claim, albeit falsely, in Ezek 28:2: אֵל אָנִי ("I am a god," the reversal in word order reflecting that the latter is a clause of categorization and the former a clause of identification). Particularly instructive is Isa 40:18: וְאֶל־מִי תְּדַמְּיוּן אֵל ("To whom will you compare Deity?"; the text goes on to challenge the reader concerning whether an idol can adequately represent God). I.e., for Isa 40:18 the question is one of how one chooses to conceive of אֵל, as an idol or as the invisible Yahweh. Normally, of course, Hb. uses אֱלֹהִים as the common word for the one God. To say that Judah wanders away with אֵל is tantamount to saying that they have embraced אֵל as a term for worship and that the resulting ambiguity has opened the door to Canaanite cultic religion.

[149] Cf. the use of רוּד in Jer 2:31, the only other certain occurrence of the verb in the *qal* stem. The root appears one time in the *hiphil* stem, in Gen 27:40, where it connotes rebellion.

pagan gods.[150] Thus the text portrays Judah as wavering in its devotion to Yahweh. They worship Yahweh under names that might be associated with orthodox Yahwism but which already indicate a turning away into the language of the Canaanite cults. What is important here is the ambiguity of this half-verse, an ambiguity that leads to two opposing translations asserting either that Judah is faithful or that Judah is apostate.[151] We should maintain this sense of ambiguity. In "wandering with" *ʾēl*, Judah is wavering in and out of orthodox Yahwism through the worship of God under ambiguous names.

This verse parallels the complaint against Ephraim in 11:7, that they call their god *ʾēl ʿal*. On the other hand, in 11:9 Yahweh declares that he is God (*ʾēl*) and not human, and that he is "holy."[152] It appears that Yahweh is affirming that he is in fact the true holy Deity, notwithstanding the people's abuse of those terms. The names themselves, in other words, are unobjectionable if understood correctly and not used as covers for apostasy.

In summary the text of Hosea 11 is structured as follows:

First Strophe	**Israel, the Exodus, and Assyria, the New Egypt**
God's Grace in the Exodus	When Israel was a child I loved him, And out of Egypt I called my son. (v. 1)

Israel's Apostasy in the Exodus	They called to them,
	    that is how they went from them.
	They kept sacrificing to Baals
	    and offering incense to idols. (v. 2)

God's Grace in the Exodus	Yet it was I who taught Ephraim to walk, taking them by their arms,

---

[150] The term קְדוֹשִׁים is simply the masculine plural of the adjective "holy." It is most often used in reference to the people of Israel, who are to be "holy" to the Lord (e.g., Lev 19:2). In Zech 14:5 it is "heavenly beings." The term apparently is used of Yahweh, the "Holy One," in Prov 9:10 (and perhaps 30:3). However, this is unusual, and it seems very odd that the plural קְדוֹשִׁים would be used for God in Hos 12:1 (Eng. 11:12) in conjunction with the singular אֵל. It is perhaps also significant that the people worship deity using the plural קְדוֹשִׁים, whereas in v. 9 he refers to himself by the singular קָדוֹשׁ. It therefore appears that in its cultus Judah had begun to use קְדוֹשִׁים as a term under which God was worshiped and that the ambiguity of this term further opened the door for polytheistic or pagan religion.

[151] Wolff gives a good defense of reading this as a positive assertion of Judah's faithfulness, and his argument principally hangs upon the syntax of וִיהוּדָה עֹד, which normally would be contrastive and translated "but Judah still ..." (*Hosea*, 209–10). But Wolff has not, to my satisfaction, successfully accounted for the strange choice of words in "wander with" and in the terms אֵל and קְדוֹשִׁים. E.g., in a context that speaks of אֵל, it is most unlikely that the קְדוֹשִׁים are faithful people and not the divine beings who filled the court of *ʾēl* (contrary to Wolff). A verdict of deliberate ambiguity in this verse is unavoidable.

[152] Using the singular קָדוֹשׁ instead of the plural.

But they did not know that I healed them. (v. 3)
With cords of a human I led them,
    with ropes of love.
And I was to them like those who raise the yoke from their
    jaws,
    I gently gave food to him. (v. 4)

**Assyria, The New
Egypt**

He shall not return to the land of Egypt,
    but Assyria will be his king,
        for they refused to repent. (v. 5)

Second Strophe

Israel, the Cities of the Plain, and a New Exodus

Destruction of
Israel's cities
because of
apostasy and
worship of ʾēl ʿal

For a sword whirls about in his cities,
    It will put an end to his boasting
        and consume their plans. (v. 6)
But my people depend upon apostasy from me,
    They call him ʾēl ʿal, "Deity Above."
    He shall not raise them up. (v. 7)

God's revulsion at
making Ephraim
into a second
Sodom and
Gomorrah, a total
annihilation,
because he is
holy ʾēl

How can I give you up, Ephraim?
    How can I surrender you, Israel?
How can I make you like Admah?
    How can I treat you like Zeboiim?
My heart is turned within me;
    my compassion is completely provoked! (v. 8)
I shall not carry out the fury of my anger.
    I shall not again destroy Ephraim.
For I am holy deity (ʾēl), and not human, in your midst.
    I shall not enter your city. (v. 9)

The new exodus

They shall come after the Lord;
    Like a lion he shall roar;
    When he roars,
his children will come trembling from the west. (v. 10)
They shall tremble like birds from Egypt,
    and like a dove from the land of Assyria.
        And I shall return them to their homes, says Yahweh.
    (v. 11)

Apostasy and
ambiguity with
ʾēl; transition
to 12:1ff.

Ephraim surrounds me with lying,
    and the house of Israel (surrounds me) with deceit.
And Judah still wanders in his relationship with ʾēl, "deity,"
    and is faithful with "holy beings." (v. 12)

¹Ephraim feeds on the wind;
  he pursues the east wind all day
  and multiplies lies and violence.
He makes a treaty with Assyria
  and sends olive oil to Egypt.
²The LORD has a charge to bring against Judah;
  he will punish Jacob according to his ways
  and repay him according to his deeds.
³In the womb he grasped his brother's heel;
  as a man he struggled with God.
⁴He struggled with the angel and overcame him;
  he wept and begged for his favor.
He found him at Bethel
  and talked with him there—
⁵the LORD God Almighty,
  the LORD is his name of renown!
⁶But you must return to your God;
  maintain love and justice,
  and wait for your God always.

⁷The merchant uses dishonest scales;
  he loves to defraud.
⁸Ephraim boasts,
  "I am very rich; I have become wealthy.
With all my wealth they will not find in me
  any iniquity or sin."

PROPHETIC COMPLAINT: JACOB AND HIS HEIRS (12:1–8) [B].   The
decision to regard 11:12 [Hb. 12:1] as the end of the previous text and 12:1
[Hb. 12:2] as the beginning of a new text requires some explanation. One could
make the case that 11:12 begins the next section and that Yahweh's oracle
closes at 11:11.[153] It certainly seems that 11:12 leads into 12:1. On the other
hand, some interpreters place a major break between 12:1 and 12:2. Thus, one
could argue that 11:12 and 12:1 go with 12:2ff.,[154] or that they both go with
11:1–11,[155] or that 11:12–12:1 are a separate unit unto themselves.[156] But one
should not put a major break between 12:1 and 12:2. Although the English at
the beginning of 12:2 ("The LORD has a charge to bring against Judah")
sounds as though it begins a new section, the Hebrew does not bear this out;

---

[153] Note that 11:11 ends with נְאֻם־יְהוָה ("the message of Yahweh") and that the Masoretic
text places a ס at the end of the verse.
[154] E.g., Wolff, *Hosea*, 205–6.
[155] E.g., NRSV.
[156] E.g., Mays, *Hosea*, 159.

12:1 belongs with 12:2.[157] Furthermore, 11:12 is plainly spoken by Yahweh, which implies that it belongs with 11:1–11. In addition 11:12 returns to the idea of worshiping God under the names *ʾēl* and "holy ones," which links it to 11:7 and 11:9. Hosea 12:1–8, however, is spoken by Hosea and not Yahweh (see 12:2). Thus a major break after 11:12 is unavoidable. On the other hand, as one often sees in the Book of Hosea, 11:12 is transitional in that it also leads into 12:1. That is, at 12:1 Hosea begins by responding to Yahweh's previous words.

In this text Hosea picks up where Yahweh breaks off, at the apostasy of Ephraim and Judah (vv. 1–2). That is, vv. 1–2 declare that both the Northern Kingdom (Ephraim, v. 1) and the Southern Kingdom (Judah, v. 2)[158] are guilty of apostasy. After that Hosea reflects upon Israel's ways in light of the story of Jacob (vv. 3–8), just as Yahweh had reflected on the current condition of Israel in light of the exodus event and the story of the destruction of the cities of the plain. Verse 2 is actually transitional; from v. 1 it completes the thought that both Israel and Judah are in rebellion, but it also begins a poem that describes Jacob's life (vv. 2–5). Here in vv. 2–5 the name Yahweh marks the beginning and ending verses. Verses 6–8 are a response to vv. 2–5; they compare the ways of the people of Israel to the ways of their ancestor, Jacob. Verse 6, however, is linked to v. 5 in the same way that v. 2 is linked to v. 1. That is, v. 5 declares that Yahweh is the name of Israel's God, and v. 6 exhorts the people to return to their God and to maintain love and justice. Sayings regarding Ephraim at vv. 1 and 8 bracket this text. This complex text therefore has the following structure, in which the arrows indicate inclusion structure:

V. 1, Ephraim ↓, linked to Judah (v. 2) and Ephraim (v. 8)

/

A: Guilt of Jacob's Offspring (vv. 1–2), both Northern and Southern Kingdoms

\

V. 2, Judah ↑, Yahweh ↓

/

---

[157] The first word of 12:2 (Hb. 12:3), וְרִיב ("and a charge"), makes it very unlikely that this begins a new major section. Although one often sees a new major section begin with וְהָיָה or וַיְהִי, it is unusual to have a simple noun with a conjunction signal a major break. Furthermore, these two verses flow together nicely, as follows:
Ephraim shepherds the wind,
    and pursues the east wind all day long.
Deceit and violence they increase,
    and a covenant with Assyria they make,
        and oil to Egypt is carried.
And a conflict Yahweh has with Judah,
    and a punishment for Jacob in accordance with his ways;
        like his deeds, he will repay him.
[158] There is no need to emend "Judah" to "Israel."

B: Story of Jacob (vv. 2–5), with v. 2 as introduction and v. 5 as conclusion

\
V. 5, Yahweh ↑ is Israel's God ↓
V. 6, Return to your God ↑

/

A′ : Guilt of Jacob's Offspring (vv. 6–8), with call to return to their God

\
V. 8, Ephraim ↑

Hosea 12 is, after chaps. 1 and 3, the most discussed chapter of the book. In order to make sense of the text, many scholars resort to emendation, sometimes on a large scale.[159] Nevertheless, the practice of keeping emendations to a minimum works well in this text.

12:1 [12:2] The translation "feed on" is incorrect here. The Hebrew word can mean to "feed on" in the sense of cattle grazing on the land, but it means to "shepherd" when used of a human. It could mean that Israel feeds on wind if Israel were here metaphorically presented as a herd of cattle or sheep,[160] but nothing in the context implies that this is the case. Rather, the following verb, "pursue," fairly rules out this option since cattle do not pursue their food. Instead, Israel is cast in the role of a shepherd who seeks to control the wind in the way that he normally controls his herds and goes in pursuit of strays. The point of the metaphor, then, is that Israel is trying to control what is by nature uncontrollable.[161] The east wind in Palestine is the destructive sirocco. Israel is here trying to manage something that is very dangerous, and as a result it will be caught up in a whirlwind. In modern terms Israel is playing with fire.[162]

The sense in which Israel tries to control the wind is explained at the end of this verse, "He makes a treaty with Assyria and sends olive oil to Egypt." That is, Israel has become involved in alliances and agreements with dangerous, powerful nations. These nations will ultimately turn and destroy them. Making a covenant implies political alliances, and sending oil implies at least commercial treaties if not also the recognition of the suzerainty of Egypt.[163] The point

---

[159] E.g., H. L. Ginsberg, "Hosea's Ephraim, More Fool Than Knave: A New Interpretation of Hosea 12:1–14," *JBL* 80 (1961): 339–47.

[160] For examples of texts where רעה describes humans metaphorically as cattle who feed off the land, see Isa 49:9; Mic 7:14; Zeph 2:7. In all these cases the nature of the metaphor is self-evident and supported by context.

[161] I cannot agree with Andersen and Freedman (*Hosea*, 603–4) that רוח and קדים are adverbial, giving the sense, "Israel shepherds (his sheep) in the wind," i.e., when conditions are not favorable. Although this translation is conceivable, it really does not illuminate the text. What would be the point of saying that Israel shepherds his sheep on a windy day?

[162] Another possibility is to take רעה in the sense of "to befriend," as do Wolff (*Hosea*, 206) and Mays (*Hosea*, 159). This too would imply that Israel is trying to come to terms with the "wind" in a way that it should not.

[163] See D. J. McCarthy, "Hosea XII 2: Covenant by Oil," *VT* 14 (1964): 215–21.

is not that Yahweh had forbidden Israel all commercial contacts with other nations but that Israel had allowed its political and economic ties to these nations to give them a false sense of security. Like someone who has tried to make a pet of a tiger, they have forgotten how dangerous these nations are.

In this context the assertion that Israel "multiplies lies and violence" is not simply a general statement that lawlessness is common. Instead, the message is that the Israelites have compromised their principles in order to accommodate relations with foreign powers. Hosea has almost taken us back to the metaphor of Israel the wayward wife who prostitutes herself for the sake of her "lovers," the gods of the nations or the nations themselves. The threat of v. 2 to punish Judah and Israel according to their "ways" and their "deeds," moreover, is very similar to Hos 4:9–10, with its reference to Israel's prostitution of itself. In the atmosphere of spiritual compromise, violence and fraud flourish.

12:2–5 [12:3–6]   The assertion that Yahweh has a complaint against Judah (v. 2) makes it very unlikely that 11:12 should be taken in a positive sense. Again, although the text calls Yahweh's charge a *rîb,* a complaint or accusation, it is not necessary to read the entire passage form-critically as a "*rîb*-motif," that is, as a legal action. To be sure, accusations appear throughout this text, as they do throughout the entire book; but this does not mean that Hosea here sets up a courtroom scene except as a passing metaphor.[164] The motif does not dominate the text, and the excursus on the life of Jacob should not be read as evidence presented in court of Israel's guilt.

Hosea here resumes the theme from 6:7–9 that Israel has inherited the worst traits of their ancestor without picking up any of the good qualities; in particular the people of Hosea's generation are untouched by grace.[165] The portrayal of the life of Jacob here is not chronological but consists of passing allusions to details of the Genesis account that are thematically arranged in order to create a portrait of the patriarch as a desperate man transformed by God. "In the womb he grasped his brother's heel" alludes to the birth of Jacob and Esau at Gen 25:26. "As a man he struggled with God. He struggled with the angel[166] and overcame him"[167] describes the wrestling at Peniel (Penuel), as presented in Genesis 32. The phrase "as a man" is a wordplay in Hebrew: it could be taken to mean "at his deception [*ʾāwen],"*

---

[164] Cf. Stuart, who takes this to be a "lawsuit" text but observes that elements in the text do not fit the normal pattern (*Hosea-Jonah,* 188). See also Mays, *Hosea,* 161.

[165] Cf. P. R. Ackroyd, "Hosea and Jacob," *VT* 13 (1963): 245–59.

[166] Davies says that Hosea plays down Jacob's victory by describing it only as a victory over an angel and not over God (*Hosea,* 274–75). A number of scholars reject מַלְאָךְ altogether as a scribal insertion.

[167] Some scholars take the angel to be the subject of וַיֻּכָל in Hos 12:4 (Eng. 5). See Mays, *Hosea,* 163. This is unlikely; in the line וַיָּשַׂר אֶל־מַלְאָךְ וַיֻּכָל one naturally reads both verbs to have the same subject rather than for the object of the first to become the subject of the second. For a more far-fetched proposal involving both emendation and alternative interpretation of the verbs, see M. Gertner, "An Attempt at an Interpretation of Hosea XII," *VT* 10 (1960): 272–84.

the term *ʾāwen* meaning "deception" or "nothingness" and also being Hosea's byword for the shrine at Bethel, Beth Aven.[168] The implied accusation is: Jacob as a man struggled with God near Bethel; the nation has rebelled against God at Beth Aven.

"He found him at Bethel and talked with him there" refers both to Jacob's vision of the heavenly stairway while he was en route to Haran and to God's second appearance to Jacob upon his return to Bethel (Gen 28:10–22; 35:6–15). That is, the line does not so much refer to one incident as make the point that *Bethel was the place where God came to Jacob.*[169] It is noteworthy that the text here calls Bethel by its right name instead of by the byword Beth Aven; at Bethel Jacob met the true God and not the god of the shrine.[170] This implicitly criticizes the decadence of the Bethel shrine to which people of Hosea's day made pilgrimages by contrasting the cult of Hosea's generation with Jacob's experience there.

Allusion to Jacob's grasping Esau's heel at their births refers to the whole history of the conflict between the two brothers. The verb *ʿāqab*, translated in the NIV as "he grasped his heel," is the root of the name "Jacob." Esau himself gave the interpretation of this name in Gen 27:36: "Isn't that why his name is called Jacob? He has supplanted [*ʿāqab*] me these two times!"[171] The word *ʿāqab* appears to have the idea of grabbing someone by the heel in order to bring that person down and take his place.[172] Jacob is thus portrayed as a man who struggled to get ahead even if it meant trying to shove aside his own brother.

Jacob's attitude, that he needed to fight for everything he had, carried over into his relationship to God. Hosea says that Jacob "struggled" [*śārâ*][173] with

---

[168] Cf. Coote, "Hosea XII," 393–94, for a good discussion of וּבְאוֹנוֹ.

[169] The *yiqtol* form יְמְצָאֶנּוּ should be taken to imply repeated action. It does not refer to a future action, contrary to Ward (*Hosea*, 210), but the presence of this verbal form in a past tense context should not be passed over in silence, as if it were a *qatal*. Cf. *GBH*, §113e.

[170] D. Kidner, *Love to the Loveless: The Message of Hosea* (Downers Grove: InterVarsity, 1981), 109. We should note that the LXX has ἐν τῷ οἴκῳ Ὤν, "in the house of On," which implies a Hebrew text בֵּת אוֹן, "Beth Aven." But it is probable that the LXX has harmonized this text with other occurrences of בֵּת אוֹן. Cf. Wolff, *Hosea*, 206–7.

[171] See also Jer 9:3. In Hos 6:8 the passive form עֲקֻבָּה מִדָּם means something like "with footprints of blood." See commentary there.

[172] A different interpretation is that of S. H. Smith, who argues that עקב here means to "seize by the genitals" as a means of supplanting his brother's position ("'Heel' and 'Thigh': The Concept of Sexuality in the Jacob-Esau Narratives," *VT* 40 [1990]: 464–73).

[173] The Hb. of 12:4 (Eng. 3) unambiguously has שׂרה, but v. 5 (Eng. 4) is more difficult. The form וַיָּשַׂר appears to be from the root שׂוּר, a word that appears in 1 Chr 20:3 with the meaning "to saw." BDB (975) suggests emending to וַיָּשַׂר as an apocopated form of שׂרה. Even so, the presence of the preposition אֶל is confusing after the previous verse used the verb with אֶת. In light of our limited knowledge of the morphology and usage of שׂרה (it only occurs here, in Gen 32:29, and possibly in Isa 28:25), significant emendation is ill-advised. Cf. Wolff (*Hosea*, 212–13) for a fairly elaborate reconstruction of the text. It appears, in fact, that Hosea has deliberately shaped these words and has even made use of unusual grammar in order to create the wordplay וישׂר אל, "and Isr[a] el."

God at Peniel, an allusion to the blessing of the angel[174] in Gen 32:29, "You have struggled *[śārâ]* with God and men." Jacob's supposition, that he could only gain what he wanted by fighting God or men to get it, seems to be vindicated in the phrase that follows, "and overcame him."

On the other hand, the following line is not compatible with the position of one who has prevailed over an adversary, "he wept and begged for his favor." This appears to refer to Gen 33:3–4, where Jacob bows seven times to Esau and then weeps with him. In the structure of Hosea's poem, begging for Esau's favor is in contrast to wrestling with Esau in the womb. However, in the normal reading of the Hosea text, one naturally takes it to mean that Jacob sought for *God's* favor, not Esau's, because the lines immediately before and after this refer to Jacob's encounters with God. "He wept and begged for his favor" therefore has a double meaning. On one level, in the chiastic structure of the poem (see discussion below), it is Jacob's encounter with Esau; on another level, in the flow of the poem, it is Jacob's encounters with God. This is thus a theological interpretation of the Genesis narrative to bring out the fact that the one from whom Jacob really sought mercy was God.

Thus v. 4 casts Jacob in the incongruous role of a victorious suppliant, who begs for grace from the angel he has defeated. Therefore this verse is also a retelling of Gen 32:25–30, in which the wounded Jacob seized the angel and refused to let him go until he gave Jacob his blessing. The Genesis text does not say that Jacob wept on this occasion, although his desire for a blessing has the air of desperation about it.[175] At that time the angel renamed him Israel. For Hosea the lesson is that Jacob the supplanter, the one who struggled for everything, was transformed into Israel the suppliant, the recipient of grace.

Because Hosea wants to present us with a theological portrayal of the transformation of Jacob, he rearranges the order of the story by placing the name "Bethel" at the end of the poem. In reality the first Bethel episode (Gen 28:10–22) took place many years earlier than the Peniel episode. It was at Bethel, however, that Jacob received from God the promise that he would inherit the promises given to his fathers Abraham and Isaac (Gen 28:13). Hosea places Bethel at the end of his retelling of the story to create a contrast between the grace Jacob received and his life of conniving, scheming, and struggling. That is, Jacob's machinations and battles for survival represented his old life, his life

---

[174] We should add that Gen 32:25 (Eng. 24) only calls Jacob's adversary a "man" (אִישׁ), but it is obtuse to fail to see that this "man" is an angelic or divine figure (cf. Gen 18:2, where the angelic figures are called "three men" [אֲנָשִׁים]). One would be well-advised not to make too much of the fact that Hosea calls this figure an "angel," as though this implied that he was drawing on a tradition distinct from the Genesis text. Contrast Mays, *Hosea,* 163.

[175] Hosea also appears to draw details from Gen 33:1–11 into his telling of the story; 33:4 says that both Jacob and Esau "wept" when they met each other, and 33:8 says that Jacob gave his brother gifts in order to "find favor" with him.

without grace, whereas his reception of the promises at Bethel represented his new life, although chronologically the first Bethel incident came prior to some of his greatest struggles.[176] Hosea has rearranged the order of the material in order to create a contrast between the old Jacob and the new Jacob, the man who received the promises at Bethel and was later renamed Israel.

The structure of this text, a chiasmus, reinforces the message that Jacob met the true God at Bethel and was converted into Israel. It can be described as follows:

A1   And a conflict Yahweh has with Judah,
A2   and a punishment for Jacob in accordance with his ways;
A3   like his deeds, he will repay him (v. 2).
   B   In the womb he (Jacob!) tripped up his brother,
      C   And in his manhood he struggled with God (v. 3).
      C'   And he (Israel!) struggled with the angel and prevailed;
   B'   He wept and sought his favor.
A1'   At Bethel he found him.
A2'   And there he spoke with him.[177]
A3'   Yahweh God of Hosts, Yahweh is his renown! (v. 4)

In this poem C and C', Jacob's encounters with God, stand at the center. Struggling with Esau in the womb (B) is the counterpart to begging Esau's favor (B'), although, as described above, B' has a double meaning in that it more profoundly refers to begging God's favor. The lines with the "A" designation begin and end with the name Yahweh (A1 and A3'). Also, both triplets begin with two parallel lines (A1 and A2, A1' and A2'), and both end with a short line giving explanation or commentary (A3 and A3').[178]

At the center of the chiasmus, therefore, is Jacob wrestling with God (C and C' in the structure of the poem). This is the pivot about which the whole story turns. Prior to this, in vv. 2–3 is Jacob the supplanter and Yahweh's wrath toward disobedient Israel. After the encounter with God there is Israel, the man whom God met and blessed at Bethel, and a doxology to Yahweh

---

[176] It is true that Jacob went to Bethel a second time according to Gen 35:6–15, but even that text refers to Gen 28:11–22 as the primary Bethel incident (see Gen 35:7). The incident of 35:6–15 was essentially a reaffirmation of 28:11–22.

[177] The word עִמָּנוּ could be translated "with him" or "with us." There probably is deliberate ambiguity here, and Hosea may have used language that brings the past experience of Jacob into the present experience of his generation. Cf. E. K. Holt, *Prophesying the Past: The Use of Israel's History in the Book of Hosea,* JSOTSup 194 (Sheffield: JSOT Press, 1994), 39.

[178] This interpretation of the text as a chiasmus follows but modifies a valuable study by W. L. Holladay, "Chiasmus, the Key to Hosea XII 3–6," *VT* 16 (1966): 53–64. My only complaints with Holladay's analysis are that he needlessly emends the text and proposes a chiasmus that is a little too elaborate to be persuasive.

(vv. 4–5). The encounters with God represent the turning points of Jacob's life and are here brought together as one conversion experience. The parentheses "(Jacob!)" in v. 3 and "(Israel!)" in v. 4 refer to the fact that the Hebrew reader could hardly fail to see the names Jacob and Israel concealed beneath the verbs of the text.[179] The reader would recognize, moreover, that Israel was the name of blessing Jacob the supplanter received after his Peniel experience.

A number of scholars look at this text as an example of "innerbiblical exegesis."[180] It is not clear that Hosea here engages in anything that we would call "exegesis," however, beyond his portrayal of Jacob weeping and begging for favor from the angel after he "overcame" him. That is, Hosea does not seek to explain any text of Genesis in a sustained, exegetical manner. Nor should his reshuffling of the order of the events of Jacob's life be taken as evidence that he was using sources that were distinct from Genesis, or that were prior to the redaction of Genesis, or that represented a tradition separate from that found in Genesis. Hosea has done nothing more than make use of the Genesis account of Jacob's life, not in chronological order but in an order that suited his rhetorical purposes.[181] Hosea 12:3–5 might well be taken as evidence that the stories in Genesis were familiar to Hosea's audience, but it tells us nothing about the redaction history of Genesis[182] or about ancient hermeneutics, except that an ancient prophet felt free to arrange a story in a manner that was appropriate for his message. On the other hand, Hosea's version of the story of Jacob does tell us that Hosea read the Genesis account to mean that Jacob the struggling conniver became Israel the recipient of grace. Thus, while we do not see the exegesis itself, we do see one specific conclusion that Hosea drew from his exegesis.

On the basis of his reading of Genesis, Hosea can proclaim, "The LORD

---

[179] Observe that in v. 4 (Eng. 3) we have עָקַב and in v. 5 (Eng. 4) we have וַיָּשַׂר אֶל, which without spaces between words would look like וישראל ("and Israel").

[180] W. J. Kaiser, Jr., develops an evangelical model ("Inner Biblical Exegesis as a Model for Bridging the 'Then' and 'Now' Gap: Hos 12:1–6," *JETS* 28 [1985]: 33–46). S. L. McKenzie operates in the documentary hypothesis framework but argues that Hosea is giving a parody of a blessing that was pronounced at Bethel in order to condemn the cult at the shrine and equate the people with the deceitfulness of Jacob ("The Jacob Tradition in Hosea 12:4–5," *VT* 36 [1983]: 311–22). L. M. Eslinger argues that the Hosea text is based on the Genesis text but has radically reinterpreted it ("Hosea 12:5a and Genesis 32:29: A Study in Inner Biblical Exegesis," *JSOT* 18 [1980]: 91–99).

[181] J. Limburg describes this as "homiletical history" (*Hosea-Micah*, IBC [Atlanta: John Knox, 1988], 45).

[182] Contra H. A. McKay, "Jacob Makes It Across the Jabbok: An Attempt to Solve the Success/Failure Ambivalence in Israel's Self-consciousness," *JSOT* 38 (1987): 3–13. McKay believes that the postexilic author of the Genesis narrative had access to fragments of the Jacob legend preserved in Hosea, Jeremiah, and tradition. See also W. D. Whitt, "The Jacob Traditions in Hosea and Their Relation to Genesis," *ZAW* 91 (1991): 18–43. Whitt asserts that Hosea is prior to Genesis and helps to explain the shaping of Genesis.

God Almighty, the LORD is his name of renown," with the meaning that this is the God whom Jacob found. The name "LORD God Almighty" (or "LORD God of Hosts") does not occur in Genesis. It appears prominently in Amos, a prophet who seems to have influenced Hosea,[183] and in a few other texts from the monarchy period.[184] In Amos the name describes the God of all the earth who judges the nations, especially Israel (3:13; 5:16; 6:14; 9:5), but who also calls upon people to repent in order that they may live (5:14–15). It is a grand name that calls to mind all the majesty and power of God, and it here contrasts with the minimal and generic name *ʾēl*, "deity," that the Israelites used in their cult (Hos 11:7,12). This was the name of the real God of Israel, the God who found Jacob and transformed him, and it is the name by which this God should be remembered.[185] The implication is that this is the God whom the Israelites have not discovered.

12:6–8 [12:7–9]   The nation of Israel continues to live like Jacob the conniver, the man without grace. Like the old Jacob, they struggle for success and seek security not in God but in wealth. Hosea calls for three things from his people: repentance, justice, and faith. "You must return to your God" uses the familiar word *šûb*, a word that here implies abandonment of the fertility cults and all that went with them and seeking grace and mercy from Yahweh. "Maintain love and justice" is shorthand for doing all that God requires while giving greatest emphasis to the more important parts of the Torah (Matt 23:23). "Wait for your God always" implies an attitude of faith that seeks security in God rather than in wealth or position and that perseveres in faith even when circumstances are difficult.[186] If Israel will repent, they will be like their ancestor in the best sense rather than in the worst sense.

The rigged scales of the merchant are proverbial for loathsome dishonesty in trade.[187] This kind of fraud, a way of cutting any corner to get ahead,[188] is in the worst traditions of the Israelite merchant's ancestor, Jacob.[189] There is

---

[183] See commentary at 4:15.

[184] The form וַיהוָה אֱלֹהֵי הַצְּבָאוֹת also appears in Amos 3:13; 6:14; 9:5. Elsewhere it is without the article (וַיהוָה אֱלֹהֵי צְבָאוֹת) as in Amos 5:14–16; 2 Sam 5:10; Jer 5:14; 15:16.

[185] Thus the text has יְהוָה זִכְרוֹ ("Yahweh is his remembrance" [i.e., Yahweh is the name by which he is to be remembered]).

[186] The verb קוה, usually in the *piel* stem, is a favorite of Isaiah, where it means to wait patiently for some good thing, and it is almost always used of the faithful waiting on God's salvation. Isaianic texts include 5:2,4,7; 8:17; 25:9; 26:8; 33:2; 40:31; 49:23; 51:5; 59:9,11; 60:9; 64:2. It appears in a smattering of other texts, e.g., Ps 25:3,5,21.

[187] Cf. Prov 11:1; 20:23, which describe the מֹאזְנֵי מִרְמָה ("rigged balances") as an abomination to Yahweh.

[188] We should note that perhaps v. 8 (Eng. 7) should be translated, "(He is) a merchant in whose hands are deceitful scales for defrauding a friend." Cf. Andersen and Freedman, *Hosea*, 617.

[189] Wolff observes that מִרְמָה, "deception," is a key word of this chapter (*Hosea*, 207–8). We might say that for Hosea מִרְמָה is the best one-word description of the old Jacob and of his offspring.

a wordplay linking v. 7 to v. 8. The word for "merchant" in v. 7 [Hb. 8] is
kĕna⁢an, a word that also means "Canaan." In v. 8 Hosea calls the prosperous merchant and upper classes "Ephraim." The point is that the successful
but unscrupulous mercantile class of Ephraim has become Canaan, that is, a
people who are as unethical as the original Canaanites.[190] These people
believe that their wealth and connections have put them out of reach of pros-
ecution; they have acquired the status of being above the law.[191] The merchant's assertion is not, "With all my wealth they will not find in me any
iniquity or sin," as in the NIV, but, "With all my wealth they will not find in
me any iniquity for which I can be held accountable."[192] The point is that
although they may escape retribution within the justice system of Israel, they
will not escape Yahweh's retribution.[193]

> [9]"I am the LORD your God,
>   [who brought you] out of Egypt;
> I will make you live in tents again,
>   as in the days of your appointed feasts.
> [10]I spoke to the prophets,
>   gave them many visions
>   and told parables through them."
>
> [11]Is Gilead wicked?
> Its people are worthless!
> Do they sacrifice bulls in Gilgal?
>   Their altars will be like piles of stones
>   on a plowed field.

---

[190] Deliberate linkage between the two is implied in beginning v. 8 (Eng. 7) with כְּנַעַן in *casus
pendens* (so giving prominence to כְּנַעַן), whereas v. 9 (Eng. 8) begins with the *wayyiqtol* sequence
וַיֹּאמֶר אֶפְרַיִם. See also Wolff, *Hosea*, 214.

[191] Hosea uses a wordplay to forge another link between Jacob and his unscrupulous offspring.
In 12:9 (Eng. 8) Ephraim boasts that he has gained אוֹן ("wealth") and can rest secure from fear of
retribution. But 12:4 (Eng. 3) asserts that Jacob, in his אוֹן ("adulthood"), struggled with God. Thus
for both Jacob and his offspring, אוֹן (which basically means "strength" but can refer to either the
prime of life or wealth) was the occasion for conflict with God.

[192] More literally, "which would be guilt." In the line לֹא יִמְצְאוּ־לִי עָוֺן אֲשֶׁר־חֵטְא the
phrase אֲשֶׁר־חֵטְא does not mean "or sin." אֲשֶׁר is a relative pronoun, and חֵטְא here has the sense
of "guilt" or that for which one may be held accountable. See, e.g., the use of חֵטְא in Lev 19:17;
22:9; Num 18:32; Deut 15:9; 23:22–23; 24:15. The last text, Deut 24:15, is particularly appropriate
regarding the charge of fraud levied against the upper classes. It warns them to pay the poor laborers their daily wages before sunset lest the laborers "cry out to the Lord against you, and you would
incur guilt" (וְהָיָה בְךָ חֵטְא, translation is NRSV).

[193] Depending on how the words were pronounced in eighth-century Israel, there may be one
other wordplay: the wealthy merchant boasts that because he has so much wealth (אוֹן) no one can
prove that he has committed any evil (עָוֺן).

DIVINE COMPLAINT: DIVINE RESOLVE OVER APOSTATE ISRAEL (12:9–
11) [A']. In this passage Yahweh briefly resumes speaking. He shifts the
focus of his complaints from the exodus to the message of the prophets, a shift
that Hosea will follow in the opening of his next complaint (vv. 12–13). Yahweh concludes his complaint with an enigmatic oracle (v. 11), an example of
the kind of speaking in "visions" and "parables" that v. 10 describes.

12:9 [12:10] Once again Yahweh declares that he will undo the exodus
and return Israel to the status of being no longer a nation. Here, however, he
speaks of a return to wilderness rather than a return to slavery. In declaring
himself to be their Savior-God, the one who came to their aid when they were
slaves in Egypt, Yahweh asserts his sovereignty over them. The NIV translation
is somewhat misleading at the end of the verse, "as in the days of your
appointed feasts." The word translated "appointed feasts" is actually singular
and refers to only one feast, the Feast of Tabernacles or Booths.[194] This was the
annual holy week in which Israel memorialized the wilderness wandering by
leaving their homes and spending a week in tents or in hastily constructed,
temporary lean-to shelters (Lev 23:33–44).[195] Probably a fair number of the
people did not relish the idea of having to move outdoors and live like this for
one week a year, and Yahweh's point is that the discomfort of the booths would
become a permanent condition. They would become, like their ancestors,
homeless wanderers. The verse looks ahead to Israel's Diaspora.

12:10 [12:11] Abruptly, Yahweh moves from the exodus and wilderness
history to the activity of the prophets and declares, "I speak by the prophets,
and I multiply visions and give parables through the prophets." The repetition
of the word "prophets" (omitted in the NIV) reinforces the fact that Yahweh
has shifted the focus of his complaint. The verbs probably should be translated
in the present tense (not past tense) because Yahweh is not here speaking of the
distant past (as in his references to the exodus) but of an ongoing activity, as
was carried on in the ministry of Hosea himself.[196] Ancient oracles often were
enigmatic or esoteric, and "parables" here almost implies "riddles." Yahweh's
point is that he has been warning the people, albeit sometimes in a puzzling
form, but they are too stubborn and too obtuse to receive the warnings. The

---

[194] The verse calls it a מוֹעֵד; it was one of the מֹעֲדֵי יְהוָה (Lev 23:44).

[195] Wolff argues that the מוֹעֵד here is not the Feast of Booths, which he regards as a late development, but refers to the actual time of wandering in the desert when Yahweh was among them in
the tent of meeting (אֹהֶל מוֹעֵד; *Hosea,* 215). See also Andersen and Freedman, *Hosea,* 618. But
כִּימֵי מוֹעֵד would be a peculiar way to refer to the wilderness period, and at any rate the shrine of
Yahweh continued to occupy the tent of meeting long after the conquest.

[196] The syntax of the verb system in poetic or prophetic texts is only partially understood, but
the sequence here—a *weqatal* and prepositional phrase (וְדִבַּרְתִּי עַל־הַנְּבִיאִים) followed by *waw*
conjunction, pronoun, object, and *qatal* form (וְאָנֹכִי חָזוֹן הִרְבֵּיתִי), followed by a *waw* conjunction, construct chain, and *yiqtol* (וּבְיַד הַנְּבִיאִים אֲדַמֶּה)—does not seem to be descriptive of a
process that is entirely in the past.

word translated "speak in parables" is sometimes rendered, "I will bring destruction" (NRSV), but this is lexically unlikely and is virtually excluded by context.[197]

12:11 [12:12]   Giving an example of the kind of "parable" that Yahweh pronounces through the prophets, v. 11 is a baffling portrayal of Israel's sin and doom. The enigmatic nature of this verse should not be smoothed out in translation (as the NIV and other versions do) but should be left intact. The verse is a prophetic riddle:

> If Gilead is deception,
>   surely they are nothing;
> In Gilgal they sacrifice bulls,
>   even their altars are like heaps of rocks on the furrows of a field.

The Book of Hosea mentions Gilead only in one other place, in 6:8, the verse that furtively alludes to Jacob in the expression "stained with footprints of blood." This brings us back to the motif of the nation Israel being like unregenerate Jacob, conniving and desperate, a theme that was again taken up in 12:3–4. Also "deception" in Hebrew is *ʾāwen*, the same word that appears in the parody of the name of Bethel, "Beth Aven."[198] Bethel was the place where Jacob saw the stairway to heaven while fleeing from Esau to Haran, and Gilead was the place where Laban caught up with Jacob as he returned with stolen property (in Rachel's possession) while returning to Canaan. In both cases Jacob had been using any means he thought necessary to get ahead of a close relative in a struggle for advantage, and in both cases Yahweh met him and gave him grace (see e.g., Gen 27:1–46; 28:10–22; 30:30–31:30). The Israelites, once again, have all of the bad qualities of Jacob (the *ʾāwen* of "Beth Aven," the footprints of blood at Gilead) but none of the grace (the vision at Bethel, the meeting of the angel at Peniel). In that condition they are "nothing."[199] That is, without Yahweh they are a nonpeople. They have forsaken the divine promises—promises that Jacob received at Bethel—that are the very basis of their national identity. As such they have no reason to continue as a nation.

---

[197] The root דמה I in the *piel* stem means to "liken," "compare," or "speak in parables." In the *niphal* stem דמה II means to "be destroyed," but there are no clear cases of its having the meaning "destroy" in the *piel* stem (see *HALOT*, 225–26). At any rate, since the verse describes how Yahweh speaks through the prophets, the meaning "speak in parables" is certain here.

[198] This also explains why the text says, "If Gilead is *ʾāwen*" instead of the grammatically correct, "If *ʾāwen* is in Gilead." By saying "Gilead = *ʾāwen*," the prophet means that the apostasy at Gilead is the same as that at Beth *ʾāwen*, that is, at Bethel.

[199] We should also recall that און could be translated "wealth" or "power." It is in this sense (albeit with a pun) that v. 4 (Eng. 3) spoke of Jacob "in his manhood" struggling with God. The Israelites would have thought of Gilead as און in the sense of "power," but actually it was nothingness. Cf. Coote, "Hosea XII," 398.

Gilgal appears in two other places in Hosea: in 4:15, where it is a shrine city like Bethel ("Beth Aven") that only leads people into apostasy, and in 9:6, where it is the paradigm of everything that is evil in Israel. The sacrifice of bulls does nothing to mollify Yahweh because the very altars of Gilgal are defiled. They are "like heaps of rocks on the furrows of a field," meaning that they are an impediment to finding God and not a means to him. Altars were characteristically made of simple, undressed stone and as such would resemble a heap of rocks. In an agricultural field, however, a heap of rocks is not a good thing but an impediment that must be removed in order for plowing, growth, and harvesting to take place. Thus Gilgal, with its religious shrines, is an obstacle to preparing a true harvest of righteousness.

¹²Jacob fled to the country of Aram;
   Israel served to get a wife,
   and to pay for her he tended sheep.
¹³The LORD used a prophet to bring Israel up from Egypt,
   by a prophet he cared for him.
¹⁴But Ephraim has bitterly provoked him to anger;
   his Lord will leave upon him the guilt of his bloodshed
   and will repay him for his contempt.

¹When Ephraim spoke, men trembled;
   he was exalted in Israel.
   But he became guilty of Baal worship and died.
²Now they sin more and more;
   they make idols for themselves from their silver,
cleverly fashioned images,
   all of them the work of craftsmen.
It is said of these people,
   "They offer human sacrifice
   and kiss the calf-idols."
³Therefore they will be like the morning mist,
   like the early dew that disappears,
   like chaff swirling from a threshing floor,
   like smoke escaping through a window.

PROPHETIC COMPLAINT: JACOB AND HIS HEIRS (12:12–13:3) [B′]. This text is divided into three parts, each of which develops further an idea from previous material. First, in 12:12–13 Hosea takes up from Yahweh's speech of 12:9–10 the themes of the exodus and of the work of the prophets, and he combines this material with the story of Jacob that he had already refashioned at 12:3–5. Second, in 12:14–13:1 he enlarges upon the theme of Ephraim's fall from power and prestige, an idea he already presented at 12:1,8. Third, in 13:2–3 he gives exposition of the riddle from 12:11, "If Gilead is deception, surely they are nothing."

12:12–13 [12:13–14] Hosea begins this section by returning to the story of Jacob, and once again he cites incidents from Jacob's life in order to make a comparison between the patriarch and his descendants. "Jacob fled to the country of Aram; Israel served to get a wife, and to pay for her he tended sheep" alludes to Gen 27:43–29:30. Here, however, Hosea takes the parallel in an altogether new direction: he compares Jacob's experience to the exodus and to the ministry of the prophets, two comparisons suggested in Yahweh's complaint (12:9–10).

Several details tie Jacob's experience in Haran to that of Israel in Egypt.[200] First, both Haran and Egypt are foreign lands that served as places of refuge, the first for Jacob the fugitive and the second for himself and his family in a time of famine. Second, Jacob worked like a slave to obtain Rachel's hand, but he was deceived by his host and ended up working fourteen years instead of the agreed upon seven. Similarly, the Israelites' confidence that Egypt was a place of safety for them was shattered when a pharaoh who did not know Joseph turned against them and enslaved them.[201] Third, the alert reader knows that Laban wanted to keep Jacob from acquiring any wealth for himself but that he was thwarted when God caused the variegated sheep to multiply and so increased Jacob's share of the flock. God thus created a situation in which Laban was eager to have Jacob leave (Gen 31:1–14). In this Yahweh delivered Jacob from the machinations of Laban just as he would later deliver Israel from Egyptians, who were also more than ready to be rid of them after Yahweh afflicted Egypt with the plagues. In both cases, moreover, the Israelites departed with the wealth of their hosts. Fourth, Hosea creates another parallel with a wordplay: Jacob "tended" (*šāmar*) sheep to get a wife (v. 12), and in the exodus Yahweh "tended" (*šāmar*) Israel through his prophet (v. 13).[202]

The "prophet" who brought Israel out of Egypt and who "tended" them

---

[200] Wolff misreads this text completely (*Hosea,* 216). He argues that fleeing to Aram serves as a metaphor for Israel's apostasy with foreign nations and gods and that serving for a wife is symbolic of the fertility cult. He writes, "The patriarch of Israel had begun his disgraceful association with the foreign woman in Aram and thus became the prototype of the condemned priesthood." But nothing in this text or any other implies that Jacob did anything wrong in taking his wife from the household of Laban (see Gen 28:1–4), and no tradition presents Rachel (or Leah) as the archetype for the cult prostitute. Actually, Jacob went to Haran to avoid marrying foreign women; cf. Rebekah's concern in Gen 27:46.

[201] Hos 12:13 (Eng. 12) and Jacob's complaint in Gen 29:25 both use the verb עבד (a term that connotes either service or slavery) to describe his work for Rachel. Exodus repeatedly uses the root עבד to describe the slavery of the Israelites in Egypt, as at Exod 1:13, "And the Egyptians ruthlessly enslaved [עבד] the Israelites."

[202] There is also a parallel in the fact that Jacob served "for a wife" (בְּאִשָּׁה) and Yahweh delivered Israel "by a prophet" (וּבְנָבִיא).

through the wilderness is self-evidently Moses.[203] There is no reason for Hosea here to refer to Moses by the title "prophet" except that Yahweh had just spoken of his work of calling to Israel through the prophets in 12:10. In picking up this term and tying it back into the theme of the exodus, Hosea identifies himself as a prophet with Moses. In rejecting Hosea, the people also were rejecting Moses.[204]

12:14–13:1 [12:15–13:1]   These two verses, with their portrayal of the crime and punishment of Ephraim, have no clear connection to the verses immediately preceding or following. Their placement here is not accidental, however, for Hosea is again taking up a theme from a prior text. In this case it is the Ephraim sayings that bracket 12:1–8. Here Ephraim's fate is regarded as not only certain but even as past (e.g., "and he died"). We should not regard this as evidence that this text comes from a later period; the past tense of the verbs is for rhetorical purposes.

Hosea first asserts that Ephraim has "provoked" Yahweh, a term that implies exasperating God through attachment to idols or pagan rites.[205] The phrase "guilt of his bloodshed" implies crimes worthy of capital punishment.[206] Hosea may be using the term metaphorically, but he most likely has actual crimes of violence in mind. The word "contempt" connotes the giving of personal insults, but here it probably refers to flagrant disregard for the Torah and especially to giving honor to Baal in the shrines of Yahweh. It is curious, however, that the text here refers to God as "his master" (NIV: "his lord").[207] The word denotes Yahweh's ownership of Ephraim but at the same time downgrades the quality of the relationship between the two parties from covenant to one of master and slave.

---

[203] Andersen and Freedman argue that the text implies that two different prophets are in view (*Hosea*, 620–22). They contend that the repetition of בְּאִשָּׁה implies that v. 13 (Eng. 12) alludes to both Rachel and Leah and thus that the repetition of וּבְנָבִיא in v. 14 (Eng. 13) implies that two prophets, Moses and one other (Elijah? Samuel?), are meant. This is unlikely and fairly pointless anyway since the identity of the second prophet is unknown and Hosea does not do anything to develop this idea. In both cases the repetition probably is for metrical reasons only. The two verses are tricola, as follows:

וַיִּבְרַח יַעֲקֹב שְׂדֵה אֲרָם/ וַיַּעֲבֹד יִשְׂרָאֵל בְּאִשָּׁה/ וּבְאִשָּׁה שָׁמָר:
וּבְנָבִיא הֶעֱלָה יְהוָה/ אֶת־יִשְׂרָאֵל מִמִּצְרָיִם/ וּבְנָבִיא נִשְׁמָר:

[204] On the other hand, there are no grounds for taking this verse with the following and drawing the conclusion that the Israelites murdered Moses. This fairly outlandish theory was proposed by E. Sellin and adopted by S. Freud, *Moses and Monotheism* (New York: Random House, 1953), 42–49. Cf. J. Lust, "Freud, Hosea, and the Murder of Moses: Hosea 12," *ETL* 65 (1989): 81–93.

[205] For such examples using the *hiphil* of כעס, see Deut 9:18 (referring to the golden calf episode); 31:29 (which says that Israel would do evil בְּמַעֲשֵׂה יְדֵיכֶם ("by provoking him with the work of your hands"); and Isa 65:3.

[206] Using the word דָּמִים, "bloodshed." Cf. Stuart, *Hosea-Jonah,* 196.

[207] Using אֲדֹנָי instead of יהוה.

Allusion to the former glory of Ephraim in 13:1[208] has a parallel in the references to the financial success of Ephraim in 12:1,8. The former was Ephraim's appraisal of its own wealth, and the latter is the prophet's admission that at one time Ephraim was indeed a formidable entity. "Ephraim," by metonymy, often stands for the whole Northern Kingdom, but here it specifically means Ephraim as the leading tribe of the north. Even so, the fall of Ephraim is representative for the fall of all the northern territory (if Ephraim could be brought down, how much more so the other northern tribes?). Hosea already looks upon Ephraim as "dead," that is, as having passed into history and with no more hope of recovery or return. The single thing to which he attributes Ephraim's fall, moreover, is the cult of Baal. For Hosea the apostasy, crime, and immorality of the people stemmed from this one fundamental deviation from God's Torah.

13:2–3 The translation of 13:2 is disputed. Instead of the NIV, one might propose the following interpretation: "And now they are repeatedly sinning, / and they make for themselves an image. // From their silver,[209] according to their skill, (they make) idols; / every one the work of craftsmen. // 'To these,' they are saying, 'sacrifice!'[210] / Humans[211] kiss calves!" The most debated feature of this text concerns the question of whether it accuses the Israelites of making human sacrifice (see NIV). Although the people of Hosea's generation may have stooped to this, two arguments tell against this interpretation. First, it seems strange that Hosea should make a passing reference to this most heinous kind of idolatry. Human sacrifice is not the sort of thing one mentions as an aside, especially if it was regularly practiced.[212]

---

[208] There is reason to question the translation "When Ephraim spoke, men trembled; he was exalted in Israel." The word רְתֵת (hapax legomenon in the OT) does appear in the Qumran text 1QH 4:33 with the meaning "dread" or "fear." However, the use of a single noun for a main clause (taking כְּדַבֵּר אֶפְרַיִם רְתֵת to mean "when Ephraim spoke, [there was] terror") is surprising. In addition, taking the *qal* form נָשָׂא as an intransitive, "he was exalted," is almost certainly wrong. One must emend to the *niphal* participle נִשָּׂא (cf. Wolff, *Hosea*, 219). Andersen and Freedman propose: "Truly He had spoken terrifyingly against Ephraim. He had lifted up (his voice) against Israel" (*Hosea*, 624, 629–30). They take the כ on כְּדַבֵּר to be asseverative, assert that the ב on בְּיִשְׂרָאֵל does double duty and means "against," and supply קוֹל with נָשָׂא. But this implies a text that is so elliptical as to be almost unintelligible. One might suggest that the line means "When Ephraim spoke, he aroused terror in Israel." But we do not know if an ancient reader would have understood רְתֵת with נָשָׂא in this way.

[209] The NIV reads מִכַּסְפָּם with מַסֵּכָה, but both the Masoretic accentuation and the meter support taking it with the following line.

[210] Both the LXX (θύσατε) and the Vg (*immolate*) support reading זֹבְחֵי as a plural imperative (זִבְחוּ). It is also possible that the text was originally the feminine singular imperative (זִבְחִי) and represents priestly instruction to the female devotees of the cults. Cf. Ward, *Hosea*, 220.

[211] Stuart correctly cites Jer 47:2 as an example of אָדָם with a plural verb (*Hosea-Jonah*, 200).

[212] The verb יֹסֵף in this verse implies that Hosea is concerned with sins that the people routinely committed and not with the occasional extreme example. One might make the case that child sacrifice is behind 9:10 (see commentary), but Hosea does not explicitly make any such charge there.

Second, the relevant portion of the Hebrew text is ungrammatical,[213] and some emending is necessary.[214] The simplest emendation, however, one that is supported in the versions,[215] eliminates from the text the idea of human sacrifice.[216] It is best to read this verse as a condemnation of the routine idolatry and apostasy of the people, especially as it occurred at Bethel.

The proposed translation suggested for v. 2 divides into three couplets. The first line, "And now they are repeatedly sinning, / and they make for themselves an image," expounds the line from 12:11, "If Gilead is ʾāwen / they are nothing." Hosea translates the enigmatic assertion that they are ʾāwen ("nothingness, deception, iniquity") to mean that they sin repeatedly. "Nothing," moreover, is sometimes code for idolatry (as at Jonah 2:9), and this may serve as a bridge to the specific charge that they worship an "image." The second line, "From their silver, according to their skill, (they make) idols; / every one the work of craftsmen," attests to the effort and expense they go to in creating their idols—a fact that increases rather than diminishes their culpability. The third line, " 'To these,' they are saying, 'sacrifice!' / Humans kiss calves!" explains how they use their idols. Under the leadership of the priests and the

---

[213] The line לָהֶם הֵם אֹמְרִים זֹבְחֵי אָדָם עֲגָלִים יִשָּׁקוּן literally translated is unintelligible: "to them they are saying sacrificers of man they kiss calves." The NIV rendering is free and unlikely; it improperly treats הֵם אֹמְרִים as a passive and so conceals the problem of whom Hosea is citing (i.e., who is the הֵם?). The הֵם probably is not some anonymous third party (no other group exists anywhere in this context) but are the leaders who, in the tradition of Jeroboam I, command the people to honor calves as their gods. Throughout Hosea the political and religious leaders of Israel are the principal opponents of the prophet. The NIV also treats זֹבְחֵי אָדָם as the predicate of a verbless clause that has no explicit subject. One might contend that לָהֶם implies a subject for this clause, but this approach would be much more persuasive if the text were syntactically consistent. Instead, Hosea switches to a *yiqtol* (imperfect) at יִשָּׁקוּן rather than maintain the parallel by using another construct participle. If the text had used two parallel participles, one could argue that it means "To them they are saying, 'Sacrificers of people! Kissers of calves!' " As it stands, this is not possible.

[214] Andersen and Freedman assert that זֹבְחֵי אָדָם plainly means "those who sacrifice humans" (*Hosea,* 632). This is correct, but it is not definitive for interpreting this verse if in fact the Hebrew needs to be emended. They translate the line, "Those who sacrifice people speak to them." This is unlikely for several reasons. First, their translation makes זֹבְחֵי אָדָם the subject of אֹמְרִים and deletes the actual subject, הֵם. Second, it is somewhat odd to have one participle immediately following another and serving as its subject. Third, if Hosea had meant "speak," he should have used the root דבר, a verb that is used absolutely, and not אמר, a verb that introduces a direct quote. Wolff translates the line, "They say to themselves, 'Those who sacrifice men kiss calves' " (*Hosea,* 219). Apart from the fact that this translation makes no sense, it is most unlikely. For "they say to themselves," one would expect בְּלִבָּם ("in their hearts"), not לָהֶם in Hb. (cf. Zech 12:5).

[215] Cf. the rendition in Vg.: *his ipsi dicunt immolate homines vitulos adorantes* (" 'To these,' they say, 'Sacrifice!' Men are worshiping calves").

[216] Another proposal is that represented by the KJV tradition, "Let the men that sacrifice kiss the calves." See also NASB. This translation, however, is hardly persuasive. It takes the construct chain זֹבְחֵי אָדָם as a partitive genitive. This kind of construction occurs in phrases such as קְטֹן בָּנָיו, "the youngest of his sons," in 1 Chr 21:17 but is an unnatural reading of our text. Cf. *GBH,* §129.

royal house, the people treat the images as the proper objects of worship and even debase themselves by kissing calves (referring to calf-idols and not to the actual animals).

We should finally observe that the exhortation to sacrifice to these images and the comment that people kiss calves calls to mind the golden calf episode of Exodus 32. In particular the proclamation "Sacrifice to these!" is analogous to the proclamation of Exod 32:8, "These are your gods, O Israel, who brought you up out of Egypt." First Kings 12:20–33, detailing Jeroboam's establishment of the shrines at Dan and Bethel, parallels the account of the golden calf but adds the point that Jeroboam established a feast at which Israel would go to Bethel and sacrifice to the calf-idols. Apparently both Hos 13:1–2 and the 1 Kings text point to a common prophetic tradition of evaluating the Bethel shrine as a repetition of the golden calf episode.[217] Thus it is all the more significant that the context in Hosea makes repeated allusions to the exodus (12:9,13; 13:4).

Verse 3 further expounds on the idea that the people have become "nothing" because of their idolatry (12:11). Morning mist, dew, smoke, and chaff are all examples of things that are insubstantial and fleeting. The translation "like smoke escaping through a window" is somewhat misleading because to the modern reader it appears that something odd is going on—we do not normally have smoke going out a window unless the house is on fire. But the "window" here is really only a chimney, which may or may not have been in the roof of an Israelite house. The chimney could be a lattice work in the wall.

Excursus: Christianity and the Second Commandment

The Second Commandment (Exod 20:4–6; Deut 5:8–10) forbids the making of an idol that has as its pattern anything in heaven, earth, or sea; and it also forbids bowing down to or worshiping the same. An idol is some kind of image that is supposed to represent God, and it may be two or three dimensional (i.e., a picture or a statue). In ancient Israel any kind of visual representation of God was forbidden, although visual art itself was not banned and even depictions of supernatural beings other than God were permitted (e.g., the cherubim above the ark of the covenant, Exod 25:18–20).

Perhaps the key passage on the nature of idolatry is Deut 4:15–19: "You saw no form of any kind the day the Lord spoke to you at Horeb out of the fire. Therefore watch yourselves very carefully, so that you do not become corrupt and make for yourselves an idol, an image of any shape, whether formed like a man or a woman, or like any animal on earth or any bird that flies in the air, or like any creature that moves along the ground or any fish in the waters below. And when you look up to the sky and see the sun, the moon and the stars—all the heavenly

---

[217] Cp. especially the line כֵּן עָשָׂה בְּבֵית־אֵל לְזַבֵּחַ לָעֲגָלִים ("This he did in Bethel, sacrificing to the calves") from 1 Kgs 12:32 with Hosea's citation of the proclamation, "Sacrifice to these!" (זְבַח, emended text) and his complaint that people kiss עֲגָלִים.

array—do not be enticed into bowing down to them and worshiping things the Lord your God has apportioned to all the nations under heaven." This passage essentially makes two points. First, Israel saw no form or pattern at Sinai (Horeb) that could be the basis for making an image. That is, God took pains to see to it that they had no reason to associate Yahweh with some visible being. Second, nothing in the universe—human or animal, animate or inanimate—should serve as the visual image of God. Humans, bulls, and the sun are all equally excluded. It almost goes without saying that for the Old Testament, and certainly for Hosea, idolatry is the great sin of Israel.[218]

Christianity has a long tradition of representing God or Jesus Christ in art form. The earliest Christian art did not use images to represent God, but it did employ abstractions, such as the *ichthus* (fish) or the dove, to symbolize the Christian faith. Fairly early in the history of the church, however, the tradition began of representing Jesus as a beardless young man, a figure derived from popular images of Apollo. Despite various iconoclastic movements (e.g., the decree against icons issued by Emperor Leo III [726], which provoked the Second Council of Nicea [787]), the use of images or icons to represent deity became common, especially in the east. A principal defender of the use of icons in Christian worship was St. John of Damascus (675–749), who drew the distinction between the "worship" *(latreia)*, which he thought should be given to God alone, and "veneration" *(proskynēsis)*, which he believed could be legitimately given to people, places, and icons. Furthermore, he claimed, the veneration was not given to the image itself but to that which the image represented. Like others who venerate icons, he also contended that the incarnation validated their use.[219]

Even so, it would be a mistake to assume that the church had anything like a uniform position. Augustine (354–430) cited with approval the comment of the Roman Varro (116–27 B.C.) that worship is done "in greater purity" without images and noted that in this the pagan philosopher approached the truth of the Christian religion.[220] A renewed opposition to the use of icons emerged with the Protestant Reformation, especially from Geneva. Calvin devoted book 1, chap. 11, of the *Institutes of the Christian Religion* to a sustained attack on the use of icons and in particular excoriated the idea that icons were the books of the unlearned.[221] The Puritan tradition of making houses of worship as plain and unadorned as possible then arose, and this practice was adopted by many of the spiritual heirs of the Reformation, notably Baptists. Thus Roman Catholic and

[218] E.g., in Hos 13:1–2 the worship of Baal and the making of images were the offenses that destroyed Ephraim. In 4:17 Ephraim is joined to idols. Hosea 8:5 calls on Israel to destroy the calf-idol.

[219] His work, Πρὸς τοὺς διαβάλλοντες τὰς ἁγίας εἰκόνας ("To those who discredit holy icons"), can be found in English as *St. John Damascene on Holy Images,* trans. M. H. Allies (London: Thomas Baker, 1898). This work translates λατρεία as "adoration" and uses the word "worship" where most iconodules would prefer "venerate." See also S. Lash, "Icons," in *A New Dictionary of Christian Theology,* ed. A. Richardson and J. Bowden (London: SCM Press, 1983), 274–75.

[220] *City of God,* 4.31.

[221] *Christian Institutes* 1.11.5.

Orthodox churches have tended to contain images of every kind—of the saints, of Mary, of Jesus, and occasionally of God the Father—while reformed churches have tended to have few or no images. The situation today, however, is more complex. It is possible to find Anglican and even Roman Catholic churches of recent vintage that are quite stark and have few or no images, while many Protestants have begun to include more pictures of Jesus in their churches (often in murals or in stained-glass windows), and almost all Protestants have abandoned entirely any scruples about putting pictures of Jesus on posters or in educational literature.

In light of the uncompromising severity of the biblical injunctions against the use of images, however, we must ask again whether such pictures are legitimate. We must clarify, however, that the question concerns only whether or not we may legitimately make images of Jesus or God, not whether we may make images of saints or even of angels. We recall again that even the tent of meeting and the ark of the covenant had representations of angels (cf. Exod 25:10–22; 26:31). For most Protestants, this writer included, the main problem with addressing prayer toward an image of a saint is not with the fact that one has a picture of a saint but with the fact that one would address prayer to a saint or angel at all, whether using an image or not. Simply put, the question before us is this: Should Christians place pictures of God (e.g., in Sistine Chapel) or Jesus in their churches, homes, and Christian literature? In my opinion, the answer is no.

The biblical prohibition against images of God is absolute and is never modified or repealed in the New Testament (see Acts 17:29–30; 1 Cor 6:9; 10:7; Gal 5:20; 1 Thes 1:9; Rev 22:15). The notion that the incarnation legitimizes the use of images of God never seems to have occurred to the apostles. In fact, it is noteworthy that in the four Gospels we do not have a single word concerning the physical appearance of Jesus. One might call this an argument from silence, but it is more than that: if the apostles had considered a picture of Jesus to be helpful for devotion or evangelism, then surely they would have given their readers some kind of guidelines for making accurate pictures. In fact, the only text that might be construed as describing Jesus' appearance (Rev 1:12–16) is so obviously symbolic (e.g., he has a sword coming out of his mouth) that one can hardly contend that it tells us what Jesus actually looks like.

In the Bible there are three methods for bringing people to an encounter with God. The first is by the word, that is, by preaching and teaching. The New Testament uses a variety of words to describe proclamation as the primary means of presenting Christ to the world.[222] This preference for the spoken word is first of

---

[222] The words include the cognates of ἀγγέλλω ("announce"), including ἀναγγέλλω ("announce, proclaim"), ἀπαγγέλλω ("announce, proclaim"), διαγγέλλω ("proclaim far and wide"), ἐξαγγέλλω ("proclaim, report"), καταγγέλλω ("proclaim [solemnly]"), προκαταγγέλλω ("announce beforehand"), and their various noun forms. The verb εὐαγγελίζομαι ("evangelize") and its cognate εὐαγγέλιον ("good news") are of central importance in the NT. Another word group, κηρύσσω ("proclaim") and κήρυγμα ("proclaimation"), also testify to the centrality of preaching in the Christian faith. When one includes the NT words related to teaching, such as διδάσκω ("teach"), κατηχέω ("instruct"), παιδεύω ("educate"), and παραδίδωμι ("pass on a tradition"), with all their noun cognates, the lexical pool that relates to the primacy of the spoken word is enormous.

all methodological, in that it means that preaching and teaching are the primary media for communicating the faith. More is at stake, however, than mere method. L. Coenen points out that in Rom 16:25, "*kērygma,* message, is already becoming hypostatized: it is Christ-preaching, as carried out by Paul."[223] In other words, the Word is sacramental. It is the means by which Christ is present with us. Thus, John can open his gospel by declaring that in the beginning was the *logos,* the Word, because it is as *logos* that God comes to us. By contrast, pictures and images have no place in the primitive Christian mission.[224] One can scarcely imagine, much less seriously argue, that the apostles placed pictures of Jesus in the early churches.

It is not difficult to understand why the *logos* and not the image is the means for propagating the faith. Pagan religions were nothing if not inclusive and syncretistic. New gods, and their images, were easily assimilated to local cults and shrines. The God proclaimed by Paul, however, had only a bare altar and could only be described as "unknown" to the Athenian crowds (Acts 17:23). He is the invisible God, the one in whom we have our being, and is nothing like an image made with gold or silver (Acts 17:28–29). Any attempt to represent him visually would bring him down to the level of all the other gods. One could argue that the missionary efforts of churches that made heavy use of icons often brought about a Christo-pagan religion in the fields they evangelized.

The second way of bringing God to people is the Eucharist. In the elements of bread and wine, the worshiper has an encounter with something that is not only visible, but that can be touched and tasted as well. Hence, it is clear that Christianity is not only a religion of the intellect but also touches the human need for something that is tangible, physically experienced, and sacred. At the same time, no one can look at the bread and seriously call it an "image" of God. Rather, as Calvin taught, the elements of communion are the vehicle whereby the Holy Spirit makes Christ present to the believer and unites the Church with her Lord in heaven.[225]

The third method of bringing God to people is through incarnational ministry. That is, our hands and feet are to take up the work of Christ in this world and so embody God for other people. Humans are created in the image of God and are meant to represent him as stewards on earth. The church, moreover, functions as the parts of the body of Christ in the world. But when the church resorts to images, it allows something else—a physical object—to supplant it in its appointed task of representing God before people. A simple illustration brings out the difference in the two methods. Protestants frequently object to the prohibition of images of Jesus on the grounds that pictures are very helpful for working with small children. "Why shouldn't we show them a picture of Jesus

---

[223] *DNTT* 3:53.

[224] To be sure, Christ is at times called the εἰκών ("image") of God, as in 2 Cor 4:4 and Col 1:15. Similarly, Heb 1:3 speaks of Christ as the χαρακτήρ ("representation") of God. However, in these texts the living Christ himself is the εἰκών of God; these passages offer no justification for making images of Christ or for communicating the gospel by showing pictures of Jesus to people.

[225] *Christian Institutes* 4.17.9–10. The whole of *Christian Institutes* 4.17 is taken up with the question of the meaning of the Lord's Supper.

blessing little children," they demand, "so that they can see how Jesus loves boys and girls?" The answer is that a better means of communicating Christ's love is already available—the teacher herself (or himself) representing Christ incarnationally to the children. By laying her hands on the child's head and making a prayer of blessing, by hugging the child and giving love, the teacher can embody Christ and teach them that Jesus blessed the children in the same way that she just did.

Images, by contrast, reduce God. An image is by nature static and not dynamic. An image of Christ fixes itself in the mind of the worshipper as representing the whole of Christ. False teaching is always a danger to the church, even where no images are used, and it usually takes the form of overemphasizing one aspect of the truth. An image, by nature, can only emphasize one aspect of Christ.

The distinction between "worship" and "veneration" is artificial and dangerous. It is a distinction that the Bible neither makes nor implicitly endorses.[226] The human heart also has difficulty maintaining this distinction in actual practice. The thing that I "venerate" and that represents God to me will inevitably in some way become God for me. Furthermore, one must ask whether the pagans and apostates to whom Hosea preached might have sought to make such a distinction in their conflicts with Hosea. After all, the people of the ancient world were not stupid; most knew that their gods transcended their images of wood and stone and gold. It was this very fact that allowed for so much syncretism in pagan religion.

The idea that images are the "books of the unlearned" fails to reckon with a fundamental aspect of the Christian faith. Training and education is a major responsibility of the church, and no church should be content to leave its people in the status of "unlearned." This does not mean that all Christians should become scholars, but one of the triumphs of the Protestant Reformation was in putting into practice the belief that all converts, men and women, should be taught to read so that they could possess and study their own copies of the Bible. Far from lifting up the illiterate, images are a means of keeping them in ignorance. Furthermore, churches ought to be places where the Scriptures are publicly read so that even the illiterate can learn its message and stories.

We should finally remind ourselves of what the prohibition of images does not mean. It does not mean the rejection of all art and symbolism, merely the rejection of images of God or Christ. Abstract symbols, such as the *ichthus* or a simple cross, are certainly permissible, and even more imaginative and ornate pictures of heroes of the faith and of angels are not prohibited. It also does not mean—and here the Puritans went too far—that churches need to be as stark as

---

[226] It is true that the LXX sometimes uses the verb προσκυνέω to describe prostrating before a king or some other human, but this hardly establishes the propriety of venerating an icon. The human before whom one bows receives the honors due to a person of high office; this is not the same as venerating an icon on the grounds that it represents God. Where προσκυνέω is directed toward God, it always means "worship," and the Bible is adamant that this kind of προσκύνησις can only be given to God and not an image. For further discussion of the meaning of προσκυνέω, see *DNTT* 2:875–79.

possible. It does not mean that worship must be nonliturgical or "low church." It only means that we take seriously the injunctions in Hosea and in the rest of the Bible that we have no right to create an image of God.[227]

⁴"But I am the LORD your God,
    [who brought you] out of Egypt.
You shall acknowledge no God but me,
    no Savior except me.
⁵I cared for you in the desert,
    in the land of burning heat.
⁶When I fed them, they were satisfied;
    when they were satisfied, they became proud;
    then they forgot me.
⁷So I will come upon them like a lion,
    like a leopard I will lurk by the path.
⁸Like a bear robbed of her cubs,
    I will attack them and rip them open.
Like a lion I will devour them;
    a wild animal will tear them apart.

⁹"You are destroyed, O Israel,
    because you are against me, against your helper.
¹⁰Where is your king, that he may save you?
    Where are your rulers in all your towns,
    of whom you said,
    'Give me a king and princes'?
¹¹So in my anger I gave you a king,
    and in my wrath I took him away.
¹²The guilt of Ephraim is stored up,
    his sins are kept on record.
¹³Pains as of a woman in childbirth come to him,
    but he is a child without wisdom;
when the time arrives,
    he does not come to the opening of the womb.

¹⁴"I will ransom them from the power of the grave;
    I will redeem them from death.
Where, O death, are your plagues?
    Where, O grave, is your destruction?

"I will have no compassion,

DIVINE COMPLAINT AND DECISION (13:4–14) [C].   Verses 4–14 constitute the last divine complaint in Hosea, with 13:15–16 being Hosea's response

---

[227] For further discussion of this issue, see J. I. Packer, *Knowing God* (Downers Grove: Inter-Varsity, 1973), 38–44.

and affirmation (note that v. 15 speaks of Yahweh in the third person). These verses together bring the accusations and complaints to a close. In chap. 14, the book will conclude by appealing to the people to return to Yahweh. For the last time the book speaks of the exodus and wilderness and of Yahweh as husband (vv. 4–5), of the impotence of the Israelite government (vv. 9–11), of Israel as a wayward wife and of the fertility cult (vv. 12–13), and of the certainty of military collapse and exile (vv. 7–8). Common themes include the guilt of Israel (vv. 12,16), drought (vv. 5–6,15), and the death of a pregnant woman and her child (vv. 13,16). Twice, Yahweh uses the "Where is …?" formula in a taunt (vv. 10,14).

In structure Yahweh's speech is two chiastic units followed by a terse, concluding line (a monocolon), as follows:[228]

First Chiasmus
1A Yahweh, at exodus, became Israel's only savior (v. 4)
    1B Yahweh saved them in the wilderness (vv. 5–6aα)
        1C Israel satisfied and apostate (vv. 6aβ–b)
    1B′ Yahweh will be beast of wilderness to them (vv. 7–8)
1A′ Israel destroyed by Yahweh, their helper (v. 9)

Second Chiasmus
2A "Where is your king?" (v. 10)
    2B Yahweh will "give" a king (v. 11)
        2C Ephraim's iniquity locked up (v. 12)
        2C′ Ephraim has travails of labor pains (v. 13)
    2B′ Yahweh will ransom from death (v. 14a)
2A′ "Where is your destructive power?" (v. 14b)

Conclusion
"Compassion is hidden from my eyes."

In the first chiasmus Yahweh as Israel's only savior (1A) contrasts with Yahweh as the "helper" who destroys Israel (1A′), just as salvation in the wilderness contrasts with being slain by the beasts of the wilderness (1B, 1B′). In the second chiasmus the taunt "Where is your king?" (2A) contrasts with the taunt against death (2A′), and the ironic giving of a king (2B) contrasts with the actual ransom from death (2B′).

13:4 The LXX version of v. 4 is expanded considerably beyond what is in the Hebrew. It reads, "I am the Lord your God, maker of the heavens and creator of earth, whose hands made all the hosts of heaven, and I did not display

---

[228] The suggestion to take this text in a chiastic fashion was made to me in a paper by Ms. Johnnye Ellison, a student at Golden Gate Baptist Theological Seminary, although I have considerably modified her original suggestion.

all these things to you so that you might go after them, and I brought you up from the land of Egypt, and you shall know no other god besides me, and there is no savior beside me." Although it is always possible that the LXX reflects a text closer to the original, one has difficulty adding this much text to the MT.[229] It is best to read this strophe as a triplet, as follows:

> But I am the Lord your God from the land of Egypt,
>> And gods other than me you shall not know.
>>> No Savior exists apart from me. (v. 4)

These lines allude to the exodus and the First Commandment, hence to the theophany at Sinai. This text (along with the prophet's response in vv. 15–16) contains the last reference to the exodus story in Hosea.[230]

Verse 4 obviously abbreviates the first of the Ten Commandments, but a significant change is from "You shall *have* no other gods" (Exod 20:3) to "You shall *know* no other gods." One should not take this as evidence for an early, alternative recension of the Decalogue. Rather, this is a deliberate modification by Hosea meant to focus attention on the significance of the word "know." All readers should be aware that "know" in Hebrew can describe the sexual experience. It is certainly not the case that one should facilely read this nuance into any text where "know" is used, but in this case, such a reading, as at least a pointer to Hosea's meaning, is justified. Here, for the last time, the book of Hosea returns to the metaphor of Israel the adulterous wife. She should "know" no other gods, but she has gone after many gods and has turned away from her one true husband. The line, "And I knew you in the wilderness," in v. 5a, further establishes that "know" in this context refers to the marriage relationship. The way that God "knows" Israel in the wilderness is as husband to wife, as Hos 2:14 (Hb. 2:16) establishes.

This allusion to the husband and wife analogy allows Hosea to develop a final portrait of the denouement of the fertility cult. Metaphorically, Israel's adultery produced a child to whom she cannot properly give birth (v. 13, see comments); on a much more gruesome and literal level, the pregnant mothers in Israel will be ripped open by Assyrian soldiers (v. 16). Mother Israel had sought to obtain children through gods other than Yahweh, and the results were catastrophic.

13:5–6aα This unit is distinguished from the first by a change in person: in the first line, God addresses Israel in the second person but then speaks about

---

[229] But one cannot dismiss the LXX as a secondary expansion, since Qumran fragment 4QXIIc tends to agree with the LXX against the MT. See the discussion in R. Fuller, "A Critical Note on Hosea 12:10 and 13:4," *RB* 98 (1991): 343–57. Fuller argues that the expanded Hebrew text in 4QXIIc is not likely to have been translated from a Greek exemplar.

[230] The line "I am the Lord your God from the land of Egypt" is elliptical. The clause אֲשֶׁר הוֹצֵאתִיךָ ("who brought you out," cf. Exod 20:2) probably is omitted for metrical purposes.

them in the third person in the second line. The format is as follows:

> And I knew[231] you in the wilderness.
> In the land of drought [v. 5] it was like their pastures. [v. 6]

The translation "in the land of drought[232] it was like their pastures" makes sense of the Hebrew text without recourse to the emendation found in the NIV and in many other interpretations.[233] The point is that even in the wilderness God so cared for them it was thought they were living in their own pasture land.

13:6aβ–b   This text draws upon Deut 8:11–12, which warns the people that they must not forget Yahweh after he has given them so many good gifts.

> And they were satisfied.
>> They were satisfied and their hearts were proud.
>> Therefore they forgot me.

The "satisfaction" is not satisfaction in the sense of having no complaints against Yahweh; it is complacency, ingratitude, and a focus on the benefits God gives instead of on God himself.

13:7–8   The next unit, vv. 7–8, is composed of three couplets. The NIV maintains this structure but for some reason rearranges the text in v. 8a.[234] The flow of the text is as follows:

> So I shall be[235] to them like a lion,
>> And like a leopard I shall lie in wait by the way. (v. 7)
> And I shall meet them like a bear whose cubs have been stolen,
>> And I shall tear open the chest covering over their heart,
> And I shall devour them there like a lion,
>> A wild beast that would rip them open. (v. 8)

---

[231] The Hb. text reads יְדַעְתִּיךָ ("I knew you"), but many interpreters and versions read this to be רְעִיתִיךָ, "I pastured you." Cf. LXX: ἐγὼ ἐποίμαινόν σε. The emendation is possible, and it leads nicely into v. 6. On the other hand, the MT is intelligible and reflects Hosea's desire to stress ידע ("know") in this text. Cf. Andersen and Freedman, *Hosea,* 634. The NIV seems to be looking for middle ground in the translation, "I cared for you."

[232] The translation of this word (תַּלְאֻבָה), a hapax legomenon in the Hebrew Bible, as "drought" is based upon an Arabic cognate. According to Davies, *Hosea,* 289–90, "there is no justification for the rendering 'burning heat'" (used in the NIV).

[233] The Hb., joining the end of v. 5 to the beginning of v. 6, is בְּאֶרֶץ תַּלְאֻבוֹת כְּמַרְעִיתָם. Interpreters usually emend כְּמַרְעִיתָם to something like כְּמוֹ רְעִיתִם ("when I pastured them"). It seems that the Masoretes erred in making בְּאֶרֶץ תַּלְאֻבוֹת part of v. 5. Instead, it should be read with v. 6, with בְּאֶרֶץ תַּלְאֻבוֹת serving as a concatenating term with בַּמִּדְבָּר in v. 5, thus allowing the first strophe to lead naturally into the second. The resulting line, "In the land of drought (it was) like their pastures" is fully intelligible with no emendation. The Hebrew text is supported by both the Vg (*iuxta pascua*) and the LXX (κατὰ τὰς νομὰς αὐτῶν).

[234] The NIV paraphrases סְגוֹר לִבָּם וְאֶקְרַע ("And I shall tear open the [chest] covering over their heart") with the less graphic "rip them open"; it also moves the verb אֶפְנֵשׁם, "I will attack them," to the second stich of 8a.

[235] The translation of this *wayyiqtol* (וָאֱהִי) as "so I shall be" is legitimate in a prophetic, poetic text such as this. Cf. McComiskey, "Hosea," 1:217.

Here Yahweh becomes a wild beast of the wilderness, which contrasts with v. 5, where he is their Savior in the wilderness. In the three couplets the first lines generally speak of the ferocity of the attacker ("like a lion," "like a bear whose cubs have been stolen," and "like a lion"). The second lines also make use of the similes of wild beasts but focus more on their actions ("I shall lie in wait by the way," "I shall tear open the chest covering over their heart," and "rip them open"). The first line of the third couplet, however, combines both elements.

The meaning of these lines is self-evident; what is surprising is that Yahweh describes himself in such ferocious, bestial terms. Here again we face Hosea's willingness to use language and metaphor that is surprising if not inappropriate to our ears. We should not assume that these similes were acceptable or unremarkable to Hosea's audience, notwithstanding the willingness of other prophets to use similar language (e.g., Amos 3:4,8; 5:19). To hear God described as beastly in his brutality—devouring human flesh like a vicious carnivore—is jolting. The purpose of such a depiction is to cut through the foggy notion of an indulgent God that their theology and ritual had given them and so awaken the audience to the reality of divine fury.

The metaphor of a bear robbed of her cubs appears elsewhere (Prov 17:12), but it is used here with deliberate purpose. Yahweh has been robbed of his children (the common people of Israel) by his wife (the woman Israel, that is, the royal and priestly leadership). She has made them to be the children of Baal. We should also note that there is a wordplay at the end of v. 7. With a slight change in pronunciation, "And like a leopard I shall lie in wait by the way" could be understood to mean, "And Assyria shall be like a leopard by the way."[236] It was Assyria that destroyed Samaria in 722.

It is curious that the four beasts of this text (lion, leopard, bear, and undefined wild beast) correspond to the four beasts of Daniel's vision (Dan 7:1–8), except that in that text the bear precedes the leopard. Also, the number four in apocalyptic texts often signifies fury upon the earth, as in the four horsemen of Rev 6:1–8. It is not unusual to find hints of apocalyptic breaking out in the midst of prophetic texts.[237] Whatever else one makes of this correspondence, the thinly concealed message is that Israel faces a whole series of onslaughts from Gentile nations, a point that is made explicit in Daniel.

13:9 The NIV has paraphrased or emended this text in a way that is difficult to justify. It is true that the Hebrew is difficult and that many versions emend to some degree, but emendation is unnecessary and unhelpful here. The verse can

---

[236] Reading אֲשׁוּר as אַשּׁוּר (cf. LXX: καὶ ὡς πάρδαλις κατὰ τὴν ὁδὸν Ἀσσυρίων). One should not take this as a case for emending the Hebrew but as a deliberate pun by the prophet. Contrary to Hubbard (*Hosea,* 217), the LXX translation is not really an error but a legitimate interpretation. Cf. also Vg.

[237] E.g., the four locusts of Joel 1:4.

be rendered: "It destroys you, Israel, for (it is) from me, from[238] your helper."

The opening Hebrew word of v. 9, "It destroys you," is often emended to read, "I destroy you" or, as in the NIV, is made into a passive ("you are destroyed"). Neither change is necessary.[239] The "it" in question is not precisely defined in the text, but vv. 7–8 describe a series of beasts that attack Israel. Although the beasts are metaphors for Yahweh, it is not difficult to regard the beasts also as representations of the hypostatized wrath of Yahweh, especially since v. 7 makes a paronomastic reference to Assyria. The "it" that destroys Israel therefore stands for the wrath of God in whatever form it takes. This judgment is from God, the one who is their only true helper. If their helper is against them, what hope of salvation do they have?

13:10–11 The taunt begins the second chiasmus, "Where is your king?" It describes the crisis in Israel in the latter days of its history, when one king followed another in rapid succession, often by assassination, and the nation looked in vain for leadership and protection. "Give me a king and princes!" reflects the desperation of people for effective rulers. This text concludes Hosea's lamentation over and derision of the deplorable condition of Israel's royal government, a theme found especially at 3:4; 7:3–7; and 8:4.

> [10]Where[240] is your king, then, that he may save you in all your cities,
> and your judges, of whom you said, "Give me a king and princes!"?
> [11]I will give you a king—in my wrath,
> and I will take (a king)—in my rage.

In this text kings, judges, and princes all describe members of the govern-

---

[238] The preposition בְ may be translated "by" or "from" in various circumstances, the latter being especially familiar in Ug. texts. See UT 10.5 and *HALOT*, 104–5. The reason the text here uses בְ (instead of the מִן that one may have expected) is that it alludes to Exod 18:4, where the text explains the name of Moses' son, Eliezer, with the words כִּי־אֱלֹהֵי אָבִי בְּעֶזְרִי וַיַּצִּלֵנִי מֵחֶרֶב פַּרְעֹה ("for the God of my father is my helper, and he has saved me from the sword of pharaoh"; on the usage of the בְ indicating apposition here, see *GBH* §133c). Reference to Exod 18:4 (1) reminds the reader that it is Yahweh who saves Israel from the sword (and thus that no salvation is possible if Yahweh is against Israel), and (2) it alludes to the context of this verse, which states that Moses had sent away his wife and two sons (Exod 18:2), a fact that forces the reader to recall that Yahweh will send his wife into exile with her children. A curious preference for the preposition בְ when used with עֵזֶר in reference to God, in texts where it would not be expected, also appears in Deut 33:26; Ps 146:5. The alternative, to translate בְ as "against," is less likely. It requires that we read "you are" into the text, an ellipsis that is less probable than the simple "it is." Andersen and Freedman's contention that the ellipsis is "you rebelled" is more improbable yet (*Hosea*, 636).

[239] The change from שִׁחֶתְךָ ("it destroys you") to the proposed שִׁחֵתִי ("I destroy you") is not terribly great, but it makes the second stich (כִּי־בִי בְעֶזְרֶךָ) virtually unintelligible and in need of significant revision. Cf. Stuart, *Hosea-Jonah*, 200, and Wolff, *Hosea*, 220–21. There is no justification for the passive translation.

[240] Scholars typically read אַיֵּה "where?" for אֱהִי in Hos 13:10 and twice in 13:14. The LXX reads ποῦ. In light of the consistency with which Hosea uses אֱהִי in this text, it seems that this is dialectical distinction rather than a scribal error. Similarly, אֱפוֹא ... אֱהִי seems to be a variant of the more familiar אַיֵּה אֵפוֹא, "where then?"

ment, and Yahweh's obvious point is that they will do Israel no good in the coming crisis of the Assyrian invasion. The phrase "in all your cities" reflects the significance of laying siege to cities in ancient warfare. To conquer a country in the Near East, an invader had to overthrow its fortified cities one by one (as described in the conquest narrative of the Book of Joshua and in the war annals of Tiglath-pileser III[241]); there is no need to emend the text.[242]

Almost all scholars and translations take the verbs of v. 11 to be past tense, notwithstanding the fact that the grammatical forms imply future tense.[243] The Vulgate is a notable exception.[244] Many argue that the story of the anointing of Saul is in view here or that more generally the text describes the whole history of the Israelite monarchy. Against this, besides the grammar of the text, v. 10 implies that Yahweh here describes the present desperation of the people for leadership and not some event from the distant past. That being the case, it is best to follow the Vulgate and render the verbs in the future tense as the answer to the prayer of v. 10. The sense of Yahweh's answer, however, is ironic. "I will give you a king—in my wrath" means that God will indeed send them a king but not the king that they expect. The king God will send is the ruler of Assyria, who comes as their conqueror. "And I will take (a king)—in my rage" means that God will remove the sitting Israelite monarch from his throne.

13:12–13 Yahweh abruptly returns to the metaphor of the woman, and in particular to the woman as bearer of children. Here, the book moves toward closure of the issue of the fertility cult. For Israelites, the great attraction of Baal was the promise of more children, calves, and crops. In response, Yahweh declares that their cult would be shut down and that the "pregnancy" of Israel would be fatal. The text could be rendered as follows:

The iniquity of Ephraim will be locked up,
    His sin will be hidden away. (v. 12)
The travails of a girl giving birth shall come to him.
    It shall be a child not "wise,"
For at the proper time it will not "stand"
    At the cervical opening. (v. 13)

As in 13:7–8, this text contains three couplets, but here only the first is truly parallel. Furthermore, the subject matter of the first couplet (sin that is locked up) differs from that of the second and third couplets, a disastrous pregnancy.

---

[241] See *ANET* 282.

[242] As is done, e.g., in Wolff, *Hosea,* 221. Contrast Stuart, *Hosea-Jonah,* 205.

[243] Although the syntax of prophetic discourse is still not fully understood, a *yiqtol* plus *weyiqtol* pattern is an unusual way to express past tense (the *weyiqtol* אֶקַּח is especially troubling for such a translation). If the verbs were past tense, they would have to refer to habitual actions, as Wolff suggests (*Hosea,* 221). It would thus mean "I would give," not, as usually translated, "I gave."

[244] *Dabo tibi regem in furore me et auferam regem in indignatione me.*

What is meant by saying that Ephraim's iniquity is "locked up" or "hidden away"? As Stuart observes, these words do not belong to the covenant curse vocabulary.[245] It is not likely that the text means that the Israelites have been concealing their guilt, since the fertility cult that Yahweh condemns was a very public part of Israelite life. Also, it makes little sense to suppose that the text portrays Israel as cherishing its guilt and carefully putting it away, like a treasure.[246] A number of scholars suggest that it is God who hides away Ephraim's guilt. But if so, to what purpose? One could argue that God is preserving the nation's guilt so that at the proper time he can fully punish the nation.[247] If so, it is a very odd metaphor; guilt is not a perishable item, like tomatoes. One does not naturally take "his sin is hidden" to mean "I will not forget his sin." For that matter, one could just as easily take the "hiding" of sin to refer to the removal of sin, as a metaphor for forgiveness, although *prima facie* this too is dubious.

The only clear analogy to this verse is the seventh vision of Zechariah (Zech 5:5–11),[248] in which the prophet sees a container that is said to contain the "iniquity in all the land." When the cover is removed, he sees a woman named "Wickedness" sitting in the container. Angels then seal the container and carry it off to "Shinar" (Babylonia) where a "house" will be built for it. This text is itself subject to various interpretations, but it is fairly certain the idea is that the evil of Israel must be returned to the land of their exile, to a pagan people who would venerate Wickedness as a goddess. That is, the return of exiles to Judah and the building of a temple for Yahweh has as its counterpart the return of iniquity to Babylonia and the building of a temple for her.[249]

It is not possible to prove that Zechariah was building upon the metaphor of Hos 13:12. Nevertheless, since the two passages are so similar, even to the point of following Hosea's practice of using a woman to symbolize the evil of Israel,[250] the Zechariah text offers the best hope for making sense of Hosea

---

[245] Stuart, *Hosea-Jonah,* 206.

[246] Thus Hubbard, *Hosea,* 220.

[247] Thus Mays, *Hosea,* 180–81, and Wolff, *Hosea,* 227–28. The main argument behind this interpretation is that the guilt of Israel is written on a scroll, and the scroll is being preserved as evidence. This interpretation follows R. Vuillenmier-Bessard, "Osée 13:12 et les manuscrits," *RevQ* 1 (1958): 281–82, who argues that צרר means to "wrap" (*enveloper*) and that צפן means to "preserve" (*conserver*), and then, on the analogy of how the Qumran sectarians preserved their manuscripts, that Hosea implies a similar activity. However, the verse says nothing about a scroll; it speaks only of iniquity and sin.

[248] There is also a more remote and dubious parallel in the Akk. incantations, which suggests that "hidden" may mean that the sins are not forgiven. See W. G. E. Watson, "Reflexes of Akkadian Incantations in *Hosea*," *VT* 34 (1984): 242–47.

[249] Thus C. Meyers and E. Meyers, *Haggai, Zechariah 1–8,* AB (New York: Doubleday, 1987), 314. See also D. L. Petersen, *Haggai, Zechariah 1–8,* OTL (Philadelphia: Westminster, 1984), 262.

[250] Another parallel is that Hosea speaks of Ephraim's עָוֹן, "iniquity," a term that also appears in Zech 5:6 (in an emendation that is all but certain, correcting the text where it has עֵינָם, "their eye").

here. Viewed in this light, Hos 13:12 is saying that the evil of Israel must be contained and removed. The verse itself does not indicate what verb tense is appropriate here, but in light of context, a future tense is probable.[251] This implies that the metaphor of the "hidden" sin stands for the coming exile, an act of judgment that is also an act of grace since it leads to the separation of Israel from Israel's sin.

There is, however, one other aspect of v. 12 that requires further examination. The word for "locked up" is used in 2 Sam 20:3 for sequestering women so that they might not have sexual relations with men.[252] This condition is analogous to Hos 2:6–7, where the woman Israel is hedged in so that she may no longer gain access to her lovers. Drawing the two together, one can conclude that the fertility cult would be "closed" in order to put an end to Israel's adultery and so that she would no longer bear children for Baal.

Some interpreters take v. 13 to mean that Ephraim would be like a baby in the womb who is so foolish that he does not know it when the time of birth has arrived,[253] an interpretation seemingly followed by the NIV. However, the verse does not mean that the travails of labor have come to the *fetus,* as though it were some kind of sign that it is time to be born. One does not speak of a fetus having labor pains. Rather, Ephraim is experiencing *the same kind of agony* that a woman in labor experiences.[254] That is, Ephraim is like the mother, not like the baby.

Furthermore, Ephraim's travail is worse than even normal labor, for (translating literally) "at the proper time it will not 'stand' at the cervical opening." While the meaning of "stand" in this context is conjectural, the most logical supposition is that this is a breech delivery. In everyday life, standing is the posture one assumes prior to walking; in the Israelite language of childbirth, therefore, "standing" would seem to describe a fetus coming into position to be born, when it turns and drops down into place prior to coming out the birth canal. Similarly, we can surmise that the phrase "unwise child" had a technical meaning in Israelite midwifery for a fetus that was not properly turned or in some other sense was not ready for birth. Otherwise, the language here is quite peculiar if not unintelligible, since no fetus

---

[251] There is really no reason for reading the *yiqtols* (imperfect forms) of vv. 11 and 13 as anything but future. Cf. Stuart, *Hosea-Jonah,* 207. Verse 12 is in effect two verbless clauses, and thus no tense is evident.

[252] Cf. צרר I in *HALOT,* 1058, which also refers to an Arabic cognate.

[253] E.g., Wolff, *Hosea,* 228.

[254] The clause חֶבְלֵי יוֹלֵדָה יָבֹאוּ לוֹ does not mean "the pangs of childbirth come for him" (NIV) as a signal to the baby but "The travails of a girl giving birth has come to him" in the sense that he would experience analogous pain. Thus the pronoun suffix לוֹ, "to him," refers to Ephraim as a nation that is suffering like a woman in labor.

is "wise" in the conventional sense of the term.[255]

Interpreted this way, the text means that Ephraim is like a woman going into labor whose child is breech, such that both the mother and child are likely to die. In Hosea's metaphor both the institutions of Israel (the mother) and her child (the people) are doomed. This is the final end of the fertility cult.

13:14 The first problem in this verse concerns whether the opening couplet is a question (as in the NIV) or a declaration (as in the KJV). If it is a question, then it is not clear whether God will actually redeem his people from death; at most, all he does is deliberate over the question. If it is a declaration, it expresses God's determination to save Israel. In favor of reading it as a question, one can argue that the wider context speaks only of judgment and that therefore a sudden promise of deliverance is incongruous. On the other hand, the second couplet at v. 14b, "Where are your plagues, death? Where is your destructive power, Sheol?" most directly relates to v. 14a and should be regarded as decisive for interpreting it. Some scholars regard v. 14b as a divine summons for death to come and unleash its plagues on Israel.[256] But analogies for taking a question beginning with "where"[257] to be a command or a call to battle are lacking in the Old Testament.[258] On the other hand, it is very common for "where" to introduce a taunt directed at an impotent enemy or god (Deut 32:37; Judg 9:38; 2 Kgs 18:34; 19:13; Pss 42:3,10; 79:10; 115:2; Isa 19:12; 36:19; 37:13; Jer 17:15; Joel 2:17; Mic 7:10). In the chiastic structure of this strophe (described above), 2A is clearly a taunt that makes use of the "Where is …?" formula (v. 10); it is very unlikely that the formula in v. 14 (2A') has an entirely different meaning. This is therefore a taunt, a poetic unit that implies the defeat of death itself. That being the case, it is unavoidable that one must take v. 14a in a declarative sense, that God intends to redeem the nation from death. Thus the two couplets conclude this strophe, as follows:

> From the power of Sheol I shall redeem them,
>   From death I shall ransom them.

---

[255] It is not necessary to take the pronoun suffix in לוֹ as the antecedent of הוּא, or assume that both pronouns refer to Ephraim. The former is Ephraim, but the latter is the metaphorical baby. In the idiom of midwifery, the statement הוּא־בֵן לֹא חָכָם may have been idiomatic for, "The child is not ready." An important element of חָכְמָה, "wisdom," is being prepared for the events of life. It is only in this sense of readiness that a child just before birth could be called חָכָם, "wise."

[256] E.g., Mays, *Hosea,* 182.

[257] The Vg translated אֱהִי as *ero* ("I will be") here and was followed by the KJV. But in v. 10 it translated the same word as *ubi* ("where"). If אֱהִי is dialectical for "where," as it appears to be, there is no reason to suppose one must either translate it as "I am" or emend, contrary to Ward, *Hosea,* 220–21.

[258] The closest analogy I have found for taking a question with "where" to be a summons or command is 2 Kgs 2:14, where Elisha strikes the water with the mantle of Elijah and calls out, "Where is the God of Elijah?" It is questionable whether one would portray God as calling on death in this manner.

Where are your barbs, death?
Where is your destructive power, Sheol?

The metaphor of death follows from the previous passage, in which Ephraim is like a woman giving birth to a breech baby, but it also describes in general terms the condition of national demise and exile. Ezekiel develops the idea of national resurrection further in his dry bones text (Ezek 37:1–14). As in Ezekiel, the message of resurrection applies first of all to the restoration of Israel, but it also looks ahead to a personal, bodily resurrection. Here, as elsewhere, the prophet develops a type. Both national and personal resurrection legitimately arise from the idea that God can restore that which has died. Paul's appropriation of this text in 1 Cor 15:55 as a celebration of the resurrection is fully warranted.[259]

We must still ask ourselves, however, about the incongruity of an oracle of salvation in the midst of a text dominated by doom. This is all the more necessary because of the monocolon that concludes Yahweh's discourse, "Compassion is hidden from my eyes." This apparent *volte-face* is not unusual, however, for the Book of Hosea. It follows the rhetorical strategy already begun in 1:6–10 in which promises of destruction and of salvation are set side by side without transition or explanation. The motif of slaying and then resurrecting Israel occurs elsewhere, as in 5:14–6:2, a text that, like 13:7–8, presents Yahweh as a devouring lion. The purpose of the strategy is to maintain the certainty of salvation in the ultimate plan of God while yet confronting Israel with the reality of their doom in a manner that does not allow for rationalistic evasion. The terse conclusion, "Compassion[260] is hidden from my eyes," disillusions any reader who may have seized upon 13:14 as meaning that calamity might not yet come after all.

[15]Even though he thrives among his brothers.
An east wind from the LORD will come,
blowing in from the desert;

---

[259] Paul does use a slightly different text. The Hb. asks where are death's barbs (דְּבָרֶיךָ; the word can also mean "plagues") and thorn (קָטָבְךָ; this could also mean "destruction," see *HALOT*, 1091–92), while the LXX asks where are death's retribution (ποῦ ἡ δίκη σου, θάνατε) and barb (κέντρον). In 1 Cor 15:5, Paul asks, "Where is your victory, death?" (ποῦ σου, θάνατε, τὸ νῖκος;) and "Where is your barb (κέντρον), death?" Apart from the different word order in Paul, it is noteworthy that he uses νῖκος ("victory") where the LXX has δίκη ("retribution"). Paul's variant is probably deliberate and meant to tie the Hosea text to the citation from Isa 25:8 in the previous verse, 1 Cor 15:54 (κατεπόθη ὁ θάνατος εἰς νῖκος ["Death has been swallowed up in victory"], a rabbinical interpretation now preserved in Aquila). See H. Conzelmann, *1 Corinthians*, Her (Philadelphia: Fortress, 1975), 292–93. Paul wanted to stress the "Christus Victor" motif in his citation of these OT texts.

[260] The word נֹחַם is a hapax legomenon, but the meaning "compassion" is fairly well established. See Wolff, *Hosea*, 222.

his spring will fail
    and his well dry up.
16His storehouse will be plundered
    of all its treasures.
The people of Samaria must bear their guilt,
    because they have rebelled against their God.
They will fall by the sword;
    their little ones will be dashed to the ground,
    their pregnant women ripped open."

PROPHETIC ANNOUNCEMENT OF JUDGMENT (13:15–16) [C']. The phrase in v. 15, "an east wind from the Lord," implies a change of speaker from Yahweh to the prophet. Here Hosea, in response to Yahweh, gives his final prophetic complaint. This text divides into three short units, v. 15a–b, vv. 15c–16a, and v. 16b. Each unit looks back to, affirms, and builds upon Yahweh's speech in 13:4–14. Indeed, it is impossible to understand Hosea's response without making reference back to Yahweh's speech.

13:15a–b The opening line of v. 15 makes little sense in the Hebrew text; it reads, "Even though he thrives (as) a son (of) brothers." The NIV rendering, "even though he thrives among his brothers," is defensible[261] but peculiar in that nothing in context tells us who the "brothers" are, nor can we see any reason for Hosea to adopt the image of thriving among brothers.[262] Translated this way, then the line has no reference point. It is better to follow recent interpreters and take this line to mean "although he thrives among the rushes."[263]

"Rushes" here is a metonymy for wetlands and pools of water, conditions in which cattle and sheep could thrive. The biblical passage to which this metaphor alludes is pharaoh's dream in Gen 41:2,18, where seven fat cows grazed among the rushes, that is, in the marshes where grass was plentiful. In Hos 13:5–6 Yahweh had spoken of Israel as a flock that thrived as well in the wilderness as if it had been in green pastures (see commentary above), a situation

---

[261] The NIV translation requires only that one take בֵּן in the sense of בֵּין, "among," on the grounds that it represents northern orthography. Cf. Andersen and Freedman, *Hosea,* 640–41. The NIV has also added "his."

[262] It is possible that "he" refers to Ephraim over against his "brothers," the other tribes, but in this text Ephraim is simply a metonymy for the whole nation. Nowhere does the text speak of the other tribes at all, much less as rivals to Ephraim. See Mays, *Hosea,* 183.

[263] This requires that we read אֲחוּ ("rushes") for אַחִים ("brothers"). For an explanation of the form of the present text, see Wolff, *Hosea,* 222, unless אַחִים is simply the plural form of אֲחוּ (as suggested in Stuart, *Hosea-Jonah,* 200). If so, no emendation is really necessary. Also בֵּן must be read as בֵּין, but this probably is a matter of regional orthography and does not demand emendation. The interpretation of Andersen and Freedman, "He became a wild one among his brothers," is unlikely (*Hosea,* 625). It requires that one posit a verb from the root פָּרָא to mean "behave like a wild ass." Translated this way, the line has no connection to its context, and it is unclear who the brothers are or why they are introduced here.

in which they forgot God. Now, although they are like cattle that grow fat among the marshlands, God will strike them with drought. The prophet is therefore responding to Yahweh's complaint in 13:5–6 with a prediction of reversion to drought. Allusion to Genesis 41 is probably not accidental. In the patriarchal history, the ancestors of Israel fled to Egypt to escape drought. After the Assyrian invasion, Israelite refugees would again flee to Egypt for refuge, but this time they would not encounter conditions that would allow them to flourish. In addition, this text looks back to the opening of the book of Hosea, where Yahweh declares that he will turn the land into a desert (Hos 2:3).

It is therefore clear that 13:15a–b forms another pair of parallel couplets, as follows:

> Although he thrives among the rushes, an east wind shall come,
> > A wind from Yahweh shall come up from the wilderness.[264]
> And it will dry up his springs,
> > And it will dehydrate his pools.

The "east wind" from Yahweh that will dry up all the pools of water alludes to the wind that drove back the Sea of Reeds and, according to Exod 14:21, turned it into a "dry land" that allowed Israel to escape pharaoh. God's work of salvation has been turned into an act of judgment. Instead of saving them from an enemy, he will open the way for the enemy to take their land, and instead of giving them water in a desert, he will parch their pastures.

13:15c No connection exists between the drying up of wetlands and the plundering of treasures;[265] thus v. 15c seems to begin a new strophe, one that goes through the first half of v. 16. In this strophe, Hosea responds to Yahweh's threats that he/Assyria would come and devour them (vv. 7–8) and that an enemy would appear whom their kings could not repel (vv. 9–11), and to the enigmatic warning that Ephraim's guilt would be "hidden" (v. 12). The general warning in v. 15c, that an enemy[266] would take away Israel's wealth, relates to the coming conquest that Yahweh had just announced (vv. 7–11). But unless this is an isolated reference to the despoiling of Israel, it is not immediately apparent why the text turns to the issue of treasuries and their plunder, an issue not raised elsewhere in context.

The solution seems to be that this text looks back to the hiding of Israel's sin (v. 12). Israel has concealed its wealth in treasuries, and this act serves as the analogue to the locking up of Ephraim's iniquity. Instead of hidden containers

---

[264] This bicolon is essentially chiastic, in which "east wind" parallels "wind from Yahweh" and "among the rushes" is in contrast with "from the wilderness."

[265] Unless the אֹוצָר is here a storehouse for grain. This is possible, but כָּל־כְּלִי חֶמְדָּה describes valuables, and the verb שׁסה would seem to connote the plundering of treasures more than the stealing of food.

[266] The הוא of v. 15c is not to be identified as the same person as that of v. 15a, that is, as Ephraim. Clearly the הוא of 15c is an enemy, either Yahweh himself or Assyria.

filled with money, there would a hidden container filled with sin. Taking the two texts together, we conclude that the people had stored up their wealth for safekeeping but that they would lose all of it. Instead, their sin would be hidden away, when they went into exile. This strophe therefore is a single line: "It shall plunder the storehouse of everything of value."

13:16 [14:1]   As if saving the worst for last, the complaints and punishments of the book of Hosea end with a brief but brutal portrayal of what conquest really entails. Terse and staccato in form, this is an unbalanced couplet with a tristich in the second line.[267]

> Samaria has become guilty,
> > for she has rebelled against her God.
> They will fall by the sword;
> > their little ones will be dashed to the ground;
> > > their pregnant women ripped open.

Hosea forges another connection with Yahweh's speech in speaking of Samaria as *guilty*[268] and *rebellious* (v. 16a), a pair of terms easily associated with the *iniquity* and *sin* of v. 12. Notably, this verse makes no direct statement to the effect that Israel's soldiers would be defeated, that their rulers would flee, or that the priests would be slaughtered, although all of this might be implied in the general assertion, "They will fall by the sword." The only two groups that the text explicitly mentions are children and pregnant women. Apart from the pathos and moral revulsion implied by the slaughter of the helpless, why end the warning section of the book with threats that focus on these particular elements of society?

Yahweh had already in the metaphor of the pregnant woman with the breech baby (v. 13) implied that both mother and child would die. What Yahweh had declared figuratively, the death of mother and child, Hosea now speaks of literally. The final outcome of the fertility cult is the carnage of babies and pregnant mothers throughout the country. The metaphor of Lady Israel and her three children, Jezreel, Lo-Ruhamah, and Lo-Ammi, has reached its denouement in a slaughter that is anything but literary and symbolic.

(3) Third Series: Exhortation for Future Grace (14:1–8)

At this point, condemnation of Israel is finished and encouragement to repent and receive grace begins. Alluding to themes and terms that have been

---

[267] Yahweh's speech also ends surprisingly, with an unexpected monocolon, "Compassion is hidden from my eyes." This is grimly appropriate for what Hosea says in v. 16, that pregnant women will be ripped open.

[268] In light of the apparent link between v. 16a and v. 12, it seems clear that, in agreement with most modern versions, וֶאְשַׁם means "be guilty" and not "be desolate," as it is translated in the LXX and Ibn Ezra (A. Lipshitz, *Ibn Ezra,* 133).

used throughout the book, first the prophet (vv. 1–3) and then Yahweh himself (vv. 4–8) exhort the nation to return to God. Healing and restoration will come, but they will come only when Israel repents.

> [1]Return, O Israel, to the LORD your God.
> Your sins have been your downfall!
> [2]Take words with you
> and return to the LORD.
> Say to him:
> "Forgive all our sins
> and receive us graciously,
> that we may offer the fruit of our lips.
> [3]Assyria cannot save us;
> we will not mount war-horses.
> We will never again say 'Our gods'
> to what our own hands have made,
> for in you the fatherless find compassion."

THE PROPHET'S CALL TO REPENT (14:1–3). **14:1–3 [14:2–4]** Hosea urges the nation to return to Yahweh, and he gives them the words that they must use as they go through this process. He has, in effect, composed a liturgy of repentance. In structure it is made of four triplets followed by a single line. It is not clear why he has chosen this pattern, but the single line at the end stands out as especially significant. One can exhibit the structure of the passage as follows:

A1 Return, Israel,
A2 to Yahweh your God,
A3 for you have stumbled in your iniquity (v. 1).[269]
B1 Take (these) words with you
B2 and return to Yahweh.
B3 Say to him:
C1 May you completely forgive iniquity,
C2 and accept (what is) good,
C3 that we may repay (you with) the fruit of our lips (v. 2).
D1 Assyria will not save us.
D2 On horses will not ride.
D3 And we will no longer say 'Our gods!' to the work of our hands.
E For in you the fatherless receive compassion (v. 3)."

With the exception of the first (A), each tricolon is governed by three verbs.[270]

---

[269] On reading this verse as a tricolon, cf. BHS text and the Masoretic accentuation.

[270] E.g., tricolon B is governed by the verbs קְחוּ, וְשׁוּבוּ, and אִמְרוּ.

The first triplet (A) is a general call to repentance, using the root *šûb* ("return, repent"). This root occurs twenty-five times in Hosea, although not always with the connotation of repentance. In 3:5 Yahweh predicts that after exile Israel would return *(šûb)* to Yahweh and to their messiah, "David." In 6:1 and 12:6 (Hb. 7), both times using *šûb*, the book encourages the nation to repent. But in 5:4 the sin of the people prevents them from repenting, and in 7:10, they refuse to repent. In chap. 14, *šûb* plays a significant role. First, Hosea again calls on the people to return to Yahweh (vv. 1–2 [Hb. 3–4]). Then, Yahweh promises, his anger will turn away *(šûb)* from them (v. 4 [Hb. 5]) and people will come again *(šûb)* to dwell under divine protection (v. 7 [Hb. 8]). It hardly needs to be stated that repentance is essential to Hosea's theology. It is of the essence of knowing God, since no restoration is possible without repentance. Sin, moreover, stands in opposition to repentance. A facile understanding of justification by faith that has no place for repentance is alien to Hosea (and, for that matter, to Paul and Jesus).

The "stumbling" *(kāšal)* of Israel (A3) also appears elsewhere in Hosea. The term describes falling into disgrace and defeat as a result of immoral or foolish behavior. In 4:5 the debauchery of the priesthood causes them to stumble. In 5:5, in a phrase virtually identical to 14:1 (Hb. 2) the upper classes stumble because of iniquity, which in context is described as a kind of hubris. This text (14:1 [Hb. 2]) uses *kāšal* in the same sense: iniquity has brought the nation into ruin. However, 14:9 (Hb. 10) asserts that Yahweh's commands will cause many to stumble *(kāšal)*. The prophetic word gives direction to the upright, but for the disobedient it is confusing and leads to ruin (cf. Matt 13:10–17).

The terse command of B3, "Take words with you," sounds quite odd, and interpreters have handled it in a variety of ways. The "words" could be vows,[271] or it may be that Hosea desires that they offer prayers and not sacrifices because their syncretism has already led them into a quasi magical view of the efficacy of animal sacrifice.[272] On the other hand, he does not categorically reject sacrificial offerings (and one might have expected something along the lines of 1 Sam 15:21 if this had been his chief concern). The simplest solution is that "bring words" is shorthand for "bring these words," the demonstrative "these" perhaps having been dropped for metrical reasons.[273] The meaning is that the people should use these words in their prayer of contrition; B3 ("Say to him") supports this interpretation of B1.

The prayer is in three parts: an appeal for forgiveness, so that the people may offer praise acceptable to God (triplet C), a renunciation of false faith (triplet D), and an appeal to the character of God (line E). The meaning of the

---

[271] Andersen and Freedman, *Hosea,* 642.

[272] See Wolff, *Hosea,* 235.

[273] Scansion in Hosea is extremely difficult, but it does seem that if one reads tricolon B with the demonstrative added (קְחוּ עִמָּכֶם הַדְּבָרִים הָאֵלֶּה), the tricolon is thrown out of balance.

opening plea for forgiveness (C1) is self-evident,[274] but C2 is more obscure because of its brevity. It is a very laconic line; it literally means only, "accept good" (the NIV translation, "receive us graciously," is unusual).[275] Some have argued that it means, "Accept (us), Good One," with "Good One" being a term for God, but this is far-fetched. The line probably simply means, "Accept what is good," with "good" referring to their prayer and praise now purged of the evil influence of Baalism.

Line C3 is equally difficult; translated verbatim it reads, "So that we may pay bulls, our lips." Keil takes this to mean "so that we may offer our lips [i.e., our prayers] as bullocks."[276] The REB, however, takes an entirely different approach and translates lines C2 and C3 as, "Accept our wealth; we shall pay our vows with the cattle of our pens."[277] Both are unlikely. It is better to follow the LXX and a number of modern interpreters and (minimally) emend the text to read, "that we may repay (you with) the fruit of our lips."[278] The "fruit of one's lips" is simply one's words or what one says.[279] The prayer here is that God will accept their words (compare line B1) as worthy praise and sacrifice (see Heb 13:15). In short, the gist of triplet C is a request that God would pardon their transgressions and accept their prayers and praise as acceptable and good rather than reject them as tarnished by sin.

D is a renunciation of false objects of faith. These are foreign nations (D1), military power (D2), and other gods (D3). For the Christian reader this text is a call to abandon faith in political power and alliances, to forsake the strength that is of the "flesh," and to reject worldviews that contradict the biblical faith. Obviously this text does not address every issue, and a strident or sectarian theology untouched by grace and disobedient to the demands for love can be highly destructive in its own way. But there can be no compromise on the issue of loyalty to our covenant God. Strictly interpreted, this tricolon demands absolute reliance upon God because it demands forsaking everything else upon

---

[274] There is a problem with the position of כָּל in כָּל־תִּשָּׂא עָוֹן, but it is probably meant to be read adverbially as "completely." Cf. *GBH* §139e: "כָּל, in some contexts, practically leads to our adverbial idea of *totally*."

[275] The basis for the NIV translation is not apparent. Davies (*Hosea*, 302) suggests that the NIV emends טוֹב to טוּב ("goodness"), but no adverbial use for טוּב is listed in either BDB or *HALOT*.

[276] C. F. Keil, *Hosea* (Grand Rapids: Eerdmans, n.d.), 163–64. Also see McComiskey, "Hosea," 1:230. This interpretation suffers from the fact that the notion of offering one's "lips" as "bulls" makes for a very harsh metaphor.

[277] I have not found any basis for translating שְׂפָתֵינוּ as "our pens," unless it is the fact that שָׂפָה can sometimes mean, "edge," as of the bank of a river. But this seems strained indeed.

[278] Cf. LXX καρπὸν χειλέων ἡμῶν ("fruit of our lips"). This requires an emendation from פָּרִים to פְּרִים. The final ם need not be dropped; Wolff (*Hosea*, 231) comments that it is an "archaic Canaanite case ending."

[279] Cf. Prov 18:20 and D. A. Garrett, *Proverbs, Ecclesiastes, and Song of Songs*, NAC (Nashville: Broadman, 1993), 166–67.

which one might depend, including one's own strength.

The last line (E), a single terse line, because of its distinctive form and brevity, stands out from the rest of this strophe and should be regarded as the linchpin of the whole. But why does it focus on Yahweh as the defender of the orphan? It is true, of course, that one aspect of God's compassionate nature is that he cares for the weak and especially for orphans and widows (Ps 68:5). But even so, this seems an unusual attribute for Hosea to single out as the very basis for Israel's prayer of repentance; there are many texts and ideas that seem more appropriate (especially Exod 34:6).

The precise form of Hosea's prayer is important: "For[280] in you the orphan receives compassion." It is not simply that God is compassionate to orphans but that the orphan seeks and finds compassion in God. The point of Hosea's prayer is that the people of Israel have become orphans. When the nation, along with its shrines, priests, kings, and military forces, is destroyed, then the general populace will be left as orphans. They will be Lo-Ammi, not my people. Their adulterous mother, the institutions of Israel, will be dead; their father, Baal, will have given them no help. But this fatherless people will turn back to their one true father, the refuge of orphans, and find shelter in him. The dispirited Diaspora of Israel must accept its position of orphan and return to Yahweh in that role and not come back as the people who proudly wear the title of the "elect of God." When that happens, Not-my-people will become the sons and daughters of the living God.

> 4"I will heal their waywardness
>   and love them freely,
>   for my anger has turned away from them.
> 5I will be like the dew to Israel;
>   he will blossom like a lily.
> Like a cedar of Lebanon
>   he will send down his roots;
> 6his young shoots will grow.
> His splendor will be like an olive tree,
>   his fragrance like a cedar of Lebanon.
> 7Men will dwell again in his shade.
>   He will flourish like the grain.
> He will blossom like a vine,
>   and his fame will be like the wine from Lebanon.
> 8O Ephraim, what more have I to do with idols?
>   I will answer him and care for him.
> I am like a green pine tree;
>   your fruitfulness comes from me."

---

[280] The opening אֲשֶׁר is best taken as shorthand for יַעַן אֲשֶׁר, "since." See Wolff, *Hosea,* 231.

YAHWEH'S RESPONSE: PROMISE (14:4–8). This strophe is divided into two parts. The first part, vv. 4–7, has precisely the same structure as vv. 1–3. That is, it is composed of four triplets and a single line. The second part, v. 8, is a pair of couplets and represents Yahweh's final word to Israel. The first part has the following structure:

A1 I will heal their apostasy,
A2   I will love[281] them freely,
A3   For my anger turns from him. (v. 4)
B1 I will be like the dew to Israel,
B2   He shall sprout like the lily,
B3   And he shall strike roots like Lebanon. (v. 5)
C1 New growth shall come,
C2   and his splendor will be like that of the olive tree,
C3   and his fragrance will be like Lebanon. (v. 6)
D1 Those who dwell in his shade shall return,
D2   And (like) grain they shall sustain (people),
D3   And they shall sprout like a vine.
E   Recollection of him is like the wine of Lebanon. (v. 7)

As in vv. 1–3, the single line at the end is critical to understanding the entire text.

14:4–7 [14:5–8] Throughout the book of Hosea, as this commentary has attempted to demonstrate, the prophet repeatedly stresses the fact that Israel is apostate (see, e.g., comments on 4:15–19; 5:3; 6:10–11; 9:10–17; 10:5–8; 11:2,7,12). Here (A1), Yahweh promises to "heal" their apostasy.[282] This metaphor implies that apostasy is more than an act of the will, but is also a kind of mental derangement (or spiritual blindness) that God himself must cure. Here, too, is the paradox of Hosea. The book repeatedly calls upon the people to choose to turn back to Yahweh, but at the same time implies that they cannot turn back without a saving act from Yahweh.

The promise to "love" them freely looks back to Yahweh's initial promise in 2:14–23 that he would woo Israel after her time in the wilderness and betroth her forever in love and compassion. The promise that his anger would turn away[283] *(šûb)* from them (A3) is a response to their repentance *(šûb)*. That

---

[281] The NIV has inserted the conjunction "and" before "love them freely," and this has the effect of obscuring the tricolon structure of v. 4 (Hb. 5). But there is no conjunction on אֹהֲבֵם.

[282] The word מְשׁוּבָה (NIV, "waywardness") is best translated as "apostasy," a technical theological word that describes defection from Yahweh, the covenants, and the truth. It is not simply a matter of occasionally going astray. In Jer 2:19 מְשׁוּבָה is described as "forsaking Yahweh your God."

[283] It is probably not necessary or even proper to translate שָׁב here as "has turned away," i.e., in the English perfect tense. The *qatal* (perfect) form here is probably aorist in the true sense of the term; that is, it is unpointed—it simply describes the action without reference to a temporal frame. Of course, it is possible that שָׁב is a participle.

Yahweh's love would be "freely" given has two implications: (1) it is by grace and thus is unearned, and (2) Yahweh's freedom to give love will no longer be hindered by their sin because he will have already removed every offense.

In the following three triplets (B, C, D), Yahweh uses a series of agricultural or pastoral images to convey the ideas of restoration and prosperity. The "dew" (B1, v. 5) signifies a return of God's favor. Dew is gentle (unlike a downpour, which can become a flood), but agriculture in Israel cannot survive without it. The evening dew waters the earth in the Levant most copiously when it is most needed, in the summer. Its absence was a calamity and could be a divine judgment (Hag 1:10). Its origin was regarded as a mystery hidden in the mind of God (Job 38:28). It is thus a fitting metaphor for grace.

Yahweh's promises to Israel encompass every aspect of opulence and health by means of metaphors derived from plant life. The lily (B2) signifies beauty. We cannot positively identify the flower here called a "lily" since the same Hebrew term (šûšan) appears to be used for a variety of flowers; one suggestion for this text is that it is the yellow iris that is also the fleur-de-lis of France.[284] Deep roots (B3) signify endurance and hardiness, and call to mind the picture of the righteous person of Ps 1:3. New growth (C1) communicates that the nation will thrive and increase, and evokes images of the renewal of life in springtime. The splendor of the olive tree (C2) probably implies wealth and well-being, since olives or olive oil served as food, fuel, medicine, and hairdressing, but it was relatively expensive. Fragrance (C3) describes the sensory pleasure associated with the renewed Israel. Instead of being a diseased or dying creature, loathsome in its decay (Hos 5:11–13), the nation would give off the scent of life. Shade (D1) implies that the nation will be a shelter for others. The term calls to mind Jesus' parable of the mustard seed, in which the kingdom of God would grow from small beginnings into a great tree that would offer its branches to the birds of the air (Luke 13:18–19). The grain and the vine (D2–D3) imply that Israel will sustain itself and others with food and drink. All in all, the text has exploited the flora of Israel to the maximum possible extent to convey a message of bounty and salvation. In addition, the pastoral metaphors are similar to the love poetry of Song of Songs. We probably should read this as the tender words by which Yahweh will woo Israel (Hos 2:14–15). Several aspects of the text, however, require special comment.

First, in v. 5 (Hb. 6) the text does not say that Israel will strike roots like a "cedar of Lebanon" (NIV) nor even like the "forest of Lebanon" (NRSV), but simply, "like Lebanon."[285] It is not unreasonable to suppose that Hosea, here as elsewhere quite elliptical, abbreviated the line by cutting the word "forest"

---

[284] *NBD*, s.v. "Plants."

[285] As is often the case, "Lebanon" has the definite article here (כַּלְּבָנוֹן), but it need not be translated.

(*ya*ᶜ*an*).[286] But it is important to note that the word he retained was "Lebanon," and this is a point to which we shall return. The same is true in v. 6 (Hb. 7), where the NIV has again added "cedar."

Second, the NIV translation at v. 6a (Hb. 7), "his young shoots will grow," is somewhat misleading since it emphasizes the growth of individual shoots. Instead, the Hebrew indicates that new growth, or shoots, will "come" or "appear" on the implied plants.[287] It is not a matter of shoots getting larger but a matter of new growth appearing on trees that had appeared dead, as after a long winter (thus C1, "New growth shall come"). Renewal of life, not increase in size, is the point.

Verse 7 (Hb. 8) is more difficult. I have translated D1 as "Those who dwell in his shade shall return."[288] The NIV, although somewhat of a paraphrase, is similar ("Men will dwell again in his shade"). Other interpreters have read the text quite differently. The REB, for example, has, "Israel will again dwell in my shadow," but this translation not only requires significant emendation of the text[289] but does not really fit the context. Throughout the passage, it is Israel—not Yahweh—that is described in a series of botanical metaphors; to place Israel in Yahweh's shade is to make Yahweh the metaphorical tree and Israel into something else.[290] But if Israel is the metaphorical tree in whose shade *others* dwell, the conceptual unity of the text is maintained and the implied expectation, that Gentiles would in the eschaton find blessing in Israel, agrees with many other prophecies of the future of the people of God.[291]

The next line (D2) is more difficult yet. The Hebrew simply reads, "They shall cause-to-live grain." This could mean, as Wolff takes it to mean, "They shall grow grain."[292] But if so, it is the only place where the Hebrew verb here has such a meaning;[293] to "make grain to live" is a strange way of saying "grow

---

[286] I.e., יַעַר.

[287] The verb is simply הלך, "go, come," and not a verb that means "grow" (e.g., גדל).

[288] Cf. the Vg and the interpretation of Ibn Ezra (Lipshitz, *Ibn Ezra*, 134).

[289] For an indication of the kind of emendation that is required, see Wolff, *Hosea*, 232.

[290] A creative but unlikely solution is found in Andersen and Freedman (*Hosea*, 647), who take יָשֻׁבוּ יֹשְׁבֵי בְצִלּוֹ יְחַיּוּ as a single line with the meaning, "Once again those who live in his shadow will flourish." But this interpretation leaves דָגָן standing by itself in front of וְיִפְרְחוּ (Andersen and Freedman force the matter by translating the following as, "They will prosper like grain," without explaining how they deal with the intervening conjunction). Their whole treatment of this verse is quite freewheeling.

[291] Beginning with Gen 12:1–3 and finding expression in numerous other texts, including Isa 2:2–4.

[292] Wolff, *Hosea*, 232. For an alternative interpretation of this verse (one that requires substantial emendation), see R. B. Coote, "Hos 14:8: 'They Who Are Filled with Grain Shall Live,'" *JBL* 93 (1974): 161–73.

[293] Cf. *HALOT*, 309. The verb חיה in the *piel* is elsewhere always used of making animals or people to live. It is difficult to see how the concept could apply to grain.

grain."[294] In addition, this translation once again turns away from the metaphorical thrust of the whole text, where Israel is symbolically portrayed under a variety of botanical images. To say simply at this point that they will become grain farmers abandons the metaphorical nature of the strophe altogether, and is indeed quite banal. The NIV translation, "He will flourish like the grain," makes sense but, as stated above, the verb means to "make (something else) live," not to "flourish." The NRSV emends the text to read, "They shall flourish as a garden." This too fits the context, but is most improbable.[295]

It is more likely that "they shall make live" (or, "they shall sustain") implies that some *people* are the unstated direct object, and that these people are probably the same group as those who "dwell in his shadow." The word "grain" then probably indicates (metaphorically) the *means by which* people will be sustained. Translated, "They (like) grain shall sustain (people)," the idea of Israel as the source of life for the world, presented in an agricultural metaphor, continues. The last line of this triplet (D3), "They shall sprout like a vine," is not problematic, and it continues the image of Israel, as a plant, giving joy to others. Here, the plant is the vine, and the implied joy is the grapes and the wine of the vine. The text again presents Israel as the agency by which God extends mercy to the world, and the metaphor of the vineyard was to become a fixture among the prophets (e.g., Isa 5:1–7; Jer 12:10; Matt 20:1–16).

The closing line (E) calls for special attention. As in 14:1–3 the structure of vv. 4–7 accentuates this line, standing apart as it does from the tricola of the rest of the strophe. In 14:3, moreover, the belief that the orphan finds compassion in God is the basis for the whole prayer of repentance that precedes it. Can the end of 14:7 have a similar function?

The NIV reads, "His fame will be like the wine from Lebanon," but "fame" is not correct. The Hebrew here means "remembrance"; Hebrew uses different words for "fame."[296] At any rate, the wine of Lebanon is a peculiar if not inappropriate analogue for the fame of a nation. It is better to translate the line as, "Recollection of him is like the wine of Lebanon." Since Yahweh is speaking, moreover, "him" must refer to Israel. The metaphor of fine wine aptly suits the idea of good memories, in that a fond memory is something to be savored. But why would Yahweh here mention his remembrance of Israel as a thing that gives him pleasure?

---

[294] If the point had been that they would grow grain, one might have expected the *hiphil* of רבה, as in וְקָרָאתִי אֶל־הַדָּגָן וְהִרְבֵּיתִי אֹתוֹ ("and I shall call to the grain and make it increase," Ezek 36:29), or the *piel* of גדל, as in Jon 4:10.

[295] Besides the unsupported emendation of דָגָן to כְּגַן ("like a garden"), it is again not clear that יְחַיּוּ can mean "they shall flourish."

[296] The Hb. word in Hosea is זֵכֶר; cf. BDB 271, which cites this as the only verse where the word can (supposedly) mean, "renown." For "fame" Hb. uses שֵׁמַע (Num 14:15; Josh 6:27; 1 Kgs 10:1; Esth 9:4) or שֵׁם (Deut 26:19; 1 Kgs 5:11; Ezek 16:14–15; 1 Chr 14:17).

Throughout the second half of Hosea, one of the standing motifs has been Yahweh's recollection of Israel's past. Sometimes the memory was pleasant, and at other times it was painful, but always the text made some connection between Israel's past and its present depravity. That is, Yahweh's memories of Israel have for the most part been a basis for condemning the nation of Hosea's generation (6:4–8; 7:15; 8:4–6; 9:1; 9:10; 9:15; 10:9–10; 10:11; 11:1–4; 12:2–4; 12:9–10; 12:12–13; 13:1–2; 13:4–6). Most tender of all, however, is Yahweh's tender memory of Israel's childhood in 11:1–4, which led to the outburst of divine compassion in v. 8: "How can I give you up, Ephraim? How can I hand you over, O Israel? How can I make you like Admah? How can I treat you like Zeboiim? My heart recoils within me; my compassion grows warm and tender."

Here in 14:7 "recollection of him is like the wine of Lebanon" has a similar function. God's memories of Israel, so often a basis of condemnation, now become the ground of their salvation. Yahweh will not forget his covenant with his people, and neither their prayer nor their historical pilgrimage has lost meaning for him. Because of his love, memory of them glows like a warm fire or, in the language of the text, has the bouquet of a fine wine. Like the sweet savor of Noah's offering (Gen 8:21), the remembrance of Israel propitiates the heart of God. This is the reason for the special place this line occupies here; God's tender memory, his faithfulness, is the foundation for the promises that precede. Rhetorically, moreover, this reference to the memory of God brings closure to the many historical reflections that permeate the Book of Hosea.

One final peculiarity of this strophe, however, requires comment. Prior to this point, the Book of Hosea does not contain a single reference to Lebanon. Suddenly, in a flurry at the end of the book, this strophe three times mentions Lebanon: Israel would strike roots like Lebanon (v. 5), would have the fragrance of Lebanon (v. 6), and memory of it would be like the wine of Lebanon (v. 7). This sudden interest in Lebanon is too striking—one could almost say that it is forced—for us to take it as simple regional color. In fact, this text goes beyond normal biblical allusion to Lebanon; the region is often celebrated for its trees, but nowhere for its wine. We must ask why the text suddenly draws our attention to Lebanon.

The name Lebanon specifically refers to the mountain range in Syria north of the Litanni river, but in the Bible it more generally describes the territory north of the Galilee region. Thus, we can assume that for Hosea's readers, "Lebanon" meant the land immediately to the north of Israel. This region was famous for its trees; from there came the wood that Hiram of Tyre delivered to Solomon for the temple (1 Kgs 5:1–12).[297] But the region

---

[297] The Ug. myth of Baal and Anat also mentions Lebanon as the region that gave timber for the temple of Baal (*ANET* 134).

also had another export to Israel—the cult of Baal. It was the Tyrian princess Jezebel, daughter of the priest-king Ethbaal, who brought into Israel a missionary force of the priests of Baal and who established shrines to him (1 Kgs 16:31–33).

It is not unreasonable to suppose that the Israelites would have associated Baal with Lebanon.[298] He was the god who came out of the mountains of the north (as Yahweh would have been regarded as the God of Sinai in the south). Furthermore, Hosea 14 refers to Lebanon as a place of almost supernatural bounty; it was a place of deep roots, or fragrances, and of fine wine. In this, we should see an allusion to the putative benefits of Baal. He was regarded as the god of fertility, a kind of Bacchus from the forests and mountains, and a bringer of plenty.

Allusions to Lebanon in this text therefore imply that all of the good things that Israel thought to get from Baal will finally come from Yahweh. He will turn their land into a fragrant paradise. In this, Yahweh repeats his earlier promise to fructify the land in a way that Baal never could (2:21–22). And it is by God's grace that Israel, once a source only of grief to the mind of God, would lose the stench of Baal and become to him like the wine of Lebanon.

14:8 [14:9]   This verse stands as a kind of internal commentary on the previous strophe and indeed on the whole book. It is God's parting word. The call, "O Ephraim, what more have I to do with idols?" does not mean that God once had business with idols but no longer does. Rather, the point is that he has already spoken as much as he can endure to speak about the gods of Canaan. Enough has been said. It is a tedious and irksome subject, and he wants to leave behind the whole matter. It is time, too, for Israel to be done with idols once and for all, so that the topic need never come up again.

The following line (NIV: "I will answer him and care for him") is rather perplexing and various interpretations have been proposed.[299] But contrary to the NIV and some other versions, there is no compelling reason to translate the line in the future tense,[300] and the second verb means not to "care

---

[298] It is also conceivable that there is a wordplay here between and לְבֵנָה ("poplar") of 4:13, one of the trees under which the Israelites had made offerings, a suggestion made by G. Morris, *Prophecy, Poetry, and Hosea*, JSOTSup 219 (1996): 88. If so, then the point is that the practice of making offerings under trees will be ended.

[299] E.g., some, following the LXX take ענה here to mean "afflict" rather than "answer" (cf. LXX, ἐταπείνωσα). Stuart (*Hosea-Jonah*) emends וַאֲשׁוּרֶנּוּ to אֲאַשְׁרֶנּוּ ("I will bless him"). The Vg translates וַאֲשׁוּרֶנּוּ as *dirigam eum* ("I will arrange him/lead him straight"), perhaps implying the *piel* of אשׁר I, "to lead." Other, less compelling suggestions, have also been offered, notably that the line means, "I am his Anat and his Asherah." Cf. Ward, *Hosea*, 228. It is probably best to take ענה to mean "answer" and read וַאֲשׁוּרֶנּוּ as the same verb in 13:7, שׁור ("wait").

[300] Note that the pattern is *qatal* followed by *weyiqtol*.

for" but to "observe (someone)."[301] The sense of the line is easier to grasp
if we translate it, "I have answered (him) and I am watching him." Yahweh
has given his answer, in this book, to the nation of Israel and now he is
watching them to see what their response will be. In keeping with the previous line, the implication is, "I have said all that I can say; now Israel must
submit."

In the final line, "I am like a green pine tree; your fruitfulness comes
from me," Yahweh applies the botanical metaphors of the preceding verses
to himself. The tree in view here (NIV: "green pine tree") appears to be a
coniferous tree with edible fruit, possibly the stone pine (*Pinus pinea*).[302] In
the ancient Near East, the tree was a common symbol of kingship, divinity,
and fertility.[303] These were the very qualities that Israel attributed to Baal.
The final appeal of the book is that all the good things that Israel has sought
in the fertility gods can be found only in Yahweh.

---

[301] The root שׁוּר II means to watch for something or someone as an animal watches for its prey
(Hos 13:7; cf. Jer 5:26), and thus implies to watch intently or look at carefully (Job 34:29; Num
23:9; 24:17). The idea of "caring for" is not implied.

[302] Cf. *NBD*, s.v. "trees."

[303] Cf. K. A. Tångberg, "'I Am Like an Evergreen Fir; From Me Comes Your Fruit': Notes on
Meaning and Symbolism in Hosea 14,9b," *SJOT* 2 (1989): 81–93.

——————— V. WISDOM POSTSCRIPT: THE ———————
RIDDLE OF HOSEA (14:9)

⁹Who is wise? He will realize these things.
  Who is discerning? He will understand them.
 The ways of the LORD are right;
  the righteous walk in them,
  but the rebellious stumble in them.

14:9 [14:10] This verse may be rightly called Hosea's "postscript" because it is not oracular; that is, it is not a declaration from Yahweh. Rather, it is a word to the reader on the subject of the task of interpretation. It should be translated as follows:

> Who is wise, that[1] he may understand these things,
>   and understanding, that he may know them?
> For the ways of Yahweh are upright;
>   and righteous people will walk in them,
>   but rebels will stumble in them.

The point is not that wise people automatically will understand Hosea (as the NIV might be taken to imply), but that *one must be wise in order to understand it*. The interpretive task calls for wisdom. In short, this verse plainly states what is obvious to any reader of the Hebrew text of Hosea: it is hard to comprehend.

This does not mean that this verse is secondary (i.e., not from Hosea). The vocabulary is Hosea's, and there is no reason to suppose that the author himself could not address the issue of the difficulty attendant to making sense of his book. Wolff, who treats it as secondary, nevertheless points out that the vocabulary is distinctively Hosea's.[2] It is better to treat this verse as a "Let the reader understand" from the prophet himself.

But why does he issue this challenge to the reader? It is clear, to begin with, that this is a book that is subtle, allusive, elliptical, and at times obscure.

---

[1] The two *weyiqtol* verbs of this verse (וְיֵדָעֵם, וְיָבֵן) both form final clauses.

[2] H. W. Wolff, *Hosea,* Her (Philadelphia: Fortress, 1974), 239. He notes that כשל is Hosean and that this verse breaks with the practice of wisdom literature by placing "rebels" (פֹּשְׁעִים) over against the "righteous" (צַדִּקִים) where wisdom literature would normally have "wicked" (רְשָׁעִים).

Although some of our troubles attendant to interpreting Hosea are no doubt due to our ignorance of the dialectical characteristics of northern Hebrew and of cultural codes and symbols, we cannot assume that eighth century B.C. Israelite readers would have comprehended Hosea without difficulty. The obscurity of this book is to some degree intentional and systematic. Illumination proceeds step-by-step. One must be "wise" in order to "understand" it and "understanding" in order to "know" it. The book offers more than simple statements of fact; it offers a journey to understanding and to God. The task of comprehending Hosea is bound up with the task of knowing God.

In this sense the words of Hosea are like the parables of Jesus. They both instruct and confuse; they both explain and disorient. They are not simply riddles, that is, word games that are interesting until the proper solutions are found and then can be laid aside like completed crossword puzzles. The meaning of the words is both on the surface and yet progressively beneath the surface. The interpretive task is a pilgrimage, the goal of which is ever more gloriously in view but never fully attained. The text invites the reader to a way of life; it is a path that leads to understanding and to God.

In the final analysis, therefore, the key to interpretation is not intelligence but submission. The enigmas of Hosea, like those of Jesus, are stumbling blocks that only anger and finally destroy those who "rebel" against God's rule. The righteous, however, find life in these same words. The strange metaphors, the passing allusions to earlier stories in the Old Testament, the paradoxical rhetorical strategy, and the confounding half-told tale of Gomer and Hosea become like choice fruits to those who rejoice in God and in the truth. To those who do not submit, they are rocks that give offense. Hosea's final message to us is this: "How do you read the words of this book? Do they enlighten or confound? Are they life or death? Your response describes not so much the state of my book as the state of your soul."

Joel

---INTRODUCTION TO JOEL---

The Book of Joel is both controversial and significant. On the one hand, its interpretation is hotly disputed. Some contend that the major theme of the book is a locust plague that swept through Judah. Others, while not denying that a locust plague was the occasion for the book, nevertheless assert that Joel recognized the locust plague as a sign and a prelude to conquest by a human army and to further eschatological events. These interpreters argue that there is an apocalyptic framework for the entire book. The date of the book is also quite uncertain. Furthermore, scholars have had reason to debate its unity. Some interpreters, in fact, consider it impossible that the author of chap. 1 also wrote chap. 3.

On the other hand, Joel draws in its short three chapters (four in Hebrew) a detailed picture of how the prophets presented and understood divine judgment, apocalyptic events, and the future of the people of God. One could fairly claim that for its size, Joel is among the most important books of the prophetic corpus. More than any other book of the Bible, Joel is the book of the day of the Lord.

1. Historical and Literary Setting

(1) Authorship

The book describes itself simply as the "word of the Lord that came to Joel son of Pethuel" (1:1). Although we know little about him, it is apparent that he was a prophet of Jerusalem and that he is the author or at least the source of the material in this book. Notwithstanding the issue of interpolations in the book (see p. 285), there is no reason to question that Joel was a real prophet and that he was responsible for this book.

(2) Chapter Divisions

The Book of Joel has four chapters in Hebrew: the English 2:28–32 constitutes the Hebrew chap. 3, and the English chap. 3 constitutes the Hebrew chap. 4. The English chapter division follows that of the Latin Vulgate. Inasmuch as this commentary is based on the NIV, it follows the English chapter division.[1]

(3) Overall Unity

Some scholars dispute the unity of Joel and see at least two authors at work. Generally, those who reject the book's unity treat 2:28–3:21 (Heb. chaps. 3–4) as apocalyptic and therefore late but see 1:1–2:27 as concerned only with a locust plague and as possibly preexilic.[2] At issue is whether one can demonstrate that the apocalyptic visions of the end of Joel have signifi-

---

[1] Footnotes that refer to the Hebrew text of the OT will refer to Hebrew versification with English equivalents where needed in brackets.

[2] T. Hiebert contends that chap. 3 (Heb. 4) is a divine warrior hymn and was composed independently of chaps. 1; 2 (on the locusts; "Joel, Book of," ABD 3:873–80). He compares Joel 3 to Exod 15:1–18; Judg 5; Pss 2; 24; 29; 68; 89; 97. Although these other divine warrior hymns tend to be fairly early, Hiebert considers Joel 3 a postexilic work on the grounds that the genre revived in the postexilic period. By contrast, Hiebert says that 1:1–2:27 focuses on a historical locust plague and may be from the seventh century. Some earlier scholars, following the work of B. Duhm, held similar positions. Many scholars are so impressed by the linguistic signs of unity that they attribute the whole to one author but regard the two halves as separate compositions having little to do with each other, except that they speak of divine judgment or day of Yahweh. See R. H. Pfeiffer, Introduction to the Old Testament (New York: Harper & Brothers, 1941), 574–75, and esp. G. Fohrer, Introduction to the Old Testament, trans. D. E. Green (Nashville: Abingdon, 1968), 428.

cant links to the locust plague at the beginning of the book.[3] The tendency to divide Joel into two halves with a separate author for each part began with M. Vernes (1872), J. W. Rothstein (1896), and B. Duhm (1875, 1911), although these scholars did not always agree about where the dividing line should be placed.[4] The position of this commentary is that the focus of Joel has already begun to shift away from locusts and toward an apocalyptic, "northern" invader in 2:1–11 (see following discussion). If the two parts of the book can be shown to be conceptually and structurally bound together, then there is no reason to doubt common authorship for the whole. Those who see only a locust plague in 1:1–2:27, however, will have difficulty linking the two halves of the prophecy and may be hard-pressed to explain wherein lies the unity of Joel, even if they maintain that a single author wrote it.[5] Nevertheless, and notwithstanding the problem of relating the locust plague of chap. 1 to the world judgment in chap. 3, one should note that quite a few scholars have found evidence for the unity of Joel.[6]

(4) Interpolations

Many scholars who hold to the essential unity of Joel nevertheless contend that there are small interpolations (later additions to the original book) in Joel. J. Bewer's analysis is particularly extravagant in this regard. He argues that Joel himself wrote only chap. 1 (excluding 1:15), chap. 2 (excluding 2:1b,2,6,10,11,27), 3:2a, and 3:9–14a. He contends that an interpolator wrote the remainder, except for 3:4–8, which was written by a third hand.[7] Bewer's

---

[3] By "apocalyptic visions" I mean the general thrust of the last part of the book: it speaks of the final judgment, the darkening of the sky, and the exaltation of Zion. I do not mean that it fully partakes of the characteristics of classic apocalyptic literature (e.g., Daniel and Revelation). J. L. Crenshaw observes that Joel lacks the bizarre creatures, heavenly journeys, angelic interpreters, divisions of history, and other features that typify a fully developed apocalyptic (*Joel*, AB [New York: Doubleday, 1995], 25).

[4] See W. S. Prinsloo, "The Unity of the Book of Joel," *ZAW* 104 (1992): 66–67. Duhm argued that the book should be divided at the end of 2:17 and asserted that Joel had written only the first half and not all of that. Others placed the division at the end of 2:27.

[5] Prinsloo has attempted to demonstrate the unity of the book on the basis of a structural analysis (*The Theology of the Book of Joel*, BZAW 163 [Berlin: Walter de Gruyter, 1985]). He argues that each section of Joel leads into the next. Prinsloo takes 2:1–11 as an "intensified version" of the locust plague and drought of chap. 1 (pp. 47–48; see also Prinsloo, "Unity," 66–81). Although his work is helpful, he is not, in my opinion, completely successful in establishing the conceptual unity of the book—it still does not make sense for a book that is concerned with an agricultural crisis involving locusts and a drought to have as its resolution the destruction of all the nations.

[6] In addition to Prinsloo's arguments, see, for example, the summary of W. Van der Meer, *Oude Woorden worden nieuw. De Opbou van het Book Joel* (1989), in Prinsloo, "Unity," 74–75. See also D. Marcus, "Nonrecurring Doublets in Joel," *CBQ* 56 (1994): 56–57, especially pp. 65–66, and J. A. Thompson, "Joel," *IB* (Nashville: Abingdon, 1956), 6:733.

[7] J. A. Bewer, "Joel," in *A Critical and Exegetical Commentary on Micah, Zephaniah, Nahum, Habakkuk, Obadiah and Joel*, ICC (Edinburgh: T & T Clark, 1911), 49–67. Bewer uses the Hebrew versification in his presentation.

analysis is arbitrary and represents the methods of an older generation of critical scholarship. Few interpreters of any persuasion today would be willing to follow him in this deflation of the text.

Quite a few scholars, however, regard 3:4–8 as an interpolation.[8] The principle reasons are that the text here seems to shift abruptly from poetry to prose and that genre and outlook of the text appear to be different. The rest of chap. 3 is apocalyptic in tone and describes the great judgment on all nations at the valley of Jehoshaphat. In 3:4–8, however, the prophet turns his attention to relatively minor disputes between the Jews and two local powers, the Philistines and Phoenicians. For many interpreters the transition is too harsh to be credible, and they conclude that a second author was at work.

This conclusion is unnecessary. To begin with, 3:4–8 can and should be read as poetry rather than prose. Also Joel 3 is not purely apocalyptic. As did most of the Old Testament prophets, Joel addressed the problems facing his own generation and saw in those problems theological parallels to eschatological events. He moved back and forth between present and future perspectives, sometimes with very little transition. This does not imply multiple authorship. All in all, no text of Joel can be shown conclusively to be an interpolation (for further details on 3:4–8, see commentary).

(5) Date of Composition

Probably no book of the Bible has had a wider range of dates assigned to it. Scholarly opinions for the date of Joel range from the early monarchy to the late postexilic period, although the early postexilic probably is the most popular option today for the date of composition. This issue obviously is tied to the issue of the unity of the book, since scholars who divide the book between two or more authors may also ascribe the different portions to different eras. This commentary concludes that no decisive grounds exist for rejecting the unity of the book and that one may safely treat all the data of the book as relevant to the date of the whole.[9]

On the face of it, the data in Joel would seem to favor a postexilic date for the book. On further analysis, however, much of the evidence is questionable or ambiguous. We thus will look at the pieces of evidence one by one and see where they lead. The most commonly cited pieces of evidence are laid out in Table 1.[10]

---

[8] For example, H. W. Wolff, *Joel and Amos,* Her (Philadelphia: Fortress, 1977), 74–75.

[9] See the discussions "Overall Unity," "Interpolations," and "Locusts or Soldiers."

[10] Data in Table 1 depend to some degree on the data in M. Treves, "The Date of Joel," *VT* 7 (1957): 149–56, but these data are cited and discussed in most commentaries and introductions. See, for example, S. R. Driver, *An Introduction to the Literature of the Old Testament,* reprint ed. (Gloucester, Mass.: Peter Smith, 1972), 310–11.

Table 1: Issues Surrounding the Date of Joel

Issue	Alleged Implication
9. Kings are not mentioned.	There were no kings; Joel is postexilic.
10. Priests and elders are the authorities in the city.	Reflects the postexilic community.
11. Focuses on Jerusalem with no mention of Northern Kingdom of Israel.	Northern Kingdom did not exist; Joel is late preexilic or postexilic.
12. Mentions walls of Jerusalem (2:7,9).	Jerusalem walls did exist; Joel is either preexilic or after Nehemiah's reform.
13. Temple exists and is functioning.	Excludes the exilic period of 586–515.
14. The Book of Joel falls between Hosea and Amos in the Hebrew canon.	The Minor Prophets are roughly arranged in chronological order. Joel is preexilic.
15. Alludes to Israelites being captives and exiles (3:1–2).	Israel has already been scattered. Joel is postexilic.
16. "All who live in the land" can gather in Jerusalem (1:14).	The population is small and local. Joel is late preexilic or postexilic.
17. Joel seems to cite other prophets (e.g., Joel 2:32 may cite Obad 17).	Joel is later than the books it cites and thus is postexilic.
18. Mentions that Jewish slaves were sold to Greeks.	Greeks were more well known to Israelites in the postexilic period. Joel is postexilic.
19. Egypt, Edom, Philistines, and Phoenicians are enemies of Jews.	Implication is disputed.
20. Mentions angelic armies (3:11).	Reflects late, apocalyptic thinking. Joel is postexilic.
21. Contains Aramaisms.	Implies postexilic origin.

1. The book never mentions a king or the royal house over Jerusalem, which would seem to indicate that there was no royal house, which would imply a postexilic date. We obviously are dealing with an argument from silence here. Although a reference to a king would have decisively placed Joel in the preexilic period, the nonmention of a king does not prove that there was no king or that Joel is postexilic. For this to be significant, one would have to show that in the context of Joel it is inconceivable that the prophet would not have spoken of the king if such a person existed. Scholars advocating a post-exilic date have tried to make this case on the grounds that the book lists various classes of society in chap. 1 and that Joel could not possibly have failed to include the royal household since it was the highest stratum of Jerusalem society. In reality, however, what Joel 1 gives us is anything but an enumeration of all segments of Jerusalem society.

The point of chap. 1 is to call people to lamentation and to dramatize the severity of the crisis by referring to a few *selected* groups of people. The text mentions drunks (1:5) because they represent the carefree consumption of the earth's bounty. It calls upon farmers because they most directly experienced the fury of the locust plague (1:11). The priests are important to Joel because they were the people who offered the daily sacrifice and libations in the temple, and this has been "cut off" (1:13). The book also calls upon brides and bridegrooms to lament (2:16; cf. 1:8) because they are normally the last people one would associate with mourning. Neither drunks, newlyweds, farmers, nor priests are presented as "social classes" at all; much less are they part of an *exhaustive* list of such classes.[11] All one can say is that the nonmention of a king leads us to wonder if in fact there was a king at the time of writing; it is hardly a decisive piece of evidence.

Some defenders of a preexilic date for Joel deal with this issue by arguing that Joel prophesied in the minority of King Joash, during the regency of Jehoiada, and thus that he had no reason to mention a king who was a mere child.[12] Apart from the fact that we have no evidence for a regency in the Book of Joel, this too is an unnecessary move. The book simply tells us nothing about the governance of Jerusalem; we have nothing to account for or explain.

2. In conjunction with the point that Joel mentions no king, many advocates of a postexilic date assert that the book treats elders and priests as the leaders of the community.[13] If correct, this would indicate fairly decisively that Joel is postexilic. In reality, however, Joel nowhere asserts or even pre-

---

[11] Cf. A. Kapelrud, *Joel Studies* (Uppsala: A. B. Lundequistska Bokhandeln, 1948), 187–89.

[12] For example, G. Archer, *A Survey of Old Testament Introduction* (Chicago: Moody, 1974), 304.

[13] For example, R. B. Dillard and T. Longman, *An Introduction to the Old Testament* (Grand Rapids: Zondervan, 1994), 365.

sumes that Jerusalem is under the governance of priests or elders. As stated above, the text mentions priests specifically in the context of temple ministry and in the role of leading in a sacred period of lamentation and prayer. This scarcely implies that they are the political leadership in the nation. Similarly, Joel calls on "elders" because they are literally old people who have long memories, not because Jerusalem is under a presbytery (1:2; see commentary). Simply put, the Book of Joel tells us nothing about the governance of Jerusalem during the time of its composition.

3. Joel does not allude to the Northern Kingdom of Israel. This is a more significant piece of evidence than the nonmention of kings. The prophets routinely spoke of the Northern Kingdom as "Ephraim" or "Samaria" (after the reign of Omri), but the Book of Joel never uses these terms and nowhere refers to this kingdom in any way. This is more than an argument from silence because Joel does use "Israel" to identify the whole people of God (3:2) without any implication that ten tribes existed as a different country. This is comparable to the practice in Chronicles (a postexilic work) of routinely representing all of the tribes as "all Israel." Although it is conceivable that Joel worked prior to the fall of Samaria and for his own reasons chose to ignore the Northern Kingdom, on balance this evidence favors a late preexilic or a postexilic date for the book. It also casts more doubt on the idea that Joel prophesied during the minority of Joash (ca. 830 B.C.).

4. Scholars who favor a postexilic date for Joel are often embarrassed at the fact that Joel describes Jerusalem as having walls, since many would prefer not to date Joel as late as after Nehemiah (who restored the walls around 444 B.C.). One maneuver is to argue that in fact Jerusalem did have at least partial walls prior to Nehemiah's work, and thus that the need for so late a date is avoided.[14] This argument does not work, however, because in Joel the walls serve as an impediment (albeit a failing one) to an attacking army. According to 2:7, this army must climb over the walls of Jerusalem to enter it. But an army would not have to scale a wall that had gaping holes in it (see commentary on 2:7). Still, we have to observe that this too is not a decisive argument (Joel's attacking army was apocalyptic and thus visionary; literal details should perhaps not be pressed). On balance, however, the mention of walls favors either a preexilic or late postexilic date in contrast to an early postexilic date.

5. The existence of temple worship excludes the exilic period, which is not a serious option anyway. Does it also demand that Joel was written either prior to the exile or after the ministry of Haggai and Zechariah (who exhorted the people to rebuild the temple around 516 B.C.)? Although it is conceivable

---

[14] For example, R. B. Dillard, "Joel," in *The Minor Prophets*, vol. 1 (Grand Rapids: Baker, 1991), 276.

that Joel is postexilic but prior to the reforms of Haggai and Zechariah, it is most unlikely. The temple was the heart and soul of Joel's religion. Worship apparently did go on at the temple site prior to its restoration, but it is difficult to imagine that Joel, who was deeply grieved that daily sacrifice had been suspended because of famine, would pass over in silence the fact that the temple itself was in ruins. A sixth-century date for Joel therefore seems out of the question (except perhaps for the first or last decade of that century). We also should note that the Book of Joel says nothing about the temple abuses that so vexed Malachi (e.g., Mal 1:6–14). While not decisive in itself, this argument from silence casts some doubt on a fifth- or fourth-century date.

6. The order of the twelve Minor Prophets is roughly chronological (e.g., Hosea is among the earliest of the twelve; and Haggai, Zechariah, and Malachi are among the latest). Joel follows Hosea and precedes Amos, and this implies that it is preexilic. But the evidence and its interpretation remain unsettled. Joel may have been inserted prior to Amos not because of chronological considerations but because of a catchword link between the end of Joel and the beginning of Amos (compare Joel 3:16 [4:16 Heb.] to Amos 1:2). The LXX, moreover, has a different order of books for the first six books of the twelve.[15] The order of the twelve in the Hebrew canon can hardly be considered decisive for dating, even in general terms. Obadiah almost certainly describes brutal crimes that took place in the course of the fall of Jerusalem, and yet in the Hebrew canon it is prior to Micah, an eighth-century work. The position of Joel in the canon may imply at most that there was a Jewish tradition and that it was written before the exile, but the evidence is far short of being conclusive.

7. Joel speaks of Yahweh returning captive and scattered Jews to their homeland (3:1–2), and thus one naturally supposes that the exile had already occurred. This assumption is not necessarily correct, however. The diaspora of the Israelites had already begun in the late preexilic period (particularly after the fall of Samaria). A partial diaspora does not imply that the Babylonian captivity had taken place. Also Deuteronomy had already predicted a dispersion of Israel (28:64), and peoples of the ancient world generally understood that the consequence of military defeat was enslavement and dispersion to other lands.[16] References to dispersion in a preexilic Joel would not have confused the original readers. At most, one can say only that references to an Israelite diaspora make an *early* preexilic date for Joel less likely.

8. The call for "all who live in the land" to gather in Jerusalem and mourn before Yahweh (1:14) implies that the population of Judah was relatively

---

[15] For an effort at accounting for the order of the twelve in the Heb. and the LXX, see T. J. Finley, *Joel, Obadiah, Amos,* WEC (Chicago: Moody, 1990), 5–6.

[16] See D. Stuart, *Hosea–Jonah,* WBC (Dallas: Word, 1987), 226.

small and did not cover a large geographic area. This fits the postexilic community, but not *only* the postexilic community. By the seventh century Judah was already a minor state in the ancient Near East. Also the call for "all" to gather may be to some extent hyperbolic; it does not necessarily envisage every living soul coming to Jerusalem. This is best taken as evidence against an early preexilic date.

9. Often two or more prophetic books in the Bible use language and phrases that strongly resemble one another. Arguments among scholars over whether prophet *A* has cited prophet *B,* or vice-versa, are notoriously difficult to settle. In most cases the evidence is simply far too ambiguous and subject to too many possible interpretations. In the case of Joel, scholars on both sides of the issue cite parallels to Joel in other prophetic books and try to demonstrate which direction the quotation has gone. Treves, for example, claims that Joel 2:2 has borrowed "a day of darkness and gloom, a day of clouds and blackness" from Zeph 1:15 and that Joel 2:3 alludes to Ezek 36:35.[17] Thus he concludes that Joel is postexilic. G. Archer, on the other hand, contends that Amos 9:13 quotes Joel 3:18 and that this shows that Joel is preexilic.[18] It is difficult, however, to make a convincing case.

The two most significant verses in Joel in this regard are 2:32 and 3:10.[19] Joel 2:32 is interesting because it is similar to Obad 17 and because the relevant line in Joel ("in Mount Zion and in Jerusalem there shall be those who escape") has the notation "as the LORD has said." This notation can be taken to imply that Joel quoted an oracle from another prophet, and thus some argue that Joel was citing Obadiah.[20] It is not clear, however, that "as the LORD has said" is meant as a pointer to a literary citation. It may be a citation of a prophetic proverb that was current at the time of Joel rather than a reference to any specific book. It may not be a citation at all but an emphatic assurance of salvation. All things considered, this verse has little value for dating Joel.[21] For further discussion see the commentary on 2:32.

Joel 3:10 is important in that it cites an expression in the reverse form from the one we are most familiar with: it says that people should beat their plowshares into swords and their pruning hooks into spears (contrast Isa 2:4 and Mic 4:3). Here the question is not who is citing whom but which form of the proverb ("swords to plowshares" or "plowshares to swords") is the original.

---

[17] Treves, "Date of Joel," 152.

[18] Archer, *Survey,* 304.

[19] For a fairly complete list of possible citations, see Crenshaw, *Joel,* 27–28.

[20] For other possible parallels between Joel and Obadiah, see S. Bergler, *Joel als Schriftinterpret,* Beiträge zur Erforschung des Alten Testaments und des antiken Judentums 16 (Frankfurt am Main: Peter Lang, 1988), 301–20. Some of the parallels he sees are noteworthy, although not necessarily decisive (e.g., וְאֶל־עַמִּי יַדּוּ גוֹרָל, Joel 4:3, with עַל יְרוּשָׁלַם יַדּוּ גוֹרָל, Obad 11).

[21] Contrast Finley, *Joel,* 8.

Joel's form of the expression probably is the earlier of the two since his expression reflects what would have been a typical call to arms at a time of mobilization (for further discussion see commentary on 3:10). This would imply, if not that Joel was written prior to Isaiah, at least that Joel was written early enough so that the original form of the proverb was still current.

10. Greeks draw attention to themselves whenever they occur in the Old Testament if only because some scholars seem to assume that no Israelite prior to the exile could have heard of Greeks. Thus they are taken to be a fairly sure sign that the books in which they appear are late. In reality, Greeks were a seafaring people who colonized the west coast of Asia Minor long before 586 B.C., and one need not be surprised to find mention of them in pre-exilic texts. What is significant is not *whether* they appear but *in what role* they appear. In Joel 3:6 the prophet assailed the Philistines and Phoenicians for taking Jews as slaves and selling them to Greeks in order to move them "far" from their homeland. What is important here is that the Greeks are presented as a *distant* people. This would tend to favor an earlier over a later date, when Greeks in significant numbers spread across the Near East as merchants and mercenaries and would not have been regarded as distant. In addition, the economic history of Greece favors a seventh-century date for Joel 3:6 since during that time frame Greek economic expansion and a severe labor shortage that accompanied it forced the Greeks to seek to acquire large numbers of slaves (for further discussion see the commentary on 3:6).

11. Various scholars have attempted to deduce the historical circumstances of Joel by looking for events in Egyptian, Edomite, Philistine, or Phoenician history that may be behind the book. On the postexilic side some scholars have been specific about what allusions to historical events they see in Joel. They have especially tried to link Joel to Persian or Ptolemaic history. Bewer, for example, states that 3:4–8 (4:4–8 Heb.) reflects events after the capture of Jerusalem by Artaxerxes Orchus around 352 B.C. but before the fall of Sidon in 348 B.C.[22] That is precision indeed! M. Treves is equally specific that the atrocities behind 3:4–8 could only have taken place during the reign of Ptolemy Soter around 320 B.C.[23]

A completely different analysis comes from G. Archer, who contends that at "no time after the reign of Joash was the kingdom of Judah faced by this particular assortment of enemies"[24] (meaning Egypt, Edom, Philistia, and Phoenicia). This assertion goes beyond what we actually know of the history of Jerusalem.

In contrast to all these scholars, one might easily conclude that Joel 3:4–8

[22] Bewer, "Joel," 61.

[23] Treves, "Date," 153.

[24] Archer, *Survey,* 305.

concerns relatively minor local incidents that in world history would have received no notice whatever. In addition, the reference to Egypt and Edom (3:19) appears to be stereotypical and may refer to *characteristic* violence from these peoples rather than to some *specific* events. If Joel had some particular atrocity in mind in 3:19, it is odd that he said so little about it. We have few reasons to attach this or any other text of Joel to known movements of ancient armies or to large-scale sieges of Jerusalem. Most recent scholars, in fact, eschew this kind of historical hypothesizing altogether.

12. Interest in angels grew during the postexilic and intertestamental periods. Thus the prayer in 3:11, "Bring down your warriors, O LORD," an apparent call for angelic intervention, would seem to reflect postexilic theology. Here too, however, the evidence is not as strong as it might seem. First of all, the text here is quite uncertain, and we cannot be sure that there was any reference to heavenly armies at all in the *Urtext* (see commentary for details). Second, the notion that Yahweh was head of a heavenly host of angels was hardly alien to preexilic Old Testament theology. Among the most common names for God is the "LORD of Hosts" (i.e., of the heavenly armies). In the later Jewish literature, by contrast, much more attention is given to *individual* angels,[25] and one could thus argue that the reference looks more preexilic than postexilic. In reality, however, Joel 3:11 contributes nothing to our understanding of the date of the book.

13. The argument that Joel contains Aramaisms and therefore is a postexilic work has been so thoroughly refuted by G. W. Ahlström that one hesitates even to mention it. Although he favors a postexilic date, Ahlström has exhaustively examined words that allegedly point to a late date and repeatedly has found occurrences of these words in earlier biblical or Ugaritic texts. He concludes, "It must be clear that many of the words and phrases having been used as arguments for a late date are not late at all."[26]

---

[25] See D. A. Garrett, *Angels and the New Spirituality* (Nashville: Broadman & Holman, 1995), 59–72.

[26] G. W. Ahlström, *Joel and the Temple Cult of Jerusalem*, VTS 21 (Leiden: Brill, 1971), 1–22. See his discussion of the verb אנח, "to sigh" (p. 2). Ahlström believes that the data point to a late preexilic or early postexilic date. He claims that בְּנֵי צִיּוֹן ("sons of Zion," Joel 2:23) cannot be earlier than the time of Jeremiah (p. 6), but his database on this phrase is so small as to be statistically meaningless (Lam 4:2; Ps 149:2; Zech 9:13). I do not believe that we can be as precise on the basis of linguistic data as Ahlström would like, but the point that most of the lexical evidence does not require a postexilic date is well founded. He finally adopts an early postexilic date on the basis of other evidence and in keeping with the thesis of his work, but he has only one piece of linguistic evidence in favor of a postexilic date. This is the uncontracted form מִן־בְּנֵי ("from the sons of"), a phrase that occurs in Joel 1:12; Lev 1:14; 14:30; Judg 10:11; and some nineteen times in Chronicles. This is, to say the least, slender evidence for dating the book, and Ahlström has not considered other explanations for the uncontracted form (e.g., that in Joel it is *metri causa*). At any rate, it is remarkable that a scholar who wants to date the book to the postexilic period, after an exhaustive study, can find so little linguistic data to support this.

In summary, clear pointers to the date of Joel are few and far between.[27] Any suggested time frame for the book should be tentative, and the interpretation of the book should not depend upon a hypothetical historical setting. On the whole I prefer a seventh-century date for the book to a late postexilic date. An early preexilic date or an early postexilic date are both even less likely alternatives. But we need not regard any date as theologically or hermeneutically troublesome. We have no clear historical context for Joel—but in Joel this is not a major obstacle to interpretation.

(6) Style

The Book of Joel uses a wide variety of rhetorical devices. J. Crenshaw has cataloged some of the techniques the book employs. These include *hendiadys* (using two words to express a single idea, as in "great and dreadful"[28] in 2:31), *merismus* (combining two antithetical ideas in order to express universality, as in "sons and daughters" in 2:28), *rhetorical questions* (as in "Are you repaying me for something I have done?" in 3:4), and *alliteration* (as in the Hebrew of 1:15, *ûkĕšōd mišadday*).[29] Joel also used *simile* and *metaphor* effectively, as when the locusts are described as a powerful "nation" in 1:6.

J. A. Thompson has identified eight functions of repetition in Joel.[30] These include the following:

1. *Emphasis.* Examples include simple repetition of the same word, as in "multitudes, multitudes" (3:14). Also Joel could use a wide variety of related words to give his message vivid imagery and emotional impact. In 2:1–11, for example, the invading army is said to "run" (2:4,9), "leap" (2:5,9), "charge," "scale," "march" (2:7), "plunge" (2:8), and "enter" (2:9).

2. *Correspondence.* Joel often used similar language to link the various events his book describes. For example, the locust plague is said to be a "dreadful day" and the "day of the LORD" (1:15). The invading army of 2:1–

---

[27] There are, of course, other suggestions for dating Joel besides those I have mentioned here. For example, F. R. Stephenson suggests that Joel 2:31 implies that a total eclipse of the sun and a total eclipse of the moon took place during Joel's ministry. He then argues that a total solar eclipse occurred in Judah only in 357 and 336 B.C. and thus that Joel must have been written about this time ("The Date of the Book of Joel," *VT* 19 [1969]: 224–29). But it is not clear that Joel was talking about an eclipse at all. The association of darkness with the day of the Lord is formulaic and stereotypical (Isa 13:10; Amos 5:18) and does not imply that any significant astronomical events occurred in Joel's lifetime. Also Joel 2:31 is prophetic and not historical.

[28] Hebrew text is 3:4, הַגָּדוֹל וְהַנּוֹרָא.

[29] Crenshaw lists other techniques as well (*Joel*, 38–39).

[30] J. A. Thompson, "Repetition in the Prophecy of Joel," in *On Language, Culture, and Religion: In Honor of Eugene A. Nida*, ed. M. Black and W. A. Smalley (The Hague: Mouton, 1974), 100–110. I have slightly altered Thompson's presentation since he uses the RSV whereas this commentary is based on the NIV. Also he takes 2:1–11 to refer to the locust plague, but I see it as a human army.

11 also comes on a "day of darkness" and "the day of the LORD" (2:1–2). The eschatological age of 2:28–32 is also the "day of the LORD" when the sun and moon go dark (2:31), and the last great battle in the valley of Jehoshaphat is the dark "day of the LORD" as well (3:14–15).

3. *Contrast.* In 2:19,22,24 Joel describes the restoration of grain, wine, oil, pastures, trees, and vineyards. This reverses the destruction of these items in 1:7,10,12,18–20. Sometimes contrast is achieved by using the same verb with a different subject. In 2:13 the prophet exhorts the people to "return" *(šûb)* to the Lord, whereas in 2:14 he hints that the Lord may "turn" (same word in Hebrew) and have pity.

4. *Climax.* The description of the attack by the enemy army in 2:1–11 reaches its climax in 2:9: "They climb into the houses; / like thieves they enter through the windows." The many references to the "day of the LORD" throughout the book prepare the reader for the account of the last judgment of chap. 3.

5. *Succession.* The text calls upon the old men to tell the story of the locust plague to their children, their children's children, and for generations to come (1:3). Joel 1:4 may describe either successive waves of locusts or the stages of growth (instars) of the locust (see commentary on 1:4). Either way the rhetorical effect of 1:4 is that Judah had been hit by successive waves of infestation.

6. *Irony.* In 3:4 God asks the Phoenicians and Philistines, "Are you repaying me for something I have done?" and then continues, "If you are paying me back, I will swiftly and speedily return on your own heads what you have done." The text goes on to describe how they will suffer the same treatment they inflicted on the Jews (3:6–8).

7. *Anaphora, Beginning a Section.* The phrase "blow the trumpet in Zion" initiates both the battle alarm of 2:1 and the liturgical call to repentance in 2:15.

8. *Epiphora, Ending a Section.* The parallel phrases "flames have burned up all the trees of the field" and "fire has devoured the open pastures" (1:19–20) concludes the account of the locust plague in chap. 1. The repeated lines "never again will my people be shamed" (2:26–27) conclude the section on the healing of the land after the locust plague. In addition, D. Marcus has investigated the phenomenon of "nonrecurring doublets" in Joel. These are short phrases that occur twice but only twice in the book. According to Marcus, there are forty-seven such doublets, and they relate complementary ideas to one another, indicate reversals, and link passages through allusions.[31]

---

[31] See Marcus, "Nonrecurring Doublets." The doublets are not always identical but are at least similar. An example of a doublet is the phrase in 2:1,15, תִּקְעוּ שׁוֹפָר בְּצִיּוֹן ("blow the trumpet in Zion").

(7) Condition of the Hebrew Text

The Hebrew text of Joel is remarkably clean. As even a brief perusal over the scarcity of textual notes in *BHS* indicates, most of the verses of the book are in good shape, and we can be confident that there are few scribal corruptions. In a handful of cases, however, emendation is possible and may be needed. Joel 1:17 is notoriously difficult, and 4:21a may require emendation. Such textual difficulties are noted in the commentary.

2. Problems in Interpretation

Although every line of Joel is naturally subject to various interpretations, two specific issues provoke major disagreements among scholars. The first revolves around the issue of whether worship at the Jerusalem temple (the "cult") was Joel's major focus. The second concerns whether Joel 2:1–11 continues the previous description of locusts from chap. 1 or whether it describes an assault by an enemy (human) army.

(1) The Cultic Interpretation

A. Kapelrud has argued that Joel was a temple or "cultic" prophet and that his central concern was with matters concerning the function and liturgy of the temple. Kapelrud argues that Joel "stood closer to the temple and the cult than many" of the prophets. For Kapelrud this is more a difference in degree than in kind, and he does not regard Joel as radically unlike the other prophets. Rather, he contends that for Joel repentance included both a penitent heart and the outward show of repentance in the temple.[32]

Even so, this perspective leads Kapelrud to some distinctive interpretations of Joel. For example, he compares Joel's prophecy of the pouring out of the Spirit (2:28–32) to Zech 12:10, which states that God would pour out a spirit of grace and supplication on the house of David and on the inhabitants of Jerusalem and that they would mourn when they looked upon the one whom "they had pierced." Kapelrud argues that the "spirit of grace" in Zech 12:10 refers to ritual penance and that the people would enter an ecstatic state and perform ceremonial dirges when they looked upon some cultic object known as the "pierced one." He then argues that in Joel, too, the pouring out of the Spirit is associated with the ecstatic rites of temple prophets. From this he imagines Joel putting in an appearance at the temple and, in the midst of a ritual that dramatized the defeat of Israel's enemies and the darkening of the sun and moon, delivering this prophecy of spiritual ecstasy.[33]

---

[32] Kapelrud, *Joel Studies*, 177, 180, 186.
[33] Ibid., 126–43.

Kapelrud also contends that Joel was influenced by the ritual mourning of the cult of Baal, a position maintained by other scholars as well. F. F. Hvidberg, for example, argues that the mourning of the virgin in 1:8 echoed the lamentation of Anat over Baal,[34] and G. W. Ahlström sees syncretism between Baalism and Yahwism here.[35]

In these and other similar musings Kapelrud and others have gone far beyond the evidence of the text. The mourning of a young woman for her beloved is an ordinary enough event that the image of 1:8 need not have been derived from mythology. We have no indication that Joel was an official "temple prophet" and little clear evidence that such individuals existed at all in ancient Israel.[36] It is true that Joel called the people to lamentation at the temple and that he was grieved at the cessation of temple sacrifice brought on by the famine conditions (Joel 1:9), but this does not mean that he stood "closer" to the temple than the other prophets or that he functioned as an official prophet for the temple. Above all, one should be careful about ascribing ritual patterns to Joel beyond what the book explicitly indicates. Apart from the improbability of the cultic interpretation Kapelrud has given Zech 12:10, there is no evidence that Joel 2:28–32 is a ritual text or has anything to do with temple ecstasy.

Ahlström argues that Joel worked in the early postexilic period and that he stood in opposition to a revived Baalism in the temple of Yahweh.[37] This interpretation is most unlikely. In spite of heroic efforts to find cultic meaning behind every conceivable word of Joel, Ahlström's thesis flounders on the fact that the book does not contain a single clear reference to Baalism or syncretism. Other scholars also have attempted to find links between Joel, cultic theology, and Ugaritic literature, but the proposals can be eccentric.[38]

---

[34] F. F. Hvidberg, *Weeping and Laughter in the Old Testament* (Leiden: Brill, 1962), cited in Crenshaw, *Joel*, 46.

[35] Ahlström, *Joel*, 48–51.

[36] See Dillard, "Joel," 239.

[37] Ahlström, *Joel*, especially pp. 27–34; 122–29.

[38] For example, O. Loretz, *Regenritual und Jahwetag im Joelbuch*, Ugaritisch–Biblische Literatur 4 (Altenberge: CIS, 1986). On the basis of a metrical analysis of the cola, Loretz sees an eight-stage evolution (*Entwicklung*) of Joel (pp. 142–43). Also he looks for Ugaritic parallels to the Book of Joel, especially in the areas of a supposed Canaanite origin for the day of Yahweh and supposed reflections in Joel of Canaanite rituals for the production of rain. He considers 1:8–10,11–12,13,14–17,18–20; 2:12–14,15–19,21–24; 4:18a (3:18a) to be the original kernel of Joel. He regards these verses as a chain of texts about drought together with rituals to induce Yahweh to send rain. Also note G. S. Ogden, "Joel 4 and Prophetic Responses to National Laments," *JSOT* 26 (1983): 97–106. Ogden considers Joel a prophetic-oracular response to ritual lamentation and thus argues that no literal locusts or droughts and no apocalyptic ideas are behind the text. In his commentary Ogden argues that Joel is a response to lamentation over the fall of Jerusalem in the sixth century (G. S. Ogden and R. R. Deutsch, "Joel," in *A Promise of Hope—A Call to Obedience*, ITC [Grand Rapids: Eerdmans, 1987], 13–14).

Having said that, we must observe that the modern, Western Protestant must be careful in interpreting Joel. No doubt the liturgy of the temple was far more important to Joel than church ritual is to many modern evangelicals. For him the repentance of the heart was inseparable from lamentation at the temple (cf. 1 Kgs 8:37–40). To read Joel with no awareness of the significance of the temple in his world is as bad or worse than exaggerating its place.

(2) Locusts or Soldiers?

Most scholars agree that Joel 1 describes an invasion of the land by a swarm of locusts. Joel 2:1–11,20, however, is subject to considerable debate. At issue is whether this is further description of the locust plague or whether the prophet used the image of the locusts to describe the sacking of the city by a human army.

Reasons for contending that 2:1–11,20 continues the account of a simple locust plague are as follows. First, its context between Joel 1, the initial account of the locus plague, and 2:21–27, which offers the hope of recovery from the locusts, implies to some readers that 2:1–11 must focus on locusts as well. Second, scholars also see several parallels between the account in 2:1–11 and the phenomena associated with locust plagues. For example, locusts leave a land looking as though it had been burned with fire (2:3); the head of a locust resembles a horse's head (2:4); and the noise of locusts is like that of cavalry or a crackling fire (2:5). The stench of a dead locust swarm is said to be overwhelming (2:20). Most important is that the enemy of Joel 2 is said to be "like" soldiers (2:7), which suggests they are not soldiers in fact.

None of these arguments can bear close scrutiny. A thorough examination of the text requires that we recognize a human army behind the imagery of 2:1–11,20. In the commentary at the appropriate verses we will develop in detail the case for seeing this as a human army. What follows here is a brief summary of the evidence.[39]

First, it is hardly surprising that descriptions of the army in 2:1–11 resemble descriptions of locusts. The locust plague of Joel's day was the occasion for his prophecy and provided the imagery. In chap. 2 a human army is described in locustlike terms simply because the locust plague was the event that prompted the prophecy in the first place.

The notion that this enemy is *like* a human army and therefore is *not* a human army is mistaken. Hebrew prophecy can use "like"[40] not to mean that the reality is *not* the analog but to describe the fulfillment of an ideal; that is,

---

[39] This material also builds upon D. A. Garrett, "The Structure of Joel," *JETS* 28 (1985): 289–97.

[40] The Hebrew particle כ.

the reality is the *absolute fulfillment* of the analog. More precisely, the reality *is* the analog in its purest, most complete form. In Joel 1:15 the locust plague brings destruction *"like* a destruction from the Almighty." This cannot mean that the destruction is not *in fact* from the Almighty; if anything, the whole burden of Joel 1 is to show that the disaster *is* from God. In Ezek 26:10 the Babylonians storm the city of Tyre *"as* men enter a city whose walls have been broken through." The point here is not that in fact the walls have *not* been breached; it is that they have been *completely broken through.* Zechariah 14:3 similarly says that Yahweh will one day fight against the nations *"as* he fights in the day of battle" (italics added).[41] The use of "like" in Joel 2:1–11 implies that this army is the absolute fulfillment of prophecies of doom. The text also uses "like" because the image of the locust plague still to some extent governs the language.

The position of 2:1–11 between the locust plague of Joel 1 and the restoration of 2:21–27 does not invalidate this interpretation. To the contrary, the structure of Joel requires that 2:1–11 move away from locusts and toward an apocalyptic crisis.[42] If there is no indication of a human army in Joel 2, then Joel 3 (Joel 4 in Heb.) becomes unintelligible. It makes no sense to move from a locust plague, to the healing of the land, and then to the destruction of all Gentile nations. Interpreted that way, it seems that the Gentiles are being punished for the locust plague that Jerusalem suffered. Why should the Gentiles suffer apocalyptic fury as retribution for a locust plague they had nothing to do with? Was Joel's nationalism so extreme that he felt he had to call down divine destruction on all nations somehow to vindicate Jerusalem after the reversal of the locust plague?[43] The final battle with the Gentile powers in Joel 3 makes sense only in a context of the Gentile powers having desecrated Jerusalem in 2:1–11. Those who interpret Joel 1–2 strictly as a locust plague and who also regard Joel 3 as a separate work written by a later author are being consistent at this point; those who try to maintain the unity of the book while contending for a "locusts only" interpretation of Joel 2 are not. In addition, the structure of Joel, as described below, perfectly fits the interpretation of 2:1–11 as a human army.

The language of 2:1–11 decisively favors reading it as an account of an assault by highly trained soldiers, although the NIV has used somewhat ambiguous language; it states that they "plunge through defenses." According to v. 8, this enemy advances unswervingly through enemy fire. The Hebrew more clearly describes the soldiers advancing through a volley of spears,

---

[41] All the verses cited use ‎כ‎ for "like" or "as."

[42] See H. Hosch, "The Concept of Prophetic Time in Joel," *JETS* 15 (1972): 31–38.

[43] To the contrary, reading 2:1–11 as a description of a human army allows one to see an implied rejection of the notion of the invulnerability of Zion. See G. V. Smith, *The Prophets as Preachers* (Nashville: Broadman & Holman, 1994), 237.

arrows, and the like.[44] Trying to hold back a swarm of locusts by shooting arrows and throwing spears would be quite absurd. In addition, the enemy scales the walls of the city, and the climax of their assault is when they invade private homes (v. 9). While there is no doubt that locusts would cling to walls and some would come into houses, these would have been nuisances and not particularly significant in a locust plague. Locusts do their real damage in the fields and gardens, not in homes. When a human army has scaled walls and entered private homes, however, that is the final sign that all defenses have failed and the city is taken.

It is also noteworthy that the Hebrew shows a shift of tense from Joel 1 to Joel 2. Joel 1 consistently uses perfect forms to describe the desolation from a locust plague that has already passed through. Joel 2, however, shifts to the Hebrew imperfect to describe another invasion that is yet to come.

Perhaps the strongest proof that Joel 2 shifts toward a human army is in v. 20, where this enemy is described as the "northerner." Locust plagues in Israel did not characteristically come from the north, and there is no logical reason to call a locust plague the "northerner." By contrast, the prophets frequently warned of the hordes of invaders who would come down from the north to sweep over the land. Despite valiant and at times desperate attempts to produce a justification for calling a locust plague the "northerner," there simply is no reason to take this as a reference to anything but a northern enemy (Assyrians, Babylonians, and others) such as the prophets frequently foretold (e.g., Jer 1:14–15; 4:6; 6:1,22; 10:22). (For more details see commentary on 2:20.)

Stuart has pointed out how carefully Joel follows the theology of Deuteronomy and in particular Deuteronomy 32.[45] This passage describes the increasing severity of hardships and calamities that would befall a disobedient Israel until at last the nation succumbed to an enemy invasion. Another significant text is Deuteronomy 28. It presents a locust plague as a prelude to a foreign invasion and captivity (vv. 38,49–68). For the informed reader of the Old Testament, locusts were a warning of worse things to come. If anything, it would have been odd for an Old Testament prophet to see swarms of locusts pass through the land and *not* regard it as a sign that foreign conquerors were coming.

Finally, P. R. Andiñach has pointed out that ancient Near Eastern literature routinely portrays human armies under the metaphor of locusts.[46] In addition to several biblical texts (Judg 6:3–5; 7:12; Jer 46:23; Nah 3:15–16), Sumer-

---

[44] The Heb. שֶׁלַח means "weapons" (e.g., spears, swords) and not the abstract "defenses." See further details in the commentary.

[45] Stuart, *Hosea–Jonah*, 228.

[46] P. R. Andiñach, "The Locusts in the Message of Joel, *VT* 42 (1992): 433–41. See also *ANET*, 144, lines 104–11, and ANETSup, 649, lines 157–60.

ian, Akkadian, and Ugaritic texts all use this imagery. It can hardly be considered strange that Joel used this metaphor.

3. Structure

The basic movement of the Book of Joel is clear. First, a locust plague in Judah is a manifestation of the day of the Lord. It is an act of judgment and a sign of further judgment to come. Second, the image of the locust invasion of the land is transformed into another image of destruction, that of the northern army sacking Jerusalem. Third, the text presents repentance and restoration as the means of healing. Rains restore the land, and the northern army is destroyed. Fourth, the image of rains coming upon the land is transformed into an image of the Spirit being poured out on all people, itself an apocalyptic sign of favor and restoration. Finally, apocalyptic fury falls upon the Gentile nations in retribution for their hatred of Israel and the despoiling of Jerusalem. Joel is consistent internally and with the message of the Torah and the other prophets.

Viewed in this way, Joel follows a simple structure of "judgment—repentance—salvation."[47] Thus one could describe the outline of Joel as follows:

I. Judgment on Jerusalem (1:1–2:11)
   A. The Locusts (1:1–20)
   B. The Northern Army (2:1–11)
II. Repentance (2:12–17)
III. Salvation (2:18–3:21)
   A. Introduction to Divine Response (2:18–19)
   B. Northern Army Destroyed (2:20)
   C. Land Restored (2:21–27)
   D. Pouring Out the Spirit (2:28–32)
   E. Judgment on Gentiles (3:1–21)

On closer examination, however, the structure of Joel is more complex than this, which is often the case. Unlike modern Western writers, the ancient Israelites were not schooled in writing according to hierarchical outlines. To seek to impose a hierarchical outline on an Old Testament passage is often tantamount to forcing an alien grid over the text. For the ancient Israelites parallelism, chiasmus, and catchwords were often more significant than hierarchy.

From the previous outline it is immediately apparent that Joel did not follow the outline a modern writer probably would use. Joel describes the destruction of the northern invader (2:20) before he gives major attention to

---

[47] For a good survey of alternative analyses of the structure of Joel, see Crenshaw, *Joel*, 29–34.

the healing of the land after the locust plague (2:21–27), even though at the beginning of the book the locust plague (1:2–20) precedes the invasion by the enemy army (2:1–11). In addition, Joel has interrupted the account of God's vengeance on the nations. He briefly describes the destruction of the northern enemy in 2:20 but then moves to an account of rains restoring the bounty of the land (2:21–27) and the Spirit coming upon all people (2:28–32) before he returns to the subject of the last battle and the final judgment against the nations at the valley of Jehoshaphat (3:1–21).

More than that, it is apparent that 2:18–19 serves a transitional role of introducing and summarizing the divine oracle of salvation that follows in 2:20–3:21. Beginning in 2:18 the whole focus of the book changes. Prior to this verse all is prophetic lamentation and appeals for repentance, but after it the entire book is an oracle of salvation from God. However, 2:18–19 are clearly transitional. Verse 18 introduces the divine decision, and v. 19 gives an advance summation of the decree. The actual decree, in its structured form, begins in 2:20 with the oracle against the northern army.[48] From all these considerations it is apparent that we must think more in terms of parallel and chiasmus than in terms of a hierarchical outline.

At the outset 1:2–2:27 shows a clear chiastic structure:

A Punishment: The Locust Plague (1:2–20)
  B Punishment: The Northern Army (2:1–11)
    C Transition: Repentance and Response (2:12–19)
  B′ Forgiveness: The Northern Army Destroyed (2:20)
A′ Forgiveness: The Locust-Ravaged Land Restored (2:21–27)

The restoration of the land in 2:21–27 parallels the destruction of the crops from chap. 1 just as the end of the northern army in 2:20 parallels the account of the sack of Jerusalem in 2:1–11. The transitional text, 2:12–19, indicates that forgiveness and salvation will come when people truly turn to God. The account of the destruction of the northern army is brief (2:20) probably because the text resumes the theme of judgment upon the Gentiles in a much larger fashion in 3:1–21. Also 2:20 specifically concerns the defeat of the invader, but chap. 3 moves beyond this to the judgment of all nations. Hence there is little need to devote much space to the destruction of the northerner in chap. 2.[49]

To comprehend further the chiastic nature of this text we must observe how 2:21–27, the healing of the land, parallels in reverse order the account of the devastation of the land in chap. 1. The promises in 2:21–22 describe the res-

[48] For further discussion see commentary on 2:18–19.
[49] For a different but chiastic analysis of 1:5–2:17, see J. Limburg, *Hosea–Micah*, IBC (Atlanta: John Knox, 1988), 61.

toration of a parched land and the provision of good pasture to the animals and also assert that the trees will again bear fruit. This reverses the lamentations of 1:18–20. Furthermore, the promises of 2:23–24 reverse the calamities of 1:5–17 (shortage of wine, oil, and grain and a general scarcity). Then the language of 2:25 closely parallels 1:4. Finally, the benediction and call to praise in 2:26–27 correspond to the introductory call to mourning in 1:2–3. This reversal of sequence confirms that 2:21–27 is a self-contained unit that answers chap. 1 (see chart). It also further indicates that 2:18–19 should be taken as introductory and that 2:20, the destruction of the northerner, answers 2:1–11.

Table 2: The Reversal of the Locust Plague

1:2–20	2:21–27
Elders are to remember, mourn, and tell the story *for generations to come* (vv. 2–3)	People will have plenty and will praise and *never again* be shamed (vv. 26–27)
The four locust swarms eat everything (v. 4)	People are repaid for the damage of the four locust swarms (v. 25)
Wine is gone and oil fails (vv. 5,10)	Wine and oil restored (v. 24b)
Grain depleted and granaries ruined (vv. 10–11,17)	Grain restored and threshing floors full (v. 24a)
Land is parched (vv. 12,17)	Rains come (v. 23)
Trees are stripped bare (vv. 12,19b)	Trees bear fruit (v. 22b)
Animals dying (vv. 18,20)	Animals have pasture (v. 22a)
Land "burned up" (vv. 19–20)	Land "not afraid" (v. 21)

There is, however, a further complication. When we examine 2:20–3:21, another chiastic structure is evident. First, the destruction of the northern invader parallels the judgment on all nations in 3:1–21. The former concerns the defeat of the invader; and the latter, the end of all Gentile power. On the other hand, a second parallel appears between 2:21–27 and 2:28–32. Specifically, the heart of the promise in 2:21–27 is that Yahweh will send rains on the dry land, but in 2:28–32 Yahweh promises to pour out his Spirit on all his people. The use of "pour out" to describe the sending of the Spirit is not accidental; Ezek 36:26–27 speaks of God "giving" the Spirit to his people. Joel, however, has used the description of *pouring out* the Spirit to draw attention to the parallel between the Spirit and the healing rains. As the rain was a sign of God's favor upon the nation in its economic distress, so the Spirit is a sign of the final vindication of Israel, the coming of the eschatological age, and the end of its reproach among the nations for all time. Thus 2:20 and 2:21–27 do double duty in the structure of the book. They both complete the chiasmus in the first part of the book and begin the chiasmus in the second part of the book.

We thus see a second chiasmus, one that overlaps the first chiasmus:

A Judgment: The Northerner Destroyed (2:20)
 B Grace: Rain Poured on the Land (2:21–27)
 B′ Grace: The Spirit Poured on All People (2:28–32)
A′ Judgment: All Nations Destroyed (3:1–21)

When we attempt to lay all this down in a single outline of the entire book, our hierarchical structures fail us, and we must resort to a more appropriate model of the text. We do best if we recognize that there are two chiastic patterns here that overlap and call the first 1 and the second 2 and develop our outline accordingly. The individual sections of chiasmus 1 are 1A, 1B, and so forth, and chiasmus 2 is similarly 2A, 2B, and so forth. When we include subdivisions in the outline, the whole works out as shown on p. 310.

4. The Theology of Joel

Considering its brevity (and perhaps its unpromising historical situation of a locust plague), the Book of Joel is remarkably rich in theological insights. Like many Old Testament prophets, Joel used the immediate crisis facing the original audience to move toward eschatological and ultimate issues. He was able to do this because the main focus of the text is not the locust plague as such but the locust plague as a manifestation of the day of the Lord.

(1) The Covenant

In Joel it is a given that all aspects of the covenant between Yahweh and Israel will be fulfilled. This implies first of all that Israel itself faces judgment for failing to keep the covenant.[50] We have already seen how passages such as Deuteronomy 28 anticipate that a series of crises, including locusts, would befall wayward Israel. The ultimate calamity would be military conquest at the hands of a foreign enemy and subsequent captivity and exile. Judgment begins with God's own people. The theology of Deuteronomy thus drives the interpretation of the locust plague in Joel.

---

[50] The word "covenant" (בְּרִית) actually never appears in Joel, but as Ahlström points out, it is a significant theological idea in Joel. He observes that preexilic prophets rarely used the word (*Joel*, 23–34).

But the covenant also implies both the compassion of God and the ultimate vindication of Israel (Deut 32:36). God is merciful, and when his people call on him, he quickly desists from punishing and heals those whom he has wounded. The Mosaic proclamation that the Lord is "compassionate and gracious" and "slow to anger, abounding in love and faithfulness" (Exod 34:6) has become the basis for Joel's hope that repentance will result in deliverance (Joel 2:13). In addition, Israel as the chosen people is the "apple of the eye" of God (Deut 32:10).[51] Gentiles who mock, attack, or despoil Israel will experience the same and worse; God will heap their atrocities back upon their own heads (Joel 3:4–8; cf. Obad 10–16; Nah 1:15). In the end God will show that he is Israel's God by bringing the whole world into judgment and allowing for no place of safety except Zion (Joel 3:19–21).

(2) The Day of the Lord

Scholars generally connect the idea of the day of the Lord with the ideology of the holy war. Passages such as Isaiah 13; 34 and Ezekiel 7 supposedly reflect ancient traditions in which Yahweh comes down as a warrior to fight for Israel. In popular eschatology this was taken to mean that the day of the Lord was always good for Israel and bad for their enemies—a position that Amos decisively rejected (Amos 5:18).[52] Whether this reconstruction is in all points correct is difficult to say,[53] but it is clear that the day of the Lord refers to dramatic action by Yahweh either to judge or to save.

The day of the Lord dominates the Book of Joel. Every major event of Joel is treated as the day of the Lord. The locust plague that initiated the book is Yahweh's "army," whose coming signals dreadful destruction from the Almighty (1:6,15). The army of 2:1–11 comes against Jerusalem on the "day of the LORD," a "day of darkness and gloom, a day of clouds and blackness" (2:1–2). This army has all the trappings of an apocalyptic enemy (see commentary on 2:1–11 for details). But the day of the Lord is also salvation for Israel. Remarkably, even the pouring out of the Spirit is accompanied by the

---

[51] That is, the pupil of his eye. God protects Israel as zealously as a man protects the pupil of his eye.

[52] The classic essay is G. von Rad, "The Origin of the Concept of the Day of Yahweh," *JSS* 4 (1959): 97–108. The main problem with this view is that the "day of the LORD" is exclusively a prophetic concept. It is not found in ancient war poetry, and there is no clear evidence that it was commonly used as some kind of battle cry. Von Rad speculates that if we possessed the ancient "Book of the Wars of Yahweh" (Num 21:14) we would find evidence for the origin and meaning of the phrase (p. 108). On the basis of Amos 5:18, however, it is clear that the phrase was popularly taken to mean the day of Israel's salvation.

[53] An alternative but less plausible view is that the יהוה יום was originally a festal or sacrificial day in Israel's cultic calendar. Ahlström interprets the יהוה יום in the context of a ritual and mythological battle between Yahweh and the forces of chaos (*Joel*, 62–97).

dreadful signs of the day of the Lord (2:30–31). The healing of the land after the locust plague also will come about because the Lord will do "great things" and "wonders" in Judah (2:21,26). Finally, the destruction of the northern enemy and the judgment of all nations is, from beginning to end, the day of the Lord. Yahweh comes down as a warrior to slaughter his enemies (2:20; 3:9–11,16). The sky grows black (3:15). Jerusalem experiences healing and vindication (3:18–21). One could correctly say that the real subject matter of Joel is the day of the Lord in all its forms.

We must recognize the paradox that the day of the Lord is at the same time one event and many events. Joel does not present some events (e.g., the locust plague) as a mere *foreshadowing* of the day of the Lord. Rather, the locust plague *is* the day of the Lord. But the invasion by the northern enemy is also the day of the Lord, and so is the pouring out of the Spirit and also the judgment of all nations. The day of the Lord is not *exclusively* any specific period of tribulation, deliverance, or final judgment. But each of these events can rightly be called the day of the Lord.

The day of the Lord refers to a decisive action of Yahweh to bring his plans for Israel to completion. This action may be an act of punishment or of salvation for Israel, but in either case it carries forward the purposes of God. The day of the Lord is thus the thematic link that binds together events as disparate as a locust plague, a foreign invasion, the gift of the Spirit empowering people of all social classes to prophesy, and the last judgment.

Simply put, Joel is seeking to persuade his audience that the plans of God are moving forward. Jerusalem must accept the calamities that come upon them as the chastisement of God and must look to him for forgiveness and protection. On the other hand, the plans of God include the final triumph of Israel. The very event that has terrified Jerusalem, the day of the Lord, is also their salvation.

Modern Christian readers should avoid interpreting every reference to clouds and darkness or to the day of the Lord as the literal end of the world. They should also be cautious about finding details of a future "great tribulation" in the Book of Joel. Such a reading of the book springs from the false premise that the day of the Lord has only a single, future reference or fulfillment. In reality, the day of the Lord is more of a theological idea than a specific event. As a theological idea it can manifest itself in human history many times and in many forms.

(3) *The Future of Zion*

Zion is connected with Jerusalem but actually transcends the geographical city. It represents the conviction that Israel is the chosen nation; that Yahweh, the God of Abraham, Isaac, and Jacob, is the one true God; and that the Davidic monarch is destined to rule all the nations of the world. When Jerusalem is humbled, it gives the nations cause to rejoice because it appears to them that their gods are higher than Israel's God or that Yahweh has simply abandoned his people. But the Lord is still God in Zion! This is the real message of Joel to his dispirited and suffering people. Like the Psalms, Joel exults in the place of Zion before God. Although brought to its knees by locusts and enemies, Zion remains the chosen city of God. It is the only place of salvation on the day of judgment (3:16).

Gentile Christian readers must acknowledge that they have come and bowed before the God of Israel in the person of Jesus Christ. They can also rejoice to have been given a share in all the promises to Israel (Eph 2:12–18). They can join the psalmist in thanking God that although once they were strangers, now they can proclaim, "We, too, were born in Zion!" (cp. Ps 87). "The LORD dwells in Zion!" (Joel 3:21).[54]

(4) A Biblical Worldview

Joel's frequent use of the themes of the covenant, the day of the Lord, and the future of Zion all reflect a mind thoroughly immersed in biblical language and the biblical view of the world. Scholars have observed how profoundly this biblicism has shaped the content of Joel. Crenshaw has aptly written:

> It seems that Joel was thoroughly familiar with a wide range of sacred tradition, either oral floating traditions or written texts. His use of words and phrases from this rich repertoire resembles that of a learned scribe, a teacher of preserved religious tradition. He draws on the ancient account of the exodus, particularly the plagues, the theophanic language, and the divine declaration to Moses of YHWH's essential attributes. He echoes the terminology of Deuteronomic threats linked to the covenant, and he is thoroughly at home in the language of holy war.[55]

The Bible calls upon readers to accept its world as their world.[56] It is not content simply to speak to us or allow us to pick and choose from among its ideas in an eclectic fashion. Rather, it demands that we see the world as it sees it and interpret events accordingly. Joel, in his treatment of a locust plague in the context of biblical theology, has modeled this kind of thinking.

(5) Natural Calamity and the Will of God

---

[54] For a good discussion of OT hermeneutics as it relates to the ultimate fulfillment of biblical prophecy, see V. S. Poythress, *Understanding Dispensationalists* (Phillipsburg, N.J.: Presbyterian & Reformed, 1994).

[55] Crenshaw, *Joel*, 36.

[56] See J. H. Sailhamer, *Introduction to Old Testament Theology* (Grand Rapids: Zondervan, 1995), 216–17.

The Book of Joel never views disaster as only a natural event or as an accident. All things are under God's control and, more specifically, relate to God's larger purposes for the world and Israel. As such, Joel contributes to our understanding of the problem of theodicy. In particular, Joel enables us to see that while disasters can be very painful and are a legitimate reason for mourning, they are always within the plan of God. There is ample reason to seek for grace here. By grace we remain in a state of repentance, and by grace we discern the larger plans for good behind our temporary setbacks and hardships. (For a more detailed discussion, see Excursus 1 in the commentary.)

(6) Ethical Questions and the Issue of Repentance

Numerous scholars have pointed out that Joel says little if anything about moral issues.[57] Many other scholars have attempted to read pronouncements about various moral issues into Joel, but these efforts have generally been futile.[58] One might contend that there is an implied mockery of drunkenness in 1:5, but this is meager indeed compared to the titanic struggles of the other prophets against the sins and the apostasy of the Jews. In fact, the issue of drunkenness itself is not the real point in 1:5 (see commentary). The question thus arises whether Joel is so concerned with either the external aspects of religion (e.g., ritual penance at the temple, 1:14) or perhaps so full of anger toward the arrogant Gentiles (chap. 3) that he is indifferent to or neglectful of the kind of spiritual issues with which the other prophets contended.

Such a reading of Joel would be misguided. First of all, although Joel commands the people to repent (2:12–19), he does not warn them that disaster will come if they refuse; he comforts a people who *already* have faced a major calamity. The population was on the verge of starvation. This was not the time for bringing up former sins or for the kind of haranguing one might give an arrogant and indifferent people. Similarly, Joel does not threaten the people with the possibility that the northern invaders *might* come; like Isaiah, he knows they *will* come (Joel 2:1–11; Isa 6:9–13; 39:5–7). Like Isa 40–55, the Book of Joel focuses on helping the people respond to the terrible events facing them.

In addition, Joel does not simply lash out in anger against the Gentiles. Rather, his portrayal of the Gentiles is part of his overall understanding of the plan of God in history in which Zion is vindicated as the only place of refuge.

The Book of Joel is not content with ritual penance only. It demands that the people turn to God with their whole hearts (2:12). They must tear their hearts and not just their garments (2:13; tearing clothes was a ritual sign of

---

[57] Stuart correctly notes that this issue has no real bearing on the date of Joel (*Hosea–Jonah*, 231).

[58] Crenshaw catalogs various failed attempts to read ethical issues into Joel (*Joel*, 40).

mourning or repentance). The structure of the book shows that healing and restoration begin only after repentance begins. The oracle of salvation (2:18–3:21) comes immediately after the prophetic call to return to God with a broken heart, which Joel assumes they will do (2:12–17).

It is not excessive to say that Joel desires the people to enter the state of grace whereby they remain repentant before God. In this Joel is not far from the New Testament understanding of grace through faith. In falling before God and depending only on the fact that he is "abounding in love" (2:13), the people abandon any pretense of righteousness or worthiness.

(7) Prophecy and the Gift of the Spirit

In the Book of Joel the gift of the Spirit is not primarily a work of God to change the hearts of his people and enable them to love God and obey his laws. This contrasts with Ezek 36:24–32, where the gift of the Spirit gives people a "new heart" (v. 26) and moves them to follow the decrees and keep the laws of God (v. 27). In Joel the gift of the Spirit instead moves people to prophetic utterances, dreams, and visions (Joel 2:28).

This does not mean, however, that Joel conceives of the gift of the Spirit simply as a private event of religious ecstasy (or that Joel would reject Ezekiel's understanding of the gift of the Spirit). In Joel the coming of the Spirit is especially an *eschatological event*. It is the sign that Yahweh is among his people and that their vindication has come. It is the evidence of salvation for Israel and of destruction for the Gentile powers. This is why the Book of Joel describes the pouring out of the Spirit as accompanied by the dark signs of the day of the Lord (2:31). It means that the end is at hand and that the judgment of the nations has begun.[59]

The pouring out of the Spirit is the great sign of the return of God to his people. It is as much proof of his favor as the drought was sign of his disfavor. A number of interpreters speak of the gift of the Spirit as the "democratization" of spiritual authority in Joel. Although there is validity in that viewpoint (young people, slaves, and women have as much of the divine anointing as the men of the ruling class), we should not miss the point that for Joel the pouring out of the Spirit is not so much an individual event as it is a national and eschatological event. It is the sign of the dawn of the messianic age, when Israel is finally vindicated.

---

[59] For further details see Excursus 2 in the commentary on the meaning of Joel 2:28–32 for the Christian reader.

─────────────── *OUTLINE OF THE BOOK* ───────────────

Title (1:1)
  I. **1A**—Judgment on Israel: Locust Plague (1:2–20)
     1. Summons to Lamentation (1:2–14)
     2. Prophetic Lamentation (1:15–20)
 II. **1B**—Judgment on Israel: Northern Army Invasion (2:1–11)
     1. Call to Sound the Alarm (2:1–2a)
     2. Description of the Army (2:2bc–9)
     3. Signs of the Day of the Lord (2:10–11)
III. **1C**—Transition: Repentance and Response (2:12–19)
     1. Invitation to Repentance (2:12–14)
     2. Summons to the Sacred Assembly (2:15–17)
     3. Introduction to the Divine Response (2:18–19)
 IV. **1B′ /2A**—Forgiveness for Israel/Judgment on Nations: Northern
     Army Destroyed (2:20)
  V. **1A′/2B**—Forgiveness for Israel: Locust Plague Reversed / Grace:
     Rain Poured on the Land (2:21–27)
     1. Summons to Celebration (2:21–24)
     2. Divine Promise of Healing (2:25–27)
 VI. **2B′**—Grace: Spirit Poured on All People (2:28–32)
     1. Gift of the Spirit (2:28–29)
     2. Signs of the Day of the Lord (2:30–31)
     3. Promise of Salvation (2:32)
VII. **2A′**—Judgment on Nations: All Nations Destroyed (3:1–21)
     1. The Valley of Jehoshaphat (3:1–3)
     2. Tyre, Sidon, and Philistia (3:4–8)
     3. Summons to All Nations (3:9–12)
     4. The Winepress of the Lord (3:13)
     5. Signs of the Day of the Lord (3:14–17)
     6. The Final State (3:18–21)

TITLE (1:1)

I. JUDGMENT ON ISRAEL: LOCUST PLAGUE (1:2–20)

   1. Summons to Lamentation (1:2–14)

     (1) Elders (1:2–4)

     (2) Drunkards (1:5–7)

     (3) General Audience (1:8–10)

     (4) Farmers (1:11–12)

     (5) Priests (1:13–14)

   2. Prophetic Lamentation (1:15–20)

TITLE (1:1)

¹The word of the LORD that came to Joel son of Pethuel.

1:1 We know nothing about Joel son of Pethuel beyond what is in this book. H. W. Wolff makes the point that the name "Joel" is especially common in the Chronicler's history and thus surmises that it became widely used in the postexilic period.[1] Of course, many of the names in the Chronicler's genealogies are from the preexilic period, and thus it is not clear that the name has chronological significance.

It seems to be standard in a commentary on Joel to mention that "Joel" means "Yahweh is God." The expositor, however, would be ill-advised to make much of this because the book does not develop this theme. It does not, for example, develop a polemic against pagan gods, such as we see in Isaiah 44.[2]

The phrase "word of the LORD" commonly introduces prophetic books (Jer 1:2; Ezek 1:3; Hos 1:1; Jonah 1:1; Mic 1:1; Zech 1:1). Its frequency, however, should not numb us to its significance. It implies first that the message is from God and therefore carries divine authority. But its presence also reminds us that we are here dealing with a specific type of literature—Hebrew prophecy—and that we need to read it according to its own rules. While there is some truth in the assertion that the Bible is as plain as a modern newspaper, the fact remains that it is not a modern newspaper. A "word of the LORD" is a

---

[1] H. W. Wolff, *Joel and Amos,* Her (Philadelphia: Fortress, 1977), 24–25.

[2] Although Joel 2:27 does touch upon this theme.

prophetic oracle, and failure to reckon with the peculiar prophetic mode of speech will inevitably result in a distorted reading of the text.

I. JUDGMENT ON ISRAEL: LOCUST PLAGUE (1:2–20)

A terrible locust plague apparently precipitated Joel's prophecy. Out of this event, which Joel saw as no less than an act of God and a manifestation of the day of the Lord, the book develops a theological program that both interprets the disaster for the prophet's generation and looks ahead to the end of the age. In the process the text shows that the "day of the LORD" is both judgment and salvation and that it appears in diverse historical events.

Joel began his message with the locust plague. His message might be summarized as follows: "What you have seen in the locusts is the day of the Lord that you have often heard the prophets foretell. It has begun not with the Gentiles but with us, the chosen people. We must realize that we are not exempt from judgment, and we must repent." Later in the book Joel will show his audience that God has not abandoned his people and that the future also holds grace for the chosen nation and judgment for the other nations. In chap. 1, however, he summoned Jerusalem to fall on its knees.

1. Summons to Lamentation (1:2–14)

Joel first called various representative groups from the nation to mourn and repent before God. He singled out old men (vv. 2–4), drunkards (vv. 5–7), farmers (vv. 11–12), and priests (vv. 13–14) and called each group to make lamentation and learn from the locust plague. It seems odd that he specified heavy drinkers along with old men, farmers, and priests, but the drunkards represent unrestrained enjoyment of the fruit of the land and thus are an appropriate target for the prophet. In designating the drunkards, Joel signified that their opportunity for overindulgence in the land's bounty was past. One section (vv. 8–10) is not addressed to any particular group but calls the entire populace to repentance (but observe that the first section, addressed to the elders, secondarily summons "all who live in the land" in v. 2).

Formally, each section follows the same general pattern. Each begins with an imperative and then summons a specific group.[3] Each section then describes the devastation left by the locusts. The last section, addressed to the

---

[3] The opening imperatives and summons are: שִׁמְעוּ (v. 2), הָחִיצוּ (v. 5), אֶלֶי (v. 8), הֹבִישׁוּ (v. 11), and חִגְרוּ (v. 13). Note that the imperative סִפְרוּ in v. 3 is not clause-initial and thus does not disrupt the pattern.

priests (vv. 13–14), somewhat breaks this pattern in that after the initial imperative, summons, and description of devastation it concludes with a series of imperatives to the effect that the priests must call a convocation of repentance (v. 14). This is a fitting end to this section and leads into vv. 15–20, where the prophet himself mourns and leads in a prayer for mercy.

(1) Elders (1:2–4)

²**Hear this, you elders;**
listen, all who live in the land.
Has anything like this ever happened in your days
or in the days of your forefathers?
³**Tell it to your children,**
and let your children tell it to their children,
and their children to the next generation.
⁴**What the locust swarm has left**
the great locusts have eaten;
what the great locusts have left
the young locusts have eaten;
what the young locusts have left
other locusts have eaten.

1:2 The double command to "hear" and "listen" implies that urgent or profound information is to follow. In Deut 32:1 this formula introduces Moses' last testimony. Hosea used it to introduce the shocking news that the priests and leaders of Israel were traps to the common people rather than being their guides (Hos 5:1). The use of a rhetorical question also reinforces the significance of what follows. "Has anything like this ever happened in your days or in the days of your forefathers?" calls attention to the astonishing severity of this particular locust plague. It was worse than anyone could remember.

The question also forces us to reckon with the meaning of "elders" in this verse. Was he referring to the "elders" as the leaders of the land or only as the oldest people in the land? Although one could answer that both are true, context implies that the point is that the elders are literally old people, not that they are leaders.[4] Only old people could answer the question of whether such a terrible locust plague had ever happened before.[5] Also the old people, as the

---

[4] Cf. D. A. Hubbard, *Joel and Amos,* TOTC (Downers Grove: InterVarsity, 1989), 42.

[5] It is incorrect to suppose that if Joel here had meant literal old people that he would have balanced זְקֵנִים with something meaning "young people" instead of with "all the inhabitants of the land." Had he said, "Listen, elders, and give ear, young ones" or the like, the merismus would imply that he was addressing all people regardless of age. But this was not his meaning. He was in effect saying, "Listen, old people, and everybody else should listen too." In other words, he specifically addressed old people here but also invited the rest of the population to consider his question. זְקֵנִים has the same ambiguity in 1:14 but refers specifically to old people in 2:16; 3:1 (Eng. 2:28), where it contrasts with young people and does (by merismus) mean "all people regardless of age."

guardians of tradition, would naturally be the ones to hand on the story of this event to the young (v. 3). It is significant that Joel only commanded the elders to remember and to teach; he did not exhort them to lead the people in any direction (contrast v. 14, where he challenged the priests to call the people together in a sacred assembly).[6] Although the lack of any mention of kings in Joel remains a problem for any who advocate a preexilic date, this verse by itself does not imply that the nation was under the governorship of elders.[7] Crenshaw appropriately translates the word here not as "elders" but as "old-timers."[8]

The point of the verse is that this locust plague is no ordinary misfortune; it is unique. The alert reader sees an echo of Deut 4:32–34 here. In that text Moses asked if anyone could remember anything since creation so wonderful as the election of Israel. Joel used the same rhetorical device to point out that God had done a new thing that was as uniquely terrible as the election of Israel was uniquely wonderful. In the locust plague he had undone creation itself. This was the day of the Lord.

1:3 Joel wanted the story of this plague to be repeated in perpetuity. D. Stuart correctly notes that locust invasions are fairly common in Palestine and generally do not drive the people to the brink of starvation. A fairly severe infestation in 1915 caused the price of wine to double; this is inconvenient, but it is hardly devastating. Also locust attacks are transitory, and recovery is often rapid. Nahum 3:17 even minimizes the significance of the Assyrians by comparing them to locusts: they are here today and gone tomorrow.[9]

Joel clearly regarded this locust plague as something special. We can be sure that it was severe enough to get the attention of all the people. Still it is the significance of this event, not its severity, that the prophet espoused. This locust plague is important because it is an eschatological catastrophe and foreshadows more to come.

This verse ironically twists the teaching of the most sacred of Israel's traditions and texts, the Passover liturgy (Exod 12:24–27) and the *Shema* (Deut 6:4–9). In these passages Moses commanded the people to repeat the story of the exodus for all generations, to keep the words of the law always before them, and to recite the law to their children. Here the people are to pass on not a story of a great deliverance or the words of the Torah but the story of Yahweh's judgment on the nation. One might also compare Exod 10:2,[10] where,

---

[6] Also when the term זְקֵנִים refers to leaders, it is often qualified in expressions such as the examples זִקְנֵי הָעָם, or זִקְנֵי הַכֹּהֲנִים. See other examples in KB[3] (Eng. ed., 1:278).

[7] Contrast R. B. Dillard, "Joel," in *The Minor Prophets* (Grand Rapids: Baker, 1991), 1:255.

[8] J. L. Crenshaw, *Joel* (New York: Doubleday, 1995), 86.

[9] D. Stuart, *Hosea–Jonah*, WBC (Dallas: Word, 1987), 232.

[10] Cf. S. Bergler, *Joel als Schriftinterpret,* Beiträge zur Erforschung des Alten Testaments und des antiken Judentums 16 (Frankfurt am Main: Peter Lang, 1988), 256–58.

immediately prior to the plague of locusts on Egypt, God promised miraculous signs "that you may show your children and grandchildren how I dealt harshly with the Egyptians." The irony, of course, is that God is now showing the same severity to Jerusalem. Still, the principle remains valid that every generation must tell the next about what God has done.

1:4 This verse, like v. 3, comprises three lines of Hebrew poetry, although the individual cola are longer and heavier here than in v. 3.[11] The heavy rhythm conveys a sense of being battered by successive waves of locusts, each one as bad as or worse than the previous. Each line also begins *yeter*, "what is left," alluding to the remnant theme but in reverse.

The precise meaning of the four Hebrew words translated "locust" in this verse is a long-standing challenge to Hebrew linguists; the problem combines etymology with entomology. In fact, the Old Testament uses no less than ten different words for locusts and grasshoppers, and the Talmud uses twenty.[12] In our text there are several possible ways of interpreting the different words. First, the terms may refer to different species of insects. The AV has "palmerworm," "locust," "cankerworm," and "caterpillar." This seems quite unlikely since everything seems to point to locusts and not to other types of insects. Second, the words may describe subspecies of grasshoppers or even grasshoppers of different colors. Third, the terms may refer to different stages of development (instars) in the life cycle of the grasshopper. Fourth, the terms may reflect regional dialectical differences. This alternative seems less likely since Joel addressed his message directly to the people of Jerusalem. Fifth, the terms could refer to four separate locust swarms that successively hit Jerusalem and its environs. In this interpretation the prophet arbitrarily attached one of the words meaning "grasshopper" to each swarm. Sixth, the terms may be synonyms that are piled up for rhetorical effect.

A number of interpreters take the position that the words here describe the instars of the locust. In this view "locust swarm"[13] is the penultimate stage of the locust, at which it is a winged grasshopper but not yet capable of flight. The "great locust"[14] is the adult locust, at which stage it flies in massive swarms. The "young locust"[15] is then the offspring of the previous generation of "great locust"; it would therefore be the larval stage, the first instar of the locust. The "other locust"[16] is therefore (supposedly) a subsequent instar of

---

[11] Note that the accent scheme in v. 3 is 3–2–3, but in v. 4 it is 4–4–4. Also note the economical use of the verb סַפֵּרוּ in v. 3, where the one verb does duty for all three cola. By contrast, the verb אָכַל is repeated in each cola of v. 4.

[12] Dillard, "Joel," 255, and Stuart, *Hosea–Joel*, 241.

[13] גָּזָם is supposedly from גזם, "to cut."

[14] Many scholars associate אַרְבֶּה with the word רַב, "many."

[15] BDB associates יֶלֶק with ילק, "to lick."

[16] BDB associates חָסִיל with חסל, "to consume."

the locust, a nymph. In this theory the land was afflicted with two generations of locusts. The first came as it was nearing the adult stage and laid its eggs while consuming the produce of the land. The second generation then consumed what was left before moving on.[17]

However neat this theory may appear, we must recognize that it is purely hypothetical. It is built upon correlation between supposed Hebrew etymologies and the life development of grasshoppers[18] and is unsupported by clear evidence. Beyond the fact that they all in some way refer to locusts, we simply do not know what these four words denote.[19]

What is certain is that the text uses the four words with remarkable rhetorical effect. The impact of the verse is that the wrath of Yahweh is inescapable; those who think they have avoided one stage of the calamity are caught by another. In this Joel 1:4 is like Amos 5:19: "It will be as though a man fled from a lion only to meet a bear, as though he entered his house and rested his hand on the wall only to have a snake bite him." The expositor of Joel, rather than give his congregation a lesson in entomology, would do well to drive home this lesson. Also the emphasis on the last remaining bits of food being consumed by the locusts reflects the story of the plague of locusts in Egypt during the exodus.[20] What God had once done to his enemies he was now doing to Jerusalem.

The number "four" also has apocalyptic significance. Nebuchadnezzar's dream and Daniel's vision both spoke of four world empires (Daniel 2; 7). Zechariah and John saw four horsemen riding across the earth (Zech 1:8; Rev 6:1–8).[21] It would be a mistake to interpret the four locusts of this verse as symbolic of four empires or the like, but it is legitimate to assert that for Joel, the locust plague itself was an apocalyptic event.

(2) Drunkards (1:5–7)

---

[17] See J. A. Thompson, "Joel's Locusts in the Light of Near Eastern Parallels," *JNES* 14 (1955): 52–55. O. R. Sellers is so confident in his etymologies (and his entomology) that he wants to emend Joel 1:4 to suit his theory ("Stages of Locust in Joel," *AJSL* 52 [1935–36]: 81–85).

[18] The term יֶלֶק, for example, is often said to mean "hopper." The explanation offered is that this is the larval instar since at this stage its wings are small and not visible.

[19] This is not to say that we do not have a great deal of information on the nature of locust plagues in Israel. For a good but brief account over the last two centuries, see F. S. Bodenheimer, "Note on Invasions of Palestine by Rare Locusts," in *Israel Exploration Journal Reader*, ed. H. M. Orlinsky (New York: KTAV, 1981), 2:1313–15.

[20] Compare this verse to Exod 10:5b (see Bergler, *Joel als Schriftinterpret*, 259). It is especially noteworthy that both verses speak of the locusts consuming (אכל) the יֶתֶר ("remaining bits") of food.

[21] Zechariah also saw a vision of four horns (Zech 1:18) and four blacksmiths (1:20), as well as a vision of four chariots (6:1), which are the "four winds of heaven" (6:5). In Revelation, John sees four living creatures (Rev 4:6), four angels at the four corners of the earth (7:1), and four angels who are bound at the river Euphrates (9:14).

⁵Wake up, you drunkards, and weep!
  Wail, all you drinkers of wine;
wail because of the new wine,
  for it has been snatched from your lips.
⁶A nation has invaded my land,
  powerful and without number;
it has the teeth of a lion,
  the fangs of a lioness.
⁷It has laid waste my vines
  and ruined my fig trees.
It has stripped off their bark
  and thrown it away,
  leaving their branches white.

1:5 Drunkards, like gluttons, use the fruit of the land in excess. The presence of drunkards (and gluttons) is evidence of bounty. Also a good harvest might be a time for heavy drinking, even for those who were not habitually excessive drinkers (Ruth 3:3,7). But now no one will be drunk for the simple reason that there is no wine[22] to drink and no harvest to celebrate.

Drunkards also suggest people who are self-indulgent and unconcerned about the things of God. Joel saw the locusts as a literal wake-up call. Weeping and wailing is generally associated with a funeral; the pleasures of the self-absorbed life have ended, and the people need to reckon with what God has done. At the same time, we should recognize that Joel did not embark on a tirade against drunkenness or alcoholism at this point. Crenshaw correctly observes that the "drinkers of wine" included virtually the entire population of the ancient world,[23] including the people of Judah. The real focus of this verse is not drunkenness in itself but the deprivation the people had suffered.

The metaphor of wine being "snatched away" (or "cut off"[24]) from the lips suggests an act that is sudden and violent. It is as though the drinker were in the very act of raising the cup to his mouth only to have it yanked from his hand. The locust plague was severe and unanticipated.

1:6 The text already begins to blur the line between literal locusts and a human army. While there is no doubt that the focus in this chapter is on the locust invasion, the locusts are here called a "nation"[25] and are said to be

---

[22] The precise meaning of עָסִיס is uncertain. It could refer to grape juice that had not yet been (but would be) fermented, or it could refer to another, very strong alcoholic drink. In either case the point is that means for getting drunk were not available. For a good discussion of this word, see Dillard, "Joel," 258.

[23] Crenshaw, *Joel*, 94.

[24] So translating כרת.

[25] The word גּוֹי is characteristically used of Gentile powers, although Prov 30:25–26 designates ants and badgers as "peoples" (עַם).

"mighty."[26] This is more than mere metaphor; for Joel the locust plague and the apocalyptic northern army shared a common source as the army of Yahweh and agent of his wrath. The use of the phrase "my land" for Judah is equally significant here; the closest parallel usage is in Ezek 38:16: "You will advance against my people Israel like a cloud that covers the land. In days to come, O Gog, I will bring you against my land, so that the nations may know me when I show myself holy through you before their eyes" (see also Isa 8:8).

Locusts do not have teeth (only vertebrates have teeth), and thus it is artificial to say that the invader "has the teeth of a lion." Some commentators state that the locust appears to have sharp teeth, or that the color of the locust or its head sometimes resembles that of a lion.[27] But concern over locust or lion physiology misses the point entirely. The lion is a stock metaphor for ferocity, and no real correspondence between lions and locusts was intended.[28]

As an image of power, the lion can occur in many contexts. In Gen 49:9, for example, the lion symbolizes the ferocity of Judah and probably of the Davidic king in particular. Here, however, the metaphor again looks to the eschatological foe, as in Isa 5:26–29: "He lifts up a banner for the distant nations. . . . Not one of them grows tired or stumbles, not one slumbers or sleeps . . . their horses' hoofs seem like flint, their chariot wheels like a whirlwind. . . . Their roar is like that of the lion, they roar like young lions" (cp. also this text from Isaiah to Joel 2:4–8). Joel's concern was not to describe locusts as such but to communicate via metaphor the theological meaning of the locust plague. It was the day of the Lord.

1:7 Here the text speaks of "my vines" and "my fig trees." A number of commentators speculate on whether the prophet or God is intended as speaker here. But since the prophet closely identified himself with God and the message anyway, this is not a particularly significant question or fruitful area for investigation. Of greater importance is that God often speaks of Judah as his "vineyard" in a context of judgment (Isa 5:1–7; Jer 2:21; Ezek 15:1–8; Matt 21:33–46). Jesus, too, described Jerusalem as a fruitless fig tree that had tested the patience of God and was destined for destruction (Luke 13:6–9). In all these cases the metaphors anticipate the destruction of Jerusalem at the hands of a "northern" army (Babylonian for Isaiah's and Ezekiel's prophecies, Roman for Jesus').

---

[26] The word עָצוּם is an adjective often used of foreign nations (e.g., Deut 4:38; 7:1; Josh 23:9; Ps 135:10).

[27] For example, T. J. Finley : "As one takes a closer look at the insects, one sees not simply 'lion's teeth,' but the very sharp 'fangs' used by the lioness for dispatching her victims" (*Joel, Obadiah, Amos,* WEC [Chicago: Moody, 1990], 24).

[28] Cf. Pss 7:2; 10:9; 17:12; 57:4; Hos 11:10; Amos 1:2; 3:4,8,12. The terms "teeth" and "fangs" also occur in parallel in Job 29:17; Ps 58:6.

Joel saw that the locusts had left the land in a pathetic state.[29] Not a leaf remained. In saying that the branches were stripped white, the text implies that there was nothing to salvage and no hope of a harvest for a long time to come.[30]

(3) General Audience (1:8–10)

8Mourn like a virgin in sackcloth
    grieving for the husband of her youth.
9Grain offerings and drink offerings
    are cut off from the house of the LORD.
The priests are in mourning,
    those who minister before the LORD.
10The fields are ruined,
    the ground is dried up;
the grain is destroyed,
    the new wine is dried up,
    the oil fails.

1:8 Grim irony pervades the image of the bride in mourning. A wedding is a community celebration; it should not be ruined by sorrow or tragedy. The bride is the image of beauty and happiness. While we do not know that brides in ancient Israel wore white, we do know that white clothes expressed joy and optimism (Eccl 9:8). But here a bride wears the black goat's hair of sackcloth, beats her breasts,[31] and mourns the death of her beloved. The sorrow and loss of an unconsummated marriage illustrates the sorrow of a lost harvest. What should have been a celebration has turned into a lamentation.

A number of scholars have puzzled over the fact that the command to mourn is feminine. Some have suggested that the subject may be the land or even the vine or fig tree, all of which are feminine.[32] But it is quite odd, if not unintelligible, to portray the land or the trees as mourning for someone else since they themselves are the victims of the locust attack. Probably the feminine gender of the verb is due to attraction to the simile "virgin," a sim-

---

[29] "Laid waste . . . and ruined" is literally "made into desolation . . . and ruin." The noun שְׁמָּה, "desolation, horror," stresses the horror or spectacle of desolation. It is always associated with divine judgment (cf. Deut 28:37; 2 Kgs 22:19; Jer 2:15; 4:7; 5:30; 8:21; 18:16). See H. J. Austel, "שׁמם," *TWOT*, 936–37. The second noun, קְצָפָה, occurs only here but is related to קֶצֶף, "wrath."

[30] Dillard points out that after a locust plague plants must divert their energy to repairing the damage ("Joel," 259). This further delays the bearing of fruit. After citing several instances of modern locust plagues and their effects, Hubbard concludes: "Joel's account is not hyperbolic but factual" (*Joel and Amos*, 45).

[31] For a good account of mourning customs, see Wolff, *Joel and Amos*, 29–30.

[32] The imperative is אֱלִי, from a verb (אלה II) that occurs only here. Proposed candidates for the subject are אֶרֶץ ("land," v. 6), גֶּפֶן ("vineyard," v. 12), and תְּאֵנָה ("fig tree," v. 12). Cf. Stuart, *Hosea–Jonah*, 243.

ile that implies that the real subject is Jerusalem or the "daughter of Zion." The prophets frequently used the latter term in texts of eschatological judgment or salvation (e.g., Isa 1:8; 62:11; Lam 2:1–18; Mic 4:10; Zech 9:9). In short, this section seems to be directed at the people of Jerusalem in general rather than to a specific group, and they are exhorted to mourn the loss of the harvest.

Against the view that it makes no sense for a "virgin" to mourn for her "husband," Wolff has pointed out that the text makes good sense against the background of Israelite marriage law. A young woman became legally bound to a man as his "wife" even before the consummation of the marriage as soon as the man paid the agreed bride-price. In such a status, legally but not yet sexually married, a woman could be called either a "virgin" or the man's "wife."[33] Mary the mother of Jesus was in such a situation at the time of Jesus' conception, and thus Joseph felt the need to "divorce" her although he had not yet had sexual relations with her (Matt 1:19). On the other hand, it may be that the word translated "virgin" here really refers to a young woman who may or may not be married. That is, she may not be a true virgin. In this case it is a young bride mourning the loss of her husband.[34]

The Hebrew word for "husband" is also the name of the god Baal, but this fact has no significance here.[35] This text does not allude to, endorse, or attack the Canaanite cult in which Anat mourns the death of Baal. For Joel this was simply a picture of a young woman grieving the loss of her fiancé.[36] The mourning for Baal commemorated the seasonal death of plants in the natural cycle of the agricultural calendar; the mourning here concerns a specific locust plague. Scholars who, tantalized by the use of common language and imagery, look for cultic parallels here, read something into Joel that is simply not there.

1:9 The cessation of regular grain offerings and libations in the temple due to lack of provisions was for Joel an appalling theological disaster. He did not include these details simply as more examples of what the locusts had done; rather, this was evidence that God had rejected his people. The Israelites were supposed to make daily offerings at the sanctuary that included lambs, grain offerings mixed with olive oil, and libations or "drink offerings" (Exod

---

[33] Wolff, *Joel and Amos*, 30.

[34] The question concerns whether בְּתוּלָה always means "virgin" or can mean simply "young woman." G. J. Wenham argues that it need not mean "virgin" (*"Betulah:* 'A Girl of Marriageable Age,'" *VT* 22 [1972]: 326–48). J. L. Crenshaw gives some credence to this argument and suggests that in Joel 1:8 this is a young woman in the early years of her marriage (*Joel*, 98).

[35] The word בַּעַל routinely means "master" or "husband" with no cultic significance.

[36] If the text had simply used the term בַּעַל, one might have had a case for a cultic reference here, albeit a weak one. But that possibility is altogether excluded by the term בַּעַל נְעוּרֶיהָ, which is properly a woman's first husband or legally betrothed fiancé.

29:38–46; Num 28:1–8). When these were "cut off" by an act of Yahweh,[37] it was as though the covenant were annulled and the daily order of creation itself were suspended.[38] Thus Joel could interpret this as the day of the Lord.

1:10 The grain was wiped out, the wine was exhausted,[39] and the oil stores had run dry. These were considered basic food requirements and signs of God's blessing (cf. 2:19,24; Deut 7:13; 11:14; 14:23; 2 Chr 31:5; 32:28; Neh 5:11; Jer 31:12; Hos 2:8,22). Supplies from the previous year's harvest were exhausted, and the people had no hope of a harvest after the locust attack. Deuteronomy 28:42 had predicted the locust plague as one of the waves of judgment that would sweep over the people: "Swarms of locusts will take over all your trees and the crops of your land." Should Israel not repent, the Lord would bring against them a nation "from far away" who would scatter them "among all nations" (Deut 28:49,64), and Israel would be without "grain, new wine or oil" (Deut 28:51; cf. Hag 1:11). Looking at the devastation from the locust plague, Joel could easily assume that the "northern army" would not be long in coming.

(4) Farmers (1:11–12)

> [11]Despair, you farmers,
>   wail, you vine growers;
> grieve for the wheat and the barley,
>   because the harvest of the field is destroyed.
> [12]The vine is dried up
>   and the fig tree is withered;

---

[37] The *hophal* of כרת is unusual; it occurs only here in the OT. A *niphal* would have communicated the simple passive idea adequately, and the *niphal* of כרת is quite common. The *hophal* implies a secondary agent: "grain offerings and drink offerings have been made to be cut off from the house of the LORD." This implies that God, through the agency of the locusts, put an end to the daily sacrifice.

[38] A daily ceremony in Egypt performed in the Middle Kingdom and afterward required that the pharaoh (or his proxy) be washed every morning in water from the sacred lake and then be robed by priests wearing the masks of Thoth and Horus. The pharaoh then approached and opened the sanctuary known as "the sky" to reveal the image of the sun god. He recited the hymn of morning worship and ceremonially awakened, washed, and fed the god. For the Egyptians this ceremony was essential to the new day, and its cessation was unthinkable. See J. E. M. White, *Ancient Egypt: Its Culture and History* (New York: Dover, 1970), 41–42. Notwithstanding the vast differences between Egyptian and Israelite religion (the Israelites did not think they needed to awaken or feed Yahweh, they had no idol to him, and so forth) the cessation of the daily sacrifice was a religious calamity for Joel. It was a disruption of the routine of creation itself.

[39] The verb הוֹבִישׁ here is from יבשׁ, "be dry," and not בושׁ, "be ashamed." E. D. Mallon observes that although one might expect the *qal* stem here, the *hiphil* serves as an "elative *hiphil*" and means, "The wine has thoroughly dried up" ("A Stylistic Analysis of Joel 1:10–12," *CBQ* 45 [1983]: 537–48). Also the phrase הוֹבִישׁ תִּירוֹשׁ has a chiastic o-i-i-o vowel pattern, and the assonance may have prompted the choice of the *hiphil* over the *qal* (pp. 542–43).

the pomegranate, the palm and the apple tree—
all the trees of the field—are dried up.
Surely the joy of mankind
is withered away.

1:11–12 The Hebrew verb *bôš* here translated "despair" means that the farmers were confounded because their efforts for the year had been for nothing. It combines the notions of shame, confusion, and chagrin. The text has an ongoing wordplay between *ybš*, "to be dry," and *bôš*, "to be ashamed or confounded." The root *ybš* appears in 1:10,12(twice),20; *bôš* appears in 1:11,12,17; and also 2:26,27.[40] The point of all this wordplay is that the ruination and withering of the crops is the external manifestation of the internal shame and distress of the people. The wordplay may indicate that the "drying up" has caused the "shame."

In specifying "farmers" and "vine growers," Joel asserted that all the major areas of the agricultural economy—grain production and horticulture ("farmers") and viticulture ("vine growers")—had been ruined. To bring home the point of the universal desolation, Joel listed representatives of every category of crop. It is not clear that the apple as we know it existed in ancient Israel. It appears more likely that the word translated "apple" is really the apricot.[41] The withering of the plants implies that in addition to locusts, the land suffered drought. Verse 17 confirms this.

Along with the harvest, the joy of the people had dried up.[42] This seems to be a metonymy of effect for cause. Urban members of our technological society may have difficulty identifying with the great celebration that a good harvest inspired, but for the ancient Israelite it was the high point of the year (cf. Deut 16:13–15). The psalmist could sing, "You have filled my heart with greater joy than when their grain and new wine abound" (Ps 4:7) because the joy of the literal harvest meant so much to the average person. This joy, Joel lamented, had perished.

---

[40] The text makes the pun all the more significant by using ambiguous *hiphil* forms. הֹבִישׁוּ in this verse could be read as a form of יָבֵשׁ, and הֹבִישׁ in v. 12c could be read as from the root בּוֹשׁ.

[41] See *ISBE*, s.v. "apple."

[42] T. Frankfort contends that כִּי in this verse can only be translated "because" (*car*), not "surely" (*oui*; cf. NIV) or "whereas" (*tandis que*; "Le כִּי de Joel I 12," *VT* 10 [1960]: 445–48). She concludes that the verse implies that the farmers and vine growers, discouraged at the damage done by the locusts, had allowed the irrigation system to fall into disrepair. She argues that this is the correct understanding of the assertion in Joel 1:12 that all the fruit trees had dried up "*because* the joy of the people has withered away." Her conclusion lacks support in the text, and scholars have not followed her suggestion. If one were to insist that the word כִּי here means "for" or "because," not "surely," the most reasonable interpretation would be that the כִּי clause looks back to v. 11a and gives the farmers an additional reason to lament because people who depended on them were suffering. At any rate, 1:20 indicates that drought had dried up even the streams and brooks wild animals used. Thus severe drought, not failure to maintain irrigation canals, was the real problem here.

Excursus: The Christian and Natural Disaster

Throughout this chapter the text consistently portrays the locust plague as an act of God. At no time does it entertain the idea that this is simply one of the crises that confront people as a matter of course. That is, the locust plague is not viewed as a "natural" event in the way that we normally understand the term. In this book disasters do not happen simply because (in this case) the natural world has grasshoppers in it and sometimes grasshoppers multiply excessively and cause great damage. Disasters happen because God chooses for them to happen. For Joel the locust plague was an "act of God" in the most literal sense. There are no accidents because God, not an impersonal "fate," governs nature. For many readers this represents an extremely troublesome view since it seems to imply that God is cruel or at least indifferent to human suffering.

Several alternative approaches to natural disasters present themselves. One is the "accident" explanation in an atheistic framework. This position claims that the presence of so much suffering in the world proves that God either will not or cannot stop it. If he will not put an end to suffering, then he is cruel; if he cannot, he is weak. In either case such disasters demonstrate either that there is no God or that he is nothing like the benevolent deity we are supposed to believe in.

Another approach is the "accident" explanation in a Christian framework. This view asserts that God is good and powerful, but that he has built certain natural laws into creation and that these laws function unremittingly except on the rare occasions that God intercedes (in a miracle) to stop them. Thus people routinely experience earthquakes, flood, famine, and plague simply because those things are a part of nature and not because God desires to see us hurt. A variant of this view is that although in some special cases disasters are divine judgments, many other disasters (perhaps the majority) are natural events.

Another Christian approach might be called the "Job's Three Friends" approach. This view affirms that God is responsible for bringing down disaster upon people but that he does so because some specific people are especially evil. In this view the righteous need not be overly concerned about such things.

Yet another Christian approach, already mentioned, is to ascribe all disasters to Satanic or human evil. People suffer because either Satan or wicked people bring trouble down upon them. In this view God always knows when Satan is about to harm people (or when evil people are about to do something destructive), but he does not intercede. Like the high gods of the pagans, God is far removed from active involvement in the affairs of this world.

This approach leads to a practical dualism. While it might affirm in theory that God can intervene and control evil, it asserts that in reality he does not. God sits high above the heavens; the world below is an arena of conflict between wicked angels and evil people on one side and elect angels and devout people on the other. Satan is regarded as an autonomous being who is free to do whatever mischief he wishes—unless he is thwarted by the works and prayers of the righteous. Someday, this theory asserts, in the eschatological consummation, God will directly act to defeat the forces of evil, but in the meantime believers must carry on a heroic struggle against the awesome power of evil. This is essentially the view of the Qumran sectarians, and it has been revived in modern evangelicalism under the guise of "spiritual warfare."[43]

All of these interpretations fail for one or more reasons. Although the Bible in some texts does present Satan bringing affliction against people, it asserts at the same time that Satan is under God's direct control (Job 1). Whether one is thinking of Satanic actions or human acts of violence (such as the bombing of a building), one cannot escape the fact that God, if our understanding of him is correct, knows all about the evil beforehand and can stop it. The argument that God is a mere passive observer makes for a hollow defense. We would not absolve a person of responsibility who knew a crime was about to be committed, had full power to stop it, and yet did nothing. We cannot save God's reputation by denying his power or sovereignty.

More than that, we must recognize that the Bible does not present God as a passive observer of human affairs who merely *permits* trouble in this world. As Amos 3:6 states, "When disaster comes to a city, has not the Lord *caused* it?" (Emphasis added.) When Joel looked upon swarms of locusts consuming the produce of his land, he did not see this as a work of the devil that Yahweh had allowed. Rather, he regarded the locusts as the agents of the wrath of God (1:15). The invading northerner is likewise the *army of Yahweh* (2:11). God, for his own purposes, so *governs* evil forces that the course of human history goes where he directs it.

The notion that only especially evil people have tragedy in their lives is the haven of the self-righteous and the smug. It contradicts the whole argument of the Book of Job as well as the common experience that calamity sometimes overtakes people who are by no means wicked.

Christians cannot take refuge in the "accident" view. While it is true that in this world things happen as a result of natural law (e.g., earthquakes happen because of plate tectonics), God is still sovereign over creation. If a person has the power to stop a disaster but chooses not to do so, then in some sense that person is responsible for the event. It is hairsplitting to say that in some way God "permitted" a tragedy to occur but that he is not responsible for what happens in his world. On the other hand, the atheist's position, that if God does not stop a disaster then he is either weak or evil, proceeds from the atheist's false sense of his own omniscience. It presumes that we fully understand the workings of the world and have the ability to limit the meaning of events to two options (God is evil or weak). There is, however, a third option: God may be doing a work of grace that we do not understand (Job 38–41).

Luke 13:1–5 and John 9:2–3 are perhaps the most important biblical texts on this subject. In Luke, Jesus asks if the Galileans "whose blood Pilate had mixed with their sacrifices" were "worse sinners" than other Galileans because they had suffered in this way. To this he adds the question of whether eighteen who were killed in an accident at the tower of Siloam were worse than all the rest. Jesus' own answer is surprising: "I tell you, no! But unless you repent, you too will all

---

[43] See D. A. Garrett, *Angels and the New Spirituality* (Nashville: Broadman & Holman, 1995), 215–33.

perish" (Luke 13:5). In John, Jesus responds to the question of whether a man was born blind because of his own or his parents' sin: "Neither this man nor his parents sinned, but this happened so that the work of God might be displayed in his life" (John 9:3).

Comparing the two, we see that in one case Jesus did attribute the calamity to judgment on sin (the Lukan text) but in the other he did not (the Johannine case). What is remarkable, however, is that *in neither case does Jesus shrink from ascribing these events to God.*

In the Lukan text Jesus avoided two common responses to tragedy. He did not ascribe these events either to accident (as he could easily have done in the case of the tower of Siloam) or to simple human sin (as he could have done in the case of Pilate killing the Galileans). Also he explicitly denied that those Galileans were worse than other people. Rather, he treated these as divine acts of punishment but made the point to his audience that *they were in dire danger of meeting the same judgment.* In effect, Jesus treated the Galilean and Siloam tragedies as tokens of wrath to come. It is likely that he was forewarning the audience of the coming siege of Jerusalem, when the walls of the city and the temple would come falling down and when other Romans would, like Pilate, spill the blood of many Jews. In this Jesus' method and message were exactly like Joel's. The Old Testament prophet saw the locust plague both as an act of judgment and as a warning of further judgments to come. The message for us is that news of distant disasters should engender, among other things, a spirit of repentance.

This is not to say that every catastrophe is punishment for sin. The John passage plainly shows that this is not the case. Here too, however, divine control of events is clear. The blindness of the man was no accident but was part of the plan of God. This agrees with the assertion of Exod 4:11: "Who gives [a man] sight or makes him blind? Is it not I, the Lord?"

The Christian response to calamity, therefore, is both to fear God and to trust him. It is to recognize that I, too, deserve the worst of what has happened to others and must *remain in a state of repentance.* On the other hand, when tragedy does strike me, it is to realize that God is not necessarily pursuing me for some sin. He is sovereign and will work all things out for his glory and our good. If we are to follow the example of Joel, then in hardship, too, we must look for the hand of God.

(5) *Priests (1:13–14)*

> [13] **Put on sackcloth, O priests, and mourn;**
>   **wail, you who minister before the altar.**
> **Come, spend the night in sackcloth,**
>   **you who minister before my God;**
> **for the grain offerings and drink offerings**
>   **are withheld from the house of your God.**
> [14] **Declare a holy fast;**
>   **call a sacred assembly.**
> **Summon the elders**
>   **and all who live in the land**

> **to the house of the LORD your God,**
> **and cry out to the LORD.**

1:13 The disaster demolished the high dignity of the priesthood. They were to remove the white garments of the priesthood in favor of the black, coarse sackcloth and reduce themselves to wailing instead of singing and to a vigil of mourning. Again the text refers to the calamity of the cessation of sacrifice in the temple.[44]

It is striking that Joel spoke of the priests as those who minister before "my God" and then called the temple the house of "your God."[45] In distinguishing the priests as those who "minister before my God," Joel reminded them of their duty to bring the needs of the people (including himself) before God. In speaking of the temple as the "house of your God" (cf. "house of the LORD your God" in v. 14), similarly, Joel implied that the priests had a special relationship to temple worship. In short, he called on them to fulfill their designated responsibilities as intercessors and leaders in worship. This implies that Joel himself was not a priest—which is significant in light of recent speculation over Joel's devotion to cultic worship.

We also should observe that a passage from the Akkadian *Hymn to Nanaya*, written during the reign of Sargon II (721–705 B.C.) parallels the call for temple prayers here. V. A. Hurowitz has given us a translation of the relevant section:

> The evil locust which destroys the crop/grain
> the wicked dwarf-locust which dries up the orchards
> which cuts off the regular offerings of the gods and goddesses—
> (Verily) Ellil listens to you, and Tutu is before you—
> may by your command it be turned to nothing.

Like Joel 1:4, this prayer uses different words for "locust" to describe the devastation wrought by the locusts, and like Joel 1:13, it laments the lack of food for offerings in the temple. Hurowitz concludes that Joel made use of traditional, liturgical language of a sort found elsewhere in the Near East in response to the locust plague of his day.[46] Although we cannot say with cer-

---

[44] The literary insensitivity of the older critical school is evident in the comments of J. A. Bewer in his assertion that v. 13c is a "doublet" of v. 9b and "not original here" ("Joel," in *A Critical and Exegetical Commentary on Micah, Zephaniah, Nahum, Habakkuk, Obadiah and Joel*, ICC [Edinburgh: T & T Clark, 1911], 85). Joel repeats key phrases and words throughout the book and in so doing draws the whole together.

[45] There is some question over whether אֱלֹהָי is the correct text here. The LXX has θεῷ with no pronoun, but the Vg has *dei mei*, "to my God." Wolff prefers the LXX. In light of אֱלֹהֵיכֶם, however, it seems that the MT is correct (*Joel and Amos*, 19).

[46] V. A. Hurowitz, "Joel's Locust Plague in Light of Sargon II's Hymn to Nanaya," *JBL* 112 (1993): 597–603.

tainty whether these two examples indicate a widespread liturgical tradition, the parallel at least shows that Joel was an ancient man who responded to the crisis in a way compatible with his own cultural background.

1:14 Four elements of Hebrew spirituality appear here. The first is that the people fasted as a vivid demonstration of their grief and remorse. Second, they came together in a "sacred assembly" to show that their sorrow was common and not private. Third, in fulfillment of Solomon's prayer of consecration for the temple (see especially 1 Kgs 8:37–40), they came to "the house of the LORD your God" to express their repentance. Fourth, they pleaded to the Lord to be their savior. Probably they chanted a psalm of community lamentation, such as Psalm 74, to voice their prayers.[47]

For the modern "low church" evangelical, the lesson here is that liturgy is not necessarily artificial, that not all spirituality is private, and that repentance can be and often should be accompanied by outward signs of sorrow (such as fasting). It is clear from Isa 58:3–6 that the prophets did not regard fasts as sure proofs of piety or as automatically effective. On the other hand, this verse implies that they did not reject fasting as artificial but instead regarded it as a genuine expression of humiliation before God.

"Summon the elders and all who live in the land" balances the opening summons to "elders" and those "who live in the land" from v. 2 and thus provides closure for this section of prophecy. As such it has no value in determining whether the elders are leaders or older people. It does, however, set the boundary for this division of the text. With this Joel finished summoning the people to lament; in the verses that follow he gave them an example of repentant lamentation.

2. Prophetic Lamentation (1:15–20)

[15]Alas for that day!
>For the day of the LORD is near;
>it will come like destruction from the Almighty.
[16]Has not the food been cut off
>before our very eyes—
joy and gladness
>from the house of our God?
[17]The seeds are shriveled
>beneath the clods.
The storehouses are in ruins,
>the granaries have been broken down,

---

[47] Cp. Joel 2:17 to Ps 74:18–19: "Remember how the enemy has mocked you, O LORD, how foolish people have reviled your name. / Do not hand over the life of your dove to wild beasts; do not forget the lives of your afflicted people forever."

for the grain has dried up.
¹⁸How the cattle moan!
The herds mill about
because they have no pasture;
even the flocks of sheep are suffering.
¹⁹To you, O LORD, I call,
for fire has devoured the open pastures
and flames have burned up all the trees of the field.
²⁰Even the wild animals pant for you;
the streams of water have dried up
and fire has devoured the open pastures.

1:15 At last the text explicitly speaks of the "day of the LORD" (cf. also 2:1,11,31; 3:14). Surprisingly, however, it speaks of the day as "near," although it is clear from this chapter that the locust plague had already occurred. Probably the temporal aspect should not be pressed; Joel did not mean that the locust plague was not the day of the Lord. By analogy when he spoke of the scourge as "*like* destruction from the Almighty" he did not mean that in reality it was *not* from God. The announcement "For the day of the LORD is near; it will come like destruction from the Almighty" may have been a stock phrase among the prophets (see especially Isa 13:6 and also Obad 15; Zeph 1:7).[48]

The prophets spoke of the day of the Lord as "near" in the context of the approach of the northern army against Jerusalem (Zeph 1:7,14; Ezek 30:3), but Isa 13:6 applies the phrase to the immanent destruction of the northern army (Babylon) itself, and Obadiah 15 uses it to describe the coming judgment of all nations.[49] Joel brought together all these themes in his book. The day of the Lord is upon the Jews in the form of the recent locust plague, but it also is imminent in the coming northern army (2:1–11). But the northern army will itself be destroyed (2:20), and all nations will face the day of the Lord (chap. 3).

1:16 Again the text laments that the food has been "cut off." First, wine was cut off from the drunkards (v. 5), and then offerings from the temple (v. 9), and now generally food is cut off from both people and beasts. Thus Joel began by specifying various groups (priests, farmers, etc.) but finally grieved even for the hunger of the animals (v. 18). This verse also draws together elements from earlier in the passage. Not only food but joy has vanished (as in v. 12). Even the house of God is destitute (as in vv. 9,13). The

---

[48] Cf. Hubbard, *Joel and Amos,* 50.

[49] For a good survey of passages dealing with the day of the Lord, see Wolff, *Joel and Amos,* 33–34. The opening phrase לַיּוֹם אֲהָהּ, "Alas for the day" (literally) occurs almost identically (using הָהּ rather than אֲהָהּ) in Ezek 30:2 announcing judgment on Egypt.

phrase "before our eyes" intensifies the bleakness of the situation: the people watched helplessly as the locusts devoured every bit of food.

1:17 According to the NIV rendering, this verse indicates that the land suffered drought in addition to the locust plague. Although that conclusion probably is correct (cf. vv. 19–20), the translation of this verse is much in doubt. The sentence "The seeds are shriveled beneath the clods" translates four words in Hebrew, but three of those four words are used only here in the Hebrew Bible.[50] Also the Hebrew actually reads "their" (not "the") with the word here translated "clods."[51] Although it is not unintelligible, it is quite odd to speak of seed rotting beneath "their clods," and we cannot be certain of the translation. The ancient versions are not consistent in rendering this line and are of no help in resolving the problems here.[52] Several emendations have been proposed. One possibility is to emend to read, "The seeds are shriveled, their threshing floor is desolate,[53] the storehouses are in ruins, the granaries have been broken down, for the grain has dried up." This emendation has the advantage of maintaining the same staccato rhythm through the entire verse.[54] M. Sprengling has attempted to translate the verse without recourse to emendation and argues that it means, "Brookbeds are parched under their banks swept hollow by torrents; / reservoirs are desolate, / pools have crumbled to ruins; / for rainclouds are barren of moisture."[55] This rendering has the advantage of describing explicitly the conditions of drought that Joel elsewhere implied, but it is quite speculative. Unfortunately, we do not have enough evidence to make a final judgment in the matter.

Still, it is clear that Joel saw a picture of complete spoliation before him. Food supplies were exhausted, and the possibility of starvation had set in.

---

[50] The line is עָבְשׁוּ פְרֻדוֹת תַּחַת מֶגְרְפֹתֵיהֶם; the hapax legomena are פְּרֻדוֹת, עָבְשׁוּ, and מֶגְרְפֹתֵיהֶם.

[51] It is not clear on what basis the NIV has rendered מֶגְרְפֹתֵיהֶם as "the clods." Wolff adopts a similar translation, apparently on the basis of the commentaries of Ibn Ezra and Radaq (see *Joel and Amos,* 19, n. z). It is translated "shovels" in KB, 494.

[52] They also tend toward the absurd. The LXX has ἐσκίρτησαν δαμάλεις ἐπὶ ταῖς φάτναις, "Heifers leap upon their mangers." In a peculiar move E. Nestle emended עָבְשׁוּ to a form of עָכַס, a word found only in Isa 3:16 with the meaning "rattle," to account for the LXX ("Miscellen: I. Joel I, 17," *ZAW* 20 [1900]: 164–65). Tg. *Jonathan,* as translated by K. J. Cathcart and R. P. Gordon, has, "The bottles of wine are decaying under their seals," although it is difficult to see how the wine would stay in bottles if the people were dying of thirst and hunger (*The Targum of the Minor Prophets,* The Aramaic Bible 14 [Wilmington: Michael Glazier, 1989], 66). See Dillard, "Joel," 267–68, for an attempt to explain the versions.

[53] *BHS* proposes this emendation (חָתּוּ גְרֹנֹתֵיהֶם) in note a.

[54] As emended every clause in the verse is just two words, a verb and subject (except for the last clause, which adds כִּי).

[55] M. Sprengling, "Joel 1, 17a," *JBL* 38 (1919): 129–41. He interprets the verse primarily on the basis of Arabic and Syriac analogies. His retranslation has not won the approval of scholars.

1:18 Several images depict unfailingly to us the horror of starvation. Among these are gaunt children, young mothers with dried, shrunken breasts, and emaciated livestock looking for food and water. The text here draws on the latter image. Like the seven lean cattle of pharaoh's dream (Gen 41:3), these cattle represent the collapse of the entire agricultural economy. Sheep can eat closer to the ground than cattle and are more adept at surviving in harsh conditions, but Joel saw that even they were at the edge of starvation.[56]

1:19 The Hebrew text emphasizes that Joel called only to Yahweh (and to no other god) for deliverance from this ecological disaster.[57] This emphasis implies a rejection of the ancient cult of Baal (or Tammuz), in which the people would call upon the fertility god to arise and send rain. Although it is a mistake to make too much of supposed parallels to the religious cults (see the comments on v. 8), it is beyond question that many of Joel's contemporaries would have responded to crisis by crying out, "To you, Baal, I call." The text reinforces the assertion that Yahweh is Lord of creation by stating in v. 20 that even wild animals look to him for relief.[58]

The "fire" here is ambiguous (cf. Amos 1:4,7,10,12,14; 2:2,5; 5:6; 7:4). It could be metaphor for the locusts, or describe the wilting effects of drought, or refer to a literal forest fire that swept over the barren, dried trees. This ambiguity allows it to serve as a symbol for all the disasters that have overtaken the land.

1:20 Previous possible allusions to drought are uncertain, but the drying up of the streams is straightforward. Joel saw that his land was in danger of becoming a barren desert. The words imply that if God did not respond to the prayer, then the "land of milk and honey" would suffer desertification. This would mean that God had abandoned his people and returned their "promised land" to chaos.

Remarkably, Joel devoted the last three verses of this lamentation to the suffering that the locusts and the drought had brought upon animals and the natural world. Here he said nothing about the starvation of people or the cessation of temple worship. Rather, he focused on deprivation suffered by the cattle and sheep, the wretched state of the woodlands and pastures, and the heartbreaking suffering of the wild animals. To be sure, the starvation of the

---

[56] Remarkably the text asserts that even the sheep "suffer punishment" (נֶאְשָׁמוּ) unless one emend to read נָשַׁמּוּ (from שׁמם), "they are desolate" (thus BHS, n. a). If the MT be read as is, it would imply that Joel understood the animal kingdom to share in the punishment that comes upon humanity (cf. also Gen 6–7), an idea that bears resemblance to Paul's assertion that the creation is groaning as it awaits redemption (Rom 8:22).

[57] Note the word order of the Hebrew: אֵלֶיךָ יְהוָה אֶקְרָא. The same words are found in Pss 28:1; 30:9[8].

[58] Note the inclusio formed by אֵלֶיךָ יְהוָה אֶקְרָא and תַּעֲרוֹג אֵלֶיךָ.

animals implied the starvation of people, but the text does not explicitly draw that conclusion here. Instead, it treats the deplorable state of the flora and fauna as pathetic in itself. This indiscriminate suffering adds pathos to the picture Joel painted throughout this chapter.

But there is another reason for the focus on domestic animals and wildlife here. This portrayal of starvation and drought gives the reader a sense that creation itself is dying. The "good" order of seedtime and harvest (Gen 1:14–18; 8:22) has been disrupted; and the variety of plants, creeping things, and beasts is receding into a chaos of dust and death. Once again there was no vegetation or plant of the field, "for the LORD God had not sent rain on the earth" (Gen 2:5). Like the darkening of the sun and the turning of the moon to blood, this is the end of all things. It is the apocalypse, the day of the Lord.

II. JUDGMENT ON ISRAEL: NORTHERN ARMY INVASION (2:1–11)

1. Call to Sound the Alarm (2:1–2a)
2. Description of the Army (2:2b–9)
3. Signs of the Day of the Lord (2:10–11)

II. JUDGMENT ON ISRAEL: NORTHERN ARMY INVASION (2:1–11)

Dramatically, unexpectedly, the reader finds that the scene has shifted entirely at 2:1. Instead of a call for lamentation over a locust plague that has already occurred and a drought that has already done its damage, the text calls the people of Jerusalem to arms to face a new threat that is about to bear down upon their walls. Surely these are not more locusts—there is nothing left for them to eat. This is a new threat and a new army. It is not insects but human warriors, and their target is not wheat, barley, or grapes so much as it is the city itself.

Many scholars maintain that these verses continue the account of the locust plague, but, as we shall see, evidence is overwhelmingly against this view. Chapter 1 consistently looks to the recent past, but 2:1–11 consistently looks to the future.[1] Attempts to account for this shift from the viewpoint of a "locust plague" interpretation of 2:1–11 are unsuccessful. J. L. Crenshaw, for example, contends that chap. 1 describes a recent locust attack but that 2:1–11 is a liturgical lament for such disasters in the *future*.[2] It is scarcely reasonable,

---

[1] Many scholars have pointed out the preponderance of perfect forms in chap. 1 in contrast to the shift to the imperfect in chap. 2.

[2] J. L. Crenshaw, *Joel* (New York: Doubleday, 1995), 129–30. Crenshaw correctly asserts: "That the two accounts cannot refer to a single locust attack is obvious from the tenses of the verbs, completed action in chapter one and future events in chapter two." He then suggests that the two accounts are liturgical: "These two versions of accomplished and imminent disaster provide distinct circumstances for penitential action." It is not clear to me whether Crenshaw believes that the liturgy of 2:1–11 originally existed separately from chap. 1 (he states that although it "possesses its own integrity, it still shares some expressions with what goes before"). Taken as a separate liturgy, no one would imagine that 2:1–11 had anything to do with locusts (but Crenshaw consistently interprets 2:1–11 as a locust plague, pp. 116–28). Be that as it may, Joel 1 prophetically calls the people to lament, but it is not itself a liturgy. Joel 2:1–11 is a cry of alarm over the coming desolation, but it too is no liturgy. Contrast the psalms of lamentation (e.g., Pss 44; 74), which are true liturgies.

however, to imagine that Israel had in its liturgical arsenal some kind of "lamentation for future locust plagues." Both grammar and content demand that a significant shift has taken place: the prophet is looking ahead now, and he sees a human army on the horizon.

This does not mean that the figure of the locust plague has been abandoned entirely in chap. 2. To the contrary, Joel used locust imagery to shape the picture of the invading army. Looking upon the locust swarm, he saw with prophetic insight not just locusts but a mass of human soldiers bearing down on his city, and he described this future army in locust-like terms. It would indeed be strange if Joel, prophesying immediately after a locust plague, had described the human army without allowing the locust analogue to influence his language. Both are armies of the Lord.

1. Call to Sound the Alarm (2:1–2a)

> **¹Blow the trumpet in Zion;**
>   **sound the alarm on my holy hill.**
> **Let all who live in the land tremble,**
>   **for the day of the LORD is coming.**
> **It is close at hand—**
> ²   **a day of darkness and gloom,**
>   **a day of clouds and blackness.**

2:1 Jerusalem, like many ancient cities, had walls and towers from which guards could be on the lookout for approaching armies. The horn is the *shofar* or ram's horn, and it, like the church bells of medieval towns, was used both to call people to worship (cf. Num 10:10) and to sound an alarm. L. C. Allen has aptly commented that the blast of the horn from the tower was "the ancient equivalent of the modern air raid siren."[3] The blowing of the ram's horn signals the coming of a (human) army but implies in this text that the people were to view this as an act of Yahweh. Joel further emphasized that this event had religious meaning by calling for an alarm not from the walls, as one would expect, but from Zion, the "holy hill" (see also 2:15). Jeremiah 4:5–6 similarly exhorts the watchmen to blow the ram's horns because Yahweh is "bringing disaster from the north."[4] Already we are in the context of a military event with theological significance.

---

[3] L. C. Allen, *The Books of Joel, Obadiah, Jonah and Micah*, NICOT (Grand Rapids: Eerdmans, 1976), 67.

[4] Note that in Jer 4:5, like Joel 2:1, the exhortation begins with the words תִּקְעוּ שׁוֹפָר (there translated "sound the trumpet"). The only significant difference is that Joel follows with בְּצִיּוֹן ("in Zion") where Jeremiah has בָאָרֶץ ("throughout the land"), but Jeremiah refers to Zion in the next verse. For other calls to alarm cf. Jer 6:1; 51:27; Hos 5:8.

Joel called on the people to tremble not because of the approaching army but because the army was a sign of the day of the Lord. The coming army, like the locusts that Judah had just experienced,[5] was a sign that the curses of Deuteronomy 28 were coming upon them in full fury. In short, they were to fear the wrath of God.

2:2a Clouds and darkness are a stock metaphor for the day of the Lord (cf. Isa 5:30; Jer 13:16; Amos 5:18–20; 8:9; Zeph 1:15), but this fact should not blind us to the theophanic significance of the language. In the exodus a "pillar of cloud" stood between the Israelites and the Egyptian chariots (Exod 14:19–20). When Yahweh gave the Ten Commandments at Sinai, the people were terrified at the thunder, lightning, and the sound of the ram's horn (Exod 20:18). Now, Joel implied, the Israelites, having failed to keep the covenant, had to face the wrath of Yahweh.

A. Kapelrud characteristically sees cultic language here. He compares the reference to cloud and darkness to Ps 97:2. Following the Scandinavian interest in myth, ritual, and the enthronement psalms, he contends that Joel reflects the cultic celebration of the New Year, with its emphasis on fertility, in which the god dies (bringing on drought) and rises again in thunderous glory prior to a time of fertility.[6] The charm of this theory seems to have passed;[7] fewer scholars today are willing to claim that the biblical Yahwism included a ritual of enthroning God as a rising fertility deity during a New Year's festival. There is no room for such ideas in this verse.

2. Description of the Army (2:2b–9)

> **Like dawn spreading across the mountains**
> > **a large and mighty army comes,**
> **such as never was of old**
> > **nor ever will be in ages to come.**
>
> [3]**Before them fire devours,**
> > **behind them a flame blazes.**
> **Before them the land is like the garden of Eden,**
> > **behind them, a desert waste—**
> > **nothing escapes them.**
> [4]**They have the appearance of horses;**

---

[5] The phrase here, כִּי־בָא יוֹם־יהוה כִּי קָרוֹב ("for the day of the LORD is coming. It is close at hand"), obviously mirrors 1:15, כִּי קָרוֹב יוֹם יהוה ("for the day of the LORD is near") followed by יָבוֹא ("it will come"). This further links the two chapters conceptually but does not prove that both refer to the same historical event.

[6] A. Kapelrud, *Joel Studies* (Uppsala: A. B. Lundequistska Bokhandeln, 1948), 72.

[7] For a good explanation and critique of this school of thought, see R. K. Harrison, *Old Testament Introduction* (Grand Rapids: Eerdmans, 1969), 993–96.

they gallop along like cavalry.
5With a noise like that of chariots
   they leap over the mountaintops,
   like a crackling fire consuming stubble,
   like a mighty army drawn up for battle.

6At the sight of them, nations are in anguish;
   every face turns pale.
7They charge like warriors;
   they scale walls like soldiers.
They all march in line,
   not swerving from their course.
8They do not jostle each other;
   each marches straight ahead.
They plunge through defenses
   without breaking ranks.
9They rush upon the city;
   they run along the wall.
They climb into the houses;
   like thieves they enter through the windows.

2:2bc The picture of the army spreading "like dawn" seems to be such a violent contrast with the preceding images of darkness and gloom that many interpreters have chosen to emend the text to read "darkness" instead.[8] The approaching dawn, after all, spreads light and not darkness. This emendation, however, is not necessary. The switch in simile from clouds and darkness to spreading dawn signals the reader that a shift has taken place in the text; the focus is moving from the general and stylized description of the day of the Lord to the specific portrayal of the coming army. The primary function of the simile of dawn is to portray the irresistible approach and massive size of the army, like morning sunlight spreading across a valley. Also armies generally move into position in the early hours before dawn in order to attack with the rising of the sun.

The verse describes this foe as a "large and mighty army" and, using a bit of hyperbole, declares it to be the most fearsome host the world has ever seen or will see.[9] Of itself, this does not establish that Joel had a human army in mind,[10] but the subsequent description shows this in fact is the meaning here.

2:3 Fire burns before and behind them in the sense that they bring destruc-

---

[8] Reading שַׁחַר instead of שָׁחַר.

[9] D. Stuart translates the last line more literally, "Nor will it again for generation after generation" (*Hosea–Jonah*, WBC [Dallas: Word, 1987], 246).

[10] Joel called the locusts a גּוֹי ("nation") that was עָצוּם וְאֵין מִסְפָּר ("powerful and without number") in 1:6; here the text describes an עַם (lit., "people") that is רַב וְעָצוּם ("large and powerful"). Neither determines the meaning of the other, but the two form one of the many cross-links in the Book of Joel.

tion with them and leave behind devastation. The Hebrew actually says that fire burns "before him" (or "it") and "after him" (or "it"). The NIV takes this to refer to the "mighty army" of v. 2 and so translates it both times as "them," which probably is correct.[11] It is possible, however, that "him" in the Hebrew text refers to God, especially since the Israelites regularly associated theophanies with fire (Exod 24:17; Num 9:15–16). Psalm 97:3 speaks of fire going out before Yahweh and devouring his enemies, and Zeph 1:18 associates fire with the day of the Lord. Dillard correctly observes, however, that it makes little difference whether one takes this as a description of Yahweh or of his army, "The army is Yahweh's, and he is its commander."[12] Notwithstanding the metaphorical language of this verse, it is also noteworthy that armies of the ancient world regularly burned the fields of lands they invaded.

The picture of the land as a "garden of Eden" self-evidently conveys the idea that it was fertile, green, and something of a paradise. The army of 2:1–11 repeats and intensifies the destructive work of the locusts (one need not assume that the army was to come immediately after the locusts, while the land was still denuded. But the language also takes us back again to the creation narrative,[13] where God brought forth a garden from what had been barren land (Gen 2:5–10). Here an act of God reduces an "Eden" to a "desert waste" in another example of the divine undoing of creation on the day of the Lord.

2:4 Interpreters who take this simply as a continuation of the description of the locust plague invariably make the case that grasshoppers somehow look like horses.[14] Be that as it may, the point here is not so much how the foe *looks* as how it affects those who see it. The army of Israel was historically an infantry army. For most of its history Israel had neither the wealth nor the terrain necessary for a significant cavalry corps. Although Solomon developed a cavalry and chariot corps (1 Kgs 10:26–28), David appears to have built his empire without them (2 Sam 8:4). In 1 Kgs 20:13–23, Ahab defeated Ben-Hadad, who had foolishly sent his chariot corps into the hill country where they would be ineffective against the Israelite infantry. The Syrians concluded that the Israelite gods were "gods of the hills" but that Syria would win a battle on the plains (where chariots could overwhelm foot soldiers). Still, the

---

[11] The question concerns the referent for the pronominal suffixes on לְפָנָיו and וְאַחֲרָיו. The NIV takes עַם as the antecedent.

[12] R. B. Dillard, "Joel," in *The Minor Prophets*, vol. 1 (Grand Rapids: Baker, 1991), 274.

[13] Scholars regularly cite Ezekiel 28 as another example of "Eden" as a metaphor for paradise. This is true insofar as it goes, but in neither case is the citation haphazard. In both the prophets allude to the Genesis narrative for specific rhetorical purposes. On Ezekiel 28 see D. A. Garrett, *Angels and the New Spirituality* (Nashville: Broadman & Holman, 1995), 39–42.

[14] T. J. Finley, for example, states that locusts "do resemble horses" (*Joel, Obadiah, Amos,* WEC [Chicago: Moody, 1990], 45).

Israelites recognized the military value of a cavalry force. Against ancient infantry troops a cavalry or chariot assault was effective beyond the actual military value of the force simply because a charge of horses terrified foot soldiers. Thus the foe has the "appearance" of horses in the sense that they unnerve the opposition in the same way that foot soldiers react when they see a cavalry charge. Stuart correctly notes that both Jeremiah and Ezekiel associated horses with the eschatological foe.[15]

2:5 When chariots in full charge erupted over the tops of hills and down onto a plain, the sound that had been muffled by the intervening hillside suddenly and deafeningly would have exploded on the people below. One can imagine troops caught in a valley who abruptly find themselves facing a mass of chariots they had neither seen nor heard. The image is one of a surprise attack and of the terror it inspires.[16] A raging grass fire similarly overwhelms the senses with sound as well as smoke and heat, and it drives people to fear and frantic helplessness.[17] Again the emotional impact of these sights and sounds, not the sights and sounds themselves, drive the imagery. In short, this army is absolutely terrifying.

The phrase "like a mighty army drawn up for battle" unfailingly draws the argument that Joel could not have said the foe was "like" an army if in fact they *were* an army (so also *like cavalry* in v. 4). This argument falls for several reasons.

First, Hebrew can use "like" in an expression that describes precisely what something is.[18] An English analogy is the expression "quit yourselves like men," an expression that does not mean that the hearers are not really men but that as men they should fulfill the ideal of manhood.[19] Joel used "like" in this way in 1:15, where he asserted that the day of the Lord was "like a destruction from the Almighty." He did not mean that it was not destruction from God but that it was the "*veritable, or ideal,* destruction from Shaddai."[20]

---

[15] Stuart, *Hosea–Jonah*, 251. See Jer 6:23 and Ezek 38:4.

[16] R. D. Patterson sees here and elsewhere in 2:1–11 allusions to the Assyrian war machine ("Joel," EBC [Grand Rapids: Eerdmans, 1985], 7:248). While I agree that a human army is described here, I do not believe the evidence is sufficiently precise to allow us to identify it as Assyrian or of any other nationality. The Assyrian identification is especially questionable since in fact the Assyrians never entered Jerusalem (see 2:9).

[17] The third line begins as the first with כְּקוֹל (lit., "like the sound of").

[18] BDB, 454, describes this use of כ as the *kaph veritatis* and explains that it expresses a thing's "correspondence with the idea which it ought to realize." Also B. K. Waltke and M. O'Connor, *IBHS* § 11.2.9b.

[19] For another example see Isa 29:1–2, which identifies Jerusalem as "Ariel" and then says it will be "like Ariel." J. A. Motyer states that Jerusalem is described as "'a veritable Ariel' *(kaph veritatis),* a place where holy wrath is aroused and active" (*The Prophecy of Isaiah* [Downers Grove: InterVarsity, 1993], 237).

[20] BDB, 454. Emphasis original.

Second, the military language throughout this chapter is too strong to be accidental or to be dismissed as metaphor. Joel's audience knew very well that the final stage of the outpouring of God's judgment upon them *after* locust plagues, as outlined in Deut 28:38–65, was warfare, defeat, and exile.

Third, we misread Joel if we think the text demands we exclusively see *either* locusts *or* a human army. On the contrary, Joel consciously drew the two ideas together here so that an army is described under the metaphor of a locust invasion. He spoke of chariots, armies drawn up for battle, and the scaling of walls, but the picture of the locust plague from chap. 1 still prompts and to some degree determines the descriptions. Thus the fact that a locust swarm may sound like wildfire and look like horses does not contradict but contributes to the vision of the fury of the northern army. The locusts were both the symbol for that army and its precursor, and Joel used language that projected both pictures into the readers' minds. To use an example from the modern world of computer-aided multimedia, it is as if we see the locusts of chap. 1 "morphing" into soldiers and cavalry before our eyes.

2:6 Before such an army people convulse in fear. The NIV's "every face turns pale" translates a Hebrew expression of uncertain meaning. Some give it the opposite meaning and translate "all faces are aglow"[21] or the like, but the NIV interpretation is preferable.[22] The Targum, curiously, has "all faces are covered with a coating of black like a pot."[23] Wolff comments that convulsing in anguish (like a woman in labor)[24] is a stock expression for the day of the Lord in Isa 13:8 and Ezek 30:16 and that it in particular alludes to the northern enemy in Jer 4:31 (see also Jer 6:24; 13:21; 22:23; 1 Thess 5:3). Wolff aptly concludes that this shows that "locusts as such are by no means meant."[25]

2:7 Once again it is a mistake to suppose that the word "like" implies that this is only a metaphor for locusts. As before, the image of the locust and the image of the soldier merge into each other.

This verse describes a highly trained, effective military force. To "charge" implies courage, determination, and physical vigor. To scale a wall implies all of these as well as training in the art of the siege. If there is any doubt about the quality of this army in the readers' minds, it is dispelled by the use of the

---

[21] Thus H. W. Wolff, *Joel and Amos,* Her (Philadelphia: Fortress, 1977), 38.

[22] The phrase כָּל־פָּנִים קִבְּצוּ פָארוּר literally means "all faces gather in פָּארוּר," the challenge being to determine the meaning of פָּארוּר. It seems to be related to the idea of a "glow" and thus for faces to gather in it presumably means that they turn pale. The phrase also appears in Nah 2:11 [10]. The ancient versions are of no help here. See Dillard, "Joel," 275.

[23] K. J. Cathcart and R. P. Gordon, *The Targum of the Minor Prophets,* The Aramaic Bible 14 (Wilmington: Michael Glazier, 1989), 68.

[24] This is the implication of יְחִילוּ as the root חוּל is used here and in the other prophetic texts (e.g., Isa 26:17–18; Mic 4:9–10).

[25] Wolff, *Joel and Amos,* 46.

terms "warriors" and "soldiers" to describe the troops[26] and the spectacle of how they do not break ranks or lose their discipline even when on the attack.[27] These are not raw recruits newly pressed into service.

Other passages also praise the prowess of the enemy eschatological army. For example, Jer 6:23 describes the northern army as follows: "They are armed with bow and spear; they are cruel and show no mercy. They sound like the roaring sea as they ride on their horses; they come like men in battle formation[28] to attack you, O Daughter of Zion."

The scaling of the walls also further implies that this is a human army. Locusts no doubt clung to walls when they infested a land, but this hardly had any significance. Locusts did their damage in the fields, not in the city. For a human army to climb the walls, however, meant that the defenses of the city were about to be breached and the people slaughtered.[29]

The mention of walls also has some bearing on the date of the book since it might mean that Jerusalem had standing walls at the time of writing. This has caused some consternation on the part of scholars who want to date the book to the early postexilic period, since the walls of Jerusalem were not repaired until the time of Nehemiah. These scholars argue that the walls of the city were not altogether thrown down prior to Nehemiah's repair work but only broken through in a few locations (since he was able to complete his work in fifty-two days, Neh 6:15). Therefore, they contend, Jerusalem did have walls during the early postexilic period, and Joel could have written at this time.[30] This argument has a serious flaw. An enemy army did not bother scaling city walls if the walls were already breached. A wall with gaping holes in it was as good as no wall at all. Joel's language implies that this wall was functioning as a defense against an enemy but that this defense was about to fail because soldiers were climbing *over* it. Hence, Joel's wall must be intact.[31]

2:8 The phalanxes of Greece and the legions of Rome were legendary for their discipline in the ranks. They could either charge precipitously or stand and face an enemy assault without bending and without a man swerving from his position. Scholars who wish to see only locusts in this verse call for a near

---

[26] The word גִּבּוֹר often describes mighty hunters, warriors, and champions (e.g., Goliath in 1 Sam 17:51). אִישׁ מִלְחָמָה (lit., "man of war") similarly is a trained soldier (as in 1 Sam 17:33).

[27] The MT reads וְלֹא יְעַבְּטוּן אֹרְחוֹתָם, literally "and they do not lend for collateral their paths." This makes no sense, unless "loaning a path" means that one soldier allows another to break ranks in front of him, and so most read יְעַבְתוּן "they do not weave their paths" (i.e., cross paths or break ranks).

[28] The expression here is כְּאִישׁ לַמִּלְחָמָה; note especially the use of the particle כְּ here, which is comparable to its use in Joel. There is no question that Jeremiah is describing a human army.

[29] Contrast Finley, *Joel, Amos, Obadiah*, 47.

[30] Thus Dillard, "Joel," 276.

[31] Of itself, this does not *prove* that Joel was written at a time when the walls were intact. It merely indicates that he *had in mind* walls that were intact.

sacrifice of the intellect; one can hardly say that locusts in a swarm do not "jostle" one another. More significantly, the NIV has somewhat misrepresented the Hebrew text in the translation, "They plunge through defenses." The text would better be translated, "They will plunge headlong through the missiles"[32] (i.e., through arrows, spears, and the like). An alternative translation is, "And [although] they will fall under the javelins, they will not break off [the attack]."[33] This rendering implies that even though some of the troops are being killed by missiles as they charge, they do not pull back from pressing the attack.

Either way, it goes without saying that no one in his right mind would shoot arrows or throw spears at a locust swarm. Attempts to find an alternative interpretation of this line that befits a locust swarm have been futile and not a little absurd.[34]

2:9 Although there can be no doubt that in the course of a locust plague the grasshoppers came into cities and houses, and that this would have been an irksome and even traumatic experience to live through (Exod 10:6), having grasshoppers in the house was not of itself particularly important. What mattered was what they did to the crops. This verse, however, stands as the climax of the description of Joel 2:1–9. In this position it indicates the goal of the invader and implies that the intrusion into houses was the final calamity. This can only mean that the invaders, while symbolically locusts, were ultimately human soldiers who had broken through to the heart of the civilian population.[35] They could dash about the city and run along the walls because the

---

[32] So translating וּבְעַד הַשֶּׁלַח יִפֹּלוּ. The noun שֶׁלַח means "a projectile type of weapon," such as a spear, or may refer to a sword. See Neh 4:17; 2 Chr 23:10; 32:5. The Ug. cognate often means "javelin." See Crenshaw, *Joel*, 26, n. 28.

[33] Taking נָפַל in the sense "to perish" rather than "to plunge ahead." The LXX reads, καὶ ἐν τοῖς βέλεσιν αὐτῶν πεσοῦνται καὶ οὐ μὴ συντελεσθῶσιν ("They will fall in their missiles and by no means be brought to a halt"). There is Ug. support for this rendering of נפל with שֶׁלַח. See Crenshaw, *Joel*, 124.

[34] Allen attempts to avoid the implication of this verse by translating שֶׁלַח as "Siloam" on the basis of Neh 3:15, where בְּרֵכַת הַשֶּׁלַח means "the Pool of Shelah" (or "Siloam"; *Joel*, 72–73). Here, however, the word is qualified by the construct בְּרֵכַת ("pool of"). A Hebrew reader would not take שֶׁלַח in Joel 2:8 to refer to the Pool of Shelah. Nor is there any conceivable reason that the prophet would describe locusts charging through this particular pool. Crenshaw carries this a step further (*Joel*, 116, 124). He takes שֶׁלַח to refer to the Siloam tunnel and translates, "They descend into a tunnel." This perhaps would not be so bizarre except that he takes the "enemy" here to be locusts! It is beyond all reason—and the most liberal poetic license—to imagine locusts descending into a tunnel to sneak into a city. D. A. Hubbard follows the same line of reasoning and seems to have lost his bearings entirely in asserting that the Siloam tunnel would be for locusts a "dramatic and effective means of entry" to Jerusalem and that once inside they would systematically loot houses (*Joel and Amos* [Downers Grove: Tyndale, 1989], 56).

[35] As Stuart observes, "Capture and destruction of houses brings to completion the conquest of a city" (*Hosea–Jonah*, 251).

defenders of the walls lay dead.

Breaking in through windows like a thief implies the idea of violation. Just as a thief has no regard for property rights or for entering a house only with the permission of the owner, so these soldiers cared nothing for the persons or property of their victims. They intruded suddenly from every direction.

3. Signs of the Day of the Lord (2:10–11)

[10]Before them the earth shakes,
    the sky trembles,
the sun and moon are darkened,
    and the stars no longer shine.
[11]The LORD thunders
    at the head of his army;
his forces are beyond number,
    and mighty are those who obey his command.
The day of the LORD is great;
    it is dreadful.
    Who can endure it?

2:10 Here the text returns to the typical language of the day of the Lord. The words do not literally describe either a locust army or a human army. While locusts may briefly darken the sky at day, they are inactive at night and do not blot out the moon and stars. Rather, the shaking of heaven and earth and the darkening of the heavenly bodies are, simply stated, the end of the world. They represent the return of chaos and the end of all the permanent, dependable structures of life on which we all depend. What, after all, could be more certain than the ground beneath our feet or the assurance that the sun will rise tomorrow and stay in its accustomed course? When the prophets asserted that heavens were shaken, they implied that creation was being undone and that the world the people knew was ending.[36]

This does not mean, however, that Joel thought that either the locust plague or the northern army literally destroyed what we would now call the solar system or brought an end to the physical universe. Rather, the message can be understood as analogous to the English expression, "Their world came to an end." When we speak in this way, we do not mean that the planet has ceased to exist but that an order in life that seemed permanent has unexpectedly collapsed, never to be rebuilt. When the Soviet Union collapsed, for example, the

---

[36] Numerous texts associate shaking of heaven and earth with theophany or with the end of creation, and the verbs רגז ("shake") and especially רעשׁ ("tremble") have become technical terms in these contexts. See Isa 13:13; Jer 4:23–26; Ezek 38:18–20; Ps 18:8[7]. B. S. Childs points out that רעשׁ has become a technical term for the return of chaos in the context of the attack by the northern invader ("The Enemy from the North and the Chaos Tradition," *JBL* 78 [1959]: 187–98).

"world" that generations of Russians had grown up with and which seemed unchanging abruptly disappeared, and people all across eastern Europe and central Asia struggled with disorientation and confusion. Deuteronomy 28:29 anticipates that the Israelites would suffer this kind of disorientation when their world collapsed: "At midday you will grope around like a blind man in the dark."[37]

For Joel the locust plague and drought did this to Judah at one level (the chaotic disruption of the agriculture patterns of life), but the northern army did it at another, even more painful level (the end of Jerusalem and the scattering of the people in diaspora). We should add that, viewed in this light, it is not mere metaphor to say that the world the Jews had known came crashing down around them. Although the language is poetic, the actual experiences hardly could have been more real and traumatic.

2:11 The prophets regularly spoke of the northern army as the army of Yahweh or as his instrument (e.g., Isa 10:5; Jer 25:9). Joel affirmed that all the powers of nature and of men were in Yahweh's hands and that nothing happened apart from his will.

To this point we have focused on the scholarly question of whether 2:1–11 concerns only locusts or looks beyond the locusts to an enemy army. This question is unavoidable, and we have argued that Joel's language and the parallels to other prophetic texts require us to see a human army here. On the other hand, this debate is somewhat skewed in that it misses the real point of Joel. His real concern was not with locusts, or enemy soldiers, or even with the last judgment: *the real subject matter of the Book of Joel is the day of the Lord.* Every event in the book is subordinated to that concept. It is here described as "great" and "dreadful" (lit. "fearful, awesome"; cf. 2:31; Mal 4:5), two words often found in the Old Testament describing the Lord.[38] When Yahweh moves, Joel asserted, the old order is inverted, the familiar disappears, and false security collapses. No one can withstand that day because there is nothing left to stand on. On the other hand, as we shall see, Yahweh brings new life and a new world into being.

---

[37] Stuart cites this verse and notes that the texts "do not identify either darkness or earthquake as curses per se" (*Hosea–Jonah*, 252).

[38] Cf. Deut 7:21; 10:17,21; 1 Chr 16:25; Neh 1:5; 4:14; 9:32; Pss 47:2[3]; 96:4; 99:3; Dan 9:4. See also Exod 14:31; 2 Kgs 17:36; Mal 1:14. An arresting sense of awe and even healthy fear are appropriate responses to the Lord.

III. TRANSITION: REPENTANCE AND RESPONSE (2:12–19)
   1. Invitation to Repentance (2:12–14)
   2. Summons to the Sacred Assembly (2:15–17)
   3. Introduction to the Divine Response (2:18–19)

III. TRANSITION: REPENTANCE AND RESPONSE (2:12–19)

To this point everything Joel has said to his people has been lamentation for pain already endured and terror over the horrors of war yet to come. The message has been untainted by hope or optimism. From 2:18 to the end of the book, however, the tone dramatically changes. There the Jews enjoy a return of prosperity, receive the Holy Spirit, and see their enemies' armies face the full fury of God. At the center of all this stands a call to repent. This call, unlike the laments of chap. 1, contains the hope of forgiveness and restoration. The message is clear: only a return to Yahweh will restore them from death to life.

1. Invitation to Repentance (2:12–14)

[12]"Even now," declares the LORD,
   "return to me with all your heart,
     with fasting and weeping and mourning."
[13]Rend your heart
   and not your garments.
Return to the LORD your God,
   for he is gracious and compassionate,
slow to anger and abounding in love,
   and he relents from sending calamity.
[14]Who knows? He may turn and have pity
   and leave behind a blessing—
grain offerings and drink offerings
   for the LORD your God.

2:12 For all that was coming to the people, Joel counseled them to react not with despair but with faith (cf. Hab 2:4). In saying that they should return "even now"[1] and in declaring this to be a word from God,[2] Joel affirmed that

---

[1] Joel uses the particle גַּם seven times, and generally it implies that what follows is contrary to expectation (e.g., 1:20).

[2] This is the only place where Joel uses the formula נְאֻם־יהוה ("a message of Yahweh").

God had not finally rejected them and that he was yet ready to heal them. The call here is for repentance,[3] an attitude of remorse for sin and a cry for forgiveness that weeping and fasting visibly express. The emotional demonstration is not just for show—the next verse shows that Joel was aware of the possibility of making a pretense of repentance through dramatic gestures. The weeping and fasting called for are appropriate indications that the people repent with their "whole hearts." In other words, they are signs that the people truly *feel* the weight of their sin and do not engage in repentance flippantly. Calvin commented that "moderate repentance will not do."[4]

2:13 Although the Old Testament several times calls on people to circumcise their hearts (cf. Deut 10:16; 30:6; Jer 4:4), this is the only place where a prophet calls on them to tear their hearts and not their garments.[5] Ritual repentance, however fervently carried out, is of no use if the heart is unchanged. A frequent criticism directed at Joel is that he was not a great ethical prophet. That is, we do not see in Joel the kind of diatribe against injustice, idolatry, or immorality that we find in the other prophets. It is undeniable that Joel was so focused on the day of the Lord that he had little room in his small book for anything else. Still he captured the very heart of biblical ethics when he demanded genuine repentance from the people. Right behavior results from true submission to God, and this is where Joel pointed. Also the exhortation to "return" to Yahweh could be a call to abandon the idols of Canaan,[6] but it is certainly a call to turn away from sin.[7]

The Old Testament frequently repeats the confession that Yahweh is "gracious and compassionate" (2 Chr 30:9; Neh 9:17,31; Pss 86:15; 103:8; Jonah 4:2). This was the language Yahweh himself used when he gave a second copy of the Ten Commandments to Moses in Exod 34:6–7. The second issuing of the tablets of the law was itself a second chance for Israel to keep the covenant. Joel in effect reminded his people that Yahweh was the God of second chances.

---

[3] The verb שׁוּב is something of a technical term for repentance. For a detailed study of this issue, see W. L. Holladay, *The Root šûbh in the Old Testament* (Leiden: Brill, 1958), especially pp. 116–57, on the "covenantal" usage of שׁוּב. The Book of Joel uses שׁוּב to describe repentance in 2:12–13. In 2:14 it describes God returning ("turn") his favor to Jerusalem. In chap. 4 (3 in Heb.) it appears in vv. 1,4,7 and means either "to return favor toward Jerusalem" or "to bring vengeance upon their enemies."

[4] J. Calvin, *A Commentary on the Prophet Joel,* trans. J. Owen (London: Banner of Truth, 1958), 48.

[5] R. B. Dillard, "Joel," in *The Minor Prophets,* vol. 1 (Grand Rapids: Baker, 1991), 280.

[6] H. W. Wolff points out that Hosea and Jeremiah used the verb שׁוּב in a context of demanding that the people abandon the gods of Canaan (*Joel and Amos,* Her [Philadelphia: Fortress, 1977], 49). See Hos 2:9[7] and Jer 4:1. Wolff does not, however, see that to be the point of Joel's use of the word.

[7] D. Stuart observes that Hos 14:1–2 captures the theological significance of the verb שׁוּב (*Hosea–Jonah,* WBC [Dallas: Word, 1987], 252).

Wolff has observed that this expression, together with "Who knows? He may turn and have pity" from v. 14, implies that Joel is here dependent on Jonah 3:9 and 4:2. This may be, for the language of the texts is remarkably similar.[8] At the same time, there is no unambiguous evidence about the direction of the borrowing, and we should hesitate about drawing conclusions from these parallels.

2:14 The phrase "Who knows?" implies divine sovereignty and freedom.[9] God has already pronounced judgment against the nation, and no one can assume that an act of repentance can force God to change his decision (Amos 5:15). On the other hand, the mercy of God is such that he yet may choose to relent. God is always free to have mercy on whom he will have mercy (Exod 33:19; Rom 9:15). We cannot force the issue through any formula or prayer. L. C. Allen notes that Joel issued "a call to faith not in a doctrinal system, but in an intensely personal God."[10] Still the overall purpose was to draw people to true repentance.[11] Wolff captures the sense of the idiom well: "The 'perhaps' of hope is appropriate to the humility of one who prays; in the proclamation of the messenger it underscores the fact that the one called to return stands, for the time being, under the message of judgment and has to face up to it."[12]

The hope is that repentance will be followed by restoration. In particular, Joel looked for a restoration of the agricultural prosperity so that they could make offerings in the temple. This would be a sign that once again they were under God's favor.

2. Summons to the Sacred Assembly (2:15–17)

[15]**Blow the trumpet in Zion,**
   declare a holy fast,
   call a sacred assembly.
[16]**Gather the people,**
   consecrate the assembly;
bring together the elders,
   gather the children,
   those nursing at the breast.
Let the bridegroom leave his room
   and the bride her chamber.

---

[8] For all practical purposes the texts are identical, the only difference being that whereas Jonah called Yahweh אֶל־חָנּוּן, Joel dropped אֶל and instead used the pronoun הוּא.

[9] Cf. F. Page, "Jonah," NAC (Nashville: Broadman & Holman, 1995), 271.

[10] L. C. Allen, *The Books of Joel, Obadiah, Jonah and Micah*, NICOT (Grand Rapids: Eerdmans, 1976), 81.

[11] Calvin speaks especially well to this point (*Joel*, 52).

[12] Wolff, *Joel and Amos*, 50.

¹⁷**Let the priests, who minister before the** LORD,
   weep between the temple porch and the altar.
Let them say, "Spare your people, O LORD.
   Do not make your inheritance an object of scorn,
   a byword among the nations.
Why should they say among the peoples,
   'Where is their God?'"

2:15 Again the text calls for the blowing of the shofar but this time for a sacred assembly and not to call for troops to man the walls (cf. 2:1). Again the people are called together for a sacred fast (1:14), but this time the purpose is not simply to wail and mourn but is in the context of hope for restoration. By linking texts together in this fashion, the prophet related the fasting and mourning of the people both to the recent locust plague and to the anticipated attack from the north.

Although the sacred assembly called for here probably was an ad hoc convocation because of the agricultural crisis, it is ironically reminiscent of the Feast of Weeks (Pentecost). This festival, described in Lev 23:15–22, celebrated the end of the grain harvest and took place seven weeks after the offering of firstfruits at Passover. In Lev 23:21 the text commands Israel to "proclaim a sacred assembly and do no regular work" at Pentecost. Joel here called upon the priests to "call a sacred assembly"[13] and demanded a cessation of all normal activity (v. 16). In a grim reversal of the normal Pentecost, this sacred assembly and cessation of labor mourned the loss of the harvest rather than celebrated an abundant harvest. It is noteworthy that the gift of the Spirit prophesied by Joel came at Pentecost (Acts 2).

2:16 Again the book calls on representative groups (1:2–14), but this time it is with a difference. Previously the text singled out individual groups for specific reasons (old men were to search their memories, drunks were to mourn the destruction of the viniculture, and so forth). Now the text calls individual groups to emphasize that the entire nation had been called to repentance (except that the call to the priests in v. 17 is distinctive). Here old men are not mentioned because they do something that specifically relates to being old but because, in conjunction with the children and the nursing babies (employing merismus[14]), their presence implies that every person in the community regardless of age should join the assembly. Similarly, the passage calls on newlyweds to join the assembly because under normal circumstances no one would expect them to do so. Also the call to the newlyweds harkens back to the previous call for Jerusalem to mourn like a virgin weep-

---

[13] Joel's terminology differs slightly from that found in Lev 23. Joel used the expressions קִרְאוּ עֲצָרָה ("proclaim a sacred assembly") and קַדְּשׁוּ קָהָל ("consecrate the assembly"), but Lev 23:21 has מִקְרָא־קֹדֶשׁ ("a sacred convocation"). The ideas obviously are similar.

[14] See Introduction, p. 294.

ing over the death of her fiancé (1:8).

It is not correct to think of the "room" and "chamber" of the bridegroom and bride as two separate rooms. Both terms refer to the room in which marriage was consummated.[15]

2:17 The call to the priests is distinctive in this section in that it singles them out for a special task—they were to intercede for the nation. It is not clear that there is specific significance to the place between the porch and the altar except that it would have been a large enough area to hold a fairly significant number of priests.[16]

The priests called on Yahweh to uphold the covenant and not abandon his people. The idea behind this is that God's name would be disgraced before the nations if he allowed his own people to fall. More than that, this was an appeal for mercy.[17]

The NIV rendering that God ought not allow his people to become "a byword among the nations"[18] is not correct.[19] The phrase can *only* mean, "Do not let the nations rule over them."[20] The call to repentance in 2:12–17 both looks back to the locusts and looks ahead to conquest by an enemy army. The

---

[15] Dillard observes that although the term חֻפָּה eventually came to mean the canopy under which marriage ceremonies were conducted, in OT times it was the chamber in which the consummation took place ("Joel," 283). See Ps 19:6[5]. The use of two separate terms in Joel is simple parallelism.

[16] Wolff, *Joel and Amos*, 51.

[17] See Calvin, *Joel*, 64.

[18] So also REB, RSV, and NRSV.

[19] See Stuart, *Hosea–Jonah*, 248, and Wolff, *Joel and Amos*, 52.

[20] Cf. NKJV. The phrase is לִמְשָׁל־בָּם גּוֹיִם in which the verb מָשַׁל ("to rule," BDB root III) marks its object with בְּ, as it commonly does. Examples include Gen 1:18; 3:16; 4:7; 37:8; 45:8,26; Deut 15:6; Josh 12:5; Judg 8:22–23; 9:2; 14:4; 15:11; 2 Sam 23:3; 1 Kgs 5:1; Isa 3:4; 19:4; 63:19; Jer 22:30; Mic 5:1; Hab 1:14; Pss 19:14; 22:29; 105:21; 106:41; Prov 16:32; Eccl 9:17; Dan 11:43. Scholars apparently are impressed by the proximity of לְחֶרְפָּה ("to reproach") and reason that the parallel requires that we read the noun מָשָׁל, a "proverb" or "byword." Allen argues that the preposition בְּ can be used in a context of mocking to mean "against them" (*Joel*, 77). Allen fails to see, however, that the grammar of the passage makes this interpretation impossible, and his extravagant translation, "Do not permit your inheritance to be ridiculed, / a swear word bandied about among the nations," is out of the question. If one were to take לִמְשָׁל as the noun מָשָׁל, then one would be left with the unintelligible, "Do not let your inheritance become a reproach, a byword against them—nations." On the other hand, the verb מָשַׁל II means "to use a proverb or simile" and not "to mock" (contra J. L. Crenshaw, *Joel* [New York: Doubleday, 1995], 142), who supplies no evidence that it may mean "to mock"), and it never takes the preposition בְּ with an object in the sense "against them." מָשָׁל II is found in Ezek 12:23; 16:44; 17:2; 18:2–3; 21:5; 24:3; Num 21:27. It is apparent that in לְחֶרְפָּה לִמְשָׁל Joel used לִמְשָׁל in the sense "to rule over" but that he has also built a paronomasia on the homonym מָשָׁל "byword" in conjunction with חֶרְפָּה. The ancient versions (LXX, Vg, Syr, and Tg) uniformly read this as meaning "to rule." The LXX, for example, translates it τοῦ κατάρξαι αὐτῶν ἔθνη.

prayer that the nations not rule over them shows that Joel had already anticipated such an event in the prophecies of 2:1–11.

3. Introduction to the Divine Response (2:18–19)

> **18**Then the LORD will be jealous for his land
>   and take pity on his people.
> **19**The LORD will reply to them:
> "I am sending you grain, new wine and oil,
>   enough to satisfy you fully;
> never again will I make you
>   an object of scorn to the nations."

Everything prior to these two verses is couched as the prophet's lamentation and his call for the people to mourn before God. Strictly speaking, God
does not speak in 1:1–2:17 (with the exception of the encouragement to
repentance in 2:12). By contrast, and notwithstanding the occasional shift to
third-person forms, all of 2:19–3:21 is a divine oracle of salvation. That is,
God is the speaker from 2:19 to the end of the book.[21] A brief perusal of the
last half of the book reveals how completely first-person verbs (with God as
subject) dominate the text.

Viewed from another perspective, however, 2:18–19 is transitional. In 2:18
God is not the speaker; rather, the prophet is announcing that Yahweh has
decided to show mercy on his people. In 2:19, after the introduction to God's
response ("The LORD will reply to them"), the text gives a proleptic summation of all that follows: God will heal the land, and he will deal with the
nations. From this perspective the actual oracles begin with the destruction of
the invader from the north (2:20) and then move on to agricultural restoration
(2:21–27), spiritual restoration (2:28–30), and the judgment on all the nations
(3:1–21). For this reason it probably is better to treat 2:18–19 as part of the
transition and view the oracles of salvation (2:20–3:21) as separate major
divisions.

2:18   The Hebrew verb forms mark a sharp transition here. The text at
this point abruptly moves from crisis and lamentation for God's people to salvation and vindication. The NIV translation (using future tense forms) is
defensible, but the text would be better rendered, "Now the LORD is jealous

---

[21] In a few places one may argue that God is not the speaker, as in 3:11b, "Bring down your
warriors, O Lord!" But the text there is quite uncertain (see commentary), and at any rate these
exceptions do not break the rule that God is the main speaker in 2:19–3:21.

for his land, and he has been moved to compassion over his people."[22]

The idiom for being "jealous for" something[23] occurs several times in the sense of people being devoted to and defending the honor of Yahweh (e.g., Num 25:13). Here, as in Ezek 39:25; Zech 1:14 and 8:2, Yahweh is zealous for the nation in the sense that he identifies himself with it, protects it, and upholds the covenant. This quality especially emerges in the context of the nations' abuse of Israel, as in Zech 1:14–15: "I am very jealous for Jerusalem and Zion, but I am very angry with the nations that feel secure. I was only a little angry [i.e., with Jerusalem], but they [i.e., the Gentiles] added to the calamity [i.e., by tormenting the Jews]." At the same time, Yahweh is motivated by pure compassion. Thus the two grounds for God's work of salvation are his covenant bond with the people and his merciful nature.

2:19 Yahweh proleptically decreed that he would undo the two curses of agricultural disaster (1:9–17) and humiliation among the Gentile powers (2:17; cf. Jer 51:51; Ezek 5:15; 22:4). This verse is proleptic in the sense that it only announces in brief what is explored in much more detail in the following verses. Restoring the grain, new wine, and oil reverses the calamity described in 1:10. Putting an end to their "reproach among the nations" implies an end to the military defeat, famine, and plague that had dogged them. It specifically looks for a restoration from exile.[24]

---

[22] The Hebrew suddenly introduces *waw*–consecutive forms here with וַיְקַנֵּא and וַיַּחְמֹל. While the *waw*-consecutive (or better, *wayyiqtol*) form is virtually a past tense in prose narrative, its use in poetic and prophetic texts is not well understood. Clearly we should not repoint the text. Probably the *wayyiqtol* forms imply that Yahweh's sudden decision to save the nation is a consequence of their repentance. They also signal that the whole direction and tone of the book is now taking a dramatic turn. They seem to imply that Yahweh had *already* decided to save Israel.

[23] Using the *piel* of קנא with the ל preposition on the object.

[24] The phrase חֶרְפָּה בַּגּוֹיִם (or a near analogy) occurs in Jer 29:18; 44:8; Ezek 5:14–15; 22:4; 36:15,30; Neh 5:9. In all the prophetic texts the context is exile (the Nehemiah text is different; it describes disgraceful behavior by the Jews). Ezekiel 36:30 does describe a return of fruition for the land, but even there the context is the return of the exiles.

IV. FORGIVENESS FOR ISRAEL/JUDGMENT ON NATIONS: NORTHERN ARMY DESTROYED (2:20)

[20]"I will drive the northern army far from you,
  pushing it into a parched and barren land,
with its front columns going into the eastern sea
  and those in the rear into the western sea.
And its stench will go up;
  its smell will rise."
Surely he has done great things.

2:20 The phrase "the northern army" (lit., "the northerner") occupies the emphatic clause initial position in Hebrew,[1] and the line could be rendered, "But the northerner shall I drive far away from you." The word "northerner" is a major conundrum for those who assert that Joel had only locusts in mind here and not a human army. It is indeed difficult to imagine how Joel could have used this term for a locust plague. Bewer finds "northerner" to be "such an unusual and improbable term for a real locust swarm" that he cannot escape the obvious conclusion that it is "an eschatological term for the enemy from the north," and therefore he advocates excising it as an interpolation.[2] His approach was typical of the older school of critical scholarship.[3] Other advocates of the locust plague interpretation, who are less willing to solve this problem with scissors, acknowledge that this term is apocalyptic and does not simply describe locusts.[4]

---

[1] וְאֶת־הַצְּפוֹנִי.

[2] J. A. Bewer, "Joel," in *A Critical and Exegetical Commentary on Micah, Zephaniah, Nahum, Habakkuk, Obadiah and Joel,* ICC (Edinburgh: T & T Clark, 1911), 51.

[3] For a thorough analysis of scholarly attempts at emending this verse, see A. Kapelrud, *Joel Studies* (Uppsala: A. B. Lundequistska Bokhandeln, 1948), 93–95. He concludes that interpreters' emendations are "definitely arbitrary in character" (p. 95).

[4] R. B. Dillard, e.g., after reviewing briefly the considerable evidence for "northerner" referring to Israel's great enemies, concludes that it has taken on apocalyptic significance and suggests that we should see a fusing of the two motifs of the "army of Yahweh" coming from the "divine abode" in the far north ("Joel," in *The Minor Prophets,* vol. 1 [Grand Rapids: Baker, 1991], 286–87). L. C. Allen similarly argues that this is an apocalyptic vision of locusts (*The Books of Joel, Obadiah, Jonah and Micah,* NICOT [Grand Rapids: Eerdmans, 1976], 88). For our purposes it is significant that these scholars cannot argue that "northerner" is a natural or self-evident metaphor for locust but must concede that we have entered the realm of apocalyptic.

The simple fact is that locust plagues attack the environs of Jerusalem from the south or southeast, not from the north. The rare exception of a locust plague arriving from the north or northeast[5] does not solve the problem. For locust plagues to acquire the nickname "northerner" in the Jerusalem dialect, they would actually have to come from the north with sufficient frequency for the term to make some kind of sense to speakers. By analogy hurricanes hit the American Gulf Coast in late summer or fall. It would be altogether unintelligible for locals to call hurricanes "the springtime storms" even if there were the occasional spring hurricane. Apart from that, we have no evidence that the people of Judah ever called locusts "northerners." By contrast, *Targum of Jonathan* explicitly interprets the line as "I will remove the people who come from the north far from you."[6]

A. Kapelrud finds evidence here to support his cultic interpretation of Joel, but it really is too far removed from the text of Joel to be convincing. He is quite impressed by the notion that Baal dwelt in Mount Zaphon in the north in the Ugaritic literature. He also can cite an occasional Old Testament text that is analogous, such as Isa 14:13, which speaks of a mountain of the gods in the remote north. From this he argues that Joel provides evidence for "an ancient dispute about which mountain was the sacred one, the original mount of the gods."[7] He sees locusts behind Joel's words, but he believes that the locusts have taken on mythological significance as forces of chaos. It probably is true that the notion of the Israelites' human enemies' being from the north armed them with apocalyptic significance in the eyes of the Israelites and that Joel and the other prophets do speak of the triumph of Zion over the mountains of the nations. Nevertheless it is going too far to describe Joel 2:20 as a contest over which mountain is the truly divine mountain, and it is quite far-fetched to speak of "northerner" as a term by which locusts portray mythical chaos.

The Bible, however, provides extensive evidence that the term "northerner" refers to an enemy (human) army. In Isaiah an army from the north terrifies Jews and Gentiles alike in the Levant (Isa 14:31; 41:25). Zephaniah saw Yahweh stretching out his hand against Assyria in the north on the day of the Lord (Zeph 2:13). The Book of Zechariah describes the captives in Babylon as dwelling "in the land of the north" (Zech 2:6–7).

The Book of Jeremiah refers extensively to the northern enemy. At the outset of the book the power about to overwhelm Judah is "a boiling pot, tilting

---

[5] Scholars here generally cite reports that the 1915 locust invasion came from the northeast. Thus T. J. Finley, *Joel, Obadiah, Amos*, WEC (Chicago: Moody, 1990), 63, and Allen, *Joel*, 88.

[6] K. J. Cathcart and R. P. Gordon, *The Targum of the Minor Prophets*, The Aramaic Bible 14 (Wilmington: Michael Glazier, 1989), 70. The Aramaic, following A. Sperber, is ודת עמא דאתי מצפונא ארחיק מנכון (*The Bible in Aramaic Based on Old Manuscripts and Printed Texts* [Leiden: Brill, 1962], 3:413).

[7] Kapelrud, *Joel Studies*, 105–8.

away from the north" which is explained as cataclysm about to come "from the north" (Jer 1:13–15). The prophecy continues to speak of "disaster" coming out of the north (4:6; 6:1; 10:22), and there is never any doubt that the text means a human army (e.g., 6:22). As in Joel, this army is all but invincible (15:12). The "northerner" for Jeremiah is none other than Nebuchadnezzar, but it is also the Babylonian army functioning as Yahweh's army (25:9). Jeremiah also taunted the Egyptians with the destruction that was to come upon them from the north (46:6,10,20,24). Remarkably, however, Jeremiah saw that even Babylon would fall prey to northern hordes (50:3,9,41; referring to the Medo-Persian coalition).

Whatever else one may make of the armies of Gog and Magog in Ezekiel, they are armies "from the far north" brought against Israel (38:15; 39:2). They are a vast horde that advances like a cloud[8] (38:15–16) and schemes to assault Jerusalem and carry away plunder (38:10–14). They will fall in the slaughter of the day of the Lord. Birds and wild animals will eat their corpses, and the Israelites will be occupied for seven months with burying the dead and for seven years with burning the equipment. The burial ground will occupy "the valley of those who travel east toward the sea" and will be so extensive that it will block the passage through (39:1–20).

The Hebrew term for "pushing it"[9] regularly appears in a context of driving a people out into exile (Deut 30:1; Jer 8:3; 16:15; 24:9; 46:28). In all of these passages it is Israel that is driven away (to the northern country in Jer 16:15), but here in Joel Yahweh drives the northerner into a wilderness, perhaps into the Negeb in the south.[10] Joel saw that a reversal would take place in which their enemies would experience the horrors they brought upon Israel.

Advocates of the position that the northerner in Joel is a locust swarm typically cite reports of how terrible the smell is when the swarm dies.[11] This is undoubtedly true, and again we observe that the northern army in Joel appears under the metaphor of locusts. Nevertheless, the stench of a slaughtered human army was at least as bad if not worse, and the prophets elsewhere describe military defeat in these terms (Amos 4:10). Isaiah 34:2–3 is especially comparable to Joel's description of the stench of the northern army: "The LORD is angry with all nations; / his wrath is upon all their armies. / He

---

[8] Had this word appeared in Joel in connection with the northern army, we would doubtless read in all the commentaries how a locust swarm resembles a cloud.

[9] The root נדח in the *hiphil* stem.

[10] M. Dahood argues that since this verse explicitly refers to north (the northern army), east (the eastern sea), and west (the western sea), then the "parched and barren land" must be the Negeb in the south ("The Four Cardinal Points in Psalm 75,7 and Joel 2,20," *Biblica* 52 [1971]: 397).

[11] For example, Dillard cites an interesting account from Augustine of Hippo ("Joel," 287). There is no disputing that a dead locust swarm does smell, however, or that this fact colored Joel's language; the question is whether he was really describing locusts here.

will totally destroy them, / he will give them over to slaughter. / Their slain
will be thrown out, / their dead bodies will send up a stench; / the mountains
will be soaked with their blood." Also the parallel is too strong to dismiss
between Ezekiel's description of the slain hordes of Gog filling the way east
to the Dead Sea (Ezek 39:11) and Joel's prophecy that the dead of the northern army would extend from east to west. Finally, we note that the language
of this verse may include specific, military terms ("front columns" and
"rear").[12] All in all, everything in this verse points toward a human army,
apocalyptic in its power and significance, whose victories represent judgment
upon Israel but whose destruction is a sign of eschatological salvation.

The NIV translation (also NRSV, REB) "surely he has done great things"
is open to question. The same phrase occurs in 2:21 except with the addition
of the subject "Yahweh." There it means "for the LORD has done great things,"
and apparently the NIV was influenced by the meaning in 2:21 in its rendering of 2:20. Of itself this would be acceptable, except that in 2:20 Yahweh
cannot be the subject. In 2:20 Yahweh is the speaker, and therefore the third-
person subject of "he has done great things" must be someone else, which the
context implies is the "northerner" (cf. NASB, "for it has done great things").
Also v. 21 begins a new strophe. "He has done great things" from v. 20 cannot
be attached to v. 21.[13] Finally, the word "surely" is not correct in either verse.
In both cases it is explanatory and means "because."[14]

The line "he has done great things" can also mean "he has acted great"[15] in
the sense of behaving with arrogance and aggression. In other words, the
phrase itself is ambiguous and can be taken in a good or a bad sense. Joel has
played upon that ambiguity by stating first that God would destroy the northerner because he had acted arrogantly (cf. NJB, "for what he made bold to
do"); then in the next verse he turned the theme to praise and reassurance by
using the same phrase in its positive sense with Yahweh as the subject.[16]

The idea that the northern foe went about its task of punishing Israel with
excessive zeal and greed and therefore itself fell under the condemnation of

---

[12] Finley observes that פָּנָיו and סֹפוֹ respectively mean "its vanguard" and "its rear guard"
(*Joel, Amos, Obadiah*, 63).

[13] Verse 21 signals a new strophe by beginning with a volitive form (אַל־תִּירְאִי). Cf. *BHS* strophic division.

[14] The word כִּי can mean "surely" in certain circumstances, but in v. 21 it introduces the *reason*
for Judah to rejoice and not to fear. In v. 20, similarly, it must be taken as the reason that Yahweh
will destroy the northern army.

[15] Thus H. W. Wolff, *Joel and Amos,* Her [Philadelphia: Fortress, 1977]. Wolff points out that
the ancient versions treat the northerner as the subject (the LXX reads, ὅτι ἐμεγάλυνε τὰ ἔργα
αὐτοῦ) and that the *hiphil* of גדל often implies haughtiness, as in Pss 35:26; 38:17[16]; 55:13[12];
Jer 48:26,42; Zeph 2:8,10; Lam 1:9; and Dan 8:4,8,11,25. The Vg renders the line in v. 20 as *quia
superbe egit* but v. 21 as *quoniam magnificavit Dominus ut faceret.*

[16] See also D. Marcus, "Nonrecurring Doublets in the Book of Joel, *CBQ* 56 (1994): 61.

Yahweh occurs elsewhere in the prophets. In Isa 10:5–7 Yahweh declares against Assyria: "Woe to the Assyrian, the rod of my anger, / in whose hand is the club of my wrath! / I send him against a godless nation, / I dispatch him against a people who anger me, / to seize loot and snatch plunder, / and to trample them down like mud in the streets. / But this is not what he intends, / this is not what he has in mind; / his purpose is to destroy, / to put an end to many nations." In v. 12 Yahweh concludes, "I will punish the king of Assyria for the willful pride of his heart and the haughty look in his eyes." Similarly, Ezek 35:13 decrees judgment on Edom because they "magnified" themselves, and Dan 8:25 speaks of an apocalyptic foe who "exalts himself" in his heart (both using the causative form of the verb *gādal,* "be great," as here).

In short, this verse describes the demise of the apocalyptic, northern army. Locusts to some degree guide the metaphors, but they are not the subject. The northerner sealed his own fate when he behaved with arrogance, something locusts surely do not do.[17]

---

[17] D. A. Hubbard devotes an extensive paragraph to arguing that the northerner refers to locusts (*Joel and Amos,* TOTC [Downers Grove: InterVarsity, 1989], 62–63). But in the very next two sentences, examining "for he has done great things," he asserts that the northerner behaved with "wanton arrogance" and committed a "crime" that merited "God's stern judgment." He seems to have forgotten that, in his interpretation, he is talking about *insects.*

V. FORGIVENESS FOR ISRAEL: LOCUST PLAGUE REVERSED/
   GRACE: RAIN POURED ON THE LAND (2:21–27)
   1. Summons to Celebration (2:21–24)
   2. Divine Promise of Healing (2:25–27)

V. FORGIVENESS FOR ISRAEL: LOCUST PLAGUE REVERSED/GRACE: RAIN POURED ON THE LAND (2:21–27)

As the *BHS* indicates, the initial command forms in this verse ("Do not fear," etc.) mark the beginning of a new strophe here. Within the larger structure of the book, this section looks back to chap. 1, the devastating locust plague and drought, and announces a reversal of the disaster. The rains will come, the grass will again be green, and the trees will bear fruit, such that the land will again flow with milk and honey. The manifold significance of the day of the Lord continues to emerge. It is not only judgment but is also reversal of judgment.

1. Summons to Celebration (2:21–24)

> ²¹ Be not afraid, O land;
>   be glad and rejoice.
> Surely the LORD has done great things.
> ²² Be not afraid, O wild animals,
>   for the open pastures are becoming green.
> The trees are bearing their fruit;
>   the fig tree and the vine yield their riches.
> ²³Be glad, O people of Zion,
>   rejoice in the LORD your God,
> for he has given you
>   the autumn rains in righteousness.
> He sends you abundant showers,
>   both autumn and spring rains, as before.
> ²⁴The threshing floors will be filled with grain;
>   the vats will overflow with new wine and oil.

2:21 The text begins with an exhortation to the land not to fear but to rejoice, then encourages animals not to fear (v. 22), and finally exhorts the people of Zion to be glad (vv. 23–24). The order generally reverses the arrangement of chap. 1, which begins with calls for the people of Zion to mourn (1:2–15) and ends with a description of the pitiful condition of the animals and land (1:16–20). Urging the land to rejoice and not be afraid obviously personifies the land.

In the Old Testament injunctions not to fear often come in speeches just before going to battle (e.g., Num 14:9; Isa 7:4). In Isaiah, however, the refrain "Do not fear"[1] (using a Hebrew phrase identical or similar to that of Joel 2:21) is a signal that redemption has come. In Isa 40:9–11 the herald is to cry out to Zion, "Do not fear!" because Yahweh himself is coming to redeem and care for his people. In Isaiah 41 God reassures Israel that he has chosen them, reminds them that their God is no powerless idol, and tells them three times (Isa 41:10,13,14) not to fear. In 43:1 he tells Israel not to fear because he has called them by his own name, and in 43:5 he again reassures them that they need not fear because he will bring the people back from exile. In 44:2–3, much as in Joel 2:21–32, he encourages them not to fear because he will pour out water on the land and his Spirit on the people. In Isa 54:4 God tells Israel not to fear because he is about to remove their reproach among the nations. In short, the Book of Isaiah addresses many of the themes that appear in Joel, including the healing of the land, the triumph over their enemies, the end of Israel's shame among the nations, the return from exile, and the gift of the Spirit. "Do not fear" is the refrain of reassurance that runs through them all. Joel's command to the land not to fear similarly signals the promise of redemption.[2]

2:22 The process of reversal continues here. The wild beasts that had been crying out in agony (1:18) receive the promise of relief, and the trees that had been stripped bare (1:7) receive new life. The personifications of land and wildlife here have none of the mythical qualities of the fertility religions, but they do emphasize the bond between the creature and the Creator and imply the dependence of the former and the sovereignty of the latter (see Luke 12:24 and Ps 147:9).

This text also implies that the redemption of humanity leads to the redemption of all creation. Just as the sin of humans brought about the alienation of the world,[3] so their reconciliation with the Creator portends a new heaven and earth. When God restores Jerusalem, the wolf and the lamb will feed together (Isa 65:17–25).

2:23 The phrase "O people of Zion" is drawn forward in the Hebrew text

---

[1] Using אַל־תִּירָא or a similar phrase, just as in Joel 2:21.

[2] The last line furnishes the reason for rejoicing; thus the particle כִּי should be translated "for" rather than "surely."

[3] Cf. K. A. Mathews, *Genesis 1–11:26,* NAC (Nashville: Broadman & Holman, 1996), 345.

to emphasize God's turning in grace toward them. The opening of the verse could be rendered, "And as for you, people of Zion, be glad and rejoice," in order to bring this emphasis out in translation.

The sending of rain reverses the drought implied in 1:17 and enables the land to recover from the locust swarms. The "autumn rains" promoted germination of the seed, and the "spring rains" came prior to harvest and enabled the grain to swell and ripen fully.

Of great interest, however, is whether the phrase "autumn rains in righteousness" should be translated "teacher of righteousness." The Hebrew is ambiguous and could mean either. Some believe that this phrase in Joel, interpreted as "teacher of righteousness" by the Qumran sectarians, led them to believe that a certain teacher who appeared among them at the very time the Jews were suffering under the Romans was the prophesied "teacher of righteousness."[4] His coming presaged the destruction of the northern hordes.[5] Against this reconstruction stands the fact that, as far as we know, the Qumran exegetes did not claim that their "teacher of righteousness" was the fulfillment of Joel 2:23.[6] Resolving the question of the interpretation of this verse in the Qumran community is made more difficult by the fact that we are still quite uncertain about the identity and function of the mysterious "teacher of righteousness" of the scrolls.[7] We need to bear in mind, however, that the conclusions of the Qumran sectarians about this verse are not normative for us. Even if they linked Joel 2:23 to their "teacher of righteousness" (and apparently they did not), this would have little bearing on what we should make of the text.

In trying to determine the correct translation of the phrase in question, "a

---

[4] Cf. Hos 10:12, וְיֹרֶה צֶּדֶק לָכֶם, which could be taken to mean "and he will teach righteousness to you."

[5] See C. Roth, "The Teacher of Righteousness and the Prophecy of Joel," *VT* 13 (1963): 91–95, and R. B. Dillard, "Joel," in *The Minor Prophets,* vol. 1 (Grand Rapids: Baker, 1991), 289. On the other hand, O. R. Sellers considers לְצְדָקָה to be a gloss inserted by a Qumran sectarian ("A Possible Old Testament Reference to the Teacher of Righteousness," *IEJ* 5 [1955]: 93–95). This is hardly likely. See H. W. Wolff, *Joel and Amos,* Her (Philadelphia: Fortress, 1977), 63–64.

[6] J. L. Crenshaw, *Joel* (New York: Doubleday, 1995), 155.

[7] The "Teacher of Righteousness" at Qumran is called מוֹרֶה צֶדֶק (or מוֹרֶה הַצֶּדֶק). Cf. J. J. Collins, "Teacher and Messiah? The One Who Will Teach Righteousness at the End of Days," in *The Community of the Renewed Covenant,* ed. E. Ulrich and J. Vanderkam (Notre Dame: University Press, 1994), 193–210. There is question about whether the מוֹרֶה צֶדֶק was an individual, messianic figure. It could refer to an office of leadership in the community that was held by many individuals. See J. Weingreen, "The Title *Moreh Sedek,*" *JSS* 6 (1961): 162–74. Weingreen resists translating the title, but his analysis implies that it simply means "bona fide leader" or the like. This would not apply to the phrase in Joel, which uses צְדָקָה rather than צֶדֶק. See also I. Rabinowitz, "The Guides of Righteousness," *VT* 8 (1958): 391–404, for another interpretation of the Qumran use of מוֹרֶה צֶדֶק. Rabinowitz contends that Joel 2:23 has nothing to do with the Qumran title. He argues that in the Joel text לְצְדָקָה is in apposition to לָכֶם, "for you," and that thus it is used concretely for "righteous people." He translates, "He gives to you, the righteous ones, rain."

teacher for righteousness" or "rains in righteousness," two contradictory pieces of evidence stand out.[8] The first is that the meaning "rains" perfectly suits the context, whereas "teacher" is discordant. Nothing in the immediate vicinity or in the wider context of the book supports the sudden appearance of a teacher here. In addition to these considerations, L. C. Allen points out that the phrase "he has given" supports the position that rains and not a teacher are meant.[9] On the other hand, notwithstanding that "righteousness" in Hebrew implies vindication or even salvation, the idea of giving "rains for righteousness" sounds harsh if not incongruous. Also several ancient versions see in this phrase a reference to a teacher.[10]

The ambiguity of the phrase is such that we must ask ourselves if we have a double entendre here. The surface or immediate meaning is that Yahweh will vindicate the Jews in the presence of the nations by sending rains to heal their land. At the same time, it seems, Joel used a wordplay to hint that the salvation of the nation would come from a teacher of righteousness. But if the book nowhere else alludes to the coming of a messianic guide, what could account for the occurrence of such an idea here?

Throughout the Book of Joel, the teachings of Deuteronomy provide the doctrinal framework for the message. We have already seen, for example, that Joel assumed with his readers that the locust plague was a sign and precursor of greater judgments to come, in particular of military defeat and exile (Deut 28:38–68). In addition to these warnings of judgment, Deuteronomy holds out the promise of a "prophet like me [Moses]" who would become Israel's guide (Deut 18:15). As J. Sailhamer points out, Deuteronomy itself asserts that this promise has gone unfulfilled (34:10).[11] If Joel has hinted here of a teacher of righteousness, it is an allusion to the eschatological prophet of salvation, the prophet for whom Israel was still waiting.[12] The messianic hope is never far from the prophetic text, and it would seem that Joel has drawn upon that promise.[13]

---

[8] The word מוֹרֶה occurs with the meaning "teach/teacher" in Job 36:22; Prov 5:13; Isa 30:20; Hab 2:18 and "rain" in Ps 84:7[6].

[9] L. C. Allen, *The Books of Joel, Obadiah, Jonah and Micah,* NICOT (Grand Rapids: Eerdmans, 1976), 93. Allen points out that in Lev 26:4 the verb נָתַן is used with "rain" as its object.

[10] The Vg, Tg, and Symmachus. The Vg has *quia dedit vobis doctorem iustitiae.* The LXX, we should add, has βρώματα εἰς δικαιοσύνην, "food for righteousness," and this has prompted some suggestions that the text be emended. See Dillard, "Joel," 289.

[11] לֹא־קָם עוֹד נָבִיא בְּיִשְׂרָאֵל כְּמֹשֶׁה means, "Never again did a prophet arise in Israel like Moses." See J. Sailhamer, *Introduction to Old Testament Theology* (Grand Rapids: Zondervan, 1995), 247, and the NRSV.

[12] Cf. T. Laetsch, *The Minor Prophets* (St. Louis: Concordia, 1956), 125.

[13] According to G. van Groningen, the reference is to "the promised seed of Abraham, about whom the prophet Moses spoke, and the antitype of all true prophets who lived in the Old Testament age" (*Messianic Revelation in the Old Testament* [Grand Rapids: Baker, 1990], 448).

The Solomonic prayer at the dedication of the temple reinforces the plausibility of a double entendre here. First Kings 8:35–36 reads (with emphasis added), "When the heavens are shut up and there is no rain because your people have sinned against you, and when they pray toward this place and confess your name and turn from their sin because you have afflicted them, then hear from heaven and forgive the sin of your servants, your people Israel. *Teach them the right way* to live, and *send rain* on the land you gave your people for an inheritance." Joel no doubt considered himself and his people to be in the very circumstance that Solomon had described. The link between right teaching and saving rain in Solomon's prayer could have led Joel to construct a paronomasia in a phrase that could mean both "rain for deliverance" and "teacher for righteousness."

Other prophets also link the ideas of rain and right teaching. Isaiah 30:20–23 promises that God would send teachers who would keep Israel from going astray as well as rains and abundant harvest. Amos compared a lack of the word of God to a drought (8:11–12) and promised a restoration that included both the resurrection of the house of David and abundant harvests (9:11–15). Isaiah 45:8 and Hos 10:12 both speak of righteousness coming down like rain. For us the link between rains and a teacher of righteousness may seem tenuous, but the prophets appear to have connected both to the divine restoration of their nation and ultimately to the messianic era.[14]

2:24 Where there was once famine and drought, there is now abundant harvest. The desolation of 1:7,10 is at an end (cf. also 2:19).

2. Divine Promise of Healing (2:25–27)

> [25]"I will repay you for the years the locusts have eaten—
>   the great locust and the young locust,
>   the other locusts and the locust swarm—
> my great army that I sent among you.
> [26]You will have plenty to eat, until you are full,
>   and you will praise the name of the LORD your God,
>   who has worked wonders for you;
> never again will my people be shamed.
> [27]Then you will know that I am in Israel,
>   that I am the LORD your God,
>   and that there is no other;
> never again will my people be shamed.

---

[14] These parallels are developed in G. W. Ahlström, *Joel and the Temple Cult of Jerusalem*, VTS 21 (Leiden: Brill, 1971), 98–110. Ahlström has a particularly good discussion of the meaning of מוֹרֶה.

2:25 This verse obviously reverses the calamity described in 1:4,6. Some scholars have suggested emending the text to read "repay double" instead of "repay for the years," but this is unlikely.[15] The word "years" implies that the effects of the locust plague and drought lasted for some time. The word order for the four locust types is different here from 1:4, and scholars who try to identify specifically each word use various means to account for the change in word order.[16]

A number of ancient interpreters even read this verse as a prophecy of military invasion. The Targum interprets it as "peoples, tongues, governments, and kingdoms," and the Greek manuscript Q has "Egyptians, Babylonians, Assyrians, Greeks, Romans."[17] Although we should not interpret this particular verse in this fashion (the phrase "my great army" looks back to 1:6), the rendering indicates that early readers saw more than locusts in the Book of Joel.

God's people experience sorrow and loss, but they also experience restoration. In the end that which is gained far outweighs that which was lost. God does not allow the years of suffering to go unrewarded. After punishment comes comfort (Isa 40:1–2), and in the end God will wipe away every tear from the eyes of his people (Rev 7:17).

2:26 The people of ancient Israel already knew that having enough to eat was not something to take for granted. The locusts and the drought of Joel's day made starvation a real possibility. For these people a good harvest and a satisfying meal would be evidence of divine favor and a true cause for praise. The "shame" that they would escape was the perception that their God had abandoned them and the need to flee to other lands as impoverished economic refugees (see Ruth 1:1).[18]

2:27 When God vindicated them, the people of Judah would know with certainty that they really are his people. The monotheistic sentiment that "there is no other" god seems to echo the powerful monotheism of Isa 43:10–11. For those who date Isaiah 40–55 to the postexilic period, this further implies a late date for Joel,[19] but for those who ascribe the entirety of Isaiah

---

[15] Reading הַשָּׁנַיִם instead of the MT, הַשָּׁנִים. Dillard observes that passages that speak of repaying double (Isa 61:7; Jer 16:18; 17:18; Zech 9:12) generally use מִשְׁנֶה ("Joel," 292). Where the word שְׁנַיִם is used for repayment of double, it is anarthrous (Exod 22:3,6,8[4,7,9]). J. A. Bewer proposes the emendation הַשְּׁמַנִים, "rich fruits," but this has nothing to commend it ("Joel," in *A Critical and Exegetical Commentary on Micah, Zephaniah, Nahum, Habakkuk, Obadiah and Joel*, ICC [Edinburgh: T & T Clark, 1911], 120).

[16] E.g., Wolff, *Joel and Amos*, 64.

[17] Dillard, "Joel," 292.

[18] Some interpreters excise לֹא־יֵבֹשׁוּ עַמִּי עוֹלָם as a dittograph from v. 27, but this is unnecessary in a book as repetitive as Joel.

[19] E.g., Wolff says that Joel "takes up Deutero-Isaianic language" (*Joel and Amos*, 65).

to the preexilic period, this clause implies nothing (one way or the other) about the date of Joel.

The saying, "Then you will know that I am the LORD your God" or the like appears repeatedly in the exodus narrative (Exod 6:7; 7:17; 8:22; 11:7; 16:6,8,12). It implies that the Lord was about to do some mighty work that would teach the Israelites a lesson about his divine power. The phrase also appears in Num 16:28,30, where the earth opened up and swallowed the rebellious sons of Korah. By this the people "knew" that the Lord was God and that Moses was his spokesperson. Ezekiel used the formula about thirty times (e.g., Ezek 6:7; 7:4,9; 11:10,12), and it appears sporadically in other Old Testament books as well (e.g., 1 Kgs 20:13,28; Isa 49:23; 60:16; Jer 44:29; cf. also John 8:28).

VI. GRACE: SPIRIT POURED ON ALL PEOPLE (2:28–32)
   1. Gift of the Spirit (2:28–29)
   2. Signs of the Day of the Lord (2:30–31)
   3. Promise of Salvation (2:32)

————— **VI. GRACE: SPIRIT POURED ON ALL PEOPLE (2:28–32)** —————

In the Hebrew Bible these five verses make up chap. 3. The phrase "and afterward" marks a major strophic division but also maintains continuity with the previous strophe.[1] The pouring out of the Spirit is distinct from but analogous to the pouring out of rain on the land. Both are saving works of the day of the Lord.

1. Gift of the Spirit (2:28–29)

28"And afterward,
   I will pour out my Spirit on all people.
Your sons and daughters will prophesy,
   your old men will dream dreams,
   your young men will see visions.
29Even on my servants, both men and women,
   I will pour out my Spirit in those days.

2:28 [3:1] The text is not specific in regard to chronology, but it implies that the gift of the Spirit would come after the nation had recovered from the agricultural and military disasters Deuteronomy had foretold. In 2 Sam 2:1; 8:1; 10:1; 13:1; 21:18, the same Hebrew phrase is translated "in the course of time." Indeed, the temporal aspect is of minimal significance here; what really matters is that this is a new and distinctive manifestation of the day of the Lord.[2]

The Bible several times associates the Holy Spirit with water or describes

---

[1] The line וְהָיָה אַחֲרֵי־כֵן is to some degree disjunctive, but the conjunctive form also links it to the preceding material.

[2] According to Acts 2:17, Peter understood this phrase in an eschatological sense and so paraphrased it as ἐν ταῖς ἐσχάταις ἡμέραις ("in the last days"). The LXX has μετὰ ταῦτα, "after these things." Peter's transformation of the text implies that he believed that he and his contemporaries had witnessed the beginning of the messianic age.

him metaphorically as something that can be poured out (Isa 44:3; Ezek 39:29; Zech 12:10; Rom 5:5). Joel easily turned this imagery to his advantage and created a parallel between the gift of rain and the pouring out of the Spirit. Amos similarly linked the image of a famine to a lack of the word of God (Amos 8:11).

The prophets often associated the Spirit with the eschatological era, but they did not always do it in precisely the same manner as did Joel. As H. W. Wolff points out, Ezekiel promised that in the age to come God would by his Spirit enable people to obey God from the heart (Ezek 36:26–27). Isaiah foretold a day when God would pour out[3] his Spirit in order to create a new community and a new people of God (32:14–18; 44:3–5).[4] In Joel, by contrast, the gift of the Spirit is prophetic. It enables people to prophesy, to experience revelatory dreams, and to see visions. These different aspects of the eschatological outpouring of the Spirit do not contradict but complement each other. The gift of the Spirit connotes direct experience with God, as in Joel, as well as the grace that enables his people to love God from the heart, as in Ezekiel. It also is the distinctive sign and mark of membership in the new people of God, as in Isaiah. In short, the coming age would be an age marked by the presence of the Spirit (contrast 1 Sam 3:1).

The Bible frequently links the Holy Spirit to prophetic or visionary experiences. The focal passage here is Num 11:24–30, in which the Spirit of God descended upon seventy elders of Israel and they all prophesied. Two of these elders, however, prophesied in the middle of the Israelite camp. Joshua, taking on the role of a religious authority, was alarmed at this development and implored Moses to put a halt to the display. To this Moses replied: "Are you jealous for my sake? I wish that all the LORD's people were prophets and that the LORD would put his Spirit on them!" (v. 29). Joel apparently envisaged the coming of the Spirit as the fulfillment of Moses' prayer.

Many other passages also associate the coming of the Spirit upon a person with ecstatic or even unnatural behavior (1 Sam 10:6; 19:20; Acts 2:15–17; 10:44–46; 19:1–6). Many texts link the prophetic gift to dreams and visions (Gen 31:10–13; 37:5–11; Isa 6; Ezek 12:27; Dan 9:24; Acts 10:9–16). On the other hand, the Bible also warns about the lying dreams and visions of false prophets (Deut 13:1–5; Jer 14:14; 23:25). The Book of Joel obviously intends here true prophetic experiences brought about by the Spirit of God. The dreams, visions, and prophecies serve to authenticate the presence of the Spirit and to draw the individual into a direct experience with God. For Joel the gift of the prophetic Spirit marked in a new way that God was establish-

---

[3] Curiously, Isaiah uses different words for "pour out" from those found in Joel. Isaiah 32:15 uses the *niphal* of ערה, whereas 44:3 uses the *qal* of יצק. Joel uses the *qal* of שׁפך.

[4] H. W. Wolff, *Joel and Amos,* Her (Philadelphia: Fortress, 1977), 66.

ing himself as the God of Israel and was putting an end to the old order.

The major characteristic of the outpouring of the Spirit is its universality. All the people of God receive the Spirit. The text specifically erases the major social distinctions of the ancient world: gender, age, and economic status. In an era in which men (not women), the old (not the young), and the landowners (not slaves) ruled society, Joel explicitly rejected all such distinctions as criteria for receiving the Holy Spirit. For Paul the fulfillment of this text is that in Christ there is neither Jew nor Greek, neither male nor female, and neither slave nor free (Gal 3:28).

In this text, however, the Spirit is universal in that he is given to all Israel (cf. Ezek 39:29; Zech 12:10) rather than to all humanity (note "*your* sons and daughters . . . *your* old men . . . *your* young men"; italics added). This does not mean, however, that Joel altogether excluded Gentiles from participation in the kingdom of God.[5] Rather, speaking to his own dispirited generation, he emphasized that Israel and not some other nation would have this great proof that God is among them. From the biblical perspective the Gentiles' reception of the Spirit does not mean that God is no longer God of Israel but that Gentiles have submitted to Israel's God. In summary, for Joel the gift of the Spirit to Israel was vindication of their status as the people of God as well as the source of their power to reconstitute as a community of obedience under God's favor. The surprising turn of events in the New Testament (Acts 10:45) has not invalidated that vision but has extended it.

2:29 [3:2] It is perhaps noteworthy that Joel, in extending the promise of the Spirit to slaves, again asserts that both males and females will receive the gift.[6] It is as though he wanted to insure that there be no possibility that a segment of society has been excluded.

2. Signs of the Day of the Lord (2:30–31)

> [30]I will show wonders in the heavens
>   and on the earth,
>   blood and fire and billows of smoke.
> [31]The sun will be turned to darkness
>   and the moon to blood
>   before the coming of the great and dreadful day of the LORD.

2:30 [3:3] Once again the text associates these events with the day of the Lord.[7] What is curious, however, is that a message of salvation, the gift of

---

[5] Note the implicit universality of "everyone" in v. 32. "Zion" as the locus of salvation in that verse implies identifying with the God of Israel.

[6] "My" in "my servants" is not in the Hebrew.

[7] D. Stuart (*Hosea–Jonah*, WBC [Dallas: Word, 1987], 261) discerns a chiastic unity to vv. 30–31 (I [= Yahweh]: sky: earth // earth portents: sky portents: Yahweh).

the Spirit, is linked with images of violence and doom. The fire and columns of smoke are traditional images of theophany (as in the pillars of cloud and fire in the exodus; Exod 13:21–22; 14:19–24; cf. also 19:16,18; 20:18),[8] but they also are apocalyptic, foreboding images, especially when combined with "blood" (e.g., Ezek 32:6–8; Rev 8:7). The mention of blood recalls the first plague on the Egyptians at the exodus (Exod 7:14–24).[9] For Joel the day of the Lord was not exclusively judgment or salvation; it was simply the coming of God to deal with people. For some this means life; for others it means death (2 Cor 2:16).

Other biblical texts associate the coming of the Spirit with judgment. John the Baptist said that the Christ would baptize with the Holy Spirit and with fire (Matt 3:11). At Pentecost the Holy Spirit came upon the people as "tongues of fire" (Acts 2:3), but in that case the fire emphasized the divine presence without apparently implying judgment. Peter, when citing this text from Joel in the course of his Pentecost sermon, included the reference to the blood, fire, and smoke even though visions of blood and smoke at least were not present. Peter appears to have interpreted the gift of the Spirit as the inauguration of the eschatological age (see excursus below).

2:31 [3:4]   As elsewhere in Joel, the darkening of the sky represents the undoing of creation (cf. 2:2,10). The great lights in the sky (Gen 1:14–19) cease to give their light. Every occurrence of the day of the Lord, be it a locust plague or the pouring out of the Spirit (cf. 1:15; 2:1,11; 3:14), is a manifestation of the great day of the Lord.

Excursus: The Interpretation of Joel 2:28–32 in the New Testament

Peter begins his Pentecost sermon by quoting Joel 2:28–32 in its entirety (Acts 2:16–21). He asserts that the glossolalia of the Christians at the temple was the fulfillment of Joel's prophecy: "This is what was spoken by the prophet Joel" (Acts 2:16). Obviously enough, however, not everything that Joel prophesied (and that Peter cited) came to pass that day. Joel spoke of dreams and visions (Joel 2:28; Acts 2:17) and of the darkening of the sun and moon[10] (Joel 2:30; Acts 2:19), but none of this took place on Pentecost. We must therefore ask ourselves what Peter meant by saying that the experience of the Christians that day fulfilled Joel's prophecy; and, more fundamentally, we must determine how the New Testament writers interpreted Joel in light of their experience of the pouring out of the Spirit.

Christians have dealt with the problem of Peter's citation of Joel in a number of ways. Classic covenant theology asserts that the Pentecost experience was

---

[8] The word here for "billows," תִּימֲרוֹת, occurs elsewhere only in Song 3:6, translated "column." The word in Exodus is עָמֻוד (cf. also Judg 20:40).

[9] Wolff argues that מוֹפְתִים ("wonders") are associated especially with the exodus (*Joel and Amos*, 68). See Deut 6:22; Jer 32:20.

[10] The Western recension omits αἷμα καὶ πῦρ καὶ ἀτμίδα καπνοῦ ("blood and fire and billows of smoke") from v. 19, but this does not really remove the problem.

indeed the fulfillment of Joel's prophecy. It has generally taken the signs in the sky in more of a spiritual than a literal sense. Some scholars suggest that the signs that accompanied Jesus' crucifixion (e.g., the darkening of the sky, Matt 27:45) fulfilled the prophecy of the darkening of the sun and moon.[11] But it is not clear how or under what hermeneutical rules the darkening of the sun and moon might be given a "spiritual" significance in the context of Peter's sermon[12] (although Joel himself did not always speak of the darkening of the sky in a context that favors a literal interpretation). Also, even though it is certain that the darkening of the sky during Jesus' crucifixion indicated that his death, too, was the day of the Lord and had great eschatological significance, it is debatable whether Peter's citation of Joel is retrospective. It does not appear that Peter was calling on his audience to recall the darkness of the crucifixion or to find some "spiritual" significance in the phrase.

Classic dispensationalism moves in the opposite direction. It claims that the Pentecost experience did not fulfill Joel's prophecy at all. Dispensationalists have argued that since the sun and moon were not darkened, Pentecost cannot be what Joel 2:28–32 anticipates. Thus Peter cited Joel's prophecy "as an *illustration* of what was taking place in his day" and as a "guarantee" of a future pouring out of the Spirit.[13] This approach, however, must contend with strong scholarly consensus that it is unacceptable to take Peter's "this is what was spoken by the prophet Joel" (Acts 2:16) as meaning that Joel illustrates the Pentecost experience or that Pentecost guaranteed some *future* pouring out the Spirit to fulfill

---

[11] Thus F. F. Bruce, *The Book of Acts*, NICNT (Grand Rapids: Eerdmans, 1954), 69.

[12] For a good but, in my view, unsuccessful attempt at a "spiritual" interpretation of this text, see A. Kerrigan, "The 'Sensus Plenior' of Joel, III, 1–5 in Act., II, 14–36," *Sacra Pagina. Miscellanea biblica congressus internationalis catholicide re biblica*. BETL 13, ed. J. Coppens (Gemblous: Editions J. Duculot, 1959), 295–313. Kerrigan sees the darkening of the sky as a metaphor for Jesus' conflict with Satan.

[13] E. S. English, ed., *The New Scofield Reference Bible* (New York: Oxford University Press, 1967), 930 (emphasis added). Many current dispensationalists, who call themselves "progressive dispensationalists," reject the illustration/analogy view and recognize the Pentecost event as the first of a two stage fulfillment of Joel. The spiritual aspects of the OT kingdom promises have been fulfilled, but the physical, national aspects await the millennium. See H. Heater, Jr., "Evidence from Joel and Amos," and D. L. Bock, "Evidence from Acts," in *A Case for Premillennialism: A New Consensus*, ed. D. K. Campbell and J. L. Townsend (Chicago: Moody, 1992), 157–64,191–94; D. L. Bock, "The Reign of the Lord Christ," in *Dispensationalism, Israel and the Church: The Search for Definition*, ed. C. A. Blaising and D. L. Bock (Grand Rapids: Zondervan, 1992), 47–49; and R. L. Saucy, *The Case for Progressive Dispensationalism* (Grand Rapids: Zondervan, 1993), 76,179,211. The progressive dispensational exposition is thus more faithful to the intent of the text than is the interpretation of its classical dispensational forebears. Indeed, the inaugurated eschatology that the progressive position espouses is very similar to the interpretation advocated here. One must question, however, whether progressive dispensationalism is truly dispensationalism, the essence of which is the separation of Israel from the church in the plan of God. Once it be granted that the fulfillment of an OT prophecy to Israel has taken place in the "Church Age," then the very linchpin of dispensational theology has been removed. Without that linchpin, the distinctive doctrines of dispensationalism (notably the "pretribulation rapture of the church") lose their principal justification. Whatever one may make of it, classic dispensationalism has theological consistency, and thus it makes for a better sparring partner than its progressive offspring.

Joel's words. Plainly and simply, Peter said that what the people saw in the temple on Pentecost was exactly what Joel anticipated.[14]

Furthermore, some dispensational interpreters have as much difficulty locating the fulfillment of Joel's prophecy in the future as they do in relating it to Pentecost. J. Walvoord, for example, contends that Joel 2:28–32 concerns Israel's future, but he is unclear on whether it is fulfilled in the "tribulation" or in the millennium. On the one hand, he contends that the tribulation period will be the time when the wonders Joel described will occur, and he argues that the ministry of the Spirit is especially important during this dark time. But on the other hand, he maintains the dispensational doctrine that the Spirit will be notable for his absence during the tribulation. In addition, he cites Joel 2:28–29 to prove that millennial believers will possess the Spirit but fails to explain whether the sky will be darkened during the millennium in keeping with vv. 30–31. He does not resolve the question of which one, the tribulation or the millennium, will be the time of the "real" fulfillment of Joel.[15]

Some interpreters, we should add, skirt around the interpretation of the darkening of the sky in Peter's citation. They contend that Peter cited these verses merely because he wanted to get to Joel 2:32, which promises that whoever calls on the name of the Lord will be saved.[16] This, too, is inadequate. Even if Peter had not cited Joel 2:29–30, we would still have to wrestle with how these verses in Joel relate to the pouring out of the Spirit. The fact that Peter *did* cite them makes it all the more imperative for us to reckon with them.

Our starting point should be that the disciples, following the preaching of John the Baptist, expected the messianic era to be accompanied by two great events: the gift of the Spirit and a great day of judgment. When questioned about the significance of his ministry, John consistently asserted that he was not the Messiah but that he only offered a token of what the Messiah would do. John baptized with water, but the Messiah would baptize "with the Holy Spirit and with fire" (Matt 3:11; Luke 3:16). These two clearly represent salvation and judgment. "Fire" is not in this passage symbolic of the saving power of the Spirit (as in the "tongues of fire" in Acts 2:3) but represents, as it often does, judgment and holy fury (as in the archetypical episode of divine judgment, the pouring of fire on Sodom and Gomorrah; Gen 19:24). As if to spell out what he meant by "fire," John illustrated his point by saying that the Messiah already has the winnowing fork in his hand and that he will gather the wheat into his granary but burn the chaff "with unquenchable fire" (Matt 3:12; Luke 3:17). In short, the dis-

---

[14] Contra R. D. Patterson, who contends that the Pentecost experience was a "corroborative pledge" to the ultimate fulfillment of the Joel prophecy in the "eschatological complex," by which he seems to mean the millennium ("Joel," 258).

[15] J. Walvoord, *The Holy Spirit* (Findlay, Ohio: Dunham, 1954), 228–34.

[16] Thus G. A. Krodel, *Acts*, Augsburg Commentary on the New Testament (Minneapolis: Augsburg, 1986), 81. Krodel believes that Luke separated the heavenly signs from the gifts of the Spirit in Luke 21:10–12,25–26 but that the citation in Acts 2:19–20 was given in order to move to the promise in v. 21 (and thus apparently has no relevance for the Pentecost experience).

ciples believed that the Messiah would pour out the Spirit on his people and pour out the wrath of God on sinners.[17]

It is significant that Peter's citation of Joel in some points differs from the Hebrew text.[18] Most significant is the change from "and afterward" in Joel 2:28 to "in the last days" in Acts 2:17.[19] By making this subtle shift, Peter signified his belief that the gift of the Spirit was a sign of the "last days," that is, the messianic era. The great age of grace and judgment has begun, and the gift of the Spirit, Peter argued, is proof of this. Elsewhere Peter maintained the doctrine that the messianic age in which we find ourselves is the long-awaited "last days" (1 Pet 1:20; 2 Pet 3:3).

Luke utilized the language and imagery of Joel throughout Acts 2 (e.g., vv. 38–39) to show that the Pentecost event was the fulfillment (at least in an inaugurated form) of the eschatological expectations of the Old Testament prophet. C. A. Evans has demonstrated numerous points of contact between the two texts. He finds twenty words in Acts 2 that also occur in Joel and several rhetorical parallels as well.[20]

It hardly matters that not all of the events of Joel's prophecy occur *at the same time*. In fact, it is not even possible, and Joel did not claim that the sky would go dark at the same moment that the Spirit was poured out. It would do little good for God to give the gift of the Spirit and the power to prophesy if on the very same day he brought the world to an end. The very fact that people would "dream dreams" implies some passage of time and not an instant or simultaneous fulfillment of the entire prophecy. No one can seriously object that Pentecost did not fulfill Joel's prophecy on the grounds that no one had yet had revelatory dreams. After all, at the time of Peter's sermon the Spirit had only come within the hour.

Peter's point was not that every detail of Joel 2:28–32 came to pass on Pentecost but that Pentecost marks the beginning of the messianic era of which Joel spoke. As far as the early Christians were concerned, the pouring out of the Spirit established that the end of the ages had come. If the Spirit had come down, it was only a matter of time before the fire would come down too. The fact that neither Joel nor Peter knew how much time might elapse between the pouring out of the

---

[17] For a good discussion of the meaning of "with fire" in this context, see R. H. Stein, *Luke*, NAC (Nashville: Broadman, 1992), 134–35, and C. A. Evans, *Luke*, NIBC (Peabody, Mass.: Hendrickson, 1990), 49. We should note that regardless of what one does with καὶ πυρί in Luke 3:16 (Matt 3:11), Luke 3:17 (Matt 3:12) clearly implies that the disciples expected judgment to be part of the messianic era.

[18] For a study of the differences between the two texts, see R. F. Zehnle, *Peter's Pentecost Discourse*, SBLMS 15 (New York: Abingdon, 1971), 28–34. Also Peter spoke of "wonders in the heaven above and signs on the earth below" (Acts 2:19), where Joel merely has "wonders in the heavens and on the earth" (Joel 2:30).

[19] Note that the LXX, in agreement with the MT (and against Peter's words), has μετὰ ταῦτα ("after these things"). Peter was not merely quoting the LXX.

[20] C. A. Evans, "The Prophetic Setting of the Pentecost Sermon," *ZNW* 74 (1983): 148–50. As an example, Evans notes that Joel 1:3 calls on the old men to tell their children, and Peter exhorted his audience that "the promise is for you and your children" (Acts 2:39).

Spirit and the final judgment is irrelevant; the important point is that the gift of the Spirit inaugurated the "end of the age," the messianic era.[21]

It follows that there is no need for a subsequent Jewish Pentecost in the tribulation or millennium to fulfill Joel's prophecy. In fact, the event of Acts 2 was a Jewish Pentecost. The "Gentile Pentecost" took place in Acts 10:44–45 when, to the astonishment of the Jews present, the Spirit came upon the Gentiles of the household of Cornelius.

This leads us to one other aspect of the messianic era, one that John the Baptist and Jesus' disciples did not initially grasp. This is the extension of salvation and full citizenship in Zion to Gentiles. Various Old Testament texts had foretold this (Isa 2:2; 51:5; Ps 87). It was Paul, however, who recognized that the Gentiles who received "the promised Holy Spirit" have been "included in Christ" along with the Jews. The barrier between the two has been broken down, and they have become "one new man out of the two" since "both have access to the Father by one Spirit." Gentiles are thus "fellow citizens" with the Jews and are becoming "a dwelling in which God lives by his Spirit" (Eph 1:13; 2:11–22). Paul understood the mystery that Gentiles are heirs together with Israel (Eph 3:6) and that this aspect of the messianic era is demonstrated by the gift of the Spirit to Gentiles.

But the fulfillment of the prophecy of Joel was in one sense altogether baffling for the early Jewish Christians. Their reading of the Scriptures had led them to believe that the gift of the Spirit would lead directly to the vindication and triumph of Israel. This, indeed, is what one might naturally expect from the Book of Joel, especially if one were to read it superficially and in isolation from other biblical teachings. To the surprise and consternation of early Jewish Christians, however, the majority of Jews continued to reject their Messiah, Jesus of Nazareth. Instead, uncircumcised Gentiles were becoming the leaders of a church in which Jews were increasingly marginalized. Far from being exalted above all nations, Jerusalem would be burned to the ground in A.D. 70. It was this situation of rising Jewish vexation over how the messianic era was actually turning out that led Paul, in about A.D. 55 or 58, to compose the letter to the Romans and in particular Romans 9–11. We are in the messianic era, and this is the fulfillment of the plan of God, Paul insisted. But what we had not foreseen, what was "mystery," was the determination of God to graft Gentiles into the Israel of God.

In summary the New Testament asserts that Joel's prophecy concerns the eschatological era and that we are now in that era. The church is not an interruption in the plan of God. This *is* the messianic age. The Spirit has come, Zion has already been exalted in that Gentiles have joined Israel in the worship of Israel's God, and the judgment of this world has begun. We await the culmination of all things.[22]

---

[21] See also R. N. Longenecker, "The Acts of the Apostles," EBC (Grand Rapids: Zondervan, 1981), 9:275–76.

3. Promise of Salvation (2:32)

[32]And everyone who calls
   on the name of the LORD will be saved;
 for on Mount Zion and in Jerusalem
   there will be deliverance,
   as the LORD has said,
 among the survivors
   whom the LORD calls.

2:32 [3:5]   This is as close as Joel came to opening the doors of salvation explicitly to Gentiles: Everyone who calls on the name of the Lord will
be saved.[23] Even here one could restrict the meaning to Jews in light of the
fact that he was addressing a Jewish audience, but such a constriction of the
meaning of the text would not be in character with the rest of the message of
the Old Testament. The eschatology of the Old Testament frequently asserts
Gentile inclusion in the eschatological kingdom. Psalm 87, as noted earlier,
says that someday Gentiles from all over the world, even from among Israel's
worst enemies, will claim Zion as their place of birth. They will claim Israel
and Israel's God as their own. Indeed, the very purpose behind the creation of
Israel was to be a blessing to many nations (Gen 12:1–3; cf. also Isa 19:23–
25). Paul appeals to Joel 2:32 as support for Gentile inclusion in the gospel
(Rom 10:12–13), and James cited Amos 9:11–12 in Acts 15:16–18.

Apart from the issue of Gentile inclusion, we see in this text that deliverance is dependent on being one who "calls on the LORD." The phrase implies
identifying Yahweh as one's own God.[24] This is not a prayer of desperation
in a moment of crisis but the consistent identification with the God of Israel.
It includes confessing him before the nations (Isa 12:4; Ps 105:1). It also
involves faithfulness to the Lord through a period of trial (Zech 13:9). Above
all else, identification with the Lord is a response to the pouring out of the
Spirit (Isa 44:3–5).

At the same time the saved are not simply those who call on the Lord but
those whom the Lord calls. As Dillard states, "This verse is one of those sub-
lime statements of Scripture which integrate in a single breath what has
always been for theologians a paradox, that tension between moral responsi-

---

[22] Prophecies concerning the future "kingdom" for Israel stress above all else that Israel would
achieve preeminence over the Gentiles—foreigners would submit to them (Isa 60:10–11), and Zion
would be exalted above all other mountains (Mic 4:1). In the NT we discover that the prophecy is
fulfilled by Gentiles coming to worship the God of Israel in the person of Jesus Christ. This at least
opens the question of whether there is any need or place for an earthly millennial kingdom.

[23] For another argument in behalf of seeing the extension of salvation to the Gentiles here, see
W. A. VanGemeren, "The Spirit of Restoration," *WTJ* 50 (1988): 81–102, especially pp. 90–93.

[24] Cf. Gen 4:26; 1 Kgs 18:24; 2 Kgs 5:11; 1 Chr 16:8; Pss 79:6; 80:18; 116:13,17; Isa 41:25;
64:7; 65:1; Jer 10:25; Zeph 3:9; Acts 9:14,21; Rom 10:13; 1 Cor 1:2.

bility and the sovereignty of God."[25] People must call on the Lord and identify with him if they are to experience his salvation; on the other hand, none can come to the Lord unless the Lord draws them (John 6:44).

The phrase "as the LORD has said" has attracted a great deal of attention. Is this to be understood as a direct quote from another prophet? If so, it would seem to be from Obadiah 17, "But on Mount Zion will be deliverance." Joel 2:32 is different only for having added "and in Jerusalem."[26] If this is in fact a direct quote of Obadiah, then one can only with great difficulty (by making Obadiah out to be a preexilic book) avoid dating Joel as a postexilic text.

On the other hand, it is doubtful that the formula "as the LORD has said" can be construed as a citation of a written text. Elsewhere in the Old Testament this phrase refers to a direct quote from Yahweh himself and not to a citation of a prophetic book.[27] By contrast, when the elders in Jer 26:18 cite the Book of Micah, they refer to it as the book of "Micah of Moresheth." Although it is possible that Joel used this formula to cite a written text, this is not the probable interpretation. It is more likely that "as the LORD has said" is an assertion that Joel's words are authentically from Yahweh, much like the more common formula "thus says the LORD."

---

[25] R. B. Dillard, "Joel," in *The Minor Prophets* (Grand Rapids: Baker, 1991), 1:298.

[26] That and the minor difference that Obad 17 has וּבְהַר where Joel has כִּי בְהַר.

[27] See Gen 21:1, where the Lord dealt with Sarah כַּאֲשֶׁר אָמָר; Exod 9:35, where Pharaoh's heart was hardened כַּאֲשֶׁר דִּבֶּר יהוה; Num 14:17, where Moses asked Yahweh to show his great power כַּאֲשֶׁר דִּבַּרְתָּ לֵאמֹר (one could take this as a textual citation of Exod 34:6–7, but it seems that the account itself requires us to take it as Moses' quotation of what he personally heard Yahweh say); and Josh 11:9, where Joshua did כַּאֲשֶׁר אָמַר־לוֹ יהוה. In every case the speaker was citing Yahweh directly and not via a written text.

VII. JUDGMENT ON NATIONS: ALL NATIONS DESTROYED (3:1–21 [4:1–21])

1. The Valley of Jehoshaphat (3:1–3 [4:1–3])
2. Tyre, Sidon, and Philistia (3:4–8 [4:4–8])
3. Summons to All Nations (3:9–12 [4:9–12])
4. The Winepress of the Lord (3:13 [4:13])
5. Signs of the Day of the Lord (3:14–17 [4:14–17])
6. The Final State (3:18–21 [4:18–21])

VII. JUDGMENT ON NATIONS: ALL NATIONS DESTROYED (3:1–21 [4:1–21])

Chapter 3 (chap. 4 in Heb.) describes a final, climactic battle with the nations of the world and Yahweh's condemnation of those nations. Depending on how one has read Joel up to this point, this is either a logical and appropriate development in the text or an abrupt change apparently unconnected to what precedes. Interpreters who contend that Joel has through chap. 2 spoken only of a locust plague on Jerusalem can only artificially tie these chapters to chap. 3. After all, the Gentile nations had nothing to do with the coming of the locust plague on Jerusalem. Earlier critical scholars were perhaps more honest in their assessment of the situation than some recent interpreters who see only locusts in chaps. 1 and 2. As early as 1872, M. Vernes declared that the subject matter was so diverse that 2:28–3:21 (chaps. 3; 4 in Heb.) could not come from the author of the earlier part of the book.[1]

The situation is altogether different, however, when one recognizes that in 2:1–11 Joel shifted away from literal locusts to destruction and captivity at the hand of the northern army, an army he described under the metaphor of a locust invasion. Viewed in this light, the movement from locusts, to the ultimate calamity of the exile, to forgiveness and restoration, and finally to the judgment on the nations is not only logical but necessary. Had Joel not included this chapter, the book would be without a resolution.

---

[1] J. A. Bewer, "Joel," in *A Critical and Exegetical Commentary on Micah, Zephaniah, Nahum, Habakkuk, Obadiah and Joel*, ICC (Edinburgh: T & T Clark, 1911), 49. Bewer himself is able to maintain the unity of the book only by excising a considerable amount of the book and by asserting that Joel wrote on "two different subjects" (pp. 50–51).

1. The Valley of Jehoshaphat (3:1–3 [4:1–3])

> ¹"In those days and at that time,
>   when I restore the fortunes of Judah and Jerusalem,
> ²I will gather all nations
>   and bring them down to the Valley of Jehoshaphat.
> There I will enter into judgment against them
>   concerning my inheritance, my people Israel,
> for they scattered my people among the nations
>   and divided up my land.
> ³They cast lots for my people
>   and traded boys for prostitutes;
> they sold girls for wine
>   that they might drink.

3:1 [4:1]   Prophetic references to "those days" and "that time" are not as chronological as they might appear. Joel, like all the prophets, has given us promises of salvation and not a timetable for the future. "Those days" refers to the salvation events of those days rather than to a historical sequence. The text in effect says that God's works of grace relate to one another in the same way that his acts of judgment relate to one another. The locust plague is the day of the Lord and therefore, theologically viewed, is part of the same event as the captivity. The healing of the land after the locust plague, the destruction of the northern army, the gift of the Spirit, and the last judgment are also all saving manifestations of the selfsame day of the Lord. On the other hand, this phrase does encourage the reader about the future. When believers see one of the promises fulfilled, they rightly feel assurance that the other promises also are drawing near. After the gift of the Spirit at Pentecost, the early Christians correctly viewed themselves as having entered the "eschatological age."

The translation "restore the fortunes," although a common rendering, is misleading. This phrase makes it sound as though the only concern was that Judah had gone through difficult times, such as an economic downturn of the sort that all nations routinely experience. "Restore the fortunes" can be taken to mean no more than "things will get better." This is not the meaning here. The phrase should be rendered either "make a restoration of Judah and

Jerusalem" or even "restore the captivity of Judah and Jerusalem."[2] In all cases where the Bible refers to the restoration of a nation, this idiom denotes restoration from captivity.[3] Joel reminded his people of the ancient promise of Deut 30:3 that Yahweh would restore his people from the coming diaspora. Their restoration would be a sign of judgment to the rest of the world.[4]

3:2 [4:2] The Old Testament several times speaks of "gathering" the nations for judgment. Especially similar to this text is Zeph 3:8—"I have decided [lit., "my decision/judgment is"] to assemble the nations, to gather the kingdoms and to pour out my wrath on them."[5] The Zephaniah prophecy, like the others, comes in a context of restoration after an exile at the hands of a foreign enemy, and it would be strange to suppose that Joel has broken the pattern by jumping directly from an account of a locust plague to the destruction of all nations.[6]

Joel probably spoke of the final judgment taking place in a valley because he was using the metaphor of a battle between Yahweh and the

---

[2] A number of scholars defend the translation "restore the fortunes" for אָשִׁיב אֶת־שְׁבוּת (following the qere). H. W. Wolff cites the Sefire stele to the effect that it means "make a restoration of" and not "restore the captivity" (Joel and Amos, Her [Philadelphia: Fortress, 1977], 76). But even "make a restoration" (unlike "restore the fortunes") can be taken to imply a return from captivity. The use of the phrase in other biblical texts indicates unambiguously that this is how the Hebrews used it. In Deut 30:2–3 Moses predicted that the Israelites in captivity (cf. 29:22–24) would repent, וְשָׁב יהוה אֱלֹהֶיךָ אֶת־שְׁבוּתְךָ, "and the LORD your God will restore your captivity." See also Ezek 16:53; 39:25. The LXX similarly translates the Joel verse as ὅταν ἐπιστρέψω τὴν αἰχμαλωσίαν "when I restore the captivity." Even in texts that speak of the agricultural devastation of the land and its final restoration, the idea of captivity is almost always conspicuous in context (see Jer 29:14; 30:3,18; 31:23; 32:42–44; 33:7,11,26; 48:47; 49:39; Ezek 29:14; Hos 6:11; Amos 9:14; Zeph 2:7; 3:20; Pss 14:7[6]; 85:2[1]; 126:4; Lam 2:14).

[3] Job 42:10 uses this idiom to describe the return of God's favor to an individual in a slightly different manner: וַיהוה שָׁב אֶת־שְׁבִית [qere שְׁבוּת] אִיּוֹב, "And Yahweh restored the reversal of Job." Even here, the context is not a simple economic restoration but healing after Job had lost all his children, his property, and his health. Psalm 53:7[6] is somewhat ambiguous but does not contradict the evidence found elsewhere. At any rate, the context of Joel 4 [3] plainly is one of conflict with the great powers of the world, and "captivity" is thus implied. Cf. Dillard, "Joel," in The Minor Prophets (Grand Rapids: Baker, 1991), 1:300.

[4] Paul also regarded the diaspora and unbelief of the Jews, as well as their salvation, as having eschatological significance. "For if their rejection is the reconciliation of the world, what will their acceptance be but life from the dead?" (Rom 11:15).

[5] Note that Zeph 3:8, like Joel 3:2, uses the verb קָבַץ, "gather," the noun גּוֹיִם, "nations," and the root שׁפט (Joel has וְנִשְׁפַּטְתִּי, "I will enter into judgment," and speaks of the valley of יְהוֹשָׁפָט; Zephaniah has מִשְׁפָּטִי, "my decision").

[6] Also Ezek 38:22 uses וְנִשְׁפַּטְתִּי (in exactly the same form as here in Joel) to describe Yahweh's destruction of the invading armies of Gog.

nations.[7] Battles are generally fought in valleys, not on mountaintops. The word "Jehoshaphat" means "Yahweh judges" and is most often identified with the famous valley of Jezreel extending from Mount Carmel past Megiddo and on to Bet Shean and the Jordan River. This valley has seen many historical battles and is often identified as the site of the Battle of Armageddon in Rev 16:16. Joel does not provide a geographical marker, however, and indeed as a symbol for the final judgment, it hardly needs specific identification. Wolff has stated it best: "The prophet knows the geographical location as little as he knows an exact date for the final conflict of Yahweh with the nations."[8]

Judgment begins with the house of God, but ultimately those of the faith are vindicated as judgment turns to vindication and God shows himself to be the guardian of his own people.[9] God guards his people as a man guards the apple (i.e., pupil) of his eye (Deut 32:10). The two specific offenses mentioned at the end of this verse (scattering the Israelites and taking their land) both refer to foreign invasion and exile.

3:3 [4:3] Obadiah 11 and Nah 3:10 both associate casting lots over refugees with the horrors that accompany capture of a city by a foreign army. Perhaps the Bible also associates Jesus with the suffering of the defeated in the casting of lots over his garments (Ps 22:18; Matt 27:35). After the capture of a city, victorious soldiers took boys and girls (older people were killed off) and sold them as slaves. The fact that the price of these slaves only bought a night with a prostitute or a little wine shows how cheaply they were regarded (cf. Amos 2:6).[10] In contrast to the behavior of these nations, Exod 21:16 forbids kidnapping people to sell them as slaves, and Deut 21:14 prohibits the sale of prisoners of war in Israel.[11]

2. Tyre, Sidon, and Philistia (3:4–8 [4:4–8])

[4]"Now what have you against me, O Tyre and Sidon and all you regions of Philistia? Are you repaying me for something I have done? If you are paying me back, I will swiftly and speedily return on your own heads what you have done.

---

[7] Contra Ahlström, *Joel and the Temple Cult of Jerusalem*, VTS 21 (Leiden: Brill, 1971), 76–77, who wants to find a cultic explanation for the mention of a valley in this text. D. A. Hubbard also notes that valleys are places of judgment in several prophets, e.g., Isa 22:10; Jer 7:31–34; 19:7; Ezek 39:11; Zech 14:4–5 (*Joel and Amos,* TOTC [Downers Grove: InterVarsity, 1989], 75.

[8] H. W. Wolff, *Joel and Amos,* Her (Philadelphia: Fortress, 1977), 76. For a thorough analysis of possible locations for the valley, see Dillard, "Joel," 300–301.

[9] The word עַמִּי ("my people") implies the covenant relationship.

[10] C. F. Keil especially sees parallels in this text to the sufferings of the Jews in the Roman wars (*The Minor Prophets* (Grand Rapids, Eerdmans, n.d.), 221–22).

[11] Pointed out in D. Stuart, *Hosea–Jonah,* WBC (Dallas: Word, 1987), 267. As Hubbard points out, "Scarcely anything rankles God more than inhumanity" (*Joel and Amos,* 75).

⁵**For you took my silver and my gold and carried off my finest treasures to your temples. ⁶You sold the people of Judah and Jerusalem to the Greeks, that you might send them far from their homeland.**

⁷**"See, I am going to rouse them out of the places to which you sold them, and I will return on your own heads what you have done. ⁸I will sell your sons and daughters to the people of Judah, and they will sell them to the Sabeans, a nation far away." The LORD has spoken.**

Many scholars believe this to be a later interpolation because of its more prosaic structure and because of how it suddenly shifts attention from the great day of judgment on all nations to some relatively minor incidents of ethnic crimes against Israel.[12] Stuart argues that it is not unusual for Joel to insert a prose section in the middle of a poetic section since (as Stuart believes) Joel did this in 2:18–20a.[13] One may question, however, why interpreters (including the NIV) persist in treating 3:4–8 [Heb. 4:4–8] as prose at all. The *BHS* analysis of these verses as poetry meets the requirements for both poetic structure (parallelism) and meter.[14]

It is hardly out of character for an Old Testament prophet to move to and fro between prophecies that have a universal, eschatological reference and those that relate specifically to incidents and concerns of their own times. On the contrary, it is the norm. Joel did this elsewhere in this chapter (v. 19), and we should not be surprised that he did it here. In short, the only reason for treating this as an interpolation is that it contradicts modern aesthetic notions about the cohesiveness of a text. From the standpoint of Old Testament prophecy, this passage is not exceptional.

3:4 [4:4] The obvious first question to ask of this text is why it singles out the Phoenicians (Tyre and Sidon) and the Philistines for condemnation. These nations did not constitute the great enemies of the north, nor would they have been a significant contingent in the gathering of nations at the "Valley of Jehoshaphat." Great powers conspicuous for their absence here (at least in terms of explicit mention) include Egypt, Babylon, Assyria, and Persia. The Greeks are mentioned not as a world empire but as an apparently distant people to whose traders the Phoenicians and Philistines sold Jewish slaves. Any reference to the Greek states of Alexander's empire here is out of the question.

At least three solutions are possible; to some degree all may be correct. First, the Phoenicians and Philistines may have in Joel's day committed atrocities against Jews about which we have no other information (cf. Amos 1:6,9). In keeping with the prophets' practice of merging events of their own time with eschatological events, Joel may have cited these recent atrocities to assure his

---

[12] For example, Bewer, "Joel," 130–31.

[13] Stuart, *Hosea–Jonah*, 265. I do not agree with the assessment that 2:18–20a is prose.

[14] So also J. A. Thompson, "Joel," IB (Nashville: Abingdon, 1956), 6:755.

people that God would avenge their suffering now and in the future. Obadiah similarly related God's punishment of the Edomites to the last judgment (Obad 15). Second, Joel may have condemned the Philistines and Phoenicians for taking advantage of the Jews' weakness while they were being crushed by the northern enemy. The obvious analogy here is again Obadiah, who denounced the Edomites for their atrocities during the fall of Jerusalem to the Babylonians. Third, Joel may have used these nations as examples specifically because they were *not* great world powers. His rhetorical purpose may have been to signal to the reader that not only the great, hated empires but even minor peoples and nations would have to face God's judgment. There is, of course, a fourth possibility. If Joel was written as early in Israel's history as some suggest, the Philistines and Phoenicians may have been the major powers confronting Israel at the time of writing (the Philistines were especially significant rivals to Israel during the late judges and early monarchy periods). So early a date for Joel, however, is unlikely.

The Philistines and Phoenicians apparently felt they had a score to settle with the Jews. What they did not reckon with, however, was that in taking vengeance on Israel they invited the vengeance of God upon themselves because God identified Israel with himself.[15] It is noteworthy that God considers attacks upon Israel to be directed at him. Jesus' words to Saul of Tarsus in Acts 9:4 make a similar connection between Christ and the Church. Elsewhere in the Old Testament, God repays the nations in proportion to how they treat Israel (see esp. Obad 15). The principle that those who bless Israel will be blessed and those who curse Israel will be cursed (Gen 12:3) has been worked out many times in history.[16]

3:5 [4:5]　Although one might be tempted to take the words "my gold" and "my silver" as metaphors for the Jewish people (mentioned in the next verse), the display of these treasures in their temples and palaces[17] establishes that this verse is talking about literal gold and silver. We do not know of any historical incidents that Joel might have had in mind here. One could postulate that the Philistines and Phoenicians joined in the plundering of the temple

---

[15] The conjunctive phrase וְגַם (NIV "now") probably should be translated "furthermore" or "moreover." It simply links the preceding strophe to what follows. It probably should not be taken as emphasizing אַתֶּם ("you"), as in "And as for you . . ." because of the intervening מָה ("what"). The expression מָה־אַתֶּם לִי (lit. "What [are] you to me?"] is used either when someone feels that another party is unjustly giving him or her injury or when someone feels that he or she is being asked to become involved in something that is not his or her business. See R. E. Brown, *The Gospel according to John I–III*, AB (New York: Doubleday, 1966), 99. The phrase here is used in the first sense, that Tyre and Sidon were wrongfully afflicting God.

[16] K. Seybold argues that this verse is useful for differentiating גְּמוּל שִׁלֵּם and הֵשִׁיב גְּמוּל (both basically meaning "avenge" or "pay back") from the verb גָּמַל, which he takes to refer to an action that stems from the willfulness of a wrongdoer ("גָּמַל," *TDOT* 3:32).

[17] The word הֵיכָל can refer to a temple or a palace.

after its destruction in 586 B.C., but the text does not necessarily imply that
this is meant (and anyway we know that the Babylonians carried off the temple treasures, and it is unlikely that they were willing to share). Probably Joel
simply alluded to incidents of plundering Jewish wealth that were known to
him but are unknown to us.[18]

3:6 [4:6]   The mention of Greeks here has no bearing on the date of Joel
except that it tends to support an earlier rather than a later date. The reason is
that sending slaves to the Greeks is here regarded as sending them "far away."
If the text were written after significant Greek expansion into the Near East,
then the presence of Greek colonies and expatriates in the Levant would have
made it impossible for anyone to regard them as a distant nation. Familiarity
shrinks our perception of distance. Those who encountered Greeks relatively
frequently would not have imagined Greece to be at the end of the world.
Here their enemies sell the Jews to Greeks specifically because that insures
that the Jews will be carried far off. In v. 8, similarly, the book promises that
one day Phoenicians and Philistines would be sold to Sabeans, another remote
people.[19]

In addition, the history of Greek slave trading tends to support a seventh-
century date for the book. J. L. Crenshaw notes that Greeks "made extensive
use of slaves on their ships, farms, vineyards, and in factories" in the period
from the eighth to sixth centuries.[20] Greek historian J. B. Bury explains that
the economic expansion of Greece during the seventh century necessitated
heavy use of slaves.[21] J. M. Myers demonstrates through archaeological evidence that the Greeks had established trading colonies in the ancient Near
East by the sixth century.[22] Although the particulars of Joel are not precise
enough for us to date the book with a high degree of confidence, this verse fits
well in the late monarchy period of Judah.[23]

Notwithstanding the question of the precise historical setting of this verse,

---

[18] 2 Chr 21:16–17 does mention that the Philistines and Arabs sacked Jerusalem during the
reign of Jehoram and carried off considerable wealth and captives.

[19] The visit of the queen of Sheba to Solomon's court was noteworthy especially because the
Sabeans were regarded as very distant. A court visit from Damascus or Moab, by contrast, would
hardly have been given special attention.

[20] J. L. Crenshaw, *Joel* (New York: Doubleday, 1995), 25. Crenshaw cites M. I. Rostovtzeff,
Social and Economic History of the Hellenistic World, vol. 1 (Oxford: University Press, 1941), as
his authority here.

[21] J. B. Bury, *A History of Greece to the Death of Alexander the Great*, 3d ed. (London: Mac-
millan, 1951), 118.

[22] J. M. Myers, "Some Considerations Bearing on the Date of Joel," *ZAW* 74 (1962): 177–95.
See especially pp. 178–85. Myers has a particularly good summary of evidence for the Greek economic expansion from the eighth to sixth centuries and the resultant need for slaves. He dates Joel
to 520 B.C., but this is, in my view, out of the question since it is hard to imagine how Joel would
have failed to mention the dilapidated state of the temple at this time.

[23] Cf. Ezek 27:13.

we should not miss the main point that the Philistines and Phoenicians followed a deliberate policy of banishing Jews from their homeland.[24] Put in modern terms, they were practicing "ethnic cleansing" in hopes that they could solve their version of the "Jewish problem." This text, in other words, was an early example of the treatment Jews would have to suffer for centuries to come.

3:7 [4:7]   Yahweh promised that the Philistines and Phoenicians would trade places with the Jews. First, he said he would "rouse them out" of the places to which they were sent. The verb here translated "rouse" (a causal form of *ʿûr*) also occurs in 3:9,12, where it means "to set troops on the march." Here it implies that Yahweh would provoke the Jews to make their way home. On the other hand, he would bring the vengeance of the Philistines and Phoenicians back on their own heads (cf. v. 4), meaning that they would suffer what they did to the Jews.

3:8 [4:8]   Specifically, the children of the Philistines and Phoenicians would go into slavery among the Sabeans. These Arab traders are known to Bible readers for the visit of the queen of Shéba to Solomon's court (1 Kgs 10:2). Ezekiel mentions them along with the far-off merchants of Tarshish (38:13) but also states that they were trading partners with the Phoenicians (27:22–23). Jeremiah 6:20 also presents them as a "distant" people. Remarkably, the text asserts that the Jews would be the agents who sold Philistines and Phoenicians into slavery. In this, God "gives them a taste of their own medicine."[25] As Stuart remarks, this probably is to be taken more rhetorically than literally. Efforts to determine what incident of Jews selling Philistine slaves Joel had in mind are speculative at best.[26]

3. Summons to All Nations (3:9–12 [4:9–12])

⁹Proclaim this among the nations:
Prepare for war!
Rouse the warriors!
Let all the fighting men draw near and attack.
¹⁰Beat your plowshares into swords
and your pruning hooks into spears.
Let the weakling say,

---

[24] This is the only possible meaning of לְמַעַן הַרְחִיקָם מֵעַל גְּבוּלָם, "in order to remove them far from their territory."

[25] Hubbard explains that "their penchant for caravan trading meant that slaves sold to them could ultimately be dispersed almost anywhere from the Indian Ocean to the East Coast of Africa. The retribution is exact: the Hebrews, who had no love for the sea, were sold to sea-peoples; the people of Phoenicia and Philistia, seasoned sea-goers, will be sold to the Sabeans, desert dwellers" (*Joel and Amos,* 76–77).

[26] Stuart, *Hosea–Jonah,* 268.

"I am strong!"
¹¹Come quickly, all you nations from every side,
    and assemble there.
Bring down your warriors, O LORD!

¹²"Let the nations be roused;
    let them advance into the Valley of Jehoshaphat,
for there I will sit
    to judge all the nations on every side.

3:9 [4:9] The text here calls for unnamed heralds to fan out to the nations and call them to battle. The tone is ironic; it does not look for a literal battle against Yahweh, but it does recall the language of Ps 2:2: "The kings of the earth take their stand, / and the rulers gather together / against the LORD / and against his Anointed One." It also reverses the language of Jer 4:6, where the people of Judah are told: "Raise the signal to go to Zion! / Flee for safety without delay! / For I am bringing disaster from the north, / even terrible destruction." Instead of the people of Judah fleeing to Zion ahead of an irresistible Gentile army, Gentile soldiers are called to rush to Zion to meet their defeat.

The irony emerges in calling for "warriors" and "fighting men" to come and do their best to attack Jerusalem. In 2:7 these terms[27] described an invincible fighting force that confronted Jerusalem; now these same soldiers are called to a battle they have no hope of winning. Before, they were described as the army of Yahweh (2:11); now they are his enemies.

3:10 [4:10] An obvious question here is whether Joel reversed the language of Isa 2:4 and Mic 4:3 ("They will beat their swords to plowshares and their spears into pruning hooks") or whether *they* have reversed *his* language. On the surface it would seem more likely that Joel has the original form of what may have been a proverbial expression. One can easily imagine a catchphrase like Joel's being passed from village to village during a time of mobilization for war. It is more difficult to conceive that a call to disarm would have had much usage. If this text reflects the "normal" meaning, that it is a proverbial call to arms, then Joel's language here cannot be regarded as distinctively apocalyptic.[28] This reconstruction, if correct, implies that the inverted form of the saying found in Isaiah and Micah must have been striking and surprising

---

[27] The terms are גִּבּוֹרִים and אַנְשֵׁי הַמִּלְחָמָה.
[28] Contrary to C. F. Mariottini, "Joel 3:10 [H 4:10]: 'Beat Your Plowshares into Swords,'" *Perspectives in Religious Studies* 14 (1987): 125–30.

to an Israelite audience.[29]

Be that as it may, the main point is that all the nations are called to mobilize for "war." In this mobilization no one is exempt. Even those who normally would be considered unfit for service are to come join the fray. In this metaphor of judgment, God has called the nations to face him in a holy war, from which none will escape.

3:11 [4:11] From the standpoint of textual criticism this is the most difficult verse in the book. The words translated "Come quickly" could be rendered "Help and come," but the NIV probably is correct to render the text in the way that it has.[30] The verb translated "and assemble" is actually a third-person form in the Hebrew text and means "and *they shall* assemble." After the preceding imperative "come quickly," this is awkward, and the NIV evidently has emended the text to read "assemble" as an imperative.[31]

The sudden shift to an imperative directed at Yahweh is also surprising in the line, "Bring down your warriors, O LORD!" The ancient versions are quite different. The Vulgate reads this to mean that the "warriors" are those of the enemy nations and that Yahweh will shatter them (rather than lead them into battle).[32] The Greek is altogether different; it reads, "Let the gentle person be a fighter."[33] If the Masoretic Text is correct that Yahweh will lead his warriors into battle, this would indicate that angelic armies will descend

---

[29] Wolff argues that Joel had not used the phrase in its original sense but had turned on its head the prophetic tradition about nations gathering at Zion in peace (e.g., Isa 2) on its head (*Joel and Amos*, 80). This strikes me as most unlikely. Dillard also asserts that Joel reversed the language of Isaiah and Micah, but he gives no rationale to justify this interpretation and seems to be working simply from prior assumption ("Joel," 306).

[30] The phrase is וּבֹ֫אוּ עֻ֫שׁוּ. The word עֻ֫שׁוּ is a hapax legomenon that could mean "to lend aid" on the basis of an Arabic cognate, but the Vg has *erumpite* ("break out"), which may reflect the Hebrew root חוּשׁ ("to hasten").

[31] Reading הִקָּבְצוּ instead of וְנִקְבָּצוּ (see *BHS* text note). On the other hand, M. Dahood argues that this is a "precative perfect" that may be translated as an imperative ("Hebrew-Ugaritic Lexicography IX," *Biblica* 52 [1971]: 343). See also *IBHS* § 32.2.2b. But one wonders why it is third person instead of second person.

[32] The Vg has *ibi occumbere faciet Dominus robustos tuos* ("there the LORD will slay your hardy [soldiers]"). Wolff proposes that the Vg reads the *hiphil* of חתת, "to shatter, terrify" rather than הַנְחַת (*Joel and Amos*, 73).

[33] ὁ πραΰς ἔστω μαχητής. L. C. Allen (*The Books of Joel, Obadiah, Jonah and Micah*, NICOT [(Grand Rapids: Eerdmans, 1976], 107) and Stuart (*Hosea–Jonah*, 265) accept this as the correct reading and argue for an original הַנֶּחֱתָת יְהִי גִּבּוֹר, with הַנֶּחֱתָת being the *niphal* participle of חתת and יְהִי being corrupted to יְהוּה. But this Hebrew retroversion is of doubtful value. It is questionable whether the LXX translators would have rendered הַנֶּחֱתָת ("the terrified one") as ὁ πραΰς. The root חתת appears fifty-six times in the OT (it is difficult to say how many of these are in the *niphal* stem since the parsing of many forms is disputed; cf. the articles on חתת in BDB and KB³). But חתת is never translated πραΰς, which appears fifteen times in the LXX. A retroversion is by nature speculative, and this one lacks any supporting evidence.

upon the Gentile powers in the day of judgment[34] as in Zech 14:5 (see also Matt 13:41, where the Son of Man sends out his angels to weed out all evil-doers from the earth). It is difficult, however, to be certain of the text of Joel here. Still, the main idea that the Gentile powers will come together to face Yahweh in battle is clear.

3:12 [4:12] The text clarifies that the battle metaphor is not to be pressed. In this verse the nations come together, but Yahweh does not have to do battle with them. Instead, he "sits" as judge (note the meaning of Jehoshaphat, "Yahweh judges").

From the New Testament perspective, on the other hand, we have to won-der if a *sensus plenior* ("more full meaning") interpretation of "Let the nations be roused" might be in order. On one level, this could be taken simply as another military metaphor for the nations to mobilize their forces and come to Yahweh's battle. But the notion of "rousing" or "awakening" the nations calls to mind the New Testament picture of the peoples of earth being awak-ened from the dead to face judgment (as in Rev 20:11–13). Joel did not explicitly speak of a resurrection or judgment of the dead, but his language in this chapter is universal and draws the apocalyptic theme of the day of the Lord to a crescendo. For the Christian reader this naturally points to the final, general judgment of the living and the dead.

Excursus: Joel as a Paradigm for the Prophetic Method

Interpreting biblical prophecy is no simple matter. Although the prophets do occasionally make straightforward predictions about a single event in the future (e.g., 1 Kgs 13:2–3), such predictions are rare. More frequently they foresee the distant future in the context of addressing a situation contemporary with them and their audience. This blurring of present and future has long baffled Christian readers. Although we affirm with the apostle Matthew that Isa 7:14 looks ahead to the virgin birth of Jesus Christ (Matt 1:23), the interpretation of Isa 7:14 in context is notoriously difficult and has taxed Christian interpreters for centuries, since it is declared to be a sign to the impious King Ahaz as he makes prepara-tions to fight a war against Syria and Samaria.[35]

In dealing with this problem, Christians have resorted to various hermeneuti-cal methods. One of the oldest techniques is allegory, whereby historical context is ignored entirely and accidental verbal parallels form the bridge between the Old and New Testaments. Numbers 23:24, for example, is taken by some to be a prophecy of the Eucharist on the grounds that it says that Israel is like a lion that "drinks the blood of his victims." Most readers, however, readily see that this

---

[34] Scholars who prefer this interpretation see this as a reflection on the ideology of the day of the Lord as a holy war. See P. D. Miller, Jr., "The Divine Council and the Prophetic Call to War," *VT* 18 (1968): 100–107.

[35] Cf. D. A. Garrett, *An Analysis of the Hermeneutics of John Chrysostom's Commentary on Isaiah 1–8 with an English Translation* (Lewiston, N.Y.: Edwin Mellen, 1992), 144–48, 214–18.

verse is merely a metaphor for ferocity and has no relationship to the Lord's Supper. Allegorism is governed only by the imagination of the interpreter and thus cannot resolve the problem of the interpretation of prophetic speech.[36]

Other interpreters, especially Roman Catholics, have invoked *sensus plenior* as the key to the interpretation of difficult prophetic texts.[37] In this model the prophet simply wrote better than he knew. Although the prophet himself may have had only his contemporary situation in mind as he spoke or wrote, the Holy Spirit so guided his choice of words that in the distant future his prophecies would be found to have a fuller meaning than he himself intended. On this hermeneutical principle Hos 11:1 ("out of Egypt I called my son") looked ahead to the flight of the holy family to Egypt not because Hosea himself foresaw this event but because he used words that readily lent themselves to being applied to this event (thus Matt 2:15). Hosea himself spoke only of the exodus event, one can argue, but by the guidance of the Spirit he used words that also looked ahead to the Messiah's sojourn in Egypt.

Although better than allegorism, however, *sensus plenior* can also lack persuasiveness. It is difficult to understand, moreover, in what sense we can say that Hos 11:1 prophesied Jesus' sojourn in Egypt if the prophet himself had no idea that his words carried that meaning. It is one thing to say that the prophets did not fully understand the significance of their words, but it is another thing entirely to say that they had no idea when or if they were making significant statements about the future.[38]

Another approach is to claim that the words of the prophets carried a "double meaning." In this view their words addressed the contemporary problems they saw and also addressed the distant future. Thus Isa 7:14 carries a double meaning of both being a sign to Ahaz in his day and also looking ahead to the virgin birth of Christ. Advocates of the double meaning method frequently employ analogies to support their case. The prophets are said to have had a "telescopic" view of the future that saw only the immediate situation and the distant fulfillment without seeing the intervening years. They are said to have seen only the "mountaintops" in the plan of God juxtaposed against one another without having seen the miles of valley between the peaks.

This view has merit as well but is terribly short on specifics. On what basis does one determine whether a specific prophecy has one, two, three, or ten fulfill-

---

[36] For a limited (but in my view unsuccessful) defense of allegorism, see M. Silva, *Has the Church Misread the Bible?* (Grand Rapids: Zondervan, 1987), 47–75.

[37] For a limited defense of *sensus plenior* exegesis from a Protestant perspective, see D. J. Moo, "The Problem of *Sensus Plenior*," in *Hermeneutics, Authority, and Canon,* ed. D. A. Carson and J. D. Woodbridge (Grand Rapids: Zondervan, 1986), 179–211. Also see W. S. LaSor, "Prophecy, Inspiration and Sensus Plenior," *TynBul* 29 (1978): 49–60; idem, "The Sensus Plenior in Biblical Interpretation," in *Scripture, Tradition, and Interpretation,* ed. W. W. Gasque and W. S. LaSor (Grand Rapids: Eerdmans, 1978), 260–77.

[38] This is not to say that *sensus plenior* has no value but that it must be invoked with care. I have used it in my interpretation of Joel 3:12. Note, however, that this verse is in a context of "last judgment" already and that the possibility of allusion to resurrection for judgment here is in keeping with the larger message of Joel's prophecy.

ments? Did the prophets themselves understand that their words had multiple meanings? Why did they not see the "gaps" between the "peaks"? If they blurred all the events through "prophetic foreshortening," does this imply that Isaiah thought that the virgin birth of the Messiah would occur during the lifetime of King Ahaz? One gets the distinct impression that the "double fulfillment" approach has little to recommend it besides a few analogies from telescopes and mountaintops.

Joel may provide the model for solving this hermeneutical puzzle. As this commentary has stressed, the actual topic of the Book of Joel is not locusts, soldiers, the Holy Spirit, or the last judgment. It is the *day of the Lord*. This is the real focus of Joel and the theme to which the book repeatedly returns. Everything that happens in Joel is a fulfillment of the day of the Lord, a term that includes both judgment and salvation. Seen in this way, the locust plague, the attack by the northern army, the deliverance from the locusts, the defeat of the northern army, the pouring out of the Spirit, and the last judgment are all manifestations of the single idea, the day of the Lord. On the other hand, it would be equally valid to say that each event in itself was the day of the Lord. The Book of Joel is not about predicting separate events, be they locust plagues or the gift of the Spirit. It is rather an exploration of the *variety of manifestations* of the *one theological theme*.

As a theological theme the day of the Lord can have greater and lesser fulfillments. The locust plague in Judah was terrible, but it is not nearly as traumatic as the last judgment. The pouring of rain on a parched land, moreover, is a promise of a greater manifestation of the day of the Lord, the pouring out of the Spirit. Understanding that the prophets deal more in theological and prophetic themes than in specific predictions allows for an openness to the future in biblical prophecy. Just as the locust plague is the day of the Lord, so many other events (e.g., the Babylonian assault on Jerusalem) can be the day of the Lord as well. This understanding of prophetic language accords well with true typological (not allegorical) interpretation.[39] To put it another way, the typological interpretation that

---

[39] The classic work on typology is L. Goppelt, *Typos: The Typological Interpretation of the Old Testament in the New,* trans. D. H. Madvig (Grand Rapids: Eerdmans, 1982). On the other hand, for an understanding of the distinctive nature of typology, one can hardly do better than E. E. Ellis, *The Old Testament in Early Christianity* (Grand Rapids: Baker, 1991), 106: "Unlike allegory, it regards the Scriptures not as verbal metaphors hiding a deeper meaning (ὑπόνοια) but as historical accounts from whose literal sense the meaning of the text arises. Unlike the 'history of religions' hermeneutic, it seeks the meaning of current, NT events not from general religious history but from the salvation-history of Israel. Unlike the use of 'type' (τύπος) in pagan and some patristic literature, which assumes a cyclical-repetitive historical process, it relates the past to the present in terms of a historical correspondence and escalation in which the divinely ordered prefigurement finds a complement in the subsequent and greater event. Like rabbinic midrash, it applies the Old Testament to contemporary situations, but it does so with historical distinctions different from those of the rabbis. Like Qumran exegesis, it gives to the Scriptures a present-time, eschatological application, but it does so with an eschatological and messianic orientation different from Qumran." Ellis goes on to observe that the NT employs a "creation typology" and a "covenant typology," and he adds that the typology is at times "synthetic" and at times "antithetic."

the apostles applied to the Old Testament was not the imposition of an alien method on the text but was in agreement with the method by which the prophets themselves addressed the future.

With this approach we can affirm that the prophets knew that their words had application beyond the specific events they confronted in their own times. They did not necessarily fully understand *how* events would unfold, but they knew *that* the prophetic themes they proclaimed would be fulfilled in various ways and times. Furthermore, even while we acknowledge that there was much that the prophets did not understand (1 Pet 1:10–11), we can affirm that they knew that the greatest fulfillments of the theological themes they proclaimed would be in the messianic age.[40]

Hosea 11:1 concerns not just the specific historical event of the exodus of Israel from Egypt but the *theological theme of exodus*, a theme that Christ had to fulfill. Isaiah 7:14 concerns the biblical idea of *the son who brings salvation* and has fulfillments both during the lifetime of King Ahaz and in the virgin birth of Christ.[41] This principle applies to many other texts as well. Second Samuel 7 is not specifically a prediction either of Solomon or of Jesus Christ; the actual topic of this text is the chosen line of David. Solomon (as well as the other kings of Judah) fulfilled this theme in a lesser sense, but Jesus Christ fulfilled it with all of its ultimate and eternal implications. Jesus Christ, we should add, prophesied in the same way. The Olivet discourse was not specifically a prediction either of the Roman destruction of Jerusalem or of the last judgment. It was, in fact, an expansion from Jesus on the theme of the day of the Lord. Both the fall of Jerusalem and the last judgment are legitimate manifestations of the day of the Lord, however, the one being a lesser fulfillment and the other being a greater fulfillment. Readers who ask which of the two Jesus was talking about are missing the point. In the same way, New Testament prophets warned of a coming antichrist, but John could already say, "Many antichrists have come" (1 John 2:18).

In Joel, therefore, we see the prophetic method at work. The prophets spoke of theological ideas with full awareness that these ideas would be fulfilled in various ways and in various times. For Joel the day of the Lord would manifest itself in many different forms. Neither we nor the New Testament writers need to

---

[40] For a survey of approaches to the NT's interpretation of the OT, see D. Bock, "Use of the Old Testament in the New," in *Foundations for Biblical Interpretation,* ed. D. S. Dockery, K. A. Mathews, R. B. Sloan (Nashville: Broadman & Holman, 1994), 97–114.

[41] In my view the birth of Maher-Shalal-Hash-Baz (Isa 8:1–10) was the immediate sign to King Ahaz of Yahweh's salvation (Isa 8:18), whereas Christ was the ultimate manifestation of the idea of the son who brings salvation. This idea has its roots in ancient Israelite culture, in which the birth of a son brought great joy because he was a "kinsman-redeemer" for the household (גֹּאֵל; see Ruth 4:14–15). Maher-Shalal-Hash-Baz grew up in the time of famine and desolation that came about because of the Assyrian invasion, but he also was a token of deliverance from Samaria and Syria (Isa 7:15–25). Christ was the true Immanuel—"God with us" (Isa 7:14; 9:1–7). Maher-Shalal-Hash-Baz was born to "the prophetess," and his birth was miraculous in the sense that Isaiah had predicted it (Isa 8:1–2). Christ's birth was miraculous in that he was born to the virgin Mary. The famous ambiguity of the term עַלְמָה ("virgin" or simply "young woman") is in my opinion deliberate.

assign arbitrarily some secondary meaning to Old Testament texts. Rather, we should seek to understand the prophetic themes the prophets proclaimed and in so doing see how all these themes have their ultimate fulfillment in Christ (Luke 24:27).

4. The Winepress of the Lord (3:13 [4:13])

¹³**Swing the sickle,**
   for the harvest is ripe.
Come, trample the grapes,
   for the winepress is full
   and the vats overflow—
so great is their wickedness!"

3:13 [4:13]   This single verse is a miniature taunt song. It derides the nations for their hostility to Yahweh and the destruction that this has brought about. Wolff notes that the word for "sickle" can mean a vintager's knife and that the word for "ripe" is literally "boil," a word that suggests the ripening of grapes.[42] Thus the entire harvest is of a vineyard (and not of grains or other crops), and the image of the swinging sickle may be inappropriate. Instead of "swing the sickle" with the implication of a wheat or barley harvest, it should be, "Send forth the harvesting knife."

The overflowing winepress suggests that the wickedness of the nations was full. In Isa 63:1–6 Yahweh treads on his enemies like a man treading out the grapes in a winepress until his feet are as red with blood as a vintager's feet would be red with grape juice. Here, however, the verbs are plural. Therefore either the heavenly armies or the armies of Jerusalem were crushing the nations. It is striking, however, that Joel would use an abundant harvest of grapes to symbolize the sin and judgment of the nations since in 1:5,12 he lamented the locusts' destruction of the vineyards of Israel. Joel turned the idea of the return of an abundant harvest in a surprising new direction: it was the harvest of God's judgment of his enemies.

5. Signs of the Day of the Lord (3:14–17 [4:14–17])

¹⁴**Multitudes, multitudes**
   in the valley of decision!
For the day of the LORD is near
   in the valley of decision.
¹⁵**The sun and moon will be darkened,**
   and the stars no longer shine.

---

[42] Wolff, *Joel and Amos*, 80. Cf. the use of בשׁל in Gen 40:10, where it refers to the ripening of grapes.

¹⁶The LORD will roar from Zion
  and thunder from Jerusalem;
  the earth and the sky will tremble.
But the LORD will be a refuge for his people,
  a stronghold for the people of Israel.

¹⁷"Then you will know that I, the LORD your God,
  dwell in Zion, my holy hill.
Jerusalem will be holy;
  never again will foreigners invade her.

3:14 [4:14] Another, perhaps more appropriate, translation, would be, "Mobs of people, mobs of people, in the Valley of Verdict." There is no opportunity of salvation here; the throngs of people are described simply as "mobs"[43] and not as individuals for whom there is any hope. The repetition of "mobs" (or "multitudes") enhances the sense that they are vast in number.[44] Once again Joel made use of common prophetic language for the northern armies (Isa 13:4; 17:12).

The word translated "decision" here is not a human decision for or against God but is God's verdict on humans and more exactly is God's condemnation of the myriad crowds.[45] In short, these are throngs of lost humanity on the day of wrath facing judgment. This verse does not describe people in a modern evangelistic setting making decisions about faith in God or Christ.[46]

Once again the text describes the day of the Lord as "near," and once again it does not mean that the day of the Lord is merely soon to come but that in the Valley of Verdict it is already upon them (see 1:15). The metaphor of warfare has almost disappeared from the text at this point; this is no battle but simply the execution of a divine judgment.

3:15 [4:15] Again the image of the darkening of the skies returns. As elsewhere, the metaphor implies the end of the world. It does not always speak of the literal destruction of earth (see 2:10,31; also Amos 8:9; Mic 3:6), but in this case it does look ahead to the final act of God in human history (cf. Isa 13:10; Ezek 32:7–8; Matt 24:29; Rev 8:12; 9:2).

3:16 [4:16] The scene suddenly shifts from the "Valley of Verdict" to Mount Zion; this is not particularly awkward since we hardly are dealing with literal geography anyway. The judgment is real, but it is not in a valley (see Rev 20:11). As the Valley of Verdict (or of Jehoshaphat) symbolizes divine

---

[43] The word הֲמוֹנִים means not just that there were many people but that they were a mob. Another appropriate rendering is "Mêlée!" (Stuart, *Hosea–Jonah*, 264).

[44] Keil, *Minor Prophets*, 228. Cf. the Hebrew of 2 Kgs 3:16.

[45] The word חָרוּץ implies a negative verdict. Wolff observes that it "connotes the irrevocably determined sentence of destruction" (*Joel and Amos*, 81). Note the related verb חרץ, "fix, determine" (cf. KB[3] Eng. ed.) in Isa 10:22–23, where it is translated "decreed."

[46] See also Dillard, "Joel," 309.

judgment on humanity, so Zion symbolizes his identification with Israel as the true people of God. The implication is that there will be no salvation outside of Israel. The prophets did not understand from this that all Gentiles are eternally damned and excluded from God's people but that the time would come when Gentiles would flee to Zion for safety and submit to the God of Israel (Isa 2:2–4). The New Testament takes up this theme. Paul said that the wall that excluded Gentiles from the covenants and promises of Israel has been broken down in Christ (Eph 2:14–3:6) and that Gentile believers have been grafted into Israel (Rom 11:17). Whenever a Gentile bows at the name of Christ, he or she is confessing that the God of Abraham, Isaac, and Jacob—the God of Zion—is the one true Lord of heaven and earth. Joel did not here mention the possibility of Gentile conversion because his purpose was to console the Jews in their suffering and assure them of final vindication. Nevertheless, the implication that there is no salvation outside of "Zion" is clear.

The line "The LORD will roar from Zion / and thunder from Jerusalem" appears also in Amos 1:2a, and this has prompted discussion about whether Amos or Joel came first. Wolff has argued that the line was original with Amos and that Joel adapted it.[47] Wolff, of course, operates from a framework of Joel's being a postexilic work. If this line were the only evidence we had, however, we would have to say that it implies that Joel is the earlier work. The reason is that for Joel the line "The LORD will roar from Zion" implied salvation for the Israelites and defeat for the nations. Indeed, we can easily imagine that "The LORD will roar from Zion" may have once served as a kind of battle cry for Israelite troops. Amos, however, has taken this customary rallying cry of Israelite triumph and has turned it *against* Israel as a warning of judgment. In Amos 1–2 the prophet began conventionally enough by declaring that the Lord would "roar" against Gentile nations but then stunned his audience by turning the same language against Judah and Israel. At the very climax of his message Amos declared to the Israelites, "Woe to you who long for the day of the LORD!" (5:18). The straightforward implication is that Joel reflects the more primitive, optimistic use of the proverbial expression about the roaring of Yahweh meaning victory for Israel. This does not necessarily mean, however, that Joel is older than Amos. Both prophets may be citing a common, more ancient formula.

3:17 [4:17] God will vindicate Israel before the nations. The promise that the Israelites themselves would understand that Yahweh was their God may indicate how discouraged Joel's generation really was. It possibly anticipates times of unbelief among the Jews before their final salvation (Rom 9–11). The language also reflects Exod 6:7, where the mighty acts of the exodus were evidence to Israel that Yahweh was their God (on "then you will

---

[47] Wolff, *Joel and Amos*, 81.

know" see comments on 2:27).

The promise that God would "dwell" *(šākan)* in Zion (cf. v. 21) also recalls the exodus, where God encamped among them at the tent of meeting, but it especially looks forward to a time when God would dwell among them not as an unclean people (Lev 16:16[48]) but as a holy people (Lev 26:11[49]). The Book of Isaiah takes up the theme of Yahweh in Zion, where the Lord who "dwells on Mount Zion" (8:18) will ultimately deliver Jerusalem from the northern foe. Isaiah 52:1–2 repeats the promise that God would redeem Zion, the "holy city," from its captivity. Zechariah 14 also anticipates the last battle and the redemption of Jerusalem from Gentile domination and promises that no "Canaanite" would be in the house of God (14:21). The promise in Joel that "never again will foreigners invade her" is analogous (it probably should be translated simply, "Never again will aliens pass through her"[50]). The idea is not that all Gentiles will be excluded (compare Zech 14:17) but that the city will be regarded as sacred territory. The language of Joel, like that of all the prophets, comes from his world and culture, but the fulfillment is eschatological and eternal. Simply put, the message for us is that no unclean person will dwell in the eternal city of God, the new Jerusalem (Heb 12:22; Rev 21:1–3,27).

6. The Final State (3:18–21 [4:18–21])

> [18]"In that day the mountains will drip new wine,
>   and the hills will flow with milk;
>   all the ravines of Judah will run with water.
> A fountain will flow out of the LORD's house
>   and will water the valley of acacias.
> [19]But Egypt will be desolate,
>   Edom a desert waste,
>   because of violence done to the people of Judah,
>   in whose land they shed innocent blood.
> [20]Judah will be inhabited forever
>   and Jerusalem through all generations.
> [21]Their bloodguilt, which I have not pardoned,
>   I will pardon."
>
> The LORD dwells in Zion!

---

[48] The verse states that Aaron had to make atonement for the sins of the people because the tent of meeting "dwelt" (שָׁכַן) among them in their uncleanness.

[49] In this verse God promises to put his "dwelling" (מִשְׁכָּן) among them.

[50] Although עָבַר could be taken as to "cross over" in the sense of "invade," this is a very weak and ambiguous verb to use to describe a military assault, had that been Joel's meaning.

3:18 [4:18] "In that day" refers to the day of the Lord (cf. Hos 2:16,18,21; Amos 8:9,13; 9:11). As in 1:5 "new wine" symbolizes not mere sufficiency but abundance. The promise that all the ravines would flow with water no doubt gave hope to a people who had seen their land parched with drought (1:12,17). The language of abundant prosperity here recalls the familiar expression that Canaan was a land flowing with milk and honey (e.g., Exod 3:8; Deut 26:15) but is even more extravagant. Amos 9:13 similarly promises that the day will come when the land will be so fertile that the "reaper will be overtaken by the plowman / and the planter by the one treading grapes" and that the mountains will drip with wine. Such language obviously is hyperbolic, but the text describes more than simple agricultural plenty because "a fountain will flow out of the LORD's house." Ezekiel 47:1–12 similarly anticipates a river of life flowing from the temple (cf. also Ps 46:4–5; Zech 14:8; Rev 22:1–2), and Jesus understood the image in a personal sense in John 7:38.

Typologically, this text develops the theme of the house of God as the source of life. The theme has four manifestations (or "fulfillments"). First, in the return from the exile the Israelites would again experience prosperity only when they gave due attention to the worship of God at the temple (Hag 1:5–11). In that sense the temple was the source of their life. Second, Jesus as the true Temple of God is the source of every blessing for the believer (John 2:21; 7:37–38a). Third, believers, individually and corporately, are the sanctuary of the Spirit and thus should bring the living waters to those around them (1 Cor 3:16; Eph 2:21; John 7:38b). Fourth, in the New Jerusalem the redeemed will drink from the fountain of the water of life (Rev 21:6).

The "valley of acacias" may have eschatological significance as well. Joel seems to have had in mind the acacias of the Kidron Valley; apparently the drought had especially parched them. But in contrast with "Valley of Jehoshaphat" and "Valley of Verdict," the valley of acacias implies a future paradise for Israel.[51]

In short, what Joel saw concerned not mere agricultural prosperity but the very dwelling of God with his people. This is the city of God. For Joel's hungry audience it was indeed the joy of seasonal rains and a good harvest. In the message of the gospel, it is the gift of the Holy Spirit and the outpouring of life from the heart. In the hope of the faithful, it is the eternal presence of God with his people, where there will be no more sorrow, tears, or hunger (Rev 7:16–17; 21:4).

3:19 [4:19] As in vv. 4–8, Joel again turned his attention to the offenses of nations of his day. In this case it was Egypt and Edom, and the offense was

---

[51] Cf. Wolff, *Joel and Amos*, 83–84.

killing innocent Jews.[52] Once again we have no basis for determining precisely what incidents Joel had in mind, although Obad 10–14, describing Edom's violence against refugees at the fall of Jerusalem, is an obvious possibility; but the text does not require or even imply that specific connection. It is noteworthy that Zech 14:18 also warns of eschatological desolation for Egypt.

The prediction of the future humiliation of Egypt and Edom serves a greater theological purpose. For the modern reader it is not too significant to read that Egypt and Edom would revert to desert conditions, but for Joel's audience it implied that their God had triumphed. In the future, the passage hints, no one will look to Egypt or the gods of Egypt for saving power, and no one will have regard for Edom. Egypt and Edom will suffer the calamity that had temporarily fallen upon Judah (Joel 2:3). Israel and Israel's God will be exalted over all the nations as well as over their gods and ideals. Egypt and Edom serve as a sign for all the nations here. This is simply another way of joining Isaiah in claiming that Mount Zion would be exalted above all mountains and all nations would stream to it to learn the true teaching of God (Isa 2:2–4). It is more than political dominance over some bygone nations and extinct cultures; it is the triumph of the gospel over every ideal, religion, or cultural identity. It is the bowing of the nations before Israel's God.

3:20 [4:20] The knowledge of God is eternal life (John 17:3). It is the presence of God among the people of the covenant that insures that Judah and Jerusalem will endure forever. We cannot say with certainty whether this verse implied eternal life to Joel's audience or whether they took it primarily as a promise that their nation would continue after the others had disappeared. Still, the ultimate fulfillment of this verse is in the eternal Jerusalem. It is that city that truly will never become desolate, suffer defeat, or endure drought. This interpretation is not a violation of the promises to historical Israel; it is their fulfillment.

3:21 [4:21] The Hebrew of v. 21a, "Their bloodguilt, which I have not pardoned, / I will pardon," is quite difficult.[53] The word translated "bloodguilt" simply means "blood." Although it obviously can refer to blood that has been shed in violence, it is not the normal way of describing the *guilt* from acts of violence. It describes the blood itself.[54] Put another way, one can *avenge blood* that has been shed (cf. Ps 79:10) or one can *forgive guilt*, but it is not clear that one can *forgive blood*, as this verse seems to imply. Also

---

[52] Hubbard says "innocent blood" here is a legal term referring to "undeserved capital punishment" (*Joel and Amos*, 83).

[53] Note the number of proposed emendations in *BHS*.

[54] The word דָּם in the singular, as we have it in this verse, generally does not move too far from the literal meaning of "blood." It does come close to describing "bloodguilt" in Deut 21:8. However, Hebrew consistently uses the plural form דָּמִים to describe the *guilt* that comes from shedding blood (e.g., Ps 51:16[14]).

while the NIV rendering is defensible, the Hebrew here is almost unnaturally terse.[55] In addition, the language here is quite close to the Hebrew phrase for the "innocent blood" of the Jews that, according to v. 19, the Egyptians and Edomites had shed.[56] This gives support to the LXX rendition, "I will avenge their blood and I will not pardon."[57]

If one takes the MT as is, the meaning is that God will forgive Israel some unknown acts of violence that he had not previously forgiven. This is possible but unusual since the text nowhere else mentions any such sins on the part of the Jews. If one emends on the basis of the LXX, as just described, the meaning is that the murderers mentioned in v. 19 finally will get the justice they deserve. Although emending is not without its problems, it is the best solution in context.[58] So interpreted, we have the following parallel structure for vv. 19–21:

A   Egypt and Edom will be *uninhabited* (v. 19a)
B   Egypt and Edom shed **innocent blood** in Judah (v. 19b)
A′   Judah will be *inhabited* forever (v. 20)
B′   God will avenge **innocent blood** (v. 21a)
A″   God will *inhabit* Zion (v. 21b)

The closing promise that Yahweh would dwell in Zion gives final vindication to the people of Jerusalem. After all their sufferings of locusts, drought, and warfare, the vow that God would dwell eternally among them is the reassurance that they were not abandoned. In God they had an eternal home because God dwells among them.

---

[55] The clause וְנִקֵּיתִי דָּמָם לֹא־נִקֵּיתִי is literally "and I will leave unpunished their blood I did not leave unpunished." This is perhaps intelligible but is harshly elliptical. Dillard aptly comments that "at first glance the verse appears to contain self-contradictory clauses" ("Joel," 313).

[56] Note that v. 19 describes the דָם־נָקִיא of the Jews; v. 21 has דָּמָם לֹא־נִקֵּיתִי. If v. 21 looks back to v. 19, this would also account for the use of דָם in v. 21 instead of דָּמִים.

[57] One could emend וְנִקֵּיתִי to וְנִקַּמְתִּי on the basis of the LXX καὶ ἐκδικήσω, as *BHS* note b suggests. Stuart proposes taking the first clause, וְנִקֵּיתִי, as a question and thus translates: "Will I leave their bloodshed unpunished? I will not leave it unpunished!" (*Hosea–Jonah*, 265). See also Dillard, "Joel," 313. This nicely avoids the need for emendation, but one may doubt whether the *weqatal* form ("*waw* conversive on a perfect tense") can have this meaning. Proponents of this rendering have failed to provide Hebrew analogies. See Allen, *Joel*, 117, for other proposals.

[58] See also Crenshaw, *Joel*, 202–3.

Selected Bibliography

Hosea Bibliography

Books and Commentaries

Allies, M. H., trans. *St. John Damascene on Holy Images.* London: Thomas Baker, 1898.

Andersen, F. I. and D. N. Freedman. *Hosea: A New Translation with Introduction and Commentary.* AB. New York: Doubleday, 1980.

Archer, G. *A Survey of Old Testament Introduction.* Chicago: Moody, 1974.

Bright, J. *A History of Israel.* 3d ed. Philadelphia: Westminster, 1981.

Brueggemann, W. *Tradition for Crisis: A Study in Hosea.* Richmond: John Knox, 1968.

Bullock, C. H. *An Introduction to the Old Testament Prophetic Books.* Chicago: Moody, 1986.

Buss, M. J. *The Prophetic Word of Hosea: A Morphological Study.* BZAW 111. Berlin: Verlag Alfred Töpelmann, 1969.

Calvin, J. *Commentaries on the Twelve Minor Prophets.* Grand Rapids: Baker, n.d.

Cassuto, U. *Biblical and Oriental Studies.* Translated by I. Abrahams. Jerusalem: Magnes, 1973.

Cohn, N. *The Pursuit of the Millennium.* London: Pimlico, 1957.

Davies, G. I. *Hosea.* NCBC. Grand Rapids: Eerdmans, 1992.

Driver, S. R. *An Introduction to the Literature of the Old Testament.* Reprint, Gloucester, Mass.: Peter Smith, 1972.

Eaton, M. A. *Hosea.* Fearn, Great Britain: Christian Focus, 1996.

Fohrer, G. *Introduction to the Old Testament.* Nashville: Abingdon, 1968.

Freud, S. *Moses and Monotheism.* New York: Random House, 1953.

Garrett, D. A. *An Analysis of the Hermeneutics of John Chrysostom's Commentary on Isaiah 1–8 with an English Translation.* Lewiston, N.Y.: Edwin Mellen, 1992.

———. *Proverbs, Ecclesiastes, and Song of Songs.* NAC. Nashville: Broadman, 1993.

———. *Rethinking Genesis.* Grand Rapids: Eerdmans, 1991.

Harper, W. R. *Amos and Hosea.* ICC. Edinburgh: T & T Clark, 1936.

Harrison, R. K. *Introduction to the Old Testament.* Grand Rapids: Eerdmans, 1969.

Hill, D. *Matthew.* New Century Bible. London: Oliphants, 1972.

Holt, E. K. *Prophesying the Past: The Use of Israel's History in the Book of Hosea.* JSOTSup 194. Sheffield: Academic Press, 1994.

Hubbard, D. A. *Hosea.* TOTC. Downers Grove: InterVarsity, 1989.

Kaufmann, Y. *The Religion of Israel.* New York: Schocken, 1960.

Keil, C. F. *Hosea.* Grand Rapids: Eerdmans, n.d.

Kidner, D. *Love to the Loveless: The Message of Hosea.* Downers Grove, IL: InterVarsity, 1981, 109.

LaSor, W. S., D. A. Hubbard, and F. W. Bush. *Old Testament Survey,* 2nd ed. Grand Rapids: Eerdmans, 1996.

Limburg, J. *Hosea–Micah.* Interpretation. Atlanta: John Knox Press, 1988.

Lipshitz: A. *The Commentary of Rabbi Ibn Ezra on Hosea: Edited from Six Manuscripts and Translated with an Introduction and Notes.* New York: Sepher-Hermon Press, 1988.

Mays, J. L. *Hosea: A Commentary.* OTL. Philadelphia: Westminster, 1969.

McComiskey, T. E. *The Minor Prophets.* Grand Rapids: Baker, 1992.

McGrath, A. E. *Luther's Theology of the Cross.* Grand Rapids: Baker, 1985.

Merrill, E. H. *Kingdom of Priests.* Grand Rapids: Baker, 1987.

Morris, G. *Prophecy, Poetry, and Hosea.* JSOTSup 219. Sheffield: Academic Press, 1996.

Noll, M. A. *The Scandal of the Evangelical Mind.* Grand Rapids: Eerdmans, 1994.

Ortlund, R. C. Jr. *Whoredom: God's Unfaithful Wife in Biblical Theology.* Grand Rapids: Eerdmans, 1996.

Östborn, G. *Yahweh and Baal.* Lund: C. W. K. Gleerup, 1956.

Packer, J. I. *Knowing God.* Downers Grove: InterVarsity, 1973.

Sherwood, Y. *The Prostitute and the Prophet: Hosea's Marriage in Literary–Theological Perspective.* JSOTSup 212. Sheffield: Academic Press, 1996.

Smith, G. V. *The Prophets as Preachers: An Introduction to the Hebrew Prophets.* Nashville: Broadman, 1994.

Stuart, D. *Hosea–Jonah.* WBC. Dallas: Word, 1987.

Thiele, E. R. *The Mysterious Numbers of the Hebrew Kings,* rev. ed. Grand Rapids: Zondervan, 1983.

Thomas Aquinas. *Summa Theologiae: Latin Text and English Translation, Introductions, Notes, Appendices and Glossaries.* Blackfriars Edition. New York: McGraw-Hill, 1963.

Ward, J. *Hosea: A Theological Commentary.* New York: Harper & Row, 1966.

Wendland, E. R. *The Discourse Analysis of Hebrew Prophetic Literature.* Lewiston, N.Y.: Mellen Biblical Press, 1995.

Westermann, C. *Basic Forms of Prophetic Speech.* Philadelphia: Westminster, 1967.

Wolff, H. W. *Hosea.* Hermeneia. Translated by G. Stansell. Philadelphia: Fortress, 1974.

Worthing, M. W. *God, Creation, and Contemporary Physics.* Minneapolis: Fortress, 1996.

Yee, G. *Composition and Tradition in the Book of Hosea.* Atlanta: Scholars Press, 1985.

Articles and Journals

Ackroyd, P. R. "Hosea and Jacob." *VT* 13 (1963): 245–59.

Arnold, P. M. "Hosea and the Sin of Gibeah." *CBQ* 51 (1989): 447–60.

Black, M. "The Theological Appropriation of the Old Testament by the New Testament." *SJT* 39 (1986): 1–17.

Boudreau, G. R. "Hosea and the Pentateuchal Traditions." JSOTSup 173 (1993): 121–32.

Buss, M. J. "Comedy and Tragedy in Hosea." *Semeia* 32 (1984): 71–82.

———. "Mari Prophecy and Hosea," *JBL* 88 (1969): 338.

Coote, R. B. Coote, "Hos 14:8: 'They who are Filled with Grain shall Live,'" *JBL* 93

(1974): 161–73.

———. "Hosea XII." *VT* 21 (1971): 389–402.

Crane, W. E. Crane, "The Prophecy of Hosea." *BSac* 89 (1932): 480–94.

Daniels, D. R. Daniels, "Is There a 'Prophetic Lawsuit' Genre?" *ZAW* 99 (1987): 339–60.

Day, J. "Pre-Deuteronomic Allusions to the Covenant in Hosea and Psalm LXXVIII." *VT* 36 (1986): 1–12.

DeRoche, M. "The Reversal of Creation in Hosea." *VT* 31 (1981): 400–409.

Dijk-Hemmes, F. van. "The Imagination of Power and the Power of Imagination: An Intertextual Analysis of Two Biblical Love Songs." *JSOT* 44 (1989): 75–88.

Driver, G. R. "Linguistic and Textual Problems: Minor Prophets. I." *JTS* 39 (1938): 154–166.

Eakin, F. E., Jr. "Yahwism and Baalism Before the Exile." *JBL* 84 (1965): 407–14.

Edelman, D. "The Meaning of *qiṭṭēr*." *VT* 35 (1985): 395–404.

Ehrlich, C. S. "The Text of Hosea 1:9." *JBL* 104 (1985): 13–19.

Eidevall, G. "Lions and Birds as Literature. Some Notes on Isaiah 31 and Hosea 11." *Scandinavian Journal of the Old Testament* 7 (1993): 78–87.

Ellison, H. L. "The Message of Hosea in the Light of His Marriage." *EvQ* 41 (1969): 3–9.

Emmerson, G. I. "A Fertility Goddess in Hosea IV 17–19?" *VT* 24 (1974): 492–97.

Eslinger, L. M. "Hosea 12:5a and Genesis 32:29: A Study in Inner Biblical Exegesis." *JSOT* 18 (1980) 91–9.

Farr, G. "The Concept of Grace in the book of Hosea." *ZAW* 70 (1958): 98–107.

Franklyn, P. N. "Oracular Cursing in Hosea 13." HAR 11 (1987): 69–80.

Freedman, D. N. "Headings in the Books of the Eighth Century Prophets." *AUSS* 25 (1987): 9–26.

Friedman, M. A. "Israel's Response in Hosea 2:17b: 'You are my Husband.'" *JBL* 99 (1980): 199–204.

Fuller, R. "A Critical Note on Hosea 12:10 and 13:4." *RB* 98 (1991): 343–57.

Gertner, M. "An Attempt at an Interpretation of Hosea XII." *VT* 10 (1960): 272–84.

Ginsberg, H. L. "Hosea's Ephraim, More Fool than Knave: A New Interpretation of Hosea 12:1–14." *JBL* 80 (1961): 339–47.

Good, E. M. "Hosea 5:8–6:6: An Alternative to Alt." *JBL* 85 (1966): 273–86.

Gordis, R. "Hosea's Marriage and Message." *HUCA* 25 (1954): 9–35.

Gordon, C. H. "Hos 2.4–5 in the Light of New Semitic Inscriptions." *ZAW* 54 (1936): 277–80.

Greenburg, M. "Ezekiel 16: A Panorama of Passions." In *Love and Death in the Ancient Near East*. Edited by J. H. Marks and R. M. Good. Guilford, Conn.: Four Quarters, 1987, 143–50.

Grossberg, D. "Multiple Meaning: Part of a Compound Literary Device in the Hebrew Bible." *East Asia Journal of Theology* 4 (1986): 77–86.

Hess, R. S. "*ādām* as 'Skin' and 'Earth': An Examination of Some Proposed Meanings in Biblical Hebrew." *TynBul* 39 (1988): 143–49.

Holladay, W. L. "Chiasmus: The Key to Hosea XII 3–6." *VT* 16 (1966): 53–64.

Houston, J. "Knowing God: The Transmission of Reformed Theology." in *Doing Theology for the People of God*. Edited by D. Lewis and A. McGrath (Downers

Grove: InterVarsity, 1996), 223–44.

Huffmon, H. B. "The Covenant Lawsuit in the Prophets." *JBL* 78 (1959): 285–95.

Irvine, S. A. Irvine, "Politics and Prophetic Commentary in Hosea 8:8–10." *JBL* 114 (1995): 292–94.

Janzen, J. G. "Metaphor and Reality in Hosea 11." *Semeia* 24 (1982): 7–44

Johansen, J. H. "The Prophet Hosea: His Marriage and Message." *JETS* 14 (1971): 179–84.

Kaiser, W. J., Jr. "Inner Biblical Exegesis as a Model for Bridging the 'Then' and 'Now' Gap: Hos 12:1–6." *JETS* 28 (1985): 33–46.

Krause, D. "A Blessing Cursed: The Prophet's Prayer for Barren Womb and Dry Breasts in Hosea 9." *In Reading Between the Texts: Intertextuality and the Hebrew Bible*. Edited by D. N. Fewell. Louisville: Westminster/John Knox, 1992, 191–202.

Kruger, Paul A. "Israel, the Harlot," *JNSL* 11 (1983): 107–16.

Lundbom, J. R. "Contentious Priests and Contentious People in Hosea IV 1–10." *VT* 36 (1986): 52–70.

———. "Poetic Structure and Prophetic Rhetoric in Hosea." *VT* 29 (1979): 300–308.

Lust, J. "Freud, Hosea, and the Murder of Moses: Hosea 12." *ETL* 65 (1989): 81–93.

Malchow, B. V. "Contrasting Views of Nature in the Hebrew Bible." *Dialog* 26 (1987): 40–43.

May, H. G. "An Interpretation of the Names of Hosea's Children." *JBL* 55 (1936): 285–91.

Mazor, Y. "Hosea 5.1–3: Between Compositional Rhetoric and Rhetorical Composition." *JSOT* 45 (1989): 119–20.

McCarthy, D. J. "Hosea XII 2: Covenant by Oil." *VT* 14 (1964): 215–21.

McComiskey, T. E. "Hosea 9:13 and the Integrity of the Masoretic Tradition in the Prophecy of Hosea." *JETS* 33 (1990): 155–60.

McKay, H. A. "Jacob Makes It across the Jabbok: An Attempt to Solve the Success/ Failure Ambivalence in Israel's Self-consciousness." *JSOT* 38 (1987): 3–13.

McKenzie, J. L. "Divine Passion in Osee." *CBQ* 17 (1955): 287–99.

McKenzie, S. L. "The Jacob Tradition in Hosea 12:4–5." *VT* 36 (1983): 311–22.

Nicholson, E. W. "Problems in Hosea VIII 13." *VT* 16 (1966): 355–58.

North, F. S. "Solution of Hosea's Marital Problems by Critical Analysis." *JNES* 16 (1957): 128–30.

O'Connor, M. "The Pseudo-sorites in Hebrew Verse." In *Perspectives on Language and Text*. Edited by E. W. Conrad and E. G. Newing. Winona Lake: Eisenbrauns, 1987. 239–53.

———. "The Pseudosorites: A Type of Paradox in Hebrew Verse." JSOTSup 40. Sheffield: Academic Press, 1987, 161–72.

Olyan, S. M. "'In the Sight of Her Lovers': On the Interpretation of *nablūt* in Hos 2,12." BZNS 36 (1992): 255–61.

Pisano, S. "'Egypt' in the Septuagint Text of Hosea." In *Tradition of the Text*. Edited by G. J. Norton and S. Pisano. Fribourg, Switzerland: Vandenhoeck & Ruprecht Göttingen, 1991, 301–8.

Ringgren, H. "The Marriage Motif in Israelite Religion." In *Ancient Israelite Religion*. Edited by P. D. Miller, Jr., P. D. Hanson, and S. D. McBride. Philadelphia: Fortress, 1987, 421–28.

Setel, T. D. "Prophets and Pornography: Female Sexual Imagery in Hosea." In *Feminist Interpretation of the Bible*. L. Russell. Philadelphia: Westminster, 1985, 86–95.

Tångberg, K. A. " 'I Am Like an Evergreen Fir; From Me Comes Your Fruit': Notes on Meaning and Symbolism in Hosea 14,9b." *Scandinavian Journal of the Old Testament* 2 (1989): 81–93.

———. "A Note on *pištî* in Hosea II, 7, 11." *VT* 27 (1977): 222–24.

Vasholz, R. I. "Gomer—Chaste or Not?" *Presbyterion* 19 (1993): 48–49.

Vogels, W. "Hosea's Gift to Gomer (Hos 3,2)." *Bib* 69 (1988): 412–21.

Waterman, L. "Hosea, Chapters 1–3, in Retrospect and Prospect." *JNES* 14 (1955): 100–109.

Watson, W. G. E. "Reflexes of Akkadian Incantations in Hosea." *VT* 34 (1984): 242–47.

Weems, R. J. "Gomer: Victim of Violence or Victim of Metaphor?" *Sem* 47 (1989): 87–104.

Whitt, W. D. "The Divorce of Yahweh and Asherah in Hos 2,4–7.12 ff." *Scandinavian Journal of the Old Testament* 6 (1992): 31–67.

———. "The Jacob Traditions in Hosea and their Relation to Genesis." *ZAW* 91 (1991): 18–43.

Wijngaards, J. "Death and Resurrection in Covenantal Context (Hos. VI 2)." *VT* 17 (1967): 226–39.

Wyrtzen, D. B. "The Theological Center of Hosea." *BibSac* 141 (1984): 315–29.

Joel Bibliography

Books and Commentaries

Ahlstrom, G. W. *Joel and the Temple Cult of Jerusalem*. VTSup 21. Leiden: Brill, 1971.

Allen, L. C. *The Books of Joel, Obadiah, Jonah and Micah*. NICOT. Grand Rapids: Eerdmans, 1976.

Bergler, S. *Joel als Schriftinterpret*. Beitrage zur des Alten Testaments und des antiken Judentums 16. Frankfurt am Main: Peter Lang, 1988.

Bewer, J. A. "Joel." In *A Critical and Exegetical Commentary on Micah, Zephaniah, Nahum, Habakkuk, Obadiah and Joel*. ICC. Edinburgh: T & T Clark, 1911.

Bodenheimer, F. S. "Note on Invasions of Palestine by Rare Locusts." In *Israel Exploration Journal Reader*. Edited by H. M. Orlinsky. New York: KTAV, 1981.

Bock, D. L. "Evidence from Acts." In *A Case for Premillennialism: A New Consensus*. Edited by D. K. Campbell and J. L. Townsend. Chicago: Moody, 1992.

———. "The Reign of the Lord Christ." In *Dispensationalism, Israel and the Church: The Search for Definition*. Edited by C. A. Blaising and D. L. Bock. Grand Rapids: Zondervan, 1992.

———. "Use of the Old Testament in the New." In *Foundations for Biblical Interpretation*. Edited by D. S. Dockery, K. A. Mathews, and R. B. Sloan. Nashville: Broadman & Holman, 1994.

Brown, R. E. *The Gospel according to John*. AB. New York: Doubleday, 1966.

Bruce, F. F. *The Book of Acts*. NICNT. Grand Rapids: Eerdmans, 1954.

Calvin, John, *A Commentary on the Prophet Joel.* Translated by J. Owen. London: Banner of Truth, 1958.

Cathcart, K. J. and Gordon, R. P. *The Targum of the Minor Prophets.* The Aramaic Bible 14. Wilmington: Michael Glazier, 1989.

Collins, J. J. "Teacher and Messiah? The One Who Will Teach Righteousness at the End of Days." In *The Community of the Renewed Covenant.* Edited by E. Ulrich and J. Vanderkam. Notre Dame: University Press, 1994.

Crenshaw, J. L. *Joel.* AB. New York: Doubleday, 1995.

Dillard, R. B. and T. Longman. *An Introduction to the Old Testament.* Grand Rapids: Zondervan, 1994.

Dillard, R. B. "Joel." In *The Minor Prophets.* Vol. 1. Grand Rapids: Baker, 1991.

Driver, S. R. *An Introduction to the Literature of the Old Testament.* Reprinted. Gloucester, Mass.: Peter Smith, 1972.

Ellis, E. E. *The Old Testament in Early Christianity.* Grand Rapids: Baker, 1991.

Evans, C. A. *Luke.* NIBC. Peabody, Mass.: Hendrickson, 1990.

———. "The Prophetic Setting of the Pentecost Sermon." *ZNW* 74 (1983): 148–50.

Finley, T. J. *Joel, Obadiah, Amos.* WEC. Chicago: Moody, 1990.

Fohrer, G. *Introduction to the Old Testament.* Translated by D. E. Green. Nashville: Abingdon, 1968.

Garrett, D. A. *An Analysis of the Hermeneutics of John Chrysostrom's Commentary on Isaiah 1–8 with an English Translation.* Lewiston, N.Y.: Edwin Mellen, 1992.

———. *Angels and the New Spirituality.* Nashville: Broadman & Holman, 1995.

Goppelt, L. *Typos: The Typological Interpretation of the Old Testament in the New.* Translated by D. H. Madvig. Grand Rapids: Eerdmans, 1982.

Groningen, G. Van. *Messianic Revelation in the Old Testament.* Grand Rapids: Baker 1990.

Heater, H. Jr. "Evidence from Joel and Amos." In *A Case for Premillennialism: A New Consensus.* Edited by D. K. Campbell and J. L. Townsend. Chicago: Moody, 1992.

Hiebert, T. "Joel, Book of." *ABD* 3. 873–80.

Holladay, W. L. *The Root subh in the Old Testament.* Leiden: Brill, 1958.

Hubbard, D. A. *Joel and Amos.* TOTC. Downers Grove: InterVarsity, 1989.

Hvidberg, F. F. *Weeping and Laughter in the Old Testament.* Leiden: Brill, 1962.

Kapelrud, A. *Joel Studies.* Uppsala: A. B. Lundequistska Bokhandeln, 1948.

Keil, C. F. *The Minor Prophets.* Grand Rapids: Eerdmans, n.d.

Krodel, G. A. *Acts.* Augsburg Commentary on the New Testament. Minneapolis: Augsburg, 1986.

———. "The Sensus Plenior in Biblical Interpretation." In *Scripture, Tradition and Interpretation.* Edited by W. W. Gasque and W. S. LaSor. Grand Rapids: Eerdmans, 1978.

Limburg, J. *Hosea–Micah.* IBC. Atlanta: John Knox, 1988.

Longnecker, R. N. "The Acts of the Apostles." EBC. Grand Rapids: Zondervan, 1981.

Loretz, O. *Regenritual und Jahwetag im Joelbuch.* Ugaritisch–Biblische Literatur 4. Altenberge: CIS, 1986.

Moo, D. J. "The Problem of Sensus Plenior." In *Hermeneutics, Authority, and Canon.* Edited by D. A. Carson and J. D. Woodbridge. Grand Rapids: Zondervan, 1986.

Motyer, J. A. *The Prophecy of Isaiah*. Downers Grove: InterVarsity, 1993.

Ogden, G. S. and R. R. Deutsch. "Joel." In *A Promise of Hope—A Call to Obedience*. ITC. Grand Rapids: Eerdmans, 1987.

Patterson, R. D. "Joel." EBC. Grand Rapids: Eerdmans, 1985.

Pfeiffer, R. H. *Introduction to the Old Testament*. New York: Harper & Brothers, 1941.

Poythress, V. S. *Understanding Dispensationalists*. Phillipsburg, N.J.: Presbyterian & Reformed, 1994.

Prinsloo, W. S. *The Theology of the Book of Joel*. BZAW. Berlin: Walter de Gruyter.

Sailhamer, J. H. *Introduction to Old Testament Theology*. Grand Rapids: Zondervan, 1995.

Saucy, R. L. The Case for Progressive Dispensationalism. Grand Rapids: Zondervan, 1993.

Silva, M. *Has the Church Misread the Bible?* Grand Rapids: Zondervan, 1987.

Smith, G. V. *The Prophets as Preachers*. Nashville: Broadman & Holman, 1994.

Stuart, D. *Hosea–Jonah*. WBC. Dallas: Word, 1987.

Thompson, J. A. "Joel." IB. Nashville: Abingdon, 1956, 6:733.

————. "Repetition in the Prophecy of Joel." In *On Language, Culture, and Religion: In Honor of Eugene A. Nida*. Edited by M. Black and W. A. Smalley. The Hague: Mouton, 1974.

Walvoord, J. *The Holy Spirit*. Findlay, Ohio: Dunham, 1954.

Wolff, H. W. *Joel and Amos*. Hermeneia. Philadelphia: Fortress, 1977.

Zehnle, R. F. *Peter's Pentecost Discourse*. SBLMS 15. New York: Abingdon, 1971.

Articles and Journals

Andinach, P. R. "The Locusts in the Message of Joel." *VT* 42 (1992): 433–41.

Child, B. S. "The Enemy from the North and the Chaos Tradition." *JBL* 78 (1959): 187–98.

Dahood, M. "The Four Cardinal Points in Psalm 75,7 and Joel 2,20." *Bib* 52 (1971): 397.

Frankfort, T. "Le כ de Joel I 12." *VT* 10 (1960): 445–48.

Garrett, D. A. "The Structure of Joel." *JETS* 28 (1985): 289–97.

Hosch, H. "The Concept of Prophetic Time in Joel," JETS 15 (1972): 31–38.

Hurowitz, V. A. "Joel's Locust Plague in Light of Sargon II's Hymn to Nanaya." *JBL* 112 (1993): 597–603.

LaSor, W. S. "Prophecy, Inspiration and Sensus Plenior." *TynBul* 29 (1978): 49–60.

Mallon, E. D. "A Stylistic Analysis of Joel 1:10–12." *CBQ* 45 (1983): 537–48.

Marcus, D. "Nonrecurring Doublets in Joel." *CBQ* 56 (1994): 56–57, 65–66.

Mariottini, C. F. "Joel 3:10 [H 4:10]: 'Beat Your Plowshares into Swords." *Perspectives in Religious Studies* 14 (1987): 125–30.

Miller, P. D., Jr. "The Divine Council and the Prophetic Call to War." *VT* 8 (1968): 100–107.

Myers, J. M. "Some Considerations Bearing on the Date of Joel." *ZAW* 74 (1962): 177–95.

Nestle, E. "Miscellen: I. Joel I, 17." *ZAW* 20 (1900): 164–65.

Ogden, G. S. "Joel 4 and Prophetic Responses to National Laments." *JSOT* 26 (1983):

Ogden, G. S. "Joel 4 and Prophetic Responses to National Laments." *JSOT* 26 (1983): 97–106.

———. "The Unity of the Book of Joel." *ZAW* 104 (1992): 66–67.

Rabinowitz, I. "The Guides of Righteousness." *VT* 8 (1958).

Rad, G. von. "The Origin of the Concept of the Day of Yahweh." *JSS* 4 (1959): 97–108.

Roth, C. "The Teacher of Righteousness and the Prophecy of Joel." *VT* 13 (1963): 91–95.

Sellers, O. R. "Stages of Locust in Joel." *AJSL* 52 (1935–36): 81–85.

———. "A Possible Old Testament Reference to the Teacher of Righteousness." *IEJ* 5 (1955): 93–95.

Sprengling, M. "Joel 1, 17a." *JBL* 38 (1919): 129–41.

Stephenson, F. R. "The Date of the Book of Joel." *VT* 19 (1969): 224–29.

Thompson, J. A. "Joel's Locusts in the Light of Near Eastern Parallels." *JNES* 14 (1955): 52–55.

Treves, M. "The Date of Joel." *VT* 7 (1957): 149–56.

VanGemeren, W. A. "The Spirit of Restoration." *WTJ* 50 (1988): 81–102.

Weingreen, J. "The Title Moreh Sedek." *JSS* 6 (1961): 162–174.

Wenham, G. J. "Betulah: 'A Girl of Marriageable Age.'" *VT* 22 (1972): 326–48.

Selected Subject Index

Person Index

411

Selected Scripture Index